THE CONTEMPORARY ESSAY

BOOKS BY DONALD HALL

Books of Poetry

Exiles and Marriages, 1955
The Dark Houses, 1958
A Roof of Tiger Lilies, 1964
The Alligator Bride: Poems New and Selected, 1969
The Yellow Room: Love Poems, 1971
The Town of Hill, 1975
Kicking the Leaves, 1978
The Happy Man, 1986
The One Day, 1988
Old and New Poems, 1990
The Museum of Clear Ideas, 1993

Books of Prose

String Too Short to Be Saved, 1961
Henry Moore, 1966
Writing Well, 1973, 1976, 1979, 1982, 1985, 1988, 1991, 1994
Dock Ellis in the Country of Baseball, 1976
Goatfoot Milktongue Twinbird, 1978
Ox-Cart Man, 1979
To Keep Moving, 1981
The Weather for Poetry, 1982
Fathers Playing Catch with Sons, 1985
The Ideal Bakery, 1987
Seasons at Eagle Pond, 1987
Poetry and Ambition, 1988
Here at Eagle Pond, 1990
Their Ancient Glittering Eyes, 1992
Life Work, 1993
Death to the Death of Poetry, 1994

Edited Works

New Poets of England and America (with R. Pack and
     L. Simpson), 1957
New Poets of England and America (Second Selection) (with R. Pack),
     1962
Contemporary American Poets, 1962, 1971
The Modern Stylists, 1968
A Choice of Whitman's Verse, 1968
American Poetry, 1970
A Writer's Reader (with D. L. Emblen), 1976, 1979, 1982, 1985, 1988,
     1991, 1994
Oxford Book of American Literary Anecdotes, 1981
To Read Literature, 1981, 1982, 1987, 1992
Claims for Poetry, 1982
Oxford Book of Children's Verse in America, 1985

THE CONTEMPORARY ESSAY

THIRD EDITION

EDITED BY

Donald Hall

BEDFORD BOOKS of ST. MARTIN'S PRESS · BOSTON

For Nan and Dick Smart

For Bedford Books
President and Publisher: Charles H. Christensen
General Manager and Associate Publisher: Joan E. Feinberg
Managing Editor: Elizabeth M. Schaaf
Developmental Editor: Jane Betz
Editorial Assistant: Andrea Goldman
Production Editor: Michelle McSweeney
Production Associate: Heidi Hood
Copyeditor: Daniel Otis
Text Design: Anna George
Cover Design: Snider Design

Manufactured in the United States of America.
9   8   7   6
f   e   d   c   b

For information, write: St. Martin's Press, Inc.
175 Fifth Avenue, New York, NY 10010

Editorial Offices: Bedford Books *of* St. Martin's Press
75 Arlington St., Boston, MA 02116

ISBN: 0–312–10138–4

ACKNOWLEDGMENTS

Edward Abbey, "Aravaipa Canyon," from *Down the River* by Edward Abbey. Copyright © 1982 by Edward Abbey. Used by permission of Dutton Signet, a division of Penguin Books USA, Inc. Photograph of author used by permission of Jay Dusard.

Margaret Atwood, "Alien Territory," from *Good Bones and Simple Murders* by Margaret Atwood. Copyright © 1983, 1992, 1994 by O. W. Toad Ltd. Used by permission of Doubleday, a division of Bantam Doubleday Dell Publishing Group, Inc. "Alien Territory" © O. W. Toad Ltd., 1992. Reprinted from *Good Bones* with the permission of Coach House Press. Copyright © O. W. Toad Ltd. Originally published in *Good Bones*, Coach House Press, 1992. Photograph of author used by permission of Anthony Loew, Inc.

Acknowledgments and copyrights are continued at the back of the book on pages 618–22, which constitute an extension of the copyright page. It is a violation of the law to reproduce these selections by any means whatsoever without the written permission of the copyright holder.

Preface
for Instructors

The Contemporary Essay is intended for composition instructors who believe, as I do, that much of the best recent writing in America is nonfiction — and who regret that more of this excellent writing does not appear in composition anthologies because it defies rhetorical or thematic classification. Instructors who use this book will demand from their students sustained attention to essays that are longer and more challenging than usual. But good prose and good thinking require each other; a composition course that demands more attentive and thoughtful reading will encourage attentive and thoughtful writing.

The Introduction for Students that follows, greatly expanded for the third edition, begins by speaking to the diversity of the writers assembled here; later, it addresses questions of reading and of modern prose style. Because today's style derives from the grandparents — who spoke eloquently on the subject of writing in the early decades of this century — we end this Introduction by gathering a few paragraphs by writers on writing: "Modern Writers on Style." Along with the earlier writers, we have included some contemporaries, essayists of this edition.

This anthology could have been three times as long without lowering its standards; my final selection of fifty essays was necessarily arbitrary. I arrived at the mix by seeking diversity in tone, in level of difficulty, in strategy, and in subject matter: *The Contemporary Essay* entertains matters of black holes and fashion, dinosaurs and eclipses, the male body and Wyoming.

Like its predecessors, this edition takes its title literally. Because we live in an age of the essay, we can assemble a collection that is both contemporary and high in quality. A few of these essays derive from the 1970s but most were published in the 1980s and 1990s. There is much to be said for studying old models; but when students of composition search for templates of a prose style, there is more to be said for using the best work of our own literary moment.

In this third edition we collect fifty essays, a few of which are brief. Many teachers told us that they wanted the options provided by short texts along with longer ones. Other teachers suggested new essays by some of our old writers. Thus, four essays in the third edition are different choices from the work of writers included in the second. All in all, twenty-six essays are new to this edition. By coincidence, half the authors here are female and half are male.

The alphabetical arrangement of the essays makes for arbitrary juxtaposition. Any rhetorical or thematic organization would belie the actual range and variety of these essays. Very few could easily associate under one topic heading; no essay exemplifies only one rhetorical device.

In both its choice of selections and its editorial apparatus, *The Contemporary Essay* tries to avoid condescension to students. I assume that students have dictionaries; I assume that the class uses a rhetoric or a handbook. Therefore, I do not footnote words easily available in dictionaries or gloss common rhetorical terms. I omit questions and writing assignments, preferring students to ask, answer, and assign their own. The Introduction gives advice about reading in general, and the headnotes supply help toward reading each essay.

Because we all like to *see* the people who address us, we add to this edition photographs of our authors.

After each selection I have written a brief Afterword, notes on the essay just read which may prove useful for some students and some teachers. These Afterwords are deliberately nonparallel: Some focus on one trick of style; others examine larger issues of structure; some address the student as reader, others the student as writer; many center on the different strategies available to the essayist. Each tries to point out something useful; none attempts to respond to a whole essay.

My debts in assembling this collection are many. I am indebted to writers and editors, to my old teachers and to colleagues at the University of Michigan where I taught for many years. I am indebted to students. In recent years, I have talked about teaching exposition with composition staffs at many colleges and universities, from Lynchburg College in Virginia to the University of Utah in Salt Lake City, from the University of New Hampshire to Pacific Lutheran in Tacoma, Washington. I wish to express my gratitude to more people than I can name. By name, I would like to thank the following instructors, who used the first and second editions and generously took the time to share their ideas: Flavia Bacarella, Herbert H. Lehman College; David Bain, Middlebury College; Ariel Balter, Tufts University; Barbara Barnard, City University of New York, Hunter College; Eileen Barrett, Boston College; Linda Bates, University of California, Davis; James Beyer, Framingham State College; Thomas L. Blanton, Central Washington University; Herbert Brenner, Gonnel Valley State University; Patricia

Brieschke, Hofstra University; Dante K. Cantrill, Idaho State University; Jo-Anne Cappeluti, California State University, Fullerton; Marlene Clarke, University of California, Davis; David Cohen, State University of New York at Buffalo; Robert Cohen, State University of New York at Stony Brook; William V. Davis, Baylor University; Patty S. Derrick, University of Maine at Fort Kent; Karen Drulener, University of Delaware; C. Annette Ducey, Rhode Island College; Lorraine Eitel, Bethel College; John Engman, St. Olaf College; David Espey, University of Pennsylvania; Kathleen Estrada-Palma, University of Maine–Orono; Michael Friedlander, Sacramento City College; David Foug, Bellevue Community College; Joan Garrett-Goodyear, Smith College; Marcia Gealy, Northwestern University; Paul Gianoli, School of the Ozarks; Joseph Green, Western Washington University; Claudia Gutwirth, Long Island University; Henry Hahn, Modesto Junior College; Robert J. Hall, College of the Sequoias; Ed Harkness, Shoreline Community College; Dale Haskell, Southeast Missouri State University; Dev Hathaway, Emporia State University; Vicki Hendricks, Broward Community College; D. Scott Hinson, University of North Carolina at Charlotte; Katherine Hoffman, Roanoke College; Nora C. Jaffe, Smith College; Allen E. Johnson, University of Pennsylvania; Brad Johnson, University of California, Berkeley; Ron Johnson, Skyline College; B. W. Jorgensen, Brigham Young University; Sabrina Kirby, Virginia Polytechnic Institute; Alice Trower Kirk, Western Oregon State College; Steve Klepetar, St. Cloud State University; Barbara Lakin, Colorado State University; Leslie Lawrence, Boston University; Paul Lehmberg, Northern Michigan University; Ruth Lepson, Boston College; Bob LeRoy, Chemeketa Community College; Carol S. Long, Willamette University; Margrit Loomis, Northeast Louisiana University; Catherine Lupori, College of St. Catherine; John McGrail, Fitchburg State College; Anne Righton Malone, University of New Hampshire; Edward A. Martin, Middlebury College; Candice Matzhe, College of the Sequoias; Robert Miles, California State University, Sacramento; Devon Miller-Duggan, University of Delaware; Patricia A. Mills, Ball State University; Jacqueline A. Mintz, University of California, Berkeley; Diana Molberg, San Francisco State University; Tam Lin Neville, Butler University; Alice P. Nunnery, Middle Tennessee State University; Kevin Oderman, Iowa State University, Ames; Scott Orme, Spokane Community College; Suzanne Owens, Ohio State University; George Peranteau, College of DuPoye; Ruth Perkins, Linn-Benton Community College; Cam A. Peterson, Oberlin College; Raymond C. Phillips, Jr., Western Maryland College; Nancy P. Pope, Webster University/Washington University; Jeanne Purdy, University of Minnesota–Morris; Dennis M. Read, Denison University; Danny Rendleman, University of Michigan, Flint; Sandra Rogosin, Western Oregon State College; Jennifer O. Rosti, Roanoke College; J. T. Scanlan, Providence College; Libby Schlagel, Adelphi University; Jocelyn A. Sheppard, State University of New York at Buffalo; Elizabeth Shull, University of Southern Maine; Maurya Simon, California Institute of Technology; Thomas Simmons, University of California, Berkeley; John C. Sisson, University of Alabama; Bill Siverly, Portland Community College; Patricia

L. Skarda, Smith College; Jonathan R. Smith, University of Virginia; Roger Sorkin, Southeastern Massachusetts University; Karyn Z. Spides, Hamline University; Karyn Sproles, State University of New York at Buffalo; Paul Strong, Alfred University; Andreas Sununu, DePauw University; Joan Taylor, University of South Carolina at Beaufort; Norma J. Tilden, Georgetown University; Sanford Tweedie, University of Wisconsin, Milwaukee; Sue Walker, University of South Alabama; Wayne Ude, Mankato State University; Anmarie Wagstaff, University of California, Davis; Eileen M. Ward, College of Dupage–Alpha; Kathleen M. Ward, University of California, Davis; Will Weaver, Bemidji State University; Jan Widmayer, Boise State University; Bronwyn T. Williams, Massachusetts Institute of Technology; Alice F. Worlsey, California State University, Stanislaus; Betsy R. Zimbalist, Washington University; John N. Zneimer, Indiana University Northwest.

More locally, I am always indebted to Jane Kenyon. I am grateful to Sharon Broughton who word-processed and to Lois Fierro who typed. At Bedford Books, I am always indebted to Charles Christensen and Joan Feinberg, who approached me about this book remembering my wistful notion of years ago. For this edition I have relied especially on the unusual, even extraordinary, help of Jane Betz and her assistant Andrea Goldman. In a time of stress for the editor, they have supplied advice, judgment, and much-needed library research. I am grateful to Ellen Darion and Steve Scipione, for many specific chores in connection with earlier editions, and to Michelle McSweeney and Elizabeth Schaaf, to Heidi Hood and Karen Baart, for taking this book through production. I am indebted to Daniel Otis, who copyedited this immense manuscript. All who care for the literature of the essay owe Robert Atwan a debt for his annual collection, *Best American Essays.*

Contents

"As Thoreau found a universe in the woods around Concord, any person whose senses are alive can make a world of any natural place, however limited it might seem, on this subtle planet of ours."

"Men's bodies are the most dangerous things on earth."

"The brutal truth is that the bulk of the white people in America never had any interest in educating black people, except as this could serve white purposes. It is not the black child's language that is in question, it is not his language that is despised: It is his experience."

xi

CONTENTS

CONTENTS

CONTENTS

THE
CONTEMPORARY
ESSAY

Introduction for Students

On These Writers and Their Work

Often one literary form dominates an era. In Shakespeare's time the play was the thing, and lyric poets and pamphleteers wrote for the stage when they turned aside from their primary work. A few decades ago, American novelists wrote novels when they could afford to but paid their bills by writing short stories for *Collier's* and the *Saturday Evening Post*. Today, novelists of similar eminence and ability — Joan Didion, Cynthia Ozick, Alice Walker, Jamaica Kincaid — become performers of the essay, for we live in the age of the essay.

In part, our age needs the essay because it requires exposition. We live in a time bewildered by the multiplicity of information; we cherish the selection and organization of information by our best writers. We live in a time that allows writers freedom to choose what they investigate, to follow their thoughts wherever they lead, and to use a variety of styles and strategies. Therefore the essay thrives, and many of our best essayists are writers for whom, as Annie Dillard puts it, the essay is "the real work." In our age, we are also fortunate to read essayists whose real work is science. Stephen Jay Gould and Stephen Hawking write brilliant prose in the service of paleontology and physics. For most of us — who are specialists, or generalists with many gaps of knowledge — the exposition of technology by gifted writers is a major necessity.

But the essay of our moment is not only exposition of information. Annie Dillard's real work is personal narrative that contains exact description of the natural world. This kind of writing, with opinions argued or suggested,

1

belongs to the older tradition of the essay. Although a few classical writers — like Plutarch in Greek, Cicero in Latin — wrote brief historical or philosophical meditations which resemble the genre, it was Michel de Montaigne in sixteenth-century France who invented the form that we know. He also invented the name, *essais*, which is modest but not *too* modest — for its suggestion of attempt or trial allows the writer freedom of tentative exploration; because the essayist does not pretend to speak the final word, she or he is at liberty to extend over unknown or speculative territory. Typically the classic essay combines personal experience with thought or opinion leading to tentative generalization — like Marianna De Marco Torgovnick, as she describes "On Being White, Female, and Born in Bensonhurst."

The contemporary essay is a house with many rooms. Trying to define *essay* so as to include everything offered in this collection, we could collapse into the negative: An essay is something in paragraphs (not poetry) that is true or supposed to be true (not fiction). But the negative is not good enough. For that matter, the contemporary essay when it is narrative and dramatic sometimes resembles a short story; look at Maxine Hong Kingston and Frank Conroy.

It is better to talk of three main traditions that characterize the contemporary essay.

There is the essay of personal experience and opinion, where the author is center stage, which can extend from the extremely personal (Gerald Early and his daughters) to the almost-objective (Hawking). See Joan Didion on water and her feelings about water. Other examples of the personal essay abound in this book: Looking at the table of contents, we can list Abbey, Berger, Carver — and keep going.

Another category of essay is primarily philosophical, intellectual, or critical — an essay that examines, argues, thinks, and makes decisions. Clearly this form resembles the essay of personal opinion, but Walker Percy wants to suggest not the opinion of one author but the truth of experience. The difference in tone is considerable. Other criticial or intellectual essays here include works by Adrienne Rich, Diane Johnson, Francine du Plessix Gray, and E. L. Doctorow.

A third type of essay is the magazine article of our day — information or exposition arranged so that we can take it in. This essay means to report on *what is there*, without apparent reference to the writer's life or opinion. See John McPhee and Sue Hubbell, for instance. However, when we read work that seems purely objective, we must remember that the instrument that measures distorts the measuring: The author chooses only a tiny proportion of the details available, and this choice expresses opinion even when the writer tries to remain out of it.

The moment we divide the essay into three parts like Caesar's Gaul, we face the fact that the largest number of essays in this book must belong to another category: NONE OF THE ABOVE, or maybe ALL OF THE ABOVE. Malcolm Cowley writes from personal experience, from opinion, but also with research and information in pursuit of a critical objectivity. In the category of humor — Molly Ivins, Ian Frazier — we find opinion, ethics by way of satire, and personal narrative or perhaps mockery of personal narrative.

The burden in making this anthology has been to choose wisely and representatively among a dazzling variety of the best. We have tried for diversity of author, style, and subject. After reading more than a thousand essays, after making a short list of a hundred and fifty, we have finally arrived at this collection. We may hope that we have chosen a range of topics and attitudes to suit and to offend practically everybody, for contemporary factual writing explores the universe, and its manners of procedure are as various as its subject matters: Writers explain, describe, narrate, argue, and reminisce about childhood, cosmology, Bosnia, the Miss America contest, rape, habits of the civilized mind, dinosaurs, apple pie, the fourteenth century, snobbishness, clothing, people named Nye, mothers, and multiple sclerosis. Nothing human is alien to the essay, nor is any method or length or degree of difficulty alien. On the one hand Walker Percy's philosophical ideas make reading him difficult, and equally rewarding for the effort. On the other hand Gary Soto on demeaning labor or Eudora Welty on a neighborhood store does not tax the philosophical mind: With these topics, difficulty would be inappropriate.

Typical strategies vary from essay to essay, partly by type — one wouldn't construct a narrative by means of analogy or definition — but also within a type. In a critical essay, Alison Lurie speaks of clothing by constructing a long and ingenious analogy to language. In an essay of argument, Richard Rodriguez describes his growing up, using personal narrative for purposes of persuasion as he discusses ethnicity and bilingualism. It pleases John McPhee to use his skill partly in self-effacement; his talent renders the author invisible behind his subject matter. On the other hand, Charles Simic has no interest in invisibility even when he writes about the suicidal nationalism of the Yugoslavia where he was born. Differences in strategy derive partly from subject matter but also from diverse abilities and obsessions. Some writers, like Annie Dillard on the eclipse, make little of their personal histories but fly the flag of personality by flaunting an idiosyncratic style.

In subjects and strategies, this book offers a diversity for study. Yet when we look at the prose of these writers from a distance — for instance, from the vantage point of another century's style — we realize that certain agreements about writing unite the distinct minds of Gretel Ehrlich and Frank Conroy, Joy Harjo and Barbara W. Tuchman. These writers agree, by and large, to use the concrete detail in place of the abstraction; to employ the active, not the passive, mood; to withhold the adjective and search for the verb. They agree to pursue clarity and vigor. And most would agree with Robert Graves (English poet, novelist, and essayist), who said some years ago: "The writing of good English is . . . a moral matter." For more on this matter, see the quotations in "Modern Writers on Style," pages 12–19.

Much good nonfiction works the way an efficient machine works, by directness that matches energy to production. A sentence is good the way an ax handle is good. Order and organization move from writer's mind to reader's by the ethic of clarity in sentence structure and transition. For good prose to aid us, both socially and psychologically, it need not speak of society or psyche; for good style, all by itself, *is* good politics and good mental hygiene. Thus John McPhee, who writes without revealing his values, contributes to ethics by the lucidity, clarity, and vigor of his exposition.

But efficiency and clarity are not the only values we derive from good style. It is true that sentences show us around the surface of the globe, lead us from one place to another; but sentences also dig beneath the earth's surface. The subjectivity of much contemporary writing — private feelings publicly exposed — provides a model for self-examination. Thus we find room not only for John McPhee but also for Annie Dillard, with whom we explore underworlds of feeling. If she did not write with the efficiency and clarity of a John McPhee, her self-exploration would reveal nothing. But because she writes with intense clarity about matters seldom regarded as clear, the light of the imagination blazes in a dark place.

On Reading Essays

We read to become more human. When we read *Gilgamesh* — the oldest surviving narrative, a Babylonian epic from 2000 B.C. — we connect with other human beings. We raise a glass across four thousand years of time and drink with our ancestors the old wine of friendship, courage, loss, and the will to survive. And in *The Contemporary Essay*, when we read Stephen Hawking on physics or Vicki Hearne on animals or Alice Walker on her mother, we find another kind of linkage. We connect not across chasms of millennia but across contemporary gaps of knowledge and experience. We read for information and pleasure together. We read to understand, to investigate, to provide background for decision, to find confirmation, to find contradiction.

We also read to learn how to write. If we study architecture, we learn in part by studying structures already designed and built. If we study basketball, we learn in part by watching other players dribble, drive to the left, and shoot. Although in learning anything we add our own flourishes, develop our talents, and overcome our drawbacks, we build on things that others did before us. For the writer of essays today, the things done are the essays written yesterday. We build on others' work and add our own uniqueness. Many professional writers, not only students in composition classes, prepare for the day's work by reading an admirable example of the kind of prose they undertake — for the example of excellence, the encouragement of brilliance, the stimulation of achievement.

Reading is as various as writing is. If we read well we read differently according to what we read. Suppose when we eat breakfast we look at a daily paper; later in the day we take on a philosophical essay, a poem, a chemistry assignment, *People* magazine, and the instructions in a box of film. If we try reading the newspaper as we should read the poem, nightfall will find us halfway through the first section. If we try reading the philosophy essay as we read *People,* the essay will pass us by. Every piece of print requires a different level of attention; good readers adjust their speed automatically when they read the first words of anything. Something tells them: "Slow down or you'll miss out!" or "Speed up or you'll bore yourself to death!"

In our education, in the culture that shapes us, we acquire unconscious habits of reading. Some habits are good, some bad. It helps to become conscious of how we read; it helps to learn appropriate reading.

A century ago, even sixty years ago, silent reading was noisier to the mental ear because people were used to hearing books read aloud. Long church services included much reading of scripture. Home entertainment was reading aloud from novels, scripture, or poetry. Public entertainment — before radio, films, or television — was lectures, debates, and dramatic recitation. In school, students memorized pieces for speaking and read aloud to their classmates. Because students practiced recitation themselves, they could not read a text in silence without considering how they would say it out loud. Unconsciously, as they read alone, they decided in what tone or with what feeling they would enunciate each word.

Mental mimicry makes for *active* reading. We cannot supply the tone of a word unless we understand its meaning. Nowadays, most of us grow up passive readers. Our passivity is encouraged by television, which provides everything for us, even a laugh track to tell us when to laugh. This collection of essays is intended for students who want more than printed television. These essays require active reading.

A few years ago I taught a composition class in which I assigned an article by Richard Rhodes called "Packaged Sentiment." This essay about greeting cards came out in *Harper's,* addressed to an audience that would expect to find such a magazine contemptuous of prefabricated emotions. But the sophisticated author took pains to explore the opposite of the preconception; he made a limited, reasonable defense of the greeting card industry. At the end of his argument, he quoted an English novelist's qualified praise of a political institution: "I celebrate [greeting] cards as E. M. Forster celebrated democracy, with a hearty two cheers." When my students came to class that morning I wrote on the blackboard: "Five minutes. Why *two* cheers?" I expected them to tell me why Rhodes's praise was incomplete. They told me something different: They told me what Rhodes found to praise about greeting cards, as if I had asked, "Why two *cheers?*"

My students were victims of passive reading. They read Rhodes's essay and accepted "two cheers" without asking themselves, "Why two rather than twelve, or one, or ten million?" When I said this much at the next meeting of the class, three or four students slapped their palms on their foreheads — the classic gesture: "How *could* I have missed that one?" These students learned a lesson; they had neglected to read actively and to note that Richard Rhodes withheld one third of the normal tribute: "Three Cheers! Hip Hip Hooray! Hip Hip Hooray! Hip Hip Hooray!"

Those students who got the point should never again forget that three is the normal number of cheers. But how would they keep from making the same kind of mistake in further reading? How would they learn to read actively, engaging the text, requiring the text to make sense? Here is a series of answers to these questions.

1. *Learn the model for active reading.* Put the author on the witness stand and make him tell not only the truth but the whole truth. Give the author the benefit of the doubt — expect him to reveal himself if you work hard at it — but be prepared on occasion to discover that the author, rather than the reader, is at fault (through illogic, a missed step in an argument, unfairness, lack of support).

2. *Adjust the speed of your reading.* Learn to adjust your reading to an appropriate speed. Most of these essays ought to be read slowly, but their demands will vary. It should take twice as long to read a page of Walker Percy as it does to read a page by Raymond Carver. (I refer to the essays by these writers in this book. Raymond Carver is sometimes, appropriately, slower reading, and Walker Percy faster.) If you tend to read quickly, learn to slow down when it is appropriate. If you tend to read slowly, make sure that your slowness results from close attention to the text, not from a wandering mind. But be neither a slow reader nor a fast one: Be an appropriate reader, adjusting your speed to the text you are reading.

3. *Take notes as you read.* Everyone should take reading notes; they help to make sure that you understand *as* you read. Pause regularly, perhaps at the end of each paragraph, at least at the end of every page or two, to inspect yourself and your text. Underline the most crucial sentences, passages with which you tentatively disagree, and phrases you need to return to. Ask yourself: Do I know where we are and how we got here? Why are we entertaining *this* subject, in *this* essay? Try to answer yourself, in a note. Write in a notebook or on the margin of the page. When you commit yourself by writing a note, often you recognize that your understanding is less secure than you had considered it.

4. *Look up what you need to know.* Learn what is appropriate to know exactly and what you can understand approximately. If an essayist on medicine refers to "the etiology of disease," we need to understand the word *etiology* to follow the sense. We turn to the dictionary. On the other hand, the essayist may refer to a particular disease by a long Latinate name, in a context where we understand that the word is an example and that the exact nature of the disease (which we could discover by scurrying from definition to

definition in a dictionary) is irrelevant to our understanding of the sentence. Learn what to look up and what not to look up; this knowledge resembles social tact. If you are in doubt, look it up, but mature readers when they read Lewis Thomas do not need to trace down *corpus callosum* in a medical dictionary. They know by the context of the essay what is happening; they know that scientific terminology suits the essayist's purpose — and that the message is the choice of scientific language, not its definition.

5. *Read and reread.* Most important: Read, reread, and reread again. When your teacher assigns an essay, read it through the first time as soon as you can. Read the headnote first; read the essay at an appropriate speed, pausing to interrogate it; take notes and underline; use a dictionary. Then read the afterword that follows the essay. Think the essay over. Consult your notes, look back at the text for difficult points, think about the whole essay — and then sleep on it. It is useful to come back to *anything* a second time after an interval, especially after sleepwork. Never write a paper or read an essay once only, at one sitting, even if it is a long sitting.

When you return to the essay a day later, reread the headnote, which should be more useful the second time. Reread the essay more slowly, now that you know its plot, and take further notes. Reread the afterword. Take notes on your notes.

6. *Make your own list.* Finally, there are problems that vary from reader to reader. Think about your *own* problems in reading, before you begin to read each essay assigned. Study your own reading to identify mistakes made in the past. ("How did I manage *not* to notice that 'two cheers' is a diminution of 'three cheers'?") When a neighbor in class finds more in an essay than you found, interrogate yourself. What in your reading prevented you from getting it all?

Keep a list, at the front of a reading notebook, of injunctions that you need to remember. "Pause after every page to summarize." "Watch for transitions." "Look up words." Toward the end of the term, maybe you can cross some injunctions off your list.

Everyone assigned this textbook knows how to read. Everyone can improve as a reader.

When we improve as readers we improve as writers. By observing Malcolm Cowley or Joyce Carol Oates or James Baldwin solve a problem in writing, be it as small as a transition or as large as any essay's whole shape, we add to our own equipment for solving problems of style and construction. By reading we also improve as human beings; we increase our ability to absorb the history of our species, preserved in the language of the tribe through time and in the language of our contemporaries in an age of the essay.

On Modern Style:
An Ethic of Clarity*

"Today's style," I said in the preface, "derives from the grandparents." Notions of style that started early in this century, common to diverse writers, were firmly fixed by midcentury and have altered little as the century comes to a close. Looking back, it is easy to discern a gradual, general agreement on what constitutes good style, but it is almost baffling to observe the strange bedfellows this agreement makes.

Ezra Pound, George Orwell, James Thurber, and Ernest Hemingway don't have much in common: a great poet who became a follower of Mussolini, a disillusioned left-wing satirist, a comic essayist and cartoonist, and a great novelist. If anything, they could represent the diversity of modern literature. Yet a common idea of good style unites them, a notion of the virtues of clarity and simplicity. This idea of style was not unknown to earlier writers, but never before had it become so pervasive and so exclusive.

Style is the manner of a sentence, not its matter. But the distinction between manner and matter is a slippery one, for manner affects matter. When *Time* used to tell us that President Truman slouched into one room, while General Eisenhower strode into another, their manner was trying to prejudice our feelings. The hotel that invites me to enjoy my favorite beverage at the Crown Room is trying not to sound crass: "Have a drink at the bar." One stylist, discussing this problem, took Caesar's "I came; I saw; I conquered," and revised it as "I arrived on the scene of the battle; I observed the situation; I won the victory." The matter is the same — if matter is ever the same, when manner changes — but Caesar's tone of arrogant dignity disappears in the pallid pedantry of the longer version; it is impossible to say that the matter is unaffected. Let us say that this kind of difference, in the two versions of Caesar, is a matter of style.

In the expression "good writing" or "good style," the word *good* has usually meant "beautiful" or "proficient" — like a good Rembrandt or a good kind of soap. In our time it has come to mean honest as opposed to fake. Bad writing happens when the writer lies to himself, to others, or to both. Probably, it is necessary to lie to oneself in order to lie to others; advertisers use the products they praise. Bad writing may be proficient; it may persuade us to buy a poor car or vote for an imbecile, but it is bad because it is tricky, false in its enthusiasm, and dishonestly motivated. It appeals to a part of us that wants to deceive itself. I am encouraged to tell myself that I am enjoying my favorite beverage when, in reality, I am only getting sloshed.

"If a man writes clearly enough any one can see if he fakes," says Hemingway. Orwell reverses the terms: "The great enemy of clear language

---

*This essay began as an introduction to *The Modern Stylists* (1968). Many of the quotations assembled in "Modern Writers on Style," which follows, were first gathered for that book.

is insincerity. . . . When there is a gap between one's real and one's declared aims, one turns as it were instinctively to long words and exhausted idioms, like a cuttlefish squirting out ink." Pound talks about the "gap between one's real and one's declared aims" as the distance between expression and meaning. In "The New Vocabularianism," Thurber speaks of the political use of clichés to hide a "menacing *Alice in Wonderland* meaninglessness." When Robert Graves claims that "the writing of good English is thus a moral matter," he means that the matter is a morality of truth-telling. Herbert Read declares that "the only thing that is indispensable for the possession of a good style is personal sincerity." We can agree, but we must add that personal sincerity is not always easy to determine, nor is it necessarily available to the will. Real aims, we must understand, are not necessarily conscious ones. The worst liars in the world may consider themselves sincere. But analysis of a writer's own style, if the writer can be smart enough, can provide a test of feelings. And certainly, many habits of bad style are bad habits of thinking as well as of feeling.

There are examples of the modern attitude toward style in older writers. Jonathan Swift, maybe the best prose writer of the language, sounds like George Orwell when he writes:

> Our English tongue is too little cultivated in this kingdom, yet the faults are nine in ten owing to affectation, not to want of understanding. When a man's thoughts are clear, the properest words will generally offer themselves first, and his own judgment will direct him in what order to place them, so as they may be best understood.

Here Swift appears tautological; clear thoughts exist *only* when they are embodied in clear words. But he goes on: "When men err against this method, it is usually on purpose" — purposes, we must add, that we often disguise from ourselves.

Aristotle in his *Rhetoric* makes a case for plainness and truth-telling. "The right thing in speaking really is that we should be satisfied not to annoy our hearers, without trying to delight them: We ought in fairness to fight our case with no help beyond the bare facts." And he anticipates the modern stylist's avoidance of unusual words: "Clearness is secured by using the words . . . that are current and ordinary." Cicero agrees with Aristotle, attacking the Sophists because they are "on the lookout for ideas that are neatly put rather than reasonable."

Yet, when we quote the master rhetorician Cicero on behalf of honest clarity we must remember that the ancients did not think of style as we do. Style until recent times has been a division of rhetoric. To learn style, students studied the types of figures of speech and the appropriateness of each to different levels of discourse — high, middle, and low. The study of style was technical rather than moral. For some writers, Latin was high and the vernacular low, but in the Renaissance the vernacular took in all levels. It is only in modern times that style divorces itself from rhetoric — rhetoric belongs to the enemy, to the advertisers and the propagandists — and becomes a matter of ethics and introspection.

Ezra Pound, like some French writers before him, makes the writer's function social. "Good writers are those who keep the language efficient. That is to say, keep it accurate, keep it clear." We must ask why this idea of the function of good style is so predominantly a modern phenomenon. Pound elsewhere speaks of the "assault," by which he means the attack upon our ears and eyes of words used dishonestly to persuade us, to convince us to buy or to believe. Never before have people been exposed to so many words — written words from newspapers and billboards and paperbacks and flashing signs and the sides of buses, and spoken words from radio and television and loudspeakers. People who wish to keep their minds clear and their feelings their own must make an effort to brush away these words like cobwebs from faces. The assault of the phony is a result of technology combined with a morality that excuses any technique useful for persuasion. The persuasion is for purposes of making money as in advertising, or winning power as in war propaganda and the slogans of politicians. Politicians have always had slogans, but never before had they the means to spread their words so widely. The cold war of rhetoric between communism and capitalism killed no great nations, but from 1950 to 1990 the air was crowded with the small corpses of good words: "democracy," "freedom," "liberty," and "liberation."

It is because of this assault that writers have become increasingly concerned with the honesty of their style to the exclusion of other qualities. Concentration on honesty is the only way to exclude the sounds of bad style that assault us all. These writers are concerned finally *to be honest about what they see, feel, and know.*

Our reading of good writers and our attempt to write like them can help to guard us against the dulling onslaught. But we can do this only if we are able to look into ourselves with some honesty. An ethic of clarity demands intelligence and self-knowledge. Really, the ethic is not only a defense against the assault (nothing good is ever merely defensive), but is a development of the same inwardness that is reflected in psychoanalysis. One cannot, after all, examine one's motives and feelings carefully if one takes a naive view that the appearance of a feeling is the reality of that feeling.

Sometimes, the assault is merely pompous. Some people say "wealthy" instead of "rich" in order to seem proper, or "home" instead of "house" in order to seem genteel. George Orwell translates a portion of Ecclesiastes into academic-pompous, for example; Sir Arthur Quiller-Couch does something similar with Hamlet's soliloquy. Years ago, James Russell Lowell ridiculed the newspapers that translated "A great crowd came to see . . ." into "A vast concourse was assembled to witness. . . ." None of these examples is so funny as a colonel's statement on television that one of our astronauts had "established visual contact" with a piece of equipment. He meant that the astronaut had *seen* it.

Comic as these pomposities are, they are signs that something has gone wrong somewhere. (My father normally spoke a perfectly good plain English, but occasionally, when he was unhappy with himself, he would fall off dreadfully; I can remember him admonishing me at dinner, "It is necessary to masticate thoroughly.") The colonel must have been worried about the intellectual respectability of the space program when he resorted to phrases like "visual contact." The woman who calls her neighbor "wealthy" instead of "rich" is worried about her social status. When we use abominable language, something has gone wrong, and it has gone wrong inside our minds and our emotions.

"The style is the man," said a French scientist. Again and again, the modern stylists repeat this idea. By people's metaphors you shall know them. When commencement orators advise students to enrich themselves culturally, chances are that they are talking more about money than poetry. When a university president says that her institution turned out 1,432 B.A.s last year, she tells us that she thinks she is running General Motors. The style is the man and the woman. Remy de Gourmont used the analogy that the bird's song is conditioned by the shape of the beak. And Paul Valery said, "What makes the style is not merely the mind applied to a particular action; it is the whole of a living system extended, imprinted, and recognizable in expression." These statements are fine, but they sound too deterministic, as if one expresses an unalterable self and can no more change the style of that self than a bird can change the shape of its beak. People are birds that can change their beaks.

A writer of bad prose, to become a writer of good prose, must alter character. We do not have to become good in terms of conventional morality, but we must become honest in the expression of ourselves, which means that we must know ourselves. There must be no gap between expression and meaning, between real and declared aims. For some people, some of the time, this simply means *not* telling deliberate lies. For most people, it means learning when they are lying and when they are not. It means learning the real names of our feelings. It means not saying or thinking, "I didn't *mean* to hurt your feelings," when we really desired to hurt. It means not saying "wealthy" or "home" or "beverage" or "perspiration" or "luncheon" for the purpose of appearing upper class or well educated. It means not using the passive mood to attribute to no one in particular opinions that we are unwilling to call our own. It means not disguising banal thinking by polysyllabic writing or the lack of feeling by clichés that purport to display feeling.

"The style is the man," and we can change ourselves by changing our styles. Prose style is the way we think and the way we understand what we feel. Frequently, we feel for one another a mixture of strong love and strong hate; if we call it love and disguise the hate to ourselves by sentimentalizing over love, we are thinking and feeling falsely or dishonestly. Style is ethics and psychology; clarity is a psychological sort of ethic, since it involves not general moral laws but truth to the individual self. The scrutiny of style is a moral and psychological study. By trying to scrutinize our own style, perhaps with the help of Orwell and Pound, Hemingway and Thurber, we try to understand ourselves. Editing our own writing, or going over in memory our own spoken words, or even inwardly examining our thought, we can ask *why* we resorted to the passive in this case or to clichés in that. When the smoke of bad prose fills the air, something is always on fire. If the style is really the human being, the style becomes an instrument for discovering and changing the human being. Language is expression of self, but language is also the instrument by which to know that self.

Modern Writers on Style

JOAN DIDION

What's so hard about that first sentence is that you're stuck with it. Everything else is going to flow out of that sentence. And by the time you've laid down the first *two* sentences, your options are all gone.

Yes, and the last sentence in a piece is another adventure. It should open the piece up. It should make you go back and start reading from page one. That's how it *should* be, but it doesn't always work. I think of writing anything at all as a kind of high-wire act. The minute you start putting words on paper you're eliminating possibilities. Unless you're Henry James.

I suppose that's part of the dynamic. I start a book and I want to make it perfect, want it to turn every color, want it to *be the world*. Ten pages in, I've already blown it, limited it, made it less, marred it. That's very discouraging. I hate the book at that point. After a while I arrive at an accommodation: Well, it's not the ideal, it's not the perfect object I wanted to make, but maybe — if I go ahead and finish it anyway — I can get it right next time. Maybe I can have another chance.

ROBERT FROST

A dramatic necessity goes deep into the nature of the sentence. Sentences are not different enough to hold the attention unless they are dramatic. No ingenuity of varying structure will do. All that can save them is the speaking tone of voice somehow entangled in the words and fastened to the page for the ear of the imagination. That is all that can save poetry from singsong, all that can save prose from itself.

The style is the man. Rather say the style is the way the man takes himself; and to be at all charming or even bearable, the way is almost rigidly prescribed. If it is with outer seriousness, it must be with inner humor. If it is with outer humor, it must be with inner seriousness. Neither one alone without the other under it will do. Robinson was thinking as much in his sonnet on Tom Hood. One ordeal of Mark Twain was the constant fear that his occluded seriousness would be overlooked. That betrayed him into his two or three books of out-and-out seriousness.

GABRIEL GARCÍA MÁRQUEZ

One of the most difficult things is the first paragraph. I have spent many months on a first paragraph and once I get it, the rest just comes out very easily. In the first paragraph you solve most of the problems with your book. The theme is defined, the style, the tone. At least in my case, the first paragraph is a kind of sample of what the rest of the book is going to be. That's why writing a book of short stories is much more difficult than writing a novel. Every time you write a short story, you have to begin all over again.

ROBERT GRAVES*

There is not, and cannot be, any permanent model of literary English; but there are everywhere obvious differences between written and spoken English. A speaker reinforces his meaning with gestures and vocal inflections, and if the people he addresses still do not understand they can ask for further explanation; whereas a writer, not enjoying either of these advantages, must formulate and observe certain literary principles if he wishes to be completely understood. Granted, he may not always wish to be so understood: A good deal of play is made in English with deliberate looseness of phrase. But the only relevant standard by which to judge any straightforward piece of prose is the ease with which it conveys its full intended sense to the readers to whom it is addressed, rather than its correctness by the laws of formal English grammar.

FRANCINE DU PLESSIX GRAY

We must all struggle against all that is curious, already-seen, fatigued, shopworn. I battle against what my admirable colleague William Gass calls "pissless prose," prose that lacks the muscle, the physicality, the gait of a good horse, for pissless prose is bodiless and has no soul. Of course this holds equally true for fiction as for essays, reporting, a letter to a friend, a book review, a decent contribution to art criticism — in sum I search for language in which faith intertwines with desire, faith that we can recapture, with erotic accuracy, that treasured memory or vision which is the object of our desire. I'm keen on the word "voluptuous," a word too seldom heard in this society founded on puritanical principles. I think back to a phrase of Julia Kristeva's, the most interesting feminist thinker of our time, who

---

*With Alan Hodge.

speaks of "the voluptuousness of family life." I would apply the same phrase to the prose I most admire, prose I can caress and nurture and linger on, diction which is nourished by the deep intimacy of familiar detail, and yet is constantly renewed by the force of the writer's love and fidelity to language.

ELIZABETH HARDWICK

I'm not sure I understand the process of writing. There is, I'm sure, something strange about imaginative concentration. The brain slowly begins to function in a different way, to make mysterious connections. Say, it is Monday, and you write a very bad draft, but if you keep on trying, on Friday, words, phrases, appear almost unexpectedly. I don't know why you can't do it on Monday, or why I can't. I'm the same person, no smarter, I have nothing more at hand. I think it's true of a lot of writers. It's one of the things writing students don't understand. They write a first draft and are quite disappointed, or often *should* be disappointed. They don't understand that they have merely begun, and that they may be merely beginning even in the second or third draft.

ERNEST HEMINGWAY

This too to remember. If a man writes clearly enough any one can see if he fakes. If he mystifies to avoid a straight statement, which is very different from breaking so-called rules of syntax or grammar to make an effect which can be obtained in no other way, the writer takes a longer time to be known as a fake and other writers who are afflicted by the same necessity will praise him in their own defense. True mysticism should not be confused with incompetence in writing which seeks to mystify where there is no mystery but is really only the necessity to fake to cover lack of knowledge or the inability to state clearly. Mysticism implies a mystery and there are many mysteries; but incompetence is not one of them; nor is overwritten journalism made literature by the injection of a false epic quality. Remember this too: All bad writers are in love with the epic.

MARY McCARTHY

I've never liked the conventional conception of "style." What's confusing is that style usually means some form of fancy writing — when people say, oh yes, so and so's such a "wonderful stylist." But if one means by style the voice, the irreducible and always recognizable and alive thing, then of course style is really everything.

H. L. MENCKEN

The American seldom believes that the trade he follows is quite worthy of his virtues and talents; he thinks that he would have adorned something far gaudier. Since it is often impossible for him to escape, or to dream plausibly of escaping, he soothes himself by pretending that he belongs to a superior section of his craft, and even invents a sonorous name to set himself off from the herd. Here we glimpse the origin of characteristic American euphemisms, e.g., *mortician* for *undertaker, realtor* for *real-estate agent, beautician* for *hairdresser, exterminating engineer* for *rat catcher,* and so on. *Realtor* was devised by a high-toned real-estate agent of Minneapolis, Charles N. Chadbourn by name, who sought a distinctive title by which he and his fellow members of the Minneapolis Real Estate Board could distinguish themselves from fly-by-night dealers in houses and lots.

GEORGE ORWELL

In our time, political speech and writing are largely the defense of the indefensible. Things like the continuance of British rule in India, the Russian purges and deportations, the dropping of the atom bombs on Japan, can indeed be defended, but only by arguments which are too brutal for most people to face, and which do not square with the professed aims of political parties. Thus political language has to consist largely of euphemism, question-begging, and sheer cloudy vagueness. Defenseless villages are bombarded from the air, the inhabitants driven out into the countryside, the cattle machine-gunned, the huts set on fire with incendiary bullets: This is called *pacification.* Millions of peasants are robbed of their farms and sent trudging along the roads with no more than they can carry: This is called *transfer of population* or *rectification of frontiers.* People are imprisoned for years without trial, or shot in the back of the neck, or sent to die of scurvy in Arctic lumber camps; this is called *elimination of unreliable elements.* Such phraseology is needed if one wants to name things without calling up mental pictures of them. Consider for instance some comfortable English professor defending Russian totalitarianism. He cannot say outright, "I believe in killing off your opponents when you can get good results by doing so." Probably, therefore, he will say something like this:

"While freely conceding that the Soviet régime exhibits certain features which the humanitarian may be inclined to deplore, we must, I think, agree that a certain curtailment of the right to political opposition is an unavoidable concomitant of transitional periods, and that the rigors which the Russian people have been called upon to undergo have been amply justified in the sphere of concrete achievement."

S. J. PERELMAN

The old apothegm that easy writing makes hard reading is as succinct as ever. I used to know several eminent writers who were given to boasting of the speed with which they created. It's not a lovable attribute, to put it mildly, and I'm afraid our acquaintanceship has languished.

KATHERINE ANNE PORTER

I've been called a stylist until I really could tear my hair out. And I simply don't believe in style. The style is you. Oh, you can cultivate a style, I suppose, if you like. But I should say it remains a cultivated style. It remains artificial and imposed, and I don't think it deceives anyone. A cultivated style would be like a mask. Everybody knows it's a mask, and sooner or later you must show yourself — or at least, you show yourself as someone who could not afford to show himself, and so created something to hide behind. Style is the man. Aristotle said it first, as far as I know, and everybody has said it since, because it is one of those unarguable truths. You do not create a style. You work, and develop yourself; your style is an emanation from your own being.

EZRA POUND

This brings us to the immorality of bad art. Bad art is inaccurate art. It is art that makes false reports. If a scientist falsifies a report either deliberately or through negligence we consider him as either a criminal or a bad scientist according to the enormity of his offence, and he is punished or despised accordingly. . . .

It is as important for the purpose of thought to keep language efficient as it is in surgery to keep tetanus bacilli out of one's bandages.

In introducing a person to literature one would do well to have him examine works where language is efficiently used; to devise a system for getting directly and expeditiously at such works, despite the smokescreens erected by half-knowing and half-thinking critics. To get at them, despite the mass of dead matter that these people have heaped up and conserved round about them in the proportion: one barrel of sawdust to each half-bunch of grapes.

Great literature is simply language charged with meaning to the utmost possible degree.

More writers fail from lack of character than from lack of intelligence. Technical solidity is not attained without at least some persistence.

GERTRUDE STEIN

Sentences and paragraphs. Sentences are not emotional but paragraphs are. I can say that as often as I like and it always remains as it is, something that is.

I said I found this out first in listening to Basket my dog drinking. And anybody listening to any dog's drinking will see what I mean.

JOHN UPDIKE

It comes down to what is language? Up to now, until this age of mass literacy, language has been something spoken. In utterance there's a minimum of slowness. In trying to treat words as chisel strokes you run the risk of losing the quality of utterance, the rhythm of utterance, the happiness. A phrase out of Mark Twain — he describes a raft hitting a bridge and says that it "went all to smash and scatteration like a box of matches struck by lightning." The beauty of "scatteration" could only have occurred to a talkative man, a man who had been brought up among people who were talking and who loved to talk himself. I'm aware myself of a certain dryness of this reservoir, this backlog of spoken talk. A Rumanian once said to me that Americans are always telling stories. I'm not sure this is as true as it once was. Where we once used to spin yarns, now we sit in front of the TV and receive pictures. I'm not sure the younger generation even knows how to gossip. But, as for a writer, if he has something to tell, he should perhaps type it almost as fast as he could talk it. We must look to the organic world, not the inorganic world, for metaphors; and just as the organic world has periods of repose and periods of great speed and exercise, so I think the writer's process should be organically varied. But there's a kind of tautness that you should feel within yourself no matter how slow or fast you're spinning out the reel.

EUDORA WELTY

At the time of writing, I don't write for my friends or myself, either; I write for *it*, for the pleasure of *it*. I believe if I stopped to wonder what So-and-so would think, or what I'd feel like if this were read by a stranger, I would be paralyzed. I care what my friends think, very deeply — and it's only after they've read the finished thing that I really can rest, deep down. But in the writing, I have to just keep going straight through with only the *thing* in mind and what it dictates.

It's so much an inward thing that reading the proofs later can be a real shock. When I received them for my first book — no, I guess it was for *Delta Wedding* — I thought, *I* didn't write this. It was a page of dialogue — I might as well have never seen it before. I wrote to my editor, John Woodburn, and told him something had happened to that page in the typesetting. He was kind, not even surprised — maybe this happens to all writers. He called me up and read me from the manuscript — word for word what the proofs said. Proofs don't shock me any longer, yet there's still a strange moment with every book when I move from the position of writer to the position of reader, and I suddenly see my words with the eyes of the cold public. It gives me a terrible sense of exposure, as if I'd gotten sunburned.

E. B. WHITE

A publisher in Chicago has sent us a pocket calculating machine by which we may test our writing to see whether it is intelligible. The calculator was developed by General Motors, who, not satisfied with giving the world a Cadillac, now dream of bringing perfect understanding to men. The machine (it is simply a celluloid card with a dial) is called the Reading-Ease

Calculator and shows four grades of "reading ease" — Very Easy, Easy, Hard, and Very Hard. You count your words and syllables, set the dial, and an indicator lets you know whether anybody is going to understand what you have written. An instruction book came with it, and after mastering the simple rules we lost no time in running a test on the instruction book itself, to see how *that* writer was doing. The poor fellow! His leading essay, the one on the front cover, tested Very Hard.

Our next step was to study the first phrase on the face of the calculator: "How to test Reading-Ease of written matter." There is, of course, no such thing as reading ease of written matter. There is the ease with which matter can be read, but that is a condition of the reader, not of the matter. Thus the inventors and distributors of this calculator get off to a poor start, with a Very Hard instruction book and a slovenly phrase. Already they have one foot caught in the briar patch of English usage.

Not only did the author of the instruction book score badly on the front cover, but inside the book he used the word "personalize" in an essay on how to improve one's writing. A man who likes the word "personalize" is entitled to his choice, but we wonder whether he should be in the business of giving advice to writers. "Whenever possible," he wrote, "personalize your writing by directing it to the reader." As for us, we would as lief Simonize our grandmother as personalize our writing.

In the same envelope with the calculator, we received another training aid for writers — a booklet called *How to Write Better*, by Rudolf Flesch. This, too, we studied, and it quickly demonstrated the broncolike ability of the English language to throw whoever leaps cocksurely into the saddle. The language not only can toss a rider but knows a thousand tricks for tossing him, each more gay than the last. Dr. Flesch stayed in the saddle only a moment or two. Under the heading "Think Before You Write," he wrote, "The main thing to consider is your *purpose* in writing. Why are you sitting down to write?" And Echo answered: Because, sir, it is more comfortable than standing up.

Communication by the written word is a subtler (and more beautiful) thing than Dr. Flesch or General Motors imagines. They contend that the "average reader" is capable of reading only what tests Easy, and that the writer should write at or below this level. This is a presumptuous and degrading idea. There is no average reader, and to reach down toward this mythical character is to deny that each of us is on the way up, is ascending. ("Ascending," by the way, is a word Dr. Flesch advises writers to stay away from. Too unusual.)

It is our belief that no writer can improve his work until he discards the dulcet notion that the reader is feeble-minded, for writing is an act of faith, not a trick of grammar. Ascent is at the heart of the matter. A country whose writers are following a calculating machine downstairs is not ascending — if you will pardon the expression — and a writer who questions the capacity of the person at the other end of the line is not a writer at all, merely a schemer. The movies long ago decided that a wider communication could be achieved by a deliberate descent to a lower level, and they walked proudly down until they reached the cellar. Now they are groping for the light switch, hoping to find the way out.

We have studied Dr. Flesch's instructions diligently, but we return for guidance in these matters to an earlier American, who wrote with more patience, more confidence. "I fear chiefly," he wrote, "lest my expression may not be *extra-vagant* enough, may not wander far enough beyond the narrow limits of my daily experience, so as to be adequate to the truth of which I have been convinced. . . . Why level downward to our dullest perception always, and praise that as common sense? The commonest sense is the sense of men asleep, which they express by snoring." .

Run that through your calculator! It may come out Hard, it may come out Easy. But it will come out whole, and it will last forever.

WILLIAM CARLOS WILLIAMS

A man writes as he does because he doesn't know any better way to do it, to represent exactly what he has to say CLEAN of the destroying, falsifying, besmutching agencies with which he is surrounded. Everything he does is an explanation. He is always trying his very best to refine his work until it is nothing else but "useful knowledge." I say everything, every minutest thing that is part of a work of art is good only when it is useful and that any other explanation of the "work" would be less useful than the work itself.

VIRGINIA WOOLF

If the essay admits more properly than biography or fiction of sudden boldness and metaphor, and can be polished till every atom of its surface shines, there are dangers in that too. We are soon in sight of ornament. Soon the current, which is the lifeblood of literature, runs slow; and instead of sparkling and flashing or moving with a quieter impulse which has a deeper excitement, words coagulate together in frozen sprays which, like the grapes on a Christmas tree, glitter for a single night, but are dusty and garish the day after. The temptation to decorate is great where the theme may be of the slightest.

EDWARD
ABBEY

B ORN IN PENNSYLVANIA, Edward Abbey (1926–1989) lived for forty years
in the Southwest, in love with the desert and with places of wild, rough beauty
like Aravaipa Canyon. Abbey discovered the West in 1948 when he arrived fresh
from the East to study at the University of New Mexico. When he died in 1989, the
way of his dying became legend. His friend Edward Hoagland (see his essay, page
249) tells the story.

> Two days before the event he decided to leave the hospital, wishing
> to die in the desert; at sunup he had himself disconnected from
> the tubes and machinery. His wife, Clarke, and three friends drove
> him as far out of town as his condition allowed. They built a
> campfire for him to look at, until, feeling death at hand, he crawled
> into his sleeping bag with Clarke. But by noon, finding he was
> still alive and possibly better, he asked to be taken home and placed
> on a mattress on the floor of his writing cabin. There he said his
> gentle good-byes.
>
> His written instructions were that he should be "transported
> in the bed of a pickup truck" deep into the desert and buried
> anonymously, wrapped in his sleeping bag, in the beautiful spot
> where his grave would never be found, with "lots of rocks" piled
> on top to keep coyotes off.

In politics Abbey liked to call himself an "agrarian anarchist." While he loved
the land and its natural flora and fauna with a passion, anger as well as love gave
energy to Edward Abbey's writing. His best-known novel, with a large underground
following, is **The Monkey Wrench Gang** (1975), in which ecovigilantes sabotage
polluters and developers. Probably his best work was done in the essay, beginning

—— Photo by Jay Dusard

with the collection Desert Solitaire *(1968) and continuing through* Abbey's Road *(1979)*, Down the River *(1982), from which we take "Aravaipa Canyon," and* Beyond the Wall *(1984).* Hayduke Lives *(1991) was his last novel, published posthumously.* Slumgullion Stew *(1984) is a reader which brings fiction and essay together. His love of the natural world attacks exploiters, developers, engineers, and scientists; his passion for mystery finds its enemy in a scientific mind that denies multiplicity. At times he writes out of passion for the natural world, almost like Solomon singing his songs. At times, like Jeremiah, he denounces the destroyers.*

The great celebrators of place in literature are rarely native to the places they celebrate; they are aliens who discover and choose the beloved place. Often they look back with contempt on their younger selves. When Edward Abbey arrived in New Mexico as a student, he tells us in an essay, he considered, "like most simpleminded Easterners" that "a cowboy was a kind of mythic hero." After a time, he no longer idolized the cowboy. Nor the cow. He told us that if he were rich enough to buy a cattle ranch, he would shoot the cattle. "Shoot them all, and stock the place with real animals, real game, real protein: elk, buffalo, pronghorn antelope, bighorn sheep, moose. And some purely decorative animals, like eagles. We need more eagles. And wolves. We need more wolves. Mountain lions and bears. Especially, of course, grizzly bears. Down in the desert, I would stock every water tank, every waterhole, every stock pond, with alligators."

Images, anecdotes, details, and exact description locate us in the loved places. Although Abbey gives us the look of things, he does not leave us with snapshots: Language embodies the precision of his looking and the passion of his advocacy.

Aravaipa Canyon

Southeast of Phoenix and northeast of Tucson, in the Pinal Mountains, is a short deep gorge called Aravaipa Canyon. It is among the few places in Arizona with a permanent stream of water and in popular estimation one of the most beautiful. I am giving away no secrets here: Aravaipa Canyon has long been well known to hikers, campers, horsemen, and hunters from the nearby cities. The federal Bureau of Land Management (BLM), charged with administration of the canyon, recently decreed it an official Primitive Area, thus guaranteeing its fame. Demand for enjoyment of the canyon is so great that the BLM has been obliged to institute a rationing program: No one camps here without a permit and only a limited number of such permits are issued.

Two friends and I took a walk into Aravaipa Canyon a few days ago. We walked because there is no road. There is hardly even a foot trail. Twelve miles long from end to end, the canyon is mostly occupied by the little river which gives it its name, and by stream banks piled with slabs of fallen rock from the cliffs above, the whole overgrown with cactus, trees, and riparian desert shrubbery.

Aravaipa is an Apache name (some say Pima, some say Papago) and the commonly accepted meaning is "laughing waters." The name fits. The stream is brisk, clear, about a foot deep at normal flow levels, churning its way around boulders, rippling over gravel bars, plunging into pools with bright and noisy vivacity. Schools of loach minnow, roundtail chub, spike dace, and Gila mudsuckers — rare and endemic species — slip and slither past your ankles as you wade into the current. The water is too warm to support trout or other varieties of what are called game fish; the fish here live out their lives undisturbed by anything more than horses' hooves and the sneaker-shod feet of hikers. (PLEASE DO NOT MOLEST THE FISH.)

The Apaches who gave the name to this water and this canyon are not around anymore. Most of that particular band — unarmed old men, women, children — huddled in a cave near the mouth of Aravaipa Canyon, were exterminated in the 1880s by a death squad of American pioneers, aided by Mexicans and Papagos, from the nearby city of Tucson. The reason for this vigilante action is obscure (suspicion of murder and cattle stealing) but the results were clear. No more Apaches in Aravaipa Canyon. During pauses in the gunfire, as the pioneers reloaded their rifles, the surviving Indians could have heard the sound of laughing waters. One hundred and twenty-five were killed, the remainder relocated in the White Mountain Reservation to the northeast. Since then those people have given us no back talk at all.

Trudging upstream and over rocky little beaches, we are no more trou-   5
bled by ancient history than are the mudsuckers in the pools. We prefer to enjoy the scenery. The stone walls stand up on both sides, twelve hundred feet high in the heart of the canyon. The rock is of volcanic origin, rosy-colored andesites and buff, golden, consolidated tuff. Cleavages and fractures across the face of the walls form perfect stairways and sometimes sloping ramps, slick as sidewalks. On the beaches lie obsidian boulders streaked with veins of quartzite and pegmatite.

The walls bristle with spiky rock gardens of formidable desert vegetation. Most prominent is the giant saguaro cactus, growing five to fifty feet tall out of crevices in the stone you might think could barely lodge a flower. The barrel cactus, with its pink fishhook thorns, thrives here on the sunny side; and clusters of hedgehog cactus, and prickly pear with names like clockface and cows-tongue, have wedged roots into the rock. Since most of the wall is vertical, parallel to gravity, these plants grow first outward then upward, forming right-angled bends near the base. It looks difficult but they do it. They like it here.

Also present are tangles of buckhorn, staghorn, chainfruit, and teddybear cholla; the teddybear cholla is a cactus so thick with spines it glistens under the sun as if covered with fur. From more comfortable niches in the rock grow plants like the sotol, a thing with sawtooth leaves and a flower stalk ten feet tall. The agave, a type of lily, is even bigger, and its leaves are long, rigid, pointed like bayonets. Near the summit of the cliffs, where the moisture is insufficient to support cactus, we see gray-green streaks of lichen clinging to the stone like a mold.

The prospect at streamside is conventionally sylvan, restful to desert-weary eyes. Great cottonwoods and sycamores shade the creek's stony shores; when we're not wading in water we're wading through a crashing autumn debris of green-gold cottonwood and dusty-red sycamore leaves. Other trees flourish here — willow, salt cedar, alder, desert hackberry, and a kind of wild walnut. Cracked with stones, the nuts yield a sweet but frugal meat. At the water's edge is a nearly continuous growth of peppery-flavored watercress. The stagnant pools are full of algae; and small pale frogs, tree-frogs, and leopard frogs leap from the bank at our approach and dive into the water; they swim for the deeps with kicking legs, quick breaststrokes.

We pass shadowy, intriguing side canyons with names like Painted Cave (ancient pictographs), Iceberg (where the sun seldom shines), and Virgus (named in honor of himself by an early settler in the area). At midday we enter a further side canyon, one called Horsecamp, and linger here for a lunch of bread, cheese, and water. We contemplate what appears to be a bottomless pool.

The water in this pool has a dark clarity, like smoked glass, transparent   10
but obscure. We see a waterlogged branch six feet down resting on a ledge but cannot see to the bottom. The water feels intensely cold to hand and foot; a few tadpoles have attached themselves to the stony rim of the pool just beneath the surface of the water. They are sluggish, barely animate. One waterbug, the kind called boatman, propels itself with limp oars down toward darkness when I extend my hand toward it.

Above the pool is a thirty-foot bluff of sheer, vesiculated, fine-grained, monolithic gray rock with a glossy chute carved down its face. Flash floods, pouring down that chute with driving force, must have drilled this basin in the rock below. The process would require a generous allowance of time — ten thousand, twenty thousand years — give or take a few thousand. Only a trickle of water from a ring of seeps° enters the pool now, on this hot still blazing day in December. Feels like 80°F; a month from now it may be freezing; in June 110°. In the silence I hear the rasping chant of locusts — that universal lament for mortality and time — here in this canyon where winter seldom comes.

The black and bottomless pool gleams in the shining rock — a sinister paradox, to a fanciful mind. To any man of natural piety this pool, this place, this silence, would suggest reverence, even fear. But I'm an apostate Presbyterian from a long-ago Pennsylvania: I shuck my clothes, jump in, and touch bottom only ten feet down. Bedrock bottom, as I'd expected, and if any Grendels° dwell in this inky pool they're not inclined to reveal themselves today.

---

seeps Small pools formed by water oozing from underground to the surface.

Grendels In the Old English epic *Beowulf*, Grendel is the monster slain by the hero, Beowulf.

We return to the Aravaipa. Halfway back to camp and the canyon entrance we pause to inspect a sycamore that seems to be embracing a boulder. The trunk of the tree has grown around the rock. Feeling the tree for better understanding, I hear a clatter of loose stones, look up, and see six, seven, eight bighorn sheep perched on the rimrock a hundred feet above us. Three rams, five ewes. They are browsing at the local salad bar — brittlebush, desert holly, bursage, and jojoba — aware of us but not alarmed. We watch them for a long time as they move casually along the rim and up a talus slope beyond, eating as they go, halting now and then to stare back at the humans staring up at them.

Once, years before, I had glimpsed a mountain lion in this canyon, following me through the twilight. It was the only mountain lion I had ever seen, so far, in the wild. I stopped, the big cat stopped, we peered at each other through the gloom. Mutual curiosity: I felt more wonder than fear. After a minute, or perhaps it was five minutes, I made a move to turn. The lion leaped up into the rocks and melted away.

We see no mountain lions this evening. Nor any of the local deer, either Sonoran whitetail or the desert mule deer, although the little heart-shaped tracks of the former are apparent in the sand. Javelina, or peccary, too, reside in this area; piglike animals with tusks, oversized heads, and tapering bodies, they roam the slopes and gulches in family bands (like the Apaches), living on roots, tubers, and innards of barrel cactus, on grubs, insects, and carrion. Omnivorous, like us, and equally playful, if not so dangerous. Any desert canyon with permanent water, like Aravaipa, will be as full of life as it is beautiful. 15

We stumble homeward over the stones and through the anklebone-chilling water. The winter day seems alarmingly short; it is.

We reach the mouth of the canyon and the old trail uphill to the roadhead in time to see the first stars come out. Barely in time. Nightfall is quick in this arid climate and the air feels already cold. But we have earned enough memories, stored enough mental-emotional images in our heads, from one brief day in Aravaipa Canyon, to enrich the urban days to come. As Thoreau found a universe in the woods around Concord, any person whose senses are alive can make a world of any natural place, however limited it might seem, on this subtle planet of ours.

"The world is big but it is comprehensible," says R. Buckminster Fuller. But it seems to me that the world is not nearly big enough and that any portion of its surface, left unpaved and alive, is infinitely rich in details and relationships, in wonder, beauty, mystery, comprehensible only in part. The very existence of existence is itself suggestive of the unknown — not a problem but a mystery.

We will never get to the end of it, never plumb the bottom of it, never know the whole of even so small and trivial and useless and precious a place as Aravaipa. Therein lies our redemption.

AFTERWORD

This essay is a classic of description. Without Abbey's visual images, his assertions would flatten themselves onto a banal page. In paragraph 17, he cites Thoreau and continues, "any person whose senses are alive can make a world of any natural place, however limited it might seem, on this subtle planet of ours." When he gives us these common words — only "alive" and "subtle" ascribe value — he has already performed for us, with exquisite skill and invention, two thousand words of acute seeing, making alive a "natural place."

At the end of an essay fertile in joyous evocation of Aravaipa Canyon, he finds and names his enemy of the day: the engineer and inventor R. Buckminster Fuller, creator of the geodesic dome, who found this world "comprehensible." For Abbey only the incomprehensible, not to mention the unpaved, survives contempt. Abbey's "wonder, beauty, mystery" — three abstract sisters — could sound naive were it not for his earlier density of detail and image. He ends his descriptive essay with the earned diction of religious thought.

BOOKS AVAILABLE IN PAPERBACK

Abbey's Road: Take the Other. New York: Dutton. *Essays.*

The Best of Edward Abbey. San Francisco: Sierra Club Books. *Essays.*

Beyond the Wall. New York: Henry Holt. *Essays.*

Black Sun. New York: Avon. *Novel.*

The Brave Cowboy. New York: Avon. *Novel.*

Desert Solitaire: A Season in the Wilderness. New York: Ballantine. *Essays.*

Down the River. New York: Dutton. *Essays.*

Edward Abbey Reader. New York: Henry Holt. *Essays.*

Fire on the Mountain. New York: Avon. *Novel.*

Fool's Progress: An Honest Novel. New York: Avon.

Good News. New York: Dutton. *Novel.*

Hayduke Lives. Boston: Little, Brown. *Novel.*

The Journey Home: Some Words in Defense of the American West. New York: Dutton. *Nonfiction.*

The Monkey Wrench Gang. New York: Avon. *Novel.*

One Life at a Time, Please. New York: Henry Holt. *Essays.*

A Voice Crying in the Wilderness (Vox Clamatis in Deserto): *Notes from a Secret Journal.* New York: St. Martin's Press. *Essays.*

MARGARET ATWOOD

*B*ORN IN OTTOWA, *Ontario (1939), Margaret Atwood did not attend school for a full year until she was eleven years old. Her father was an entomologist who worked for the Canadian government (her mother was a dietician), and the family moved every April into the backwoods of Quebec, where her father studied insects until November. A good deal of the bush works itself into Atwood's writing.*

At sixteen she decided that writing would be her life: "It was suddenly the only thing I wanted to do." Best known as a novelist — The Edible Woman *(1969),* Surfacing *(1972),* Lady Oracle *(1976),* Life Before Man *(1979),* Bodily Harm *(1982),* The Handmaid's Tale *(1985), and* Cat's Eye *(1989) — she first published as a poet, and in 1987 Houghton Mifflin published a new* Selected Poems *in two volumes. Like many freelance writers, Margaret Atwood has tried her hand at other genres as well: children's books, collections of short stories (*Dancing Girls, *1977;* Bluebeard's Egg, *1983), anthologies of Canadian poetry, television plays — and of course the essay. Her essay collection,* Second Words, *appeared in 1982. In 1993 she published her most recent novel,* The Robber Bride.

In 1994, the Michigan Quarterly Review *published an issue devoted to the male body, from which we take "Alien Territory" as well as John Updike's "The Disposable Rocket" (p. 571). When an MQR issue on the female body appeared back in 1990, Joyce Carol Oates chose the paired essays by Atwood and Updike for the annual collection* Best American Essays 1991. *Surely the two are aware, writing their essays, that they collaborate as friendly adversaries.*

When she decided to become a writer, Atwood remembers, she "was scared to death for a couple of reasons. For one thing, I was Canadian, and the prospects for being a Canadian and a writer, both at the same time, in 1960, were dim. The only

Photo by Anthony Loew

writers I had encountered in high school had been dead and English . . . but it was more complicated than that, because, in addition to being a Canadian, I was also a woman." In her life's work, she has of course converted these prospective limitations into a double blessing. Prejudice invited energetic response. From the vantage point of a Canadian woman, she writes books that leave modifiers behind (adjectives like Southern *poet* or Swiss *novelist* are diminutives; subcategories, small pools) for the largest ocean of literature.

In 1972, she published a book on Canadian letters, Survival, *which provoked controversy; certainly her feminist novels have engendered the same. Firsthand perceptions of oppression and bias have widened in later work into concern about more general political repressiveness. One critic suggests that Atwood's bias against bias is inherited: "Before Margaret Atwood's ancestors emigrated to Canada, one of them — a certain Mary Webster of Connecticut — was accused of witchcraft and hanged. But when the town fathers came around the next day to cut her down, Webster was still alive (either miraculously or thanks to the ineptitude of her accusers); because of the principles of double jeopardy, she was allowed to go free. . . . As a writer who has managed both to make a devastating attack on contemporary American political trends and to get critical acclaim for it, Atwood apparently inherited old Mary's neck."*

The United States has been important in Margaret Atwood's life not only as *enemy or potential enemy. Her writing is popular here as it is in England. When she went to Massachusetts after her Canadian college, she learned about her own country by living outside it. Ten thousand writers, exiled by choice, for study, or for pleasure, have learned who they were only by leaving the place that made them — and by returning with new eyes.*

Alien Territory

[handwritten annotation: Red rivers = blood / wish-wash, wish-wash = heartbeat / birth]

1

He conceives himself in alien territory. Not his turf — alien! Listen! The rushing of the red rivers, the rustling of the fresh leaves in the dusk, always in the dusk, under the dark stars, and the wish-wash, wish-wash of the heavy soothing sea, which becomes — yes! — the drums of the natives, beating, beating, louder, faster, lower, slower. Are they hostile? Who knows, because they're invisible.

He sleeps and wakes, wakes and sleeps, and suddenly all is movement and suffering and terror and he is shot out gasping for breath into blinding light and a place that's even more dangerous, where food is scarce and two enormous giants stand guard over his wooden prison. Shout as he might, rattle the bars, nobody comes to let him out. One of the giants is boisterous and hair-covered, with a big stick; the other walks more softly but has two enormous bulgy comforts which she selfishly refuses to detach and give away, to him. Neither of them looks anything like him, and their language is incomprehensible.

Aliens! What can he do? And to make it worse, they surround him with animals — bears, rabbits, cats, giraffes — each one of them stuffed and, evidently, castrated, because although he looks and looks, all they have at best is a tail. Is this the fate the aliens have in store for him, as well?

Where did I come from? he asks, for what will not be the first time. *Out of me,* the bulgy one says fondly, as if he should be pleased. Out of *where*? Out of *what*? He covers his ears, shutting out the untruth, the shame, the pulpy horror. It is not to be thought, it is not to be borne!

No wonder that at the first opportunity he climbs out the window and   5
joins a gang of other explorers, each one of them an exile, an immigrant, like himself. Together they set out on their solitary journeys.

What are they searching for? Their homeland. Their true country. The place they came from, which can't possibly be here.

obsession with penis size

2

All men are created equal, as someone said who was either very hopeful or very mischievous. What a lot of anxiety could have been avoided if he'd only kept his mouth shut.

Sigmund was wrong about the primal scene: Mom and Dad, keyhole version. That might be upsetting, true, but there's another one:

Five guys standing outside, pissing into a snowbank, a river, the underbrush, pretending not to look down. Or maybe *not* looking down: gazing upward, at the stars, which gives us the origin of astronomy. Anything to avoid comparisons, which aren't so much odious as intimidating.

And not only astronomy: quantum physics, engineering, laser technol-   10
ogy, all numeration between zero and infinity. Something safely abstract, detached from you; a transfer of the obsession with size to anything at all. Lord, Lord, they measure everything: the height of the Great Pyramids, the rate of fingernail growth, the multiplication of viruses, the sands of the sea, the number of angels that can dance on the head of a pin. And then it's only a short step to proving that God is a mathematical equation. Not a person. Not a body, Heaven forbid. Not one like yours. Not an earthbound one, not one with size and therefore pain.

When you're feeling blue, just keep on whistling. Just keep on measuring. Just don't look down.

3

The history of war is a history of killed bodies. That's what war is: bodies killing other bodies, bodies being killed.

Some of the killed bodies are those of women and children, as a side effect you might say. Fallout, shrapnel, napalm, rape and skewering, anti-personnel devices. But most of the killed bodies are men. So are most of those doing the killing.

Why do men want to kill the bodies of other men? Women don't want to kill the bodies of other women. By and large. As far as we know.

Here are some traditional reasons: Loot. Territory. Lust for power. Hormones. Adrenaline high. Rage. God. Flag. Honor. Righteous anger. Revenge. Oppression. Slavery. Starvation. Defense of one's life. Love; or, a desire to protect the women and children. From what? From the bodies of other men. 15

What men are most afraid of is not lions, not snakes, not the dark, not women. Not any more. What men are most afraid of is the body of another man.

Men's bodies are the most dangerous things on earth.

4

On the other hand, it could be argued that men don't have any bodies at all. Look at the magazines! Magazines for women have women's bodies on the covers, magazines for men have women's bodies on the covers. When men appear on the covers of magazines, it's magazines about money, or about world news. Invasions, rocket launches, political coups, interest rates, elections, medical breakthroughs. *Reality.* Not *entertainment.* Such magazines show only the heads, the unsmiling heads, the talking heads, the decision-making heads, and maybe a little glimpse, a coy flash of suit. How do we know there's a body, under all that discreet pinstriped tailoring? We don't, and maybe there isn't.

What does this lead us to suppose? That women are bodies with heads attached, and men are heads with bodies attached? Or not, depending.

You can have a body, though, if you're a rock star, an athlete, or a gay model. As I said, *entertainment.* Having a body is not altogether serious. 20

5

Or else too serious for words.

The thing is: Men's bodies aren't dependable. Now it does, now it doesn't, and so much for the triumph of the will. A man is the puppet of his body, or vice versa. He and it make tomfools of each other: It lets him down. Or up, at the wrong moment. Just stare hard out the schoolroom window and recite the multiplication tables and pretend this isn't happening! Your face at least can be immobile. Easier to have a trained dog, which will do what you want it to, nine times out of ten.

The other thing is: Men's bodies are detachable. Consider the history of statuary: The definitive bits get knocked off so easily, through revolution or prudery or simple transportation, with leaves stuck on for substitutes, fig or grape; or in more northern climates, maple. A man and his body are soon parted.

In the old old days, you became a man through blood. Through incisions, tattoos, splinters of wood; through an intimate wound, and the refusal to flinch. Through being beaten by older boys, in the dormitory, with a wooden paddle you were forced to carve yourself. The torments varied, but they were all torments. *It's a boy,* they cry with joy. *Let's cut some off!*

Every morning I get down on my knees and thank God for not creating 25 me a man. A man so chained to unpredictability. A man so much at the mercy of himself. A man so prone to sadness. A man who has to take it like a man. A man, who can't fake it.

In the gap between desire and enactment, noun and verb, intention and infliction, *want* and *have,* compassion begins.

6

Bluebeard ran off with the third sister, intelligent though beautiful, and shut her up in his palace. *Everything here is yours, my dear,* he said to her. *Just don't open the small door. I will give you the key; however I expect you not to use it.*

Believe it or not, this sister was in love with him, even though she knew he was a serial killer. She roamed over the whole palace, ignoring the jewels and the silk dresses and the piles of gold. Instead she went through the medicine cabinet and the kitchen drawers, looking for clues to his uniqueness. Because she loved him, she wanted to understand him. She also wanted to cure him. She thought she had the healing touch.

Women who love mad men

alluring, exciting men — only get into trouble

But she didn't find out a lot. In his closet there were suits and ties and matching shoes and casual wear, some golf outfits and a tennis racquet, and some jeans for when he wanted to rake up the leaves. Nothing unusual, nothing kinky, nothing sinister. She had to admit to being a little disappointed.

Men who don't know the power of their own bodies

She found his previous women quite easily. They were in the linen closet, neatly cut up and ironed flat and folded, stored in mothballs and lavender. Bachelors acquire such domestic skills. The women didn't make much of an impression on her, except the one who looked like his mother. That one she took out with rubber gloves on and slipped into the incinerator in the garden. *Maybe it was his mother,* she thought. *If so, good riddance.*

She read through his large collection of cookbooks, and prepared the dishes on the most-thumbed pages. At dinner he was politeness itself, pulling out her chair and offering more wine and leading the conversation around to topics of the day. She said gently that she wished he would talk more about his feelings. He said that if she had his feelings, she wouldn't want to talk about them either. This intrigued her. She was now more in love with him and more curious than ever.

Well, she thought, *I've tried everything else; it's the small door or nothing. Anyway, he gave me the key.* She waited until he had gone to the office or wherever it was he went, and made straight for the small door. When she opened it, what should be inside but a dead child. A small dead child with its eyes wide open.

It's mine, he said, coming up behind her. *I gave birth to it. I warned you. Weren't you happy with me?*

It looks like you, she said, not turning around, not knowing what to say. She realized now that he was not sane in any known sense of the word, but she still hoped to talk her way out of it. She could feel the love seeping out of her. Her heart was dry ice.

It is me, he said sadly. *Don't be afraid.*

Where are we going? she said, because it was getting dark, and there was suddenly no floor.

Deeper, he said.

7

Those ones. Why do women like them? They have nothing to offer, none of the usual things. They have short attention spans, falling-apart clothes, old beat-up cars, if any. The cars break down, and they try to fix them, and don't succeed, and give up. They go on long walks, from which they forget to return. They prefer weeds to flowers. They tell trivial fibs. They perform clumsy tricks with oranges and pieces of string, hoping desperately that someone will laugh. They don't put food on the table. They don't make money. Don't, can't, won't.

They offer nothing. They offer the great clean sweep of nothing, the unseen sky during a blizzard, the dark pause between moon and moon. They offer their poverty, an empty wooden bowl; the bowl of a beggar, whose gift is to ask. Look into it, look down deep, where potential coils like smoke, and you might hear anything. Nothing has yet been said.

They have bodies, however. Their bodies are unlike the bodies of other men. Their bodies are verbalized. *Mouth, eye, hand, foot,* they say. Their bodies have weight, and move over the ground, step by step, like yours. Like you they roll in the hot mud of the sunlight, like you they are amazed by morning, like you they can taste the wind, like you they sing. *Love,* they say, and at the time they always mean it, as you do also. They can say *lust* as well, and *disgust;* you wouldn't trust them otherwise. They say the worst things you have ever dreamed. They open locked doors. All this is given to them for nothing.

They have their angers. They have their despair, which washes over them like gray ink, blanking them out, leaving them immobile, in metal kitchen chairs, beside closed windows, looking out at the brick walls of deserted factories, for years and years. Yet nothing is with them; it keeps faith with them, and from it they bring back messages:

Hurt, they say and suddenly their bodies hurt again, like real bodies. *Death,* they say, making the word sound like the backwash of a wave. Their bodies die, and waver, and turn to mist. And yet they can exist in two worlds at once: lost in earth or eaten by flames, and here. In this room, when you re-say them, in their own words.

But why do women like them? Not *like,* I mean to say: *adore.* (Remember, that despite everything, despite all I have told you, the rusted cars, the greasy wardrobes, the lack of breakfasts, the hopelessness, remain the same.)

Because if they can say their own bodies, they could say yours also. Because they could say *skin* as if it meant something, not only to them but to you. Because one night, when the snow is falling and the moon is blotted out, they could put their empty hands, their hands filled with poverty, their beggar's hands, on your body, and bless it, and tell you it is made of light.

AFTERWORD

Atwood is a poet and a novelist first, which may be why she called her essay collection Second Words. In her essay on the male body — or about the creatures who inhabit male bodies — she tells stories, using her first words of image and symbol. Atwood thinks about her topic with her primary tools of narrative and metaphor. Imagining herself in a male body at the beginning, she makes woman into landscape or geography. This is a figure for femininity that feminists have learned to deplore because it leaves women insentient, reserving mentality for males. Atwood is known for her irony.

"Men's bodies are the most dangerous things on earth." Atwood's essay, despite its mockery, makes strong statements. "Every morning I get down on my knees and thank God for not creating me a man." Yet look at how the essay ends. Atwood is of two minds, as most of us are — about anything serious. Her poetic and narrative structure, abjuring reasonable argument, embodies the many sides of her feelings.

BOOKS AVAILABLE IN PAPERBACK

Bluebeard's Egg and Other Stories. New York: Fawcett Books. Short stories.

Bodily Harm. New York: Bantam. Novel.

Cat's Eye. New York: Bantam. Novel.

The Circle Game. Toronto: University of Toronto Press–Anansi. Poetry.

Dancing Girls and Other Stories. New York: Bantam. Short stories.

The Edible Woman. New York: Warner. Novel.

For the Birds. Willowdale, Ontario: Firefly Books. Nonfiction.

The Handmaid's Tale. New York: Fawcett Books. Novel.

Journals of Suzanna Moodie: Poems. New York: Oxford University Press.

Lady Oracle. New York: Fawcett Books. Novel.

Life Before Man. Orlando: Holt, Rinehart & Winston. Novel.

Power Politics. Toronto: University of Toronto Press–Anansi. Nonfiction.

The Robber Bride. New York: Doubleday. Novel.

Selected Poems, 1965–1975. Boston: Houghton Mifflin.

Selected Poems II: Poems Selected and New, 1976–1986. Boston: Houghton Mifflin.

Surfacing. New York: Fawcett Books. Novel.

Wilderness Tips. New York: Bantam. Short stories.

JAMES
BALDWIN

WHEN JAMES BALDWIN *died of cancer in 1987, in France where he lived much of his adult life, his death was front-page news. For decades he had been a leading literary spokesman of American black experience, without modification one of our leading writers. One critic said that Baldwin, "more than any other writer, . . . can make one begin to feel what it is really like to have a black skin in a white man's world; and he is especially expert at evoking, not merely the brutally overt physical confrontations between black and white, but the subtle unease that lurks beneath all traffic between the colors."*

He was born in Harlem (1924), a native son of the American black ghetto. He was also born a writer, as near as anybody can be. "I began plotting novels at about the time I learned to read," he once wrote. "My first professional triumph . . . occurred at the age of twelve or thereabouts, when a short story I had written about the Spanish Revolution won some sort of prize in an extremely short-lived church newspaper. I remember the story was censored by the lady editor, though I don't remember why, and I was outraged."

A series of fellowships supported Baldwin when he was young — a Saxton when he was only twenty-one in 1945, a Rosenwald in 1948, a Guggenheim in 1954, a Partisan Review *fellowship in 1956, and support from the Ford Foundation in 1959. His first novel was the autobiographical* Go Tell It on the Mountain *(1953), followed by the essay collection* Notes of a Native Son *(1955). Many novels followed, and many essays.* The Fire Next Time *(1963) was a crucial document in the struggle for civil rights that occupied the sixties before the Vietnam War took center stage. Although he felt fiction to be his calling, outrage led James Baldwin into nonfiction. "One writes out of one thing only — one's own experience," he said. "Everything depends on how relentlessly one forces from this experience the last drop, sweet or bitter, it can possibly give. This is the only real concern of the artist, to recreate out of the disorder of life that order which is art."*

Baldwin was also a playwright, notably of Blues for Mr. Charlie *(1964), and author of short stories. His second novel was* Giovanni's Room *(1956), followed by* Another Country *in 1962. Black with a large white readership, homosexual, an American frequently domiciled in France, Baldwin lived in many worlds. In the sixties he was criticized by black leaders; Eldridge Cleaver spoke of his "agonizing, total hatred of blacks." Langston Hughes, the great writer of the Harlem Renaissance, did not agree with Cleaver but said of Baldwin — what has become almost a commonplace — that "he is much better at provoking thought in an essay than he is in arousing emotion in fiction."*

This essay appeared in the New York Times *in 1979.*

If Black English Isn't a Language, Then Tell Me, What Is?

The argument concerning [the use] or [the status] or [the reality] of black English is rooted in American history and has absolutely nothing to do with the question the argument supposes itself to be posing. The argument has nothing to do with language itself but with the *role* of language. Language, incontestably, reveals the speaker. Language, also, far more dubiously, is meant to define the other — and, in this case, the other is refusing to be defined by a language that has never been able to recognize him.

People evolve a language in order to describe and thus control their circumstances, or in order not to be submerged by a reality that they cannot articulate. (And, if they cannot articulate it, they *are* submerged.) A Frenchman living in Paris speaks a subtly and crucially different language from that of the man living in Marseilles; neither sounds very much like a man living in Quebec; and they would all have great difficulty in apprehending what the man from Guadeloupe, or Martinique, is saying, to say nothing of the man from Senegal — although the "common" language of all these areas is French. But each has paid, and is paying, a different price for this "common" language, in which, as it turns out, they are not saying, and cannot be saying, the same things: They each have very different realities to articulate, or control.

What joins all languages, and all men, is the necessity to confront life, in order, not inconceivably, to outwit death: The price for this is the acceptance, and achievement, of one's temporal identity. So that, for example, though it is not taught in the schools (and this has the potential of becoming a political issue) the south of France still clings to its ancient and musical Provençal, which resists being described as a "dialect." And much of the tension in the Basque countries, and in Wales, is due to the Basque and Welsh determination not to allow their languages to be destroyed. This determination also feeds the flames in Ireland for among the many indignities the Irish have been forced to undergo at English hands is the English contempt for their language.

It goes without saying, then, that language is also a political instrument, means and proof of power. It is the most vivid and crucial key to identity: It reveals the private identity, and connects one with, or divorces one from, the larger, public, or communal identity. There have been, and are, times, and places, when to speak a certain language could be dangerous, even fatal. Or, one may speak the same language, but in such a way that one's antecedents are revealed, or (one hopes) hidden. This is true in France, and is absolutely true in England: The range (and reign) of accents on that damp little island make England coherent for the English and totally incomprehensible for everyone else. To open your mouth in England is (if I may use black English) to "put your business in the street": You have confessed your parents, your youth, your school, your salary, your self-esteem, and alas, your future.

Now, I do not know what white Americans would sound like if there had never been any black people in the United States, but they would not sound the way they sound. *Jazz*, for example, is a very specific sexual term, as in *jazz me, baby*, but white people purified it into the Jazz Age. *Sock it to me*, which means, roughly, the same thing, has been adopted by Nathaniel Hawthorne's descendants with no qualms or hesitations at all, along with *let it all hang out* and *right on! Beat to his socks*, which was once the black's most total and despairing image of poverty, was transformed into a thing called the Beat Generation, which phenomenon was, largely, composed of *uptight*, middle-class white people, imitating poverty, trying to *get down*, to get *with it*, doing their *thing*, doing their despairing best to be *funky*, which we, the blacks, never dreamed of doing — we *were* funky, baby, like *funk* was going out of style.

Now, no one can eat his cake, and have it, too, and it is late in the day to attempt to penalize black people for having created a language that permits the nation its only glimpse of reality, a language without which the nation would be even more *whipped* than it is.

I say that this present skirmish is rooted in American history, and it is. Black English is the creation of the black diaspora. Blacks came to the United States chained to each other, but from different tribes: Neither could speak the other's language. If two black people, at that bitter hour of the world's history, had been able to speak to each other, the institution of chattel slavery could never have lasted as long as it did. Subsequently, the slave was given, under the eye, and the gun, of his master, Congo Square, and the Bible —

or, in other words, and under these conditions, the slave began the formation of the black church, and it is within this unprecedented tabernacle that black English began to be formed. This was not, merely, as in the European example, the adoption of a foreign tongue, but an alchemy that transformed ancient elements into a new language: *A language comes into existence by means of brutal necessity, and the rules of the language are dictated by what the language must convey.*

There was a moment, in time, and in this place, when my brother, or my mother, or my father, or my sister, had to convey to me, for example, the danger in which I was standing from the white man standing just behind me, and to convey this with a speed, and in a language, that the white man could not possibly understand, and that, indeed, he cannot understand, until today. He cannot afford to understand it. This understanding would reveal to him too much about himself, and smash that mirror before which he has been frozen for so long.

Now, if this passion, this skill, this (to quote Toni Morrison) "sheer intelligence," this incredible music, the mighty achievement of having brought a people utterly unknown to, or despised by "history" — to have brought this people to their present, troubled, troubling, and unassailable and unanswerable place — if this absolutely unprecedented journey does not indicate that black English is a language, I am curious to know what definition of language is to be trusted.

A people at the center of the Western world, and in the midst of so 10 hostile a population, has not endured and transcended by means of what is patronizingly called a "dialect." We, the blacks, are in trouble, certainly, but we are not doomed, and we are not inarticulate because we are not compelled to defend a morality that we know to be a lie.

The brutal truth is that the bulk of the white people in America never had any interest in educating black people, except as this could serve white purposes. It is not the black child's language that is in question, it is not his language that is despised: It is his experience. A child cannot be taught by anyone who despises him, and a child cannot afford to be fooled. A child cannot be taught by anyone whose demand, essentially, is that the child repudiate his experience, and all that gives him sustenance, and enter a limbo in which he will no longer be black, and in which he knows that he can never become white. Black people have lost too many black children that way.

And, after all, finally, in a country with standards so untrustworthy, a country that makes heroes of so many criminal mediocrities, a country unable to face why so many of the nonwhite are in prison, or on the needle, or standing, futureless, in the streets — it may very well be that both the child, and his elder, have concluded that they have nothing whatever to learn from the people of a country that has managed to learn so little.

AFTERWORD

Among the old rhetorical patterns of language — devices for thinking that include comparison and contrast, cause and effect, example, process analysis, classification and division — maybe none sounds so boring as definition: "An apple is a spheroid fruit consisting of skin, pulp, and core with seeds. . . ."

But definition can be used for argument, even for polemic, as James Baldwin shows in this essay. To begin with, he defines language by asserting that a language enacts itself by its purposes: "People evolve a language in order to describe and thus control their circumstances, or in order not to be submerged by a reality that they cannot articulate." Utility, not history, provides definition.

The linguist and traveler Baldwin supplies examples from other cultures, within francophone and anglophone cultures, to develop ideas and values intrinsic to his definition. Definition becomes argument as the role of black English supports an indictment of racism. Language is experience, and "It is not the black child's language that is . . . despised: It is his experience."

BOOKS AVAILABLE IN PAPERBACK

The Amen Corner. New York: Dell. *Play.*

Another Country. New York: Dell. *Novel.*

The Devil Finds Work. New York: Dell. *Essays.*

The Evidence of Things Not Seen. New York: Henry Holt. *Nonfiction.*

The Fire Next Time. New York: Dell. *Essays.*

Giovanni's Room. New York: Dell. *Novel.*

Go Tell It on the Mountain. New York: Dell. *Novel.*

Going to Meet the Man. New York: Dell. *Short stories.*

If Beale Street Could Talk. New York: Dell. *Novel.*

Jimmy's Blues: Selected Poems. New York: St. Martin's Press.

Just Above My Head. New York: Dell. *Novel.*

No Name in the Street. New York: Dell. *Nonfiction.*

Nobody Knows My Name. New York: Dell. *Essays.*

Notes of a Native Son. Boston: Beacon Press. *Essays.*

One Day When I Was Lost. New York: Dell. *Play.*

Tell Me How Long the Train's Been Gone. New York: Dell. *Novel.*

JOHN
BERGER

*J*OHN BERGER'S MIND *investigates and creates, using his many talents as painter, art critic, novelist, and poet. Born in London (1926), he served in the British army at the end of World War II, then attended art school in London. He has worked as a painter and as a teacher of drawing, exhibiting his own work in many English galleries. In periodicals, on television, and in many books and collections of essays — among them* Permanent Red: Essays in Seeing *(1960),* The Success and Failure of Picasso *(1965),* The Moment of Cubism *(1969),* The Look of Things *(1972),* The Sense of Sight *(1985) — he has developed a Marxist criticism of art that derives and values painting in relation to society and history.* Ways of Seeing *was a television series that became a book in 1972. He has written books of poems and three screenplays and has translated from the German. He has also published novels, beginning with* A Painter of Our Time *(1958), most notably* G *(1972), which won both the Booker Prize and the James Tait Black Memorial Prize. In 1993, he brought out a 1964 novel,* Corker's Freedom, *published for the first time in the United States. He has also made books of social documentation with the aid of photographer Jean Mohr:* A Fortunate Man *(1982) records the life and work of a physician in rural England, with observations on politics and society.* A Seventh Man *(1975) mixes Mohr's photographs and Berger's prose on the subject of migrant workers in Europe.* Keeping a Rendezvous *(1991) is a recent gathering of critical pieces.*

In his art criticism, fiction, and essays Berger's Marxism continually investigates the impact of society and economics on the individual life. This autobiographical essay about his mother and her death is more personal, less argumentative, than most of his work. We found it in the Threepenny Review.

———— Photo by Jean Mohr

Her Secrets

FOR KATYA

From the age of five or six I was worried about the death of my parents. The inevitability of death was one of the first things I learnt about the world on my own. Nobody else spoke of it yet the signs were so clear.

Every time I went to bed — and in this I am sure I was like millions of other children — the fear that one or both my parents might die in the night touched the nape of my neck with its finger. Such a fear has, I believe, little to do with a particular psychological climate and a great deal to do with nightfall. Yet since it was impossible to say: You won't die in the night, will you? (when Grandmother died, I was told she had gone to have a rest, or — this was from my uncle who was more outspoken — that she had passed over), since I couldn't ask the real question and I sought a reassurance, I invented — like millions before me — the euphemism: See you in the morning! To which either my father or mother, who had come to turn out the light in my bedroom, would reply: See you in the morning, John.

After their footsteps had died away, I would try for as long as possible not to lift my head from the pillow so that the last words spoken remained, trapped like fish in a rock-pool at low tide, between my pillow and ear. The implicit promise of the words was also a protection against the dark. The words promised that I would not (yet) be alone.

Now I'm no longer usually frightened by the dark and my father died ten years ago and my mother a month ago at the age of ninety-three. It would be a natural moment to write an autobiography. My version of my life can no longer hurt either of them. And the book, when finished, would be there, a little like a parent. Autobiography begins with a sense of being alone. It is an orphan form. Yet I have no wish to do so. All that interests me about my past life are the common moments. The moments — which if I relate them well enough — will join countless others lived by people I do not personally know.

Six weeks ago my mother asked me to come and see her; it would be the last time, she said. A few days later, on the morning of my birthday, she believed she was dying. Open the curtains, she asked my brother, so I can see the trees. In fact, she died the following week.

On my birthdays as a child, it was my father rather than she who gave me memorable presents. She was too thrifty. Her moments of generosity were at the table, offering what she had bought and prepared and cooked and served to whoever came into the house. Otherwise she was thrifty. Nor did she ever explain. She was secretive, she kept things to herself. Not for

5

46

her own pleasure, but because the world would not forgive spontaneity, the world was mean. I must make that clearer. She didn't believe life was mean — it was generous — but she had learnt from her own childhood that survival was hard. She was the opposite of quixotic — for she was not born a knight and her father was a warehouse foreman in Lambeth. She pursed her lips together, knitted her brows as she calculated and thought things out and carried on with an unspoken determination. She never asked favors of anyone. Nothing shocked her. From whatever she saw, she just drew the necessary conclusions so as to survive and to be dependent on nobody. If I were Aesop, I would say that in her prudence and persistence my mother resembled the agouti.° (I once wrote about an agouti in the London zoo, but I did not then realize why the animal so touched me.) In my adult life, the only occasions on which we shouted at each other were when she estimated I was being quixotic.

When I was in my thirties she told me for the first time that, ever since I was born, she had hoped I would be a writer. The writers she admired when young were Bernard Shaw, J. M. Barrie, Compton Mackenzie, Warwick Deeping, E. M. Dell. The only painter she really admired was Turner — perhaps because of her childhood on the banks of the Thames.

Most of my books she didn't read. Either because they dealt with subjects which were alien to her or because — under the protective influence of my father — she believed they might upset her. Why suffer surprise from something which, left unopened, gives you pleasure? My being a writer was unqualified for her by what I wrote. To be a writer was to be able to see to the horizon where, anyway, nothing is ever very distinct and all questions are open. Literature had little to do with the writer's vocation as she saw it. It was only a by-product. A writer was a person familiar with the secrets. Perhaps in the end she didn't read my books so that they should remain more secret.

If her hopes of my becoming a writer — and she said they began on the night after I was delivered — were eventually realized, it was not because there were many books in our house (there were few) but because there was so much that was unsaid, so much that I had to discover the existence of on my own at an early age: death, poverty, pain (in others), sexuality . . .

These things were there to be discovered within the house or from its windows — until I left for good, more or less prepared for the outside world, at the age of eight. My mother never spoke of these things. She didn't hide the fact that she was aware of them. For her, however, they were wrapped secrets, to be lived with, but never to be mentioned or opened. Superficially this was a question of gentility, but profoundly, of a respect, a secret loyalty to the enigmatic. My rough and ready preparation for the world did not include a single explanation — it simply consisted of the principle that events carried more weight than the self.

---

agouti   A rodent about the size of a rabbit.

Thus, she taught me very little — at least in the usual sense of the term: she a teacher about life, I a learner. By imitating her gestures I learnt how to roast meat in the oven, how to clean celery, how to cook rice, how to choose vegetables in a market. As a young woman she had been a vegetarian. Then she gave it up because she did not want to influence us children. Why were you a vegetarian? I once asked her, eating my Sunday roast, much later when I was first working as a journalist. Because I'm against killing. She would say no more. Either I understood or I didn't. There was nothing more to be said.

In time — and I understand this only now writing these pages — I chose to visit abattoirs in different cities of the world and to become something of an expert concerning the subject. The unspoken, the unfaceable beckoned me. I followed. Into the abattoirs and, differently, into many other places and situations.

The last, the largest, and the most personally prepared wrapped secret was her own death. Of course I was not the only witness. Of those close to her, I was maybe the most removed, the most remote. But she knew, I think, with confidence that I would pursue the matter. She knew that if anybody can be at home with what is kept a secret, it was me, because I was her son whom she hoped would become a writer.

The clinical history of her illness is a different story about which she herself was totally uncurious. Sufficient to say that with the help of drugs she was not in pain, and that, thanks to my brother and sister-in-law who arranged everything for her, she was not subjected to all the mechanical ingenuity of aids for the artificial prolongation of life.

Of how many deaths — though never till now of my own mother's —   15
have I written? Truly we writers are the secretaries of death.

She lay in bed, propped up by pillows, her head fallen forward, as if asleep.

I shut my eyes, she said, I like to shut my eyes and think. I don't sleep though. If I slept now, I wouldn't sleep at night.

What do you think about?

She screwed up her eyes which were gimlet sharp and looked at me, twinkling, as if I'd never, not even as a small child, asked such a stupid question.

Are you working hard? What are you writing?   20

A play, I answered.

The last time I went to the theater I didn't understand a thing, she said. It's not my hearing that's bad though.

Perhaps the play was obscure, I suggested.

She opened her eyes again. The body has closed shop, she announced. Nothing, nothing at all from here down. She placed a hand on her neck. It's a good thing, make no mistake about it, John, it makes the waiting easier.

On her bedside table was a tin of handcream. I started to massage her   25
left hand.

Do you remember a photograph I once took of your hands? Working hands, you said.

No, I don't.

Would you like some more photos on your table? Katya, her grand-daughter, asked her.

She smiled at Katya and shook her head, her voice very slightly broken by a laugh. It would be *so* difficult, so difficult, wouldn't it, to choose.

She turned towards me. What exactly are you doing?   30

I'm massaging your hand. It's meant to be pleasurable.

To tell you the truth, dear, it doesn't make much difference. What plane are you taking back?

I mumbled, took her other hand.

You are all worried, she said, especially when there are several of you. I'm not. Maureen asked me the other day whether I wanted to be cremated or buried. Doesn't make one iota of difference to me. How could it? She shut her eyes to think.

For the first time in her life and in mine, she could openly place the   35
wrapped enigma between us. She didn't watch me watching it, for we had the habits of a lifetime. Openly she knew that at that moment her faith in a secret was bound to be stronger than any faith of mine in facts. With her eyes still shut, she fingered the Arab necklace I'd attached round her neck with a charm against the evil eye. I'd given her the necklace a few hours before. Perhaps for the first time I had offered her a secret and now her hand kept looking for it.

She opened her eyes. What time is it?

Quarter to four.

It's not very interesting talking to me, you know. I don't have any ideas any more. I've had a good life. Why don't you take a walk.

Katya stayed with her.

When you are very old, she told Katya confidentially, there's one thing   40
that's very very difficult — it's very difficult to persuade other people that you're happy.

She let her head go back onto the pillow. As I came back in, she smiled.

In her right hand she held a crumpled paper handkerchief. With it she dabbed from time to time the corner of her mouth when she felt there was the slightest excess of spittle there. The gesture was reminiscent of one with which, many years before, she used to wipe her mouth after drinking Earl Grey tea and eating watercress sandwiches. Meanwhile with her left hand she fingered the necklace, cushioned on her forgotten bosom.

Love, my mother had the habit of saying, is the only thing that counts in this world. Real love, she would add, to avoid any factitious misunder-standing. But apart from that simple adjective, she never added anything more.

AFTERWORD

"Truly we writers are the secretaries of death."

John Berger's prose is straightforward, a glass of water compared with the rich, complex, personal styles of writers like Annie Dillard and Edward Abbey, who multiply metaphors and visual images. But when Berger requires it, he invents the metaphor or analogy that situates tone or value by its comparison. It is ordinary to note how writers speak often about death; Berger does not say anything so watery. He makes the writer an amanuensis taking down the spoken words of death the dictator.

Other examples, in this essay almost without metaphor, make themselves equally prominent by adding excellence to rarity: When he was a child thinking in bed of his parents' potential deaths, "fear . . . touched the nape of my neck with its finger," or "the most personally prepared wrapped secret was her own death."

BOOKS AVAILABLE IN PAPERBACK

About Looking. New York: Pantheon. *Nonfiction.*

And Our Faces, My Heart, Brief as Photos. New York: Pantheon. *Nonfiction.*

Art in Revolution. New York: Pantheon. *Nonfiction.*

Corker's Freedom. New York: Writers & Readers. *Novel.*

The Foot of Clive. New York: Writers & Readers. *Novel.*

G. New York: Pantheon. *Novel.*

Lilac and Flag. New York: Pantheon. *Novel.*

A Painter of Our Time. New York: Writers & Readers. *Novel.*

Permanent Red: Essays in Seeing. New York: Writers & Readers.

Pig Earth. New York: Pantheon. *Novel.*

The Sense of Sight. New York: Pantheon. *Nonfiction.*

A Seventh Man. New York: Writers & Readers. *Nonfiction.*

The Success and Failure of Picasso. New York: Pantheon. *Nonfiction.*

Ways of Seeing. New York: Penguin. *Nonfiction.*

RAYMOND CARVER

*R*AYMOND CARVER (1938–1988) *was as responsible as anyone for the resurgence of the American short story in the 1980s. The literature of the short story virtually begins with Poe and Hawthorne, and in the twentieth century Americans have continued to serve the genre: Hemingway, Faulkner, Welty, Porter, Flannery O'Connor, Updike. But until recently it had become axiomatic among publishers that even the best book of stories would find no readers. Carver helped to change things; his collections of stories were best-sellers in America, England, and all over the world — translated into Japanese, French, and half a dozen other languages. His collections are* Will You Please Be Quiet, Please? *(1976),* What We Talk About When We Talk About Love *(1981), and* Cathedral *(1983) followed in 1988 by a volume of new and selected stories,* Where I'm Calling From. *In 1983 he collected a miscellany,* Fires: Essays, Poems, Stories. *"My Father's Life" appeared in* Esquire *in 1984. Always a poet, Carver in 1987 published* In a Marine Light, *a selection of his best poems.*

After his death, his publisher issued a last collection of poems, A New Path to the Waterfall *(1989). In 1993 Robert Altman made a film* Short Cuts, *by amalgamating several Carver stories; he was nominated for an Academy Award as best director.*

As a writer of fiction, Carver was called a minimalist, for his stories were usually lean, spare, and bleak. Many stories narrate moments in the lives of people who have failed, often passive and depressed; many of his characters are heavy drinkers, out of work, out of love, separated, or divorced. From this relentless material Carver makes his art; his ear for the way people speak is devastating: "Will you please be quiet, please?"

Photo by Marion Ettlinger

Himself an alcoholic for many years — he stopped drinking in 1977 — Carver started writing when he was nineteen or twenty and began taking classes with the late novelist John Gardner at Chico State College in northern California. His successes were rare, occasional stories in Esquire *or in annual anthologies, until late in the seventies. Despite his sudden international celebrity, he never wavered from his dedication to the art of writing. Most of the year he and Tess Gallagher — also a poet, essayist, and short-story writer — lived in the small town of Port Angeles in the state of Washington, where they wrote and Carver fished for salmon. In 1987 Carver underwent an operation for lung cancer, and in 1988 the cancer returned to his brain. He continued writing stories and poems until he died that summer.*

My Father's Life

My dad's name was Clevie Raymond Carver. His family called him Raymond and friends called him C. R. I was named Raymond Clevie Carver, Jr. I hated the "Junior" part. When I was little my dad called me Frog, which was okay. But later, like everybody else in the family, he began calling me Junior. He went on calling me this until I was thirteen or fourteen and announced that I wouldn't answer to that name any longer. So he began calling me Doc. From then until his death, on June 17, 1967, he called me Doc, or else Son.

When he died, my mother telephoned my wife with the news. I was away from my family at the time, between lives, trying to enroll in the School of Library Science at the University of Iowa. When my wife answered the phone, my mother blurted out, "Raymond's dead!" For a moment, my wife thought my mother was telling her that I was dead. Then my mother made it clear *which* Raymond she was talking about and my wife said, "Thank God. I thought you meant *my* Raymond."

My dad walked, hitched rides, and rode in empty boxcars when he went from Arkansas to Washington State in 1934, looking for work. I don't know whether he was pursuing a dream when he went out to Washington. I doubt it. I don't think he dreamed much. I believe he was simply looking for steady work at decent pay. Steady work was meaningful work. He picked apples for a time and then landed a construction laborer's job on the Grand Coulee Dam. After he'd put aside a little money, he bought a car and drove back to Arkansas to help his folks, my grandparents, pack up for the move west. He said later that they were about to starve down there, and this wasn't meant as a figure of speech. It was during that short while in Arkansas, in a town called Leola, that my mother met my dad on the sidewalk as he came out of a tavern.

"He was drunk," she said. "I don't know why I let him talk to me. His eyes were glittery. I wish I'd had a crystal ball." They'd met once, a year or so before, at a dance. He'd had girlfriends before her, my mother told me. "Your dad always had a girlfriend, even after we married. He was my first and last. I never had another man. But I didn't miss anything."

They were married by a justice of the peace on the day they left for Washington, this big, tall country girl and a farmhand-turned-construction worker. My mother spent her wedding night with my dad and his folks, all of them camped beside the road in Arkansas.

In Omak, Washington, my dad and mother lived in a little place not much bigger than a cabin. My grandparents lived next door. My dad was still working on the dam, and later, with the huge turbines producing electricity and the water backed up for a hundred miles into Canada, he stood in the crowd and heard Franklin D. Roosevelt when he spoke at the construction site. "He never mentioned those guys who died building that dam," my dad said. Some of his friends had died there, men from Arkansas, Oklahoma, and Missouri.

He then took a job in a sawmill in Clatskanie, Oregon, a little town alongside the Columbia River. I was born there, and my mother has a picture of my dad standing in front of the gate to the mill, proudly holding me up to face the camera. My bonnet is on crooked and about to come untied. His hat is pushed back on his forehead, and he's wearing a big grin. Was he going in to work or just finishing his shift? It doesn't matter. In either case, he had a job and a family. These were his salad days.

In 1941 we moved to Yakima, Washington, where my dad went to work as a saw filer, a skilled trade he'd learned in Clatskanie. When war broke out, he was given a deferment because his work was considered necessary to the war effort. Finished lumber was in demand by the armed services, and he kept his saws so sharp they could shave the hair off your arm.

After my dad had moved us to Yakima, he moved his folks into the same neighborhood. By the mid-1940s the rest of my dad's family — his brother, his sister, and her husband, as well as uncles, cousins, nephews, and most of their extended family and friends — had come out from Arkansas. All because my dad came out first. The men went to work at Boise Cascade, where my dad worked, and the women packed apples in the canneries. And in just a little while, it seemed — according to my mother — everybody was better off than my dad. "Your dad couldn't keep money," my mother said. "Money burned a hole in his pocket. He was always doing for others."

The first house I clearly remember living in, at 1515 South Fifteenth Street, in Yakima, had an outdoor toilet. On Halloween night, or just any night, for the hell of it, neighbor kids, kids in their early teens, would carry our toilet away and leave it next to the road. My dad would have to get somebody to help him bring it home. Or these kids would take the toilet and stand it in somebody else's backyard. Once they actually set it on fire. But ours wasn't the only house that had an outdoor toilet. When I was old enough to know what I was doing, I threw rocks at the other toilets when

I'd see someone go inside. This was called bombing the toilets. After a while, though, everyone went to indoor plumbing until, suddenly, our toilet was the last outdoor one in the neighborhood. I remember the shame I felt when my third-grade teacher, Mr. Wise, drove me home from school one day. I asked him to stop at the house just before ours, claiming I lived there.

I can recall what happened one night when my dad came home late to find that my mother had locked all the doors on him from the inside. He was drunk, and we could feel the house shudder as he rattled the door. When he'd managed to force open a window, she hit him between the eyes with a colander and knocked him out. We could see him down there on the grass. For years afterward, I used to pick up this colander — it was as heavy as a rolling pin — and imagine what it would feel like to be hit in the head with something like that.

It was during this period that I remember my dad taking me into the bedroom, sitting me down on the bed, and telling me that I might have to go live with my Aunt LaVon for a while. I couldn't understand what I'd done that meant I'd have to go away from home to live. But this, too — whatever prompted it — must have blown over, more or less, anyway, because we stayed together, and I didn't have to go live with her or anyone else.

I remember my mother pouring his whiskey down the sink. Sometimes she'd pour it all out and sometimes, if she was afraid of getting caught, she'd only pour half of it out and then add water to the rest. I tasted some of his whiskey once myself. It was terrible stuff, and I don't see how anybody could drink it.

After a long time without one, we finally got a car, in 1949 or 1950, a 1938 Ford. But it threw a rod the first week we had it, and my dad had to have the motor rebuilt.

"We drove the oldest car in town," my mother said. "We could have had a Cadillac for all he spent on car repairs." One time she found someone else's tube of lipstick on the floorboard, along with a lacy handkerchief. "See this?" she said to me. "Some floozy left this in the car."

Once I saw her take a pan of warm water into the bedroom where my dad was sleeping. She took his hand from under the covers and held it in the water. I stood in the doorway and watched. I wanted to know what was going on. This would make him talk in his sleep, she told me. There were things she needed to know, things she was sure he was keeping from her.

Every year or so, when I was little, we would take the North Coast Limited across the Cascade Range from Yakima to Seattle and stay in the Vance Hotel and eat, I remember, at a place called the Dinner Bell Cafe. Once we went to Ivar's Acres of Clams and drank glasses of warm clam broth.

In 1956, the year I was to graduate from high school, my dad quit his job at the mill in Yakima and took a job in Chester, a little sawmill town in northern California. The reasons given at the time for his taking the job had to do with a higher hourly wage and the vague promise that he might, in a few years' time, succeed to the job of head filer in this new mill. But I think, in the main, that my dad had grown restless and simply wanted to try his luck elsewhere. Things had gotten a little too predictable for him in Yakima. Also, the year before, there had been the deaths, within six months of each other, of both his parents.

But just a few days after graduation, when my mother and I were packed to move to Chester, my dad penciled a letter to say he'd been sick for a while. He didn't want us to worry, he said, but he'd cut himself on a saw. Maybe he'd got a tiny sliver of steel in his blood. Anyway, something had happened and he'd had to miss work, he said. In the same mail was an unsigned postcard from somebody down there telling my mother that my dad was about to die and that he was drinking "raw whiskey."

When we arrived in Chester, my dad was living in a trailer that belonged 20 to the company. I didn't recognize him immediately. I guess for a moment I didn't want to recognize him. He was skinny and pale and looked bewildered. His pants wouldn't stay up. He didn't look like my dad. My mother began to cry. My dad put his arm around her and patted her shoulder vaguely, like he didn't know what this was all about, either. The three of us took up life together in the trailer, and we looked after him as best we could. But my dad was sick, and he couldn't get any better. I worked with him in the mill that summer and part of the fall. We'd get up in the mornings and eat eggs and toast while we listened to the radio, and then go out the door with our lunch pails. We'd pass through the gate together at eight in the morning, and I wouldn't see him again until quitting time. In November I went back to Yakima to be closer to my girlfriend, the girl I'd made up my mind I was going to marry.

He worked at the mill in Chester until the following February, when he collapsed on the job and was taken to the hospital. My mother asked if I would come down there and help. I caught a bus from Yakima to Chester, intending to drive them back to Yakima. But now, in addition to being physically sick, my dad was in the midst of a nervous breakdown, though none of us knew to call it that at the time. During the entire trip back to Yakima, he didn't speak, not even when asked a direct question. ("How do you feel, Raymond?" "You okay, Dad?") He'd communicate, if he communicated at all, by moving his head or by turning his palms up as if to say he didn't know or care. The only time he said anything on the trip, and for nearly a month afterward, was when I was speeding down a gravel road in Oregon and the car muffler came loose. "You were going too fast," he said.

Back in Yakima a doctor saw to it that my dad went to a psychiatrist. My mother and dad had to go on relief, as it was called, and the county paid for the psychiatrist. The psychiatrist asked my dad, "Who is the President?" He'd had a question put to him that he could answer. "Ike," my dad said. Nevertheless, they put him on the fifth floor of Valley Memorial Hospital and began giving him electroshock treatments. I was married by then and about to start my own family. My dad was still locked up when my wife went into this same hospital, just one floor down, to have our first baby. After she had delivered, I went upstairs to give my dad the news. They let me in through a steel door and showed me where I could find him. He was sitting on a couch with a blanket over his lap. *Hey,* I thought. *What in hell is happening to my dad?* I sat down next to him and told him he was a grand-father. He waited a minute and then said, "I feel like a grandfather." That's all he said. He didn't smile or move. He was in a big room with a lot of other people. Then I hugged him, and he began to cry.

Somehow he got out of there. But now came the years when he couldn't work and just sat around the house trying to figure what next and what he'd done wrong in his life that he'd wound up like this. My mother went from job to crummy job. Much later she referred to that time he was in the hospital, and those years just afterward, as "when Raymond was sick." The word *sick* was never the same for me again.

In 1964, through the help of a friend, he was lucky enough to be hired on at a mill in Klamath, California. He moved down there by himself to see if he could hack it. He lived not far from the mill, in a one-room cabin not much different from the place he and my mother had started out living in when they went west. He scrawled letters to my mother, and if I called she'd read them aloud to me over the phone. In the letters, he said it was touch and go. Every day that he went to work, he felt like it was the most important day of his life. But every day, he told her, made the next day that much easier. He said for her to tell me he said hello. If he couldn't sleep at night, he said, he thought about me and the good times we used to have. Finally, after a couple of months, he regained some of his confidence. He could do the work and didn't think he had to worry that he'd let anybody down ever again. When he was sure, he sent for my mother.

He'd been off from work for six years and had lost everything in that 25 time — home, car, furniture, and appliances, including the big freezer that had been my mother's pride and joy. He'd lost his good name too — Raymond Carver was someone who couldn't pay his bills — and his self-respect was gone. He'd even lost his virility. My mother told my wife, "All during that time Raymond was sick we slept together in the same bed, but we didn't have relations. He wanted to a few times, but nothing happened. I didn't miss it, but I think he wanted to, you know."

During those years I was trying to raise my own family and earn a living. But, one thing and another, we found ourselves having to move a lot. I couldn't keep track of what was going down in my dad's life. But I did have a chance one Christmas to tell him I wanted to be a writer. I might as well have told him I wanted to become a plastic surgeon. "What are you going to write about?" he wanted to know. Then, as if to help me out, he said, "Write about stuff you know about. Write about some of those fishing trips we took." I said I would, but I knew I wouldn't. "Send me what you write," he said. I said I'd do that, but then I didn't. I wasn't writing anything about fishing, and I didn't think he'd particularly care about, or even necessarily understand, what I was writing in those days. Besides, he wasn't a reader. Not the sort, anyway, I imagined I was writing for.

Then he died. I was a long way off, in Iowa City, with things still to say to him. I didn't have the chance to tell him good-bye, or that I thought he was doing great at his new job. That I was proud of him for making a comeback.

My mother said he came in from work that night and ate a big supper. Then he sat at the table by himself and finished what was left of a bottle of whiskey, a bottle she found hidden in the bottom of the garbage under some coffee grounds a day or so later. Then he got up and went to bed, where my mother joined him a little later. But in the night she had to get up and make a bed for herself on the couch. "He was snoring so loud I couldn't sleep," she said. The next morning when she looked in on him, he was on his back with his mouth open, his cheeks caved in. *Graylooking,* she said. She knew he was dead — she didn't need a doctor to tell her that. But she called one anyway, and then she called my wife.

Among the pictures my mother kept of my dad and herself during those early days in Washington was a photograph of him standing in front of a car, holding a beer and a stringer of fish. In the photograph he is wearing his hat back on his forehead and has this awkward grin on his face. I asked her for it and she gave it to me, along with some others. I put it up on my wall, and each time we moved, I took the picture along and put it up on another wall. I looked at it carefully from time to time, trying to figure out some things about my dad, and maybe myself in the process. But I couldn't. My dad just kept moving further and further away from me and back into time. Finally, in the course of another move, I lost the photograph. It was then that I tried to recall it, and at the same time make an attempt to say something about my dad, and how I thought that in some important ways we might be alike. I wrote the poem when I was living in an apartment house in an urban area south of San Francisco, at a time when I found myself, like my dad, having trouble with alcohol. The poem was a way of trying to connect up with him.

Photograph of My Father in His Twenty-Second Year

October. Here in this dank, unfamiliar kitchen
I study my father's embarrassed young man's face.
Sheepish grin, he holds in one hand a string
of spiny yellow perch, in the other
a bottle of Carlsberg beer.

In jeans and flannel shirt, he leans
against the front fender of a 1934 Ford.
He would like to pose brave and hearty for his posterity,
wear his old hat cocked over his ear.
All his life my father wanted to be bold.

But the eyes give him away, and the hands
that limply offer the string of dead perch
and the bottle of beer. Father, I love you,
yet how can I say thank you, I who can't hold my liquor
     either
and don't even know the places to fish.

The poem is true in its particulars, except that my dad died in June and not October, as the first word of the poem says. I wanted a word with more than one syllable to it to make it linger a little. But more than that, I wanted a month appropriate to what I felt at the time I wrote the poem — a month of short days and failing light, smoke in the air, things perishing. June was summer nights and days, graduations, my wedding anniversary, the birthday of one of my children. June wasn't a month your father died in.

After the service at the funeral home, after we had moved outside, a woman I didn't know came over to me and said, "He's happier where he is now." I stared at this woman until she moved away. I still remember the little knob of a hat she was wearing. Then one of my dad's cousins — I didn't know the man's name — reached out and took my hand, "We all miss him," he said, and I knew he wasn't saying it just to be polite.

I began to weep for the first time since receiving the news. I hadn't been able to before. I hadn't had the time, for one thing. Now, suddenly, I couldn't stop. I held my wife and wept while she said and did what she could do to comfort me there in the middle of that summer afternoon.

I listened to people say consoling things to my mother, and I was glad that my dad's family had turned up, had come to where he was. I thought I'd remember everything that was said and done that day and maybe find a way to tell it sometime. But I didn't. I forgot it all, or nearly. What I do remember is that I heard our name used a lot that afternoon, my dad's name and mine. But I knew they were talking about my dad. *Raymond, these* people kept saying in their beautiful voices out of my childhood. *Raymond.*

[handwritten annotation: symbolic of his manhood]

AFTERWORD

The poet Marianne Moore talked about poetry written "in plain American that dogs and cats can read" — though she did not succeed in writing it. Raymond Carver, whether he wrote a story, a poem, or an essay, chose the common and unpretentious word, the demotic over the literary. Nineteen out of twenty writers in this book would have used "father's" for the second word of this essay. Few of them would have said, five sentences into the story, "which was okay."

Now, the avoidance of affectation can be affectation itself, but Carver was too good a writer to catch himself in any bear trap. Two lines after "okay" he tells us that he "announced" something to his father, where "said" would have done the job: Carver controlled an ironic tone by elevating the diction, attributing a touch of pomposity to his younger self's speech.

With his spare, bare, demotic style, Carver did wonders: The precision of the death date makes its own announcement at the end of the first paragraph, and the second paragraph introduces difficult themes — duplication of father and son, relations of wife and mother — by means of a laconic, bizarre anecdote.

BOOKS AVAILABLE IN PAPERBACK

Carver Country: The World of Raymond Carver. New York: Arcade. *Short stories.*

Cathedral. New York: Random House–Vintage. *Short stories.*

Fires: Essays, Poems, Stories. New York: Random House–Vintage.

A New Path to the Waterfall: Poems. New York: Grove/Atlantic.

No Heroics, Please: Uncollected Writings. New York: Random House. *Short stories.*

Ultramarine. New York: Random House–Vintage. *Poetry.*

What We Talk About When We Talk About Love. New York: Random House–Vintage. *Short stories.*

Where I'm Calling From. New York: Random House–Vintage. *Short stories.*

Where Water Comes Together with Other Water. New York: Random House–Vintage. *Poetry.*

Will You Please Be Quiet, Please? New York: David McKay. *Short stories.*

JUDITH ORTIZ COFER

JUDITH ORTIZ COFER was born in Puerto Rico in 1952 and came to the United States four years later. Her father, in the U.S. Navy, was stationed at the Brooklyn Navy Yard, and she grew up alternating residences. Her firm sense of family and place on the island contrasted with feelings of alienation in New Jersey.

Living now in Athens, Georgia, she has written for Glamour *and the* Keynon Review, *and has received fellowships from the National Endowment for the Arts and the arts councils of two states. She has published two books of poems, a novel, and the book from which we take this essay,* Silent Dancing, *which is subtitled* A Partial Remembrance of a Puerto Rican Childhood. *Cofer's lucid language of recollection adds to American literature textures and values from an Hispanic source.*

She has written, "The 'infinite variety' and power of language interest me. I never cease to experiment with it. As a native Puerto Rican, my first language was Spanish. It was a challenge, not only to learn English, but to master it enough to teach it and — the ultimate goal — to write poetry in it." Most recently, Judith Ortiz Cofer has collected poetry and prose together in The Latin Deli *(1993), continuing her exploration of the lives of Puerto Rican immigrants to the United States.*

Primary Lessons

My mother walked me to my first day at school at La Escuela Segundo Ruiz Belvis, named after the Puerto Rican patriot born in our town. I remember yellow cement with green trim. All the classrooms had been painted these colors to identify them as government property. This was true all over the Island. Everything was color-coded, including the children, who wore uniforms from first through twelfth grade. We were a midget army in white and brown, led by the hand to our battleground. From practically every house in our barrio emerged a crisply ironed uniform inhabited by the savage creatures we had become over a summer of running wild in the sun.

At my grandmother's house where we were staying until my father returned to Brooklyn Yard in New York and sent for us, it had been complete chaos, with several children to get ready for school. My mother had pulled my hair harder than usual while braiding it, and I had dissolved into a pool of total self-pity. I wanted to stay home with her and Mamá, to continue listening to stories in the late afternoon, to drink *café con leche* with them, and to play rough games with my many cousins. I wanted to continue living the dream of summer afternoons in Puerto Rico, and if I could not have it, then I wanted to go back to Paterson, New Jersey, back to where I imagined our apartment waited, peaceful and cool for the three of us to return to our former lives. Our gypsy lifestyle had convinced me, at age six, that one part of life stops and waits for you while you live another for a while — and if you don't like the present, you can always return to the past. Buttoning me into my stiff blouse while I tried to squirm away from her, my mother attempted to explain to me that I was a big girl now and should try to understand that, like all the other children my age, I had to go to school.

"What about him?" I yelled pointing at my brother who was lounging on the tile floor of our bedroom in his pajamas, playing quietly with a toy car.

"He's too young to go to school, you know that. Now stay still." My mother pinned me between her thighs to button my skirt, as she had learned to do from Mamá, from whose grip it was impossible to escape.

"It's not fair, it's not fair. I can't go to school here. I don't speak Spanish." 5
It was my final argument, and it failed miserably because I was shouting my defiance in the language I claimed not to speak. Only I knew what I meant by saying in Spanish that I did not speak Spanish. I had spent my early childhood in the United States, where I lived in a bubble created by my Puerto Rican parents in a home where two cultures and languages became one. I learned to listen to the English from the television with one ear while I heard my mother and father speaking in Spanish with the other. I thought I was an ordinary American kid — like the children on the shows

I watched — and that everyone's parents spoke a secret second language at home. When we came to Puerto Rico right before I started first grade, I switched easily to Spanish. It was the language of fun, of summertime games. But school — that was a different matter.

I made one last desperate attempt to make my mother see reason: "Father will be very angry. You know that he wants us to speak good English." My mother, of course, ignored me as she dressed my little brother in his play-clothes. I could not believe her indifference to my father's wishes. She was usually so careful about our safety and the many other areas that he was forever reminding her about in his letters. But I was right, and she knew it. Our father spoke to us in English as much as possible, and he corrected my pronunciation constantly — not "jes" but "y-es." Y-es, sir. How could she send me to school to learn Spanish when we would be returning to Paterson in just a few months?

But, of course, what I feared was not language, but loss of freedom. At school there would be no playing, no stories, only lessons. It would not matter if I did not understand a word, and I would not be allowed to make up my own definitions. I would have to learn silence. I would have to keep my wild imagination in check. Feeling locked into my stiffly starched uniform, I only sensed all this. I guess most children can intuit their loss of childhood's freedom on that first day of school. It is separation anxiety too, but mother is just the guardian of the "playground" of our early childhood.

The sight of my cousins in similar straits comforted me. We were marched down the hill of our barrio where Mamá's robin-egg-blue house stood at the top. I must have glanced back at it with yearning. Mamá's house — a place built for children — where anything that could be broken had already been broken by my grandmother's early batch of offspring (they ranged in age from my mother's oldest sisters to my uncle who was six months older than me.) Her house had long since been made childproof. It had been a perfect summer place. And now it was September — the cruelest month for a child.

La Mrs., as all the teachers were called, waited for her class of first-graders at the door of the yellow and green classroom. She too wore a uniform: It was a blue skirt and a white blouse. This teacher wore black high heels with her "standard issue." I remember this detail because when we were all seated in rows she called on one little girl and pointed to the back of the room where there were shelves. She told the girl to bring her a shoebox from the bottom shelf. Then, when the box had been placed in her hands, she did something unusual. She had the little girl kneel at her feet and take the pointy high heels off her feet and replace them with a pair of satin slippers from the shoe box. She told the group that every one of us would have a chance to do this if we behaved in her class. Though confused about the prize, I soon felt caught up in the competition to bring *La Mrs.* her slippers in the morning. Children fought over the privilege.

Our first lesson was English. In Puerto Rico, every child has to take twelve years of English to graduate from school. It is the law. In my parents' 10 school days, all subjects were taught in English. The U.S. Department of Education had specified that as a U.S. territory, the Island had to be "Americanized," and to accomplish this task, it was necessary for the Spanish language to be replaced in one generation through the teaching of English in all schools. My father began his school day by saluting the flag of the United States and singing "America" and "The Star-Spangled Banner" by rote, without understanding a word of what he was saying. The logic behind this system was that, though the children did not understand the English words, they would remember the rhythms. Even the games the teacher's manuals required them to play became absurd adaptations. "Here We Go Round the Mulberry Bush" became "Here We Go Round the Mango Tree." I have heard about the confusion caused by the use of a primer in which the sounds of animals were featured. The children were forced to accept that a rooster says *cockadoodledoo,* when they knew perfectly well from hearing their own roosters each morning that in Puerto Rico a rooster says *cocorocó.* Even the vocabulary of their pets was changed; there are still family stories circulating about the bewilderment of a first-grader coming home to try to teach his dog to speak in English. The policy of assimilation by immersion failed on the Island. Teachers adhered to it on paper, substituting their own materials for the texts, but no one took their English home. In due time, the program was minimized to the one class in English per day that I encountered when I took my seat in *La Mrs.*'s first grade class.

Catching us all by surprise, she stood very straight and tall in front of us and began to sing in English:

Pollito	—	Chicken
Gallina	—	Hen
Lápiz	—	Pencil
Y Pluma	—	Pen.

"Repeat after me, children: Pollito — Chicken," she commanded in her heavily accented English that only I understood, being the only child in the room who had ever been exposed to the language. But I too remained silent. No use making waves or showing off. Patiently *La Mrs.* sang her song and gestured for us to join in. At some point it must have dawned on the class that this silly routine was likely to go on all day if we did not "repeat after her." It was not her fault that she had to follow the rule in her teacher's manual stating that she must teach English *in* English, and that she must not translate, but merely repeat her lesson in English until the children "begin to respond" more or less "unconsciously." This was one of the vestiges of the regimen followed by her predecessors in the last generation. To this day I can recite "Pollito — Chicken" mindlessly, never once pausing to visualize chicks, hens, pencils, or pens.

I soon found myself crowned "teacher's pet" without much effort on my part. I was a privileged child in her eyes simply because I lived in "Nueva York," and because my father was in the navy. His name was an old one in our pueblo, associated with once-upon-a-time landed people and long-gone money. Status is judged by unique standards in a culture where, by definition, everyone is a second-class citizen. Remembrance of past glory is as good as titles and money. Old families living in decrepit old houses rank over factory workers living in modern comfort in cement boxes — all the same. The professions raise a person out of the dreaded "sameness" into a niche of status, so that teachers, nurses, and everyone who went to school for a job were given the honorifics of *El Míster* or *La Mrs.* by the common folks, people who were likely to be making more money in American factories than the poorly paid educators and government workers.

My first impressions of the hierarchy began with my teacher's shoe-changing ceremony and the exaggerated respect she received from our parents. *La Mrs.* was always right, and adults scrambled to meet her requirements. She wanted all our schoolbooks covered in the brown paper now used for paper bags (used at that time by the grocer to wrap meats and other foods). That first week of school the grocer was swamped with requests for paper which he gave away to the women. That week and the next, he wrapped produce in newspapers. All school projects became family projects. It was considered disrespectful at Mamá's house to do homework in privacy. Between the hours when we came home from school and dinner time, the table was shared by all of us working together with the women hovering in the background. The teachers communicated directly with the mothers, and it was a matriarchy of far-reaching power and influence.

There was a black boy in my first-grade classroom who was also the   15
teacher's pet but for a different reason than I: I did not have to do anything to win her favor; he would do anything to win a smile. He was as black as the cauldron that Mamá used for cooking stew and his hair was curled into tight little balls on his head — *pasitas*, like little raisins glued to his skull, my mother had said. There had been some talk at Mamá's house about this boy; Lorenzo was his name. I later gathered that he was the grandson of my father's nanny. Lorenzo lived with Teresa, his grandmother, having been left in her care when his mother took off for "Los Nueva Yores" shortly after his birth. And they were poor. Everyone could see that his pants were too big for him — hand-me-downs — and his shoe soles were as thin as paper. Lorenzo seemed unmindful of the giggles he caused when he jumped up to erase the board for *La Mrs.* and his baggy pants rode down to his thin hips as he strained up to get every stray mark. He seemed to relish playing the little clown when she asked him to come to the front of the room and sing his phonetic version of "o-bootifool, forpashios-keeis," leading the class in our incomprehensible tribute to the American flag. He was a bright, loving child, with a talent for song and mimicry that everyone commented on. He should have been chosen to host the PTA show that year instead of me.

At recess one day, I came back to the empty classroom to get something. My cup? My nickel for a drink from the kiosk man? I don't remember. But I remember the conversation my teacher was having with another teacher. I remember because it concerned me, and because I memorized it so that I could ask my mother to explain what it meant.

"He is a funny *negrito*, and, like a parrot, he can repeat anything you teach him. But his Mamá must not have the money to buy him a suit."

"I kept Rafaelito's First Communion suit; I bet Lorenzo could fit in it. It's white with a bow-tie," the other teacher said.

"But, Marisa," laughed my teacher, "in that suit, Lorenzo would look like a fly drowned in a glass of milk."

Both women laughed. They had not seen me crouched at the back of the 20 room, digging into my schoolbag. My name came up then.

"What about the Ortiz girl? They have money."

"I'll talk to her mother today. The superintendent, *El Americano* from San Juan, is coming down for the show. How about if we have her say her lines in both Spanish and English?"

The conversation ends there for me. My mother took me to Mayagüez and bought me a frilly pink dress and two crinoline petticoats to wear underneath so that I looked like a pink and white parachute with toothpick legs sticking out. I learned my lines, "Padres, maestros, Mr. Leonard, bienvenidos/Parents, teachers, Mr. Leonard, welcome. . . ." My first public appearance. I took no pleasure in it. The words were formal and empty. I had simply memorized them. My dress pinched me at the neck and arms, and made me itch all over.

I had asked my mother what it meant to be a "mosca en un vaso de leche," a fly in a glass of milk. She had laughed at the image, explaining that it meant being "different," but that it wasn't something I needed to worry about.

AFTERWORD

To look or feel simple, good prose must be cunning in its construction. Look at the way Judith Ortiz Cofer opens her essay by playing with changes on color. It is charming to remember, from the first day of school, the yellow and the green; this is how we remember things. But then the reader learns, as if it were an innocent statement of fact, that these colors identify government property. We are now ready to hear: "Everything was color-coded, including the children" — and to understand Cofer's fundamental contrast between regimentation and liberty. In another writer who provided the information about government color codes, we might react against the whining noise of complaint. Cofer lets the facts work upon her reader without appearing coercive.

BOOKS AVAILABLE IN PAPERBACK

The Line of the Sun. Athens: University of Georgia Press. *Novel.*

Silent Dancing: A Partial Remembrance of a Puerto Rican Childhood. Houston: Arte Público Press. *Essays.*

FRANK
CONROY

*F*RANK CONROY *(b. 1936) grew up in the East, mostly under conditions of poverty, then attended Haverford College in Pennsylvania. He is a jazz pianist, and from time to time has supported himself as a musician. In 1982 he became director of the literature program at the National Endowment for the Arts, and in 1987 director of the writing program at the University of Iowa.*

Stop Time (1967) was the marvelous memoir-as-novel by which Conroy entered the literary scene, writing a reminiscent prose rich with detail, exact and bright though miniature with distance, like the landscape crafted behind model trains. For a long time he published no further books, but then in 1985 he collected his short stories in Midair, *and in 1994 he published a novel,* Body and Soul.

"Think About It" has an unusual provenance. In a letter, Conroy writes that soon after he arrived at Iowa, "the dean asked me to address the graduating class of the College of Liberal Arts. Now like every writer I loathe writing for free. . . . I read it at an indoor commencement at the huge basketball arena — so big the words echoed back at me while I spoke, like some political thing. I felt like Mussolini." Later a friend showed a copy to Lewis Lapham, editor of Harper's, *who printed it, whence it was reprinted first in a* Best American Essays *volume and now in* The Contemporary Essay.

Think About It

When I was sixteen I worked selling hot dogs at a stand in the Fourteenth Street subway station in New York City, one level above the trains and one below the street, where the crowds continually flowed back and forth. I worked with three Puerto Rican men who could not speak English. I had no Spanish, and although we understood each other well with regard to the tasks at hand, sensing and adjusting to each other's body movements in the extremely confined space in which we operated, I felt isolated with no one to talk to. On my break I came out from behind the counter and passed the time with two old black men who ran a shoeshine stand in a dark corner of the corridor. It was a poor location, half hidden by columns, and they didn't have much business. I would sit with my back against the wall while they stood or moved around their ancient elevated stand, talking to each other or to me, but always staring into the distance as they did so.

As the weeks went by I realized that they never looked at anything in their immediate vicinity — not at me or their stand or anybody who might come within ten or fifteen feet. They did not look at approaching customers once they were inside the perimeter. Save for the instant it took to discern the color of the shoes, they did not even look at what they were doing while they worked, but rubbed in polish, brushed, and buffed by feel while looking over their shoulders, into the distance, as if awaiting the arrival of an important person. Of course there wasn't all that much distance in the underground station, but their behavior was so focused and consistent they seemed somehow to transcend the physical. A powerful mood was created, and I came almost to believe that these men could see through walls, through girders, and around corners to whatever hyperspace it was where whoever it was they were waiting and watching for would finally emerge. Their scattered talk was hip, elliptical, and hinted at mysteries beyond my white boy's ken, but it was the staring off, the long, steady staring off, that had me hypnotized. I left for a better job, with handshakes from both of them, without understanding what I had seen.

Perhaps ten years later, after playing jazz with black musicians in various Harlem clubs, hanging out uptown with a few young artists and intellectuals, I began to learn from them something of the extraordinarily varied and complex riffs and rituals embraced by different people to help themselves get through life in the ghetto. Fantasy of all kinds — from playful to dangerous — was in the very air of Harlem. It was the spice of uptown life.

Only then did I understand the two shoeshine men. They were trapped in a demeaning situation in a dark corner in an underground corridor in a filthy subway system. Their continuous staring off was a kind of statement, and kind of dance. Our bodies are here, went the statement, but our souls are receiving nourishment from distant sources only we can see. They were powerful magic dancers, sorcerers almost, and thirty-five years later I can still feel the pressure of their spell.

The light bulb may appear over your head, is what I'm saying, but it   5 may be a while before it actually goes on. Early in my attempts to learn jazz piano, I used to listen to recordings of a fine player named Red Garland, whose music I admired. I couldn't quite figure out what he was doing with his left hand, however; the chords eluded me. I went uptown to an obscure club where he was playing with his trio, caught him on his break, and simply asked him. "Sixths," he said cheerfully. And then he went away.

I didn't know what to make of it. The basic jazz chord is the seventh, which comes in various configurations, but it is what it is. I was a self-taught pianist, pretty shaky on theory and harmony, and when he said sixths I kept trying to fit the information into what I already knew, and it didn't fit. But it stuck in my mind — a tantalizing mystery.

A couple of years later, when I began playing with a bass player, I discovered more or less by accident that if the bass played the root and I played a sixth based on the fifth note of the scale, a very interesting chord involving both instruments emerged. Ordinarily, I suppose I would have skipped over the matter and not paid much attention, but I remembered Garland's remark and so I stopped and spent a week or two working out the voicings, and greatly strengthened my foundations as a player. I had remembered what I hadn't understood, you might say, until my life caught up with the information and the light bulb went on.

I remember another, more complicated example from my sophomore year at the small liberal-arts college outside Philadelphia. I seemed never to be able to get up in time for breakfast in the dining hall. I would get coffee and a doughnut in the Coop instead — a basement area with about a dozen small tables where students could get something to eat at odd hours. Several mornings in a row I noticed a strange man sitting by himself with a cup of coffee. He was in his sixties, perhaps, and sat straight in his chair with very little extraneous movement. I guessed he was some sort of distinguished visitor to the college who had decided to put in some time at a student hangout. But no one ever sat with him. One morning I approached his table and asked if I could join him.

"Certainly," he said. "Please do." He had perhaps the clearest eyes I had ever seen, like blue ice, and to be held in their steady gaze was not, at first, an entirely comfortable experience. His eyes gave nothing away about himself while at the same time creating in me the eerie impression that he was looking directly into my soul. He asked a few quick questions, as if to put me at my ease, and we fell into conversation. He was William O. Douglas from the Supreme Court, and when he saw how startled I was he said, "Call me Bill. Now tell me what you're studying and why you get up so late in the morning." Thus began a series of talks that stretched over many weeks. The fact that I was an ignorant sophomore with literary pretensions who knew nothing about the law didn't seem to bother him. We talked about everything from Shakespeare to the possibility of life on other planets. One day I mentioned that I was going to have dinner with Judge Learned Hand. I explained that Hand was my girlfriend's grandfather. Douglas nodded, but I could tell he was surprised at the coincidence of my knowing the chief judge of the most important court in the country save the Supreme Court itself. After fifty years on the bench Judge Hand had become a famous man, both in and out of legal circles — a living legend, to his own dismay. "Tell him hello and give him my best regards," Douglas said.

Learned Hand, in his eighties, was a short, barrel-chested man with a large, square head, huge, thick, bristling eyebrows, and soft brown eyes. He radiated energy and would sometimes bark out remarks or questions in the living room as if he were in court. His humor was sharp, but often leavened with a touch of self-mockery. When something caught his funny bone he would burst out with explosive laughter — the laughter of a man who enjoyed laughing. He had a large repertoire of dramatic expressions involving the use of his eyebrows — very useful, he told me conspiratorially, when looking down on things from behind the bench. (The court stenographer could not record the movement of his eyebrows.) When I told him I'd been talking to William O. Douglas, they first shot up in exaggerated surprise, and then lowered and moved forward in a glower. 10

"*Justice* William O. Douglas, young man," he admonished. "Justice Douglas, if you please." About the Supreme Court in general, Hand insisted on a tone of profound respect. Little did I know that in private correspondence he had referred to the Court as "The Blessed Saints, Cherubim and Seraphim," "The Jolly Boys," "The Nine Tin Jesuses," "The Nine Blameless Ethiopians," and my particular favorite, "The Nine Blessed Chalices of the Sacred Effluvium."

Hand was badly stooped and had a lot of pain in his lower back. Martinis helped, but his strict Yankee wife approved of only one before dinner. It was my job to make the second and somehow slip it to him. If the pain was particularly acute he would get out of his chair and lie flat on the rug, still talking, and finish his point without missing a beat. He flattered me by asking for my impression of Justice Douglas, instructed me to convey his warmest regards, and then began talking about the Dennis case, which he described as a particularly tricky and difficult case involving the prosecution of eleven leaders of the Communist party. He had just started in on the First Amendment and free speech when we were called in to dinner.

William O. Douglas loved the outdoors with a passion, and we fell into the habit of having coffee in the Coop and then strolling under the trees down toward the duck pond. About the Dennis case, he said something to this effect: "Eleven Communists arrested by the government. Up to no good, said the government; dangerous people, violent overthrow, etc. First Amendment, said the defense, freedom of speech, etc." Douglas stopped walking. "Clear and present danger."

"What?" I asked. He often talked in a telegraphic manner, and one was expected to keep up with him. It was sometimes like listening to a man thinking out loud.

"Clear and present danger," he said. "That was the issue. Did they   15
constitute a clear and present danger? I don't think so. I think everybody
took the language pretty far in Dennis." He began walking, striding along
quickly. Again, one was expected to keep up with him. "The FBI was all
over them. Phones tapped, constant surveillance. How could it be clear and
present danger with the FBI watching every move they made? That's a
ginkgo," he said suddenly, pointing at a tree. "A beauty. You don't see those
every day. Ask Hand about clear and present danger."

I was in fact reluctant to do so. Douglas's argument seemed to me to be
crushing — the last word, really — and I didn't want to embarrass Judge
Hand. But back in the living room, on the second martini, the old man asked
about Douglas. I sort of scratched my nose and recapitulated the conversation by the ginkgo tree.

"What?" Hand shouted. "Speak up, sir, for heaven's sake."

"He said the FBI was watching them all the time so there couldn't be a
clear and present danger," I blurted out, blushing as I said it.

A terrible silence filled the room. Hand's eyebrows writhed on his face
like two huge caterpillars. He leaned forward in the wing chair, his face
settling, finally, into a grim expression. "I am astonished," he said softly, his
eyes holding mine, "at Justice Douglas's newfound faith in the Federal
Bureau of Investigation." His big, granite head moved even closer to mine,
until I could smell the martini. "I had understood him to consider it a
politically corrupt, incompetent organization, directed by a power-crazed
lunatic." I realized I had been holding my breath throughout all of this, and
as I relaxed, I saw the faintest trace of a smile cross Hand's face. Things are
sometimes more complicated than they first appear, his smile seemed to say.
The old man leaned back. "The proximity of the danger is something to
think about. Ask him about that. See what he says."

I chewed the matter over as I returned to campus. Hand had pointed out   20
some of Douglas's language about the FBI from other sources that seemed
to bear out his point. I thought about the words "clear and present danger,"
and the fact that if you looked at them closely they might not be as simple
as they had first appeared. What degree of danger? Did the word "present"
allude to the proximity of the danger, or just the fact that the danger was
there at all — that it wasn't an anticipated danger? Were there other hidden
factors these great men were weighing of which I was unaware?

But Douglas was gone, back to Washington. (The writer in me is tempted
to create a scene here — to invent one for dramatic purposes — but of course
I can't do that.) My brief time as a messenger boy was over, and I felt a
certain frustration, as if, with a few more exchanges, the matter of *Dennis v.
United States* might have been resolved to my satisfaction. They'd left me
high and dry. But, of course, it is precisely because the matter did not resolve
that has caused me to think about it, off and on, all these years. "The
Constitution," Hand used to say to me flatly, "is a piece of paper. The Bill
of Rights is a piece of paper." It was many years before I understood what
he meant. Documents alone do not keep democracy alive, nor maintain the

state of law. There is no particular safety in them. Living men and women, generation after generation, must continually remake democracy and the law, and that involves an ongoing state of tension between the past and the present which will never completely resolve.

Education doesn't end until life ends, because you never know when you're going to understand something you hadn't understood before. For me, the magic dance of the shoeshine men was the kind of experience in which understanding came with a kind of click, a resolving kind of click. The same with the experience at the piano. What happened with Justice Douglas and Judge Hand was different, and makes the point that understanding does not always mean resolution. Indeed, in our intellectual lives, our creative lives, it is perhaps those problems that will never resolve that rightly claim the lion's share of our energies. The physical body exists in a constant state of tension as it maintains homeostasis, and so too does the active mind embrace the tension of never being certain, never being absolutely sure, never being done, as it engages the world. That is our special fate, our inexpressibly valuable condition.

AFTERWORD

Frank Conroy is a story teller, and Stop Time *is memoir salted with fiction. People tell stories to entertain, to brag, to complain, to preserve — and also as tools for thinking. "Think About It" tells anecdotes, with the skill of a novelist, about delayed perception, about moments when "the light bulb went on." Conroy's efficient and deft storytelling allows us to experience understanding in the author's mind, first by action, then by puzzlement — the beginning of thought — and finally in an epiphany of insight. This essay provides a model for learning the world through experience and questioning — by thought, in effect — and generalizes by the variety of its contexts: race and society, jazz music, law and social prominence.*

He doesn't sound like Mussolini. Because this is an essay of advice, it partly resembles the traditional commencement address, but in its language it is intimate rather than cold and public. Compare this essay with Ursula K. Le Guin's commencement address on page 329.

BOOKS AVAILABLE IN PAPERBACK

Midair. New York: Penguin. *Short stories.*
Stop Time. New York: Penguin. *Novel.*

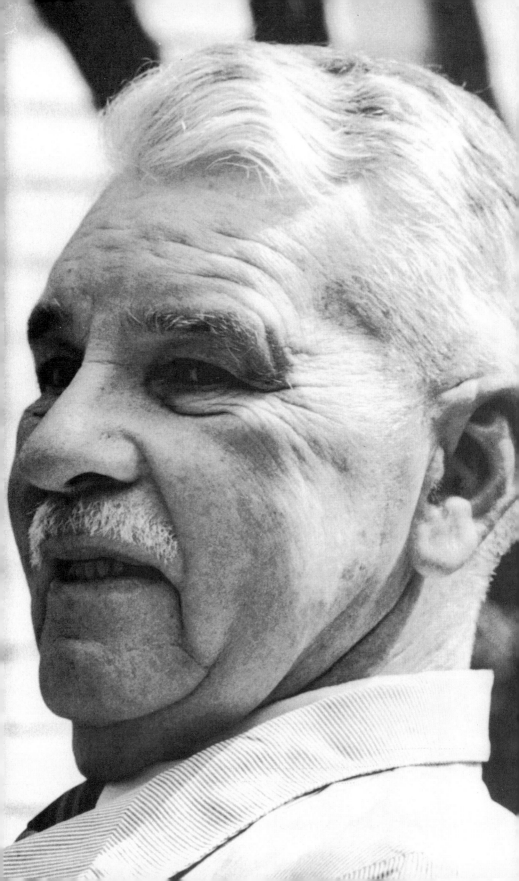

MALCOLM
COWLEY

M AYBE MALCOLM COWLEY (1898–1989) lived long enough to look back *on "The View from 80" as youthful work. Vigorous essays continued to emerge from his Connecticut house, often memorials to younger writers, now dead, whom Cowley befriended at the beginnings of their careers. His affectionate, acute reminiscence of the novelist and short-story writer John Cheever appeared in the* Sewanee Review *in 1983.*

Cowley had much to look back on. He drove an ambulance during World War I, interrupting his studies at Harvard, and when he graduated in 1920 he returned to France, where literary Americans lived as expatriates in those days. Cowley published his first book of poems, Blue Juniata, *in 1929 — and almost forty years later he used the same title for his collected poems. Back in the United States he became an editor at the* New Republic *and a freelance writer. He was literary advisor for the Viking Press and edited Viking Portables of Hemingway and Faulkner. He wrote many books about writers and writing.* Exile's Return *is the best known, chronicling the expatriate generation Cowley belonged to. It appeared first in 1934 and, extensively revised, in 1951.*

Age did not slow him down. Who's Who *listed five books published by Cowley after the age of seventy, almost as many as he published before the age of seventy. His later books, criticism and literary reminiscence, include* A Second Flowering *(1973),* And I Worked at the Writer's Trade *(1978), and* The Dream of the Golden Mountains *(1980). In 1981 he received the Gold Medal of the American Academy of Arts and Letters.*

It was appropriate. Cowley was an old-fashioned man of letters — poet, essayist, editor — which was what he set out to be. "I believed, first of all, that the only respectable ambition for a man of letters was to be a man of letters — not exclusively

Photo by Robert Cowley

a novelist, an essayist, a dramatist, but rather one who adopts the whole of literature as his province. . . . I believed that the man of letters, while retaining his own point of view, which was primarily that of the poet, should concern himself with every department of human activity, including science, sociology, and revolution."

It made good sense for the editors of Life *magazine to ask him in 1978 to write about turning eighty — a commission that prompted "The View from 80." Later the essay became the first chapter of a book with the same title, which makes a metaphor of age as vantage point. Cowley wrote as a traveler reporting on a landscape many of us will not live to visit. As a writer he knew how to gather and assemble varied material. In this essay Cowley includes research on the literature and scholarship of old age as well as his personal experience of the phenomenon. His attitude toward old age shows itself both in direct statement and, by implication, in the mountaintop he wrote from.*

The View from 80

They gave me a party on my 80th birthday in August 1978. First there were cards, letters, telegrams, even a cable of congratulation or condolence; then there were gifts, mostly bottles; there was catered food and finally a big cake with, for some reason, two candles (had I gone back to very early childhood?). I blew the candles out a little unsteadily. Amid the applause and clatter I thought about a former custom of the Northern Ojibwas when they lived on the shore of Lake Winnipeg. They were kind to their old people, who remembered and enforced the ancient customs of the tribe, but when an old person became decrepit, it was time for him to go. Sometimes he was simply abandoned, with a little food, on an island in the lake. If he deserved special honor, they held a tribal feast for him. The old man sang a death song and danced, if he could. While he was still singing, his son came from behind and brained him with a tomahawk.

That was quick, it was dignified, and I wonder whether it was any more cruel, essentially, than some of our civilized customs or inadvertences in disposing of the aged. I believe in rites and ceremonies. I believe in big parties for special occasions such as an 80th birthday. It is a sort of belated bar mitzvah, since the 80-year-old, like a Jewish adolescent, is entering a new stage of life; let him (or her) undergo a *rite de passage*, with toasts and a cantor. Seventy-year-olds, or septuas, have the illusion of being middle-aged, even if they have been pushed back on a shelf. The 80-year-old, the octo, looks at the double-dumpling figure and admits that he is old. That last act has begun, and it will be the test of the play.

He has joined a select minority that numbers, in this country, 4,842,000 persons (according to Census Bureau estimates for 1977), or about two percent of the American population. Two-thirds of the octos are women, who have retained the good habit of living longer than men. Someday you, the reader, will join that minority, if you escape hypertension and cancer, the two killers, and if you survive the dangerous years 75 to 79, when half the survivors till then are lost. With advances in medicine, the living space taken over by octos is growing larger year by year.

To enter the country of age is a new experience, different from what you supposed it to be. Nobody, man or woman, knows the country until he has lived in it and has taken out his citizenship papers. Here is my own report, submitted as a road map and guide to some of the principal monuments.

The new octogenarian feels as strong as ever when he is sitting back in $\qquad$ 5 a comfortable chair. He ruminates, he dreams, he remembers. He doesn't want to be disturbed by others. It seems to him that old age is only a costume assumed for those others; the true, the essential self is ageless. In a moment he will rise and go for a ramble in the woods, taking a gun along, or a fishing rod, if it is spring. Then he creaks to his feet, bending forward to keep his balance, and realizes that he will do nothing of the sort. The body and its surroundings have their messages for him, or only one message: "You are old." Here are some of the occasions on which he receives the message:

- when it becomes an achievement to do thoughtfully, step by step, what he once did instinctively
- when his bones ache
- when there are more and more little bottles in the medicine cabinet, with instructions for taking four times a day
- when he fumbles and drops his toothbrush (butterfingers)
- when his face has bumps and wrinkles, so that he cuts himself while shaving (blood on the towel)
- when year by year his feet seem farther from his hands
- when he can't stand on one leg and has trouble pulling on his pants
- when he hesitates on the landing before walking down a flight of stairs
- when he spends more time looking for things misplaced than he spends using them after he (or more often his wife) has found them
- when he falls asleep in the afternoon
- when it becomes harder to bear in mind two things at once
- when a pretty girl passes him in the street and he doesn't turn his head
- when he forgets names, even of people he saw last month ("Now I'm beginning to forget nouns," the poet Conrad Aiken said at 80)
- when he listens hard to jokes and catches everything but the snapper
- when he decides not to drive at night anymore
- when everything takes longer to do — bathing, shaving, getting dressed or undressed — but when time passes quickly, as if he were gathering speed while coasting downhill. The year from 79 to 80 is like a week when he was a boy.

Those are some of the intimate messages. "Put cotton in your ears and pebbles in your shoes," said a gerontologist, a member of that new profession dedicated to alleviating all maladies of old people except the passage of years. "Pull on rubber gloves. Smear Vaseline over your glasses, and there you have it: instant aging." Not quite. His formula omits the messages from the social world, which are louder, in most cases, than those from within. We start by growing old in other people's eyes, then slowly we come to share their judgment.

I remember a morning many years ago when I was backing out of the parking lot near the railroad station in Brewster, New York. There was a near collision. The driver of the other car jumped out and started to abuse me; he had his fists ready. Then he looked hard at me and said, "Why, you're an old man." He got back into his car, slammed the door, and drove away, while I stood there fuming. "I'm only 65," I thought. "He wasn't driving carefully. I can still take care of myself in a car, or in a fight, for that matter."

My hair was whiter — it may have been in 1974 — when a young woman rose and offered me her seat in a Madison Avenue bus. That message was kind and also devastating. "Can't I even stand up?" I thought as I thanked her and declined the seat. But the same thing happened twice the following year, and the second time I gratefully accepted the offer, though with a sense of having diminished myself. "People are right about me," I thought while wondering why all those kind gestures were made by women. Do men now regard themselves as the weaker sex, not called upon to show consideration? All the same it was a relief to sit down and relax.

A few days later I wrote a poem, "The Red Wagon," that belongs in the record of aging:

> For his birthday they gave him a red express wagon
> with a driver's high seat and a handle that steered.
> His mother pulled him around the yard.
> "Giddyap," he said, but she laughed and went off
> to wash the breakfast dishes.
>
> "I wanta ride too," his sister said,
> and he pulled her to the edge of a hill.
> "Now, sister, go home and wait for me,
> but first give a push to the wagon."
>
> He climbed again to the high seat,
> this time grasping that handle-that-steered.
> The red wagon rolled slowly down the slope,
> then faster as it passed the schoolhouse
> and faster as it passed the store,
> the road still dropping away.
> Oh, it was fun.
>
> But would it ever stop?
> Would the road always go downhill?

The red wagon rolled faster
Now it was in strange country.
It passed a white house he must have dreamed about,
deep woods he had never seen,
a graveyard where, something told him, his sister was buried.

Far below
the sun was sinking into a broad plain.

The red wagon rolled faster.
Now he was clutching the seat, not even trying to steer.
Sweat clouded his heavy spectacles.
His white hair streamed in the wind.

Even before he or she is 80, the aging person may undergo another 10
identity crisis like that of adolescence. Perhaps there had also been a middle-aged crisis, the male or the female menopause, but the rest of adult life
he had taken himself for granted, with his capabilities and failings. Now,
when he looks in the mirror, he asks himself, "Is this really me?" — or he
avoids the mirror out of distress at what it reveals, those bags and wrinkles.
In his new makeup he is called upon to play a new role in a play that must
be improvised. André Gide, that long-lived man of letters, wrote in his
journal, "My heart has remained so young that I have the continual feeling
of playing a part, the part of the 70-year-old that I certainly am; and the
infirmities and weaknesses that remind me of my age act like a prompter,
reminding me of my lines when I tend to stray. Then, like the good actor I
want to be, I go back into my role, and I pride myself on playing it well."

In his new role the old person will find that he is tempted by new vices,
that he receives new compensations (not so widely known), and that he may
possibly achieve new virtues. Chief among these is the heroic or merely
obstinate refusal to surrender in the face of time. One admires the ships that
go down with all flags flying and the captain on the bridge.

Among the vices of age are avarice, untidiness, and vanity, which last
takes the form of a craving to be loved or simply admired. Avarice is the
worst of those three. Why do so many old persons, men and women alike,
insist on hoarding money when they have no prospect of using it and even
when they have no heirs? They eat the cheapest food, buy no clothes, and
live in a single room when they could afford better lodging. It may be that
they regard money as a form of power; there is a comfort in watching it
accumulate while other powers are dwindling away. How often we read of
an old person found dead in a hovel, on a mattress partly stuffed with
bankbooks and stock certificates! The bankbook syndrome, we call it in our
family, which has never succumbed.

Untidiness we call the Langley Collyer syndrome. To explain, Langley
Collyer was a former concert pianist who lived alone with his 70-year-old
brother in a brownstone house on upper Fifth Avenue. The once fashionable
neighborhood had become part of Harlem. Homer, the brother, had been an

admiralty lawyer, but was now blind and partly paralyzed; Langley played for him and fed him on buns and oranges, which he thought would restore Homer's sight. He never threw away a daily paper because Homer, he said, might want to read them all. He saved other things as well and the house became filled with rubbish from roof to basement. The halls were lined on both sides with bundled newspapers, leaving narrow passageways in which Langley had devised booby traps to catch intruders.

On March 21, 1947, some unnamed person telephoned the police to report that there was a dead body in the Collyer house. The police broke down the front door and found the hall impassable; then they hoisted a ladder to a second-story window. Behind it Homer was lying on the floor in a bathrobe; he had starved to death. Langley had disappeared. After some delay, the police broke into the basement, chopped a hole in the roof, and began throwing junk out of the house, top and bottom. It was 18 days before they found Langley's body, gnawed by rats. Caught in one of his own booby traps, he had died in a hallway just outside Homer's door. By that time the police had collected, and the Department of Sanitation had hauled away, 120 tons of rubbish, including, besides the newspapers, 14 grand pianos and the parts of a dismantled Model T Ford.

Why do so many old people accumulate junk, not on the scale of Langley   15 Collyer, but still in a dismaying fashion? Their tables are piled high with it, their bureau drawers are stuffed with it, their closet rods bend with the weight of clothes not worn for years. I suppose that the piling up is partly from lethargy and partly from the feeling that everything once useful, including their own bodies, should be preserved. Others, though not so many, have such a fear of becoming Langley Collyers that they strive to be painfully neat. Every tool they own is in its place, though it will never be used again; every scrap of paper is filed away in alphabetical order. At last their immoderate neatness becomes another vice of age, if a milder one.

The vanity of older people is an easier weakness to explain, and to condone. With less to look forward to, they yearn for recognition of what they have been: the reigning beauty, the athlete, the soldier, the scholar. It is the beauties who have the hardest time. A portrait of themselves at twenty hangs on the wall, and they try to resemble it by making an extravagant use of creams, powders, and dyes. Being young at heart, they think they are merely revealing their essential persons. The athletes find shelves for their silver trophies, which are polished once a year. Perhaps a letter sweater lies wrapped in a bureau drawer. I remember one evening when a no-longer athlete had guests for dinner and tried to find his sweater. "Oh, that old thing," his wife said. "The moths got into it and I threw it away." The athlete sulked and his guests went home early.

Often the yearning to be recognized appears in conversation as an innocent boast. Thus, a distinguished physician, retired at 94, remarks casually that a disease was named after him. A former judge bursts into chuckles as he repeats bright things that he said on the bench. Aging scholars complain in letters (or one of them does), "As I approach 70 I'm becoming avid of honors, and such things — medals, honorary degrees, etc. — are only passed around among academics on a *quid pro quo* basis (one hood capping another)." Or they say querulously, "Bill Underwood has ten honorary doctorates and I have only three. Why didn't they elect me to . . . ?" and they mention the name of some learned society. That search for honors is a harmless passion, though it may lead to jealousies and deformations of character, as with Robert Frost in his later years. Still, honors cost little. Why shouldn't the very old have more than their share of them?

To be admired and praised, especially by the young, is an autumnal pleasure enjoyed by the lucky ones (who are not always the most deserving). "What is more charming," Cicero observes in his famous essay *De Senectute*, "than an old age surrounded by the enthusiasm of youth! . . . Attentions which seem trivial and conventional are marks of honors — the morning call, being sought after, precedence, having people rise for you, being escorted to and from the forum. . . . What pleasures of the body can be compared to the prerogatives of influence?" But there are also pleasures of the body, or the mind, that are enjoyed by a greater number of older persons.

Those pleasures include some that younger people find hard to appreciate. One of them is simply sitting still, like a snake on a sun-warmed stone, with a delicious feeling of indolence that was seldom attained in earlier years. A leaf flutters down; a cloud moves by inches across the horizon. At such moments the older person, completely relaxed, has become a part of nature — and a living part, with blood coursing through his veins. The future does not exist for him. He thinks, if he thinks at all, that life for younger persons is still a battle royal of each against each, but that now he has nothing more to win or lose. He is not so much above as outside the battle, as if he had assumed the uniform of some small neutral country, perhaps Liechtenstein or Andorra. From a distance he notes that some of the combatants, men or women, are jostling ahead — but why do they fight so hard when the most they can hope for is a longer obituary? He can watch the scrounging and gouging, he can hear the shouts of exultation, the moans of the gravely wounded, and meanwhile he feels secure; nobody will attack him from ambush.

Age has other physical compensations besides the nirvana of dozing in the sun. A few of the simplest needs become a pleasure to satisfy. When an old woman in a nursing home was asked what she really liked to do, she answered in one word: "Eat." She might have been speaking for many of her fellows. Meals in a nursing home, however badly cooked, serve as climactic moments of the day. The physical essence of the pensioners is being renewed at an appointed hour; now they can go back to meditating or to watching TV while looking forward to the next meal. They can also look forward to sleep, which has become a definite pleasure, not the mere interruption it once had been.

Here I am thinking of old persons under nursing care. Others ferociously guard their independence, and some of them suffer less than one might expect from being lonely and impoverished. They can be rejoiced by visits

20

and meetings, but they also have company inside their heads. Some of them are busiest when their hands are still. What passes through the minds of many is a stream of persons, images, phrases, and familiar tunes. For some that stream has continued since childhood, but now it is deeper; it is their present and their past combined. At times they conduct silent dialogues with a vanished friend, and these are less tiring — often more rewarding — than spoken conversations. If inner resources are lacking, old persons living alone may seek comfort and a kind of companionship in the bottle. I should judge from the gossip of various neighborhoods that the outer suburbs from Boston to San Diego are full of secretly alcoholic widows. One of those widows, an old friend, was moved from her apartment into a retirement home. She left behind her a closet in which the floor was covered wall to wall with whiskey bottles. "Oh, those empty bottles!" she explained. "They were left by a former tenant."

Not whiskey or cooking sherry but simply giving up is the greatest temptation of age. It is something different from a stoical acceptance of infirmities, which is something to be admired. At 63, when he first recognized that his powers were failing, Emerson wrote one of his best poems, "Terminus":

> It is time to be old,
> To take in sail: —
> The god of bounds,
> Who sets to seas a shore,
> Came to me in his fatal rounds,
> And said: "No more!
> No farther shoot
> Thy broad ambitious branches, and thy root.
> Fancy departs: no more invent;
> Contract thy firmament
> To compass of a tent."

Emerson lived in good health to the age of 79. Within his narrowed firmament, he continued working until his memory failed; then he consented to having younger editors and collaborators. The givers-up see no reason for working. Sometimes they lie in bed all day when moving about would still be possible, if difficult. I had a friend, a distinguished poet, who surrendered in that fashion. The doctors tried to stir him to action, but he refused to leave his room. Another friend, once a successful artist, stopped painting when his eyes began to fail. His doctor made the mistake of telling him that he suffered from a fatal disease. He then lost interest in everything except the splendid Rolls-Royce, acquired in his prosperous days, that stood in the garage. Daily he wiped the dust from its hood. He couldn't drive it on the road any longer, but he used to sit in the driver's seat, start the motor, then back the Rolls out of the garage and drive it in again, back twenty feet and forward twenty feet; that was his only distraction.

I haven't the right to blame those who surrender, not being able to put myself inside their minds or bodies. Often they must have compelling reasons, physical or moral. Not only do they suffer from a variety of ailments, but also they are made to feel that they no longer have a function in the community. Their families and neighbors don't ask them for advice, don't really listen when they speak, don't call on them for efforts. One notes that there are not a few recoveries from apparent senility when that situation changes. If it doesn't change, old persons may decide that efforts are useless. I sympathize with their problems, but the men and women I envy are those who accept old age as a series of challenges.

For such persons, every new infirmity is an enemy to be outwitted, an 25 obstacle to be overcome by force of will. They enjoy each little victory over themselves, and sometimes they win a major success. Renoir was one of them. He continued painting, and magnificently, for years after he was crippled by arthritis; the brush had to be strapped to his arm. "You don't need your hand to paint," he said. Goya was another of the unvanquished. At 72 he retired as an official painter of the Spanish court and decided to work only for himself. His later years were those of the famous "black paintings" in which he let his imagination run (and also of the lithographs, then a new technique). At 78 he escaped a reign of terror in Spain by fleeing to Bordeaux. He was deaf and his eyes were failing; in order to work he had to wear several pairs of spectacles, one over another, and then use a magnifying glass; but he was producing splendid work in a totally new style. At 80 he drew an ancient man propped on two sticks, with a mass of white hair and beard hiding his face and with the inscription "I am still learning."

Giovanni Papini said when he was nearly blind, "I prefer martyrdom to imbecility." After writing sixty books, including his famous *Life of Christ*, he was at work on two huge projects when he was stricken with a form of muscular atrophy. He lost the use of his left leg, then of his fingers, so that he couldn't hold a pen. The two big books, though never to be finished, moved forward slowly by dictation; that in itself was a triumph. Toward the end, when his voice had become incomprehensible, he spelled out a word, tapping on the table to indicate letters of the alphabet. One hopes never to be faced with the need for such heroic measures.

"Eighty years old!" the great Catholic poet Paul Claudel wrote in his journal. "No eyes left, no ears, no teeth, no legs, no wind! And when all is said and done, how astonishingly well one does without them!"

Yeats is the great modern poet of age, though he died — I am now tempted to say — as a mere stripling of 73. His reaction to growing old was not that of a stoic like Emerson or Cicero, bent on obeying nature's laws and the edicts of Terminus, the god "Who sets to seas a shore"; it was that of a romantic rebel, the Faustian° man. He was only 61 when he wrote (in "The Tower"):

Faustian In German legend, Faust sells his soul to the devil in return for ultimate knowledge and eternal youth.

What shall I do with this absurdity —
O heart, O troubled heart — this caricature,
Decrepit age that has been tied to me
As to a dog's tail?

At 68 he began to be worried because he wasn't producing many new poems. Could it be, he must have wondered, that his libido had lost its force and that it was somehow connected with his imagination? He had the Faustian desire for renewed youth, felt almost universally, but in Yeats's case with a stronger excuse, since his imagination was the center of his life. A friend told him, with gestures, about Dr. Steinach's then famous operation designed to rejuvenate men by implanting new sex glands. The operation has since fallen into such medical disfavor that Steinach's name is nowhere mentioned in the latest edition of *The Encyclopaedia Britannica*. But Yeats read a pamphlet about it in the Trinity College library, in Dublin, and was favorably impressed. After consulting a physician, who wouldn't say yes or no, he arranged to have the operation performed in a London clinic; that was in May 1934.

Back in Dublin he felt himself to be a different man. Oliver St. John Gogarty, himself a physician, reports a conversation with Yeats that took place the following summer. "I was horrified," he says, "to hear when it was too late that he had undergone such an operation. 'On both sides?' I asked.

"'Yes,' he acknowledged.

"'But, why on earth did you not consult anyone?'

"'I read a pamphlet.'

"'What was wrong with you?'

"'I used to fall asleep after lunch.'"

It was no use making a serious answer to Gogarty the jester. He tells us in his memoir of Yeats that the poet claimed to have been greatly benefited by the operation, but adds, "I have reason to believe that this was not so. He had reached the age when he would not take 'Yes' for an answer." Gogarty's judgment as a physician was probably right; the poet's physical health did not improve and in fact deteriorated. One conjectures that the operation may have put an added strain on his heart and thus may have shortened his life by years. Psychologically, however, Yeats was transformed. He began to think of himself as "the wild old wicked man," and in that character he wrote dozens of poems in a new style, direct, earthy, and passionate. One of them reads:

You think it horrible that lust and rage
Should dance attention upon my old age;
They were not such a plague when I was young;
What else have I to spur me into song?

False remedies are sometimes beneficial in their own fashion. What artists would not sacrifice a few years of life in order to produce work on a level with Yeats's *Last Poems*? Early in January 1939, he wrote to his friend Lady Elizabeth Pelham:

I know for certain that my time will not be long. . . . I am happy, and I think full of energy, of an energy I had despaired of. It seems to me that I have found what I wanted. When I try to put all into a phrase I say, "Man can embody truth but he cannot know it." I must embody it in the completion of my life.

His very last poem, and one of the best, is "The Black Tower," dated the 21st of that month. Yeats died a week after writing it.

AFTERWORD

In the book that began with this essay, Malcolm Cowley surveyed the litera-ture of aging. The Latin orator and statesman Cicero wrote about old age, in De Senectute, *when he was merely middle-aged. He avoided the conditions of advanced age, in a fashion commonplace during the civil wars that established the Roman Empire, by having his head cut off. Another essayist of the aging process was Michel de Montaigne, four hundred years ago the inventor of the essay as we know it, who wrote about old age when he was forty-seven. Montaigne's* essais *emphasized by their name (from the French for "trial" or "test") the tentative, modest, and personal: a prose composition on a subject, setting forth the author's opinion or experience; an endeavor or an attempt (in gesture) without appearing to deem itself the last word on the subject.*

Malcolm Cowley's essay is classic in form — but it does not appear so. It appears informal, personal ("They gave me a party . . ."); it carries its considerable infor-mation with a light touch. Even the beginning example of the Northern Ojibwas, a zinger of an opening, drops into place with a modest if dreadful humor. From this example he is able to move into consideration of our own culture's treatment of the old and deftly deposit some useful statistics. These numbers are useful: They also provide a stone foundation of apparent objectivity upon which the essay can con-struct the frailer house of private testimony. For Cowley the analogy is not archi-tectural but geographical, "the country of old age."

Beginning with paragraph 5, the heart of this essay is personal observation, experience wittily recounted: the feeling of growing old. A personal voice addresses us; readers with imagination or compassion respond to the voice that touches them. The first anecdote of paragraph 5 gives a new habitation and a name to an old insight. Then Cowley lists messages, as he calls them, visually isolating them as if they were telegrams. Or the list resembles a free verse poem, each line rhythmically distinct and grammatically variant, each beginning with a parallel "when." This is the device of the list, notes of detail and experience spread out on the page. Paragraph 6 alludes to a vivid anecdote of aging's effects, then uses it as a transition from the internal sensations of age to the sensations of the outside world's response to the old.

The structure of a good essay appears casual, like a person talking, while it executes the designs of art. Between Gide and the painters and writers who triumph over the adversity of aging — positive models — Cowley inserts a series of bad models, terrors, and warnings. He uses a trinity of abstractions — avarice, untidiness, vanity — and specifies or particularizes by different methods — by example, by anecdote, and by allusion — generalized stories of greed or miserliness, the Collyer brothers, and vanity in several forms, including a reference to the aging Robert Frost.

When we finish the essay — or more likely when we finish it a second time, sleep on it for two nights, and glance at it again to refresh our minds — we understand that we have been manipulated and we are happy about it: The apparently rambling ruminations of an agreeable old sort turn out to be the art of a scrupulous writer.

BOOKS AVAILABLE IN PAPERBACK

The Dream of the Golden Mountains: Remembering the 1930s. New York: Penguin. *Nonfiction.*

Exile's Return: A Literary Odyssey of the 1920s. New York: Penguin. *Nonfiction.*

A Second Flowering: Works and Days of the Lost Generation. New York: Penguin. *Nonfiction.*

JOAN
DIDION

J OAN DIDION is a fifth-generation Californian, born in Sacramento (1934), who took her B.A. at Berkeley and lives in Los Angeles. Between college and marriage to the writer John Gregory Dunne, she lived in New York for seven years, where she worked as an editor for Vogue *and wrote essays for the* National Review *and the* Saturday Evening Post. *In California, Didion and Dunne separately write novels and magazine articles and collaborate on screenplays. Didion's novels are* Run River *(1963),* Play It as It Lays *(1970),* A Book of Common Prayer *(1977), and* Democracy *(1984). Her collections of essays are* Slouching Towards Bethlehem *(1968),* The White Album *(1979), from which we have taken this selection, and* After Henry *(1992). She published* Salvador *in 1983, in 1987* Miami.

Joan Didion is one of our best nonfiction writers. She describes the alien, simple California she grew up in and the southern California where she now lives — a landscape of drive-ins and orange groves, ocean and freeway, the Manson murders and ordinary, domestic, adulterous homicide. She has done witness to the turmoils of the decades, especially the sixties — drugs, Vietnam, and personal breakdown. Expertly sensitive and inventive with language, she is most talented in the representation of hysteria. While her book about El Salvador mentions politics, it is essentially the record of a sensibility, sensitive to fear, exposed to an atmosphere that engenders it: "Terror is the given of the place."

Much of Didion's journalism derives from interviews. She has written of herself: "My only advantage as a reporter is that I am so physically small, so temperamentally unobtrusive, and so neurotically inarticulate that people tend to forget that my presence runs counter to their best interests. And it always does. That is one last thing to remember: writers are always selling somebody out."

Photo by Quintana Roo Dunne

In an essay called "Why I Write," she remembers how she tried to think in abstractions when she was an undergraduate at the University of California. "I failed. My attention veered inexorably back to the specific, to the tangible. . . . I would try to contemplate the Hegelian dialectic and would find myself concentrating instead on a flowering pear tree outside my window." She was a particularist, not an abstractionist; finally, her particulars are not the world outside the window but the words she puts on the page. She is a writer, obsessed by the language she manipulates: "Grammar is a piano I play by ear. . . . All I know about grammar is its infinite power. To shift the structure of a sentence alters the meaning of that sentence, as definitely and inflexibly as the position of a camera alters the meaning of the object photographed."

Holy Water

Some of us who live in arid parts of the world think about water with a reverence others might find excessive. The water I will draw tomorrow from my tap in Malibu is today crossing the Mojave Desert from the Colorado River, and I like to think about exactly where that water is. The water I will drink tonight in a restaurant in Hollywood is by now well down the Los Angeles Aqueduct from the Owens River, and I also think about exactly where that water is: I particularly like to imagine it as it cascades down the 45-degree stone steps that aerate Owens water after its airless passage through the mountain pipes and siphons. As it happens my own reverence for water has always taken the form of this constant meditation upon where the water is, of an obsessive interest not in the politics of water but in the waterworks themselves, in the movement of water through aqueducts and siphons and pumps and forebays and afterbays and weirs and drains, in plumbing on the grand scale. I know the data on water projects I will never see. I know the difficulty Kaiser had closing the last two sluiceway gates on the Guri Dam in Venezuela. I keep watch on evaporation behind the Aswan in Egypt. I can put myself to sleep imagining the water dropping a thousand feet into the turbines at Churchill Falls in Labrador. If the Churchill Falls Project fails to materialize, I fall back on waterworks closer at hand — the tailrace at Hoover on the Colorado, the surge tank in the Tehachapi Mountains that receives California Aqueduct water pumped higher than water has ever been pumped before — and finally I replay a morning when I was seventeen years old and caught, in a military-surplus life raft, in the construction of the Nimbus Afterbay Dam on the American River near Sacramento. I remember that at the moment it happened I was trying to open a tin of anchovies with capers. I recall the raft spinning into the narrow chute through which the river had been temporarily diverted. I recall being deliriously happy.

I suppose it was partly the memory of that delirium that led me to visit, one summer morning in Sacramento, the Operations Control Center for the California State Water Project. Actually so much water is moved around California by so many different agencies that maybe only the movers themselves know on any given day whose water is where, but to get a general picture it is necessary only to remember that Los Angeles moves some of it, San Francisco moves some of it, the Bureau of Reclamation's Central Valley Project moves some of it, and the California State Water Project moves most of the rest of it, moves a vast amount of it, moves more water farther than has ever been moved anywhere. They collect this water up in the granite keeps of the Sierra Nevada and they store roughly a trillion gallons of it behind the Oroville Dam and every morning, down at the Project's headquarters in Sacramento, they decide how much of their water they want to move the next day. They make this morning decision according to supply and demand, which is simple in theory but rather more complicated in practice. In theory each of the Project's five field divisions — the Oroville, the Delta, the San Luis, the San Joaquin, and the Southern divisions — places a call to headquarters before nine A.M. and tells the dispatchers how much water is needed by its local water contractors, who have in turn based their morning estimates on orders from growers and other big users. A schedule is made. The gages open and close according to schedule. The water flows south and the deliveries are made.

In practice this requires prodigious coordination, precision, and the best efforts of several human minds and that of a Univac 418. In practice it might be necessary to hold large flows of water for power production, or to flush out encroaching salinity in the Sacramento–San Joaquin Delta, the most ecologically sensitive point on the system. In practice a sudden rain might obviate the need for a delivery when that delivery is already on its way. In practice what is being delivered here is an enormous volume of water, not quarts of milk or spools of thread, and it takes two days to move such a delivery down through Oroville into the Delta, which is the great pooling place for California water and has been for some years alive with electronic sensors and telemetering equipment and men blocking channels and diverting flows and shoveling fish away from the pumps. It takes perhaps another six days to move this same water down the California Aqueduct from the Delta to the Tehachapi and put it over the hill to Southern California. "Putting some over the hill" is what they say around the Project Operations Control Center when they want to indicate that they are pumping Aqueduct water from the floor of the San Joaquin Valley up and over the Tehachapi Mountains. "Pulling it down" is what they say when they want to indicate that they are lowering a water level somewhere in the system. They can put some over the hill by remote control from this room in Sacramento with its Univac and its big board and its flashing lights. They can pull down a pool in the San Joaquin by remote control from this room in Sacramento with its locked doors and its ringing alarms and its constant printouts of data from sensors out there in the water itself. From this room in Sacramento the whole system takes on the aspect of a perfect three-billion-dollar hydraulic toy, and in certain ways it is. "LET'S START DRAINING QUAIL AT 12:00" was the 10:51 A.M. entry on the electronically recorded communications log the day I visited the Operations Control Center. "Quail" is a reservoir in Los Angeles County with a gross capacity of 1,636,018,000 gallons. "OK" was the response recorded in the log. I knew at that moment that I had missed the only vocation for which I had any instinctive affinity: I wanted to drain Quail myself.

Not many people I know carry their end of the conversation when I want to talk about water deliveries, even when I stress that these deliveries affect their lives, indirectly, every day. "Indirectly" is not quite enough for most people I know. This morning, however, several people I know were affected not "indirectly" but "directly" by the way the water moves. They had been in New Mexico shooting a picture, one sequence of which required a river deep enough to sink a truck, the kind with a cab and a trailer and fifty or sixty wheels. It so happened that no river near the New Mexico location was running that deep this year. The production was therefore moved today to Needles, California, where the Colorado River normally runs, depending upon releases from Davis Dam, eighteen to twenty-five feet deep. Now. Follow this closely: Yesterday we had a freak tropical storm in Southern California, two inches of rain in a normally dry month, and because this rain flooded the fields and provided more irrigation than any grower could possibly want for several days, no water was ordered from Davis Dam.

No orders, no releases.

Supply and demand.

As a result the Colorado was running only seven feet deep past Needles today, Sam Peckinpah's° desire for eighteen feet of water in which to sink a truck not being the kind of demand anyone at Davis Dam is geared to meet. The production closed down for the weekend. Shooting will resume Tuesday, providing some grower orders water and the agencies controlling the Colorado release it. Meanwhile many gaffers, best boys, cameramen, assistant directors, script supervisors, stunt drivers, and maybe even Sam Peckinpah are waiting out the weekend in Needles, where it is often 110 degrees at five P.M. and hard to get dinner after eight. This is a California parable, but a true one.

I have always wanted a swimming pool, and never had one. When it became generally known a year or so ago that California was suffering severe drought, many people in water-rich parts of the country seemed

5

Sam Peckinpah American film director (1925–1984).

obscurely gratified, and made frequent reference to Californians having to brick up their swimming pools. In fact a swimming pool requires, once it has been filled and the filter has begun its process of cleaning and recirculating the water, virtually no water, but the symbolic content of swimming pools has always been interesting: A pool is misapprehended as a trapping of affluence, real or pretended, and of a kind of hedonistic attention to the body. Actually a pool is, for many of us in the West, a symbol not of affluence but of order, of control over the uncontrollable. A pool is water, made available and useful, and is, as such, infinitely soothing to the western eye.

It is easy to forget that the only natural force over which we have any control out here is water, and that only recently. In my memory California summers were characterized by the coughing in the pipes that meant the well was dry, and California winters by all-night watches on rivers about to crest, by sandbagging, by dynamite on the levees, and flooding on the first floor. Even now the place is not all that hospitable to extensive settlement. As I write a fire has been burning out of control for two weeks in the ranges behind the Big Sur coast. Flash floods last night wiped out all major roads into Imperial County. I noticed this morning a hairline crack in a living-room tile from last week's earthquake, a 4.4 I never felt. In the part of California where I now live aridity is the single most prominent feature of the climate, and I am not pleased to see, this year, cactus spreading wild to the sea. There will be days this winter when the humidity will drop to ten, seven, four. Tumbleweed will blow against my house and the sound of the rattlesnake will be duplicated a hundred times a day by dried bougainvillea drifting in my driveway. The apparent ease of California life is an illusion, and those who believe the illusion real live here in only the most temporary way. I know as well as the next person that there is considerable transcendent value in a river running wild and undammed, a river running free over granite, but I have also lived beneath such a river when it was running in flood, and gone without showers when it was running dry.

"The West begins," Bernard DeVoto wrote, "where the average annual rainfall drops below twenty inches." This is maybe the best definition of the West I have ever read, and it goes a long way toward explaining my own passion for seeing the water under control, but many people I know persist in looking for psychoanalytical implications in this passion. As a matter of fact I have explored, in an amateur way, the more obvious of these implications, and come up with nothing interesting. A certain external reality remains, and resists interpretation. The West begins where the average annual rainfall drops below twenty inches. Water is important to people who do not have it, and the same is true of control. Some fifteen years ago I tore a poem by Karl Shapiro from a magazine and pinned it on my kitchen wall. This fragment of paper is now on the wall of a sixth kitchen, and crumbles a little whenever I touch it, but I keep it there for the last stanza, which has for me the power of a prayer:

It is raining in California, a straight rain
Cleaning the heavy oranges on the bough,
Filling the gardens till the gardens flow,
Shining the olives, tiling the gleaming tile,
Waxing the dark camellia leaves more green,
Flooding the daylong valleys like the Nile.

I thought of those lines constantly on the morning in Sacramento when I went to visit the California State Water Project Operations Control Center. If I had wanted to drain Quail at 10:51 that morning, I wanted, by early afternoon, to do a great deal more. I wanted to open and close the Clifton Court Forebay intake gate. I wanted to produce some power down at the San Luis Dam. I wanted to pick a pool at random on the Aqueduct and pull it down and then refill it, watching for the hydraulic jump. I wanted to put some water over the hill and I wanted to shut down all flow from the Aqueduct into the Bureau of Reclamation's Cross Valley Canal, just to see how long it would take somebody over at Reclamation to call up and complain. I stayed as long as I could and watched the system work on the big board with the lighted checkpoints. The Delta salinity report was coming in on one of the teletypes behind me. The Delta tidal report was coming in on another. The earthquake board, which has been desensitized to sound its alarm (a beeping tone for Southern California, a high-pitched tone for the north) only for those earthquakes which register at least 3.0 on the Richter Scale, was silent. I had no further business in this room and yet I wanted to stay the day. I wanted to be the one, that day, who was shining the olives, filling the gardens, and flooding the daylong valleys like the Nile. I want it still.

AFTERWORD

Somewhere Didion writes: "A place belongs forever to whoever claims it hardest, remembers it most obsessively, wrenches it from itself, shapes it, renders it, loves it so radically that he really makes it in his image." Whatever she speaks of, she will always discover the extreme; the middle way does not interest her. (Even as a child, "I can recall disapproving of the golden mean. . . .") Surely we can imagine a middling essay on water, all statistics and predictions, which would interest nobody. Information in "Holy Water" supplies a frame, and we would miss it if it were not there, but it is not the essay's heart. With Didion, information is the ephemeral flesh; feeling is the skeleton that endures. She will not work herself up to write unless "the extremes show up."

This extremity is a matter of personal feeling, it requires the letter "I." Feeling requires someone to do it. In her essay called "Why I Write," Didion says, "In many ways writing is the act of saying I, of imposing oneself on people, of saying listen to me, see it my way, change your mind."

BOOKS AVAILABLE IN PAPERBACK

After Henry. New York: Random House–Vintage. *Essays.*
Play It as It Lays. New York: Farrar, Straus & Giroux. *Novel.*
Run River. New York: Random House–Vintage. *Novel.*
Salvador. New York: Random House–Vintage. *Nonfiction.*
Slouching Towards Bethlehem. New York: Farrar, Straus & Giroux. *Essays.*
The White Album. New York: Farrar, Straus & Giroux. *Essays.*

ANNIE
DILLARD

*A*NNIE DILLARD *(b. 1945) grew up in Pittsburgh and attended Hollins College in Virginia, where she completed her B.A. and M.A. She has taught at Western Washington University and currently teaches at Wesleyan University in Connecticut. But she has worked mostly as a writer. A book of poems,* Tickets for a Prayer Wheel, *appeared in 1974. In the same year she published* Pilgrim at Tinker Creek, *her first prose — an example of the ecstatic natural observation that makes up her best work. The book won a Pulitzer Prize. In 1977 she published* Holy the Firm *and early in 1982 a work of literary theory called* Living by Fiction. *Later in the same year she collected her essays into* Teaching a Stone to Talk. Encounters with Chinese Writers *appeared in 1984. In 1987 she published* An American Childhood, *her energetic and lively and thoughtful memoir of growing up in Pittsburgh; the book is funny and profound, with acute observations of the beginnings of consciousness and self-consciousness. In 1989 she wrote* The Writing Life, *a reminiscence and speculation on her art, and in 1992 a novel called* The Living.

Book reviewers often deride miscellaneous collections of work from periodicals, as if a book that preserves magazine pieces must be ephemeral. Annie Dillard writes a note at the front of Teaching a Stone to Talk, *to make sure that no one misunderstands her own attitude toward this work: "This is not a collection of occasional pieces, such as a writer brings out to supplement his real work; instead, this is my real work. . . ."*

The ellipsis at the quotation's end omits Annie Dillard's last words: "such as it is." Such as it is, Annie Dillard's real work reaches a level of imagination we usually associate not with the essay but with poetry and fiction. Her mind combines qualities not often found together: an almost insatiable curiosity about details of the natural world, science, and thought together with a spiritual appetite, a visionary's or mystic's seeking through religious study and meditation. Combining these qualities, she becomes a major writer of American prose.

Like all writers, Dillard encounters difficulties writing. Every time she tries, she says, "There's just some prohibitive and fatal flaw in the structure. And that's where most people quit. You just have to hang on." Handing essays back to a class of students not long ago, she said, "I hand back these miserable things — that's O.K. I knew they'd be miserable. . . . The assignment was to write a brilliant essay. The assignment is always to write a brilliant essay." It is the assignment she gave herself, and fulfilled, when she wrote "Total Eclipse," from Teaching a Stone to Talk. *Dillard's curiosity, observation, narrative, description, and vision bring to this volume a model of the modern essay.*

Total Eclipse

I

It had been like dying, the sliding down the mountain pass. It had been like the death of someone, irrational, that sliding down the mountain pass and into the region of dread. It was like slipping into fever, or falling down that hole in sleep from which you wake yourself whimpering. We had crossed the mountains that day, and now we were in a strange place — a hotel in central Washington, in a town near Yakima. The eclipse we had traveled here to see would occur early in the next morning.

I lay in bed. My husband, Gary, was reading beside me. I lay in bed and looked at the painting on the hotel room wall. It was a print of a detailed and lifelike painting of a smiling clown's head, made out of vegetables. It was a painting of the sort which you do not intend to look at, and which, alas, you never forget. Some tasteless fate presses it upon you; it becomes part of the complex interior junk you carry with you wherever you go. Two years have passed since the total eclipse of which I write. During those years I have forgotten, I assume, a great many things I wanted to remember — but I have not forgotten that clown painting or its lunatic setting in the old hotel.

The clown was bald. Actually, he wore a clown's tight rubber wig, painted white; this stretched over the top of his skull, which was a cabbage. His hair was bunches of baby carrots. Inset in his white clown makeup, and in his cabbage skull, were his small and laughing human eyes. The clown's glance was like the glance of Rembrandt in some of the self-portraits: lively, knowing, deep, and loving. The crinkled shadows around his eyes were string beans. His eyebrows were parsley. Each of his ears was a broad bean.

His thin, joyful lips were red chili peppers; between his lips were wet rows of human teeth and a suggestion of a real tongue. The clown print was framed in gilt and glassed.

To put ourselves in the path of the total eclipse, that day we had driven five hours inland from the Washington coast, where we lived. When we tried to cross the Cascades range, an avalanche had blocked the pass.

A slope's worth of snow blocked the road; traffic backed up. Had the 5 avalanche buried any cars that morning? We could not learn. This highway was the only winter road over the mountains. We waited as highway crews bulldozed a passage through the avalanche. With two-by-fours and walls of plywood, they erected a one-way, roofed tunnel through the avalanche. We drove through the avalanche tunnel, crossed the pass, and descended several thousand feet into central Washington and the broad Yakima valley, about which we knew only that it was orchard country. As we lost altitude, the snows disappeared; our ears popped; the trees changed, and in the trees were strange birds. I watched the landscape innocently, like a fool, like a diver in the rapture of the deep who plays on the bottom while his air runs out.

The hotel lobby was a dark, derelict room, narrow as a corridor, and seemingly without air. We waited on a couch while the manager vanished upstairs to do something unknown to our room. Beside us on an overstuffed chair, absolutely motionless, was a platinum-blond woman in her forties wearing a black silk dress and a strand of pearls. Her long legs were crossed; she supported her head on her fist. At the dim far end of the room, their backs toward us, sat six bald old men in their shirtsleeves, around a loud television. Two of them seemed asleep. They were drunks. "Number six!" cried the man on television. "Number six!"

On the broad lobby desk, lighted and bubbling, was a ten-gallon aquarium containing one large fish; the fish tilted up and down in its water. Against the long opposite wall sang a live canary in its cage. Beneath the cage, among spilled millet seeds on the carpet, were a decorated child's sand bucket and matching sand shovel.

Now the alarm was set for six. I lay awake remembering an article I had read downstairs in the lobby, in an engineering magazine. The article was about gold mining.

In South Africa, in India, and in South Dakota, the gold mines extend so deeply into the earth's crust that they are hot. The rock walls burn the miners' hands. The companies have to air-condition the mines; if the air conditioners break, the miners die. The elevators in the mine shafts run very slowly, down, and up, so the miners' ears will not pop in their skulls. When the miners return to the surface, their faces are deathly pale.

Early the next morning we checked out. It was February 26, 1979, a 10 Monday morning. We would drive out of town, find a hilltop, watch the eclipse, and then drive back over the mountains and home to the coast. How familiar things are here; how adept we are; how smoothly and professionally we check out! I had forgotten the clown's smiling head and the hotel lobby as if they had never existed. Gary put the car in gear and off we went, as off we have gone to a hundred other adventures.

It was dawn when we found a highway out of town and drove into the unfamiliar countryside. By the growing light we could see a band of cirro-stratus clouds in the sky. Later the rising sun would clear these clouds before the eclipse began. We drove at random until we came to a range of unfenced hills. We pulled off the highway, bundled up, and climbed one of these hills.

I I

The hill was five hundred feet high. Long winter-killed grass covered it, as high as our knees. We climbed and rested, sweating in the cold; we passed clumps of bundled people on the hillside who were setting up telescopes and fiddling with cameras. The top of the hill stuck up in the middle of the sky. We tightened our scarves and looked around.

East of us rose another hill like ours. Between the hills, far below, was the highway which threaded south into the valley. This was the Yakima valley; I had never seen it before. It is justly famous for its beauty, like every planted valley. It extended south into the horizon, a distant dream of a valley, a Shangri-la. All its hundreds of low, golden slopes bore orchards. Among the orchards were towns, and roads, and plowed and fallow fields. Through the valley wandered a thin shining river; from the river extended fine, frozen irrigation ditches. Distance blurred and blued the sight, so that the whole valley looked like a thickness or sediment at the bottom of the sky. Directly behind us was more sky, and empty lowlands blued by distance, and Mount Adams. Mount Adams was an enormous, snow-covered volcanic cone rising flat, like so much scenery.

Now the sun was up. We could not see it; but the sky behind the band of clouds was yellow, and, far down the valley, some hillside orchards had lighted up. More people were parking near the highway and climbing the hills. It was the West. All of us rugged individuals were wearing knit caps and blue nylon parkas. People were climbing the nearby hills and setting up shop in clumps among the dead grasses. It looked as though we had gathered on hilltops to pray for the world on its last day. It looked as though we had all crawled out of spaceships and were preparing to assault the valley below. It looked as though we were scattered on hilltops at dawn to sacrifice virgins, make rain, set stone stelae in a ring. There was no place out of the wind. The straw grasses banged our legs.

Up in the sky where we stood the air was lusterless yellow. To the west the sky was blue. Now the sun cleared the clouds. We cast rough shadows on the blowing grass; freezing, we waved our arms. Near the sun, the sky was bright and colorless. There was nothing to see.

15

It began with no ado. It was odd that such a well-advertised public event should have no starting gun, no overture, no introductory speaker. I should have known right then that I was out of my depth. Without pause or preamble, silent as orbits, a piece of the sun went away. We looked at it through welders' goggles. A piece of the sun was missing; in its place we saw empty sky.

I had seen a partial eclipse in 1970. A partial eclipse is very interesting. It bears almost no relation to a total eclipse. Seeing a partial eclipse bears the same relation to seeing a total eclipse as kissing a man does to marrying him, or as flying in an airplane does to falling out of an airplane. Although the one experience precedes the other, it in no way prepares you for it. During a partial eclipse the sky does not darken — not even when 94 percent of the sun is hidden. Nor does the sun, seen colorless through protective devices, seem terribly strange. We have all seen a sliver of light in the sky; we have all seen the crescent moon by day. However, during a partial eclipse the air does indeed get cold, precisely as if someone were standing between you and the fire. And blackbirds do fly back to their roosts. I had seen a partial eclipse before, and here was another.

What you see in an eclipse is entirely different from what you know. It is especially different for those of us whose grasp of astronomy is so frail that, given a flashlight, a grapefruit, two oranges, and fifteen years, we still could not figure out which way to set the clocks for daylight saving time. Usually it is a bit of a trick to keep your knowledge from blinding you. But during an eclipse it is easy. What you see is much more convincing than any wild-eyed theory you may know.

You may read that the moon has something to do with eclipses. I have never seen the moon yet. You do not see the moon. So near the sun, it is as completely invisible as the stars are by day. What you see before your eyes is the sun going through phases. It gets narrower and narrower, as the waning moon does, and, like the ordinary moon, it travels alone in the simple sky. The sky is of course background. It does not appear to eat the sun; it is far behind the sun. The sun simply shaves away; gradually, you see less sun and more sky.

The sky's blue was deepening, but there was no darkness. The sun was 20 a wide crescent, like a segment of tangerine. The wind freshened and blew steadily over the hill. The eastern hill across the highway grew dusky and sharp. The towns and orchards in the valley to the south were dissolving into the blue light. Only the thin river held a trickle of sun.

Now the sky to the west deepened to indigo, a color never seen. A dark sky usually loses color. This was a saturated, deep indigo, up in the air. Stuck up into that unworldly sky was the cone of Mount Adams, and the alpenglow was upon it. The alpenglow is that red light of sunset which holds out on snowy mountaintops long after the valleys and tablelands are dimmed. "Look at Mount Adams," I said, and that was the last sane moment I remember.

I turned back to the sun. It was going. The sun was going, and the world was wrong. The grasses were wrong; they were platinum. Their every detail of stem, head, and blade shone lightless and artificially distinct as an art photographer's platinum print. This color has never been seen on earth. The hues were metallic; their finish was matte. The hillside was a nineteenth-century tinted photograph from which the tints had faded. All the people you see in the photograph, distinct and detailed as their faces look, are now dead. The sky was navy blue. My hands were silver. All the distant hills' grasses were finespun metal which the wind laid down. I was watching a faded color print of a movie filmed in the Middle Ages; I was standing in it, by some mistake. I was standing in a movie of hillside grasses filmed in the Middle Ages. I missed my own century, the people I knew, and the real light of day.

I looked at Gary. He was in the film. Everything was lost. He was a platinum print, a dead artist's version of life. I saw on his skull the darkness of night mixed with the colors of day. My mind was going out; my eyes were receding the way galaxies recede to the rim of space. Gary was light-years away, gesturing inside a circle of darkness, down the wrong end of a telescope. He smiled as if he saw me; the stringy crinkles around his eyes moved. The sight of him, familiar and wrong, was something I was remembering from centuries hence, from the other side of death: Yes, *that* is the way he used to look, when we were living. When it was our generation's turn to be alive. I could not hear him; the wind was too loud. Behind him the sun was going. We had all started down a chute of time. At first it was pleasant; now there was no stopping it. Gary was chuting away across space, moving and talking and catching my eye, chuting down the long corridor of separation. The skin on his face moved like thin bronze plating that would peel.

The grass at our feet was wild barley. It was the wild einkorn wheat which grew on the hilly flanks of the Zagros Mountains, above the Euphrates valley, above the valley of the river we called *River*. We harvested the grass with stone sickles, I remember. We found the grasses on the hillsides; we built our shelter beside them and cut them down. That is how he used to look then, that one, moving and living and catching my eye, with the sky so dark behind him, and the wind blowing. God save our life.

From all the hills came screams. A piece of sky beside the crescent sun was detaching. It was a loosened circle of evening sky, suddenly lighted from the back. It was an abrupt black body out of nowhere; it was a flat disk; it was almost over the sun. That is when there were screams. At once this disk of sky slid over the sun like a lid. The sky snapped over the sun like a lens cover. The hatch in the brain slammed. Abruptly it was dark night, on the land and in the sky. In the night sky was a tiny ring of light. The hole where the sun belongs is very small. A thin ring of light marked its place. There was no sound. The eyes dried, the arteries drained, the lungs hushed. There was no world. We were the world's dead people rotating and orbiting 25 around and around, embedded in the planet's crust, while the earth rolled down. Our minds were light-years distant, forgetful of almost everything. Only an extraordinary act of will could recall to us our former, living selves and our contexts in matter and time. We had, it seems, loved the planet and loved our lives, but could no longer remember the way of them. We got the light wrong. In the sky was something that should not be there. In the black sky was a ring of light. It was a thin ring, an old, thin silver wedding band, an old, worn ring. It was an old wedding band in the sky, or a morsel of bone. There were stars. It was all over.

III

It is now that the temptation is strongest to leave these regions. We have seen enough; let's go. Why burn our hands any more than we have to? But two years have passed; the price of gold has risen. I return to the same buried alluvial beds and pick through the strata again.

I saw, early in the morning, the sun diminish against a backdrop of sky. I saw a circular piece of that sky appear, suddenly detached, blackened, and backlighted; from nowhere it came and overlapped the sun. It did not look like the moon. It was enormous and black. If I had not read that it was the moon, I could have seen the sight a hundred times and never thought of the moon once. (If, however, I had not read that it was the moon — if, like most of the world's people throughout time, I had simply glanced up and seen this thing — then I doubtless would not have speculated much, but would have, like Emperor Louis of Bavaria in 840, simply died of fright on the spot.) It did not look like a dragon, although it looked more like a dragon than the moon. It looked like a lens cover, or the lid of a pot. It materialized out of thin air — black, and flat, and sliding, outlined in flame.

Seeing this black body was like seeing a mushroom cloud. The heart screeched. The meaning of the sight overwhelmed its fascination. It obliterated meaning itself. If you were to glance out one day and see a row of mushroom clouds rising on the horizon, you would know at once that what you were seeing, remarkable as it was, was intrinsically not worth remarking. No use running to tell anyone. Significant as it was, it did not matter a whit. For what is significance? It is significance for people. No people, no significance. This is all I have to tell you.

In the deeps are the violence and terror of which psychology has warned us. But if you ride these monsters deeper down, if you drop with them farther over the world's rim, you find what our sciences cannot locate or name, the substrate, the ocean or matrix or ether which buoys the rest, which gives goodness its power for good, and evil its power for evil, the unified field: our complex and inexplicable caring for each other, and for our life together here. This is given. It is not learned.

The world which lay under darkness and stillness following the closing 30 of the lid was not the world we know. The event was over. Its devastation lay around about us. The clamoring mind and heart stilled, almost indifferent, certainly disembodied, frail, and exhausted. The hills were hushed, obliterated. Up in the sky, like a crater from some distant cataclysm, was a hollow ring.

You have seen photographs of the sun taken during a total eclipse. The corona fills the print. All of those photographs were taken through telescopes. The lenses of telescopes and cameras can no more cover the breadth and scale of the visual array than language can cover the breadth and simultaneity of internal experience. Lenses enlarge the sight, omit its context, and make of it a pretty and sensible picture, like something on a Christmas card. I assure you, if you send any shepherds a Christmas card on which is printed a three-by-three photograph of the angel of the Lord, the glory of the Lord, and a multitude of the heavenly host, they will not be sore afraid. More fearsome things can come in envelopes. More moving photographs than those of the sun's corona can appear in magazines. But I pray you will never see anything more awful in the sky.

You see the wide world swaddled in darkness; you see a vast breadth of hilly land, and an enormous, distant, blackened valley; you see towns' lights, a river's path, and blurred portions of your hat and scarf; you see your husband's face looking like an early black-and-white film; and you see a sprawl of black sky and blue sky together, with unfamiliar stars in it, some barely visible bands of cloud, and over there, a small white ring. The ring is as small as one goose in a flock of migrating geese — if you happen to notice a flock of migrating geese. It is one 360th part of the visible sky. The sun we see is less than half the diameter of a dime held at arm's length.

The Crab Nebula, in the constellation Taurus, looks, through binoculars, like a smoke ring. It is a star in the process of exploding. Light from its explosion first reached the earth in 1054; it was a supernova then, and so bright it shone in the daytime. Now it is not so bright, but it is still exploding. It expands at the rate of seventy million miles a day. It is interesting to look through binoculars at something expanding seventy million miles a day. It does not budge. Its apparent size does not increase. Photographs of the Crab Nebula taken fifteen years ago seem identical to photographs of it taken yesterday. Some lichens are similar. Botanists have measured some ordinary lichens twice, at fifty-year intervals, without detecting any growth at all. And yet their cells divide; they live.

The small ring of light was like these things — like a ridiculous lichen up in the sky, like a perfectly still explosion 4,200 light-years away: it was interesting, and lovely, and in witless motion, and it had nothing to do with anything.

It had nothing to do with anything. The sun was too small, and too cold, and too far away, to keep the world alive. The white ring was not enough. It was feeble and worthless. It was as useless as a memory; it was as off kilter and hollow and wretched as a memory.

When you try your hardest to recall someone's face, or the look of a place, you see in your mind's eye some vague and terrible sight such as this. It is dark; it is insubstantial; it is all wrong.

The white ring and the saturated darkness made the earth and the sky look as they must look in the memories of the careless dead. What I saw, what I seemed to be standing in, was all the wrecked light that the memories of the dead could shed upon the living world. We had all died in our boots on the hilltops of Yakima, and were alone in eternity. Empty space stoppered our eyes and mouths; we cared for nothing. We remembered our living days wrong. With great effort we had remembered some sort of circular light in the sky — but only the outline. Oh, and then the orchard trees withered, the ground froze, the glaciers slid down the valleys and overlapped the towns. If there had ever been people on earth, nobody knew it. The dead had forgotten those they had loved. The dead were parted one from the other and could no longer remember the faces and lands they had loved in the light. They seemed to stand on darkened hilltops, looking down.

IV

We teach our children one thing only, as we were taught: to wake up. We teach our children to look alive there, to join by words and activities the life of human culture on the planet's crust. As adults we are almost all adept at waking up. We have so mastered the transition we have forgotten we ever learned it. Yet it is a transition we make a hundred times a day, as, like so many will-less dolphins, we plunge and surface, lapse and emerge. We live half our waking lives and all of our sleeping lives in some private, useless, and insensible waters we never mention or recall. Useless, I say. Valueless, I might add — until someone hauls their wealth up to the surface and into the wide-awake city, in a form that people can use.

I do not know how we got to the restaurant. Like Roethke, "I take my waking slow." Gradually I seemed more or less alive and already forgetful. It was now almost nine in the morning. It was the day of a solar eclipse in central Washington, and a fine adventure for everyone. The sky was clear; there was a fresh breeze out of the north.

The restaurant was a roadside place with tables and booths. The other 40 eclipse-watchers were there. From our booth we could see their cars' California license plates, their University of Washington parking stickers. Inside the restaurant we were all eating eggs or waffles; people were fairly shouting and exchanging enthusiasms, like fans after a World Series game. Did you see . . . ? Did you see . . . ? Then somebody said something which knocked me for a loop.

A college student, a boy in a blue parka who carried a Hasselblad, said to us, "Did you see that little white ring? It looked like a Life Saver. It looked like a Life Saver up in the sky."

And so it did. The boy spoke well. He was a walking alarm clock. I myself had at that time no access to such a word. He could write a sentence, and I could not. I grabbed that Life Saver and rode it to the surface. And I had to laugh. I had been dumbstruck on the Euphrates River, I had been dead and gone and grieving, all over the sight of something which, if you could claw your way up to that level, you would grant looked very much like a Life Saver. It was good to be back among people so clever; it was good to have all the world's words at the mind's disposal, so the mind could begin its task. All those things for which we have no words are lost. The mind — the culture — has two little tools, grammar and lexicon: a decorated sand bucket and a matching shovel. With these we bluster about the continents and do all the world's work. With these we try to save our very lives.

There are a few more things to tell from this level, the level of the restaurant. One is the old joke about breakfast. "It can never be satisfied, the mind, never." Wallace Stevens wrote that, and in the long run he was right. The mind wants to live forever, or to learn a very good reason why not. The mind wants the world to return its love, or its awareness; the mind wants to know all the world, and all eternity, and God. The mind's sidekick, however, will settle for two eggs over easy.

The dear, stupid body is as easily satisfied as a spaniel. And, incredibly, the simple spaniel can lure the brawling mind to its dish. It is everlastingly funny that the proud, metaphysically ambitious, clamoring mind will hush if you give it an egg.

Further: While the mind reels in deep space, while the mind grieves or 45 fears or exults, the workaday senses, in ignorance or idiocy, like so many computer terminals printing out market prices while the world blows up, still transcribe their little data and transmit them to the warehouse in the skull. Later, under the tranquilizing influence of fried eggs, the mind can sort through this data. The restaurant was a halfway house, a decompression chamber. There I remembered a few things more.

The deepest, and most terrifying, was this: I have said that I heard screams. (I have since read that screaming, with hysteria, is a common reaction even to expected total eclipses.) People on all the hillsides, including, I think, myself, screamed when the black body of the moon detached from the sky and rolled over the sun. But something else was happening at that same instant, and it was this, I believe, which made us scream.

The second before the sun went out we saw a wall of dark shadow come speeding at us. We no sooner saw it than it was upon us, like thunder. It roared up the valley. It slammed our hill and knocked us out. It was the monstrous swift shadow cone of the moon. I have since read that this wave shadow moves 1,800 miles an hour. It was 195 miles wide. No end was in sight — you saw only the edge. It rolled at you across the land at 1,800 miles an hour, hauling darkness like plague behind it. Seeing it, and knowing it was coming straight for you, was like feeling a slug of anesthetic shoot up your arm. If you think very fast, you may have time to think, "Soon it will hit my brain." You can feel the deadness race up your arm; you can feel the appalling, inhuman speed of your own blood. We saw the wall of shadow coming, and screamed before it hit.

This was the universe about which we have read so much and never before felt: the universe as a clockwork of loose spheres flung at stupefying, unauthorized speeds. How could anything moving so fast not crash, not veer from its orbit amok like a car out of control on a turn?

Less than two minutes later, when the sun emerged, the trailing edge of the shadow cone sped away. It coursed down our hill and raced eastward over the plain, faster than the eye could believe; it swept over the plain and dropped over the planet's rim in a twinkling. It had clobbered us, and now it roared away. We blinked in the light. It was as though an enormous, loping god in the sky had reached down and slapped the earth's face.

Something else, something more ordinary, came back to me along about 50 the third cup of coffee. During the moments of totality, it was so dark that drivers on the highway below turned on their cars' headlights. We could see the highway's route as a strand of lights. It was bumper-to-bumper down there. It was eight-fifteen in the morning, Monday morning, and people were driving into Yakima to work. That it was as dark as night, and eerie as hell, an hour after dawn, apparently meant that in order to *see* to drive to work, people had to use their headlights. Four or five cars pulled off the road. The rest, in a line at least five miles long, drove to town. The highway ran between hills; the people could not have seen any of the eclipsed sun at all. Yakima will have another total eclipse in 2086. Perhaps, in 2086, businesses will give their employees an hour off.

From the restaurant we drove back to the coast. The highway crossing the Cascades range was open. We drove over the mountain like old pros. We joined our places on the planet's thin crust; it held. For the time being, we were home free.

Early that morning at six, when we had checked out, the six bald men were sitting on folding chairs in the dim hotel lobby. The television was on. Most of them were awake. You might drown in your own spittle, God knows, at any time; you might wake up dead in a small hotel, a cabbage head watching TV while snows pile up in the passes, watching TV while the chili peppers smile and the moon passes over the sun and nothing changes and nothing is learned because you have lost your bucket and shovel and no longer care. What if you regain the surface and open your sack and find, instead of treasure, a beast which jumps at you? Or you may not come back at all. The winches may jam, the scaffolding buckle, the air conditioning collapse. You may glance up one day and see by your headlamp the canary keeled over in its cage. You may reach into a cranny for pearls and touch a moray eel. You yank on your rope; it is too late.

Apparently people share a sense of these hazards, for when the total eclipse ended, an odd thing happened.

When the sun appeared as a blinding bead on the ring's side, the eclipse was over. The black lens cover appeared again, backlighted, and slid away. At once the yellow light made the sky blue again; the black lid dissolved and vanished. The real world began there. I remember now: We all hurried away. We were born and bored at a stroke. We rushed down the hill. We found our car; we saw the other people streaming down the hillsides; we joined the highway traffic and drove away.

We never looked back. It was a general vamoose, and an odd one, for when we left the hill, the sun was still partially eclipsed — a sight rare enough, and one which, in itself, we would probably have driven five hours to see. But enough is enough. One turns at last even from glory itself with a sigh of relief. From the depths of mystery, and even from the heights of splendor, we bounce back and hurry for the latitudes of home.

55

AFTERWORD

A writer can choose to build emotion toward a climax, gradually increasing tempo, but Annie Dillard starts at full throttle with "It had been like dying, that sliding down the mountain pass." She compares moving downhill to the extremity of death. Note, however, that her intensity of feeling and her grandeur of metaphor — fever, falling into a hole; illness and sleep and death; later madness — do not preclude exposition, slipped in like an afterthought: "The eclipse we had traveled here to see. . . ."

The third paragraph contains Dillard's description of the tasteless, horrid, fascinating vegetable-clown, making it into a literary symbol — a device to embody what we lack words to say outright. (A French poet called the symbol "a new word.") The symbolic writer gathers a complex of feelings and sensations into images or narrative. This vegetable-clown horrifies by violating nature; so does the total eclipse, during which (paragraph 23) Dillard looks at her husband: "He was in the film. Everything was lost. He was a platinum print, a dead artist's version of life. I saw on his skull the darkness of night mixed with the colors of day. My mind was going out."

BOOKS AVAILABLE IN PAPERBACK

An American Childhood. New York: HarperCollins. *Nonfiction.*

Encounters with Chinese Writers. Middletown, Conn.: Wesleyan University Press. *Nonfiction.*

Holy the Firm. New York: HarperCollins. *Nonfiction.*

The Living. New York: HarperCollins. *Novel.*

Living by Fiction. New York: HarperCollins. *Nonfiction.*

Pilgrim at Tinker Creek. New York: HarperCollins. *Essays.*

Teaching a Stone to Talk. New York: HarperCollins. *Essays.*

Tickets for a Prayer Wheel. New York: HarperCollins. *Poetry.*

The Writing Life. New York: HarperCollins. *Nonfiction.*

E. L.
DOCTOROW

E. *L. DOCTOROW was born in New York (1931), where he now lives, but went to school in Ohio, majoring in philosophy at Kenyon College. For many years he worked as an editor for publishing firms in New York while he wrote fiction. His first novel,* Welcome to Hard Times, *appeared in 1960. In* The Book of Daniel *(1971), he made fiction out of contemporary history and politics, using as his source the trial and execution of Julius and Ethel Rosenberg, convicted as spies for the Soviet Union. With* Ragtime *(1975) he brought historical characters into his fiction while rendering the early twentieth century with humor and outrage together. Characters like Harry Houdini and Sigmund Freud turned up in* Ragtime's *pages along with figures of fiction.*

Subsequent novels — Loon Lake *(1980),* Lives of the Poets *(1984),* World's Fair *(1985), and especially* Billy Bathgate *(1990) — have won literary prizes and placed Doctorow at the forefront of contemporary American fiction. His work always concerns itself with American society and politics — as his first essay collection makes clear; we take "False Documents" from* Jack London, Hemingway, and the Constitution *(1993).*

The New York Times Magazine *told a story about Doctorow, falsity, and the facts. His first novel was set in the Dakota Territory late in the nineteenth century. After publication, Doctorow received a letter from a very old lady in Texas, who wrote, "Young man, when you said that Jenks enjoyed for his dinner the roasted haunch of a prairie dog, I knew you'd never been west of the Hudson. Because the haunch of a prairie dog wouldn't fill a teaspoon." Doctorow claims that he answered her, "That's true of prairie dogs today, Madam, but in the 1870s . . ."*

False Documents

Fiction is a not entirely rational means of discourse. It gives to the reader something more than information. Complex understandings, indirect, intuitive, and nonverbal, arise from the words of the story, and by a ritual transaction between reader and writer, instructive emotion is generated in the reader from the illusion of suffering and experience not his own. A novel is a printed circuit through which flows the force of a reader's own life.

Sartre in his essay "Literature and Existentialism" says: "Each book is a recovery of the totality of being. . . . For this is quite the final goal of art: to recover this world by giving it to be seen as it is, but as if it had its source in human freedom."

Certainly I know that I would rather read a sentence such as this from Nabokov's *The Gift* —

> As he crossed toward the pharmacy at the corner he involuntarily turned his head because of a burst of light that had ricocheted from his temple, and saw, with that quick smile with which we greet a rainbow or a rose, a blindingly white parallelogram of sky being unloaded from the van — a dresser with mirror, across which, as across a cinema screen, passed a flawlessly clear reflection of boughs, sliding and swaying not arboreally, a human vacillation, produced by the nature of those who were carrying this sky, these boughs, this gliding facade.

— whose occasion is in question, whose truth I cannot test, than a sentence such as this from the rational mentality of the *New York Times* —

> The navy has announced base consolidations and other actions that it said would eliminate five hundred civilian jobs and sixteen military positions at an annual savings of about five million dollars.

— whose purposes are immediately clear, and with regard to whose truth I am completely credulous.

As a writer of fiction I could make the claim that a sentence spun from the imagination, i.e., a sentence composed as a lie, confers upon the writer a degree of perception or acuity or heightened awareness, but in any event some additional usefulness, that a sentence composed with the most strict reverence for fact does not. In any event, what can surely be distinguished here are two kinds of power in language, the power of the navy's announcement residing in its manifest reference to the verifiable world — let us call that *the power of the regime* — and the power of Nabokov's description

116

inhering in a private or ideal world that cannot be easily corroborated or verified — let us call that *the power of freedom.*

Immediately I have to wonder if this formulation is too grandiose — the power of the regime and the power of freedom. But it is true that we live in an industrial society which counts its achievements from the discoveries of science and which runs on empirical thinking and precise calculations. In such a society language is conceived primarily as the means by which facts are communicated. Language is seen as a property of facts themselves — their persuasive property. We are taught that facts are to be distinguished from feeling and that feeling is what we are permitted for our rest and relaxation when the facts get us down. This is the bias of scientific method and empiricism by which the world reveals itself and gives itself over to our control insofar as we recognize the primacy of fact-reality. We all kick the rock to refute Berkeley.

So what I suppose I mean by *the power of the regime* is first of all the modern consensus of sensibility that could be called *realism*, which, since there is more than epistemology to this question of knowing the world, may be defined as the business of getting on and producing for ourselves what we construe as the satisfaction of our needs — and doing it with standards of measure, market studies, contracts, tests, polls, training manuals, office memos, press releases, and headlines.

But I shall go further: If we are able to recognize and name any broad consensus of sensibility we are acknowledging its rule. Anything which governs us must by necessity be self-interested and organized to continue itself. Therefore I have to conclude that the regime of facts is not from God but man-made, and, as such, infinitely violable. For instance, it used to be proposed as a biological fact that women were emotionally less stable and intellectually less capable than men. What we proclaim as the discovered factual world can be challenged as the questionable world we ourselves have painted — the cultural museum of our values, dogmas, assumptions, that prescribes for us not only what we may like and dislike, believe and disbelieve, but also what we may be permitted to see and not to see.

And so I am led to affirm my phraseology. There is a regime language that derives its strength from what we are supposed to be and a language of freedom whose power consists in what we threaten to become. And I'm justified in giving a political character to the nonfictive and fictive uses of language because there is conflict between them.

It is possible there was a time in which the designative and evocative functions of language were one and the same. I remember being taught that in school. The sun was Zeus's chariot in fact as well as fiction — the chariot was metaphor and operative science at one and the same time. The gods have very particular names and powers and emotions in Homer. They go about deflecting arrows, bringing on human rages, turning hearts, and controlling history. Nevertheless there really was a Troy and a Trojan war. Alone among the arts, literature confuses fact and fiction. In the Bible the natural and supernatural flow into each other, man and God go hand in hand. Even so, there are visible to our own time volcanoes that are pillars of fire by night and pillars of cloud by day.

I conclude there must have been a world once in which the act of telling a story was in itself a presumption of truth. It was not necessarily a better world than our own, but as a writer of fiction I can see the advantages to my craft of not having a reader question me and ask if what I've written is true — that is, if it really happened. In our society there is no presumption of truth in the art of storytelling except in the minds of children. We have complex understandings of the different functions of language and we can all recognize the aesthetic occasion and differentiate it from a "real" one. This means to me that literature is less a tool for survival than it once was. In ancient times, presumably, the storyteller got a spot near the fire because the story he told defined the powers to which the listener was subject and suggested how to live with them. Literature was as valuable as a club or a sharpened bone. It bound the present to the past, the visible with the invisible, and it helped to compose the community necessary for the continuing life of its members.

In Walter Benjamin's brilliant essay "The Story Teller: Reflections on the Works of Nikolai Leskov," we're told that storytelling in the Middle Ages was primarily a means of giving counsel. The resident master craftsmen and traveling journeymen worked together in the same room and stories passed between them in the rhythm of their work. Thus each story was honed by time and many tellers. If the story was good, the counsel was valuable and therefore the story was true. "The art of story telling is coming to an end," Benjamin says, writing in 1936. "Less and less frequently do we encounter people with the ability to tell a tale properly. . . . One reason for this is obvious: Experience has fallen in value. . . . We are not richer but poorer in communicable experience."

For our sins, Benjamin implies, we have the novelist, an isolated individual who gives birth to his novel whole, himself uncounseled and without the ability to counsel others. "In the midst of life's fullness, the novel gives evidence of the profound perplexity of the living," he says. "The first great novel, *Don Quixote,* teaches how the spiritual greatness, the boldness, the helpfulness, of one of the noblest of men, Don Quixote, are completely devoid of counsel and do not contain the slightest scintilla of wisdom."

But I am interested in the ways, not peculiar to itself, that *Don Quixote* does its teaching. And of special significance I think is Cervantes' odd claim that he cannot be considered the author of his book. In Part 1, Chapter 9, for instance, he introduces the Don's adventures that follow by claiming to have come across an account of them, on parchment, by an Arab historian, in a marketplace in Toledo. "I bought all the parchments for half a real," he confides. "But if the merchant had had any sense and had known how much I wanted them he might have demanded and got more than six reales from the sale."

I look at another great early fiction, *Robinson Crusoe,* and see that it is treated by its author in much the same way. There is a Robinson Crusoe and this is his memoir, and Daniel Defoe has only edited this book for him. As editor, Defoe can assure us, with all the integrity naturally falling to his profession, that the story is true. "The editor believes the thing to be a just history of fact," he says. "Neither is there any appearance of fiction in it."

So both of these classic practitioners dissociate themselves from the work, apparently as a means of gaining authority for the narrative. They use other voices than their own in the composition and present themselves not as authors but as literary executors. In the excellent phrase of Kenneth Rexroth, they adopt the convention of the "false document."

I'm not familiar enough with their publishing histories to know the degree of gullibility with which these false documents were originally received by their readers. Certainly the parodic intentions of *Don Quixote* were explicit. But the romances of chivalry and pastoral love that punctuate the narrative stand in contrast to the realistic humiliations of the Don. Cervantes complains at the beginning of Part 2 of *Don Quixote* that other writers have, subsequent to the great success of Part One, written their own histories of the same person. In fact, he has Quixote and Sancho Panza review their representations in the piratical works, thus conferring upon themselves an additional falsely documented reality. But let us grant Cervantes' audience, and Defoe's as well, a gullibility no greater than ironic appreciation: In order to have its effect, a false document need only be possibly true. The transparency of the pretense does not damage it. A man named Alexander Selkirk, who had been a castaway, was famous in Defoe's London, and all the English readers needed to know to read *Crusoe* and to believe it was that there were others who could have had Selkirk's experience. . . .

Of course every fiction is a false document in that compositions of words are not life. But I speak specifically of the novelist's act of creative disavowal by which the text he offers takes on some additional authority because he did not write it, or latterly, because he claims it was impossible to write it.

I come back for a moment to *Robinson Crusoe:* As a false document it interests me enormously. It was published at a time when the life adventures of Alexander Selkirk had been well broadcast in London for several years. In fact, Selkirk's autobiography had been published and there is reason to believe Defoe actually interviewed him. Selkirk was a clearly unstable, tormented individual. His months alone on an island had so wrecked what equanimity he had that when he was restored to London he immediately built himself a cave in his garden, and he lived in the cave and sulked and raged, an embarrassment to his family and a menace to his neighbors. Defoe turned this disturbed person into the stout, resolute Englishman (Crusoe), a genius at survival by the grace of his belief in God and in the white European race.

And inevitably, Crusoe the composition has obscured Selkirk the man, whose great gift to civilization, we see now, was in providing Daniel Defoe the idea for a story. The story tells what happens when an urban Englishman is removed from his environment and plunked down in nature. What happens is that he defines the national character.

But the point about this first of the great false documents in English is 20 that at the moment of its publication there was an indwelling of the art in the real life, everyone in London who read *Crusoe* knew about Selkirk, there was intervention, a mixing-up of the historic and the aesthetic, the real and the possibly real. And what was recovered was the state of wisdom that existed, for Walter Benjamin, before fact and fiction became ontologically differentiated — that is, when it was possible for fiction to give counsel.

The novelist deals with his isolation by splitting himself in two, creator and documentarian, teller and listener, conspiring to pass on the collective wisdom in its own language, disguised in its own enlightened bias, that of the factual world.

It is not a bad system, but it gets the writer into trouble. To offer facts to the witness of the imagination and pretend they are real is to commit a kind of regressive heresy. The language of politicians, historians, journalists, and social scientists always presumes a world of fact discovered, and, like a religious tenet, the presumption is held more fiercely the more it is seen to be illusory.

Fiction writers are at best inconvenient, like some old relative in mismatching pants and jacket who knocks on our door during a dinner party to remind us from what we come. Society has several ways of dealing with this inconvenience. The writer is given most leeway in the Western democracies which are the most industrially advanced. In these countries, where empiricism works so well as to be virtually unassailable, the writer-nuisance is relegated to the shadow world of modern aesthetics or culture, a nonintegral antiuniverse with reflections of power rather than power, with a kind of shamanistic potence at best, subject to the whims of gods and spirits, an imitation with words of the tangible real world of act and event and thunder.

In those countries which are not advanced industrial democracies the writer is treated with more respect. In Burma or Iran or Chile or Indonesia or the Soviet Union, it is understood that a writer using the common coin of the political speech or the press release or the newspaper editorial to compose facts in play has the power to do harm. He is recognized to have discovered the secret the politician is born knowing: that good and evil are construed, that there is no outrage, no monstrousness that cannot be made reasonable and logical and virtuous, and no shining act that cannot be turned to disgrace — with language.

Thus the American Center of PEN, the organization of novelists, poets, 25 essayists, editors, and publishers, finds it necessary to distribute each year a poster entitled WRITERS IN PRISON. This poster, which is very large, simply lists the writers who are currently locked in cells or insane asylums or torture chambers in various countries around the world — who are by their being and profession threats to the security of political regimes. The imprisonment of writers is common in countries of the right and of the left, it doesn't seem to matter what the ideology. I know from the novelist Alexander Solzhenitsyn about the Gulag Archipelago, the network of Soviet prison camps and secret police in Siberia, but I know too from Reza Baraheni, the Iranian novelist and poet, about the Iranian secret police, SAVAK, and the torture of artists and intellectuals in Iranian prisons. Wherever citizens are seen routinely as enemies of their own government, writers are routinely seen to be the most dangerous enemies.

So that in most countries of the world literature is politics. All writers are by definition engagé. Even if they are timid gentle souls who write pastoral verses on remote farms, the searchlight will seek them out.

In this country we are embarrassed or angered by the excesses of repression of foreign petty tyrants and murderous bureaucracies. But apart from the excesses, the point of view is hardly unprecedented. Elizabethan writers lived in the shadow of the Tower and when Plato proposed his ideal republic he decreed that poets were to be outlawed. Part of our problem, as Americans, in failing to apprehend the relationship of art and politics is, of course, our national good fortune. . . . Our primary control of writers in the United States does not have to be violent — it operates on the assumption that aesthetics is a limited arena where, according to the rules, we may be shocked or threatened, but only in fun. The novelist need not be taken seriously because his work appeals largely to young people, women, intellectuals, and other pampered minorities, and, lacking any real currency, is not part of the relevant business of the nation.

If these thoughts were a story, the story would tell of a real tangible world and the writer's witness of that world in which some writers occasionally, by the grace of God, cause the real world to compose itself according to the witness, as our faces compose themselves in our mirrors.

However I detect a faint presumption of romance in my attitude, and I have to wonder why I suspect myself of being less than hospitable to the forms of nonfictive discourse, as if they were a team from another city. Nonfiction enjoys the sort of authority that has not easily been granted fiction since Walter Benjamin's storytellers traded their last tales. On the other hand it does give up something for the privilege; it is dulled by the obligation to be factual. This is acknowledged by the people who would not pick up a novel but who say of a particularly good biography or history that it reads like one.

Perhaps I feel that the nonfictive premise of a discoverable factual world 30 is in itself a convention no less hoary than Cervantes' Arab historian.

Consider those occasions — criminal trials in courts of law — when society arranges with all its investigative apparatus to apprehend factual reality. Using the tested rules of evidence and the accrued wisdom of our system of laws, we determine the guilt or innocence of defendants and come to judgment. Yet the most important trials in our history, those which reverberate in our lives and have most meaning for our future, are those in which the judgment is called into question: Scopes, Sacco and Vanzetti, the Rosenbergs. Facts are buried, exhumed, deposed, contradicted, recanted. There is a decision by the jury and, when the historical and prejudicial context of the decision is examined, a subsequent judgment by history. And the trial shimmers forever with just that perplexing ambiguity characteristic of a true novel. . . .

"There are no facts in themselves," said Nietzsche. "For a fact to exist we must first introduce meaning." When a physicist invents an incredibly sophisticated instrument to investigate subatomic phenomena, he must wonder to what degree the instrument changes or creates the phenomena it reports. This problem was elucidated by Werner Heisenberg as the Principle of Uncertainty. At the highest level of scruple and reportorial disinterest there is the intrusive factor of an organized consciousness. At lower levels, in law, in political history, the intrusion is not instrumental but moral: Meaning must be introduced, and no judgment does not carry the passion of the judge.

We all know examples of history that doesn't exist. We used to laugh at the Russians, who in their encyclopedias attributed every major industrial invention to themselves. We knew how their great leaders who had fallen out of favor were erased from their history texts. We were innocent then: Our own school and university historians had done just the same thing to whole peoples who lived and died in this country but were seriously absent from our texts: Afro-American, Native American, Chinese. There is no history except as it is composed. There are no failed revolutions, only lawless conspiracies. All history is contemporary history, says Benedetto Croce in *History as the Story of Liberty:* "However remote in time events may seem to be, every historical judgment refers to present needs and situations." That is why history has to be written and rewritten from one generation to another. The act of composition can never end.

What is a historical fact? A spent shell? A bombed-out building? A pile of shoes? A victory parade? A long march? Once it has been suffered it maintains itself in the mind of witness or victim, and if it is to reach anyone else it is transmitted in words or on film and it becomes an image, which, with other images, constitutes a judgment. I am well aware that some facts, for example, the systematic murder by the Nazis and their client states of six million men, women, and children, are so indisputably monstrous as to seem to stand alone. But history shares with fiction a mode of mediating the world for the purpose of introducing meaning, and it is the cultural authority from which they both derive that illuminates those facts so that they can be perceived.

Facts are the images of history, just as images are the facts of fiction.   35

Of course it happens that the people most skeptical of history as a nonfictive discipline are the historians themselves. E. H. Carr, in his famous essay "The Historian and His Facts," speaks of history "as a continuous process of interaction" between the writer of history and his facts. Carr also quotes the American historian Carl Becker, who said: "The facts of history do not exist for any historian until he has created them." Neither man would be surprised by the tentative conclusions of the structuralist critic Roland Barthes, who, in an essay entitled "Historical Discourse," attempts to find the specific linguistic features that differentiate factual and imaginary narrative. "By structures alone," Barthes concludes, "historical discourse is essentially a product of ideology, or rather of imagination." In other words a visitor from another planet could not by study of the techniques of discourse distinguish composed fiction from composed history. The important stylistic device of composed history, the chaste or objective voice, one that gives no clues to the personality of the narrator, Barthes says, "turns out to be a particular form of fiction." (Teachers of English know that form as Realism.)

So that as a novelist considering this particular nonfictive discipline I could claim that history is a kind of fiction in which we live and hope to survive, and fiction is a kind of speculative history, perhaps a superhistory, by which the available data for the composition are seen to be greater and more various in their sources than the historian supposes.

At issue is the human mind, which has to be shocked, seduced, or otherwise provoked out of its habitual stupor. Even the biblical prophets knew they had to make it new. They shouted and pointed their fingers to heaven, but they were poets too, and dramatists. Isaiah walked abroad naked and Jeremiah wore a yoke around his neck to prophesy deportation and slavery, respectively, to their soon-to-be-deported-and-enslaved countrymen. Moral values are inescapably aesthetic. In the modern world it is the moral regime of factual reality that impinges on the provinces of art. News magazines present the events of the world as an ongoing weekly serial. Weather reports are constructed on television with exact attention to conflict (high pressure areas clashing with lows), suspense (the climax of tomorrow's weather prediction coming after the commercial), and other basic elements of narrative. The creating, advertising, packaging, and marketing of factual products is unquestionably a fictional enterprise. The novelist looking around him has inevitably to wonder why he is isolated by his profession when everywhere the factualists have appropriated his techniques and even brought a kind of exhaustion to the dramatic modes by the incessant exploitation of them.

Nevertheless, there is something we honor in the character of a journalist — whatever it is that makes him value reportorial objectivity and assure us at the same time that it is an unattainable ideal. We recognize and trust that combination of passion and humility. It is the religious temperament.

The virtues of the social sciences are even more appealing to us. Sociolo- 40 gists and social psychologists not only make communion with facts but in addition display the scientific method of dealing with them. The tale told by the social scientists, the counsel given, is nonspecific, collated, and subject to verification. Because they revise each other's work constantly and monitor themselves, as novelists do not, and are like a democracy in that the rule of this or that elevated theorist is subject to new elections every few years, we find them ingenuous and trustworthy. Today we read the empirical fictions of Konrad Lorenz or Oscar Lewis, B. F. Skinner or Eric Erikson, as we used to read Dickens and Balzac, for pleasure and instruction. The psychologists' and sociologists' compositions of facts seem less individualistic and thus more dependable than any random stubborn vision of which the novelist is capable. They propose to understand human character or to define it as a function of ethnic background, sexuality, age, economic class, and they produce composite portraits like those done in a police station — bad art, but we think we see someone we recognize. It is at least a possibility that the idea of human beings as demographic collections of traits, or as loci of cultural and racial and economic events, is exactly what is needed in our industrial society to keep the machines going. We have in such concepts as "complex," "sublimation," "repression," "identity crisis," "object relations," "borderline," and so on, the interchangeable parts of all of us. In this sense modern psychology is the industrialization of storytelling.

I am thus led to the proposition that there is no fiction or nonfiction as we commonly understand the distinction: There is only narrative.

But it is a novelist's proposition, I can see that very well. It is in my interest to claim that there is no difference between what I do and what everyone else does. I claim as I pull everyone else over to my side of the mirror that there is nothing between the given universe and our attempt to mediate it, there is no real power, only some hope that we might deny our own contingency.

And I am led to an even more pugnacious view — that the development of civilizations is essentially a progression of metaphors.

The novelist's opportunity to do his work today is increased by the power of the regime to which he finds himself in opposition. As clowns in the circus imitate the aerialists and tightrope walkers, first for laughs and then so that it can be seen that they do it better, we have it in us to compose false documents more valid, more real, more truthful than the "true" documents of the politicians or the journalists or the psychologists. Novelists know explicitly that the world in which we live is still to be formed and that reality is amenable to any construction that is placed upon it. It is a world made for liars and we are born liars. But we are to be trusted because ours is the only profession forced to admit that it lies — and that bestows upon us the mantle of honesty. "In a writer's eyes," said Emerson, "anything which can be thought can be written; the writer is the faculty of reporting and the universe is the possibility of being reported." By our independence of all institutions, from the family to the government, and with no responsibility to defend them from their own hypocrisy and murderousness, we are a valuable resource and an instrument of survival. There is no nonfictive discipline that does not rule out some element of the human psyche, that does not restrict some human energy and imprison it, that does not exclude some monstrous phantom of human existence. Unlike the politicians, we take office first and then create our constituencies, and that is to be a shade more arrogant than the politicians. But our justification and redemption is in emulating the false documents that we universally call our dreams. For dreams are the first false documents, of course: They are never real, they are never factual; nevertheless they control us, purge us, mediate our baser natures, and prophesy our fate.

AFTERWORD

E. L. Doctorow says that this essay gives "fullest expression" to his idea that "those who make history write it, just as those who write it make it." Known as a man of the left (in a conservative country), Doctorow is an old-fashioned liberal who distrusts regimes, not to mention regime writing. Note the contrast of styles in his long paragraph 3. It is common to think of style as clothing that covers or conceals nakedness. Doctorow like most artists insists that language is the thing itself and not decoration.

History, we presume, is factual — but E. L. Doctorow finds such an assumption naive. "Facts are the images of history, just as images are the facts of fiction." The literary conviction that one tells the truth by telling lies — maybe one tells truth only by telling lies — seems to fly in the face of the modern insistence on fact as information. But "there is no fiction or nonfiction as we commonly understand the distinction: There is only narrative."

Paragraph 5: "We all kick the rock to refute Berkeley." How can you refute a campus of the University of California or a town across the bay from San Francisco? How do you know when to look something up? If your dictionary or encyclopedia doesn't help you connect any "Berkeley" to any rock, what do you do next? What kind of a book might help you, if you looked up the word "rock"?

BOOKS AVAILABLE IN PAPERBACK

Billy Bathgate. New York: HarperCollins. *Novel.*

The Book of Daniel. New York: Random House–Vintage. *Novel.*

Lives of the Poets: Six Stories and a Novella. New York: Avon.

Loon Lake. New York: Random House–Vintage. *Novel.*

Ragtime. New York: Random House–Vintage. *Novel.*

Welcome to Hard Times. New York: Random House–Vintage. *Novel.*

World's Fair. New York: Random House–Vintage. *Novel.*

ANDRE
DUBUS

*A*NDRE DUBUS *was born in Louisiana (1936). After five years in the Marine
Corps, leaving as a captain, he attended the Writers Workshop in Iowa where
he wrote and published a novel called* The Lieutenant *("It's now out of print and
it ought to be; it should have been a novella"). His best works are short stories, set
mostly with a background of working class Massachusetts, where he moved to in
1966. The scenes of his imagination are the old mill towns of the Merrimack Valley.*

*In 1986, Dubus lost a leg when a car struck him after he stopped to help motorists
stranded on an interstate north of Boston. A woman and her brother were standing
beside her car, which had just struck an abandoned motorcycle. Dubus led the two
across the speed lane, toward the median, but paused to wave down an oncoming
car. Unaccountably, the approaching car swerved and hit all three people, injuring
Dubus and the woman, killing her brother.*

*Dubus's memory of the accident is unclear. He learned from his doctor that he
had saved the woman's life by pushing her away, shortly before the impact. "Now I
can never be angry at myself for stopping that night," Dubus wrote after he heard
what he had done. "I am forever a cripple, but I am alive, and I am a father and a
husband, and in 1987 I am sitting in the sunlight of June and writing this."*

*Gradually and surely, Dubus's reputation has grown. PEN gave him an award
in 1987, and the American Academy in 1988 — the same year in which he received
the five-year support of a MacArthur Fellowship. Some of his titles are* Adultery
and Other Choices *(1977),* Finding a Girl in America *(1980),* The Last Worthless Evening *(1986), and* Selected Stories *(1988).* Broken Vessels *(1991) is a
collection of essays.*

*One of Dubus's writing habits is uncommon. When he has finished a draft to
his satisfaction, he tapes it and listens. "I recommend it to everybody. I think most*

_____ Photo by Marion Ettlinger

ANDRE DUBUS

writers do what I do, which is to sit down every day and read everything you've written up until where you left off the day before. So some paragraphs you've read a hundred times, and you're not really reading them anymore. When you read them aloud, it involves your body and it awakens some focus."

Imperiled Men

He was a navy pilot in World War II and in Korea, and when I knew him in 1961 for a few months before he killed himself he was the Commander of the Air Group aboard the USS *Ranger*, an aircraft carrier, and we called him by the acronym CAG. He shot himself with his .38 revolver because two investigators from the Office of Naval Intelligence came aboard ship while we were anchored off Iwakuni in Japan and gave the ship's captain a written report of their investigation of CAG's erotic life. CAG was a much-decorated combat pilot, and his duty as a commander was one of great responsibility. The ship's executive officer, also a commander, summoned CAG to his office, where the two investigators were, and told him that his choices were to face a general court-martial or to resign from the navy. Less than half an hour later CAG was dead in his stateroom. His body was flown to the United States; we were told that he did not have a family, and I do not know where he was buried. There was a memorial service aboard ship, but I do not remember it; I only remember a general sadness like mist in the passageways.

I did not really know him. I was a first lieutenant then, a career marine; two years later I would resign and become a teacher. On the *Ranger* I was with the marine detachment; we guarded the planes' nuclear weapons stored below decks, ran the brig, and manned one of the antiaircraft gun mounts. We were fifty or so enlisted men and two officers among a ship's crew of about three thousand officers and men. The Air Group was not included in the ship's company. They came aboard with their planes for our seven-month deployment in the western Pacific. I do not remember the number of pilots and bombardier-navigators, mechanics and flight controllers, and men who worked on the flight deck, but there were plenty of all, and day and night you could hear planes catapulting off the front of the deck and landing on its rear.

The flight deck was 1,052 feet long, the ship weighed 81,000 tons fully loaded, and I rarely felt its motion. I came aboard in May for a year of duty, and in August we left our port in San Francisco Bay and headed for Japan. I had driven my wife and three young children home to Louisiana, where they would stay during the seven months I was at sea, and every day I

incredible pressure, responsibility

longed for them. One night on the voyage across the Pacific I sat in the wardroom drinking coffee with a lieutenant commander at one of the long tables covered with white linen. The wardroom was open all night because men were always working. The lieutenant commander told me that Soviet submarines tracked us, they recorded the sound of our propellers and could not be fooled by the sound of a decoy ship's propellers, and that they even came into San Francisco Bay to do this; our submarines did the same with Soviet carriers. He said that every time we tried in training exercises to evade even our own submarines we could not do it, and our destroyers could not track and stop them. He said, "So if the whistle blows we'll get a nuclear fish up our ass in the first thirty minutes. Our job is to get the birds in the air before that. They're going to Moscow." *always being observed, can never escape, there is no evasion, no movement or action is hidden/concealed*

"Where will they land afterward?"
"They won't. They know that." *men who accept the possibility of death*

The voyage to Japan was five or six weeks long because we did not go directly to Japan; the pilots flew air operations. Combat units are always training for war, but these men who flew planes, and the men in orange suits and ear protectors who worked on the flight deck during landings and takeoffs, were engaging in something not at all as playful as marine field exercises generally were. They were imperiled. One pilot told me that from his fighter-bomber in the sky the flight deck looked like an aspirin tablet. On the passage to Japan I became friendly with some pilots drinking coffee in the wardroom, and I knew what CAG looked like because he was CAG. He had dark skin and alert eyes, and he walked proudly. Then in Japan I sometimes drank with young pilots. I was a robust twenty-five-year-old, one of two marine officers aboard ship, and I did not want to be outdone at anything by anyone. But I could not stay with the pilots; I had to leave them in the bar, drinking and talking and laughing, and make my way back to the ship to sleep and wake with a hangover. Next day the pilots flew; if we did not go to sea, they flew from a base on land. Once I asked one of them how he did it.

"The pure oxygen. Soon as you put on the mask, your head clears."

It was not simply the oxygen, and I did not understand any of these wild, brave, and very efficient men until years later when I read Tom Wolfe's *The Right Stuff.*

It was on that same tour that I saw another pilot die. I worked below decks with the marine detachment, but that warm gray afternoon the entire ship was in a simulated condition of war, and my part was to stand four hours of watch in a small turret high above the ship. I could move the turret in a circular way by pressing a button, and I looked through binoculars for planes or ships in the 180-degree arc of our port side. On the flight deck planes were taking off; four could do this in quick sequence. Two catapults launched planes straight off the front of the ship, and quickly they rose and climbed. The third and fourth catapults were on the port side where the flight deck angled sharply out to the left, short of the bow. From my turret I looked down at the ship's bridge and the flight deck. A helicopter flew low

very succinct language

129

near the ship, and planes were taking off. On the deck were men in orange suits and ear protectors; on both sides of the ship, just beneath the flight deck, were nets for these men to jump into, to save themselves from being killed by a landing plane that veered or skidded or crashed. One night I'd inspected a marine guarding a plane on the flight deck; we had a sentry there because the plane carried a nuclear bomb. I stepped from a hatch into the absolute darkness of a night at sea and into a strong wind that lifted my body with each step. I was afraid it would lift me off the deck and hurl me into the sea, where I would tread water in that great expanse and depth while the ship went on its way; tomorrow they would learn that I was missing. I found the plane and the marine; he stood with one arm around the cable that held the wing to the deck.

In the turret I was facing aft when it happened: Men in orange were at the rear of the flight deck, then they sprinted forward, and I rotated my turret toward the bow and saw a plane in the gray sea and an orange-suited pilot lying facedown in the water, his parachute floating beyond his head, moving toward the rear of the ship. The plane had dropped off the port deck and now water covered its wing, then its cockpit, and it sank. The pilot was behind the ship; his limbs did not move, his face was in the sea, and his parachute was filling with water and starting to sink. The helicopter hovered low and a sailor on a rope descended from it; he wore orange, and I watched him coming down and the pilot floating and the parachute sinking beneath the waves. There was still some length of parachute line remaining when the sailor reached the pilot; he grabbed him; then the parachute lines tightened their pull and drew the pilot down. There was only the sea now beneath the sailor on the rope. Then he ascended.

I shared a stateroom with a navy lieutenant, an officer of medical administration, a very tall and strong man from Oklahoma. He had been an enlisted man, had once been a corpsman aboard a submarine operating off the coast of the Soviet Union, and one night their periscope was spotted, destroyers came after them, and they dived and sat at the bottom and listened by sonar to the destroyers' sonar trying to find them. He told me about the sailor who had tried to save the pilot. In the dispensary they gave him brandy, and the sailor wept and said he was trained to do that job, and this was his first time, and he had failed. Of course he had not failed. No man could lift another man attached to a parachute filled with water. Some people said the helicopter had not stayed close enough to the ship while the planes were taking off. Some said the pilot was probably already dead; his plane dropped from the ship, and he ejected himself high into the air, but not high enough for his parachute to ease his fall. This was all talk about the mathematics of violent death; the pilot was killed because he flew airplanes from a ship at sea.

He was a lieutenant commander, and I knew his face and name. As he was being catapulted, his landing gear on the left side broke off and his plane skidded into the sea. He was married; his widow had been married before, also to a pilot who was killed in a crash. I wondered if it were her bad luck to meet only men who flew; years later I believed that whatever in their spirits made these men fly also drew her to them.

I first spoke to CAG at the officers' club at the navy base in Yokosuka. The officers of the Air Group hosted a party for the officers of the ship's company. We wore civilian suits and ties, and gathered at the club to drink. There were no women. The party was a matter of protocol, probably a tradition among pilots and the officers of carriers; for us young officers it meant getting happily drunk. I was doing this with pilots at the bar when one of them said, "Let's throw CAG into the pond."

He grinned at me, as I looked to my left at the small shallow pond with pretty fish in it; then I looked past the pond at CAG, sitting on a soft leather chair, a drink in his hand, talking quietly with two or three other commanders sitting in soft leather chairs. All the pilots with me were grinning and saying yes, and the image of us lifting CAG from his chair and dropping him into the water gave me joy, and I put my drink on the bar and said, "Let's *go*."

I ran across the room to CAG, grabbed the lapels of his coat, jerked him   15
up from his chair, and saw his drink spill onto his suit; then I fell backward to the floor, still holding his lapels, and pulled him down on top of me. There was no one else with me. He was not angry yet, but I was a frightened fool. I released his lapels and turned my head and looked back at the laughing pilots. Out of my vision the party was loud, hundreds of drinking officers who had not seen this, and CAG sounded only puzzled when he said, "What's going on?"

He stood and brushed at the drink on his suit, watching me get up from the floor. I stood not quite at attention but not at ease either. I said, "Sir, I'm Marine Lieutenant Dubus. Your pilots fooled me." I nodded toward them at the bar, and CAG smiled. "They said, 'Let's throw CAG into the pond.' But, sir, the joke was on me."

He was still smiling.

"I'm very sorry, sir."

"That's all right, Lieutenant."

"Can I get the Commander another drink, sir?"   20

"Sure," he said, and told me what he was drinking, and I got it from the bar, where the pilots were red-faced and happy, and brought it to CAG, who was sitting in his chair again with the other commanders. He smiled and thanked me, and the commanders smiled; then I returned to the young pilots and we all laughed.

Until a few months later, on the day he killed himself, the only words I spoke to CAG after the party were greetings. One night I saw him sitting with a woman in the officers' club, and I wished him good evening. A few times I saw him in the ship's passageways; I recognized him seconds before the features of his face were clear: He had a graceful, athletic stride that dipped his shoulders. I saluted and said, "Good morning, sir" or "Good afternoon, sir." He smiled as he returned my salute and greeting, his eyes and voice mirthful, and I knew that he was seeing me again pulling him out of his chair and down to the floor, then standing to explain myself and apologize. I liked being a memory that gave him sudden and passing amusement.

On a warm sunlit day we were anchored off Iwakuni, and I planned to go with other crew members on a bus to Hiroshima. I put on civilian clothes and went down the ladder to the boat that would take us ashore. I was not happily going to Hiroshima; I was going because I was an American, and I felt that I should look at it and be in it. I found a seat on the rocking boat, then saw CAG in civilian clothes coming down the ladder. There were a few seats remaining, and he chose the one next to me. He asked me where I was going, then said he was going to Hiroshima, too. I was relieved and grateful; while CAG was flying planes in World War II, I was a boy buying savings stamps and bringing scrap metal to school. On the bus he would talk to me about war, and in Hiroshima I would walk with him and look with him, and his seasoned steps and eyes would steady mine. Then from the ship above us the officer of the deck called down, "CAG?"

CAG turned and looked up at him, a lieutenant junior grade in white cap and short-sleeved shirt and trousers.

"Sir, the executive officer would like to see you."

I do not remember what CAG said to me. I only remember my disappointment when he told the boat's officer to go ashore without him. All I saw in CAG's face was the look of a man called from rest back to his job. He climbed the ladder, and soon the boat pulled away.

Perhaps when I reached Hiroshima CAG was already dead; I do not remember the ruins at ground zero or what I saw in the museum. I walked and looked, and stood for a long time at a low arch with an open space at the ground, and in that space was a stone box that held the names of all who died on the day of the bombing and all who had died since because of the bomb. That night I ate dinner ashore, then rode the boat to the ship, went to my empty room, climbed to my upper bunk, and slept for only a while, till the quiet voice of my roommate woke me: "The body will be flown to Okinawa."

I looked at him standing at his desk and speaking into the telephone.

"Yes. A .38 in the temple. Yes."

I turned on my reading lamp and watched him put the phone down. He was sad, and he looked at me. I said, "Did someone commit suicide?"

"CAG."

"CAG?"

I sat up.

"The ONI investigated him."

Then I knew what I had not known I knew, and I said, "Was he a homosexual?"

"Yes."

My roommate told me the executive officer had summoned CAG to his office, shown him the report, and told him that he could either resign or face a general court-martial. Then CAG went to his room. Fifteen minutes later the executive officer phoned him; when he did not answer, the executive officer and the investigators ran to his room. He was on his bunk, shot in the right temple, his pilot's .38 revolver in his hand. His eyelids fluttered; he was unconscious but still alive, and he died from bleeding.

"They *ran*?" I said. "They *ran* to his room?"

Ten years later one of my shipmates came to visit me in Massachusetts; we had been civilians for a long time. In my kitchen we were drinking beer, and he said, "I couldn't tell you this aboard ship, because I worked in the legal office. They called CAG back from that boat you were on because he knew the ONI was aboard. His plane was on the ground at the base of Iwakuni. They were afraid he was going to fly it and crash into the sea and they'd lose the plane."

All three thousand of the ship's crew did not mourn. Not every one of the hundreds of men in the Air Group mourned. But the shock was general and hundreds of men did mourn, and each morning we woke to it, and it was in our talk in the wardroom and in the passageways. In the closed air of the ship it touched us, and it lived above us on the flight deck and in the sky. One night at sea a young pilot came to my room; his face was sunburned and sad. We sat in desk chairs, and he said, "The morale is very bad now. The whole Group. It's just shot."

"Did y'all know about him?"

"We all knew. We didn't care. We would have followed him into hell."

Yes, they would have followed him; they were ready every day and every night to fly with him from a doomed ship and follow him to Moscow, to perish in their brilliant passion.

AFTERWORD

In June of 1993, Harper's *printed Andre Dubus's reminiscence, from his Marine Corps days, only a few months after President Clinton outraged the opposition when he tried lifting the ban against gays in the military. Doubtless the controversy recalled this tragic story to Andre Dubus.*

Dubus holds nothing back from the reader. In the first sentence of the first paragraph we learn that a navy pilot, veteran and leader, committed suicide. At the end of the second sentence we learn that he killed himself because his "erotic life" was exposed; we do not need great sophistication to guess the nature of the erotic life. No one killed himself over the Tailhook scandal.

Making an argument without appearing to argue, Dubus establishes CAG's manliness or heroism. Paragraph 2 puts the Air Group in its special place. Paragraph 3, and the two lines of dialogue that come out of it, establish the routine heroism expected of CAG and his pilots. Ironically, it is a courage made manifest by suicide presumed in the line of duty. Such a notion is not the only irony in the paragraph. The idiom describing the carrier's fate, in a Russian attack, alludes in its slang to sodomy: "If the whistle blows we'll get a nuclear fish up our ass in the first thirty minutes."

In paragraph 9, Dubus tells the story of how he "saw another pilot die." In the story of this pilot's death, in the guilt and regret of his would-be savior, and even in the sinking of his airplane under the waves, Dubus foreshadows details toward the end of the story. See the last words of paragraph 39: "They were afraid he was going to fly it and crash into the sea and they'd lose the plane." For that matter, after the suicide by a .38 pistol, the morale of the Group is low; as a young pilot puts it, "It's just shot."

BOOKS AVAILABLE IN PAPERBACK

Adultery and Other Choices. Boston: David R. Godine. *Short stories.*

Broken Vessels. Boston: David R. Godine. *Essays.*

Finding a Girl in America. Boston: David R. Godine. *Short stories.*

Selected Stories. New York: Random House–Vintage. *Short stories.*

Separate Flights. Boston: David R. Godine. *Short stories.*

The Times Are Never So Bad. Boston: David R. Godine. *Short stories.*

GERALD
EARLY

*G*ERALD EARLY *(b. 1952) teaches English and directs the African and Afro-American Studies Program at Washington University in St. Louis. His essay* collections include Tuxedo Junction: Essays on American Culture *(1990) and* The Culture of Bruising *(1994), which is subtitled,* Essays Toward a Definition of Literature, Prizefighting, and Modern American Culture.

"Life with Daughters: Watching the Miss America Pageant" came out in the Kenyon Review. *Early edits collections of essays, his work appears in the annual* Best American Essays *volumes, and he teaches a course called "The Art of the Essay."*

Life with Daughters:
Watching the
Miss America Pageant

The theater is an expression of our dream life — of our unconscious aspirations.
— DAVID MAMET, "A Tradition of the Theater as Art," *Writing in Restaurants*

Aunt Hester went out one night, — where or for what I do not know, — and happened to be absent when my master desired her presence.
— FREDERICK DOUGLASS, *Narrative of the Life of Frederick Douglass*

Adults, older girls, shops, magazines, newspapers, window signs — all the world had agreed that a blue-eyed, yellow-haired, pink-skinned doll was what every girl child treasured.
— TONI MORRISON, *The Bluest Eye*

It is now fast become a tradition — if one can use that word to describe a habit about which I still feel a certain amount of shamefacedness — for our household to watch the Miss America contest on television every year. The source of my embarrassment is that this program remains, despite its attempts in recent years to modernize its frightfully antique quality of "women on parade," a kind of maddeningly barbarous example of the persistent, hard, crass urge to sell: from the plugs for the sponsor that are made a part of the script (that being an antique of fifties and sixties television; the show does not remember its history so much as it seems bent on repeating it) to the constant references to the success of some of the previous contestants and the reminders that this is some sort of scholarship competition, the program has all the cheap earnestness of a social uplift project being played as a musical revue in Las Vegas. Paradoxically, it wishes to convince the public that it is a common entertainment while simultaneously wishing to convey that it is more than mere entertainment. The Miss America pageant is the worst sort of "Americanism," the soft smile of sex and the hard sell of toothpaste and hair dye ads wrapped in the dreamy ideological gauze of "making it through one's own effort." In a perverse way, I like the show; it is the only live television left other than sports, news broadcasts, performing arts awards programs, and speeches by the president. I miss live TV. It was the closest thing to theater for the masses. And the Miss America contest is as it has been for some time, the most perfectly rendered theater in our culture, for it so perfectly captures what we yearn for: a low-class ritual, a polished restatement of vulgarity, that wants to open the door to high-class respectability by way of plain middle-class anxiety and ambition. Am I doing all right? the contestants seem to ask in a kind of reassuring, if numbed, way. The contest brings together all the American classes in a show-biz spectacle of classlessness and tastelessness.

My wife has been interested in the Miss America contest since childhood, and so I ascribe her uninterrupted engagement with America's cultural passage into fall (Miss America, like college and pro football, signifies for us as a nation the end of summer; the contest was invented, back in 1921, by Atlantic City merchants to prolong the summer season past Labor Day) as something mystically and uniquely female. She, as a black woman, had a long-standing quarrel with the contest until Vanessa Williams was chosen the first black Miss America in September 1983. Somehow she felt vindicated by Williams for all those years as a black girl in Dallas, watching white women win the crown and thumb their noses at her, at her blackness, at her straightened hair, her thick lips, her wide nose. She played with white Barbie dolls as a little girl and had, I suppose, a "natural," or at least an under-standable and predictable, interest in seeing the National White Barbie Doll chosen every year because for such a long time, of course, the Miss America contest, with few exceptions, was a totemic preoccupation with and repre-sentation of a particularly stilted form of patriarchal white supremacy. In short, it was a national white doll contest. And well we know that every black girl growing up in the fifties and early sixties had her peculiar love-hate affair with white dolls, with mythicized white femininity. I am re-minded of this historical instance: Everyone knows that in the *Brown* versus *Topeka Board of Education* case (the case that resulted in the Supreme Court decision to integrate public schools) part of the sociological evidence used by the plaintiffs to show the psychological damage suffered by blacks be-cause of Jim Crow was an account by Kenneth Clarke of how, when offered a choice between a black doll and a white doll, little black girls invariably chose the white doll because they thought it "prettier."

On the front page of the January 6, 1962, *Pittsburgh Courier,* a black weekly, is a picture of a hospitalized black girl named Connie Smith holding a white doll sent to her by Attorney General Robert Kennedy. Something had occurred between 1954, when the Supreme Court made its decision, and 1962 which made it impossible for Kennedy to send the girl a black doll, and this impossibility was to signal, ironically, that the terms of segregation and the terms of racial integration, the very icon of them, were to be exactly the same. Kennedy could not send the girl a black doll, as it would have implied, in the age of integration, that he was, in effect, sending her a Jim Crow toy, a toy that would emphasize the girl's race. In the early sixties such a gesture would have been considered condescending. To give the black girl a white doll in the early sixties was to mainstream the black girl into the culture, to say that she was worthy of the same kind of doll that a white girl would have. But how can it be that conservatism and liberalism, segregation and integration, could produce, fantastically, the same results, the identical iconography: a black girl hugging a white doll because everyone thinks it is best for her to have it? How can it be that at one time the white doll is the sign of the black girl's rejection and inferiority and fewer than ten years later it is the sign of her acceptance and redemption? Those who are knowledgeable about certain aspects of the black mind or the collective black consciousness realize, of course, that the issues of segregation and integration, of conservatism and liberalism, of acceptance and rejection, of redemption and inferiority, are all restatements of the same immovable and relentless reality of the meaning of American blackness; that this is all a matter of the harrowing and compelling intensity that is called, quaintly, race pride. And in this context, the issue of white dolls, this fetishization of young white feminine beauty, and the complexity of black girlhood becomes an unresolved theme stated in a strident key. Blacks have preached for a long time about how to heal their daughters of whiteness: In the November 1908 issue of *The Colored American Magazine,* E. A. Johnson wrote an article entitled, "Negro Dolls for Negro Babies," in which he said, "I am convinced that one of the best ways to teach Negro children to respect their own color would be to see to it that the children be given colored dolls to play with. . . . To give a Negro child a white doll means to create in it a prejudice against its own color, which will cling to it through life." Lots of black people believed this and, for all I know, probably still do, as race pride, or the lack thereof, burns and crackles like a current through most African-American public and private discourse. Besides, it is no easy matter to wish white dolls away.

A few years ago I was thumbing through an album of old family photographs and saw one of me and my oldest sister taken when I was four and she was nine. It struck me, transfixed me really, as it was a color photo and most of the old family pictures taken when I was a boy were black-and-white because my mother could not afford to have color pictures developed. We, my sister and I, are sitting on an old stuffed blue chair and she is holding a white doll in her hand, displaying it for the picture. I remember the occasion very well, as my sister was to be confirmed in our small, all-black Episcopal church that day, and she was, naturally, proud of the moment and wanted to share it with her favorite toy. That, I remembered, was why these were color pictures. It was a special day for the family, a day my mother wanted to celebrate by taking special pictures. My mother is a very dark woman who has a great deal of race pride and often speaks about my sisters' having black dolls. I was surprised, in looking at the picture recently, that they ever owned a white one, that indeed a white one had been a favorite.

My wife grew up — enjoyed the primary years of black girlhood, so to speak — during the years 1954 through 1962; she was about five or six years younger than my oldest sister. She lived in a southern state, or a state that was a reasonable facsimile of a southern state. She remembers that signs for colored and white bathrooms and water fountains persisted well into the mid-sixties in Texas. She remembers also Phyllis George, the Miss America from Denton, Texas, who went on to become a television personality for several years. She has always been very interested in George's career, and she has always disliked her. "She sounds just like a white girl from Texas," my wife likes to say, always reminding me that while both blacks and whites in Texas have accents, they do not sound alike. George won the contest in 1971, my wife's freshman year at the University of Pennsylvania and around the time she began to wear an Afro, a popular hairstyle for young black women in the days of "our terrible blackness" or "our black terribleness." It was a year fraught with complex passages into black womanhood for her. To think that a white woman from Texas should win the Miss America title that year! For my wife, the years of watching the Miss America contest were nothing more, in some sense continue to be nothing more, than an expression of anger made all the worse by the very unconscious or semiconscious nature of it. But if the anger has been persistent, so has her enormous capacity to "take it"; for in all these years it has never occurred to her to refuse to watch because, like the black girl being offered the white doll, like all black folk being offered white gifts, she has absolutely no idea how that is done, and she is not naive enough to think that a simple refusal would be an act of empowerment. Empowerment comes only through making demands of our bogeymen, not by trying to convince ourselves we are not tormented. Yet, paradoxically, among blacks there is the bitter hope that a simplistic race pride will save us, a creed that masks its complex contradictions beneath lapping waves of bourgeois optimism and bourgeois anguish; for race pride clings to the opposing notions that the great hope (but secret fear) of an African-American future is, first, that blacks will always remain black and, second, that the great fear (but secret hope) of an African-American future is that blacks will not always remain black but evolve into something else. Race pride, which at its most insistent argues that blackness is everything, becomes, in its attempt to be the psychological quest for sanity, a form of dementia that exists as a response to that form of white dementia that says blackness is nothing. Existing as it does as a reactive force battling against a white preemptive presumption, race pride begins to take on the vices of an unthinking dogma and the virtues of a disciplined religious faith, all in the same instance. With so much at stake, race pride becomes both the act of making a virtue of a necessity and making a necessity of a virtue and, finally, making a profound and touching absurdity of both virtue and necessity. In some ways my wife learned her lessons well in her youth: She never buys our daughters white dolls.

My daughters, Linnet, age ten, and Rosalind, age seven, have become staunch fans of beauty contests in the last three years. In that time they have watched, in their entirety, several Miss America pageants, one Miss Black America contest, and one Miss USA. At first, I ascribed this to the same impulse that made my wife interested in such events when she was little: something secretly female, just as an interest in professional sports might be ascribed to something peculiarly male. Probably it is a sort of resentment that black girls harbor toward these contests. But that could not really be the case with my daughters. After all, they have seen several black entrants in these contests and have even seen black winners. They also have black dolls.

Back in the fall of 1983 when Vanessa Williams became Miss America, we, as a family, had our picture taken with her when she visited St. Louis. We went, my wife and I, to celebrate the grand moment when white American popular culture decided to embrace black women as something other than sexual subversives or fat, kindly maids cleaning up and caring for white families. We had our own, well, royalty, and royal origins mean a great deal to people who have been denied their myths and their right to human blood. White women reformers may be ready to scrap the Miss America contest. (And the contest has certainly responded to the criticism it has been subjected to in recent years by muting some of the fleshier aspects of the program while, in its attempts to be even more the anxiety-ridden middle-class dream-wish, emphasizing more and more the magic of education and scholarly attainments.) It is now the contest that signifies the quest for professionalism among bourgeois women, and the first achievement of the professional career is to win something in a competition. But if there is a movement afoot to bring down the curtain finally on Miss America, my wife wants no part of it: "Whites always want to reform and end things when black people start getting on the gravy train they've been enjoying for years. What harm does the Miss America contest do?" None, I suppose, especially since black women have been winning lately.

Linnet and Rosalind were too young when we met Vanessa Williams to recall anything about the pictures, but they are amazed to see themselves in a bright, color Polaroid picture with a famous person, being part of an event which does not strike a chord in their consciousness because they cannot remember being alive when it happened. I often wonder if they attach any significance to the pictures at all. They think Vanessa is very pretty, prettier than their mother, but they attach no significance to being pretty — that is to say, no real value; they would not admire someone simply because he or she was good-looking. They think Williams is beautiful, but they do not wish that she was their mother. And this issue of being beautiful is not to be taken lightly in the life of a black girl. About two years ago Linnet started coming home from school wishing aloud that her hair was long and blond so that she could fling it about, the way she saw many of her white classmates doing. As she attends a school that is more than 90 percent white, it seemed inevitable to my wife that one of our daughters would become sensitive about her appearance. At this time Linnet's hair was not straightened and she wore it in braids. Oddly, despite the fact that she wanted a different hairstyle that would permit her hair to "blow in the wind," so to speak, she vehemently opposed having it straightened, although my wife has straightened hair, after having worn an Afro for several years. I am not sure why Linnet did not want her hair straightened; perhaps, after seeing her teenage cousin have her hair straightened on several occasions, the process of hair straightening seemed distasteful or disheartening or frightening. Actually, I do not think Linnet wanted to change her hair to be beautiful; she wanted to be like everyone else. But perhaps this is simply wishful thinking here or playing with words because Linnet must have felt her difference as being a kind of ugliness. Yet she is not a girl who is subject to illusion. Once, about a year earlier, when she had had a particularly rough day in school, I told her, in a father's patronizing way with a daughter, that I thought she was the most beautiful girl in the world. She looked at me strangely when I said that and then replied matter-of-factly: "I don't think I'm beautiful at all. I think I'm just ordinary. There is nothing wrong with that, is there, Daddy? Just to be ordinary?" "Are you unhappy to be ordinary?" I asked. She thought for a moment, then said quietly and finally, "No. Are you?"

Hair straightening, therefore, was not an option and would not have been even if Linnet had wanted it, because my wife was opposed to having Linnet's hair straightened at her age. At first, Linnet began going to school with her hair unbraided. Unfortunately, this turned out to be a disastrous hairdo, as her hair shrank during the course of a day to a tangled mess. Finally, my wife decided to have both Linnet and Rosalind get short Afro haircuts. Ostensibly, this was to ease the problem of taking swim lessons during the summer. In reality, it was to end Linnet's wishes for a white hairstyle by, in effect, foreclosing any possibility that she could remotely capture such a look. Rosalind's hair was cut so that Linnet would not feel that she was being singled out. (Alas, the trials of being both the second and the younger child!) At first, the haircuts caused many problems in school. Some of the children — both black and white — made fun of them. Brillo heads, they were called, and fungus and Afro heads. One group of black girls at school refused to play with Linnet. "You look so ugly with that short hair," they would say. "Why don't you wear your hair straight like your mom. Your mom's hair is so pretty." Then, for the first time, the girls were called niggers by a white child on their school bus, although I think neither the child nor my daughters completely understood the gravity of that obscenity. People in supermarkets would refer to them as boys unless they were wearing dresses. Both girls went through a period when they suffered most acutely from that particularly American disease, that particularly African-American disease, the conjunction of oppression and exhibitionistic desire: self-consciousness. They thought about their hair all the time. My wife called the parents of the children who teased them. The teasing stopped for the most part, although a few of the black girls remained so persistent that the white school counselor suggested that Linnet's and Rosalind's hair be straightened. "I'm white," he said, "and maybe I shouldn't get into this, but they might feel more comfortable if they wore a different hairstyle." My wife angrily rejected that bit of advice. She had them wear dresses more often to make them look unmistakably like girls, although she refused out of hand my suggestion of having their ears pierced. She is convinced that pierced ears are just a form of mutilation, primitive tattooing or scarring passing itself off as something fashionable. Eventually, the girls became used to their hair. Now, after more than a year, they hardly think about it, and even if Linnet wears a sweat suit or jeans, no one thinks she is a boy because she is budding breasts. Poor Rosalind still suffers on occasion in supermarkets because she shows no outward signs of sexual maturity. Once, while watching Linnet look at her mother's very long and silken straight hair, the hair that the other black girls at school admire, always calling it pretty, I asked her if she would like to have hers straightened.

"Not now," she said. "Maybe when I'm older. It'll be something   10 different."

"Do you think you will like it?" I asked.

"Maybe," she said.

And in that "maybe," so calmly and evenly uttered, rests the complex contradictions, the uneasy tentative negotiations of that which cannot be compromised yet can never be realized in this flawed world as an ideal; there is, in that "maybe," the epistemology of race pride for black American women so paradoxically symbolized by their straightened hair. In the February 1939 issue of the *Atlantic Monthly*, a black woman named Kimbal Goffman (possibly a pseudonym) wrote an essay entitled "Black Pride" in which she accused blacks of being ashamed of their heritage and, even more damningly in some of her barbs obviously aimed at black women, of their looks:

> Why are so many manufacturers becoming rich through the manufacture of bleaching preparations? Why are hair-straightening combs found in nearly every Negro home? Why is the following remark made so often to a newborn baby, when grandma or auntie visits it for the first time? "Tell Mother she must pinch your nose every morning. If she doesn't, you're gonna have a sure 'nough darky nose."

According to Goffman, blacks do not exploit what society has given them; they are simply ashamed to have what they have, tainted as it is with being associated with a degraded people, and long to be white or to have possessions that would accrue a kind of white status. In the essay, blacks in general receive their share of criticism but only black women are criticized in a gender-specific way that their neurotic sense of inferiority concerning physical appearance is a particularly dangerous form of reactionism as it stigmatizes each new generation. According to Goffman, it is black women, because they are mothers, who perpetuate their sense of inferiority by passing it on to their children. In this largely Du Boisian argument, Goffman advises, "Originality is the backbone of all progress." And, in this sense, originality means understanding blackness as something uncontrolled or uninfluenced by what whites say it is. This is the idealism of race pride that demands both purity and parity. Exactly one year later, in the February 1940 issue of the *Brown American*, a black magazine published in Philadelphia, Lillian Franklin McCall wrote an article about the history of black women beauty shop owners and entrepreneurs entitled "Appointment at Seven." The opening paragraph is filled with dollar signs:

> The business of straightening milady's insistent curls tinkles cash registers in the country to the tune of two million and a half dollars a year. And that covers merely the semi-monthly session with the hairdresser for the estimated four million of Eve's sepia adult daughters by national census. Today there is a growing trend to top off the regular, "Shampoo and wave," with a facial; and, perhaps, a manicure. New oil treatments and rinses prove a lure, too, so milady finds her beauty budget stepped up from approximately $39 yearly for an average $1.25 or $1.50 "hair-do," to $52.00 per year if she adds a facial to the beauty rite, and $10 more, for the manicure.

In a Booker T. Washington tone, McCall goes on to describe how the establishment of a black beauty culture serves as a source of empowerment for black women:

> Brown business it is, in all its magnitude, for Miss Brown America receives her treatments from the hands of Negro beauticians, and her hair preparations and skin creams come, usually, from Negro laboratories.

She then tells the reader that leading companies in this field were founded by black women: Madam C. J. Walker, Mrs. Annie Turbo Malone, Madame Sara Spencer Washington. And one is struck by the absences that this essay evokes, not only in comparison to Goffman's piece but also to Elsie Johnson McDougald's major manifesto on black women, "The Task of Negro Womanhood," that appeared in Alain Locke's seminal 1925 anthology of African-American thought, *The New Negro*. In McDougald's piece, which outlines all the economic status and achievements of black women at the time, there is absolutely no mention of black beauty culture, no mention of Madame C. J. Walker, although her newspaper ads were among the biggest in black newspapers nationwide during the twenties. (And why did McDougald not mention black women's beauty workers and businesspeople culture along with the nurses, domestics, clerks, and teachers she discusses at length? It can scarcely be because she, as a trained and experienced writer on black sociological matters, did not think of it.)[1] It is not simply money or black woman's industry or endeavor that makes the black woman present or a presence; it is beauty culture generally which finally brings her into

---

[1]Richard Wright tells a story in his 1956 account of the Bandung conference, entitled *The Color Curtain,* that emphasizes the absence of the black woman. He relates how a white woman journalist knocks on his hotel room door during the course of the conference and confides the strange behavior of her roommate — a black woman journalist from Boston. Her roommate walks around in the middle of the night and the white woman often covertly spies her in "a dark corner of the room . . . bent over a tiny blue light, a very low and a very blue flame. . . . It seemed like she was combing her hair, but I wasn't sure. Her right

being, and specifically, her presence is generated by her hair. What for one black woman writer, Goffman, is an absence and thus a sign of degradation, is for another a presence and a sign of economic possibilities inherent in feminine aesthetics.

What did I see as a boy when I passed the large black beauty shop on Broad and South Streets in Philadelphia where the name of its owner, Adele Reese, commanded such respect or provoked such jealousy? What did I see there but a long row of black women dressed immaculately in white tunics, washing and styling the hair of other black women. That was a sign of what culture, of what set of politics? The sheen of those straightened heads, the entire enterprise of the making of black feminine beauty: Was it an enactment of a degradation inspirited by a bitter inferiority or was it a womanly laying on of hands where black women were, in their way, helping themselves to live through and transcend their degradation? As a boy, I used to watch and wonder as my mother straightened my sisters' hair every Saturday night for church on Sunday morning. Under a low flame on the stove, the hot comb would glow dully; from an open jar of Apex bergamot hair oil or Dixie Peach, my mother would extract blobs and place them on the back of one hand, deftly applying the oil to strands of my sisters' hair with the other. And the strange talk about a "light press" or a "heavy press" or a "close press" to get the edges and the ends; the concern about the hair "going back" if caught in the rain. Going back where, I wondered. To Africa? To the bush? And the constant worry and vigil about burning, getting too

---

arm was moving and now and then she would look over her shoulder toward my bed." The white woman thinks that the black woman is practicing voodoo. But Wright soon explains that the black woman is simply straightening her hair.

> "But why would she straighten her hair? Her hair seems all right" [the white woman journalist asks].
> "Her hair is all right. But it's not straight. It's kinky. But she does not want you, a white woman, to see her when she straightens her hair. She would feel embarrassed — "
> "Why?"
> "Because you were born with straight hair, and she wants to look as much like you as possible. . . ."
> The woman stared at me, then clapped her hands to her eyes and exclaimed: "Oh!"
> I leaned back and thought: Here in Asia, where everybody was dark, the poor American Negro woman was worried about the hair she was born with. Here, where practically nobody was white, her hair would have been acceptable; no one would have found her "inferior" because her hair was kinky; on the contrary, the Indonesians would perhaps have found her different and charming.

The conversation continues with an account of the black woman's secretive skin-lightening treatments. What is revealing in this dialogue which takes on both political and psychoanalytic proportions is the utter absence of the black woman's voice, her presence. She is simply the dark, neurotic ghost that flits in the other room while the black male and the white female, both in the same room, one with dispassionate curtness and the other with sentimentalized guilt, consider the illness that is enacted before them as a kind of bad theater. Once again, the psychopathology of the black American is symbolized by the black woman's straightened hair, by her beauty culture. [Early's note.]

close to the scalp. I can remember hearing my sisters' hair sizzle and crackle as the comb passed through with a kind of pungent smell of actually burning hair. And I, like an intentional moth, with lonely narrow arcs, hovered near this flame of femininity with a fascinated impertinence. Had I witnessed the debilitating nullity of absence or was it the affirmation of an inescapable presence? Had I witnessed a mutilation or a rite of devotion? Black women's hair is, I decided even as a boy, unintelligible. And now I wonder, is the acceptance of the reigns of black women as Miss America a sign that black beauty has become part of the mainstream culture? Is the black woman now truly a presence?

We, I and my wife and our daughters, sat together and watched the latest 15
Miss America contest. We did what we usually do. We ate popcorn. We laughed at all the talent numbers, particularly the ones when the contestants were opera singers or dancers. We laughed when the girls tried to answer grand social questions — such as "How can we inspire children to achieve and stay in school?" or "How can we address the problem of mainstreaming physically disadvantaged people?" — in thirty seconds. In fact, as Rosalind told me after the show, the main reason my daughters watch the Miss America pageant is that "it's funny." My daughters laugh because they cannot understand why the women are doing what they are doing, why they are trying so hard to please, to be pleasing. This must certainly be a refreshing bit of sanity, as the only proper response for such a contest is simply to dismiss it as hilarious; this grandiose version of an elocution, charm school, dance and music recital, which is not a revelation of talent but a reaffirmation of bourgeois cultural conditioning. And this bit of sanity on my daughters' part may prove hopeful for our future, for our American future, for our African-American future, if black girls are, unlike my wife when she was young, no longer angry. When it was announced that Miss Missouri, Debbye Turner, the third black to be Miss America, was the winner, my children were indifferent. It hardly mattered to them who won, and a black woman's victory meant no more than if any other contestant had prevailed. "She's pretty," Linnet said. She won two dollars in a bet with my wife, who did not think it possible that another black Miss America would be chosen. "Vanessa screwed up for the whole race," she told me once. "It's the race burden, the sins of the one become the original sins of us all." Linnet said simply, "She'll win because she is the best." Meritocracy is still a valid concept with the young.] *qualifier, not necessarily true for him*

For me, it was almost to be expected that Miss Turner would win. First, she received more precontest publicity than any other contestant in recent years, with the possible exception of the black woman who was chosen Miss Mississippi a few years ago. Second, after the reign of Vanessa Williams, one would think that the Miss America powers that be very much wanted to have another black win and have a successful reign so that the contest itself could both prove its good faith (to blacks) and forestall criticism from white feminists and liberals (who are always put in a difficult position when the object of their disapproval is a black woman). As with the selection of

Williams, the contest gained a veneer of postmodernist social and political relevance not only by selecting a black again but by having an Asian, a kidney donor, and a hearing-impaired woman among the top ten finalists. This all smacks of affirmative action or let's-play-fair-with-the-underrepresented doctrine, which, as Miss Virginia pointed out after the contest, smacks of politics. But the point she missed, of course, is the point that all people who oppose affirmative action miss. The selection process for the Miss America contest has always been political. Back in the days when only white college women, whose main interest in most instances was a degree in MRS, could win, the contest was indeed just as political as it is now, a clear ideological bow to both patriarchal ideals and racism. It is simply a matter of which politics you prefer, and while no politics are perfect, some are clearly better than others. But in America, it must be added, the doctrine of fair play should not even be graced with such a sophisticated term as "political." It is more our small-town, bourgeois Christian, muscular myth of ethical rectitude, the tremendous need Americans feel to be decent. So Miss Turner is intended to be both the supersession of Vanessa Williams — a religious vet student whose ambitions are properly, well, postmodernist Victorianism, preach do-goodism, evoke the name of God whenever you speak of your ambitions, and live with smug humility — and the redemption of the image of black women in American popular culture, since the Miss America contest is one of the few vehicles of display and competition for women in popular culture.

And if my daughters have come to one profound penetration of this cultural rite, it is that the contest ought to be laughed at in some ways, as most of the manifestations of popular culture ought to be for being the shoddy illusions that they are. For one always ought to laugh at someone or a group of someones who are trying to convince you that nothing is something — and that is not really the same as someone trying to convince you that you can have something for nothing, because in the popular culture business, the price for nothing is the same as the price for something; this "nothing is something" is, in fact, in most cases what the merchandising of popular culture is all about. (But as Mother reminded me as a boy: Nothing is nothing and something is something. Accept no substitutes!) For my children, the contest can be laughed at because it is so completely meaningless to them; they know it is an illusion despite its veneer as competition. And it is that magical word, competition, which is used over and over again all night long by the host and hostesses of the Miss America show (a contest, like most others these days, from the SATs to professional sports, that is made up of a series of competitions within the framework of larger competitions in such a pyramid that the entire structure of the outside world, for the bourgeois mind, is a frightful maze, a strangulating skein of competitions), that is the touchstone of reality, the momentous signifier that the sponsors of the pageant hope will give this extravaganza new significance and new life. For everything that we feel is important now is a matter of competition, beating out someone else for a prize, for some cheap prestige, a moment of notice before descending to cipherhood again; competition ranging from high culture (literary prizes, which seem to be awarded every day in the week, and classical music competitions for every instrument in a symphony orchestra, because of course for high culture one can never have enough art) to midculture (the entire phenomenon of American education, from academic honors to entrance requirements for prestigious schools, because of course for the middle class one can never have enough education or enough professionalism) to low culture (playing the lottery and various forms of gambling, because of course for the lower class one can never hope enough for money). And the more stringent and compulsively expressed the competition is (and the Miss America contest has reached a new height of hysteria in both the stridency and compulsion of the competition), the more legitimate and noteworthy it is.

Everyone in our culture wants to win a prize. Perhaps that is the grand lesson we have taken with us from kindergarten in the age of the perversions of Dewey-style education: Everyone gets a ribbon, and praise becomes a meaningless narcotic to soothe egoistic distemper. And in our bourgeois coming-of-age, we simply crave more and more ribbons and praise, the attainment of which becomes all the more delightful and satisfying if they are gotten at someone else's expense. Competition, therefore, becomes in the end a kind of laissez-faire psychotherapy that structures and orders our impossible rages of ambition, our rages to be noticed. But competition does not produce better people (a myth we have swallowed whole); it does not even produce better candidates; it simply produces more desperately grasping competitors. The "quality" of the average Miss America contestant is not significantly better now than it was twenty-five years ago, although the desires of today's contestants may meet with our approval (who could possibly disapprove of a black woman who wishes to be a vet in this day of careerism as the expression of independence and political empowerment), but then the women of twenty-five years ago wanted what their audiences approved of as well. That is not necessarily an advance or progress; that is simply a recognition that we are all bound by the mood and temper of our time. So, in this vast competition, this fierce theatrical warfare where all the women are supposed to love their neighbor while they wish to beat her brains out, this warfare so pointedly exposed before the nation, what we have chosen is not the Royal American Daughter (although the contest's preoccupation with the terminology of aristocracy mirrors the public's need for such a person as the American princess) but rather the Cosmopolitan Girl. As the magazine ad states:[2]

> Can a girl be too busy? I'm taking seventeen units at Princeton, pushing on with my career during vacations and school breaks, study singing and dancing when I can, try never to lose

---

[2]Jacques Barzun, "Culture High and Dry," *The Culture We Deserve* (Middletown, Conn.: Wesleyan University Press, 1989). [Early's note.]

track of my five closest chums, steal the time for Michael
Jackson and Thomas Hardy, work for an antidrug program for
kids and, oh yes, I hang out with three horses, three cats, two
birds and my dog, Jack. My favorite magazine says "too busy"
just means you don't want to miss anything. . . . I love that
magazine. I guess you can say I'm That Cosmopolitan Girl.

When one reads about these women in the Miss America contest, that is
precisely what they sound like: the Cosmopolitan Girl who knows how to
have serious fun, and she has virtually nothing with which to claim our
attention except a moralistic bourgeois diligence. To use a twenties term: She
sounds "swell." She is an amalgam of both lead characters portrayed by
Patty Duke on her old TV show: the studious, serious kid and the "typical"
wacky but good-hearted suburban teenager, or, to borrow Ann Douglas's
concept, she is the Teen Angel: the bourgeois girl who can do everything, is
completely self-absorbed with her leisure, and has a heart of gold. Once
again, with the Miss America contest we have America's vehement preoccupation with innocence, with its inability to deal with the darkness of youth,
the darkness of its own uselessly expressed ambition, the dark complexity
of its own simplistic morality of sunshine and success, the darkness, righteous rage, and bitter depth of its own daughters. Once again, when the new
Miss America, victorious and smiling, walks down the runway, we know
that runway, that victory march, to be the American catwalk of supreme
bourgeois self-consciousness and supreme illusion. We are still being told
that nothing is something.

Nonetheless, the fact that Miss Turner won struck both my wife and me
as important, as something important for the race. We laughed during the
contest, but we did not laugh when she was chosen. We wanted her to win
very much; it is impossible to escape that need to see the race uplifted, to
thumb your nose at whites on a competition. It is impossible for blacks not
to want to see their black daughters elevated to the platforms where white
women are. Perhaps this tainted desire, an echoing "Ballad of the Brown
Girl" that resounds in the unconscious psyche of all black people, is the
unity of feeling which is the only race pride blacks have ever had since they
became Americans; for race pride for the African American, finally, is something that can only be understood as existing on the edge of tragedy and
history and is, finally, that which binds both together to make the African
American the darkly and richly complicated person he or she is. In the end,
both black women magazine writers quoted earlier were right: Race pride
is transcending your degradation while learning to live in it and with it. To
paraphrase an idea of Dorothy Sayers, race pride must teach blacks that they
are not to be saved *from* degradation but saved *in* it.

A few days after the contest I watched both my daughters playing [20]
Barbies, as they call it. They squat on the floor on their knees, moving their
dolls around through an imaginary town and in imaginary houses. I decided
to join them and squatted down too, asking them the rules of their game,
which they patiently explained as though they did not mind having me, the

strange adult, invade their children's world. I told them it was hard for me to squat and asked if I could simply sit down, but they said that one always plays Barbies while squatting. It was a rule that had to be obeyed. As they went along, explaining relationships among their myriad dolls and the several landscapes, as complicated a genealogy as anything Faulkner ever dreamed up, a theater as vast as the entire girlhood of the world, they told me that one particular black Ken doll and one particular black Barbie doll were married and that the dolls had a child. Then Rosalind held up a white doll that someone, probably a grandparent, had given them (my wife is fairly strict on the point of our daughters' not having white dolls, but I guess a few have slipped through), explaining that this doll was the daughter of the black Ken and Barbie.

"But," I said, "how could two black dolls have a white daughter?"

"Oh," said Rosalind, looking at me as if I were an object deserving of only her indulgent pity, "we're not racial. That's old-fashioned. Don't you think so, Daddy? Aren't you tired of all that racial stuff?"

Bowing to that wisdom which, it is said, is the only kind that will lead us to Christ and to ourselves, I decided to get up and leave them to their play. My knees had begun to hurt and I realized, painfully, that I was much too old, much too at peace with stiffness and inflexibility, for children's games.

AFTERWORD

Not many essays begin with three epigraphs. (Note: not epitaphs, not epigrams.) Aspiration, desire, treasure; dream and absence. Like titles, epigraphs can be useful to an essay: setting a tone, citing authority.

In his second and third paragraphs, Early writes about the changing significance of white dolls in connection with black children. The language of literature constantly reminds us to stay alert to the inside gestures of words. Language serves first to embody, then to identify irony, the self-cancellation of feeling and import. Think of the circle of euphemism whereby "colored" was condescending decades ago, and now "people of color" has become not only acceptable but even correct. We are tactless, or stupid, when we use a word — or other language, like the color of a doll's skin — in outdated usage, after society has reversed an implication.

Literature — including this essay — exists to reveal the real dazzling complexity of our lives and feelings. Logic says that a thing cannot be true and untrue at the same time. Literature knows better and shows it happening, affirming both sides of a contradiction. Early assembles in this essay innumerable contradictions — male and female, black and white, past and present. The essay comes to no pat conclusion — essays are not required to vote this way or that — but in its domestic anecdotes, and in Early's brilliant and modest commentary, this essay illuminates conjunctions of dilemma.

BOOKS AVAILABLE IN PAPERBACK

How the War in the Streets Is Won: Poems of a Black American's Journey into Himself. St. Louis: Time Being Books.

Tuxedo Junction: Essays on American Culture. Hopewell, N.J.: Ecco Press.

GRETEL
EHRLICH

G RETEL EHRLICH *was born in Santa Barbara (1946), where her father raised breed mares and rode the professional horse show circuit. Now she rides rough, cowboying in Wyoming. She went to college at Bennington in Vermont, at the UCLA film school, and at the New School for Social Research in New York City. In 1976 when she was thirty, she arrived in Wyoming for the first time, to film a documentary for PBS on sheepherders, while the man she loved, her partner on the film, was dying of cancer in New York. "The tears came and lasted for two years."*

But when the tears ended, Wyoming was still there. Ehrlich fell in love with the land and later married a rancher, with whom she shares a small ranch in the Big Horn Basin ten miles from a paved road. After making films and publishing two collections of poetry, Ehrlich turned to prose. This essay appears in The Solace of Open Spaces *(1985), which critics called a prose equivalent to the photographs of Ansel Adams. She has written a novel,* Heart Mountain *(1988), and in 1991 she collected more essays in* Islands, the Universe, Home.

"Landscape does not exist without an observer," she has written, "without a human presence." The vivid language of "The Solace of Open Spaces" makes a landscape palpable for the reader; Ehrlich is also alert to the men and women of her Wyoming, products of the rough indomitable land.

The Solace of Open Spaces

It's May and I've just awakened from a nap, curled against sagebrush the way my dog taught me to sleep — sheltered from wind. A front is pulling the huge sky over me, and from the dark a hailstone has hit me on the head. I'm trailing a band of two thousand sheep across a stretch of Wyoming badlands, a fifty-mile trip that takes five days because sheep shade up in hot sun and won't budge until it's cool. Bunched together now, and excited into a run by the storm, they drift across dry land, tumbling into draws like water and surge out again onto the rugged, choppy plateaus that are the building blocks of this state.

The name Wyoming comes from an Indian word meaning "at the great plains," but the plains are really valleys, great arid valleys, sixteen hundred square miles, with the horizon bending up on all sides into mountain ranges. This gives the vastness a sheltering look.

Winter lasts six months here. Prevailing winds spill snowdrifts to the east, and new storms from the northwest replenish them. This white bulk is sometimes dizzying, even nauseating, to look at. At twenty, thirty, and forty degrees below zero, not only does your car not work, but neither do your mind and body. The landscape hardens into a dungeon of space. During the winter, while I was riding to find a new calf, my jeans froze to the saddle, and in the silence that such cold creates I felt like the first person on earth, or the last.

Today the sun is out — only a few clouds billowing. In the east, where the sheep have started off without me, the benchland tilts up in a series of eroded red-earthed mesas, planed flat on top by a million years of water; behind them, a bold line of muscular scarps rears up ten thousand feet to become the Big Horn Mountains. A tidal pattern is engraved into the ground, as if left by the sea that once covered this state. Canyons curve down like galaxies to meet the oncoming rush of flat land.

To live and work in this kind of open country, with its hundred-mile 5 views, is to lose the distinction between background and foreground. When I asked an older ranch hand to describe Wyoming's openness, he said, "It's all a bunch of nothing — wind and rattlesnakes — and so much of it you can't tell where you're going or where you've been and it don't make much difference." John, a sheepman I know, is tall and handsome and has an explosive temperament. He has a perfect intuition about people and sheep. They call him "Highpockets," because he's so long-legged; his graceful stride matches the distances he has to cover. He says, "Open space hasn't affected me at all. It's all the people moving in on it." The huge ranch he was born on takes up much of one county and spreads into another state; to put 100,000 miles on his pickup in three years and never leave home is

156

not unusual. A friend of mine has an aunt who ranched on Powder River and didn't go off her place for eleven years. When her husband died, she quickly moved to town, bought a car, and drove around the States to see what she'd been missing.

Most people tell me they've simply driven through Wyoming, as if there were nothing to stop for. Or else they've skied in Jackson Hole, a place Wyomingites acknowledge uncomfortably because its green beauty and chic affluence are mismatched with the rest of the state. Most of Wyoming has a "lean-to" look. Instead of big, roomy barns and Victorian houses, there are dugouts, low sheds, log cabins, sheep camps, and fence lines that look like driftwood blown haphazardly into place. People here still feel pride because they live in such a harsh place, part of the glamorous cowboy past, and they are determined not to be the victims of a mining-dominated future.

Most characteristic of the state's landscape is what a developer euphemistically describes as "indigenous growth right up to your front door" — a reference to waterless stands of salt sage, snakes, jack rabbits, deerflies, red dust, a brief respite of wildflowers, dry washes, and no trees. In the Great Plains the vistas look like music, like Kyries° of grass, but Wyoming seems to be the doing of a mad architect — tumbled and twisted, ribboned with faded, deathbed colors, thrust up and pulled down as if the place had been startled out of a deep sleep and thrown into a pure light.

I came here four years ago. I had not planned to stay, but I couldn't make myself leave. John, the sheepman, put me to work immediately. It was spring, and shearing time. For fourteen days of fourteen hours each, we moved thousands of sheep through sorting corrals to be sheared, branded, and deloused. I suspect that my original motive for coming here was to "lose myself" in new and unpopulated territory. Instead of producing the numbness I thought I wanted, life on the sheep ranch woke me up. The vitality of the people I was working with flushed out what had become a hallucinatory rawness inside me. I threw away my clothes and bought new ones; I cut my hair. The arid country was a clean slate. Its absolute indifference steadied me.

Sagebrush covers fifty-eight thousand square miles of Wyoming. The biggest city has a population of fifty thousand, and there are only five settlements that could be called cities in the whole state. The rest are towns, scattered across the expanse with as much as sixty miles between them, their populations two thousand, fifty, or ten. They are fugitive-looking, perched on a barren, windblown bench, or tagged onto a river or a railroad, or laid out straight in a farming valley with implement stores and a block-long Mormon church. In the eastern part of the state, which slides down into the Great Plains, the new mining settlements are boomtowns, trailer cities, metal knots on flat land.

Kyries Short prayers, beginning *Kyrie eleison* ("Lord, have mercy"), often sung or chanted.

Despite the desolate look, there's a coziness to living in this state. There 10
are so few people (only 470,000) that ranchers who buy and sell cattle know
one another statewide; the kids who choose to go to college usually go to
the state's one university, in Laramie; hired hands work their way around
Wyoming in a lifetime of hirings and firings. And despite the physical
separation, people stay in touch, often driving two or three hours to another
ranch for dinner.

Seventy-five years ago, when travel was by buckboard or horseback,
cowboys who were temporarily out of work rode the grub line — drifting
from ranch to ranch, mending fences or milking cows, and receiving in
exchange a bed and meals. Gossip and messages traveled this slow circuit
with them, creating an intimacy between ranchers who were three and four
weeks' ride apart. One old-time couple I know, whose turn-of-the-century
homestead was used by an outlaw gang as a relay station for stolen horses,
recall that if you were traveling, desperado or not, any lighted ranch house
was a welcome sign. Even now, for someone who lives in a remote spot,
arriving at a ranch or coming to town for supplies is cause for celebration.
To emerge from isolation can be disorienting. Everything looks bright, new,
vivid. After I had been herding sheep for only three days, the sound of the
camp tender's pickup flustered me. Longing for human company, I felt a
foolish grin take over my face; yet I had to resist an urgent temptation to
run and hide.

Things happen suddenly in Wyoming, the change of seasons and
weather; for people, the violent swings in and out of isolation. But good-
naturedness is concomitant with severity. Friendliness is a tradition. Strangers passing on the road wave hello. A common sight is two pickups stopped
side by side far out on a range, on a dirt track winding through the sage.
The drivers will share a cigarette, uncap their Thermos bottles, and pass a
battered cup, steaming with coffee, between windows. These meetings summon up the details of several generations, because, in Wyoming, private
histories are largely public knowledge.

Because ranch work is a physical and, these days, economic strain, being
"at home on the range" is a matter of vigor, self-reliance, and common sense.
A person's life is not a series of dramatic events for which he or she is
applauded or exiled but a slow accumulation of days, seasons, years, fleshed
out by the generational weight of one's family and anchored by a land-
bound sense of place.

In most parts of Wyoming, the human population is visibly outnumbered
by the animal. Not far from my town of fifty, I rode into a narrow valley
and startled a herd of two hundred elk. Eagles look like small people as they
eat car-killed deer by the road. Antelope, moving in small, graceful bands,
travel at sixty miles an hour, their mouths open as if drinking in the space.

The solitude in which westerners live makes them quiet. They telegraph 15
thoughts and feelings by the way they tilt their heads and listen; pulling
their Stetsons into a steep dive over their eyes, or pigeon-toeing one boot

over the other, they lean against a fence with a fat wedge of Copenhagen beneath their lower lips and take in the whole scene. These detached looks of quiet amusement are sometimes cynical, but they can also come from a dry-eyed humility as lucid as the air is clear.

Conversation goes on in what sounds like a private code; a few phrases imply a complex of meanings. Asking directions, you get a curious list of details. While trailing sheep I was told to "ride up to that kinda upturned rock, follow the pink wash, turn left at the dump, and then you'll see the water hole." One friend told his wife on roundup to "turn at the salt lick and the dead cow," which turned out to be a scattering of bones and no salt lick at all.

Sentence structure is shortened to the skin and bones of a thought. Descriptive words are dropped, even verbs; a cowboy looking over a corral full of horses will say to a wrangler, "Which one needs rode?" People hold back their thoughts in what seems to be a dumbfounded silence, then erupt with an excoriating perceptive remark. Language, so compressed, becomes metaphorical. A rancher ended a relationship with one remark: "You're a bad check," meaning bouncing in and out was intolerable, and even coming back would be no good.

What's behind this laconic style is shyness. There is no vocabulary for the subject of feelings. It's not a hangdog shyness, or anything coy — always there's a robust spirit in evidence behind the restraint, as if the earth-dredging wind that pulls across Wyoming had carried its people's voices away but everything else in them had shouldered confidently into the breeze.

I've spent hours riding to sheep camp at dawn in a pickup when nothing was said; eaten meals in the cookhouse when the only words spoken were a mumbled "Thank you, ma'am" at the end of dinner. The silence is profound. Instead of talking, we seem to share one eye. Keenly observed, the world is transformed. The landscape is engorged with detail, every movement on it chillingly sharp. The air between people is charged. Days unfold, bathed in their own music. Nights become hallucinatory; dreams, prescient.

Spring weather is capricious and mean. It snows, then blisters with heat. There have been tornadoes. They lay their elephant trunks out in the sage until they find houses, then slurp everything up and leave. I've noticed that melting snowbanks hiss and rot, viperous, then drip into calm pools where ducklings hatch and livestock, being trailed to summer range, drink. With the ice cover gone, rivers churn a milkshake brown, taking culverts and small bridges with them. Water in such an arid place (the average annual rainfall where I live is less than eight inches) is like blood. It festoons drab land with green veins; a line of cottonwoods following a stream; a strip of alfalfa; and, on ditch banks, wild asparagus growing.

I've moved to a small cattle ranch owned by friends. It's at the foot of the Big Horn Mountains. A few weeks ago, I helped them deliver a calf who was stuck halfway out of his mother's body. By the time he was freed, we could see a heartbeat, but he was straining against a swollen tongue for air.

Mary and I held him upside down by his back feet, while Stan, on his hands and knees in the blood, gave the calf mouth-to-mouth resuscitation. I have a vague memory of being pneumonia-choked as a child, my mother giving me her air, which may account for my romance with this windswept state.

If anything is endemic to Wyoming, it is wind. This big room of space is swept out daily, leaving a bone yard of fossils, agates, and carcasses in every stage of decay. Though it was water that initially shaped the state, wind is the meticulous gardener, raising dust and pruning the sage.

I try to imagine a world in which I could ride my horse across uncharted land. There is no wilderness left; wildness, yes, but true wilderness has been gone on this continent since the time of Lewis and Clark's overland journey.

Two hundred years ago, the Crow, Shoshone, Arapaho, Cheyenne, and Sioux roamed the intermountain West, orchestrating their movements according to hunger, season, and warfare. Once they acquired horses, they traversed the spines of all the big Wyoming ranges — the Absarokas, the Wind Rivers, the Tetons, the Big Horns — and wintered on the unprotected plains that fan out from them. Space was life. The world was their home.

What was life-giving to Native Americans was often nightmarish to 25 sodbusters who had arrived encumbered with families and ethnic pasts to be transplanted in nearly uninhabitable land. The great distances, the shortage of water and trees, and the loneliness created unexpected hardships for them. In her book *O Pioneers!*, Willa Cather gives a settler's version of the bleak landscape:

> The little town behind them had vanished as if it had never been, had fallen behind the swell of the prairie, and the stern frozen country received them into its bosom. The homesteads were few and far apart; here and there a windmill gaunt against the sky, a sod house crouching in a hollow.

The emptiness of the West was for others a geography of possibility. Men and women who amassed great chunks of land and struggled to preserve unfenced empires were, despite their self-serving motives, unwitting geographers. They understood the lay of the land. But by the 1850s the Oregon and Mormon trails sported bumper-to-bumper traffic. Wealthy landowners, many of them aristocratic absentee landlords, known as remittance men because they were paid to come West and get out of their families' hair, overstocked the range with more than a million head of cattle. By 1885 the feed and water were desperately short, and the winter of 1886 laid out the gaunt bodies of dead animals so closely together that when the thaw came, one rancher from Kaycee claimed to have walked on cowhide all the way to Crazy Woman Creek, twenty miles away.

Territorial Wyoming was a boy's world. The land was generous with everything but water. At first there was room enough, food enough, for everyone. And, as with all beginnings, an expansive mood set in. The young cowboys, drifters, shopkeepers, schoolteachers, were heroic, lawless, generous, rowdy, and tenacious. The individualism and optimism generated during those times have endured.

John Tisdale rode north with the trail herds from Texas. He was a college-educated man with enough money to buy a small outfit near the Powder River. While driving home from the town of Buffalo with a buckboard full of Christmas toys for his family and a winter's supply of food, he was shot in the back by an agent of the cattle barons who resented the encroachment of small-time stockmen like him. The wealthy cattlemen tried to control all the public grazing land by restricting membership in the Wyoming Stock Growers Association, as if it were a country club. They ostracized from roundups and brandings cowboys and ranchers who were not members, then denounced them as rustlers. Tisdale's death, the second such cold-blooded murder, kicked off the Johnson County cattle war, which was no simple good-guy-bad-guy shoot-out but a complicated class struggle between landed gentry and less affluent settlers — a shocking reminder that the West was not an egalitarian sanctuary after all.

Fencing ultimately enforced boundaries, but barbed wire abrogated space. It was stretched across the beautiful valleys, into the mountains, over desert badlands, through buffalo grass. The "anything is possible" fever — the lure of any new place — was constricted. The integrity of the land as a geographical body, and the freedom to ride anywhere on it, were lost.

I punched cows with a young man named Martin, who is the great-grandson of John Tisdale. His inheritance is not the open land that Tisdale knew and prematurely lost but a rage against restraint.

Wyoming tips down as you head northeast; the highest ground — the Laramie Plains — is on the Colorado border. Up where I live, the Big Horn River leaks into difficult, arid terrain. In the basin where it's dammed, sandhill cranes gather and, with delicate legwork, slice through the stilled water. I was driving by with a rancher one morning when he commented that cranes are "old-fashioned." When I asked why, he said, "Because they mate for life." Then he looked at me with a twinkle in his eyes, as if to say he really did believe in such things but also understood why we break our own rules.

In all this open space, values crystalize quickly. People are strong on scruples but tenderhearted about quirky behavior. A friend and I found one ranch hand, who's "not quite right in the head," sitting in front of the badly decayed carcass of a cow, shaking his finger and saying, "Now, I don't want you to do this ever again!" When I asked what was wrong with him, I was told, "He's goofier than hell, just like the rest of us." Perhaps because the West is historically new, conventional morality is still felt to be less important than rock-bottom truths. Though there's always a lot of teasing and sparring, people are blunt with one another, sometimes even cruel, believing honesty is stronger medicine than sympathy, which may console but often conceals.

The formality that goes hand in hand with the rowdiness is known as the Western Code. It's a list of practical do's and don'ts, faithfully observed.

161

A friend, Cliff, who runs a trapline in the winter, cut off half his foot while chopping a hole in the ice. Alone, he dragged himself to his pickup and headed for town, stopping to open the ranch gate as he left, and getting out to close it again, thus losing, in his observance of rules, precious time and blood. Later, he commented, "How would it look, them having to come to the hospital to tell me their cows had gotten out?"

Accustomed to emergencies, my friends doctor each other from the vet's bag with relish. When one old-timer suffered a heart attack in hunting camp, his partner quickly stirred up a brew of red horse liniment and hot water and made the half-conscious victim drink it, then tied him onto a horse and led him twenty miles to town. He regained consciousness and lived.

The roominess of the state has affected political attitudes as well. Ranchers keep up with world politics and the convulsions of the economy but are basically isolationists. Being used to running their own small empires of land and livestock, they're suspicious of big government. It's a "don't fence me in" holdover from a century ago. They still want the elbow room their grandfathers had, so they're strongly conservative, but with a populist twist. ³⁵

Summer is the season when we get our "cowboy tans" — on the lower parts of our faces and on three fourths of our arms. Excessive heat, in the nineties and higher, sends us outside with the mosquitoes. In winter we're tucked inside our houses, and the white wasteland outside appears to be expanding, but in summer all the greenery abridges space. Summer is a go-ahead season. Every living thing is off the block and in the race: battalions of bugs in flight and biting; bats swinging around my log cabin as if the bases were loaded and someone had hit a home run. Some of summer's high-speed growth is ominous: Larkspur, death camas, and green greasewood can kill sheep — an ironic idea, dying in this desert from eating what is too verdant. With sixteen hours of daylight, farmers and ranchers irrigate feverishly. There are first, second, and third cuttings of hay, some crews averaging only four hours of sleep a night for weeks. And, like the cowboys who in summer ride the night rodeo circuit, nighthawks make daredevil dives at dusk with an eerie whirring sound like a plane going down on the shimmering horizon.

In the town where I live, they've had to board up the dance-hall windows because there have been so many fights. There's so little to do except work that people wind up in a state of idle agitation that becomes fatalistic, as if there were nothing to be done about all this untapped energy. So the dark side to the grandeur of these spaces is the small-mindedness that seals people in. Men become hermits; women go mad. Cabin fever explodes into suicides, or into grudges and lifelong family feuds. Two sisters in my area inherited a ranch but found they couldn't get along. They fenced the place in half. When one's cows got out and mixed with the other's, the women went at each other with shovels. They ended up in the same hospital room but never spoke a word to each other for the rest of their lives.

After the brief lushness of summer, the sun moves south. The range grass is brown. Livestock is trailed back down from the mountains. Water holes begin to frost over at night. Last fall Martin asked me to accompany him on a pack trip. With five horses, we followed a river into the mountains behind the tiny Wyoming town of Meeteetse. Groves of aspen, red and orange, gave off a light that made us look toasted. Our hunting camp was so high that clouds skidded across our foreheads, then slowed to sail out across the warm valleys. Except for a bull moose who wandered into our camp and mistook our black gelding for a rival, we shot at nothing.

One of our evening entertainments was to watch the night sky. My dog, a dingo bred to herd sheep, also came on the trip. He is so used to the silence and empty skies that when an airplane flies over he always looks up and eyes the distant intruder quizzically. The sky, lately, seems to be much more crowded than it used to be. Satellites make their silent passes in the dark with great regularity. We counted eighteen in one hour's viewing. How odd to think that while they circumnavigated the planet, Martin and I had moved only six miles into our local wilderness and had seen no other human for the two weeks we stayed there.

At night, by moonlight, the land is whittled to slivers — a ridge, a river, 40 a strip of grassland stretching to the mountains, then the huge sky. One morning a full moon was setting in the west just as the sun was rising. I felt precariously balanced between the two as I loped across a meadow. For a moment, I could believe that the stars, which were still visible, work like cooper's bands, holding together everything above Wyoming.

Space has a spiritual equivalent and can heal what is divided and burdensome in us. My grandchildren will probably use space shuttles for a honeymoon trip or to recover from heart attacks, but closer to home we might also learn how to carry space inside ourselves in the effortless way we carry our skins. Space represents sanity, not a life purified, dull, or "spaced out" but one that might accommodate intelligently any idea or situation.

From the clayey soil of northern Wyoming is mined bentonite, which is used as a filler in candy, gum, and lipstick. We Americans are great on fillers, as if what we have, what we are, is not enough. We have a cultural tendency toward denial, but, being affluent, we strangle ourselves with what we can buy. We have only to look at the houses we build to see how we build *against* space, the way we drink against pain and loneliness. We fill up space as if it were a pie shell, with things whose opacity further obstructs our ability to see what is already there.

AFTERWORD

Bad writers are niggardly, using in a given essay only what they think they need — *holding back, refusing to loosen largess of detail or feeling. On the other hand, the best writers are spendthrift, throwing into the moment's essay (poem, story) everything they know* — *heaping up details, overwhelming us with their riches and convictions. The saver loses and the spender gains: Only when the well is emptied may it fill again; the careful conserver waters no meadow but dries the desert.*

Gretel Ehrlich has written many essays about these open spaces; she never holds back and she always has more to tell us. This essay is urgent, written almost entirely in the present tense. (Departures into varieties of past tense explain themselves; nothing is accidental in good prose.) We feel the writer's happy urge to share the gold, to convince us of the wonders of her place and the life lived in it. She has the knack of quick motion from one example — *or season or animal* — *to another, usually without overt transition or development. "Eagles look like small people as they eat car-killed deer by the road," she tells us, giving scene and story we might like more of. But her relentless, quick motion onward excites the reader while it carries Ehrlich's excitement: "Antelope, moving in small, graceful bands, travel at sixty miles an hour, their mouths open as if drinking in the space."*

The eagles are "like small people"; we see the look of the antelope's mouth "open as if drinking in the space." Images thrive on comparisons. Elsewhere, with more rapid motion, she glides from music to architecture: "In the Great Plains the vistas look like music, like Kyries of grass, but Wyoming seems to be the doing of a mad architect — *tumbled and twisted, ribboned with faded, deathbed colors, thrust up and pulled down as if the place had been startled out of a deep sleep and thrown into a pure light."*

BOOKS AVAILABLE IN PAPERBACK

Arctic Heart: A Poem Cycle. Santa Barbara: Capra Press.

Drinking Dry Clouds: Stories from Wyoming. Santa Barbara: Capra Press. *Short stories.*

Heart Mountain. New York: Penguin. *Novel.*

Islands, the Universe, Home. New York: Penguin. *Essays.*

The Solace of Open Spaces. New York: Penguin. *Essays.*

To Touch the Water. Boise: Ahsahta Press. *Poetry.*

IAN
FRAZIER

*I*AN FRAZIER *has only one absolute rule when it comes to writing. "I quit every day at seven o'clock, buy a quart of beer, and watch TV." He follows this discipline on Canal Street in Manhattan, where he lives these days, having started out from Lake Erie some years ago (b. Cleveland, 1951). As an undergraduate at Harvard University, he wrote for the* Lampoon, *which has cradled many American writers: Robert Benchley, Robert Sherwood, George Plimpton, John Updike.*

"Dating Your Mom" is the title essay of Frazier's first collection, which is hysterical and which places him in a grand tradition of American satirists and zanies. For the past fifty years many of these writers, like Frazier, have written for the New Yorker, *where Frazier is also on the staff. A second collection of essays, reportage rather than humor or satire, is called* Nobody Better, Better than Nobody *(1987).* Great Plains, *which is indeed an account of the American great plains, appeared in 1989.*

Dating Your Mom

In today's fast-moving, transient, rootless society, where people meet and make love and part without ever really touching, the relationship every guy already has with his own mother is too valuable to ignore. Here is a grown, experienced, loving woman — one you do not have to go to a party or a singles bar to meet, one you do not have to go to great lengths to get to know. There are hundreds of times when you and your mother are thrown together naturally, without the tension that usually accompanies court-ship — just the two of you, alone. All you need is a little presence of mind to take advantage of these situations. Say your mom is driving you down-town in the car to buy you a new pair of slacks. First, find a nice station on the car radio, one that she likes. Get into the pleasant lull of freeway driving — tires humming along the pavement, air-conditioner on max. Then turn to look at her across the front seat and say something like, "You know, you've really kept your shape, Mom, and don't think I haven't no-ticed." Or suppose she comes into your room to bring you some clean socks. Take her by the wrist, pull her close, and say, "Mom, you're the most fascinating woman I've ever met." Probably she'll tell you to cut out the foolishness, but I can guarantee you one thing: She will never tell your dad. Possibly she would find it hard to say, "Dear, Piper just made a pass at me," or possibly she is secretly flattered, but, whatever the reason, she will keep it to herself until the day comes when she is no longer ashamed to tell the world of your love.

Dating your mother seriously might seem difficult at first, but once you try it I'll bet you'll be surprised at how easy it is. Facing up to your intention is the main thing: You have to want it bad enough. One problem is that lots of people get hung up on feelings of guilt about their dad. They think, Oh, here's this kindly old guy who taught me how to hunt and whittle and dynamite fish — I can't let him go on into his twilight years alone. Well, there are two reasons you can dismiss those thoughts from your mind. First, *every* woman, I don't care who she is, prefers her son to her husband. That is a simple fact; ask any woman who has a son, and she'll admit it. And why shouldn't she prefer someone who is so much like herself, who repre-sents nine months of special concern and love and intense physical close-ness — someone whom she actually created? As more women begin to ex-press the need to have something all their own in the world, more women are going to start being honest about this preference. When you and your mom begin going together, you will simply become part of a natural and inevitable historical trend.

Second, you must remember this about your dad: You have your mother, he has his! Let him go put the moves on his own mother and stop messing with yours. If his mother is dead or too old to be much fun anymore, that's not your fault, is it? It's not your fault that he didn't realize his mom for the woman she was, before it was too late. Probably he's going to try a lot of emotional blackmail on you just because you had a good idea and he never did. Don't buy it. Comfort yourself with the thought that your dad belongs to the last generation of guys who will let their moms slip away from them like that.

Once your dad is out of the picture — once he has taken up fly-tying, joined the Single Again Club, moved to Russia, whatever — and your mom has been wooed and won, if you're anything like me you're going to start having so much fun that the good times you had with your mother when you were little will seem tame by comparison. For a while, Mom and I went along living a contented, quiet life, just happy to be with each other. But after several months we started getting into some different things, like the big motorized stroller. The thrill I felt the first time Mom steered me down the street! On the tray, in addition to my Big Jim doll and the wire with the colored wooden beads, I have my desk blotter, my typewriter, an in-out basket, and my name plate. I get a lot of work done, plus I get a great chance to people-watch. Then there's my big, adult-sized highchair, where I sit in the evening as Mom and I watch the news and discuss current events, while I paddle in my food and throw my dishes on the floor. When Mom reaches to wipe off my chin and I take her hand, and we fall to the floor in a heap — me, Mom, highchair, and all — well, those are the best times, those are the very best times.

It is true that occasionally I find myself longing for even more — for things I know I cannot have, like the feel of a firm, strong, gentle hand at the small of my back lifting me out of bed into the air, or someone who could walk me around and burp me after I've watched all the bowl games and had about nine beers. Ideally, I would like a mom about nineteen or twenty feet tall, and although I considered for a while asking my mom to start working out with weights and drinking Nutrament, I finally figured, Why put her through it? After all, she is not only my woman, she is my best friend. I have to take her as she is, and the way she is is plenty good enough for me.

5

AFTERWORD

An anonymous pamphlet, published in 1729, suggested that the best solution for overpopulation and poverty in Ireland, which would also provide healthy nutrition, was to cook and eat Irish children. Jonathan Swift's "A Modest Proposal for Preventing the Children of Poor People in Ireland from Being a Burden to Their Parents . . . " argued its thesis with a calm logic that fooled, and therefore outraged, some of its readers; others recognized that they read, in the form of satire, a passionate attack on England and its landlords who exploited the "Poor People in Ireland."

Ian Frazier at the end of his essay departs into fiction; at least, one would like to think so. Earlier this essay advances an argument, as logically as Swift, which implies notions about the condition of the male psyche in America. Frazier begins the essay with a string of clichés — "In today's fast-moving, transient, rootless society" — and makes judgment throughout by means of prose style; he parodies the language of self-help, the jargon of pop psychology.

BOOKS AVAILABLE IN PAPERBACK

Dating Your Mom. New York: Penguin. *Nonfiction.*
Great Plains. New York: Penguin. *Nonfiction.*

PAUL
FUSSELL

A FTER MANY YEARS *of teaching English at Rutgers University, Paul Fussell (b. 1924) moved to a chair in English literature at the University of Pennsylvania. Born in California, the son of a millionaire, he did his undergraduate work at Pomona College. He saw combat in World War II as an infantry officer, was wounded, and returned to do his Ph.D. at Harvard. He wrote two books on eighteenth-century literature and* Poetic Meter and Poetic Form *(1965, revised 1979). In* The Great War and Modern Memory *(1975) he investigated the British experience of World War I, especially the books in which that war found its way into literature.* The Great War and Modern Memory *won Fussell the National Book Critics Circle Award and the National Book Award in 1976. He has written many articles and book reviews for magazines, especially for* Harper's *and the* New Republic *(which published "Notes on Class" in 1980). These essays are collected in* The Boy Scout Handbook and Other Observations *(1982). Fussell edited* The Norton Book of Travel *in 1987; more recently he has published* Thank God for the Atom Bomb and Other Essays *(1988),* Wartime: Understanding and Behavior in the Second World War *(1989), and* BAD, or The Dumbing of America *(1991).*

Paul Fussell is a historian of society and the imagination whose field of investigation is largely literature. In "Notes on Class" he makes ironic commentary on the class structure of our country. Because we lack the rigid social hierarchies of some European countries, with aristocracies of ancient fortunes and inherited titles, we sometimes pretend that our society is classless. Fussell — whose book on the subject, Class: A Guide Through the American Status System, *was published in 1983 — writes about the American class system with wit and sarcasm.*

Notes on Class

If the dirty little secret used to be sex, now it is the facts about social class. No subject today is more likely to offend. Over thirty years ago Dr. Kinsey° generated considerable alarm by disclosing that despite appearance, one-quarter of the male population had enjoyed at least one homosexual orgasm. A similar alarm can be occasioned today be asserting that despite the much-discussed mechanism of "social mobility" and the constant redistribution of income in this country, it is virtually impossible to break out of the social class in which one has been nurtured. Bad news for the ambitious as well as the bogus, but there it is.

Defining class is difficult, as sociologists and anthropologists have learned. The more data we feed into the machines, the less likely it is that significant formulations will emerge. What follows here is based not on interviews, questionnaires, or any kind of quantitative technique but on perhaps a more trustworthy method — perception. Theory may inform us that there are three classes in America, high, middle, and low. Perception will tell us that there are at least nine, which I would designate and arrange like this:

> Top Out-of-Sight
> Upper
> Upper Middle
>
> —
>
> Middle
> High-Proletarian
> Mid-Proletarian
> Low-Proletarian
>
> —
>
> Destitute
> Bottom Out-of-Sight

In addition, there is a floating class with no permanent location in this hierarchy. We can call it Class X. It consists of well-to-do hippies, "artists," "writers" (who write nothing), floating bohemians, politicians out of office, disgraced athletic coaches, residers abroad, rock stars, "celebrities," and the shrewder sort of spies.

The quasi-official division of the population into three economic classes called high-, middle-, and low-income groups rather misses the point, because as a class indicator the amount of money is not as important as the

---

Dr. Kinsey Alfred Charles Kinsey (1894–1956), author of studies of the sexual life of humans based on 18,500 personal interviews. Founded the Institute for Sex Research in 1947.

source. Important distinctions at both the top and bottom of the class scale arise less from degree of affluence than from the people or institutions to whom one is beholden for support. For example, the main thing distinguishing the top three classes from each other is the amount of money inherited in relation to the amount currently earned. The Top Out-of-Sight Class (Rockefellers, du Ponts, Mellons, Fords, Whitneys) lives on inherited capital entirely. Its money is like the hats of the Boston ladies who, asked where they got them, answer, "Oh, we *have* our hats." No one whose money, no matter how ample, comes from his own work, like film stars, can be a member of the Top Out-of-Sights, even if the size of his income and the extravagance of his expenditure permit him temporary social access to it.

Since we expect extremes to meet, we are not surprised to find the very lowest class, Bottom Out-of-Sight, similar to the highest in one crucial respect: It is given its money and kept sort of afloat not by its own efforts but by the welfare machinery or the prison system. Members of the Top Out-of-Sight Class sometimes earn some money, as directors or board members of philanthropic or even profitable enterprises, but the amount earned is laughable in relation to the amount already possessed. Membership in the Top Out-of-Sight Class depends on the ability to flourish without working at all, and it is this that suggests a curious brotherhood between those at the top and the bottom of the scale.

It is this also that distinguishes the Upper Class from its betters. It lives on both inherited money and a salary from attractive, if usually slight, work, without which, even if it could survive and even flourish, it would feel bored and a little ashamed. The next class down, the Upper Middle, may possess virtually as much as the two above it. The difference is that it has earned most of it, in law, medicine, oil, real estate, or even the more honorific forms of trade. The Upper Middles are afflicted with a bourgeois sense of shame, a conviction that to live on the earnings of others, even forebears, is not entirely nice.

The Out-of-Sight Classes at top and bottom have something else in common: They are literally all but invisible (hence their name). The façades of Top Out-of-Sight houses are never seen from the street, and such residences (like Rockefeller's upstate New York premises) are often hidden away deep in the hills, safe from envy and its ultimate attendants, confiscatory taxation and finally expropriation. The Bottom Out-of-Sight Class is equally invisible. When not hidden away in institutions or claustrated in monasteries, lamaseries, or communes, it is hiding from creditors, deceived bail-bondsmen, and merchants intent on repossessing cars and furniture. (This class is visible briefly in one place, in the spring on the streets of New York City, but after this ritual yearly show of itself it disappears again.) When you pass a house with a would-be impressive façade addressing the street, you know it is occupied by a mere member of the Upper or Upper Middle Class. The White House is an example. Its residents, even on those occasions when they are Kennedys, can never be classified as Top Out-of-Sight but only Upper Class. The house is simply too conspicuous, and temporary residence there usually constitutes a come-down for most of its occupants. It is a hopelessly Upper- or Upper-Middle-Class place.

Another feature of both Top and Bottom Out-of-Sight Classes is their anxiety to keep their names out of the papers, and this too suggests that socially the president is always rather vulgar. All the classes in between Top and Bottom Out-of-Sight slaver for personal publicity (monograms on shirts, inscribing one's name on lawn-mowers and power tools, etc.), and it is this lust to be known almost as much as income that distinguishes them from their Top and Bottom neighbors. The High- and Mid-Prole Classes can be recognized immediately by their pride in advertising their physical presence, a way of saying, "Look! We pay our bills and have a known place in the community, and you can find us there any time." Thus hypertrophied house-numbers on the front, or house numbers written "Two Hundred Five" ("Two Hundred and Five" is worse) instead of 205, or flamboyant house or family names blazoned on façades, like "The Willows" or "The Polnickis."

(If you go behind the façade into the house itself, you will find a fairly trustworthy class indicator in the kind of wood visible there. The top three classes invariably go in for hardwoods for doors and paneling; the Middle and High-Prole Classes, pine, either plain or "knotty." The knotty-pine "den" is an absolute stigma of the Middle Class, one never to be overcome or disguised by temporarily affected higher usages. Below knotty pine there is plywood.)

Façade study is a badly neglected anthropological field. As we work down from the (largely white-painted) banklike façades of the Upper and Upper Middle Classes, we encounter such Middle and Prole conventions as these, which I rank in order of social status:

Middle

1. A potted tree on either side of the front door, and the more pointy and symmetrical the better.
2. A large rectangular picture-window in a split-level "ranch" house, displaying a table-lamp between two side curtains. The cellophane on the lampshade must be visibly inviolate.
3. Two chairs usually metal with pipe arms, disposed on the front porch as a "conversation group," in stubborn defiance of the traffic thundering past.

High-Prole

4. Religious shrines in the garden, which if small and understated, are slightly higher class than

Mid-Prole

5. Plaster gnomes and flamingos, and blue or lavender shiny spheres supported by fluted cast-concrete pedestals.

Low-Prole

6. Defunct truck tires painted white and enclosing flower beds. (Auto tires are a grade higher.)
7. Flower-bed designs worked in dead light bulbs or the butts of disused beer bottles.

The Desitute have no façades to decorate, and of course the Bottom Out-of-Sights, being invisible, have none either, although both these classes can occasionally help others decorate theirs — painting tires white on an hourly basis, for example, or even watering and fertilizing the potted trees of the Middle Class. Class X also does not decorate its façades, hoping to stay loose and unidentifiable, ready to relocate and shape-change the moment it sees that its cover has been penetrated.

In this list of façade conventions an important principle emerges. Organic [10] materials have higher status than metal or plastic. We should take warning from Sophie Portnoy's° aluminum venetian blinds, which are also lower than wood because the slats are curved, as if "improved," instead of classically flat. The same principle applies, as *The Preppy Handbook* has shown so effectively, to clothing fabrics, which must be cotton or wool, never Dacron or anything of that prole kind. In the same way, yachts with wood hulls, because they must be repaired or replaced (at high cost) more often, are classier than yachts with fiberglass hulls, no matter how shrewdly merchandised. Plastic hulls are cheaper and more practical, which is precisely why they lack class.

As we move down the scale, income of course decreases, but income is less important to class than other seldom-invoked measurements: for example, the degree to which one's work is supervised by an omnipresent immediate superior. The more free from supervision, the higher the class, which is why a dentist ranks higher than a mechanic working under a foreman in a large auto shop, even if he makes considerably more money than the dentist. The two trades may be thought equally dirty: It is the dentist's freedom from supervision that helps confer class upon him. Likewise, a high-school teacher obliged to file weekly "lesson plans" with a principal or "curriculum coordinator" thereby occupies a class position lower than a tenured professor, who reports to no one, even though the high-school teacher may be richer, smarter, and nicer. (Supervisors and Inspectors are titles that go with public schools, post offices, and police departments: The student of class will need to know no more.) It is largely because they must report that even the highest members of the naval and military services lack social status: They all have designated supervisors — even the chairman of the Joint Chiefs of Staff has to report to the president.

Class is thus defined less by bare income than by constraints and insecurities. It is defined also by habits and attitudes. Take television watching.

Sophie Portnoy   A character in Philip Roth's novel *Portnoy's Complaint* (1969).

The Top Out-of-Sight Class doesn't watch at all. It owns the companies and pays others to monitor the thing. It is also entirely devoid of intellectual or even emotional curiosity: It *has* its ideas the way it has its money. The Upper Class does look at television but it prefers camp offerings, like the films of Jean Harlow or Jon Hall. The Upper Middle Class regards TV as vulgar except for the highminded emissions of National Educational Television, which it watches avidly, especially when, like the Shakespeare series, they are the most incompetently directed and boring. Upper Middles make a point of forbidding children to watch more than an hour a day and worry a lot about violence in society and sugar in cereal. The Middle Class watches, preferring the more "beautiful" kinds of non-body-contact sports like tennis or gymnastics or figure-skating (the music is a redeeming feature here). With High-, Mid-, and Low-Proles we find heavy viewing of the soaps in the daytime and rugged body-contact sports (football, hockey, boxing) in the evening. The lower one is located in the Prole classes the more likely one is to watch "Bowling for Dollars" and "Wonder Woman" and "The Hulk" and when choosing a game show to prefer "Joker's Wild" to "The Family Feud," whose jokes are sometimes incomprehensible. Destitutes and Bottom Out-of-Sights have in common a problem involving choice. Destitutes usually "own" about three color sets, and the problem is which three programs to run at once. Bottom Out-of-Sights exercise no choice at all, the decisions being made for them by correctional or institutional personnel.

The time when the evening meal is consumed defines class better than, say, the presence or absence on the table of ketchup bottles and ashtrays shaped like little toilets enjoining the diners to "Put Your Butts Here." Destitutes and Bottom Out-of-Sights eat dinner at 5:30, for the Prole staff on which they depend must clean up and be out roller-skating or bowling early in the evening. Thus Proles eat at 6:00 or 6:30. The Middles eat at 7:00, the Upper Middles at 7:30 or, if very ambitious, at 8:00. The Upper and Top Out-of-Sights dine at 8:30 or 9:00 or even later, after nightly protracted "cocktail" sessions lasting usually around two hours. Sometimes they forget to eat at all.

Similarly, the physical appearance of the various classes defines them fairly accurately. Among the top four classes thin is good, and the bottom two classes appear to ape this usage, although down there thin is seldom a matter of choice. It is the three Prole classes that tend to fat, partly as a result of their use of convenience foods and plenty of beer. These are the classes too where anxiety about slipping down a rung causes nervous overeating, resulting in fat that can be rationalized as advertising the security of steady wages and the ability to "eat out" often. Even "Going Out for Breakfast" is not unthinkable for Proles, if we are to believe that they respond to the McDonald's TV ads as they're supposed to. A recent magazine ad for a diet book aimed at Proles stigmatizes a number of erroneous assumptions about body weight, proclaiming with some inelegance that "They're all a crock." Among such vulgar errors is the proposition that "All Social Classes Are Equally Overweight." This the ad rejects by noting quite accurately:

Your weight is an advertisement of your social standing. A
century ago, corpulence was a sign of success. But no more.
Today it is the badge of the lower-middle-class, where obesity
is *four times* more prevalent than it is among the upper-middle
and middle classes.

It is not just four times more prevalent. It is at least four times more visible, as
any observer can testify who has witnessed Prole women perambulating shopping malls in their bright, very tight jersey trousers. Not just obesity but the
flaunting of obesity is the Prole sign, as if the object were to give maximum
aesthetic offense to the higher classes and thus achieve a form of revenge.

Another physical feature with powerful class meaning is the wearing of 15
plaster casts on legs and ankles by members of the top three classes. These
casts, a sort of white badge of honor, betoken stylish mishaps with frivolous
but costly toys like horses, skis, snowmobiles, and mopeds. They signify a
high level of conspicuous waste in a social world where questions of un-
payable medical bills or missed working days do not apply. But in the matter
of clothes, the Top Out-of-Sight is different from both Upper and Upper
Middle Classes. It prefers to appear in new clothes, whereas the class just
below it prefers old clothes. Likewise, all three Prole classes make much of
new garments, with the highest possible polyester content. The question
does not arise in the same form with Destitutes and Bottom Out-of-Sights.
They wear used clothes, the thrift shop and prison supply room serving as
their Bonwit's and Korvette's.

This American class system is very hard for foreigners to master, partly
because most foreigners imagine that since America was founded by the
British it must retain something of British institutions. But our class system
is more subtle than the British, more a matter of gradations than of blunt
divisions, like the binary distinction between a gentleman and a cad. This
seems to lack plausibility here. One seldom encounters in the United States
the sort of absolute prohibitions which (half-comically, to be sure) one is
asked to believe define the gentleman in England. Like these:

> A gentleman never wears brown shoes in the city, or
> A gentleman never wears a green suit, or
> A gentleman never has soup at lunch, or
> A gentleman never uses a comb, or
> A gentleman never smells of anything but tar, or
> "No gentleman can fail to admire Bellini"
>   — W. H. AUDEN

In America it seems to matter much less the way you present yourself —
green, brown, neat, sloppy, scented — than what your backing is — that is,
where your money comes from. What the upper orders display here is no
special uniform but the kind of psychological security they derive from
knowing that others recognize their freedom from petty anxieties and trivial
prohibitions.

"Language most shows a man," Ben Jonson used to say. "Speak, that I may see thee." As all acute conservatives like Jonson know, dictional behavior is a powerful signal of a firm class line. Nancy Mitford so indicated in her hilarious essay of 1955, "The English Aristocracy," based in part on Professor Alan S. C. Ross's more sober study "Linguistic Class-Indicators in Present-Day English." Both Mitford and Ross were interested in only one class demarcation, the one dividing the English Upper Class ("U," in their shorthand) from all below it ("non-U"). Their main finding was that euphemism and genteelism are vulgar. People who are socially secure risk nothing by calling a spade a spade, and indicate their top-dog status by doing so as frequently as possible. Thus the U-word is *rich,* the non-U *wealthy.* What U-speakers call *false teeth* non-U's call *dentures.* The same with *wigs* and *hairpieces, dying* and *passing away* (or *over*).

For Mitford, linguistic assaults from below are sometimes so shocking that the only kind reaction of a U-person is silence. It is "the only possible U-response," she notes, "to many embarrassing modern situations: the ejaculation of 'cheers' before drinking, for example, or 'It was so nice seeing you' after saying good-bye. In silence, too, one must endure the use of the Christian name by comparative strangers. . . . " In America, although there are more classes distinguishable here, a linguistic polarity is as visible as in England. Here U-speech (or our equivalent of it) characterizes some Top Out-of-Sights, Uppers, Upper Middles, and Class X's. All below is a waste land of genteelism and jargon and pretentious mispronunciation, pathetic evidence of upward social scramble and its hazards. Down below, the ear is bad and no one has been trained to listen. Culture words especially are the downfall of the aspiring. Sometimes it is diphthongs that invite disgrace, as in *be-yóu-ti-ful.* Sometimes the aspirant rushes full-face into disaster by flourishing those secret class indicators, the words *exquisite* and *despicable,* which, like another secret sign, *patina,* he (and of course she as often) stresses on the middle syllable instead of the first. High-class names from cultural history are a frequent cause of betrayal, especially if they are British, like Henry Purcell. In America non-U speakers are fond of usages like "Between he and I." Recalling vaguely that mentioning oneself last, as in "He and I were there," is thought gentlemanly, they apply that principle uniformly, to the entire destruction of the objective case. There's also a problem with *like.* They remember something about the dangers of illiteracy its use invites, and hope to stay out of trouble by always using *as* instead, finally saying things like "He looks as his father." These contortions are common among young (usually insurance or computer) trainees, raised on Leon Uris° and *Playboy,* most of them Mid- or High-Proles pounding on the firmly shut doors of the Middle Class. They are the careful, dark-suited first-generation aspirants to American respectability and (hopefully, as they would put it) power. Together with their deployment of the anomalous nominative case on all occasions goes their preference for jargon (you can hear them going at it on

---

Leon Uris   Popular American novelist, author of *Exodus* (1958) and *Trinity* (1976).

airplanes) like *parameters* and *guidelines* and *bottom lines* and *funding, dialogue, interface,* and *lifestyles.* Their world of language is one containing little more than smokescreens and knowing innovations. "Do we gift the Johnsons, dear?" the corporate wife will ask the corporate husband at Christmas time.

Just below these people, down among the Mid- and Low-Proles, the complex sentence gives trouble. It is here that we get sentences beginning with elaborate pseudogenteel participles like "Being that it was a cold day, the furnace was on." All classes below those peopled by U-speakers find the gerund out of reach and are thus forced to multiply words and say, "The people in front of him at the theater got mad due to the fact that he talked so much" instead of "His talking at the theater annoyed the people in front." (But *people* is not really right: *individuals* is the preferred term with non-U speakers. Grander, somehow.) It is also in the domain of the Mid- and Low-Prole that the double negative comes into its own as well as the superstitious avoidance of *lying* because it may be taken to imply telling untruths. People are thus depicted as always *laying* on the beach, the bed, the grass, the sidewalk, and without the slightest suggestion of their performing sexual exhibitions. A similar unconscious inhibition determines that *set* replace *sit* on all occasions, lest low excremental implications be inferred. The ease with which *sit* can be interchanged with the impolite word is suggested in a Second World War anecdote told by General Matthew Ridgway. Coming upon an unidentifiable head and shoulders peeping out of a ditch near the German border, he shouted, "Put up your hands, you son of a bitch!" to be answered, so he reports, "Aaah, go sit in your hat."

All this is evidence of a sad fact. A deep class gulf opens between two 20 current generations: the older one that had some Latin at school or college and was taught rigorous skeptical "English," complete with the diagramming of sentences; and the younger one taught to read by the optimistic look-say method and encouraged to express itself — as the saying goes — so that its sincerity and well of ideas suffer no violation. This new generation is unable to perceive the number of syllables in a word and cannot spell and is baffled by all questions of etymology (it thinks *chauvinism* has something to do with gender aggressions). It cannot write either, for it has never been subjected to tuition in the sort of English sentence structure which resembles the sonata in being not natural but artificial, not innate but mastered. Because of its misspent, victimized youth, this generation is already destined to fill permanently the middle-to-low slots in the corporate society without ever quite understanding what devilish mechanism has prevented it from ascending. The disappearance of Latin as an adjunct to the mastery of English can be measured by the rapid replacement of words like *continuing* by solecisms like *ongoing.* A serious moment in cultural history occurred a few years ago when gasoline trucks changed the warning word on the rear from *Inflammable* to *Flammable.* Public education had apparently produced a population which no longer knew *In-* as an intensifier. That this happened at about the moment when every city was rapidly running up a "Cultural Center" might make us laugh, if we don't cry first. In another few generations Latinate words will be found only in learned writing, and the spoken language will have returned to the state it was in before the revival of learning. Words like *intellect* and *curiosity* and *devotion* and *study* will have withered away together with the things they denote.

There's another linguistic class-line, dividing those who persist in honoring the nineteenth-century convention that advertising, if not commerce itself, is reprehensible and not at all to be cooperated with, and those proud to think of themselves not as skeptics but as happy consumers, fulfilled when they can image themselves as functioning members of a system by responding to advertisements. For U-persons a word's succeeding in an ad is a compelling reason never to use it. But possessing no other source of idiom and no extra-local means of criticizing it, the subordinate classes are pleased to appropriate the language of advertising for personal use, dropping brand names all the time and saying things like "They have some lovely fashions in that store." In the same way they embrace all subprofessional euphemisms gladly and employ them proudly, adverting without irony to hair stylists, sanitary engineers, and funeral directors in complicity with the consumer world which cynically casts them as its main victims. They see nothing funny in paying a high price for an article and then, after a solemn pause, receiving part of it back in the form of a "rebate." Trapped in a world wholly defined by the language of consumption and the hype, they harbor restively, defending themselves against actuality by calling habitual drunkards *people with alcohol problems,* madness *mental illness,* drug use *drug abuse,* building lots *homesites,* houses *homes* ("They live in a lovely $250,000 home"), and drinks *beverages.*

Those delighted to employ the vacuous commercial "Have a nice day" and those who wouldn't think of saying it belong manifestly to different classes, no matter how we define them, and it is unthinkable that those classes will ever melt. Calvin Coolidge said that the business of America is business. Now apparently the business of America is having a nice day. Tragedy? Don't need it. Irony? Take it away. Have a nice day. Have a nice day. A visiting Englishman of my acquaintance, a U-speaker if there ever was one, has devised the perfect U-response to "Have a nice day": "Thank you," he says, "but I have other plans." The same ultimate divide separates the two classes who say respectively when introduced, "How do you do?" and "Pleased to meet you." There may be comity between those who think *prestigious* a classy word and those who don't, but it won't survive much strain, like relations between those who think *momentarily* means in a moment (airline captain over loudspeaker: "We'll be taking off momentarily, folks") and those who know it means for a moment. Members of these two classes can sit in adjoining seats on the plane and get along fine (although there's a further division between those who talk to their neighbors in planes and elevators and those who don't), but once the plane has emptied, they will proceed toward different destinations. It's the same with those who conceive that *type* is an adjective ("He's a very classy type person") and those who know it's only a noun or verb.

The pretense that either person can feel at ease in the presence of the other is an essential element of the presiding American fiction. Despite the lowness of the metaphor, the idea of the melting pot is high-minded and noble enough, but empirically it will be found increasingly unconvincing. It is our different language habits as much as anything that makes us, as the title of Richard Polenberg's book puts it, *One Nation Divisible*.

Some people invite constant class trouble because they believe the official American publicity about these matters. The official theory, which experience is constantly disproving, is that one can earn one's way out of his original class. Richard Nixon's behavior indicated dramatically that this is not so. The sign of the Upper Class to which he aspired is total psychological security, expressed in loose carriage, saying what one likes, and imperviousness to what others think. Nixon's vast income from law and politics — his San Clemente property aped the style of the Upper but not the Top Out-of-Sight Class, for everyone knew where it was, and he wanted them to know — could not alleviate his original awkwardness and meanness of soul or his nervousness about the impression he was making, an affliction allied to his instinct for cunning and duplicity. Hammacher Schlemmer might have had him specifically in mind as the consumer of their recently advertised "Champagne Recork": "This unusual stopper keeps 'bubbly' sprightly, sparkling after uncorking ceremony is over. Gold electro-plated." I suspect that it is some of these same characteristics that made Edward Kennedy often seem so inauthentic a member of the Upper Class. (He's not Top Out-of-Sight because he chooses to augment his inheritance by attractive work.)

What, then, marks the higher classes? Primarily a desire for privacy, if 25 not invisibility, and a powerful if eccentric desire for freedom. It is this instinct for freedom that may persuade us that inquiring into the American class system this way is an enterprise not entirely facetious. Perhaps after all the whole thing has something, just something, to do with ethics and aesthetics. Perhaps a term like *gentleman* still retains some meanings which are not just sartorial and mannerly. Freedom and grace and independence: It would be nice to believe those words still mean something, and it would be interesting if the reality of the class system — and everyone, after all, hopes to rise — should turn out to be a way we pay those notions a due if unwitting respect.

AFTERWORD

Fussell amuses himself and his readers by hanging this essay on the hook of social class. Although he starts by referring to "the facts about social class," he writes without making use of facts. When he mentions Rockefellers and du Ponts, he could as well speak of Morgans and Vanderbilts; his proper names are exemplary and illustrative. If we hear about welfare on the one hand and unmentionably huge incomes on the other, we hear nothing of numbers or dollar amounts.

Maybe Fussell isn't writing about class at all, but the suggestion of class allows him a structure. Any device that categorizes, even something as foolish as the horoscope, allows us a tentative framework to think with; if we then gather useful insights, we can always deconstruct the framework.

This light essay is about manners or about style; it is not about inherited wealth or power, about accents or clubs — instruments of exclusion that perpetuate families connected by marriage into a system.

For Fussell class *is behavior, permissible or derisory. This essay sounds like a feature in a fashion magazine, playing the perpetual game of who's in, who's out. To be sure, there's a difference between people who studied Latin at school and people who didn't, a generation later. But if, say, these generations both attended Choate and Yale, it is questionable to say that the difference between them is class.*

BOOKS AVAILABLE IN PAPERBACK

Abroad: British Literary Traveling Between the Wars. New York: Oxford University Press. *Nonfiction.*

BAD, or the Dumbing of America. New York: Touchstone Books. *Nonfiction.*

Class: A Guide Through the American Status System. New York: Simon & Schuster. *Nonfiction.*

Poetic Meter and Poetic Form. New York: Random House.

The Rhetorical World of Augustan Humanism: Ethics and Imagery from Swift to Burke. Ann Arbor: University of Michigan Press. *Nonfiction.*

Samuel Johnson and the Life of Writing. New York: Norton. *Nonfiction.*

Thank God for the Atom Bomb and Other Essays. New York: Ballantine.

Wartime: Understanding and Behavior in the Second World War. New York: Oxford University Press. *Nonfiction.*

STEPHEN
JAY GOULD

STEPHEN JAY GOULD *(b. 1941), whose essays delight and instruct the non-scientist in the byways of natural history, dedicated* Ever Since Darwin *(1977) to his father, "who took me to see the tyrannosaurus when I was five." Maybe the child's visit to a museum formed the whole life.*

Gould is a paleontologist who teaches geology, biology, and history of science at Harvard University. After graduating from Antioch College in 1963, he took his Ph.D. at Columbia University. He is an evolutionist. He writes that his essays "range broadly from planetary and geological to social and political history, but they are united . . . by the common thread of evolutionary theory — Darwin's version." Author of a long book called Ontogeny and Phylogeny *(1977) and of* The Mismeasure of Man *(1981), which attacks methods of quantifying intelligence, he has collected volumes of brief scientific essays, mostly from his column, "This View of Life," in* Natural History *magazine.* Ever Since Darwin *was the first collection, and he followed it with* The Panda's Thumb *(1980),* Hen's Teeth and Horse's Toes *(1983), and* The Flamingo's Smile *(1985), from which we take the essay printed here. In 1987 he collected his book reviews and miscellaneous writing in* An Urchin in the Storm: Essays About Books and Ideas. *More recently he has published* Time's Arrow, Time's Cycle *(1987);* Wonderful Life *(1989);* Bully for Brontosaurus *(1991); and* Eight Little Piggies *(1993). Among other honors, he has won a National Book Award and become a MacArthur Prize fellow.*

Writing in the New York Times Book Review *about three great scientific essayists (T. H. Huxley, J. B. S. Haldane, and P. B. Medawar), Gould listed the qualities he admired in terms that we can apply to Gould himself: "All write about the simplest things and draw from them a universe of implications. . . . All maintain an unflinching commitment to rationality amid the soft attractions of an uncritical*

Photo by Eleanor Gould

187

mysticism. . . . All demonstrate a deep commitment to the demystification of science by cutting through jargon; they show by example rather than exhortation that the most complex concepts can be rendered intelligible to everyone."

Early in the 1980s Gould was diagnosed to suffer from mesothelioma, a form of cancer which usually — as he quickly discovered by research — terminates its victim in about eight months. Gould's case was discovered early and proved amenable to treatment. "I simply had to see my children grow up," he said, "and it would be perverse to come this close to the millennium and then blow it." During months of grave illness, weight loss, and debilitating chemotherapy, Gould continued teaching and writing. He appears completely recovered.

In one of Gould's essays he writes, "I have never been able to raise much personal enthusiasm for disembodied theory. Thus, when I wish to explore the explanatory power of evolutionary theory, . . . I write about apparent oddities resolved by Darwin's view — dwarf male anglerfishes parasitically united with females, wasps that paralyze insects to provide a living feast for their larvae, young birds that kill their siblings by simply pushing them outside a ring of guano." Although Gould may choose these "oddities" for their explanatory function, the reader glimpses in his writing, alongside the enthusiastic explainer, a five-year-old who looks with joy and wonder at the immense skeleton of a dinosaur.

Sex, Drugs, Disasters, and the Extinction of Dinosaurs

Science, in its most fundamental definition, is a fruitful mode of inquiry, not a list of enticing conclusions. The conclusions are the consequence, not the essence.

My greatest unhappiness with most popular presentations of science concerns their failure to separate fascinating claims from the methods that scientists use to establish the facts of nature. Journalists, and the public, thrive on controversial and stunning statements. But science is, basically, a way of knowing — in P. B. Medawar's apt words, "the art of the soluble." If the growing corps of popular science writers would focus on *how* scientists develop and defend those fascinating claims, they would make their greatest possible contribution to public understanding.

Consider three ideas, proposed in perfect seriousness to explain that greatest of all titillating puzzles — the extinction of dinosaurs. Since these three notions invoke the primally fascinating themes of our culture — sex, drugs, and violence — they surely reside in the category of fascinating claims. I want to show why two of them rank as silly speculation, while the other represents science at its grandest and most useful.

Science works with testable proposals. If, after much compilation and scrutiny of data, new information continues to affirm a hypothesis, we may accept it provisionally and gain confidence as further evidence mounts. We can never be completely sure that a hypothesis is right, though we may be able to show with confidence that it is wrong. The best scientific hypotheses are also generous and expansive: They suggest extensions and implications that enlighten related, and even far distant, subjects. Simply consider how the idea of evolution has influenced virtually every intellectual field.

Useless speculation, on the other hand, is restrictive. It generates no   5
testable hypothesis, and offers no way to obtain potentially refuting evidence. Please note that I am not speaking of truth or falsity. The speculation may well be true; still, if it provides, in principle, no material for affirmation or rejection, we can make nothing of it. It must simply stand forever as an intriguing idea. Useless speculation turns in on itself and leads nowhere; good science, containing both seeds for its potential refutation and implications for more and different testable knowledge, reaches out. But, enough preaching. Let's move on to dinosaurs, and the three proposals for their extinction.

1. Sex: Testes function only in a narrow range of temperature (those of mammals hang externally in a scrotal sac because internal body temperatures are too high for their proper function). A worldwide rise in temperature at the close of the Cretaceous period caused the testes of dinosaurs to stop functioning and led to their extinction by sterilization of males.
2. Drugs: Angiosperms (flowering plants) first evolved toward the end of the dinosaurs' reign. Many of these plants contain psychoactive agents, avoided by mammals today as a result of their bitter taste. Dinosaurs had neither means to taste the bitterness nor livers effective enough to detoxify the substances. They died of massive overdoses.
3. Disasters: A large comet or asteroid struck the earth some 65 million years ago, lofting a cloud of dust into the sky and blocking sunlight, thereby suppressing photosynthesis and so drastically lowering world temperatures that dinosaurs and hosts of other creatures became extinct.

Before analyzing these three tantalizing statements, we must establish a basic ground rule often violated in proposals for the dinosaurs' demise. *There is no separate problem of the extinction of dinosaurs.* Too often we divorce specific events from their wider contexts and systems of cause and effect. The fundamental fact of dinosaur extinction is its synchrony with the demise of so many other groups across a wide range of habitats, from terrestrial to marine.

The history of life has been punctuated by brief episodes of mass extinction. A recent analysis by University of Chicago paleontologists Jack Sepkoski and Dave Raup, based on the best and most exhaustive tabulation of data ever assembled, shows clearly that five episodes of mass dying stand well above the "background" extinctions of normal times (when we consider all mass extinctions, large and small, they seem to fall in a regular 26-million-year cycle). The Cretaceous debacle, occurring 65 million years ago and separating the Mesozoic and Cenozoic eras of our geological time scale, ranks prominently among the five. Nearly all the marine plankton (single-celled floating creatures) died with geological suddenness; among marine invertebrates, nearly 15 percent of all families perished, including many previously dominant groups, especially the ammonites (relatives of squids in coiled shells). On land, the dinosaurs disappeared after more than 100 million years of unchallenged domination.

In this context, speculations limited to dinosaurs alone ignore the larger phenomenon. We need a coordinated explanation for a system of events that includes the extinction of dinosaurs as one component. Thus it makes little sense, though it may fuel our desire to view mammals as inevitable inheritors of the earth, to guess that dinosaurs died because small mammals ate their eggs (a perennial favorite among untestable speculations). It seems most unlikely that some disaster peculiar to dinosaurs befell these massive beasts — and that the debacle happened to strike just when one of history's five great dyings had enveloped the earth for completely different reasons.

The testicular theory, an old favorite from the 1940s, had its root in an interesting and thoroughly respectable study of temperature tolerances in the American alligator, published in the staid *Bulletin of the American Museum of Natural History* in 1946 by three experts on living and fossil reptiles — E. H. Colbert, my own first teacher in paleontology; R. B. Cowles; and C. M. Bogert.

The first sentence of their summary reveals a purpose beyond alligators: 10 "This report describes an attempt to infer the reactions of extinct reptiles, especially the dinosaurs, to high temperatures as based upon reactions observed in the modern alligator." They studied, by rectal thermometry, the body temperatures of alligators under changing conditions of heating and cooling. (Well, let's face it, you wouldn't want to try sticking a thermometer under a 'gator's tongue.) The predictions under test go way back to an old theory first stated by Galileo in the 1630s — the unequal scaling of surfaces and volumes. As an animal, or any object, grows (provided its shape doesn't change), surface areas must increase more slowly than volumes — since surfaces get larger as length squared, while volumes increase much more rapidly, as length cubed. Therefore, small animals have high ratios of surface to volume, while large animals cover themselves with relatively little surface.

Among cold-blooded animals lacking any physiological mechanism for keeping their temperatures constant, small creatures have a hell of a time keeping warm — because they lose so much heat through their relatively large surfaces. On the other hand, large animals, with their relatively small surfaces, may lose heat so slowly that, once warm, they may maintain effectively constant temperatures against ordinary fluctuations of climate. (In fact, the resolution of the "hot-blooded dinosaur" controversy that burned so brightly a few years back may simply be that, while large dinosaurs possessed no physiological mechanism for constant temperature, and were not therefore warm-blooded in the technical sense, their large size and relatively small surface area kept them warm.)

Colbert, Cowles, and Bogert compared the warming rates of small and large alligators. As predicted, the small fellows heated up (and cooled down) more quickly. When exposed to a warm sun, a tiny fifty-gram (1.76-ounce) alligator heated up one degree Celsius every minute and a half, while a large alligator, 260 times bigger at thirteen thousand grams (28.7 pounds), took seven and a half minutes to gain a degree. Extrapolating up to an adult ten-ton dinosaur, they concluded that a one-degree rise in body temperature would take eighty-six hours. If large animals absorb heat so slowly (through their relatively small surfaces), they will also be unable to shed any excess heat gained when temperatures rise above a favorable level.

The authors then guessed that large dinosaurs lived at or near their optimum temperatures; Cowles suggested that a rise in global temperatures just before the Cretaceous extinction caused the dinosaurs to heat up beyond their optimal tolerance — and, being so large, they couldn't shed the unwanted heat. (In a most unusual statement within a scientific paper, Colbert and Bogert then explicitly disavowed this speculative extension of their empirical work on alligators.) Cowles conceded that this excess heat probably wasn't enough to kill or even to enervate the great beasts, but since testes often function only within a narrow range of temperature, he proposed that this global rise might have sterilized all the males, causing extinction by natural contraception.

The overdose theory has recently been supported by UCLA psychiatrist Ronald K. Siegel. Siegel has gathered, he claims, more than two thousand records of animals who, when given access, administer various drugs to themselves — from a mere swig of alcohol to massive doses of the big H. Elephants will swill the equivalent of twenty beers at a time, but do not like alcohol in concentrations greater than 7 percent. In a silly bit of anthropocentric speculation, Siegel states that "elephants drink, perhaps, to forget . . . the anxiety produced by shrinking rangeland and the competition for food."

Since fertile imaginations can apply almost any hot idea to the extinction of dinosaurs, Siegel found a way. Flowering plants did not evolve until late in the dinosaurs' reign. These plants also produced an array of aromatic, amino-acid-based alkaloids — the major group of psychoactive agents. Most mammals are "smart" enough to avoid these potential poisons. The alkaloids simply don't taste good (they are bitter); in any case, we mammals have livers happily supplied with the capacity to detoxify them. But, Siegel speculates, perhaps dinosaurs could neither taste the bitterness nor detoxify the substances once ingested. He recently told members of the American Psychological Association: "I'm not suggesting that all dinosaurs OD'd on plant drugs, but it certainly was a factor." He also argued that death by overdose may help explain why so many dinosaur fossils are found in contorted positions. (Do not go gentle into that good night.)

Extraterrestrial catastrophes have long pedigrees in the popular literature of extinction, but the subject exploded again in 1979, after a long lull, when the father-son, physicist-geologist team of Luis and Walter Alvarez proposed that an asteroid, some 10 kilometers in diameter, struck the earth sixty-five million years ago (comets, rather than asteroids, have since gained favor. Good science is self-corrective).

The force of such a collision would be immense, greater by far than the megatonnage of all the world's nuclear weapons. In trying to reconstruct a scenario that would explain the simultaneous dying of dinosaurs on land and so many creatures in the sea, the Alvarezes proposed that a gigantic dust cloud, generated by particles blown aloft in the impact, would so darken the earth that photosynthesis would cease and temperatures drop precipitously. (Rage, rage against the dying of the light.) The single-celled photosynthetic oceanic plankton, with life cycles measured in weeks, would perish outright, but land plants might survive through the dormancy of their seeds (land plants were not much affected by the Cretaceous extinction, and any adequate theory must account for the curious pattern of differential survival). Dinosaurs would die by starvation and freezing; small, warm-blooded mammals, with more modest requirements for food and better regulation of body temperature, would squeak through. "Let the bastards freeze in the dark," as bumper stickers of our chauvinistic neighbors in sunbelt states proclaimed several years ago during the Northeast's winter oil crisis.

All three theories, testicular malfunction, psychoactive overdosing, and asteroidal zapping, grab our attention mightily. As pure phenomenology, they rank about equally high on any hit parade of primal fascination. Yet one represents expansive science, the others restrictive and untestable speculation. The proper criterion lies in evidence and methodology; we must probe behind the superficial fascination of particular claims.

How could we possibly decide whether the hypothesis of testicular frying is right or wrong? We would have to know things that the fossil record cannot provide. What temperatures were optimal for dinosaurs? Could they avoid the absorption of excess heat by staying in the shade, or in caves? At what temperatures did their testicles cease to function? Were late Cretaceous climates ever warm enough to drive the internal temperatures of dinosaurs close to this ceiling? Testicles simply don't fossilize, and how could we infer their temperature tolerances even if they did? In short, Cowles's hypothesis is only an intriguing speculation leading nowhere. The most damning statement against it appeared right in the conclusion of Colbert, Cowles, and Bogert's paper, when they admitted: "It is difficult to advance any definite arguments against this hypothesis." My statement may seem paradoxical — isn't a hypothesis really good if you can't devise any arguments against it? Quite the contrary. It is simply untestable and unusable.

Siegel's overdosing has even less going for it. At least Cowles extrapolated his conclusion from some good data on alligators. And he didn't completely violate the primary guideline of siting dinosaur extinction in the context of a general mass dying — for rise in temperature could be the root cause of a general catastrophe, zapping dinosaurs by testicular malfunction and different groups for other reasons. But Siegel's speculation cannot touch the extinction of ammonites or oceanic plankton (diatoms make their own food with good sweet sunlight; they don't OD on the chemicals of terrestrial plants). It is simply a gratuitous, attention-grabbing guess. It cannot be tested, for how can we know what dinosaurs tasted and what their livers could do? Livers don't fossilize any better than testicles.

The hypothesis doesn't even make any sense in its own context. Angiosperms were in full flower ten million years before dinosaurs went the way of all flesh. Why did it take so long? As for the pains of a chemical death recorded in contortions of fossils, I regret to say (or rather I'm pleased to note for the dinosaurs' sake) that Siegel's knowledge of geology must be a bit deficient: Muscles contract after death and geological strata rise and fall with motions of the earth's crust after burial — more than enough reason to distort a fossil's pristine appearance.

The impact story, on the other hand, has a sound basis in evidence. It can be tested, extended, refined, and, if wrong, disproved. The Alvarezes did not just construct an arresting guess for public consumption. They proposed their hypothesis after laborious geochemical studies with Frank Asaro and Helen Michael had revealed a massive increase of iridium in rocks deposited right at the time of extinction. Iridium, a rare metal of the platinum group, is virtually absent from indigenous rocks of the earth's crust; most of our iridium arrives on extraterrestrial objects that strike the earth.

The Alvarez hypothesis bore immediate fruit. Based originally on evidence from two European localities, it led geochemists throughout the world to examine other sediments of the same age. They found abnormally high amounts of iridium everywhere — from continental rocks of the western United States to deep sea cores from the South Atlantic.

Cowles proposed his testicular hypothesis in the mid-1940s. Where has it gone since then? Absolutely nowhere, because scientists can do nothing with it. The hypothesis must stand as a curious appendage to a solid study of alligators. Siegel's overdose scenario will also win a few press notices and fade into oblivion. The Alvarezes' asteroid falls into a different category altogether, and much of the popular commentary has missed this essential distinction by focusing on the impact and its attendant results, and forgetting what really matters to a scientist — the iridium. If you talk just about asteroids, dust, and darkness, you tell stories no better and no more entertaining than fried testicles or terminal trips. It is the iridium — the source of testable evidence — that counts and forges the crucial distinction between speculation and science.

The proof, to twist a phrase, lies in the doing. Cowles's hypothesis has generated nothing in thirty-five years. Since its proposal in 1979, the Alvarez hypothesis has spawned hundreds of studies, a major conference, and attendant publications. Geologists are fired up. They are looking for iridium at all other extinction boundaries. Every week exposes a new wrinkle in the scientific press. Further evidence that the Cretaceous iridium represents extraterrestrial impact and not indigenous volcanism continues to accumulate. As I revise this essay in November 1984 (this paragraph will be out of date when the book is published), new data include chemical "signatures" of other isotopes indicating unearthly provenance, glass spherules of a size and sort produced by impact and not by volcanic eruptions, and high-pressure varieties of silica formed (so far as we know) only under the tremendous shock of impact.

My point is simply this: Whatever the eventual outcome (I suspect it will be positive), the Alvarez hypothesis is exciting, fruitful science because it generates tests, provides us with things to do, and expands outward. We are having fun, battling back and forth, moving toward a resolution, and extending the hypothesis beyond its original scope.

As just one example of the unexpected, distant cross-fertilization that good science engenders, the Alvarez hypothesis made a major contribution to a theme that has riveted public attention in the past few months — so-called nuclear winter. In a speech delivered in April 1982, Luis Alvarez calculated the energy that a ten-kilometer asteroid would release on impact. He compared such an explosion with a full nuclear exchange and implied that all-out atomic war might unleash similar consequences.

This theme of impact leading to massive dust clouds and falling temperatures formed an important input to the decision of Carl Sagan and a group of colleagues to model the climatic consequences of nuclear holocaust. Full nuclear exchange would probably generate the same kind of dust cloud and darkening that may have wiped out the dinosaurs. Temperatures would drop precipitously and agriculture might become impossible. Avoidance of nuclear war is fundamentally an ethical and political imperative, but we must know the factual consequences to make firm judgments. I am heartened by a final link across disciplines and deep concerns — another criterion, by the way, of science at its best:[1] A recognition of the very phenomenon that made our evolution possible by exterminating the previously dominant dinosaurs and clearing a way for the evolution of large mammals, including us, might actually help to save us from joining those magnificent beasts in contorted poses among the strata of the earth.

---

[1]This quirky connection so tickles my fancy that I break my own strict rule about eliminating redundancies from [this essay]. . . . [Gould's note.]

AFTERWORD

Dinosaurs endure in the imagination. When Gould elsewhere deplores the boom in dinosaurs, he sounds like a romantic: "The problem now is there's no sense of wonder about dinosaurs. There's no mystery . . . they're on every street corner — I mean — dinosaurs are just a phase you go through, like firemen and policemen."

Happily Gould remains in his dinosaur phase. Much newspaper talk about dinosaurs concerns theories of their extinction, and Gould's theory here is one of many. I do not choose it because it proves its point, establishing at last the wording of the dinosaur's death certificate. I choose it for its spritely clear argument and its prose. Gould writes like a writer and thinks like a scientist.

Gould writes to present scientific thought: "My greatest unhappiness with most popular presentations of science concerns their failure to separate fascinating claims from the methods that scientists use to establish the facts of nature. . . . If the growing corps of popular science writers would focus on how *scientists develop and defend those fascinating claims, they would make their greatest possible contribution to public understanding."*

BOOKS AVAILABLE IN PAPERBACK

Bully for Brontosaurus: Reflections in Natural History. New York: Norton. *Essays.*

Eight Little Piggies. New York: Norton. *Essays.*

Ever Since Darwin: Reflections in Natural History. New York: Norton. *Essays.*

The Flamingo's Smile: Reflections in Natural History. New York: Norton. *Essays.*

Hen's Teeth and Horse's Toes: Further Reflections in Natural History. New York: Norton. *Essays.*

The Mismeasure of Man. New York: Norton. *Nonfiction.*

Ontogeny and Phylogeny. Cambridge: Harvard University Press. *Nonfiction.*

The Panda's Thumb: More Reflections in Natural History. New York: Norton. *Essays.*

Time's Arrow, Time's Cycle: Myth and Metaphor in the Discovery of Geological Time. Cambridge: Harvard University Press. *Nonfiction.*

An Urchin in the Storm: Essays About Books and Ideas. New York: Norton. *Essays.*

Wonderful Life: The Burgess Shale and the Nature of History. New York: Norton. *Nonfiction.*

FRANCINE
DU PLESSIX
GRAY

F RANCINE du PLESSIX GRAY (b. 1930) came to the United States from
France when she was eleven. Her late introduction to English inspired her.
"The challenge of a new language in one's adolescence! Think of Conrad — he was
eighteen or nineteen when he learned English. Learning a language beyond the
nursery years turns you into both a soldier and a lover."

Novelist, journalist, essayist, Gray attended Bryn Mawr College for two years,
then Black Mountain College in North Carolina in the early 1950s — a great
experimental school which included, among students and faculty, Robert Mother-
well, Charles Olson, Josef Albers, Merce Cunningham, Robert Rauschenberg, and
Robert Creeley. Her novels are Lovers and Tyrants (1976), World Without End
(1981), and October Blood (1985). She reported for UPI for a few years, worked
for Art in America, and has written articles for the New Yorker, the New York
Review of Books, Vogue, Saturday Review, and the New Republic. Adam and
Eve in the City (1987) collects her essays, including this one. Her biography of
Louise Colet, Rage and Fire (1994), is her latest work.

Gray is the rare writer who delights in acknowledging the help of her editors,
especially when she writes journalism. "I love authority," she said in an interview
with Contemporary Authors. "I love to work with editors. . . . I love suggestions;
I love being corrected and improved. I'll remain a perennial student until the day I
die." It is possible that all writers, on their most honest days, would admit to being
perpetual students.

Gray is married to a painter, has two children, and lives in Connecticut.

———— Photo by Sigrid Estrada

On Friendship

I saw Madame Bovary at Bloomingdale's the other morning, or rather, I saw many incarnations of her. She was hovering over the cosmetic counters, clutching the current issue of *Cosmopolitan*, whose cover line read "New Styles of Coupling, Including Marriage." Her face already ablaze with numerous products advertised to make her irresistible to the opposite sex, she looked anguished, grasping, overwrought, and terribly lonely. And I thought to myself: Poor girl! With all the reams of literature that have analyzed her plight (victimized by double standards, by a materialistic middle-class glutting on the excesses of romantic fiction), notwithstanding all these diagnoses, one fact central to her tragic fate has never been stressed enough: Emma Bovary had a faithful and boring husband and a couple of boring lovers — not so intolerable a condition — but she did not have a friend in the world. And when I think of the great solitude which the original Emma and her contemporaries exude, one phrase jumps to my mind. It comes from an essay by Francis Bacon, and it is one of the finest statements ever penned about the human need for friendship: "Those who have no friends to open themselves unto are cannibals of their own hearts."

In the past years the theme of friendship has been increasingly prominent in our conversations, in our books and films, even in our college courses. It is evident that many of us are yearning with new fervor for this form of bonding. And our yearning may well be triggered by the same disillusionment with the reign of Eros that destroyed Emma Bovary. Emma was eating her heart out over a fantasy totally singular to the Western world, and only a century old at that: the notion that sexual union between men and women who believe that they are passionately in love, a union achieved by free choice and legalized by marriage, tends to offer a life of perpetual bliss and is the most desirable human bond available on earth. It is a notion bred in the same frenzied climate of the romantic epoch that caused countless young Europeans to act like the characters of their contemporary literature. Goethe's *Werther* is said to have triggered hundreds of suicides. Numerous wives glutted on the fantasies of George Sand's heroines demanded separations because their husbands were unpoetic. And Emma Bovary, palpitating from that romantic fiction which precurses our current sex manuals in its outlandish hopes for the satiation of desire, muses in the third week of her marriage: Where is "the felicity, the passion, the intoxication" that had so enchanted her in the novels of Sir Walter Scott?

This frenzied myth of love which has also led to the downfall of Cleopatra, Juliet, Romeo, and King Kong continues to breed, in our time, more garbled thinking, wretched verse, and nonsensical jingles than any emotion under the sun: "All You Need Is Love," or as we heard it in our high-school days, "Tell me you'll love me forever, if only tonight." As Flaubert put it, we are all victims of romanticism. And if we still take for granted its cult of heterosexual passion, it is in part because we have been victimized, as Emma was, by the propaganda machine of the Western novel. It was the power and the genius of the novel form to fuse medieval notions of courtly love with the idealization of marriage that marked the rise of the eighteenth-century middle class. (By "romantic love," I mean an infatuation that involves two major ingredients: a sense of being "enchanted" by another person through a complex process of illusion, and a willingness to totally surrender to that person.)

One hardly needs a course in anthropology to realize that this alliance of marriage and romantic love is restricted to a small segment of the Western world, and would seem sheer folly in most areas of this planet. The great majority of humans — be it in China, Japan, Africa, India, the Moslem nations — still engage in marriages prearranged by their elders or dictated by pragmatic reasons of money, land, tribal politics, or (as in the Socialist countries) housing shortages. Romantically motivated marriage as the central ingredient of the good life is almost as novel in our own West. In popular practice, it remained restricted to a narrow segment of the middle class until the twentieth century. And on the level of philosophical reflection, it was always friendship between members of the same sex, never any bonding of sexual affection, which from Greek times to the Enlightenment was held to be the cornerstone of human happiness. Yet this central role allotted to friendship for two thousand years has been progressively eroded by such factors as the nineteenth-century exaltation of instinct; science's monopoly on our theories of human sentiment; the massive eroticizing of society; and that twentieth-century celebration of the body that reaches its peak in the hedonistic solitude of the multiple orgasm.

To Aristotle, friendship can be formed only by persons of virtue: A man's 5 capacity for friendship is the most accurate measure of his virtue; it is the foundation of the state, for great legislators care even more for friendship than they care for justice. To Plato, as we know, passionate affection untainted by physical relations is the highest form of human bonding. To Cicero, *Amicitia* is more important than either money, power, honors, or health because each of these gifts can bring us only one form of pleasure, whereas the pleasures of friendship are marvelously manifold; and friendship being based on equity, the tyrant is the man least capable of forming that bond because of his need to wield power over others. Montaigne's essay, along with Bacon's, is the most famous of many that glorify our theme in the Renaissance. And like the ancients, he stresses the advantages of friendship over any kind of romantic and physical attachment. Love for members of the opposite sex, in Montaigne's words, is "an impetuous and fickle flame, undulating and variable, a fever flame subject to fits and lulls." Whereas the fire of friendship produces "a general and universal warmth, moderate and even," and will always forge bonds superior to those of marriage because marriage's continuance is "constrained and forced, depending on factors other than our free will."

[handwritten margin note: history of thought on friendship]

A century later, even La Rochefoucauld, that great cynic who described the imperialism of the ego better than any other precursor of Freud, finds that friendship is the only human bond in which the tyrannical cycle of our self-love seems broken, in which "we can love each other even more than love ourselves." One of the last classic essays on friendship I can think of before it loses major importance as a philosophical theme is by Ralph Waldo Emerson. And it's interesting to note that by mid-nineteenth century, the euphoric absolutes which had previously described this form of bonding are sobered by many cautious qualifications. A tinge of modern pragmatism sets in. Emerson tends to distrust any personal friendship unless it functions for the purpose of some greater universal fraternity.

Yet however differently these thinkers focused on our theme, they all seemed to reach a consensus on the qualities of free will, equity, trust, and selflessness unique to the affection of friendship. They cannot resist comparing it to physical passion, which yearns for power over the other, seeks possession and the state of being possessed, seeks to devour, breeds on excess, can easily become demonic, is closely allied to the death wish, and is often a form of agitated narcissism quite unknown to the tranquil, balanced rule of friendship. And rereading the sagas of Tristan and Iseult, Madame Bovary, and many other romantic lovers, it is evident that their passions tend to breed as much on a masturbatory excitement as on a longing for the beloved. They are in love with love, their delirium is involved with a desire for self-magnification through suffering, as evidenced in Tristan's words, "Eyes with joy are blinded. I myself am the world." There is confrontation, turmoil, aggression, in the often militaristic language of romantic love: Archers shoot fatal arrows or unerring shafts; the male enemy presses, pursues, and conquers; women surrender after being besieged by amorous assaults. Friendship on the other hand is the most pacifist species in the fauna of human emotions, the most steadfast and sharing. No wonder then that the finest pacifist ideology in the West was devised by a religious group — the Quakers — which takes as its official name the Religious Society of Friends; the same temperate principle of fraternal bonding informs that vow demanded by the Benedictine Order — the Oath of Stability — which remains central to the monastic tradition to this day. No wonder, also, that the kind of passionate friendship shared by David and Jonathan has inspired very few masterpieces of literature, which seem to thrive on tension and illicitness. For until they were relegated to dissecting rooms of the social sciences, our literary views of friendship tended to be expressed in the essay form, a cool, reflective mode that never provided friendship with the motive, democratic, propagandistic force found by Eros in novel, verse, and stage. To this day, friendship totally resists commercial exploitation, unlike the vast businesses fueled by romantic love that support the couture, perfume, cosmetic, lingerie, and pulp-fiction trades.

One should note, however, that most views of friendship expressed in the past twenty centuries of Western thought have dealt primarily with the male's capacity for affection. And they tend to be extremely dubious about the possibility of women ever being able to enjoy genuine friendship with members of their own sex, not to speak of making friends with male peers. Montaigne expressed a prejudice that lasts well into our day when he wrote, "The ordinary capacity of women is inadequate for that communion and fellowship which is the nurse of that sacred bond, nor does their soul feel firm enough to endure the strain of so tight and durable a knot." It is shocking, though not surprising, to hear prominent social scientists paraphrase that opinion in our own decades. Konrad Lorenz and Lionel Tiger, for instance, seem to agree that women are made eminently unsociable by their genetic programming; their bondings, in Lorenz's words, "must be considered weak imitations of the exclusively male associations." Given the current vogue for sociobiology, such assertions are often supported by carefully researched papers on the courtship patterns of Siberian wolves, the prevalence of eye contact among male baboons, and the vogue for gangbanging among chimpanzees.

Our everyday language reflects the same bias: "Fraternity" is a word that goes far beyond its collegiate context and embraces notions of honor, dignity, loyalty. "Sorority" is something we might have belonged to as members of the University of Oklahoma's bowling team in the early 1950s. So I think it is high time that the same feminist perspective that has begun to correct the biases of art history and psychoanalysis should be brought to bear on this area of anthropology. We have indeed been deprived of those official, dramatically visible rites offered to men in pub, poolroom, Elks, hunting ground, or football league. And having been brought up in a very male world, I'm ashamed to say it took me a decade of feminist consciousness to realize that the few bonding associations left to twentieth century women — garden clubs, church suppers, sewing circles (often derided by men because they do not deal with power) — have been activities considerably more creative and life-enhancing than the competition of the poolroom, the machismo of beer drinking, or the bloodshed of hunting.

Among both sexes, the rites and gestures of friendship seemed to have been decimated in the Victorian era, which brought a fear of homosexuality unprecedented in the West. (They also tended to decrease as rites of heterosexual coupling became increasingly permissive.) Were Dr. Johnson and James Boswell° gay, those two men who constantly exhibited their affection for each other with kisses, tears, and passionate embraces? I suspect they were as rabidly straight as those tough old soldiers described by Tacitus begging for last kisses when their legion broke up. Since Freud, science has tended to dichotomize human affection along lines of deviance and normalcy, genitality and platonic love, instead of leaving it as a graduated spectrum of emotion in which love, friendship, sensuality, sexuality, can freely flow into each other as they did in the past. This may be another facet

10

Dr. Johnson and James Boswell Samuel Johnson (1709–1784), quintessential English man of letters, whose fast friendship with James Boswell (1740–1795) resulted in Boswell's *Life of Samuel Johnson,* which immortalized Johnson as a brilliant, witty conversationalist.

of modern culture that has cast coolness and self-consciousness on our gestures of friendship. The 1960s brought us some hope for change, both in its general emotional climate and in our scientists' tendency to relax their definitions of normalcy and deviance. For one of the most beautiful signs of that decade's renewed yearning for friendship and community, particularly evident among the groups who marched in civil-rights or antiwar demonstrations, was the sight of men clutching, kissing, embracing each other unabashedly as Dr. Johnson and James Boswell.

Which leads me to reflect on the reasons why I increasingly turn to friendship in my own life: In a world more and more polluted by the lying of politicians and the illusions of the media, I occasionally crave to hear and to tell the truth. To borrow a beautiful phrase from Friedrich Nietzsche, I look upon my friend as "the beautiful enemy" who alone is able to offer me total candor. I look for the kind of honest friend Emma Bovary needed: one who could have told her that her lover was a jerk.

Friendship is by its very nature freer of deceit than any other relationship we can know because it is the bond least affected by striving for power, physical pleasure, or material profit, most liberated from any oath of duty or of constancy. With Eros the *body* stands naked, in friendship our *spirit* is denuded. Friendship, in this sense, is a human condition resembling what may be humanity's most beautiful and necessary lie — the promise of an afterlife. It is an almost celestial sphere in which we most resemble that society of angels offered us by Christian theology, in which we can sing the truth of our inner thoughts in relative freedom and abundance. No wonder then that the last contemporary writers whose essays on friendship may remain classics are those religiously inclined, scholars relatively unaffected by positivism or behaviorism, or by the general scientificization of human sentiment. That marvelous Christian maverick, C. S. Lewis, tells us: "Friendship is unnecessary, like philosophy, like art, like the universe itself (since God did not *need* to create). It has no survival value; rather it is one of those things that give value to survival." And the Jewish thinker Simone Weil focuses on the classic theme of free consent when she writes: "Friendship is a miracle by which a person consents to view from a certain distance, and without coming any nearer, the very being who is necessary to him as food."

The quality of free consent and self-determination inherent in friendship may be crucial to the lives of twentieth-century women beginning their vocations. But in order to return friendship to an absolutely central place in our lives, we might have to wean ourselves in part from the often submissive premises of romantic passion. I suspect that we shall always need some measure of swooning and palpitating, of ecstasy and trembling, of possessing and being possessed. But, I also suspect that we've been bullied and propagandized into many of these manifestations by the powerful modern organism that I call the sexual-industrial complex and that had an antecedent in the novels that fueled Emma Bovary's deceitful fantasies. For one of the most treacherous aspects of the cult of romantic love has been its complex idealization and exploitation of female sexuality. There is now a new school of social scientists who are militantly questioning the notion that Western romantic love is the best foundation for human bonding, and their criticism seems much inspired by feminist perspectives. The Australian anthropologist Robert Brain, for instance, calls romantic love "a lunatic relic of medieval passions . . . the handmaiden of a moribund capitalistic culture and of an equally dead Puritan ethic."

What exactly would happen if we women remodeled our concepts of ideal human bonding on the ties of friendship and abandoned the premises of enchantment and possession? Such a restructuring of our ideals of happiness could be extremely subversive. It might imply a considerable de-eroticizing of society. It could bring about a minor revolution against the sexual-industrial complex that brings billions of dollars to thousands of men by brainwashing us into the roles of temptress and seductress, and estranges us from the plain and beautiful Quaker ideal of being a sister to the world. How topsy-turvy the world would be! Dalliance, promiscuity, all those more sensationalized aspects of the Women's Movement that were once seen as revolutionary might suddenly seem most bourgeois and old-fashioned activities. If chosen in conditions of rigorous self-determination, the following values, considered up to now as reactionary, could suddenly become the most radical ones at hand: Virginity. Celibacy. Monastic communities. And that most endangered species of all, fidelity in marriage, which has lately become so exotically rare that it might soon become very fashionable, and provide the cover story for yet another publication designed to alleviate the seldom-admitted solitude of swinging singles: "Mick Jagger Is into Fidelity."

AFTERWORD

The classic essay takes a single topic for its title — "On Generosity," "Courage," "Old Age" — and meditates around and about it: reminiscing, quoting, generalizing, supplying anecdote and detail, running off on tangents. Both Cicero and Montaigne wrote on friendship. At the end of her first paragraph, Gray quotes another great essayist — quotation is characteristic of the classic essay — and continues citing the great in chronological order: Plato, Cicero, Montaigne, Bacon, La Rochefoucauld, Emerson. . . .

Quotation makes a music of authority, and for the literary reader a reencounter with old friends. But there are dangers. Notice that for Gray every author quoted contributes to the structure of thought; none seems only decorative, pasted onto a structure to prettify it or disguise it. Sometimes an inexperienced writer uses quotations to pad an essay or merely to cover a shaky structure. Reading quotations without structural function, the reader leaps to the conclusion that the Reference Room bulks too large in the essay. Bartlett, Oxford, Penguin, and Mencken have supported many a diffident essayist and editorial writer.

At the start it seems that this essay might have been called "Against Love" rather than "On Friendship." Often it's bad tactics to praise hotdogs by slandering hamburgers, but maybe the name of LOVE is loud enough in the land so that Gray is shrewd to introduce friendship by knocking love off its pedestal.

BOOKS AVAILABLE IN PAPERBACK

Lovers and Tyrants. New York: Norton. *Novel.*

Soviet Women: Walking the Tightrope. New York: Doubleday. *Nonfiction.*

DONALD
HALL

D ONALD HALL *was born in Connecticut in 1928 and lives in New Hampshire, on the farm where his mother and grandmother were born, married to
poet Jane Kenyon. He makes his living as a freelance writer. Principally a poet, he
started writing prose with a memoir,* String Too Short to Be Saved *(1961), and
now writes for the* Atlantic, *the* New Yorker, Yankee, Esquire, Playboy, *and*
Sports Illustrated. *"A Ballad of the Republic" was commissioned for a centenary
edition (1988) of the poem "Casey at the Bat."*

Some of his essay collections are Fathers Playing Catch with Sons *(1985),*
Seasons at Eagle Pond *(1987), and* Death to the Death of Poetry *(1994). Books
of poems include* The One Day *(1988),* Old and New Poems *(1990), and* The
Museum of Clear Ideas *(1993). In his long essay* Life Work *(1993), Hall revealed,
to universal distaste, that he rises at four in the morning and writes until nightfall
in a continuous abandoned joyous frenzy of work.*

A Ballad of
the Republic

Somewhere the sun is shining, and somewhere children shout, and somewhere someone is writing, "Casey at One Hundred." A century ago, on June 3, 1888, a twenty-five-year-old Harvard graduate, one-poem poet Ernest Lawrence Thayer, published "Casey at the Bat" in the pages of the *San Francisco Examiner*. I suppose it's the most popular poem in our country's history, if not exactly in its literature. Martin Gardner collected twenty-five sequels and parodies to print in his prodigy of scholarship, *The Annotated Casey at the Bat* (1967; rev. 1984). Will the next Casey bat clean-up in the St. Petersburg Over-Ninety Softball League? Perhaps, instead, we will hear of a transparent Casey on an Elysian diamond, shade swinging the shadow of a bat while wraith pitcher uncoils phantom ball. Or spheroid, I should say.

The author of this people's poem was raised in Worcester, Massachusetts: gentleman and scholar, son of a mill owner. At Harvard he combined scholastic and social eminence, not always feasible on the banks of the Charles. A bright student of William James in philosophy, he graduated magna cum laude and delivered the Ivy Oration at graduation. On the other hand, he was editor of the *Lampoon*, for which traditional requirements are more social than literary; he belonged to Fly, a club of decent majesty. It is perhaps not coincidence, considering Victorian Boston's social prejudices, that Thayer's vainglorious mock hero carries an Irish name.

After his lofty graduation, Thayer drifted about in Europe. One of his Harvard acquaintances had been young William Randolph Hearst, business manager of the *Lampoon*, expelled from Harvard for various pranks while Thayer was pulling a magna. The disgraced young Hearst was rewarded by his father with editorship of the *San Francisco Examiner*, where he offered Thayer work as humorous columnist. By the time "Casey" appeared, Thayer had left California to return to Worcester, where he later managed a mill for his father and studied philosophy in his spare time.

He received five dollars for "Casey" and never claimed reward for its hundreds of further printings. By all accounts, "Casey"'s author found his notoriety problematic. As with all famous nineteenth-century recitation pieces — "The Night Before Christmas," "Backward Turn Backward O Time in Thy Flight" — other poets claimed authorship, which annoyed Thayer first because he *did* write it and second because he wasn't especially proud of it. There was the additional annoyance that old ballplayers continually asserted themselves the *original* Casey of the ballad: Thayer insisted that he made the poem up. The author of "Casey at the Bat" died in Santa Barbara in 1940 without ever doing another notable thing.

The poem's biography is richer than the poet's: At first "Casey" blushed 5
unseen, wasting its sweetness on the desert air, until an accident blossomed
it into eminence. In New York De Wolf Hopper, a young star of comic opera,
was acting in *Prince Methusalem.* On August 15, 1888, management invited
players from the New York Giants and the Chicago White Stockings to
attend a performance, and Hopper gave thought to finding a special bit that
he might perform in the ballplayers' honor. His friend the novelist Archibald
Clavering Gunter, recently returned from San Francisco, showed him a
clipping from the *San Francisco Examiner.*

In Hopper's autobiography, he noted that when he "dropped my voice
to B-flat, below low C, at 'the multitude was awed,' I remember seeing Buck
Ewing's gallant mustachios give a single nervous twitch." Apparently Hopper's recitation left everyone in the house twitching for joy, and not only the
Giants' hirsute catcher. For the rest of his life, Hopper repeated his performance by demand, no matter what part he sang or played, doomed to recite
the poem (five minutes and forty seconds) an estimated ten thousand times
before his death in 1935. As word spread from Broadway, the poem was
reprinted in newspapers across the country, clipped out, memorized, and
performed for the millions who would never hear De Wolf Hopper. Eventually the ballad was set to music, made into silent movies, and animated
into cartoons; radio broadcast it, there were recordings by Hopper and
others, and William Schuman wrote an opera called *The Mighty Casey* (pre-
miere 1953).

When he first recited the poem, Hopper had no notion who had written
it. Thayer had signed it "Phin.", abbreviating his college nickname of Phinny.
Editors reprinted the poem anonymously or made up a reasonable name.
When Hopper played Worcester early in the 1890s, he met the retiring
Thayer — and poet recited poem for actor, as Hopper later reported, without
a trace of elocutionary ability.

There are things in any society that *we always knew.* We do not remember
when we first heard about Ground Hog Day, or the rhyme that reminds us
Thirty Days Hath September. Who remembers first hearing "Casey at the
Bat"? Although I cannot remember my original exposure, I remember many
splendid renditions from early in my life by the great ham actor of my
childhood. My New Hampshire grandfather, Wesley Wells, was locally renowned for his powers of recitation — for speaking pieces, as we called it.
He farmed bad soil in central New Hampshire: eight Holsteins, fifty sheep,
a hundred chickens. In the tie-up for milking, morning and night, he leaned
his bald head into warm Holstein ribs and recited poems with me as audience; he kept time as his hands pulled blue milk from long teats. When he
got to the best part, he let go the nozzles, leaned back in his milking chair,
spread his arms wide and opened his mouth in a great O, the taught gestures
of elocution. He spellbound me as he set out the lines on warm cowy air:
"But there is no joy in Mudville — mighty Casey has struck out!" The old
barn (with its whitewash over rough boards, with its spiderwebs and straw,

209

with its patched harness and homemade ladders and pitchforks shiny from decades of hand-labor) paused in its shadowy hugeness and applauded again the ringing failure of the hero.

If he had not recited it for me lately, I reminded him. He recited a hundred other poems also, a few from Whittier and Longfellow but mostly poems from newspapers by poets without names. I don't suppose he knew "Ernest Lawrence Thayer" or the history of the poem, but "Casey" itself was as solid as the rocks in his pasture. The word that left Broadway and traveled was: *This poem is good to say out loud.* Earlier, the same news had brought intelligence of Edgar Allan Poe's "The Raven" and Bret Harte's "The Heathen Chinee." Public schooling once consisted largely of group memorization and recitation. The *New England Primer* taught theology and the alphabet together: "In Adam's fall/ We sinned all" through "Zacchaeus he/ Did climb a tree/ His Lord to see." Less obviously the *Primer* instilled pleasures of rhyme and oral performance. When we decided fifty and sixty years ago that rote memorization was bad teaching, we threw out not only the multiplication table but also "Barbara Frietchie." Recitation of verse was turned over to experts.

Earlier, for two hundred years at least, recitation and performance took 10 center stage in the one-room schools; but it did not end there. In the schools, recitation-as-performance — not merely memorization to retain information — climbed toward competitive speaking, elimination and reward on Prize Speaking Day, when the athletes of elocution recited in contest before judges. The same athletes did not stop when school stopped, and recitation exfoliated into the adult world as a major form of entertainment. Hamlets and cities alike formed clubs meeting weekly for mutual entertainment that variously included singing, playing the violin or the piano, recitation, and political debate. In the country towns and villages, which couldn't afford to hire Mr. Hopper to entertain them (nor earlier Mr. Emerson to instruct and inspire them), citizens made their own Lyceums and Chautauquas.° In my grandfather's South Danbury, New Hampshire, young people founded the South Danbury Debating and Oratorical Society. Twice a month they met for programs that began with musical offerings and recitations, paused for coffee and doughnuts, and concluded with a political debate, like: "Resolved: That the United States should Cease from Territorial Expansion."

While recitation thrived the recitable poem became a way of entertaining ideas and each other, of exposing or exercising public concerns. Poetry in the United States was briefly a public art. But after the Great War came cars, radios, and John Dewey; recitation departed, and poets have been blamed, ever since, for losing their audience. The blame is unfair, because the connection between poetry and a mass audience was brief, nor did it work for all poetry. John Donne never had a great audience; neither did George

---

Lyceums and Chautauquas   Associations providing public lectures, concerts, and entertainment.

Herbert nor Andrew Marvell, nor in America Walt Whitman or Emily Dickinson. These poets made poems with a fineness of language that required sophisticated reading, and from most readers silent reading not to mention rereading.

All the same, *some* nineteenth-century poets wrote poems both popular and fine — without being as popular as baseball or as fine as Gerard Manley Hopkins. This moment was the fragile age of elocution. Some poets wrote variously — turning in one direction to talk to the people, and in another to talk to the ages. Longfellow's best work — the *Divine Comedy* sonnets, "The Jewish Cemetery at Newport" — is dense, sophisticated, adult poetry of the second order. But in his nationalist fervor he also wrote epics of the Republic's prehistory like *Evangeline*, or lyrics of the common life like "The Village Blacksmith." Making these poems, he made recitation pieces; without intending to, he wrote poems for children and for entertainment. When Whittier made "Barbara Frietchie" in his abolitionist passion, he made willy-nilly a patriotic poem to recite in schools. Meantime Walt Whitman — who had notions about poetry for the people — went relatively unread as he went largely unrecited. Mind you, he showed he could turn his hand to the recitation piece: "O Captain My Captain" is poetically inferior to "Casey."

The twin phenomena of recitation and the popular poem thrived in England at the same time, and Macaulay's *The Lays of Ancient Rome* turned up on American school readers and on prize speaking days. The public Tennyson, laureate not melancholic, wrote verses often memorized for performance; lyrical Wordsworth and bouncy Browning served as well. There were many English sources, even for "Casey at the Bat": Thayer remembered looking into W. S. Gilbert's *Bab Ballads* before composing "Casey."

At my grammar school in the 1930s we memorized American poets: Whitman for "O Captain My Captain," Joaquin Miller's "Columbus," something by James Whitcomb Riley. The trajectory of the recitation piece, of which "Casey" is a late honorable example, began its descent early. James Whitcomb Riley scored hits with "Little Orphant Annie" and others, but Riley was mostly hokum. Then there was Eugene Field, whose "Little Boy Blue" is gross sentimentality accomplished with skill; then there is Ella Wheeler Wilcox; then there is Edgar Lee Guest. (The Canadian Robert Service is a late recitable anomaly.) Vachel Lindsay and Carl Sandburg were themselves performers who seldom gave rise to performance in others; they led from recitation toward the poetry reading. There are poets today as sentimental and popular as Edgar Guest but they write free verse and no one recites them.

The tradition of recitation survives only in backwaters, like Danbury, 15 New Hampshire. If you come to our elementary school on Prize Speaking Day and sit in the school cafeteria-gymnasium-assembly, a miniature elocutionist may break your heart reciting "Little Boy Blue," or you may watch a stout ten-year-old outfielder, straight out of central casting, begin: "The outlook wasn't brilliant for the Mudville nine that day . . ."

Among the thousands of pieces memorized and recited, in the Age of Elocution, few survive. Why "Casey at the Bat"? For a hundred years this mock heroic ballad has lurked alive at the edges of American consciousness. It has endured past the culture that spawned it. When an artifact like this clownish old poem persists for a century, surviving not only its moment but its natural elocutionary habitat, there must be reasons. There must be public reasons for public endurance.

We might as well ask: Why has baseball survived? Neither the Black Sox scandal nor the crash nor two World Wars nor the National Football League have ended the game of baseball. Every year more people buy tickets to sit in wooden seats over a diamond of grass — or in plastic seats over plastic grass, as may be. Doubtless we need to ask: *Has* baseball survived? Casey's game pitted town against town with five thousand neighbors watching. Maybe the descendant of Casey's game is industrial league softball played under the lights by teams wearing rainbow acrylics. These days when we speak of baseball we mostly mean the Major Leagues, millionaire's hardball, where our box seats place us half a mile from a symmetrical petrochemical field. Do we watch the game that Mudville watched?

Yes.

As "Casey at the Bat" survives the culture of recitation, the game's shape and import survive its intimate origins. Not without *change:* If the five thousand ghosts of the Mudville crowd, drinking a Mississippi of blood to turn solid, reconstituted themselves on a Friday night at Three Rivers Stadium to witness combat between Cincinnati's team and Pittsburgh's, they would gape in spiritual astonishment at the zircon-light of a distant diamond under velvet darkness, at the pool-table green of imitation grass, at amenities of Lite, at the wave, at the skin color of many players, at tight uniforms, and at a scoreboard that showed moving pictures of what just happened.

But in their ectoplasmic witness they would also observe the template of an unaltered game. They would watch a third baseman move to his left, stopping the ball with his chest, picking the ball up to throw the runner out; or a second baseman flipping underhand to a shortstop pivoting toward first for the double play, or an outfielder charging a line drive while setting himself to throw. Above all, they would see a pitcher facing a batter late in the game with men on base. They would see a clean-up man approaching the batter's box with defiance curling his lip. "Casey at the Bat" survives — to begin with — because it crystallizes baseball's moment, the medallion carved at the center of the game, where pitcher and batter confront each other.

There are other reasons, literary and historical. When a poem is so popular, one needs to quote Mallarmé again, and observe that poems are made of words. "Casey"'s language is a small consistent comic triumph of irony. The diction is mock heroic, big words for small occasions: When a few fans go home in the ninth inning, they depart not in discouragement or disdain but "in deep despair." The remaining five thousand require a learned allusion: In his *Essay on Man,* Alexander Pope wrote that "Hope springs eternal in the human breast," and Thayer of course knew the source of his saw; but Pope like Shakespeare is largely composed of book titles and proverbs: Thayer uses Pope not as literary allusion but as appeal to common knowledge by way of common elevated sentiment.

Elevation is fundamental: Despite the flicker of hope, the crowd is a "grim multitude" — language appropriate to Milton's hell — and if the hero is mocked, hero-worshippers are twice mocked. Thayer's poetic similes are Homeric — as if Achilles faced Hector instead of Casey the pitcher. (If Casey is not quite Achilles, at least he is Ajax.) Imagery of noise, loud in Homer and his echo Virgil, rouses Thayer to exalted moments: A yell "rumbled through the valley, it rattled in the dell;/ It knocked upon the mountain and recoiled upon the flat." This yell is cousin to the "roar/ Like the beating of the stormwaves on a stern and distant shore." It is noise again when Thayer's crowd reacts to a called strike: " 'Fraud!' cried the maddened thousands, and echo answered fraud." These days at Fenway Park the bleacherites divide themselves for a rhythmic double chant, but they do not say "Fraud." When they feel polite they cry "Less filling" and echo answers "Tastes great."

Possibly crowds were not chanting "Fraud" in the 1880s either. It was a major form of Victorian humor to elevate diction over circumstance. Mr. Micawber soared into periphrastic euphemism to admit that he as in debt; W. C. Fields was an orotund low-comedy grandson. For a hundred years it was witty or amusing to call kissing osculation, and to refer to a house as a domicile. If somebody missed our tone, we sounded pompous, but usually people understood us: When we enjoyed something common or vulgar (like baseball) we could show a humorous affection for it, yet retain our superiority, by calling the ball a spheroid.

This habit of language has not entirely disappeared, but more and more it looks like an Anglophile or academic *tic.* The late poet and renowned advocate of baseball, Marianne Moore, always talked this way, never more than when she spoke of the game. When she identified the Giants' pitcher, "Mr. Mathewson," we are told that she noted: "I've read his instructive book on the art of pitching, and it's a pleasure to note how unerringly his execution supports his theories." Another St. Louis poet was T. S. Eliot, born the same year as "Casey," and like Moore expert in the humor of a polysyllabic synonym for a homely word. Eliot is the most eminent poet influenced by "Casey at the Bat." *Old Possum's Book of Practical Cats* includes "Growltiger's Last Stand," conflation of Custer and Casey, written in metrical homage and in allusion: "Oh there was joy in Wapping when the news flew through the land. . . ." Growltiger is a vicious fellow, racist or at least nationalist ("But most of Cats of foreign race his hatred has been vowed"), and loathed by felines of an Asian provenance. Absorbed in romantic adventure he is surrounded by a "fierce Mongolian horde," captured, and made to walk the plank.

The author of *Four Quartets* and "The Love Song of J. Alfred Prufrock" 25 grew up in the age of recitation; we could be certain that he knew "Casey" even if "Growltiger" were not written in homage. Like many poets he could write high or low, wide or narrow; unlike some poets, when he wrote for children he recognized that he was doing it.

Mockery is "Casey"'s point, with humor to soften the blow. After the crowd (which is us), the great Casey himself takes the brunt of our laughter. His name is the poem's mantra, repeated twenty-two times, often twice in a line: As he puffs with vainglory, "Defiance gleamed in Casey's eye, a sneer curled Casey's lip." The hero's role is written in the script of gesture. After five stanzas of requisite exposition, we catch sight of the rumored Casey in the sixth stanza: "There was ease in Casey's manner. . . ." By this phrase we are captured and the double-naming locks us in: "There was pride in Casey's bearing and a smile on Casey's face." We know the smile's message, and we know how Casey doffs his cap. Casey is Christlike: It is "With a smile of Christian charity" that he "stilled the rising tumult"; if we remember that this metaphoric storm occurs at sea ("the beating of the stormwaves"), we may understand that Casey's charity earns its adjective.

And every time we hear "Casey at the Bat," the hero strikes out. We require this failure.

Not all of us. My grandfather with his sanguine temperament always regretted that Casey struck out. He memorized the sequels and tried them all, especially "The Volunteer." In Clarence P. MacDonald's poem, printed in the *San Francisco Examiner* in 1908, the home team plays with no bench; behind in the game, it loses its catcher to an injury, and the captain calls for a substitute from the stands: A gray-headed volunteer finishes the game as catcher and his home run wins the game in the ninth. Besieged by teammates and fans to reveal his identity, the weeping stranger proclaims: "I'm mighty Casey who struck out just twenty years ago."

Wonderful.

But it won't do. None of the triumphant sequels will do. None show the 30 flair of Thayer's ballad, its vigorous bumpety heptameter and mostly well-earned rhymes, or its consistently overplayed language. Most important, none celebrates failure. Casey may strike out: Casey's failure is the poem's success.

When Thayer first published "Casey at the Bat" in 1888, it bore a subtitle seldom reprinted: "A Ballad of the Republic." Once we lived in heroic times: once — and then again. When we suffer wars and undertake explorations we require heroes, and Jeb Stuart must gallop behind Union lines, Lindbergh fly the Atlantic, Davey Crockett enter the wilderness alone, Washington endure Valley Forge, the *Merrimack* attack the *Monitor*, Neil Armstrong step on the moon, and U.S. stand for Ulysses S., Unconditional Surrender, *and* the United States.

The Civil War, which ripped the country apart, began the work of stitching it together again. (One small agent of integrity was baseball, as blue and gray troops played the game at rest and even in prison camps, even North against South as legend tells us.) For five years North and South lived through the triumphs and disaster of heroes. Although nameless boys charged stone walls blazing with rifle fire, we concentrated our attention on heroic leaders, from dandified cavalrymen to dignified generals. Sons born to veterans, late in the sixties and early in the seventies, were christened Forrest, Jackson, Sherman, Grant, Lee, Bedford, Beauregard. . . .

But hero-worship is dangerous and needs correction, especially in a democracy if we will remain democratic. To survive hero-worship we mock our heroes; if we don't we become their victims. Odysseus came home to slay the suitors; Ulysses S. allowed them to fatten on our larder: Heroic governance became disaster as the triumphant General turned into the ruinous President. Many other heroes struck out. When the romantic vainglorious George Custer, with his shoulder-length hair, made combat with Geronimo in 1876, Growltiger walked the plank. Affluence and corruption, defeat and corruption bred irony. Violence of reconstruction and violence of antireconstruction eventually encouraged detachment from crowd passion.

Whatever young Thayer had in mind, writing his Ballad of the Republic, 1888 was a presidential year. We elected the mighty Benjamin Harrison president, a former officer of the Union Army, who took the job in a deal and installed as Secretary of State the notorious James G. Blaine. De Tocqueville stands behind this poem as much as Homer does. Democracies choose figures to vote in and out of office — to argue over, to ridicule: We do not want gods or kings — that's why we crossed the ocean west — but human beings, fallible like us.

We pretend to forgive failure; really we celebrate it. Bonehead Merkle 35 lives forever and Bill Maserowski's home run diminishes in memory. We fail, we all fail, we fail all our lives. The best hitters fail, two out of three at-bats. If from time to time we succeed, our success is only a prelude to further failure — and success's light makes failure darker still. Triumph's pleasures are intense but brief; failure remains with us forever, a featherbed, a mothering nurturing common humanity. With Casey we all strike out. Although Bill Buckner won a thousand games with his line drives and brilliant fielding, he will endure in our memories in the ninth inning of the sixth game of the World Series, one out to go, as the ball inexplicably, ineluctably, and eternally rolls between his legs.

DONALD HALL

AFTERWORD

*Baseball is my favorite pastime, and poetry my chosen work; when a publisher
planned a centennial edition of "Casey at the Bat," it was not surprising that my
name came up. Barry Moser painted the pictures, and I wrote the Afterword for
Casey at the Bat: A Centennial Edition (1988).*

*To prepare for the essay, I read the poem over many times, took notes about my
associations with the poem, and pondered the history of recitation. I read Martin
Gardner and others about Ernest Lawrence Thayer, De Wolf Hopper, and the poem's
popularity. "Casey"'s subtitle led me to political or social notions, relating the poem
to the gilded age. Notes, notes, notes. Putting my notes in order, I made a quick and
dirty first draft (many writers do a slower, more nearly finished first draft, because
it works best for them; not for me) and a laborious second draft (order; focus; cutting)
and seven or eight further drafts. My drafts became easier as the essay progressed;
they became mere tidying. Before book publication, I sold this essay to the* New York
Times Book Review; *it was too long for the space available, so they cut it —
removing with deft precision anything that resembled an idea.*

*My problem in writing this piece, which was also my opportunity, was the
amalgamation of many different subjects into one essay. I arrived at my structure
by discovering transitions — ways to move from place to place by legitimate association or by turn of phrase, in order to make one discourse out of literary criticism,
biography, social and historical ideas, anecdotes of education, personal reminiscence,
popular cultural history, and psychological speculation. To move from an account of
the poem's popularity to the history of recitation was easy (paragraph 8); then I could
move to reasons for reciting* this *poem (paragraph 16) which allowed me scope to
speak of its language and its cultural or historical implications; finally — from
history to the individual — I could speculate on "Casey" and the American psyche.*

*The structure pleases me, when I look at the essay again. A poem that I enjoy
became an excuse for me to revisit things — baseball, recitation, American history,
and grandfathers — that I like to write about.*

BOOKS AVAILABLE IN PAPERBACK

The Bone Ring: Verse Play. Brownsville, Oreg.: Story Line Press. *Poetry.*

Fathers Playing Catch with Sons. New York: Farrar, Straus & Giroux. *Essays.*

Goatfoot Milktongue Twinbird. Ann Arbor: University of Michigan Press. *Essays.*

Here at Eagle Pond. Boston: Houghton Mifflin. *Essays.*

Life Work. Boston: Beacon Press. *Nonfiction.*

The Museum of Clear Ideas. New York: Ticknor & Fields. *Poetry.*

Old and New Poems. New York: Ticknor & Fields.

The One Day. New York: Ticknor & Fields. *Poetry.*

Ox-Cart Man. New York: Viking Children's Books. *Children's Book.*

Poetry and Ambition: Essays, 1982–1988. Ann Arbor: University of Michigan Press.

Seasons at Eagle Pond. New York: Ticknor & Fields. *Essays.*

String Too Short to Be Saved. Boston: David R. Godine. *Nonfiction.*

To Keep Moving: Essays, 1959–1969. Geneva, N.Y.: Hobart & William Smith Press.

The Weather for Poetry: Essays, Reviews, and Notes on Poetry. Ann Arbor: University of Michigan Press.

JOY
HARJO

JOY HARJO lives in Albuquerque, where she is a professor of English at the University of New Mexico. Born in Tulsa, Oklahoma, in 1951, she is a member of the Creek (also known as Muscogee) tribe. She is a poet, an editor, an essayist, an author of works for children, and a saxophonist who leads her own band called Poetic Justice. As a poet she received a fellowship from the National Endowment for the Arts. Her books of poems include The Last Song *(1973),* What Moon Drove Me to This *(1980),* She Had Some Horses *(1983), and* In Mad Love and War *(1990).*

Family Album

FOR MY COUSIN JOHN JACOBS, 1918–1991,
WHO WILL ALWAYS BE WITH ME.

I felt as if I had prepared for the green corn ceremony my whole life. It's nothing I can explain in print; besides, no explanation would fit in the English language. All I can say is that it is central to the mythic construct of the Muscogee people (otherwise known as "Creek"), a rite of resonant renewal, of forgiveness.

Photo by Paul Abdoo, Photographer/Denver, Colo.

219

The drive to Tallahassee grounds in northeastern Oklahoma with my friends Helen and Jim Burgess and Susan Williams was filled with stories. Stories here are as thick as the insects singing. We were part of the ongoing story of the people. Helen and I had made a promise to take part together in a ceremony that ensures that survival of the people, a link in the epic story of grace. The trees and tall reedlike grasses resounded with singing.

There's nothing quite like it anywhere else I've been, and I've traveled widely. The most similar landscape is in Miskito country in northeastern Nicaragua. I thought I was home once again as I walked with the Miskito people who had suffered terrible destruction of their homeland from both sides of the war. The insects singing provided a matrix of complex harmonies which shift cells in the body that shape imagination. I imagine a similar insect language in a place I've dreamed in west Africa. In summer in Oklahoma it's as if insects shape the world by songs. Their collective punctuation helps the growing corn remember the climb to the sun.

Our first stop on the way to the grounds was Holdenville to visit one of my favorite older cousins and his wife, John and Carol Jacobs. They would meet us later at the grounds. We traded gifts and stories, ate a perfectly fried meal at the Dairy Queen, one of the few restaurants open in a town hit hard by economic depression. I always enjoy visiting and feasting with these, my favorite relatives, and I feel at home in their house, a refuge surrounded with peacocks, dogs, and well-loved cats, guarded by giant beneficent spirits disguised as trees.

Across the road an oil well pumps relentlessly. When I was a child in 5 Oklahoma, the monster insect bodies of the pumping wells terrified me. I would duck down in the car until we passed. Everyone thought it was funny. I was called high-strung and imaginative. I imagined the collapse of the world, as if the wells were giant insects without songs, pumping blood from the body of Earth. I wasn't far off from the truth.

My cousin John, who was more like a beloved uncle, gave me two photographs he had culled for me from family albums. I had never before seen my great-grandparents on my father's side in photographs; this was the first time. I held them in my hand as reverberations of memory astounded me beyond language. I believe stories are encoded in the DNA spiral and call each cell into perfect position. Sound tempered with emotion and meaning propels the spiral beyond three dimensions.

I recognized myself in this photograph. I saw my sister, my brothers, my son and daughter. My father lived once again at the wheel of a car, my father who favored Cadillacs and Lincolns, cars he was not always able to afford but sacrificed to own because he was compelled by the luxury of well-made vehicles, sung to by the hum of a finely constructed motor. He made sure his cars were well-greased and perfectly tuned. That was his favorite music.

I was not surprised, yet I was shocked, to recognize something I always knew. The images of my great-grandmother Katie Menawe, my great-grandfather Marsie Harjo, my grandmother Naomi, my aunts Lois and Mary, and my uncle Joe were always inside me, as if I were a soul catcher made of a crystal formed from blood. I had heard the names, the stories, and perhaps it was because of the truth of those stories and what the names conveyed that the images had formed, had propelled me into the world. My grandchildren and great-grandchildren will see a magnification of themselves in their grandparents. It's implicit in the way we continue, the same as corn plants, the same as stars or the cascades of insects singing in summer. The old mystery of division and multiplication will always lead us to the root.

I think of my Aunt Lois's admonishments about photographs. She said a photograph can steal your soul. I believe it's true, for an imprint remains behind, forever locked in paper and chemicals. Perhaps the family will always be touring somewhere close to the border, dressed in their Sunday best, acutely aware of the soul stealer that Marsie Harjo hired to photograph them, steadying his tripod to the right of the road. Who's to say they didn't want something left to mark time in that intimate space, a place they could be in forever as a family, the world drenched in sienna?

Nothing would ever be the same again. The family is ever present, as is the photographer, unnamed except for his visual arrangement. I wonder whether he was surprised to see rich Indians. 10

Both of my great-grandparents' parents were part of the terrible walk of the Muscogee Nation from Alabama to Indian territory, where they were settled on land bordered by what is now Tulsa on the north, the place where my brothers, sister, and I were born. The people were promised that if they made this move they would be left alone by the U.S. Government, which claimed it needed the tribal homelands for expansion. But within a few years

white settlers were once again crowding Indian lands, and in 1887 the Dawes Act, sometimes better known as the Allotment Act, was made law.

This act undermined one of the principles that had always kept the people together: that land was communal property which could not be owned. With the Dawes Act, private ownership of land was forced on the people. Land that supposedly belonged in perpetuity to the tribe was divided into plots, allotted to individuals. What was "left over" was opened for white settlement. But this did not content the settlers who proceeded by new laws, other kinds of trickery, and raw force to take over allotments belonging to the Muscogee and other tribes.

On December 1, 1905, oil was struck in Glenpool, Oklahoma. This was one of the richest pools of oil discovered in Oklahoma, which at its height produced forty million barrels annually. Marsie Harjo's allotted land was here. He was soon a rich man, as were many other Indian people whose allotted land lay over lakes of oil. This intensified the land grab. Many tribal members were swindled of their land, killed for money. It's a struggle that is still played out in the late twentieth century.

Oil money explains the long elegant car Marsie Harjo poses in with his family. In the stories I've been told, he always loved Hudsons. This may or may not be a Hudson. The family was raised in luxury. My grandmother Naomi and my aunt Lois both received their B.F.A. degrees in art and were able to take expensive vacations at a time when many people in this country were suffering economic deprivation. They also had an African-American maid, whose name was Susie. I've tried to find out more about her. I do know she lived with the family for many years and made the best ice cream.

There is an irony here because Marsie Harjo was also half or nearly half   15 African-American. Another irony is the racism directed toward African Americans and African blood in recent years by a tribe whose members originally accepted Africans and often welcomed them as relatives. Humanity was respected above color or ownership. The acceptance of African-American slavery came with the embrace of European-American cultural values. It was then we also began to hate ourselves for our darkness. It's all connected; this attitude towards ownership of land has everything to do with how human beings are treated, with the attitude toward all living things.

There are many ironies in this vision of the family of my great-grandparents, which is my family — a vision that explodes the myth of being Indian in this country for non-Indian and Indian alike. I wonder at the interpretation of the image of this Muscogee family in a car only the wealthy could own by another Muscogee person, or by another tribal person, or by a non-Indian anywhere in this land. This image challenges the popular culture's image of "Indian," an image that fits no tribe or person. I mean to question those accepted images, images that have limited us to cardboard cutout figures, without blood, tears, or laughter.

There were many photographs of this family. I recently sent my cousin Donna Jo Harjo a photograph of her father Joe as a child of about five. He was dressed in a finely made suit and driving a child's-size scale model of a car. She's never lived in this kind of elegance. She lives on her salary as a sorter for a conglomerate nut-and-dried-fruit company in northern California. She has a love for animals, especially cats. Our clan is the Tiger Clan. She also is a great lover of horses. I wonder at this proliferation of photographs and think of the diminishment of the family in numbers to this present generation.

One of the photographs is a straight-on shot of my great-grandparents and two Seminole men dressed traditionally. The Seminoles in their turbans are in stark contrast to my grandparents, especially to Marsie Harjo, who is stately and somewhat stiff with the fear of god in his elegant white-man's clothes, his Homburg hat.

He was quite an advanced thinker and I imagine he repressed what he foresaw for the Muscogee people. I don't think anyone would have believed him. He was a preacher, a Creek Baptist minister. He represents a counterforce to traditional Muscogee culture and embodies a side of the split in our tribe since Christianity, since the people were influenced by the values of European culture. The dividing lines are the same several hundred years later.

My great-grandfather was in Stuart, Florida, to "save" the Seminole   20 people, as he did every winter. He bought a plantation there and, because he hated pineapples, he had every one of the plants dug up and destroyed. Another story I've often heard says he also owned an alligator farm. I went to Stuart last spring on my way to Miami and could find no trace of the mission or the plantation anywhere in the suburban mix of concrete, glass, and advertisements. I had only memories that are easier to reach in a dimension that is as alive and living as the three dimensions we know with our five senses.

My great-grandmother Katie Menawe is much more hidden in this photograph. She is not in the driver's seat, and not next to the driver but in the very back of the car, behind her four children. Yet she quietly presides over everything as she guards her soul from the intrusive camera. I have the sense that Marsie boldly entered the twentieth century ahead of everyone else, while Katie reluctantly followed. I doubt she ever resolved the split in her heart. I don't know too much about her. She and her siblings were orphaned. They were schooled and boarded for some time at Eufaula Indian School. I don't know how old she was when she married Marsie Harjo. Her sister Ella, a noted beauty queen, was my cousin John's mother.

The name "Menawe" is one of those names in the Muscogee tribe that is charged with memory of rebellion, with strength in the face of terrible destruction. Tecumseh came looking for Menawe when he was building his great alliance of nations in the 1800s. Menawe was one of the leaders of the Red Stick War, an armed struggle against the U.S. Government and Andrew Jackson's demand for western settlement of the Muscogee tribes. The fighting forces were made up of Creeks, Seminoles, and Africans. Not many survived the struggle.

The Seminoles successfully resisted colonization by hiding in the Floridian swamps. They beat the United States forces who were aided by other tribes, including other Creeks who were promised land and homes for their help. The promises were like other promises from the U.S. government. For their assistance, the Indian troops were forced to walk to Indian Territory like everyone else, to what later became the state of Oklahoma.

Menawe stayed in Alabama. He was soon forced west, but not before he joined with Jackson's forces to round up Seminoles for the move to Oklahoma. My cousin John said Menawe died on the trail. I know that he died of a broken heart. I have a McKenney Hall print of Menawe, an original hand-colored lithograph dated 1848. Katie has the eyes and composure of this man who was her father.

By going to Tallahassee grounds to join in traditional tribal ceremony, I was taking my place in the circle of relatives. I was one more link in the concatenation of ancestors. Close behind me are my son and daughter, behind them my granddaughter. Next to me, interlocking the pattern, are my cousins, my aunts and uncles. We dance together in this place of knowing beyond the physical dimensions of space, much denser than the chemicals and paper of photographs. It is larger than mere human memory, than any destruction we have walked through to come to this ground of memory.

Time can never be stopped; rather, it is poised to make a leap into knowing or a field of questions. I understood this as we stompdanced in the middle of the night, as the stars whirred in the same pattern overhead, as they had been when Katie, Marsie, and the children lived beneath them. I heard time resume as the insects took up their singing once more to guide us through memory. The old Hudson heads to the east of the border of the photograph. For the Muscogee, East is the place of origins, the place the People emerged from so many hundreds of years ago. It is also a place of return.

AFTERWORD

We reprint this essay with its photographs, as it originally appeared in the Progressive *in 1992. Since the invention of photography, many magazines have specialized in the photographic essay, in which words and pictures carry equal weight. The illustrated essay is a form that amalgamates different arts, like the song with its wedding of poetry and music.*

Harjo's "Family Album" refers to photography in its title, and photographs provide the writer a passage into her topic. If we tried reading this essay without its family portraits, we would substitute our own family pictures out of imagination or recollection. The actual photographs reduce our imaginative participation and magnify our concentration on particulars.

Harjo's essay falls into two parts, which we might label Affection and Anger. (Think of the title of her recent book of poems, In Mad Love and War.*) When she writes with loving nostalgia of family and tribe — the green corn ceremony and an Oklahoma summer where "it's as if insects shape the world by songs" — she uses a lyrical language that is gorgeous, clear, and touching. In her animated universe, trees are "giant beneficent spirits" and oil wells are "insects without songs, pumping blood from the body of Earth." Insects, metaphorical and real, bulk large in this essay.*

By the time Harjo concludes "Family Album," she has progressed from affectionate feelings, located in memory's images, to outrage over the oppression of her people. She ends by returning to lyrical images, circling back as a writer must do — "the insects took up their singing once more" — but in the meantime she has delivered a forceful argument. Without the affection of her descriptive opening paragraph, readers would not be so responsive to her reasonable rage.

BOOKS AVAILABLE IN PAPERBACK

In Mad Love and War. Middletown, Conn.: Wesleyan University Press. *Poetry.*

Secrets from the Center of the World. (with photographs by Stephan Strom) Tucson: University of Arizona Press. *Poetry.*

She Had Some Horses. New York: Thunder's Mouth. *Poetry.*

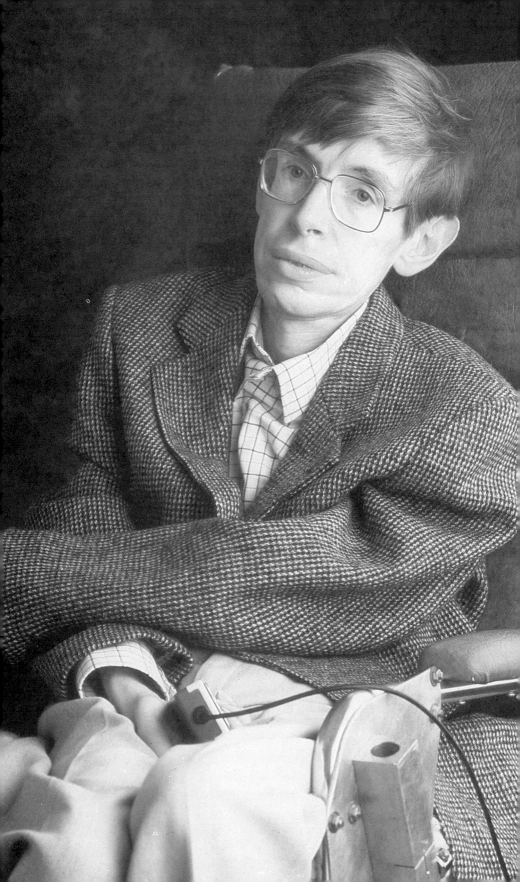

STEPHEN
HAWKING

S TEPHEN HAWKING (b. 1942) has been called the greatest living theoretical physicist. As a child he was interested in mechanics, good at taking things apart — he says in an autobiographical essay — but not so good at putting them together. He went to Oxford at seventeen, majored in physics, and figures in retrospect that over his three years of college he averaged one hour of work a day. Still, he took first class honors and went on to graduate study at Cambridge, where he was diagnosed with ALS, the motor neuron disease known in the United States as Lou Gehrig's disease, which is progressive and incurable.

Nonetheless, Hawking continued his scientific research, married, fathered children, taught, and worked in cosmology and general relativity, inventing mathematical processes. "From 1970 to 1974 I worked mainly on black holes. . . . Since 1974 I have been working on combining general relativity and quantum mechanics into a consistent theory." His mind functions out of a ruined body; he is unable to walk or feed himself or speak, able only to move his fingers slightly — enough therefore to calculate and write, even to synthesize speech. "I can either speak what I have written or save it on disk. I can then print it out or call it back and speak it sentence by sentence. Using this system I have written two books. . . ."

A Brief History of Time (1988) sold something like six million copies. We take this essay from its sequel, a collection of lectures, essays, and radio programs called Black Holes and Baby Universes and Other Essays (1993). Hawking delivered this essay as a lecture at the Sigma Club seminar at the University of Cambridge in April of 1990.

Is Everything
Determined?

In the play *Julius Caesar*, Cassius tells Brutus, "Men at some times are masters of their fate." But are we really masters of our fate? Or is everything we do determined and preordained? The argument for preordination used to be that God was omnipotent and outside time, so God would know what was going to happen. But how then could we have any free will? And if we don't have free will, how can we be responsible for our actions? It can hardly be one's fault if one has been preordained to rob a bank. So why should one be punished for it?

In recent times, the argument for determinism has been based on science. It seems that there are well-defined laws that govern how the universe and everything in it develops in time. Although we have not yet found the exact form of all these laws, we already know enough to determine what happens in all but the most extreme situations. Whether we will find the remaining laws in the fairly near future is a matter of opinion. I'm an optimist: I think there's a fifty-fifty chance that we will find them in the next twenty years. But even if we don't, it won't really make any difference to the argument. The important point is that there should exist a set of laws that completely determines the evolution of the universe from its initial state. These laws may have been ordained by God. But it seems that He (or She) does not intervene in the universe to break the laws.

The initial configuration of the universe may have been chosen by God, or it may itself have been determined by the laws of science. In either case, it would seem that everything in the universe would then be determined by evolution according to the laws of science, so it is difficult to see how we can be masters of our fate.

The idea that there is some grand unified theory that determines everything in the universe raises many difficulties. First of all, the grand unified theory is presumably compact and elegant in mathematical terms. There ought to be something special and simple about the theory of everything. Yet how can a certain number of equations account for the complexity and trivial detail that we see around us? Can one really believe that the grand unified theory has determined that Sinead O'Connor will be the top of the hit parade this week, or that Madonna will be on the cover of *Cosmopolitan*?

A second problem with the idea that everything is determined by a grand unified theory is that anything we say is also determined by the theory. But why should it be determined to be correct? Isn't it more likely to be wrong, because there are many possible incorrect statements for every true one? Each week, my mail contains a number of theories that people have sent me. They are all different, and most are mutually inconsistent. Yet presumably the grand unified theory has determined that the authors think they were correct. So why should anything I say have any greater validity? Aren't I equally determined by the grand unified theory?

A third problem with the idea that everything is determined is that we feel that we have free will — that we have the freedom to choose whether to do something. But if everything is determined by the laws of science, then free will must be an illusion, and if we don't have free will, what is the basis for our responsibility for our actions? We don't punish people for crimes if they are insane, because we have decided that they can't help it. But if we are all determined by a grand unified theory, none of us can help what we do, so why should anyone be held responsible for what they do?

These problems of determinism have been discussed over the centuries. The discussion was somewhat academic, however, as we were far from a complete knowledge of the laws of science, and we didn't know how the initial state of the universe was determined. The problems are more urgent now because there is the possibility that we may find a complete unified theory in as little as twenty years. And we realize that the initial state may itself have been determined by the laws of science. What follows is my personal attempt to come to terms with these problems. I don't claim any great originality or depth, but it is the best I can do at the moment.

To start with the first problem: How can a relatively simple and compact theory give rise to a universe that is as complex as the one we observe, with all its trivial and unimportant details? The key to this is the uncertainty principle of quantum mechanics, which states that one cannot measure both the position and speed of a particle to great accuracy; the more accurately you measure the position, the less accurately you can measure the speed, and vice versa. This uncertainty is not so important at the present time, when things are far apart, so that a small uncertainty in position does not make much difference. But in the very early universe, everything was very close together, so there was quite a lot of uncertainty, and there were a number of possible states for the universe. These different possible early states would have evolved into a whole family of different histories for the universe. Most of these histories would be similar in their large-scale features. They would correspond to a universe that was uniform and smooth, and that was expanding. However, they would differ on details like the distribution of stars and, even more, on what was on the covers of their magazines. (That is, if those histories contained magazines.) Thus the complexity of the universe around us and its details arose from the uncertainty principle in the early stages. This gives a whole family of possible histories for the universe. There would be a history in which the Nazis won the Second World War, though the probability is low. But we just happen to live in a history in which the Allies won the war and Madonna was on the cover of *Cosmopolitan*.

I now turn to the second problem: If what we do is determined by some grand unified theory, why should the theory determine that we draw the right conclusions about the universe rather than the wrong ones? Why should anything we say have any validity? My answer to this is based on Darwin's idea of natural selection. I take it that some very primitive form of life arose spontaneously on earth from chance combinations of atoms. This early form of life was probably a large molecule. But it was probably not DNA, since the chances of forming a whole DNA molecule by random combinations are small.

The early form of life would have reproduced itself. The quantum un- 10 certainty principle and the random thermal motions of the atoms would mean that there were a certain number of errors in the reproduction. Most of these errors would have been fatal to the survival of the organism or its ability to reproduce. Such errors would not be passed on to future genera- tions but would die out. A very few errors would be beneficial, by pure chance. The organisms with these errors would be more likely to survive and reproduce. Thus they would tend to replace the original, unimproved organisms.

The development of the double helix structure of DNA may have been one such improvement in the early stages. This was probably such an advance that it completely replaced any earlier form of life, whatever that may have been. As evolution progressed, it would have led to the develop- ment of the central nervous system. Creatures that correctly recognized the implications of data gathered by their sense organs and took appropriate action would be more likely to survive and reproduce. The human race has carried this to another stage. We are very similar to higher apes, both in our bodies and in our DNA; but a slight variation in our DNA has enabled us to develop language. This has meant that we can hand down information and accumulated experience from generation to generation, in spoken and eventually in written form. Previously, the results of experience could be handed down only by the slow process of it being encoded into DNA through random errors in reproduction. The effect has been a dramatic speed-up of evolution. It took more than three billion years to evolve up to the human race. But in the course of the last ten thousand years, we have developed written language. This has enabled us to progress from cave dwellers to the point where we can ask about the ultimate theory of the universe.

There has been no significant biological evolution, or change in human DNA, in the last ten thousand years. Thus, our intelligence, our ability to draw the correct conclusions from the information provided by our sense organs, must date back to our cave dweller days or earlier. It would have been selected for on the basis of our ability to kill certain animals for food and to avoid being killed by other animals. It is remarkable that mental qualities that were selected for these purposes should have stood us in such good stead in the very different circumstances of the present day. There is probably not much survival advantage to be gained from discovering a grand unified theory or answering questions about determinism. Nevertheless, the intelligence that we have developed for other reasons may well ensure that we find the right answers to these questions.

I now turn to the third problem, the questions of free will and responsibility for our actions. We feel subjectively that we have the ability to choose who we are and what we do. But this may just be an illusion. Some people think they are Jesus Christ or Napoleon, but they can't all be right. What we need is an objective test that we can apply from the outside to distinguish whether an organism has free will. For example, suppose we were visited by a "little green person" from another star. How could we decide whether it had free will or was just a robot, programmed to respond as if it were like us?

The ultimate objective test of free will would seem to be: Can one predict the behavior of the organism? If one can, then it clearly doesn't have free will but is predetermined. On the other hand, if one cannot predict the behavior, one could take that as an operational definition that the organism has free will.

One might object to this definition of free will on the grounds that once we find a complete unified theory we will be able to predict what people will do. The human brain, however, is also subject to the uncertainty principle. Thus, there is an element of the randomness associated with quantum mechanics in human behavior. But the energies involved in the brain are low, so quantum mechanical uncertainty is only a small effect. The real reason why we cannot predict human behavior is that it is just too difficult. We already know the basic physical laws that govern the activity of the brain, and they are comparatively simple. But it is just too hard to solve the equations when there are more than a few particles involved. Even in the simpler Newtonian theory of gravity, one can solve the equations exactly only in the case of two particles. For three or more particles one has to resort to approximations, and the difficulty increases rapidly with the number of particles. The human brain contains about 10^{26} or a hundred million billion billion particles. This is far too many for us ever to be able to solve the equations and predict how the brain would behave, given its initial state and the nerve data coming into it. In fact, of course, we cannot even measure what the initial state was, because to do so we would have to take the brain apart. Even if we were prepared to do that, there would just be too many particles to record. Also, the brain is probably very sensitive to the initial state — a small change in the initial state can make a very large difference to subsequent behavior. So although we know the fundamental equations that govern the brain, we are quite unable to use them to predict human behavior.

This situation arises in science whenever we deal with the macroscopic system, because the number of particles is always too large for there to be any chance of solving the fundamental equations. What we do instead is use effective theories. These are approximations in which the very large number of particles are replaced by a few quantities. An example is fluid mechanics.

A liquid such as water is made up of billions of billions of molecules that themselves are made up of electrons, protons, and neutrons. Yet it is a good approximation to treat the liquid as a continuous medium, characterized just by velocity, density, and temperature. The predictions of the effective theory of fluid mechanics are not exact — one only has to listen to the weather forecast to realize that — but they are good enough for the design of ships or oil pipelines.

I want to suggest that the concepts of free will and moral responsibility for our actions are really an effective theory in the sense of fluid mechanics. It may be that everything we do is determined by some grand unified theory. If that theory has determined that we shall die by hanging, then we shall not drown. But you would have to be awfully sure that you were destined for the gallows to put to sea in a small boat during a storm. I have noticed that even people who claim that everything is predestined and that we can do nothing to change it look before they cross the road. Maybe it's just that those who don't look don't survive to tell the tale.

One cannot base one's conduct on the idea that everything is determined, because one does not know what has been determined. Instead, one has to adopt the effective theory that one has free will and that one is responsible for one's actions. This theory is not very good at predicting human behavior, but we adopt it because there is no chance of solving the equations arising from the fundamental laws. There is also a Darwinian reason that we believe in free will: A society in which the individual feels responsible for his or her actions is more likely to work together and survive to spread its values. Of course, ants work well together. But such a society is static. It cannot respond to unfamiliar challenges or develop new opportunities. A collection of free individuals who share certain mutual aims, however, can collaborate on their common objectives and yet have the flexibility to make innovations. Thus, such a society is more likely to prosper and to spread its system of values.

The concept of free will belongs to a different arena from that of fundamental laws of science. If one tries to deduce human behavior from the laws of science, one gets caught in the logical paradox of self-referencing systems. If what one does could be predicted from the fundamental laws, then the fact of making that prediction could change what happens. It is like the problems one would get into if time travel were possible, which I don't think it ever will be. If you could see what is going to happen in the future, you could change it. If you knew which horse was going to win the Grand National, you could make a fortune by betting on it. But that action would change the odds. One only has to see *Back to the Future* to realize what problems could arise.

This paradox about being able to predict one's actions is closely related 20 to the problem I mentioned earlier: Will the ultimate theory determine that we come to the right conclusions about the ultimate theory? In that case, I argued that Darwin's idea of natural selection would lead us to the correct answer. Maybe the correct answer is not the right way to describe it, but natural selection should at least lead us to a set of physical laws that work fairly well. However, we cannot apply those physical laws to deduce human behavior for two reasons. First, we cannot solve the equations. Second, even if we could, the fact of making a prediction would disturb the system. Instead, natural selection seems to lead to us adopting the effective theory of free will. If one accepts that a person's actions are freely chosen, one cannot then argue that in some cases they are determined by outside forces. The concept of "almost free will" doesn't make sense. But people tend to confuse the fact that one may be able to guess what an individual is likely to choose with the notion that the choice is not free. I would guess that most of you will have a meal this evening, but you are quite free to choose to go to bed hungry. One example of such confusion is the doctrine of diminished responsibility: the idea that persons should not be punished for their actions because they were under stress. It may be that someone is more likely to commit an antisocial act when under stress. But that does not mean that we should make it even more likely that he or she commit the act by reducing the punishment.

One has to keep the investigation of the fundamental laws of science and the study of human behavior in separate compartments. One cannot use the fundamental laws to deduce human behavior, for the reasons I have explained. But one might hope that we could employ both the intelligence and the powers of logical thought that we have developed through natural selection. Unfortunately, natural selection has also developed other characteristics, such as aggression. Aggression would have given a survival advantage in cave dweller days and earlier and so would have been favored by natural selection. The tremendous increase in our powers of destruction brought about by modern science and technology, however, has made aggression a very dangerous quality, one that threatens the survival of the whole human race. The trouble is, our aggressive instincts seem to be encoded in our DNA. DNA changes by biological evolution only on a time scale of millions of years, but our powers of destruction are increasing on a time scale for the evolution of information, which is now only twenty or thirty years. Unless we can use our intelligence to control our aggression, there is not much chance for the human race. Still, while there's life, there's hope. If we can survive the next hundred years or so, we will have spread to other planets and possibly to other stars. This will make it much less likely that the entire human race will be wiped out by a calamity such as a nuclear war.

To recapitulate: I have discussed some of the problems that arise if one believes that everything in the universe is determined. It doesn't make much difference whether this determination is due to an omnipotent God or to the laws of science. Indeed, one could always say that the laws of science are the expression of the will of God.

I considered three questions: First, how can the complexity of the universe and all its trivial details be determined by a simple set of equations? Alternatively, can one really believe that God chose all the trivial details, like who should be on the cover of *Cosmopolitan*? The answer seems to be that the uncertainty principle of quantum mechanics means that there is not just a single history for the universe but a whole family of possible histories. These histories may be similar on very large scales, but they will differ greatly on normal, everyday scales. We happen to live on one particular history that has certain properties and details. But there are very similar intelligent beings who live on histories that differ in who won the war and who is Top of the Pops. Thus, the trivial details of our universe arise because the fundamental laws incorporate quantum mechanics with its element of uncertainty or randomness.

The second question was: If everything is determined by some fundamental theory, then what we say about the theory is also determined by the theory — and why should it be determined to be correct, rather than just plain wrong or irrelevant? My answer to this was to appeal to Darwin's theory of natural selection: Only those individuals who drew the appropriate conclusions about the world around them would be likely to survive and reproduce.

The third question was: If everything is determined, what becomes of free will and our responsibility for our actions? But the only objective test of whether an organism has free will is whether its behavior can be predicted. In the case of human beings, we are quite unable to use the fundamental laws to predict what people will do, for two reasons. First, we cannot solve the equations for the very large number of particles involved. Second, even if we could solve the equations, the fact of making a prediction would disturb the system and could lead to a different outcome. So as we cannot predict human behavior, we may as well adopt the effective theory that humans are free agents who can choose what to do. It seems that there are definite survival advantages to believing in free will and responsibility for one's actions. That means this belief should be reinforced by natural selection. Whether the language-transmitted sense of responsibility is sufficient to control the DNA-transmitted instinct of aggression remains to be seen. If it does not, the human race will have been one of natural selection's dead ends. Maybe some other race of intelligent beings elsewhere in the galaxy will achieve a better balance between responsibility and aggression. But if so, we might have expected to be contacted by them, or at least to detect their radio signals. Maybe they are aware of our existence but don't want to reveal themselves to us. That might be wise, given our record.

In summary, the title of this essay was a question: Is everything determined? The answer is yes, it is. But it might as well not be, because we can never know what is determined.

AFTERWORD

Richard Wilbur wrote a short story called "A Game of Catch" in which a boy taunts other boys by saying, "I made you do that" — whatever they do. In "Design," Robert Frost made a sonnet about an insect trapped by a spider's web, an arrangement he tentatively describes as "design of darkness to appall"; then he qualifies this line with a greater darkness: "If design govern in a thing so small."

Men and women have always searched for reasons to explain how things came to be as they are. In ancient epic poems the gods intervened. In some versions of religion — as in Calvinism — God has determined everything that happens, and we have no freedom at all. Materialistic minds also seek to feel determined or controlled — without the expedient of God — presumably because of the terror that no design govern in a thing so small. We place our fates, or our faiths, in the motions of planets at our birth, in conspiracy theories of politics and economics, or in a naive scientism: Once the first atom bumped another atom, every subsequent bump (including me writing these sentences and you reading them) has been determined by an inevitable sequence of cause and effect.

Are we free or are we bound? It is a perennial all-night argument in the dormitory. Hawking sets forth the old questions forthrightly as he begins his talk — delivered, presumably, by his synthesizer with its American accent. He proceeds quickly to his own subject, the grand unified theory of the universe. His essay does not provide the big bang of a conclusion, but the meditations of a great scientist on an eternal human concern.

BOOK AVAILABLE IN PAPERBACK

A Brief History of Time. New York: Bantam. *Nonfiction.*

VICKI
HEARNE

*V*ICKI HEARNE *is a fellow at Yale University. Most of her teaching life, she has worked with other species: Does experience of animal training modify the creative writing workshop?*

Hearne has trained dogs in obedience and for hunting and tracking; she has also trained their owners. She has trained show horses, wolves, and one goat. Born (1946) in Texas, she grew up mainly in California, where she graduated from the University of California at Riverside and attended Stanford University on a writing fellowship. She has published two collections of poetry, Nervous Horses *(1980) and* In the Absence of Horses *(1984), and a novel,* The White German Shepherd *(1988). For a while she wrote a newspaper column about animals for the* Los Angeles Times, *and she has written essays for many magazines, especially* Harper's, *where "What's Wrong with Animal Rights" originally appeared. As an undergraduate she followed an interest in philosophy; her essays brim with allusion to Nietzsche, Wittgenstein, and the contemporary philosopher Stanley Cavell. She married a philosopher who teaches at Yale and lives with him and her animals in Connecticut.*

Her Adam's Task *(1986), subtitled* Calling Animals by Name, *is a philosophical, combative, and learned account of horses and dogs with attention to the psychology and values of animals. A brilliant human mind encounters the minds of animals and tries not only to teach the animals but to learn from them — to hear, as she understands it, "the stories they tell." She continues telling their stories in* Bandit: Dossier of a Dangerous Dog *(1991) and* Animal Happiness *(1994). In the photo on the opposite page, Bandit is pictured with Hearne.*

———— Photo by Enrico Ferorelli

What's Wrong with Animal Rights

Not all happy animals are alike. A Doberman going over a hurdle after a small wooden dumbbell is sleek, all arcs of harmonious power. A basset hound cheerfully performing the same exercise exhibits harmonies of a more lugubrious nature. There are chimpanzees who love precision the way musicians or fanatical housekeepers or accomplished hypochondriacs do; others for whom happiness is a matter of invention and variation — chimp vaudevillians. There is a rhinoceros whose happiness, as near as I can make out, is in needing to be trained every morning, all over again, or else he "forgets" his circus routine, and in this you find a clue to the slow, deep, quiet chuckle of his happiness and to the glory of the beast. Happiness for Secretariat is in his ebullient bound, that joyful length of stride. For the draft horse or the weight-pull dog, happiness is of a different shape, more awesome and less obviously intelligent. When the pulling horse is at its most intense, the animal goes into himself, allocating all of the educated power that organizes his desire to dwell in fierce and delicate intimacy with that power, leans into the harness, and MAKES THAT SUCKER MOVE.

If we are speaking of human beings and use the phrase "animal happiness," we tend to mean something like "creature comforts." The emblems of this are the golden retriever rolling in the grass, the horse with his nose deep in the oats, the kitty by the fire. Creature comforts are important to animals — "Grub first, then ethics" is a motto that would describe many a wise Labrador retriever, and I have a pit bull named Annie whose continual quest for the perfect pillow inspires her to awesome feats. But there is something more to animals, a capacity for satisfactions that come from work in the fullest sense — what is known in philosophy and in this country's Declaration of Independence as "happiness." This is a sense of personal achievement, like the satisfaction felt by a good wood-carver or a dancer or a poet or an accomplished dressage horse. It is a happiness that, like the artist's, must come from something within the animal, something trainers call "talent." Hence, it cannot be imposed on the animal. But it is also something that does not come *ex nihilo*. If it had not been a fairly ordinary thing, in one part of the world, to teach young children to play the pianoforte, it is doubtful that Mozart's music would exist.

Happiness is often misunderstood as a synonym for pleasure or as an antonym for suffering. But Aristotle associated happiness with ethics — codes of behavior that urge us toward the sensation of getting it right, a kind of work that yields the "click" of satisfaction upon solving a problem or surmounting an obstacle. In his *Ethics*, Aristotle wrote, "If happiness is activity in accordance with excellence, it is reasonable that it should be in accordance with the highest excellence." Thomas Jefferson identified the capacity for happiness as one of the three fundamental rights on which all others are based: "life, liberty, and the pursuit of happiness."

I bring up this idea of happiness as a form of work because I am an animal trainer, and work is the foundation of the happiness a trainer and an animal discover together. I bring up these words also because they cannot be found in the lexicon of the animal-rights movement. This absence accounts for the uneasiness toward the movement of most people, who sense that rights advocates have a point but take it too far when they liberate snails or charge that goldfish at the county fair are suffering. But the problem with the animal-rights advocates is not that they take it too far; it's that they've got it all wrong.

Animal rights are built upon a misconceived premise that rights were   5
created to prevent us from unnecessary suffering. You can't find an animal-rights book, video, pamphlet, or rock concert in which someone doesn't mention the Great Sentence, written by Jeremy Bentham in 1789. Arguing in favor of such rights, Bentham wrote: "The question is not, Can they *reason?* nor, can they *talk?* but, can they suffer?"

The logic of the animal-rights movement places suffering at the iconographic center of a skewed value system. The thinking of its proponents — given eerie expression in a virtually sadopornographic sculpture of a tortured monkey that won a prize for its compassionate vision — has collapsed into a perverse conundrum. Today the loudest voices calling for — demanding — the destruction of animals are the humane organizations. This is an inevitable consequence of the apotheosis of the drive to relieve suffering: Death is the ultimate release. To compensate for their contradictions, the humane movement has demonized, in this century and the last, those who made animal happiness their business: veterinarians, trainers, and the like. We think of Louis Pasteur as the man whose work saved you and me and your dog and cat from rabies, but antivivisectionists of the time claimed that rabies increased in areas where there were Pasteur Institutes.

An antirabies public relations campaign mounted in England in the 1880s by the Royal Society for the Prevention of Cruelty to Animals and other organizations led to orders being issued to club any dog found not wearing a muzzle. England still has her cruel and unnecessary law that requires an animal to spend six months in quarantine before being allowed loose in the country. Most of the recent propaganda about pit bulls — the crazy claim that they "take hold with their front teeth while they chew away with their rear teeth" (which would imply, incorrectly, that they have double jaws) — can be traced to literature published by the Humane Society of the United States during the fall of 1987 and earlier. If your neighbors want your dog or horse impounded and destroyed because he is a nuisance — say the dog barks, or the horse attracts flies — it will be the local Humane Society to whom your neighbors turn for action.

In a way, everyone has the opportunity to know that the history of the humane movement is largely a history of miseries, arrests, prosecutions, and death. The Humane Society is the pound, the place with the decompression chamber or the lethal injections. You occasionally find worried letters about this in Ann Landers's column.

Animal-rights publications are illustrated largely with photographs of two kinds of animals — "Helpless Fluff" and "Agonized Fluff," the two conditions in which some people seem to prefer their animals, because any other version of an animal is too complicated for propaganda. In the introduction to his book *Animal Liberation,* Peter Singer says somewhat smugly that he and his wife have no animals and, in fact, don't much care for them. This is offered as evidence of his objectivity and ethical probity. But it strikes me as an odd, perhaps obscene underpinning for an ethical project that encourages university and high school students to cherish their ignorance of, say, great bird dogs as proof of their devotion to animals.

I would like to leave these philosophers behind, for they are inept connoisseurs of suffering who might revere my Airedale for his capacity to scream when subjected to a blowtorch but not for his wit and courage, not for his natural good manners that are a gentle rebuke to ours. I want to celebrate the moment not long ago when, at his first dog show, my Airedale, Drummer, learned that there can be a public place where his work is respected. I want to celebrate his meticulousness, his happiness upon realizing at the dog show that no one would stoop down upon him and swamp him with the goo-goo excesses known as the "teddy-bear complex" but that people actually got out of his way, gave him room to work. I want to say, "There can be a six-and-a-half-month-old puppy who can care about accuracy, who can be fastidious, and whose fastidiousness will be a foundation for courage later." I want to say, "Leave my puppy alone!"

I want to leave the philosophers behind, but I cannot, in part because the philosophical problems that plague academicians of the animal-rights movement are illuminating. They wonder, do animals have rights or do they have interests? Or, if these rightists lead particularly unexamined lives, they dismiss that question as obvious (yes, of course animals have rights, prima facie) and proceed to enumerate them, James Madison style. This leads to the issuance of bills of rights — the right to an environment, the right not to be used in medical experiments — and other forms of trivialization.

The calculus of suffering can be turned against the philosophers of festering flesh, even in the case of food animals, or exotic animals who perform in movies and circuses. It is true that it hurts to be slaughtered by man, but it doesn't hurt nearly as much as some of the cunningly cruel arrangements meted out by "Mother Nature." In Africa, 75 percent of the lions cubbed do not survive to the age of two. For those who make it to two, the average age at death is ten years. Asali, the movie and TV lioness, was still working at age twenty-one. There are fates worse than death, but twenty-one years of a close working relationship with Hubert Wells, Asali's

242

trainer, is not one of them. Dorset sheep and polled Herefords would not exist at all were they not in a symbiotic relationship with human beings.

A human being living in the "wild" — somewhere, say, without the benefits of medicine and advanced social organization — would probably have a life expectancy of from thirty to thirty-five years. A human being living in "captivity" — in, say, a middle-class neighborhood of what the Centers for Disease Control call a Metropolitan Statistical Area — has a life expectancy of seventy or more years. For orangutans in the wild in Borneo and Malaysia, the life expectancy is thirty-five years; in captivity, fifty years. The wild is not a suffering-free zone or all that frolic-some a location.

The question asked by animal-rights activists are flawed, because they are built on the concept that the origin of rights is in the avoidance of suffering rather than in the pursuit of happiness. The question that needs to be asked — and that will put us in closer proximity to the truth — is not, do they have rights? or, what are those rights? but rather, what is a right?

Rights originate in committed relationships and can be found, both intact 15
and violated, wherever one finds such relationships — in social compacts, within families, between animals, and between people and nonhuman animals. This is as true when the nonhuman animals in question are lions or parakeets as when they are dogs. It is my Airedale whose excellencies have my attention at the moment, so it is with reference to him that I will consider the question, what is a right?

When I imagine situations in which it naturally arises that A defends or honors or respects B's rights, I imagine situations in which the relationship between A and B can be indicated with a possessive pronoun. I might say, "Leave her alone, she's my daughter" or "That's what she wants, and she is my daughter. I think I am bound to honor her wants." Similarly, "Leave her alone, she's my mother." I am more tender of the happiness of my mother, my father, my child, than I am of other people's family members; more tender of my friends' happinesses than your friends' happinesses, unless you and I have a mutual friend.

Possession of a being by another has come into more and more disrepute, so that the common understanding of one person possessing another is slavery. But the important detail about the kind of possessive pronoun that I have in mind is reciprocity: If I have a friend, she has a friend. If I have a daughter, she has a mother. The possessive does not bind one of us while freeing the other; it cannot do that. Moreover, should the mother reject the daughter, the word that applies is "disown." The form of disowning that most often appears in the news is domestic violence. Parents abuse children; husbands batter wives.

Some cases of reciprocal possessives have built-in limitations, such as "my patient / my doctor" or "my student / my teacher" or "my agent / my client." Other possessive relations are extremely limited but still remarkably binding: "my neighbor" and "my country" and "my president."

The responsibilities and the ties signaled by reciprocal possession typically are hard to dissolve. It can be as difficult to give up an enemy as to give up a friend, and often the one becomes the other, as though the logic of the possessive pronoun outlasts the forms it chanced to take at a given moment, as though we were stuck with one another. In these bindings, nearly inextricable, are found the origin of our rights. They imply a possessiveness but also recognize an acknowledgment by each side of the other's existence.

The idea of democracy is dependent on the citizens' having knowledge 20 of the government; that is, realizing that the government exists and knowing how to claim rights against it. I know this much because I get mail from the government and see its "representatives" running about in uniforms. Whether I actually have any rights in relationship to the government is less clear, but the idea that I do is symbolized by the right to vote. I obey the government, and, in theory, it obeys me, by counting my ballot, reading the *Miranda* warning to me, agreeing to be bound by the Constitution. My friend obeys me as I obey her; the government "obeys" me to some extent, and, to a different extent, I obey it.

What kind of thing can my Airedale, Drummer, have knowledge of? He can know that I exist and through that knowledge can claim his happinesses, with varying degrees of success, both with me and against me. Drummer can also know about larger human or dog communities than the one that consists only of him and me. There is my household — the other dogs, the cats, my husband. I have had enough dogs on campuses to know that he can learn that Yale exists as a neighborhood or village. My older dog, Annie, not only knows that Yale exists but can tell Yalies from townies, as I learned while teaching there during labor troubles.

Dogs can have elaborate conceptions of human social structures, and even of something like their rights and responsibilities within them, but these conceptions are never elaborate enough to construct a rights relationship between a dog and the state, or a dog and the Humane Society. Both of these are concepts that depend on writing and memoranda, officers in uniform, plaques and seals of authority. All of these are literary constructs, and all of them are beyond a dog's ken, which is why the mail carrier who doesn't also happen to be a dog's friend is forever an intruder — this is why dogs bark at mailmen.

It is clear enough that natural rights relations can arise between people and animals. Drummer, for example, can insist, "Hey, let's go outside and do something!" if I have been at my computer several days on end. He can both refuse to accept various of my suggestions and tell me when he fears for his life — such as the time when the huge, white flapping flag appeared out of nowhere, as it seemed to him, on the town green one evening when we were working. I can (and do) say to him either, "Oh, you don't have to worry about that" or, "Uh oh, you're right, Drum, that guy looks dangerous." Just as the government and I — two different species of organism — have developed improvised ways of communicating, such as the vote, so Drummer and I have worked out a number of ways to make our expressions known. Largely through obedience, I have taught him a fair amount about how to get responses from me. Obedience is reciprocal; you cannot get responses from a dog to whom you do not respond accurately. I have enfranchised him in a relationship to me by educating him, creating the conditions by which he can achieve a certain happiness specific to a dog, maybe even specific to an Airedale, inasmuch as this same relationship has allowed me to plumb the happiness of being a trainer and writing this article.

Instructions in this happiness are given terms that are alien to a culture in which liver treats, fluffy windup toys, and miniature sweaters are confused with respect and work. Jack Knox, a sheepdog trainer originally from Scotland, will shake his crook at a novice handler who makes a promiscuous move to praise a dog, and will call out in his Scottish accent, "Eh! Eh! Get back, get BACK! Ye'll no be abusin' the dogs like that in my clinic." America is a nation of abused animals, Knox says, because we are always swooping at them with praise, "no gi'ing them their freedom." I am reminded of Rainer Maria Rilke's account in which the Prodigal Son leaves — has to leave — because everyone loves him, even the dogs love him, and he has no path to the delicate and fierce truth of himself. Unconditional praise and love, in Rilke's story, disenfranchise us, distract us from what truly excites our interest.

In the minds of some trainers and handlers, praise is dishonesty. Paradoxically, it is a kind of contempt for animals that masquerades as a reverence for helplessness and suffering. The idea of freedom means that you do not, at least not while Jack Knox is nearby, helpfully guide your dog through the motions of, say, herding over and over — what one trainer called "explainy-wainy." This is rote learning. It works tolerably well on some handlers, because people have vast unconscious minds and can store complex preprogrammed behaviors. Dogs, on the other hand, have almost no unconscious minds, so they can learn only by thinking. Many children are like this until educated out of it.

If I tell my Airedale to sit and stay on the town green, and someone comes up and burbles, "What a pretty thing you are," he may break his stay to go for a caress. I pull him back and correct him for breaking. Now he holds his stay because I have blocked his way to movement but not because I have punished him. (A correction blocks one path as it opens another for desire to work; punishment blocks desire and opens nothing.) He holds his stay now, and — because the stay opens this possibility of work, new to a heedless young dog — he watches. If the person goes on talking, and isn't going to gush with praise, I may heel Drummer out of his stay and give him an "Okay" to make friends. Sometimes something about the person makes Drummer feel that reserve is in order. He responds to an insincere approach by sitting still, going down into himself, and thinking, "This person has no business pawing me. I'll sit very still, and he will go away." If the person doesn't take the hint from Drummer, I'll give the pup a little backup by saying, "Please don't pet him, he's working," even though he was not under any command.

The pup reads this, and there is a flicker of a working trust now stirring in the dog. Is the pup grateful? When the stranger leaves, does he lick my hand, full of submissive blandishments? This one doesn't. This one says nothing at all, and I say nothing much to him. This is a working trust we are developing, not a mutual congratulation society. My backup is praise enough for him; the use he makes of my support is praise enough for me.

Listening to a dog is often praise enough. Suppose it is just after dark and we are outside. Suddenly there is a shout from the house. The pup and I both look toward the shout and then toward each other: "What do you think?" I don't so much as cock my head, because Drummer is growing up, and I want to know what he thinks. He takes a few steps toward the house, and I follow. He listens again and comprehends that it's just Holly, who at fourteen is much given to alarming cries and shouts. He shrugs at me and goes about his business. I say nothing. To praise him for this performance would make about as much sense as praising a human being for the same thing. Thus:

A. What's that?
B. I don't know. [Listens] Oh, it's just Holly.
A. What a goooooood human being!
B. Huh?

This is one small moment in a series of like moments that will culminate in an Airedale who on a Friday will have the discrimination and confidence required to take down a man who is attacking me with a knife and on Saturday clown and play with the children at the annual Orange Empire Dog Club Christmas party.

People who claim to speak for animal rights are increasingly devoted to 30 the idea that the very keeping of a dog or a horse or a gerbil or a lion is in and of itself an offense. The more loudly they speak, the less likely they are to be in a rights relation to any given animal, because they are spending so much time in airplanes or transmitting fax announcements of the latest Sylvester Stallone antifur rally. In a 1988 *Harper's* forum, for example, Ingrid Newkirk, the national director of People for the Ethical Treatment of Animals, urged that domestic pets be spayed and neutered and ultimately phased out. She prefers, it appears, wolves — and wolves someplace else — to Airedales and, by a logic whose interior structure is both emotionally and intellectually forever closed to Drummer, claims thereby to be speaking for "animal rights."

She is wrong. I am the only one who can own up to my Airedale's inalienable rights. Whether or not I do it perfectly at any given moment is no more refutation of this point than whether I am perfectly my husband's mate at any given moment refutes the fact of marriage. Only people who know Drummer, and whom he can know, are capable of this relationship. PETA and the Humane Society and the ASPCA and the Congress and NOW — as institutions — do have the power to affect my ability to grant rights to Drummer but are otherwise incapable of creating conditions or laws or rights that would increase his happiness. Only Drummer's owner has the power to obey him — to obey who he is and what he is capable of — deeply enough to grant him rights and open up the possibility of happiness.

AFTERWORD

Hearne's eclectic and resourceful mind — alluding to philosophers, novelists, and etymologies — pulls everything into her ken. The membrane of sophisticated discourse is allusion. If the first sentence of Vicki Hearne's essay rings no bells, the reader has missed something. The reader has not missed a step in an argument — and may continue to read the essay without hindrance — but a cross-reference to the beginning of a great novel. If the reader recognizes the allusion, fine; but suppose the sentence rings a faint bell, as if something is almost quoted. Look in a book of quotations under the heading of "happy." In my library three out of six such books led to the source.

"There are chimpanzees who love precision the way musicians or fanatical housekeepers or accomplished hypochondriacs do." If this notion of a chimpanzee sounds too anthropomorphic to you, look at her arguments in Adam's Task; *she anticipates objections. One of Hearne's habits in writing is to anticipate objections; sometimes her exposition reads like dialogue.*

BOOKS AVAILABLE IN PAPERBACK

Adam's Task: Calling Animals by Name. New York: Random House–Vintage. *Essays.*

Bandit: Dossier of a Dangerous Dog. New York: HarperCollins. *Essays.*

In the Absence of Horses. Princeton: Princeton University Press. *Poetry.*

EDWARD
HOAGLAND

*E*DWARD HOAGLAND *(b. 1932) published his first novel two years after graduating from college. He spent a decade writing novels and short stories and more recently has concentrated on essays for* Harper's, *the* Atlantic, *and other magazines, editorials for the* New York Times, *and books of travel. His book-length journal of time spent in British Columbia is called* Notes from the Century Before *(1965).* African Calliope *(1979) is subtitled* A Journey to the Sudan, *and there are essay collections —* The Courage of Turtles *(1971),* Walking the Dead Diamond River *(1973),* Red Wolves and Black Bears *(1976),* The Tugman's Passage *(1982) and, in 1992,* The Final Fate of the Alligators *and* Balancing Acts, *from which we take this essay.*

Hoagland worked with a traveling circus when he was young and later used the experience in a novel. Mostly he has worked as a writer. He returns to particular themes or topics: New York tugboats, tugboat captains, tugboat crews; animals; and life in the woods. He divides his time as well as his prose between Manhattan, where he lives with his family during the school year, and a small town in remote northern Vermont, where the Hoagland family spends its summers. Reading this author's essays, one flips back and forth between the wilderness of the north country and the wilderness of city streets.

Hoagland's work as an essayist is celebratory. He says somewhere that writers either "prefer subject matter that they rejoice in or subject matter they deplore and wish to savage with ironies. . . . I'm of the first type." He celebrates without heaping sugar on, and he is capable of irony, but joy is his major note — not merely joy in subject matter, writing happily about what makes you happy, but joy in the act of writing. Joy and caprice together make the shape of "Learning to Eat Soup."

Photo by Thomas Victor

Learning to Eat Soup

Learning to eat soup: Like little boats that go out to sea, I push my spoon ahead of me.

At my parents' wedding in Michigan, one of Mother's uncles leaned over before the cake cutting and whispered to her, "Feed the brute and flatter the ass." The uncles threw rice at them as they jumped into their car, and Dad, after going a mile down the road, stopped and silently swept it out. That night, before deflowering each other (both over thirty), they knelt by the bed to consecrate the experience.

To strike a balance is everything. If a person sings quietly to himself on the street, people smile with approval; but if he talks, it's not all right; they think he's crazy. The singer is presumed to be happy and the talker unhappy, which counts heavily against him. . . . To strike a balance: If, for example, walking in the woods, we flake off a bit of hangnail skin and an ant drags this bonanza away, we might say that the ants were feasting on human flesh, but probably wouldn't. On the other hand, if a man suffers a heart attack there and festers undiscovered, then we would.

Baby inside M.'s stomach feels like the popping and simmering of oatmeal cooking, as I lay my hand across. Pain, "a revelation to me like fireworks, those comets that whirl," she says in the labor room. She lies like a boy under stress in the canoe-shaped cot, the nurses gathering gravely, listening to the baby's heartbeat through the stethoscope between contractions — heart like a drumbeat sounded a block away. Baby, with bent monkey feet, is born still in its sac. Doctor is unlocatable. The interns gather. A nurse picks up both phones simultaneously and calls him with urgency. The crowd, the rooting and cheering in the delivery room — as if the whole world were gathered there — after the solitary labor room.

Very old people age somewhat as bananas do.   5

Two Vietcong prisoners: An American drew crosses on their foreheads, one guy's cross red, other guy's green, to distinguish which was the target and which the decoy to be thrown out of the helicopter to make the target talk.

Winter travel: Snowbanks on river ice means thin ice because snow layers shield the ice from the cold. And water is always wearing it away from underneath; therefore keep on the *inside* of curves and away from all cut-banks, where the current is fast. Travel on barest ice and avoid obstacles like rocks and drift piles sticking through, which also result in a thinning of the cover. Gravel bars may dam the river, causing overflows, which "smoke" in cold weather like a fire, giving some warning before you sink through the slush on top and into the overflow itself. Overflows also can occur in slow sections of the river where the ice is thick and grinds against itself. A special danger area is the junction of incoming creeks whose whirlpools have kept the water open under a concealment of snow. If the water level falls abruptly, sometimes you can walk on the dry edges of the riverbed under solid ice which remains on top as though you were in a tunnel, but that can be dangerous because bears enjoy following such a route too.

You butter a cat's paws when moving it to a new home, so it can find its way back after going out exploring the first time.

My friend Danny Chapman, the Ringling Bros. clown, had a sliding, circus sort of face, like the eternal survivor, marked by the sun, wind, pain, bad luck, and bad dealings, the standard lusts and equivocations, like a stone that the water has slid over for sixty years. Face was much squarer when not in august-clown blackface, its seams smudged by reacting to all he'd seen, and holding so many expressions in readiness that none could be recognized as characteristic of him.

Success in writing, versus painting, means that your work becomes   10 *cheaper,* purchasable by anybody.

The *New York Times* is a vast democratic souk in which every essayist can find a place to publish his or her voice. But otherwise, for a native New Yorker with proud and lengthy ties to the city, it's not so easy. The *New York Review of Books* is published by a group of sensibilities that give the impression of having been born in this metropolis but of wishing they were Londoners instead. And the *New Yorker* traditionally has been the home of writers and editors born in Columbus, Ohio — who yearned so much to seem like real New Yorkers that their city personalities in print had an artificial, overeager sophistication and snobbery.

I ride my stutter, posting over its jolts, swerving with it, guiding it, if never "mastering" it.

At the annual sports show at the New York Colosseum: "Stay straight with sports," says a poster, a picture of a girl wearing a T-shirt with that slogan over her breasts. An exhibitor tells me he just saw two men fondling each other in the men's room — "It just turns your stomach." A woman wearing a huge odd-looking hat made of dried pheasants' heads is cooing affectionately at a cageful of pheasants. A skinning contest is held in which three taxidermists go to work on the carcasses of three Russian boars.

"If two people are in love they can sleep on the blade of a knife."

Karl Wheeler used a baby bottle until he was five years old, whereupon   15
his mother said to him, "That's your last bottle, Karl. When you break that
one you'll never get another one!" and he began to toss it idly in the air to
catch it, but missed.

First white men in British Columbia sold some of the Indians their
names: Ten dollars for a fine name like O'Shaughnessy, five dollars for the
more modest Harris.

At six A.M. I shoot a porcupine in the garage (knew about it from seeing
Bimbo vomit from a fear reaction after his many tangles with porcupines).
It goes under the building to die but not too far for a rake to reach. I take
it to Paul Brooks's house. In his freezer he has woodchucks, beaver, bear,
deer, bobcat, and porcupine meat (he is a man living only on Social Security),
and he cleans it for me. We see it's a mama with milk in her breasts. His
mouth fills with saliva as he works; he's also preparing a venison roast for
lunch, with garlic salt, Worcestershire sauce, pepper, onions, etc. Says this
time of year, first of June, the woodchucks are light as your hat, the winter
has been so long for them; you can feel their thin legs. Porcupine liver is a
delicacy, the rest not so much. The porcupine had been chewing at my
garage for the salts; I eat the porcupine; therefore I'm eating my garage —
dark drumsticks that night by kerosene lamp. Game tastes herby even
without herbs — best is bobcat and muskrat, in my experience, not counting
big meats like moose. One countryman we know had his ashes scattered on
his muskrat pond. The porcupine had chattered its teeth and rattled its poor
quiver of quills as I approached with my gun. Was so waddly it could not
even limp properly when badly wounded. Lay on its side gurgling, choking,
and sighing like a man dying.

At the Freifields' one-room cabin, with snowshoes hung under steep
roof, I read Larry's father's hectic journal, written in Austro-English, of
desperate orphanhood on the Austrian-Russian front in WWI. He, adopted
by the rival armies as they overran the town, living in the trenches with
them, living off stolen crusts otherwise, surviving the bombardments, dodging the peasants who hated Jews, but cherished by Austrian soldiers, who
then were killed — saw one's legs blown off just after he'd changed places
with him. That night peed in his pants in the trench and froze himself to the
ground.

"Old Bet," the first circus elephant in America, was bought by Hachaliah
Bailey from an English ship captain in 1815 but was shot eventually by
religious fanatics in Connecticut as resembling the biblical Behemoth of the
Book of Job (as indeed she did).

My first overtly sexual memory is of me on my knees in the hallway 20
outside our fifth-grade classroom cleaning the floor, and Lucy Smith in a
white blouse and black skirt standing above me, watching me.
My first memory is of being on a train which derailed in a rainstorm in
Dakota one night when I was two — and of hearing, as we rode in a hay
wagon toward the distant weak lights of a little station, that a boy my age
had just choked to death from breathing mud. But maybe my first real
memory emerged when my father was dying. I was thirty-five and I
dreamed so incredibly vividly of being dandled and rocked and hugged by
him, being only a few months old, giggling helplessly and happily.

Had supper at a local commune where they have a fast turnover and
have made life hard. They buy twenty-dollar used cars instead of spending
two hundred dollars, use kerosene instead of the electricity they have, and
a team of horses to plow. They got 180 gallons of maple syrup out of their
trees, but they washed 1,400 sugaring pails in the bathtub in cold water,
never having put in a hot-water heater. Much husky embracing, like wres-
tlers; and before they eat their supper they have Grace, where twenty-some
people clasp hands around the table, meditating and squeezing fingers.
Bread bakes on a puffy wood stove. Rose hips and chili peppers hang from
the ceiling on strings, other herbs everywhere and pomegranates and jars of
basic grains. The toilet is a car on blocks up the hill. Supper is a soup bowl
full of rice and chard and potato pancakes with two sour sauces and apple
butter, yogurt for dessert; and we drink from mason jars of water passed
around. And the final "course" is dental floss, which everybody solemnly
uses. A dulcimer is played with the quill of a feather, accompanied by bongo
drums. The women ended the public festivities by each announcing where
she was going to sleep that night, which bedroom or which hayloft, in case
anyone wished to join her. Clothing is heaped in a feed bin near the bottom
of the stairs, and everybody is supposed to reach in in the morning and remove
the first items that fit them and come to hand, without regard for which
particular sex the clothes were originally made for. The saddest moment of
the evening for me was when a little girl came around to her mother carrying a hairbrush in her hand and asking to be put to bed. The mother lost
her temper. "Why run to me?" she said. "Everybody in this room is your
parent. Anybody can brush your hair and tell you a story and put you to bed."

Manhattan, now 14,310 acres, was 9,800.

Bernard Malamud speaks of writing as a battle: "go to paper" with a
novel. At age sixty-one is trying to "write wise," a new aim, and hard. Being
between books, I say I'm in a period of withdrawal and inaction like that of
a snake that is shedding its skin.

On the crest of Moose Mountain is an old birch growing low and twisty 25
out of the ruins of a still older, bigger bole, surrounded by ferns, and it's
there that the deer that feed in my field bed down during the day.

There is a whole literary genre that consists, first, of foolish writing and then later capitalizing upon the foolishness by beating one's breast and crying *mea culpa*. Why *was* I a white Black Panther, a drug swallower, a jackbooted feminist, a jet-set-climbing novelist, a 1940s Communist? How interesting and archetypal of me to have shared my generation's extremes.

Busybodies are called in Yiddish *kochleffl*, "cooking spoon," because they stir people up.

The hollow in the center of the upper lip is where "the angel touched you and told you to forget what you had seen in heaven."

Wife of F.'s uncle, to prevent him from going to work one morning when she preferred he stay home, set the alarm so that it seemed it was too late for him to make the train when he woke. But he did rush so terribly he got to the station, and there collapsed and died, and she, only twenty-seven, never remarried.

Joyce consulted Jung, who diagnosed his poor daughter as incurably 30 schizophrenic partly on the evidence of her brilliant, obsessive punning. Joyce remarked that he, too, was a punner. "You are a deep-sea diver," said Jung. "She is drowning."

The cure for stuttering of holding stones in one's mouth works because of the discomfort of them rattling against one's teeth. Stones from a crocodile's stomach were thought to be best.

Amerigo Vespucci said that Indian women enlarged their lovers' sexual parts by applying venomous insects to them.

After losing her virginity at seventeen, she felt unstoppered on the street, like a hollow tube, as though the wind could blow right through her.

The sea, at the village of Soya on Hokkaido island in 1792, was so fertile that twelve quarts of dry rice could be bartered for 1,200 herring, 100 salmon, 300 trout, or 3 sealskins.

How Davy Crockett kept warm when lost in the woods one night: 35 climbing thirty feet up a smooth tree trunk and sliding down.

Am drunk from a soft-shell-crab lunch with Random House's Joe Fox, but stutter so vigorously with William Shawn as to obscure both from him and myself my drunkenness — stutter through it and give myself time to recall names like Numeiry and Assad, necessary to win Shawn's backing for the trip to Africa. He, as reported, is excessively solicitous of my comfort and state of mind; insulated and jittery; heated by electric heater (in August), yet fanned by electric fan; in his shirtsleeves, and immediately suggests I remove my coat. He has an agonized, bulging baby's head with swallowed-up eyes, like that of the tormented child in Francis Bacon's painting *The Scream*. Questions me effectively, however, on my knowledge of the Sudan and the prospects for a salable article there. Says OK. I go to 42nd St. and watch screwing to relax — crazily enough, less is charged to see live souls (twenty-five cents) than for a porno flick — then walk home. Lunch the next day with Alfred Kazin, my old teacher (and the day after that with Barthelme, who has just broken through a writing block, he says, and is therefore more cheerful and sober than I have seen him in a considerable while; says women's movement will produce changes as profound as the abolition of slavery). Kazin as always is a veritable tumult of impressions, like H. S. Commager and other busy intellectuals I have liked, but in Kazin's case it is enormously in earnest and felt. Expresses hurt at Bellow's recent inexplicable anger. Otherwise an outpouring of talk about his new book on the forties, when he published his first book and met the literary figures of the day. Played violin with drunken Alan Tate. Advances the idea that William James, a hero of his, is a better direct heir of Emerson than Thoreau; also the view that students now resent the fact that a professor knows more than they do, want him to learn along with them in class, as in group therapy, and when caught out on homework facts, get offended instead of trying to fake through, as in the old days. On Ph.D. orals, the candidates seem to have no favorite poem, no poem they can quote from, when he asks them for one at the end.

I like Easterners more than Westerners but Western geography more than Eastern geography; and I like the country more than the city, but I like city people more than country people.

Essays, the most conversational form, have naturally drawn me, who have a hard time speaking with my actual mouth.

Tail end of hurricane rains buckets, flooding Barton River. Then the sky clears with nearly full moon, and I hear the deer whickering and whanging to one another gleefully, the mountain behind them gigantic and white.

Bellow says in Jerusalem journal that "light may be the outer garment of 40 God."

Oil spills seem to attract aquatic birds; the sheen may resemble schooling fish. Also, oil slicks calm the surface, look like a landing area.

Roth speaks of his debt to both Jean Genet and the Fugs for *Portnoy*. Roth a man who wears his heart on his sleeve, thus rather vulnerable to insult and injury; part of his exceptional generosity. Tells story of man bleeding in front of God but trying to hide blood from His sight apologetically.

William Gaddis: jockeylike, narrow-boned, fastidious Irishman, clever and civilized, with none of the usual hangdog bitterness of the neglected writer.

Warhol: keen, Pan face with tight manipulated skin that makes it ageless except for his eyes. Bleached hair hanging to his leather collar. Fame based upon being immobile.

Pete Hamill, bursting personality, does columns in half an hour, movie 45 script in three weeks, discipline based upon not drinking till day's stint is through. Fewer bar brawls now, more empathetic, though still lives from a suitcase. "Irish Ben Hecht," he laughs.

Malamud: not at all the "Jewish businessman's face" I'd heard about, but a sensitive, gentle face, often silent or dreamy at Podhoretz's, disagreeing with the host and Midge, but holds his tongue and hugs him at the end with professional gratitude to an editor who once published him. When he speaks, his voice is young, light, and quick, an enthusiast's, idealist's. Hurt by attacks on him in *Jerusalem Post,* for dovishness. Extremely solicitous of me, as kind in his way as Bellow, though style of it is modulated lower. Both of us distressed by Israeli's grinning description of Arab prisoners being beaten up. William Phelps says he thinks the Palestinians probably have a point but that he's not interested in hearing what it is. Podhoretz mentions Israel's "Samson option," pulling everything down, and makes fun of Malamud's "ego" when he's left.

Grace Paley: short, stocky woman who at first sight on the Sarah Lawrence campus I mistook for the cleaning woman; asked her where the men's room was. We rode rubbing knees throughout that semester in the back seat of a car pool. She'd been marching in protests since high school (Ethiopia and Spanish civil war), but her exhilaration at being arrested in Washington peace march in midterm reminded me of my own exuberance at completing the hard spells of army basic training. Yes, we were good enough!

Heard MacLeish at YMHA. Afterward unrecovered yet from defeat of his play *Scratch* on B'way. Sweetness and bounce of his voice, however, is unchanged in twenty years; sounds forty, a matinee tenor, and the old lilt to his rhetoric. Face like a sachem's, too wise, too heroic, with a public man's nose. Talks of friendships with Joyce and Hemingway and imitates Sandburg's *O* very well. Talks of Saturday Club in Boston where monthly Harlow Shapley debated Robert Frost. Reminisces of artillery lieutenant days in World War I, "making the world safe for democracy," where his brother was killed. Five years later he and other nondead *did* die a bit when they realized it had been a "commercial" war and they had been lied to. He is a man of Hector-type heroes. Says Andrew Marvell poem was written while going home from Persia after his father's death.

Berryman given five-thousand-dollar prize at the Guggenheim reading, wearing a graybeard's beard which hides tieless collar. Reads best "Dream Songs," plus two sonnets and Rilke, Ralph Hodgson, and eighteenth-century Japanese poet. Emphatically, spoutingly drunk, reads with frail man's grotesqueries, contortions, and his own memorable concoction of earnestness, coyness, staginess, name dropping, and absolutely forceful, rock-bottom directness. Becomes louder and louder at the end of this floodlighted moment after long years of obscurity and hardship. Here was the current Wild Man, people thought, successor to Pound, there being one to a generation, though many others may have been reminded of Dylan Thomas as he fell into the arms of Robert Lowell, punching him affectionately, when he finished. His whole life was thereupon paraded before him, when old mistresses and chums and students like me came up, expecting recognition, and one of his old wives, presenting him with a son whom obviously he hadn't laid eyes on for a long while. He boomed with love and guilt, with repeated thanks for letters informing him that So-and-so had had a child or remarried, till one was wearied of watching. One felt guilty too, as though competing for his attention with the neglected son. I felt Berryman had not long to live and I ought to be content with my memories of him and lessons learned and not join in the hounding of him. Nevertheless, I did go next afternoon to the Chelsea Hotel, with bronze plaques outside memorializing other tragic figures, like Thomas and Brendan Behan. He'd said the son would be there, so I was afraid that, like my last visit with Bellow, I would be taking time away from a son who needed to see him much more. But the son had left — all that remained was a note in Ann B.'s handwriting. Instead a *Life* photographer and reporter were talking with him, plying him with drinks, though he was holding back dignifiedly, talking of fame, of Frost, and his own dog Rufus. Frost was a shit who tried to hurt him, but he quoted the wonderful couplet about God forgiving our little faux pas if we forgive Him His great big joke on us. Is bombastic in his total commitment to words. Legs look very small, but chest inflates with importance of uttering snatches of poems, till he collapses in coughs. Rubs beard and hair exhaustedly, recklessly spendthrift with his strength, and begins harder drinking; leads me to bar, where waiter, thinking from his red face and thin clothing that he is a bum, won't serve him till he lays a ten-dollar bill on the table. I soon leave, but he was hospitalized within a couple of days. "Twinkle" was his favorite word at this time. He used it for commentary, by itself, and irony, or expostulation, quoting an enemy like Oscar Williams, then merely adding a somber "Twinkle."

Turgenev's brain was the heaviest ever recorded, 4.7 pounds; three is average.

Child's tale about a man who suffered from shortness of breath. Afraid he would run out, he blew up a bunch of balloons as an extra supply for emergencies. Blew up so many that he floated away holding on to them.

Updike comes to U. of Iowa for first workshop session in three years (hasn't really taught for sixteen years) but handles himself in a classy manner nevertheless, and very well prepared with students' manuscripts beforehand, and in the exhilaration of reading his own work in front of one thousand people in McBride Hall (which we call Mammal Hall because it's part of Nat'l Hist. Museum), freely sheds his private-person role that had made him a bit stiff before, when he'd refused even a newspaper interview. Signs autograph cards for eleven-year-old boys and physics texts for Japanese students and mimeo forms for students with nothing better to offer him. Wife is ample, attractive woman with large, intense face, obviously both loving and sexy, a relaxed, close companion — he is wearing a wedding ring and ignoring the ambitious students who show up for his morning class wearing cocktail dresses. We talk of Africa — both finishing Africa books — and classmates and lit. hierarchies. He mentions Cheever's drunkenness — once he had to dress him after a party like dressing a father. Our mothers are same age. "Poor Johnny," his said, watching a TV program about senility with him recently.

Updike says he quit teaching years ago because he "felt stupid," seeing only one way to write a given story properly, not the endless alternatives students proposed in discussions.

Indians used to scratch small children with mouse teeth fastened to a stick as a punishment for crying in front of white men. (White man, of course, a "skinned" man.)

Short stories tend to be boat-shaped, with a lift at each end, to float.   55

Richard Yates says art is a result of a quarrel with oneself, not others.

Five toes to a track means it's wild, four toes means cat or dog.

Writers customarily write in the morning and try to make news, make love, or make friends in the afternoon. But alas, I write all day.

Bellow says he spent the first third of his life absorbing material, the second third trying to make himself famous, and the last third trying to evade fame.

"A woman without a man is like a fish without a bicycle": T-shirt.   60

People say they'll take a dip in the sea as if it were like dipping into a book, but I nearly drowned in surf's riptide off Martha's Vineyard's South Beach. Repeatedly changed swimming strokes to rest myself as I struggled in the water, surf too loud to shout over, and I'm too nearsighted to see where to shout to. Reaching beach, I sprawled for an hour before moving further. Spent next day in bed, next week aching.

New England is "pot-bound," says Charlton Ogburn; thus superfertile.

Petrarch, climbing Mount Ventoux in 1336, began the Renaissance by being the first learned man ever to climb a mountain only for the view.

Rahv told Roth, "You can't be both Scott Fitzgerald and Franz Kafka."

People who marry their great loves sometimes wish they'd married their best friends; and vice versa.   65

Trapeze artists some days complain "there's too much gravity," when a change of the weather or the magnetic field affects their bodies. Elvin Bale bought his heel-hook act from Geraldine Soules, who after a fall started doing a dog act instead. Soules had, in turn, bought it from Vander Barbette, who, walking funny after *his* fall, had become a female impersonator and trainer of circus showgirls.

In old-time Georgia you ate mockingbird eggs for a stutter; boiled an egg for jaundice and went and sat beside a red-ant anthill and ate the white and fed the yolk to the ants. For warts, you bled them, put the blood on grains of corn, and fed that to a chicken. Fiddlers liked to put a rattlesnake rattle inside their fiddles.

The fifties are an interim decade of life, like the thirties. In the thirties one still has the energy of one's twenties, combined with the judgment (sometimes) of the forties. In the fifties one still has the energy of one's forties, combined with the composure of the sixties.

The forties are the old age of youth and the fifties are the youth of old age.

Adage: "God sends meat, the Devil sends cooks."   70

Carnival stuntman whom Byron Burford banged the drum for used to swallow live rats and Ping-Pong balls, upchucking whichever ones the crowd asked for first. Stunned the rats with cigar smoke before he swallowed them.

> *The intellect of man is forced to choose*
> *Perfection of the life, or of the work,*
> *And if it take the second must refuse*
> *A heavenly mansion, raging in the dark.*
> — YEATS "Choice"

Lying to my lieutenant as a private at Fort Sam Houston as to whether I'd shaved that morning before inspection, or only the night before — he reaching out and rubbing his hand down my face.

Glenn Gould liked to practice with the vacuum cleaner on, to hear "the skeleton of the music."

Nature writers, I sometimes think, are second only to cookbook writers in being screwed up.

Deer follow moose in these woods, says Toad. I say maybe they look like father (mother) figures to them.

At Academy-Institute ceremonial, the big scandal is Ellison's lengthy introduction of Malamud for a prize and Barbara Tuchman's brutal interruption of it. Stegner very youthful, as befits an outdoorsman. Cowley very food-hungry as always, as befits a 1930s survivor. Commager tells my wife that his daughter loved me and so he loved me. Lots of cold-faced ambitious poets cluster around each other and Northrop Frye; Galway seems likably unaffected and truthful next to them. Ditto Raymond Carver. Ellison had tried to speak of blacks and Jews.

Joe Flaherty's line for the Brooklyn Bridge: "the Irish gangplank."

Whale mother's milk would stain the sea after she was harpooned, and the calf would circle the ship forlornly. "I do not say that John or Jonathan will realize all this," said Thoreau, in finishing *Walden;* and that's the central and tragic dilemma as the environmental movement fights its rearguard battles.

In starving midwinter, foxes catch cats by rolling on their backs like a kitten ready to play.

Warblers average eight thousand or ten thousand songs a day in spring; vireo twenty thousand. Woodchucks wag their tails like a dog. Blue jays like to scare other birds by imitating a red-shouldered hawk.

My bifocals are like a horse's halter, binding the lower half of my eyes to the day's work.

At my frog pond a blue heron circles low overhead while a brown-muzzled black bear clasps chokecherry bushes and eats off them thirty yards away from me.

Only six hours old, a red calf stumbles toward the barn, as mother is herded in by Hugh Stevens on ATV vehicle, and is eventually tied to its mother's stanchion with hay twine, while a six-inch red tab of its previous cord hangs from its belly. It's as shiny as a new pair of shoes, its deerlike hooves perfectly formed, including the dew claws. Mother and calf had had a brief wild idyll under the summer sky before they were discovered by Hugh — the last sky this vealer will ever see.

Crocodiles yawn to cool themselves in hot weather, but coyotes yawn as   85
an agonistic device. Mice yawn from sleepiness, as people do, but we also yawn from boredom, which is to say contempt — agonistic again.

Old people seem wise because they have grown resigned and because they remember the axioms, even if they've forgotten the data.

"When you come to the end of your life, make sure you're used up."

I trust love more than friendship, which is why I trust women more than men.

"All hat and no cows." Or, "Big hat, no cattle": Texas saying.

"Eat with the rich, laugh with the poor."   90

Buying a new car after thirteen years, I discover why country people like to keep the old one about the yard. First, it makes the house look occupied. Second, it's a nesting site for ducks and geese and a shelter for chickens during the day. Third, it reminds you of *you*.

AFTERWORD

The essay, as defined in this book and by Edward Hoagland, includes the opinions and therefore the person of the essayist. Yet the essayist learns ways to present himself without appearing narcissistic. Try not to begin paragraphs with "I." Even if you almost begin the paragraph with "I" — as in, "Later, I" — you have avoided the ego pronoun's visual prominence by placing it in a tucked-in starting place of the paragraph.

Sometimes, avoidance of "I" is more egotistical than "I," as when a sporting figure speaks of himself in the third person; asked what he eats for breakfast, a third baseman replies, "Wade Boggs eats chicken livers for breakfast."

The New York Times *book critic Christopher Lehman-Haupt, reviewing essays by Edward Hoagland, noted, "The typical Hoagland essay announces his subject, broaches it, and at once collapses sideways into the author's delight and curiosity in things, catching us up so readily in its apparently free associations and random anecdotes that we quickly forget the starting point and hardly care to remember."*

Yes, but . . . whoa! *"Learning to Eat Soup"* is nothing but *"free association and random anecdotes."* Maybe that's the first attraction, for writer and reader alike: at last, an essay without a structure! No argument, no definition, no description, no narrative, no process analysis, no Who? Why? What? When? Where?

So what holds it together? Its randomness?

The editor has reserved, until now, his knowledge of the provenance of this essay. Edward Hoagland writes in a letter: " *'Learning to Eat Soup'* was compiled in response to a request for a journal selection." On a trip to Italy Hoagland brought with him his five-hundred page journal, twenty years in the making, and made selections.

Is it possible that nothing is random, that everything is determined, that indeterminate human thought is impossible, that one thing always leads to another?

BOOKS AVAILABLE IN PAPERBACK

Balancing Acts. New York: Simon & Schuster. *Essays.*

The Courage of Turtles: Fifteen Essays by Edward Hoagland. New York: Lyons & Burford.

The Final Fate of Alligators. Santa Barbara: Capra Press. *Essays.*

Heart's Desire: The Best of Edward Hoagland. New York: Summit Books. *Essays.*

Red Wolves and Black Bears. New York: Penguin Books. *Essays.*

Walking the Dead Diamond River. New York: Lyons & Burford. *Essays.*

SUE
HUBBELL

S UE HUBBELL (b. 1935) commutes between the District of Columbia, where she keeps a husband, and Missouri, where she keeps bees on a farm in the Ozarks. Her essays turn up in the New York Times, Smithsonian, *and the* New Yorker — *where we found this piece of pie research. She has published four books:* A Country Year: Living the Questions *(1986),* A Book of Bees and How to Keep Them *(1988),* On This Hilltop *(1991), and* Broadsides from the Other Orders: A Book of Bugs *(1993).*

The Great American Pie Expedition

Nobody needs drug-store ice cream; pie is good enough for anybody.
— SINCLAIR LEWIS, *"Main Street"*

Easy as pie. It's easy to make good, tasty, comforting, serviceable pie. Of course, excellent pie is harder to make, and harder to find, but excellence is always rare. The Shaker Lemon Pie served at Shaker Village of Pleasant Hill, near Harrodsburg, Kentucky, is an excellent pie. The Shakers invented this

___ Photo by Nancy Stacel

pie back in the early 1800s, when they began trading goods they grew or manufactured for the few necessities they couldn't produce. Lemons, which they considered an important item in a healthy diet, were one of the "world's goods" they needed. Their lemons came all the way from New Orleans and were so dear that the Shakers believed it a sin to waste any part of them, so they devised a recipe that would use the whole lemon.

Pie from that recipe is served in the public dining room of the Trustees' House at Shaker Village. The pie has a beautifully browned crust — surprisingly thick, but so light and flaky that it shatters under a fork. Inside is a generous lemon custard, with bits of lemon pulp and rind throughout. The sourness of the lemon plays off the sweetness of the custard in an altogether delicious way. It is a pretty pie, too. Here is the way to make both the crust and the filling. The recipes are from *We Make You Kindly Welcome,* a cookbook available at the restaurant.

Crust for a 9-Inch Pie

  2 C. flour
  1 tsp. salt
 $^2/_3$ C. plus 4 tbsp. shortening
  4 tbsp. cold water

Mix flour and salt. Cut shortening into flour until it forms very small balls. Sprinkle in water, a tbsp. at a time, while mixing lightly with a fork until the flour is moistened. Mix it into a ball that cleans the bowl. Do not overwork the dough. Roll out on floured board.

(The less you handle dough, the better; handling toughens it. A good crust must be crisp, even at the risk of being a bit crumbly.)

Shaker Lemon Pie

  2 large lemons with very thin rinds
  4 eggs, well beaten
  2 C. sugar
     Crust for pie

Slice lemons as thin as paper, rind and all. Combine with sugar; mix well. Let stand 2 hours, or preferably overnight, blending occasionally. Add beaten eggs to lemon mixture; mix well. Turn into 9-inch pie shell, arranging lemon slices evenly. Cover with top crust. Cut several slits near center. Bake at 450° for 15 minutes. Reduce heat to 375° and bake for about 20 minutes or until silver knife inserted near edge of pie comes out clean. Cool before serving.

Pleasant Hill is on U.S. 68, the Harrodsburg Road, which winds past prosperous looking horse farms, curving through stratified rock as it dips down to cross the Kentucky River. There have been no Shakers at Shaker Village since 1923, but it has been restored to its bucolic picturesqueness. After eating the excellent lemon pie, I went back to my car and let my dog, Tazzie, out for a run. We found a sheepy hillside and sprawled out on it, soaking up the early-spring sunshine. Tazzie, who is mostly German shepherd but with soft edges, gazed decorously at the sheep, sniffed the air, and rolled over on her back in the short grass, kicking her feet lazily in the air. I lay on my back, too, staring at fluffy clouds and listening to meadowlarks.

My family has always been a pie family. When my son, Brian, was in high school, he spent more time hitchhiking around the country with friends than I or those in loco parentis at his boarding school ever knew. He and his friends seldom had much money, but they always had enough in their jeans to buy pie and coffee. Fifteen years and more later, he is still an expert on pie in astonishing places. A few years ago, I was driving across the country with him and his wife, Liddy, when, in a small town in Kentucky, an abstracted look came across his face. He said to Liddy, who was driving, "If you'll turn left at the stop sign and then go two blocks, there's a place that has really good pecan pie." We did, and there was. We sat there eating pie and drinking coffee, and, caffeine coursing through our veins, we spun a plan. Someday we would drive around the country on back roads and eat pie. It would be the Great American Pie Expedition. Their lives, alas, are now regulated by jobs, but mine grows freer and more unruly with each passing year, so Tazzie and I had undertaken the pie expedition. We were on its final leg; during the previous summer and autumn, we had been eating pie — some good, some bad, some indifferent — through Pennsylvania, southern New England, and on into Maine, where the blueberry and raspberry pies are glorious. Now we were heading west, through the cream-pie belt.

Before setting out on the initial trip that summer, I had wanted to estab-   5
lish some sort of standard for the expedition — a federal benchmark. I was in Washington, D.C., where I live for part of the year, so my husband and I went to lunch at the United States Senate Family Dining Room, which prides itself on its pie — particularly its pecan pie — nearly as much as it does on its bean soup. It seemed our patriotic duty to order, in addition to the pecan, the Senate Apple Pie, and only fair to add the special of the day, Senate Chocolate Mousse Pie. The last-named turned out to be a triumph of the imitation-food industry, and the apple pie was more government issue than federal benchmark. Both it and the pecan had been warmed up, though not, thank heaven, in a microwave oven. The microwave oven is one of the worst enemies that pie has in restaurant kitchens these days. I remember especially a piece of raspberry pie in Maine that had been microwaved to death. The hot raspberries, all integrity gone, oozed sadly out of the crust, and the pie had a faintly bitter aftertaste. Freshly made, warm pie is one of life's

better things, but after it cools it should be allowed to grow old gently rather than brought back to an unnatural warmth. Our government-issue apple pie was no worse than many apple pies I was to sample on the road, but certainly no better. It contained too much cornstarch filling and too few apples, and those present were flaccid and tasteless. The pecan was a marginal improvement, but so cloying that it would have benefitted from the quarter cup of brandy a friend of mine always adds to pecan-pie filling to cut its sweetness.

A few days later, Tazzie and I headed west and north in search of better pie. In western Maryland, on U.S. 40 at Sideling Hill, we drove through a magnificent roadcut, which is sometimes shown in geology textbooks; it is a place where a great part of the earth's history is laid out. There are signs along the roadside: NO PARKING. NO CLIMBING. No gawking, no looking, don't be interested in what there is to see. When I had driven through there with Brian and Liddy on our trip a few years back, the State of Maryland wasn't so prohibitive, and we had parked, climbed, gawked.

Tazzie and I followed U.S. 40 north into Pennsylvania, stopping by the bank of a stream for Tazzie to run and for me to have a cup of coffee from the Thermos. It was June, and the cow parsnip would soon be in bloom; daisies and buttercups already were. Wild geranium was everywhere. A blackbird, pert and sweet-voiced, was singing. "There's a cabbage white," I told Tazzie, "and there's a tiger swallowtail." I was trying to interest her in butterflies, but she paid them no attention whatever.

I sat sipping my coffee and thinking about pie. Meat pies, according to the Columbia Encyclopedia, have been around since the days of the Romans, but no one mentions fruit pies — or any dessert pies — until the fifteenth century. Even after that, no one ate very much pie until the New World was settled. Americans were the first to understand what pie could be. For instance, the English had been making what they called pompion by cutting a hole in the side of a pumpkin, extracting the seeds and the filaments, stuffing the cavity with apples, and baking the whole. New Englanders improved on this, combining the apples and pumpkin and putting them in a proper pastry. Then they eliminated the apples and added milk, eggs, spices, and molasses to the mashed, stewed pumpkin. Molasses, the colonists' substitute for sugar, was so important for pies that on several occasions a New England town put off its celebration of Thanksgiving for a week or more in anticipation of a shipment of molasses from the West Indies.

Americans discovered that other tasty pies could be made from materials at hand. A mock-cherry pie could be made with Cape Cod cranberries (spiced with raisins from Spain). Vermont pie was made with apples — a fruit successfully transplanted from England — and syrup cooked down from the sap of maple trees. Pie has never been more loved than in nineteenth-century America, where it was not simply dessert but also a normal part of breakfast. The food writer Evan Jones quotes a contemporary observer as noting that in northern New England "all the hill and country towns were full of women who would be mortified if visitors caught them without pie in the house," and that the absence of pie at breakfast "was more noticeable than the scarcity of the Bible." I knew a farmer in Iowa who died at the age of ninety-three a contented man, for he had eaten pie at breakfast every day of his life.

Herrings Family Restaurant is on U.S. 40 — on the eastern outskirts of 10 Uniontown, Pennsylvania. It is called a family restaurant not because it is OK to wear blue jeans there or because the food is moderately priced (although both these things are true), but because the Herring family runs it. I sat in a rosy-orange plastic booth and had a home-style platter of beef stew, and after eating it I hoped that the pies would be as good. There was a choice: banana, coconut, peanut-butter, lemon, cherry-cream, blackberry, apple, cherry, raisin, and peach. A friend had recommended the banana pie, so I ordered that, but I couldn't resist ordering blackberry, too. The waitress looked amused. "I never had anyone order two pieces of pie before," she said. The crust on both pies was superb. The banana was still a little warm, and the filling spilled onto the plate. The bananas had been mashed before cooking, so there was pulp throughout instead of discrete slices. It was a good pie, but the blackberry was even better — tart and beautifully seedy. It was dense with fruit and had just as much filler as was needed, no more. The maker of the pies was pointed out to me — a slim, bespectacled young man. He blushed when I congratulated him on his pie-baking abilities, and told me that he sometimes made the pies but his relatives also made them. "The whole family works at the business," he said. "Grandpap started it. We all work in it." He pointed to the waitress. "She's my cousin."

"We make pies every day," his cousin said as I paid my check. "Doughnuts, too. And bread. And we eat all of them, but we stay skinny."

In the days that followed, I remembered fondly the pie at Herrings, for I had pies so middling as to be not worth reporting and one that was bad enough to be notable. I would not have been cross about this particular peach pie if pie had not been so boasted of on the restaurant's menu, and if it had not been peach season. I had asked for the apricot pie, which I'd heard good things about, but apricot was not available the day I was there, and since it was the height of the peach harvest I didn't think I could go wrong ordering peach pie. The crust was tasteless and thick and rested heavily in the stomach. The cook had been stingy with the peaches, which were suspended in a gluelike filling. I've had bad peach pie *out* of season — I remember especially one canned-peach pie in El Reno, Oklahoma — but during peach season it is hard not to make a good peach pie. Fresh peaches should be sliced and sweetened with enough white or brown sugar to make them pleasant to the taste. Egg yolk mixed with flour is a good thickener for peach pie, and after the thickener, sugar, and peaches have been lightly combined they should be heaped up roundly in an unbaked shell, topped with more crust, and baked. Toward the end of the baking, the pie should be removed briefly from the oven and the top crust brushed with a bit of egg white and sprinkled with sugar and cinnamon; the pie is then returned to the oven to brown prettily. That's all there is to it.

Of course, the underpinning of that pie — the crust — should be adequate. A New York man I know who thinks about pie a great deal says that pie judgments are sexually dimorphic. He believes that women judge a pie by its crust, men by its filling. That's so, says my friend Abby, because women know that the crust is the hardest part to make. That's *not* so, says my friend Linda, who loves both parts too much but eats only the filling, in the vain hope that most of the calories have settled in the crust. The truth is that a good pie can be ruined by a bad crust but a good crust cannot save a bad pie. A crust can be only so good, anyway. It should show off the pie and not call a lot of attention to itself. On my pie expedition I often found that restaurant cooks used frozen pie shells rather than making crusts themselves. In many cases, that was probably a mercy, because if left to their own devices they would make worse. Once, after I had eaten a memorably bad piece of cherry pie in a café in West Virginia the cook and the waitress sat down in my booth to talk. I asked the cook how she made the crust, which was thick and soggy. She told me that it was made of Crisco, flour, and milk. I've had a few bad milk crusts, and I don't use milk myself. Seldom has there been a week in my adult life when I haven't made a pie, and the following is the crust I use more often than any other. It is easy to make, crisp in a way that flakier crusts can't be, and shows off many pie fillings to advantage.

Dough for a Two-Crust Pie

2   C. flour
1   tsp. salt
$^{1}/_{2}$ C. cooking oil
$^{1}/_{4}$ C. water

Mix flour and salt in a bowl and make a hollow in center of the mixture. Quickly blend water and oil together in a cup and pour into hollow in flour-salt mixture. Combine ingredients quickly and lightly with a few strokes of a spoon. Pinch dough in half and roll out each half between two sheets of waxed paper. Peel off top layer of paper. Invert dough into pie pan and remove second layer of waxed paper.

On several occasions in the course of my expedition I stopped at the Mount Nittany Inn, which is just north of Tusseyville on Pennsylvania Route 144, hoping to have its special peanut-butter pie. A man whose pie sense I trust had urged me to try it. "Just don't think about it too much," he said. "Once you get over the idea of it, it's really terrific." But each time I went there the peanut-butter pie was not available, for one reason or another. The inn's proprietor agreed that it was a wonderful pie; his wife made it, he told me, but he didn't know how. "She makes the peanut butter all creamy, and then she freezes it," he said. "But I don't know what all she puts into it. A lot of stuff. Cheese, maybe?" I do hope not. In an effort not to think about *that*, I finally ordered, on my third stop, the inn's walnut pie, which was very good indeed. The crust was perfect, and the filling was similar to that of a good pecan pie, with black walnuts substituted for the pecans. The whole was topped with cream, whipped gently. It was satisfying, but not satisfying enough to drive the peanut-butter pie from my mind. I wish I could stop thinking about it.

I also failed to have the famous sour-cream raisin pie at the Potato City 15
Motor Inn, in Potter County, Pennsylvania. That harsh, empty country, on the northern edge of the state, comes into its own in winter, during hunting and snow seasons. In daisy time, the Potato City Motor Inn is a quiet, unvisited place and serves up no sour-cream raisin pie. I asked the waitress which of the three pies available that day I should order. "None of 'em," she said. The Potato City Motor Inn was originally built as a place for potato growers to meet. Dr. E. L. Nixon, uncle to Himself, was involved in the beginnings of Potato City, where he crossbred potatoes and developed new strains. The cavernous dining rooms of the inn were empty when I was there. I would have liked at least to see the nearby ice mine, "a deep mountainside shaft" that "for no apparent reason forms heavy ice beginning in the spring," according to my Pennsylvania road map, which adds, "In winter the ice disappears." But it was closed. Potter County was in commercial diapause, so we drove on.

I stopped to feed Tazzie in a spruce woods, where bracken grew among the trees. While she ate, I watched clouds of blue butterflies — spring azures — squeezing into nearly opened blackberry blossoms to lay their eggs. We drove east on U.S. 6, a gentle road that wound through small towns filled with well-kept late-nineteenth-century houses surrounded by poppies. In between towns, wild blue phlox and buttercups were in bloom. I heard an Eastern wood pewee calling *pee-a-weeee, peee-a-wee*. But the pie was indifferent until the X-Trail Restaurant, in Mansfield, at the intersection of U.S. 6 and Business Route U.S. 15. The X-Trail is a cheerful, unpretentious restaurant, painted blue, with crisp blue-and-white curtains at mullioned windows. It serves good pie baked in deep-dish pie pans, which is just the way pies should be baked. (These pans are hard to find — something I discovered while shopping for one as a birthday present for Michael, my stepson, who has become interested in pie-making. But a few stores still stock them, and any serious pie-maker should have one.) The X-Trail's coconut-cream pie was cool enough to cut so I ordered some. It was a delicate pie, a handsome pie — monochrome, with white meringue floating on a cream-white filling whose very pallor guaranteed that no packaged mix had been used. The crust was crisp, clean, distinct. The waitress told me that it was the restaurant's most favored pie — even more popular than the black-raspberry pie, which I also sampled, and which was stuffed with juicy berries.

I asked at each of my stops which pie was the most popular, and usually it was the coconut-cream. Coconut-cream is a good year-round pie. My friend Charlie, a Republican, is a pie conservative, and he doesn't believe in cream pies. The only real pies, he says, are of berries or other fruit, but he thinks that no one makes even fruit pies very well anymore. "You're not going to find good apple pie anywhere," he told me. I hoped he was wrong, but as the summer progressed it seemed possible that he might not be. When in doubt, I always ordered apple pie, and it was almost always as bad as the government-issue pie I'd had back in Washington — or worse. With such a standard, small wonder that gardeners with a lot of green tomatoes on their hands at the end of the season and with frost imminent tell us that green-tomato pie is just as good as apple any day.

Charlie wouldn't have approved of the chocolate-meringue pie I had at the Hotel Wyalusing, in Wyalusing, Pennsylvania, just off U.S. 6, by the Susquehanna River. I did. It was made of bittersweet chocolate so rich that the memory of Droste chocolate apples came to me. The meringue was as brown as a toasted marshmallow and so flat and neat that it must have been spread with a knife. I would have enjoyed staying at the Hotel Wyalusing. It was a pleasant place — a former stagecoach stop lovingly restored, its brick front cleaned and its gingerbread woodwork, balconies, and dormers painted pale olive and buff yellow — but I wanted to eat pie at a New Jersey diner, and I wanted to get on to New York City to pick up a sweet-potato pie from Hugh Nelms, the president and corn-breadist of Hoecake International, so I drove on.

I discovered on my pie expedition that making a schedule was often a mistake. Certainly it was this time, because twenty-five miles west of New York City a tractor-trailer rig had tumbled over, and as a result all of northern New Jersey was in gridlock. I coasted, usually in neutral, across the state, reading the *Times* from page 1 through the classifieds, seldom passing the one-mile-per-hour mark. Pie at a diner was the first part of the plan to be abandoned, but I did want that sweet-potato pie. Abby had been telling me about it for years. She said that Nelms sells his pie every Sunday in fine weather at the open-air market at Seventy-seventh Street and Columbus Avenue. It is, she told me, a beautiful pie to look at, and a pie so tasty that she can't resist buying it in the six-inch-wide, hand-held version and eating it on the spot.

I tried to break away to the north, thinking I might come into the city 20 from a different direction, but there had been a two-car collision somewhere in Connecticut, and that made the northern roads sluggish, too. Pie thoughts faded, and all I could think of was escape. I fled to the wilds of western Massachusetts and took stock. Sweet-potato pie would have to be added to my list of pies not sampled: Nittany peanut-butter, sour-cream raisin, apricot, sweet-potato. I don't like shoofly pie — a pie that has always reminded me of sweetened library paste — and wasn't even going to try eating that. I do like Key-lime, but Florida was not on my route. Nor was Colorado, though a friend recommended the black-bottom pie in Denver. Nor Wisconsin, where there was said to be a strawberry pie so good that it was impossible to eat only one piece.

The next day was better. It was a golden, sunny morning, and beside the Connecticut River at Turners Falls, Massachusetts, I stopped in a park filled with bluebells to give Tazzie a short run. A friendly woman was walking her dog, who was part hound, part black Lab, and Tazzie fell in love with him. While our dogs played, the woman and I talked, and she told me about the Shady Glen, a restaurant on the main street of Turners Falls, where a friend of hers went once a day to eat chocolate-cream pie. The Shady Glen is a wide, squat, hospitable café. Inside are cheerful yellow booths and a wide selection of pies. I ordered the squash pie. It was my first of the season, nicely spiced with nutmeg and set off by a firm, crisp crust.

Diner chic is spreading, but it has not yet come to the Miss Florence Diner, on State Route 9, in Florence, Massachusetts, a vestigial outcropping of the more uptown-looking Alexander's Taproom. Miss Florence appears to have been there a long time and looks as though it would outlast Alexander's. It serves a thick, sincere apple pie — not an exceptional pie but a good pie. The apple pie at Allen Brothers Farm Market, on U.S. 5, in Westminster, Vermont, *is* exceptional. The indoor farm stand smelled of good things from the bakery the day I was there, but the fragrance of fresh apple pies dominated all. ("Thy breath is like the steame of apple-pyes," Robert Greene wrote in 1589.) I bought a whole one and a slab of Vermont Cheddar to go with it, and then I drove down to Boston, where I was going to meet my husband and stay with Brian and Liddy, who live there.

It was an apple pie almost beyond praise. "This pie is good enough for breakfast," Liddy said reverently. The crust set it off well, and the apples — Lodis, in this case — were superb. Some of their skins had escaped the peeler and were in the pie, an addition that the four of us liked, but when I talked later to Alice Porter, the Allens' baker, she was a bit embarrassed about them. Tim Allen, a second-generation apple grower, says Northern Spies make the best apple pie, and that's the variety Mrs. Porter uses when they're in season. When they're not, she uses Lodis or Cortlands.

Allens' Piecrust

  2   C. flour
$^3/_4$ C. shortening
$1^1/_2$ tsp. sugar
  1   tsp. salt
  1   egg
  1   tbsp. vinegar
$^1/_4$ C. water

Mix dry ingredients in a bowl and cut in shortening with a pastry blender. In a separate bowl beat together egg, vinegar, and water. Mix with dry ingredients and refrigerate dough for at least two hours before rolling out. Makes a 9-inch two-crust pie.

Allens' Apple-Pie Filling

    4 C. sliced apples
    $^1/_2$ to $^3/_4$ C. sugar, depending upon tartness of apples
    $^1/_2$ tsp. cinnamon
    $^1/_4$ tsp. nutmeg
    2 tbsp. flour

Mix flour, sugar, and spices. Add to apples and mix lightly. Pour into unbaked pie shell. Dot with butter. Cover with top crust. Brush top with whole egg beaten with a little milk. Bake at 325° for 35 to 40 minutes or until browned.

Charlie, there's your pie.

In Maine, I settled into a routine of raspberry and blueberry pie, and each one was better than the one before it, which makes them very difficult to write about. The raspberry I remember with the greatest fondness is one I bought at the Village One Stop, in Lovell, in the western part of the state. One stop indeed: liquor, worms, gas, grain, groceries, lunch counter. A sign over the lunch counter, hand-lettered, said PLEASE EAT OR WE'LL BOTH STARVE. I asked the young woman behind the counter about pie. She pointed to a man in a plaid flannel shirt sitting on a stool at the far end. "Talk to him — he just finished baking them."

"You have pie?" I asked him. 25

"Yep."

"What kind?"

"Pineapple. Blackberry. Raspberry."

"Raspberry sounds good."

Silence. 30

"May I have some?"

"Well . . . they're awful warm to cut. You want a whole pie?"

"Please."

The whole pie was five dollars and eighty-five cents. I bought it and a copy of the *Boston Globe*. The man smiled, faintly, and said, "Have a nice one. I mean a day, I guess. Have a nice day."

The warm pie filled the car with its fragrance. Tazzie and I drove north 35 on State Route 5. The bracken at the roadside had the hint of bronze that says fall is on its way. The air and the sunlight agreed. We threaded in and out among logging trucks and finally pulled in at a rest stop, beside a lake where a loon was calling. A hand-carved sign on a post said that the spot was not maintained by any government agency and asked me to take away my trash. A reasonable request. The entreaty was signed by E. Littlefield — presumably the person who had mowed the grass so neatly and painted the blue picnic table, which was sheltered by a maple tree. Tazzie checked out the lakeshore, and I joined her, balancing on the rocks there. The late-morning sun made the wavelets glisten, their shimmer set off by the dark greens of spruce, fir, and pine that ringed the lake. I spread my *Globe* out on the picnic table, poured coffee from my Thermos, and took out the pie. It was nicely browned and had little slash marks in the crust to let the steam escape. The edges were lovingly crimped, and the crust broke apart under my fork in delicious shattery flakes. The filling was no sweeter than it needed to be. It tasted of fresh raspberries and summer sunshine. I read my *Globe* and listened to the loon and ate pie. Thank you, E. Littlefield.

We resumed our drive north, but the blue sky and the sunshine prompted us to stop beside the Sunday River. Tazzie made friends with a man in sweatshirt and jeans who was peering at trees in a puzzled way. He asked if I had a field guide to trees with me. I did. We talked trees, and he told me that he had just begun learning to identify trees and birds and was driving around the country trying to learn the names of all he saw. Splendid man. I asked him if he'd like five-sixths of a really good raspberry pie. He said yes, and I gave it to him.

One afternoon, we stopped beside the Kennebec River, below the town of Skowhegan and its falls. Tazzie pounced on crickets, catching none. I watched damselflies. Clouds thickened and turned gray as they floated up from the southwest. Goldenrod and aster, the yellow and purple of summer's end, bloomed around us. I could hear a chain saw somewhere. All along the roads I'd been driving, I'd seen serious, multicord woodpiles. Winter is never far from the thoughts of people who live in north country.

Tazzie, who takes more interest in rocks than most dogs do, and certainly more than is good for her teeth, fetched numbers of them out of the Kennebec and laid them neatly on the bank, sometimes sticking her entire head underwater in a most undoglike fashion. We drove on through towns whose front lawns were bright with mountain ash, through Passadumkeag, through Mattawamkeag — which is to say that we were on our way to Aroostook, or The County, as Down Easters call it. And there, in Houlton, I found the Elm Tree Diner, on the southwestern edge of town, on U.S. Alternate 2. It specialized in homemade pies, and it was a busy place, with table-filled additions that were signs of its commercial success. The blueberry pie had a thick but light crust. The berries were sparingly sweetened and little cooked; they maintained their integrity and berryish freshness so well that they brought back the memory of a sunny day when Brian, then twelve, and his father and I walked up Cadillac Mountain and stuffed ourselves with blueberries that we picked as we climbed.

I would have liked to buy pie in Wytopitlock, but there was none to be had, so I stopped in front of a boarded-up general store (FOR SALE), amid an unkempt patch of orange hawkweed, red clover, and pesky ripe burdock waiting for a chance to entangle itself in Tazzie's fur. There I ate a piece of French apple pie that I'd had the foresight to buy at the Elm Tree Diner. It is the same pie that in Pennsylvania is called Dutch apple pie — a single-crust apple pie topped with a crumbly mixture of brown sugar, flour, and butter (the "dowdy" of apple pandowdy). This French apple, however, was much better than any of its Pennsylvania Dutch relatives that I had sampled. It was generously filled with apples, and was pleasantly tart. It is always a mistake to sweeten these pies much, because the crumbly dowdy is sweet enough, and needs the sharp fruit contrast to be at its best.

Never play cards with a man named Doc, never eat at a place called 40 Mom's, and never go to bed with anyone who has more troubles than you do, Nelson Algren advised. I discovered an exception in the case of a place called Mom's on U.S. 1, in Harrington, where I met Liddy and Brian for a travelling pie party. We ordered strawberry-rhubarb, apple, and blueberry pies and shared them. The strawberry-rhubarb was out of season but good nevertheless, and the apple was good, too, with a lovely ooze-browned back to its crust. The blueberry was the best I'd had so far. The crust was good — thick but not heavy — and the fresh blueberries that filled it were wild ones, sparkling and tangy. And then there was the blueberry pie we had at Duffy's, in East Orland, which was the last one I ate and the best one of all. The legend on the cover of Duffy's menu sounds a bit truculent:

WELCOME TO DUFFY'S
WE HERE AT DUFFY'S ARE A
NATIVE ORIENTATED RESTAURANT
WE AREN'T FUSSY
AND WE'RE CERTAINLY NOT FANCY.
IF YOU ARE,
ELLSWORTH IS 12 MILES EAST
AND
BUCKSPORT IS 7 MILES WEST.
YOURS TRULY,
DUFFY

Even so, Duffy's is a welcoming sort of place, with geranium-filled window boxes. We ordered graham-cracker pie first. "You know what banana-cream pie is?" the waitress asked. "Well, it's like that, without the bananas." That's not quite accurate. It was more like a custard pie on a graham-cracker crust, topped with whipped cream and sprinkled with graham-cracker crumbs. Quite good, and much better than most custard pies, which are at best sweet, modest little things. But the three of us gave the blueberry pie gold stars all around. The crust had been pinched up into extreme points, and was delicious. The local blueberries were delicious, too, and their flavor was enhanced by the generous addition of cinnamon.

In season, though, all blueberry pies are good. A few years ago, I was visiting a nonbaking friend, who asked me to make one. The oven wasn't working, but we thought we might be able to bake it on the covered outdoor grill, over a wood fire. There was no pie pan, but perhaps I could make do with an aluminum cake pan. There was no rolling pin or waxed paper, so I used a water glass to roll out the pie dough between two pieces of brown paper cut from a grocery bag. There were, however, plenty of fresh wild blueberries, and there was sugar and cinnamon and a lemon, which I cut up and added to the filling. The pie that came off the grill had rather too thick a crust, and it had cooked unevenly, and it tasted of wood smoke, but it wasn't a *bad* pie; the blueberries were too good for that.

I had two other pies of note in Maine. The Farmington Diner, under the sign of fork and spoon transverse, was on State Route 4, on the south side of Farmington; it laid out logger-sized meals and good pie. The lunch special the day I was there was two thick pork chops cut from a very large pig, a platter of carrots, a platter of mashed potatoes and gravy, and a soup bowl full of applesauce. I made tiny inroads on the food, and realizing that I'd badly neglected lemon-meringue pie I ordered a wedge of it. It came accompanied by coffee in a sturdy mug that fitted amiably into my hand. My eyes told me that the pie filling was too yellow to be anything but a mix, but my taste buds said they didn't care: It was a good, classic diner pie — lots of loft to the meringue, and the crust a bit relaxed. Real lemon-meringue pie is too delicate and too ephemeral to be served in a diner, and too fussy to make for a diner cook to be happy with it.

The Milbridge House, in Milbridge, near the intersection of U.S. 1 and U.S. Alternate 1, serves a tasty and unusual pie. It is called Nantucket Cranberry Pie, and the recipe was brought up to Maine by Greg Charczuk, who owns the restaurant, when he moved from New Jersey. I copied it from the stained scrap of paper that his wife, Helen, uses when she makes it.

Nantucket Cranberry Pie

      3 C. fresh cranberries
         Sugar to coat berries
$^1/_2$ C. chopped walnuts
      1 C. flour
$1^1/_4$ tsp. baking powder
$^1/_8$ tsp. salt
$^1/_4$ C. shortening
      1 C. sugar
      1 egg
$^1/_3$ C. milk
$^1/_2$ tsp. vanilla
$^1/_8$ tsp. almond extract

Rinse cranberries, and dredge with sugar. Pour into greased 10-inch pie pan, leaving excess sugar in bowl. Add chopped walnuts to cranberries. Cream shortening with 1 C. sugar. Add dry ingredients alternately with mixture of egg, milk, vanilla, and almond. Spoon and spread over cranberries and walnuts. Bake at 350° for 25 to 30 minutes.

This is a fine pie, but, because the crust is cakelike and all on top, there will be pie conservatives who won't accept it. I will. If a creative and artful cook invents something and calls it pie, I'll call it pie. Let the crabbed formalists make their categories; I wouldn't like to miss something as lovely as this cranberry-walnut pie — an echo of the colonists' mock-cherry — or the banana-puddin' pie, which will make its appearance later.

My autumn was a busy one, and then the snows came, so it wasn't until 45 the highways cleared in early springtime that Tazzie and I headed south from Washington on the pie roads.

Just south of Buffalo Gap, Virginia, on State Route 42, I came upon Our Place. It was part house, part restaurant, and was presided over by Betty Wade, a blond, comfortable woman with an easy smile. She showed me the back living room, where her daughters used to play until they were old enough to help out in the restaurant. Thirteen years ago, she told me, she and her husband bought the restaurant, and she started cooking there using *The Better Homes and Gardens Cook Book*, just as she did at home. "I wasn't sure folks would like my cooking," she said. "But they did. I didn't have to change anything." It seemed like the right kind of place to order butterscotch pie. I did, and watched the waitress slip quarters into the Wurlitzer.

> Shoe string, you ain't got no
> money.
> Shoe string, you cain't hang
> around here.
> Shoe string, you got your hat on
> back'ards.

My pie arrived. It was a trim, neat, light-brown wedge on a crisp crust, topped with daintily browned meringue. Home cooking: I am back in the nineteen-forties, hungry as only an eight-year-old can be with supper still half an hour away. I am standing in front of the open door of a refrigerator — a big one, with gently sloping shoulders. Inside, on the shelf next to the ice-cube-tray compartment, is a row of tall stemmed dessert glasses, each one filled with its own golden dollop of butterscotch pudding. I count. There are five, and five of us will sit down to supper. There is no way I can winkle one out of the refrigerator without drawing down maternal wrath. I can't remember what happened after that. I can't even remember eating the butterscotch pudding after finishing my nice vegetables. All I can remember is the yearning. I'm glad to be an adult. As I leave, George Jones is wailing from the Wurlitzer:

> The last thing I gave her was
> the bird,
> And she returned the favor with
> a few selected words.

We drove on. State Route 42 is my kind of road, playing tag with a little river that glistened in the sunlight. Well-tended farms are tucked in among the hills. We stopped at a wayside, superior in every respect to interstate rest stops, and Tazzie ran about, sampling the river, snuffling expectantly at the newly softened ground. A nuthatch in a sycamore at the river edge called *whoink . . . whoink* as he surveyed the bark for edibles. I leaned against the same tree and soaked up the wan sunshine, glad to be on the road, glad to be driving south to meet the springtime.

Pie called, and we got back in the car and went west on U.S. 60, a more peaceable road than the distant but parallel interstate. In Grayson, Kentucky, on Main Street, I stopped at the City Café, in accordance with pie rules I have formulated over the years for the Middle West. Rule 1: Pie is good in 85 percent of the eating establishments that are between two other buildings. Rule 2: Good pie may often be had near places where meadowlarks sing. If you follow these two rules in the Middle West you will find yourself at the City Café or its like. A restaurant like this makes it unnecessary for a town to have anything but a bland local newspaper. Nearly all the citizens gather there early in the morning for breakfast or coffee and the exchange of news and gossip. By 8:30 A.M., whatever has happened during the past twenty-four hours has been talked over. These cafés have a pressed-metal ceiling, sometimes covered with insulating panels, and dark imitation-wood panelling on the walls. Oil paintings by local artists are often displayed there for sale. The doors open early — by five or five-thirty. Fresh-baked pie is ready by nine-thirty or ten. The coffee drinkers are replaced by the dinner crowd not long after (away from cities, dinner is the noontime meal), and by two the pie is gone and the restaurant is closed for the day.

There was a Mountain Dew sign in front of the City Café. A poster in 50 the window promoted a local wrestling match. Inside were an imitation-brick carpet and imitation-woodgrain tables. Everything was imitation except the food. I ordered pecan pie. It was exceptional — solid, with good texture. The filling was rich and eggy tasting but not overpoweringly sweet. The pecans on top were chopped, glazed, brown. Wilma Berry, a big woman with a pleasant face and a curly hairdo, was the waitress and owner of the café. She was happy to share her recipe, adapted from *What's Cooking in Kentucky*:

Palestene Layne's Pecan Pie

    1 tsp. vanilla
    3 eggs, slightly beaten
    1 C. corn syrup, light or dark
  $^1/_2$ tsp. salt
  $^1/_2$ C. white sugar
  $^1/_2$ C. brown sugar
    2 C. coarsely chopped pecans
    1 unbaked 9-inch, deep-dish pie shell

Blend well, but do not overbeat, vanilla, eggs, corn syrup, salt, sugar. Stir in pecans. Pour into pie shell. Bake approximately 50 minutes in preheated 350° oven, or until knife comes out clean.

The Beaver Dam Café was on the main street of Beaver Dam, Kentucky, just off U.S. 231, and was nestled between the Style Shop and Catalyst Management, Ltd. The sign outside said "HOME OF GOOD FOOD." Inside, imitation-needlepoint placemats said:

Cherish Yesterday
Dream of Tomorrow
Live Today

Nice, I thought; the Beaver Dam Café would have good pie. The possibilities, according to the menu, were interesting: cherry, pinto-bean, pecan, banana-pudding, and (Sundays only) buttermilk. It wasn't Sunday, nor was the pinto-bean ready, so I asked the waitress what I should order. "We sure do brag on our banana-puddin' pie," she said. I ordered banana-puddin' pie. It was fresh from the kitchen, chock-full of bananas, and so warm and relaxed that it had to be served in a bowl. The manager — a birdlike, wary little woman — said she'd be happy to give me the recipe but not her name. "What if someone tried to make it and didn't like it?" she asked. I am able to reassure her. Over the past months, my stepson has been committing pie courtship. He and his friend Barbara have been having pie dates, making pies from the recipes I brought back from my expedition. They tell me that the pecan and apple pies were the best all around and Shaker lemon the prettiest and most flavorful, but that the banana-puddin' pie was the most fun.

Beaver Dam Café
Banana-Puddin' Pie

4 eggs, separated
3$^1/_2$ C. milk
$^1/_4$ C. flour
$^1/_4$ tsp. salt
1$^3/_4$ C. sugar
4 tbsp. butter or margarine
2$^1/_2$ tsp. vanilla
    Vanilla wafers
    Bananas

Beat egg yolks with milk and add to mixture of flour, salt, and 1$^1/_2$ C. sugar. Cook in a double boiler over medium heat until thickened. Remove from heat and stir in butter and vanilla. In the bottom of a loaf pan put a layer of vanilla wafers and then a layer of sliced bananas. Pour one half of the custard over them. Repeat. Whip egg whites until stiff, adding $^1/_4$ C. sugar near the end. Spoon meringue on top of pie and bake in 425° oven until meringue is slightly browned.

A generation ago in the Ozarks, where I farm, pies also served romance — and an unlikely adjunct, school finance — in what were known as pie suppers. Back in those days of one-room schools in rural areas with a poor tax base, pie suppers were an annual autumn event. Young women would bake the best, the prettiest, the fanciest pies they could and take them to the school in the evening for young men to bid on. The top bidder would earn not only the pie but the right to eat it with its baker. The money from the auction funded the school. The young women would try to mark their pies in such a way that certain young men would recognize them, and Ozark folklore is full of stories about men who created emotional havoc by bidding — perhaps mistakenly, perhaps not — on the "wrong" pie.

In addition to Pie Rules 1 and 2, there is another, which applies to the entire country. Rule 3: Never eat pie within one mile of an interstate highway. This rule eliminates pie in most fast-food restaurants and in most truck stops, which are usually also franchises these days. I once violated Rule 3 and had a disappointing piece of gooseberry pie at a much-recommended truck stop just off Interstate 70, between Kansas City and St. Louis. But now I thought I had better check out the small, independent truck stops, so I visited the Wyatt Junction Truck Stop, just west of the Mississippi River, on U.S. 60. A sign on the wall said:

WELCOME TO
WYATT JUNCTION TRUCK STOP
TRUCKER'S NOTICE
ALL COFFEE FREE WITH
THE PURCHASE OF DIESEL FUEL
THANK YOU FOR COMING
HAVE
A
NICE
DAY

I ordered the dinner special: chicken-fried steak, fried bread, deep-fried okra, French-fried potatoes, and a tossed salad made almost entirely of fried bacon. A trucker in a black leather jacket came in looking enormously pleased and announced to no one in particular that he'd passed his sweetie about two hundred miles back and left her behind. He hoped she wasn't frosted. He put a quarter in the jukebox:

> The last thing I gave her was
> the bird,
> And she returned the favor with
> a few selected words. . . .
> Then left two streaks of Firestone
> smokin' on the street.

Sweetie pulled up and climbed out of her own eighteen-wheeler. She saunteted in. She had a fluffy shock of black hair and was wearing tight jeans, high-heeled red shoes, and a black leather jacket to match his. She glared at him and ordered Royal Crown Cola and apple pie. If she could, I could. I told the waitress to hold the R.C. but lemme have some pie. It was very like that served in the United States Senate Family Dining Room.

281

I was just a bit bilious by the time that I got to my farm, in southern Missouri, so I spent a couple of days there sucking on soda crackers and letting Tazzie visit her favorite places down by the river. I had heard about Opal Wheeler's Pie Factory, on U.S. 63, south of West Plains, but I'd never been there, and I enlisted the help of my friend Nancy for a pie foray. Nancy is a little bitty skinny woman who runs a health-food store and talks a lot about bean sprouts. She is always ready to try something new, however, and is a woman of considerable enthusiasm. We drove down U.S. 63 and found the Pie Factory, a cheery, small ten-sided building with white walls and red-trimmed windows. It would have been easy to miss, because it sits back from the road and has only a small, hand-painted sign to call attention to itself. Opal Wheeler is a grandmotherly-looking woman with a warm smile. She had been in the restaurant business for years before she and her sister drove by the newly constructed building in 1985. Her sister, who understood Opal's love of baking, pointed to it and said, "Opal, wouldn't that make a cute little pie factory?" Opal agreed, rented the place, put up the sign, and set to work. She starts rolling out pie dough on the counter in the center of the building each morning at about five-thirty. She is usually done baking by eleven, and the rest of the day she sells pies — sometimes whole, sometimes by the slice with coffee.

The day Nancy and I were there she had apple, apple-raisin, raisin, pecan, cherry, apricot, blueberry, pineapple-cream, peach-cream, cherry-cream, icebox mixed-fruit, strawberry-rhubarb, gooseberry, lemon-meringue, chocolate, coconut, banana, chocolate-delight (chocolate, pecans, cream cheese, single crust, whipped topping), lemon-delight, pecan-delight, and strawberry. I ordered a cup of coffee and told Nancy she could order whatever she wanted if she would talk to me about it. She began with a wedge each of apricot, apple-raisin, cherry, icebox mixed-fruit, and strawberry. And a cup of tea. "Oh, look," she said. "The crusts are sprinkled with sugar and browned. Pretty. . . . This apricot is too mooshy. . . . The apple-raisin is superior, though. I think it's the best one. . . . No, the cherry is the best — tart, lots of cherries, not much gooey filling. . . . No, maybe the mixed-fruit is my favorite. It's got a single crust, then a layer of cream cheese, then cherries with fresh pineapple. And this whipped topping! Wow! Can this lady make pies!"

"Anything else appeal to you?" I asked.

"Well, maybe I'll try a piece of lemon-meringue."

I watched in admiration as she ate that, too. Opal Wheeler freshened my coffee. I asked Nancy again which pie was best.

"How can I choose?" she asked. "Each one is a jewel."

"Nancy," I said, "you run a health-food store."

"Yeah, isn't it wonderful? She can make good pies out of stuff like this. I mean, white flour, white sugar, solid shortening? Maybe she could make the crusts out of whole-wheat flour. Oh, well, it just shows you what a talented cook can do."

Nancy left with an entire chocolate-delight pie in a box. She was happy, in perfect health, looking not one ounce fatter. And I was happy. I had always hoped that pies were good for us — a hope that had been encouraged by an article in the *Weekly World News* of October 27, 1987. I've long thought that there is a supermarket-tabloid headline designed to sucker every man, woman, or child at least once. Mine was "Snickers and Twinkies Make You Healthy, Says Food Expert," touting an article declaring that there was "more nutrition in a Snickers bar or a Twinkie than in an apple." Might I not therefore assume, after watching Nancy tuck into her pies, that apple pie was the healthiest way to eat an apple?

In western Missouri, the good pie places thin out. The town cafés have 65 become Daylight Donut outlets, to the detriment of both pies and doughnuts, but just at the border of Oklahoma I had an unexpectedly dainty and tasty chocolate pie at the Corners Minimart Motel & Café, on U.S. 60. The chocolate filling rested on a flavorful crust and was topped with a perfect, delicate meringue. Outside, prickly pear grew on the sunny, south side of the restaurant, where there was a big white box with a sign on it that said:

CAUTION

BABY RATTLERS

Hints of the West.

Once I had crossed the Oklahoma line, I began seeing red-tailed hawks hunting high in the air above the road. It had been a long time since I'd heard a meadowlark sing. In one small town after another, waitresses in the cafés shook their heads when I asked for pie, and offered cobbler instead. "And mighty good cobbler it is, too," a customer informed me in the Hot Biscuit Café, in Vinita. But I drove on. There were sandburs at the rest stops, and Tazzie whimpered when she got them in her feet. The sun was warm. Spring had been in Oklahoma for some time. The sky opened up. I could see forever. The road threaded between hills covered with prairie grass, and someplace between Bartlesville and Ponca City I realized that I was in the West. I rolled down all the windows. *Ky-y-y-yr* screamed a red-tail overhead. I leaned out the window and the wind blew and tugged at my hair. "*Ky-y-yr*," I screamed back. Fun. Can't do that on the interstate. The road was empty, and I was in love with driving. Out of nowhere, an Oklahoma trooper came up behind me and pulled me over. He reminded me that the speed limit was still fifty-five off the interstate, and gave me a "courtesy" ticket. Nice young man. Troopers know pie, so I asked him where he went to get it. He blushed a little, took off his hat, scratched his head, and thought awhile. Then, by way of explanation, he said, in his slow drawl, "Sorry, Ma'am, but you're in cobbler country now."

AFTERWORD

Rhetoricians have it that a recipe is an example of process analysis. Certainly an essay that divides pies is also an attempt at division, not to mention classification by pie type and pie quality. Still, the skeleton of this essay is narrative, travel beautified by the flesh of description. This essay includes all sorts of writing — mixed fruit, pumpkin, and mince.

William Least Heat-Moon wrote a book called Blue Highways, *driving on less-traveled roads. John Steinbeck roamed the country in a pickup accompanied by a dog in* Travels with Charley. *The search for perfection in pie — pie in the sky, as it were — will do as well as any other excuse. Someone called Sue Hubbell's crusty epic an "unreheated American Odyssey."*

People who love to eat love to talk about eating. When Sue Hubbell eats one piece of pie it reminds her of a hundred others. People who take food for granted turn the conversation to food only when they are hungry; with others, a surfeit of good food serves to remind us of Great Dinners We Have Known. Some of us can stay up all night speaking of romaine lettuces, a paté devoured at Pigall's in Cincinnati in 1972, and hotdogs at the adjacent ballpark.

Good essays may be written in venom — see Vidal; see Mencken — but it seems clear that often the most engaging language comes from writers in love with their subjects: with baseball, with prose style, with the immortal soul, with Jane Austen, with hairdos, with the great American slice of pie.

BOOKS AVAILABLE IN PAPERBACK

A Book of Bees and How to Keep Them. New York: Ballantine. *Nonfiction.*

Broadsides from the Other Orders: A Book of Bugs. New York: Random House. *Nonfiction.*

A Country Year: Living the Questions. New York: HarperCollins. *Essays.*

MOLLY
IVINS

*M*OLLY IVINS (b. 1948) is a Texan, a progressive in politics, a feminist admirer of men who love whiskey and women, and the funniest political writer of our day. She has been employed by a number of newspapers, including the Minneapolis Tribune *and the* New York Times, *most memorably by the late* Dallas Times-Herald. She writes a monthly column for the Progressive *and frequent dispatches for the* Nation, Mother Jones, *and the* Fort Worth Star-Telegram. In 1991 she first collected her columns under the title Molly Ivins Can't Say That, Can She? In 1993 she followed it with Nothin' But Good Times Ahead, *from which we take these columns.*

She is celebrated for common sense, down-home Texas straight talk, raunchiness, and keen intelligence. Her greatest honors, she likes to say, are two: The Minneapolis police force named its mascot pig after her, and she was once banned from the campus of Texas A & M. Like many a regional genius, she put in time as an alien. Molly Ivins graduated from Smith College in Northampton, Massachusetts, did a journalism degree at Columbia University, and studied for a year in Paris, France.

Three Columns

Sleazy Riders

"Texas political ethics" is not an oxymoron. Our guys have 'em. They just tend to have an overdeveloped sense of the extenuating circumstance.

Remember when Bill Clements was asked why he'd lied about approving payments to Southern Methodist University football players and replied, "Well, there was never a Bible in the room. . . ."? There was that to be considered, wasn't there?

Remember when a crusty state senator named Bill Moore was caught carrying a bill that would directly benefit his own company and said, "I'd just make a little bit of money, I wouldn't make a whole lot. . . ."? You see? These things are complicated.

When you've got Louisiana on one side and Mexico on another, the sleaze standard is high, but we're holding our own. Look what became of the last six Speakers — three got indicted, two got defeated, one got shot. One of the indictees, Billy Clayton, got in trouble for taking five thousand dollars in cash from a lobbyist, which he said he meant to return, honest, but it just somehow slipped his mind. He got off. If there's one thing a Texas Speaker has got to know, it's how to explain himself.

The definitive statement on Texas political ethics — source unknown, but often quoted by Texas liberals — is: "If you can't take their money, drink their whiskey, screw their women, and vote against 'em anyway, you don't belong in the legislature." But things are getting better. We seldom pay them off in cash anymore. They want their money the legal way, as campaign contributions.

In the not-so-distant past, they were more up-front about it. Two state senators were holed up in the Driskill Hotel, drinkin' whiskey and "interviewin' secretaries." Comes a *knock-knock-knock* on the door, and it's the lobbyist for the chiropractors. He offers both senators two hundred dollars to vote for the chiropractors' bill. One guy takes the money, the bill comes up, and lo and behold, he votes against it. This is bad Texas political ethics: You're supposed to stay bought. The chiropractor lobbyist is some pissed. He stalks up to the senator and demands to know what happened. "Doctors offered me four hundred to vote against you," said the senator. The lobbyist started to cuss that senator up one side and down the other. "Look," the senator argued, "you knew I was weak when I took the two hundred."

The late pol Woodrow Bean of El Paso, God rest him, used to tell the story of the time a court appointed him to defend a young robber who had made off with the loot with the cops right on his heels. Woody interviews this kid in the hoosegow, gets the directions to where the loot is stashed, drives out there, and helps himself to a very generous fee. As he drives away, he says aloud, "Woodrow Wilson Bean, you are skatin' on the thin edge of ethics." Then he drives awhile further and says, "Woodrow Wilson Bean, ethics is for young lawyers."

Occasionally things get so bad that the press bestirs itself into a state of high dudgeon and the citizenry gets aroused. Then all the pols run for cover and talk about reform, only they pronounce it *"ree-*form," as in, "We're gonna have us some *ree-*form around here," just to let each other know they aren't really serious. Back in 1973, when they were supposed to be cleaning up the mess from the Sharpstown scandal, the House chamber was the scene of a performance by the Apache Belles from Tyler Junior College. The highlight came when six Belles turned their derrieres toward the lawmakers, revealing letters spelling out *R-E-F-O-R-M.* Texas voters, knowing better than to expect the Lege to put an end to sleaze, have resorted to their own ways of dealing with it, which sometimes take the form of voting half the Legislature out of office and more often result in electing folks who are god-awful rich in the hope that they or their ancestors have already stolen all they need.

But the scandals go on. Since Sharpstown we've had Brilab and Gibgate and a list of sleaze du jours too long to recount. Who can forget the time Bo Pilgrim, the East Texas chicken magnate, walked onto the floor of the senate during a special session in 1989 and started handing out checks for ten thousand dollars — payee blank — to any senator who would take one? Seven took the money, but five gave it back when the story broke. Still, it was technically legit. That's Texas ethics for you. The real scandal isn't what's illegal — it's what's legal.

– The Texas Observer, February 1993

Get a Knife, Get a Dog, but Get Rid of Guns

Guns. Everywhere guns.   10

Let me start this discussion by pointing out that I am not antigun. I'm proknife. Consider the merits of the knife.

In the first place, you have to catch up with someone in order to stab him. A general substitution of knives for guns would promote physical fitness. We'd turn into a whole nation of great runners. Plus, knives don't ricochet. And people are seldom killed while cleaning their knives.

As a civil libertarian, I, of course, support the Second Amendment. And I believe it means exactly what it says:

A well-regulated militia being necessary to the security of a free state, the right of the people to keep and bear arms shall not be infringed. Fourteen-year-old boys are not part of a well-regulated militia. Members of wacky religious cults are not part of a well-regulated militia. Permitting unregulated citizens to have guns is destroying the security of this free state.

I am intrigued by the arguments of those who claim to follow the judi-   15
cial doctrine of original intent. How do they know it was the dearest wish

of Thomas Jefferson's heart that teenage drug dealers should cruise the cities of this nation perforating their fellow citizens with assault rifles? Channeling?

There is more hooey spread about the Second Amendment. It says quite clearly that guns are for those who form part of a well-regulated militia, that is, the armed forces, including the National Guard. The reasons for keeping them away from everyone else get clearer by the day.

The comparison most often used is that of the automobile, another lethal object that is regularly used to wreak great carnage. Obviously, this society is full of people who haven't enough common sense to use an automobile properly. But we haven't outlawed cars yet.

We do, however, license them and their owners, restrict their use to presumably sane and sober adults, and keep track of who sells them to whom. At a minimum, we should do the same with guns.

In truth, there is no rational argument for guns in this society. This is no longer a frontier nation in which people hunt their own food. It is a crowded, overwhelmingly urban country in which letting people have access to guns is a continuing disaster. Those who want guns — whether for target shooting, hunting, or potting rattlesnakes (get a hoe) — should be subject to the same restrictions placed on gun owners in England, a nation in which liberty has survived nicely without an armed populace.

The argument that "guns don't kill people" is patent nonsense. Anyone   20 who has ever worked in a cop shop knows how many family arguments end in murder because there was a gun in the house. Did the gun kill someone? No. But if there had been no gun, no one would have died. At least not without a good foot race first. Guns do kill. Unlike cars, that is all they do.

Michael Crichton makes an interesting argument about technology in his thriller *Jurassic Park*. He points out that power without discipline is making this society into a wreckage. By the time someone who studies the martial arts becomes a master — literally able to kill with bare hands — that person has also undergone years of training and discipline. But any fool can pick up a gun and kill with it.

"A well-regulated militia" surely implies both long training and long discipline. That is the least, the very least, that should be required of those who are permitted to have guns, because a gun is literally the power to kill. For years I used to enjoy taunting my gun-nut friends about their psychosexual hang-ups — always in a spirit of good cheer, you understand. But letting the noisy minority in the NRA force us to allow this carnage to continue is just plain insane.

I do think gun nuts have a power hang-up. I don't know what is missing in their psyches that they need to feel they have the power to kill. But no sane society would allow this to continue.

Ban the damn things. Ban them all.

You want protection? Get a dog.   25

— *Fort Worth Star-Telegram*, March 9, 1993

'Twas a Fine Spring Day
to Air Out Attitudes

Well, the gay folks had a fine march in Washington, D.C., but I think they missed a couple of bets. State senator Jack Gordon of Florida suggests that they should have stopped en route and had a ceremony thanking the feds for naming that fine new building right there on Pennsylvania Avenue after one of their own. That's the J. Edgar Hoover Building.

Speaking of whom, there was a great example of why we don't want to force gays to stay in the closet.

And I would have liked to have seen a banner reading, BAN HETERO-SEXUALS FROM THE MILITARY — REMEMBER TAILHOOK. I trust you all took a look at the charming little report on that incident.

I suspect that finally ventilating all the myths and misconceptions about gays is a useful exercise, even for those who would prefer not to think about them. "I have nothing against gays," my mother is fond of saying. "I just wish they'd stay in the closet." But we all know by now — or should — that that state of affairs was cruel and unjust and led to terrible abuses.

Of all the odd misperceptions current about homosexuality, perhaps the oddest is that it is a choice, that people choose to be homosexual. That strikes me as so patently silly. Did any of us who are straight choose to be heterosexual? When? Did we wake up one morning when we were fifteen and say, "Gosh, I think I'll be a heterosexual"? For heaven's sakes, how can anyone believe that people choose to be homosexual? "I think it would be a lot of fun to be called *queer* and *sissy* for the rest of my life, so I think I'll be gay."

Last time I checked, the experts were still leaning toward the view that homosexuality is multicausational (isn't that a dandy word?). Most gay people I know believe they were literally born that way, that it's like being left-handed or brown-eyed. But in at least some cases, there is apparently some developmental influence as well.

The best description I ever heard of sexual orientation came from Dr. John Money of the Johns Hopkins University, who used to draw it on a horizontal scale going from one to ten, with one being completely homosexual and ten being completely heterosexual. Money says that very few people are either one or ten and about as few are at five (totally bisexual). Most of us fall into a clump ranging from about six to eight, while there's a smaller clump of homosexuals ranging from about four to two.

Because homosexuality occurs in many species of animals (stickleback fish always struck me as the strangest case) and because it has appeared in all human cultures throughout history, we must conclude that it is what statisticians call a "normal aberrant" (and isn't that a dandy phrase?).

I actually saw a letter to the editor last week declaring that homosexuality is a symptom of the decadence and decline of civilization and that it didn't exist among primitive people such as American Indians. *Au contraire,* as we say in Lubbock. Aside from the insult to Indians, there were indeed gay Indians before the white man came, and at least in the Plains tribes, they were regarded as sort of endearingly special.

Among the less charming counterdemonstrators at the Washington 35 march was the group from Kansas carrying signs saying, GOD HATES FAGS and DEATH TO FAGS. It is true that the Old Testament contains an injunction against homosexuality; it's in the same list of laws given when the Hebrews were a wandering desert people and were forbidden to eat shellfish. I always thought Christians were supposed to be followers of Jesus Christ, and Jesus' injunctions to love one another — to love even the despised and the out- cast — could scarcely be clearer. Hate is not a Christian value.

And, of course, there are the gay fundamentalists. We all know of scan- dals involving gay preachers, and if you wonder what it's like to grow up gay in a religious environment that stigmatizes gays, I commend to you a truly funny book called *Strange Angel — The Gospel According to Benny Joe* by Ben Davis, who grew up near Dallas and would have become a fundamen- talist preacher had it not been for his sexual orientation. The book's affec- tionate look at fundamentalist religion is worth the price for that alone (it is published by Corona Publishing, San Antonio).

As a matter of law, I do not see that we have any choice but to seek to ensure that gays have full civil rights. They are citizens; they pay taxes; as Jesse Jackson said the day of the march, no one gives them a break on April 15. They serve honorably in the military, ban or no ban; the Sixth Army's soldier of the year marched Sunday in Washington.

It has been my observation that some gay people are absolutely wonder- ful human beings, and some are complete you-know-whats, and most are somewhere in between. Depressingly like heterosexuals. So I suggest we all grow up and get over our small-town prejudices. (I can never remember whether it was "Queers wear red on Friday" or "green on Thursday." Lord, didn't we grow up with some silly ideas?) In our fair land, no one can force us to be tolerant. But neither can prejudice be allowed to keep people out of jobs for which they are qualified.

I suppose some people will continue to feel entitled to hate gays. As the psychiatrists have been telling us for a long time, hating them seems to be a function of being afraid that you might be one yourself.

— Fort Worth Star-Telegram, April 27, 1993

AFTERWORD

Newspaper columns are topical, which means that we seldom find them in essay collections. Molly Ivins has been writing columns and telling stories about the Texas state legislature since she started publishing. It is unfair, as we know, to generalize from a particular. Molly Ivins's method multiplies particulars so rapidly that we are dazzled into accepting an implied generalization; and to hell with being fair.

In other columns here, Ivins argues about two issues of the day: gun control and homosexuals in the military. She salts her logic with humor — "people are seldom killed while cleaning their knives" — and especially with the humor that follows implications to logical extremes. Referring to the Second Amendment, she asks, "How do they know it was the dearest wish of Thomas Jefferson's heart that teenage drug dealers should cruise the cities of this nation perforating their fellow citizens with assault rifles? Channeling?"

You don't doubt where Molly Ivins stands; ambiguity is not a flag she flies. "Ban the damn things. Ban them all." She has invented a speech that is Texas country-talk surreptitiously fed by underground intellectual streams, talk that is hilarious, exaggerated, clear, exact, and purely Molly Ivins. No one I know, writing about homophobia, more tellingly pillories the notion that homosexuality is a wicked choice of behavior. When she finds that she cannot avoid a word like "multicausational," difficult to accommodate to her tone, she uses it anyway and removes the problem by asking, "Isn't that a dandy word?"

BOOKS AVAILABLE IN PAPERBACK

Molly Ivins Can't Say That, Can She? New York: Random House–Vintage. *Essays.*
Nothin' But Good Times Ahead. New York: Random House–Vintage. *Essays.*

DIANE
JOHNSON

*D*IANE JOHNSON (b. 1934) took her B.A. at the University of Utah and her
Ph.D. at the University of California at Los Angeles. She now lives in
Berkeley, occasionally teaches at the University of California at Davis, and writes
novels, biographies, and essays. She is married to a pulmonologist and has four
children by an earlier marriage. In 1987 she was awarded a $250,000 Harold and
Mildred Strauss Living Award so that she can devote all her time to writing. The
latest of her seven novels are Persian Nights *(1987) and* Health and Happiness
(1990). She has written a biography of mystery writer Dashiell Hammett. Her
essays, mostly book reviews enlarged by generality, appear in the New York Review
of Books *and the* New York Times Book Review. *"Rape" comes from her essay*
collection Terrorists and Novelists *(1982), a title that expresses not only Diane*
Johnson's range but also her desire to connect extremes of social reality and the
printed page.

Johnson's prose, as in "Rape," creates reasonable discourse about subjects to
which reason is seldom applied. Sometimes we belittle the word intellectual, *assum-*
ing that intellect is useful in evading or denying the emotional facts of life. Some-
times we are right. But Johnson's intellect does its proper task, in a lucid progress
of good sentences that sort unpleasant matters into discernible units, subject to the
clarification of mind. Biographer and novelist, as well as critic and essayist, she
brings to her essays not only the orderly progress of ideas but story and image.

Rape

No other subject, it seems, is regarded so differently by men and women as rape. Women deeply dread and resent it to an extent that men apparently cannot recognize; it is perhaps the ultimate and essential complaint that women have to make against men. Of course men may recognize that it is wrong to use physical force against another person, and that rape laws are not prosecuted fairly, and so on, but at a certain point they are apt to say, "But what was she doing there at that hour anyway?" or "Luckily he didn't really hurt her," and serious discussion ceases.

Women sense — indeed, are carefully taught to feel — that the institution of rape is mysteriously protected by an armor of folklore, Bible tales, legal precedents, specious psychological theories. Most of all it seems protected by a rooted and implacable male belief that women want to be raped — which most women, conscientiously examining their motives, maintain they do not — or deserve to be raped, for violation of certain customs governing dress or behavior, a strange proposition to which women are more likely to accede.

While women can all imagine themselves as rape victims, most men know they are not rapists. So incidents that would be resented on personal grounds if happening to their "own" women do not have even the intrinsic interest for them of arguments on principle against military intervention in the political destiny of foreign nations, as in Vietnam, where the "rape" of that country was referred to in the peace movement and meant defoliation of crops. But unlike the interest in the political destiny of Vietnam, which greatly diminished when the danger to American males, via the draft, was eliminated, rape is an abiding concern to women.

Even if they don't think about it very much, most have incorporated into their lives routine precautions along lines prescribed by the general culture. From a woman's earliest days she is attended by injunctions about strangers, and warnings about dark streets, locks, escorts, and provocative behavior. She internalizes the lessons contained therein, that to break certain rules is to invite or deserve rape. Her fears, if not entirely conscious, are at least readily accessible, and are continually activated by a vast body of exemplary literature, both traditional and in the daily paper. To test this, ask yourself, if you are a woman, or ask any woman what she knows about Richard Speck, the Boston Strangler, and "that thing that happened over on —— Street last week," and you will find that she has considerable rape literature by heart.

It seems important, in attempting to assess the value or seriousness of Susan Brownmiller's polemic on rape (*Against Our Will*), to understand that there are really two audiences for it, one that will know much of what she has to say already, and another that is ill equipped by training or sympathy to understand it at all. This likely accounts for a certain unevenness of tone, veering from indignation to the composed deployment of statistics in the manner of a public debater. It is not surprising that women began in the past few years by addressing their complaints about rape to one another, not to men, and one infers that the subject is still thought to be of concern only to women. It remains to be seen what if any rhetorical strategies will prove to be of value in enlisting the concern of men.

That rape is aggressive, hostile, and intended to exact female submission, and that it is the extreme expression of underlying shared masculine attitudes, is, I think, most women's intuition of the subject, even women who have not been raped but who have tacitly accepted that this is how men are. Women who have in fact been raped (more than 255,000 each year) are certain of it after the indifference, disbelief, and brutality of police, doctors, judges, jurors, and their own families. That the actual rapists, making examples of a few women, in effect frighten and control all women seems obvious, even inarguable.

What is left to be explained, though neither Brownmiller nor Jean MacKellar, in another recent book on rape (*Rape: The Bait and the Trap*), can satisfactorily explain it, is what this primal drama of domination and punishment is about, exactly. Both books communicate an impression of an escalating conflict, with the increasing collective force of female anger and indignation about rape not only effecting some changes in judiciary and police procedures and even, perhaps, in popular attitudes, but also effecting an increase in anxiety about the subject, exemplified by the obligatory rape scenes in current movies and best sellers. Perhaps it is even female anger that is effecting an increase in rape itself, as if, whatever is at stake in this ancient hostility, it is now the rapist who has his back to the wall.

It is not too extreme to say that Brownmiller's book is exceedingly distressing, partly because it is exceedingly discouraging; it is a history of the failure of legal schemes and social sciences to improve society, at least society as viewed from a female perspective; it is the history of the failure of the social sciences even to address themselves to the peculiar mystery of male aggression toward those weaker than themselves. This failure seems in turn to demonstrate the powerlessness of human institutions before the force of patently untrue and sinister myths, whose ability to reflect, but also to determine, human behavior seems invincible. The disobedient Eve, the compliant Leda,° the lying wife of Potiphar° are still the keys to popular assumptions about women.

But Brownmiller's book is also distressing in another way that wicked myths and scary stories are distressing, that is, because they are meant to be. Here in one handy volume is every admonitory rape story you were ever

---

Leda Impregnated by Zeus, who came to her in the form of a swan.
Wife of Potiphar In Genesis, the wife of a wealthy Egyptian. She tries to seduce Joseph and, when she fails, accuses him of trying to seduce her.

told, horrifying in the way that propaganda is horrifying and also titillating just in the way that publishers hope a book will be titillating. Brownmiller is trapped in the fallacy of imitative form, and by the duplicitous powers of literature itself to contain within it its own contradictions, so that the exemplary anecdotes from Red Riding Hood to Kitty Genovese to the Tralala scene in *Last Exit to Brooklyn* must appeal at some level to the instincts they illustrate and deprecate. The book may be criticized for an emotional tone that is apparently impossible to exclude from an effective work on a subject so inaccessible to rational analysis. Because rape is an important topic of a potentially sensational and prurient nature, it is too bad that the book is not a model of surpassing tact and delicacy, unassailable learning and scientific methodology. Instead it is probably the book that was needed on this subject at this time, and may in fact succeed where reticence has failed to legitimate the fundamental grievance of women against men.

Much of the book is devoted to an attempt to locate in history the reasons 10 for rape, but inquiry here is fruitless because though history turns up evidence, it offers little explanation. One learns merely that rape has been with us from earliest times, that it is associated variously with military policy, with ideas of property and possession (to rape someone's wife was interpreted as the theft of something from him), with interracial struggles and complicated tribal and class polarities of all kinds (masters and slaves, cowboys and Indians), with intrasexual power struggles, as in the rape of young or weak men in prison by gangs of stronger ones, and within families, by male relatives of young girls or children.

None of these patterns is, except in one respect, wholly consistent with the others, but viewed together they induce a kind of dispirited resignation to natural law, from which are derived the supposed constants of human nature, maybe including rape. The respect in which violations of conquered women in Bangladesh and of Indian (or white) women in pioneer America, or of men in prison, are alike is that they all dramatize some authority conflict. In war between groups of males, women are incidental victims and prizes, but in the back of the car the dispute arises between a man and a woman on her own behalf. The point at issue seems to be "maistrye," as the Wife of Bath° knew; and the deepest lessons of our culture have inculcated in both sexes the idea that he is going to prevail. This in turn ensures that he usually does, but the central question of why it is necessary to have male mastery remains unanswered, and perhaps unasked. Meantime, the lesson of history seems to elevate the right of the male to exact obedience and inflict punishment to the status of immutable law.

Anthropology seems to support this, too, despite Brownmiller's attempts to find a primitive tribe (the obligingly rape-free Arapesh) to prove otherwise. Rather inconsistently, she conjectures that the origin of monogamy lies in the female's primordial fear of rape and consequent willingness to attach

---

Wife of Bath   A bawdy character in Chaucer's *Canterbury Tales.*

herself to some male as his exclusive property. If this is so, it would be the only instance in which the female will has succeeded in dictating social arrangements. In any case, alternate and better hypotheses exist for the origin of the family, generally that it developed for the protection of the young. The insouciance of Brownmiller's generalizations invites cavil and risks discrediting her book, and with it her subject. Granting that a primitive tribe can be found to illustrate any social model whatever, one would like to know just what all the anthropological evidence about rape is. If rape is the primordial norm; if, as Lévi-Strauss° says, women were the first currency; if male humans in a state of nature run mad raping, unlike chimpanzees, who we are told do not, is rape in fact aberrant? Perhaps it is only abhorrent.

It seems evident that whatever the facts of our nature, it is our culture that leads women in some degree to collaborate in their own rape, an aspect of the matter that men seem determined to claim absolves *them* from responsibility. Perhaps this is implicit in the assumptions about male power they are heir to. But every woman also inherits assumptions about female submission. In even the simplest fairy tale, the vaguely sexual content of the punishment needs no elaboration: Every woman darkly knows what really happened to Red Riding Hood in the woods — and to Grandmother, too, for that matter. Most women do not go into the woods alone, but the main point is that the form of the prohibition as it is expressed in most stories is not "Do not go into the woods lest you be raped," but "Obey me by not going into the woods or you *will* be raped."

Thus the idea of sexual punishment for disobedience is learned very early, and is accepted. Who has done this to you, Desdemona?° "Nobody; I myself, farewell," says Desdemona meekly as she dies. Everyone feels that Carmen,° that prick-tease, is "getting what she deserves," poor Lucrece's° suicide is felt to be both noble and tactful, maybe Anna Karenina's° too. So if a woman is raped, she feels, besides outrage, deep guilt and a need to find out what she has done "wrong" to account for it, even if her sin is only one of omission; for example, concerned citizens in Palo Alto were told a few days ago that "Sometimes women are raped because of carelessness."

To the extent that a woman can convince a jury that she was neither 15 careless nor seductive, her attacker may be found guilty and she may be absolved from guilt, but more often in rape trials something is found in her

---

Lévi-Strauss Claude Lévi-Strauss (b. 1908), French anthropologist.

Desdemona In Shakespeare's play *Othello*, wife of the title character. She is murdered by Othello when he mistakenly believes that she was unfaithful to him.

Carmen In the French tale and the opera by George Bizet, Carmen is a seductive Spanish gypsy who is stabbed by her jilted lover.

Lucrece In Roman legend, Lucrece stabs herself after telling her father and her husband that she has been raped.

Anna Karenina The title character in Tolstoy's novel who commits suicide after her adulterous love affair goes awry.

behavior to "account" for her fate. The point is that whatever the circumstances of a rape, social attitudes and legal processes at the present time
make the victim guilty of her own rape. Even the most innocent victim is
likely to be told by her mother, "I told you never to walk home alone," and
this is sometimes the attitude of an entire population, as in Bangladesh,
where thousands of raped wives were repudiated by their husbands.

The unfortunate rape victim is in some ways worse off the more "feminine," the better socialized, she is, for she will have accepted normal social
strictures: Do not play rough, do not make noise or hit. Then she will be
judged at the trial of her attacker on the extent to which she has struggled,
hit, bitten (though she would not be expected to resist an armed robber).
Not to struggle is to appear to want to be raped. In the courtroom men
pretend not to understand the extent to which cultural inhibitions prevent
women from resisting male force, even moral force, though in the parking
lot they seem to understand it very well.

In the practical world, who are the rapists, who are the raped, what is
to be done? It is here that Brownmiller's account is most interesting and
most disturbing. Both Brownmiller and MacKellar agree on the statistical
particulars: The rape victim is most likely a teenaged black girl but she may
be a woman of any age, and she will know her attacker to some extent in
about half of the cases. The rapist is the same sort of person as other violent
offenders: young, uneducated, unemployed, likely black or from another
deprived subculture; the rapist is *not* the shy, hard-up loner living with his
mother, victim of odd obsessions; a quarter of all rapes are done in gangs
or pairs.

The sociology of rapists has some difficult political implications, as
Brownmiller, to judge from the care with which she approaches it, is well
aware. She traces the complicated history of American liberalism and Southern racism which has led to the present pass, in which people who have
traditionally fought for human freedom seem committed to obstructing
freedom for women. Historically, she reminds us, the old left, and the Communist Party in particular,

> understood rape as a political act of subjugation only when the
> victim was black and the offender was white. White-on-white
> rape was merely "criminal" and had no part in their Marxist
> canon. Black-on-black rape was ignored. And black-on-white
> rape, about which the rest of the country was phobic, was
> discussed in the oddly reversed world of the Jefferson School
> as if it never existed except as a spurious charge that "the state"
> employed to persecute black men.

Meantime, circumstances have changed; folk bigotry, like folk wisdom, turns
out to contain a half-truth, or grain of prescience; and the black man has
taken to raping. Now

> the incidence of actual rape combined with the looming spectre
> of the black man as rapist to which the black man in the name

of his manhood now contributes, must be understood as a control mechanism against the freedom, mobility, and aspirations of all women, white and black. The crossroads of racism and sexism had to be a violent meeting place. There is no use pretending it doesn't exist.

It is at this crossroads that the problem appears most complex and most insoluble. Not only rapists, but also people more suavely disguised as right-thinking, like the ACLU and others associated with the civil-rights movement, still feel that protection of black men's rights is more important than injustice to women, whether white or black. Black men and white women are in effect pitted against one another in such a way as to impede the progress of both groups, and in particular to conceal and perpetuate the specific victimization of black women. Various studies report that blacks do up to 90 percent of rapes, and their victims are 80 to 90 percent black women, who now must endure from men of their own race what they historically had to endure from whites. A black girl from the ages of ten to fifteen is twelve times more likely than others to be a victim of this crime.

In this situation, which will win in the long run, sexism or racism? Who 20 are the natural antagonists? It seems likely, on the evidence, that sexism, being older, will prevail.

The MacKellar/Amir book, a short, practical manual about rape, something to be used perhaps by jurors or counselors, gives a picture of the crime and of the rapist which is essentially the same as Brownmiller's. But MacKellar's advice, when compared with Brownmiller's, is seen to be overlaid by a kind of naive social optimism. What can women do? They can avoid hitchhiking; they can be better in bed: "If women were less inhibited with their men the sense of depravity that their prudishness inspires might be reduced," as if it were frustrated middle-class husbands who were out raping; authorities can search out those "many youngsters warped by a brutish home life [who] can still be recuperated for a reasonably good adult life if given therapy in time"; "Education. Education helps to reduce rape."

Maybe. But does any evidence exist to suggest that any of this would really help? Brownmiller has found none, but I suppose she would agree with MacKellar that for America's violent subcultures we must employ "the classical remedies of assimilating the people in these subcultures, economically and socially, in opportunities for education, jobs, and decent housing," and change the fundamental values of American society. "As long as aggressive, exploitive behavior remains the norm, it can be expected that individuals will make these errors and that the weaker members of society will be the victim."

Until aggressive, exploitive behavior is not the norm, a few practical measures are being suggested. The LEAA study, MacKellar, and Brownmiller are all in favor of prosecuting rape cases and of punishing rapists. Brownmiller feels the punishment should suit the crime, that it should be made similar to penalties for aggravated assault, which it resembles. MacKellar feels that the penalty should fit the criminal: "a nineteen-year-old unemployed black with a fourth-grade education and no father, whose uptight, superreligious mother has, after a quarrel, kicked him out of the home, should not be judged by the same standard nor receive the same kind of sentence as a white middle-aged used-car salesman, twice divorced, who rapes a girl he picks up at a newsstand during an out-of-town convention." She does not, by the way, say who should get the stiffer sentence, and I can think of arguments either way.

Both agree that corroboration requirements and courtroom questions about a victim's prior sexual history should be eliminated, and in this the government-sponsored study for the Law Enforcement Assistance Administration (*Rape and Its Victims*) also agrees. At present the established view holds that whether or not a raped girl is a virgin or is promiscuous is germane to the issue of whether a forced act of sexual intercourse has occurred in a given case. This reflects the ancient idea that by violating male standards of female chastity, a woman forfeits her right to say no.

The LEAA study found that prosecutors' offices in general were doing 25 little to urge the revision of outdated legal codes, and that the legal system is in fact impeding reform. It observes (in a nice trenchant style that makes better reading than most government reports) that

> since rapists have no lobby, the major opposition to reform measures can be expected from public defenders, the defense bar in general, and groups, such as the American Civil Liberties Union, that are vigilant with respect to the rights of criminal defendants.

The conclusion one cannot help coming to is that whatever is to be done about rape will have to be done by women primarily. Brownmiller feels that law enforcement must include 50 percent women. She finds it significant that whereas male law-enforcement authorities report 15 or 20 percent of rape complaints to be "unfounded," among the ones they actually bother to write down, women investigators find only 2 percent of such reports to be unfounded, exactly the number of unfounded reports of other violent crimes. Apparently the goal of male-female law enforcement is not without its difficulties; women police officers in Washington, D.C., recently have complained that their male patrol-car partners are attempting to force them to have sexual intercourse. Since these women are armed with service revolvers, we may soon see an escalation of what appears to be the Oldest Conflict.

MacKellar and the LEAA report both favor some sort of rape sentencing by degree, as in murder, with rape by a stranger constituting first-degree rape, and third degree taking cognizance of situations in which the victim may be judged to have shared responsibility for initiating the situation that led to the rape — for instance, hitchhiking. This is a compromise that would be unacceptable to feminist groups who feel that a woman is no more responsible for a rape under those circumstances than a man would be thought to be who was assaulted in the same situation.

It is likely that the concept of penalty by degree, with its concession to history, will prevail here, but one sees the objection on principle. While men continue to believe that men have a right to assert their authority over women by sexual and other means, rape will continue, and this in turn suggests two more measures. One is control of pornography, which Brownmiller argues is the means by which the rape ethic is promulgated. In spite of objections about censorship and about the lack of evidence that pornography and violence are related, Brownmiller's argument here is a serious one. She also feels that women should learn self-defense, if only to give them increased self-confidence and awareness of their bodies. But it is easy to see that this is yet another way in which the female might be made to take responsibility for being raped. If a woman learns karate and is raped anyway, the question will become, why hadn't she learned it better?

Surely the definition of civilization is a state of things where the strong refrain from exercising their advantages over the weak. If men can be made to see that the abolition of sexual force is necessary in the long-term interest of making a civilization, then they may cooperate in implementing whatever measures turn out to be of any use. For the short term, one imagines, the general effect of female activism about rape will be to polarize men and women even more than nature has required. The cooperation of state authorities, if any, may ensue from their perception of rape, especially black-on-white rape, as a challenge to white male authority (as in the South). This in turn may produce an unlikely and ominous coalition of cops and feminists, and the generally severer prosecution and sentencing which we see as the current response to other forms of violent crime. But do we know that rapists will emerge from the prisons — themselves centers of homosexual rape — any less inclined to do it again?

Meantime, one feels a certain distaste for the congratulatory mood surrounding proposed law-enforcement reforms devoted entirely to making the crime less miserable for the victim while denying or concealing the complicity of so many men in its perpetuation. This implies a state of things worthy of a society described by Swift.°

AFTERWORD

"Rape" is an essay-review. A book review, narrowly conceived, tells us what's in a book and how good or bad it is. An essay-review — common in the New York Review of Books, *sometimes in the* New Yorker, *and in literary quarterlies — reports on a book but also assembles the essayist's own thoughts on the subject matter of the book. Sometimes an essayist-reviewer hardly touches on the book which is*

Swift Jonathan Swift (1667–1745), English author best known for *Gulliver's Travels,* which satirically depicted the political and social structure of the day.

nominally the subject or dismisses it to substitute his or her own subjects. Some examples seem pure egotism, but the form — as Diane Johnson uses it — can be valuable: The reader gets two for the price of one.

Notice how Diane Johnson, writing about outrage, avoids the language of out-rage. In her opening paragraph she refers to actions — specific like Richard Speck's multiple murders, general like the quotidian omnipresence of rape — without using potent words, like outrage. *The acts named are sufficient; the rhetoric of outrage would obscure the thing itself. A rule of thumb: When a writer represents an action morally neutral, like a total eclipse of the sun, the writer's language may embody extremities of violence, ecstasy, and pain. When a writer deals with the morally evil, or with the saintly, understatement suffices; perhaps it is requisite.*

BOOKS AVAILABLE IN PAPERBACK

Dashiell Hammett: A Life. New York: Fawcett Books. *Nonfiction.*
Persian Nights. New York: Fawcett Books. *Novel.*

JAMAICA
KINCAID

*J*AMAICA KINCAID *was born in Antigua, West Indies, in 1949, and came to the United States in 1966 as family help. Briefly attending Franconia College in New Hampshire, she worked at odd jobs until she began contributing to the* New Yorker, *joining its staff in 1976.* At the Bottom of the River *(1983) collects her short stories. Her novels are* Annie John *(1985),* Lucy *(1990), and* Autobiography of My Mother *(1994). She has written a long essay about Antigua and colonialism called* A Small Place *(1988).*

"Flowers of Evil" came out in the New Yorker *as a gardening column. The* New Yorker *has published much of her fiction, and when the editors assigned Kincaid a column on gardening, they knew that she would not take her subject matter as a boundary.*

Kincaid lives in Vermont now, with her composer husband and their two children, in a climate that demands ingenuity from the gardener.

Flowers of Evil

The way you think and feel about gardens and the things growing in them — flowers, vegetables — I can see must depend on where you come from, and I don't mean the difference in opinion and feeling between a person from Spain and a person from England but a difference like this:

> The implements of the little feast had been disposed upon the lawn of an old English country-house, in what I should call the perfect middle of a splendid summer afternoon. Part of the afternoon had waned, but much of it was left, and what was left was of the finest and rarest quality. Real dusk would not arrive for many hours; but the flood of summer light had begun to ebb, the air had grown mellow, the shadows were long upon the smooth, dense turf. . . . The great still oaks and beeches flung down a shade as dense as that of velvet curtains; and the place was furnished, like a room, with cushioned seats, with rich-colored rugs, with the books and papers that lay upon the grass.

And this:

> The smooth, stoneless drive ran between squat, robust conifers on one side and a blaze of canna lilies burning scarlet and amber on the other. Plants like that belonged to the cities. They had belonged to the pages of my language reader, to the yards of Ben and Betty's uncle in town. Now, having seen it for myself because of my Babamukuru's kindness, I too could think of planting things for merrier reasons than the chore of keeping breath in the body. I wrote it down in my head: I would ask Maiguru for some bulbs and plant a bed of those gay lilies on the homestead. In front of the house. Our home would answer well to being cheered up by such lovely flowers. Bright and cheery, they had been planted for joy. What a strange idea that was. It was a liberation, the first of many that followed from my transition to the mission.

The first quotation is from Henry James's novel *The Portrait of a Lady*, and it can be found isolated in a book called *Pleasures of the Garden: Images from the Metropolitan Museum of Art*, by Mac Griswold, beneath a painting by Pierre Bonnard called *The Terrace at Vernon*. The painting is rich, rich, rich: rich in color (a profusion of reds, oranges, yellows, blues, greens), rich in material things, rich in bounty from the land. And the quotation itself, with its "little feast," its luxurious observations "splendid summer afternoon" and "flood of summer light," could have been written only by a person who comes from a place where the wealth of the world is like a skin, a natural part of the body, a right, assumed, like having two hands and on them five fingers each.

It is the second quotation that immediately means something to me, especially this: "Bright and cheery, they had been planted for joy. What a strange idea that was." These sentences are from a novel called *Nervous Conditions*, by a woman from Zimbabwe named Tsitsi Dangarembga, and I suppose it is a coming-of-age novel (and really, most people who come from the far parts of the world who write books write at some point about their childhood — I believe it is a coincidence); but the book is also a description of brutality, foreign and local. There are the ingredients for a garden — a plot of land, a hoe, some seeds — but they do not lead to little feasts; they lead to nothing or they lead to work, and not work as an act of self-definition, self-acclaim, but work as torture, work as hell. And so it is quite appropriate that the young narrator — her name is Tambu — finds in the sight of things growing just for the sheer joy of it liberation.

And what is the relationship between gardening and conquest? Is the conqueror a gardener and the conquered the person who works in the field? The climate of southern Africa is not one that has only recently become hospitable to flowering herbs, and so it is quite possible (most likely) that the ancestors of this girl Tambu would have noticed them and cultivated them, not only for their medicinal value but also for the sheer joy of seeing them all by themselves in their loveliness, in afternoons that were waning, in light that had begun to ebb. At what moment was this idea lost? At what moment does such ordinary, everyday beauty become a luxury, then something forgotten?

When the Spanish marauder Hernando Cortez and his army invaded   5
Mexico, they met "floating gardens . . . teeming with flowers and vegetables, and moving like rafts over the waters"; as they looked down on the valley of Mexico, seeing it for the first time, a "picturesque assemblage of water, woodland, and cultivated plains, its shining cities and shadowy hills, was spread out like some gay and gorgeous panorama before them," and "stretching far away at their feet were seen noble forests of oak, sycamore, and cedar, and beyond, yellow fields of maize and the towering maguey, intermingled with orchards and blooming gardens"; there were "flowers, which, with their variegated and gaudy colors, form the greatest attraction of our greenhouses"; and again, "Extensive gardens were spread . . . filled with fragrant shrubs and flowers, and especially with medicinal plants. No country has afforded more numerous species of these last . . . and their virtues were perfectly understood by the Aztecs, with whom medical botany may be said to have been studied as a science." (All this is from *The Conquest of Mexico*, by William H. Prescott, and it is the best history of conquest I have ever read.) Quite likely, within a generation most of the inhabitants of this place (Mexico), spiritually devastated, would have lost touch with that strange idea — things planted for no other reason than the sheer joy of it.

Certainly if after the conquest an Aztec had gone into a shop and said "It's my husband's birthday. I would like to give him some flowers. May I have a bunch of cocoxochitl, please?" no one would have been able to help her, because cocoxochitl was no longer the name of that flower. It had become the dahlia. In its place of origin (Mexico, Central America), the people who lived there had no dahliamania, no Dahlia Societies, no dinner-plate-size dahlia, no peony-, no anemone-, no ball-shaped-, no water-lily-, no pompon-flowered dahlia. The flower seems to have been appreciated and cultivated for its own sake and for its medicinal value (urinary-tract disorders — cocoxichitl means "water pipes") and as animal fodder. And understandably, beautiful as this flower would have appeared to these people, there were so many other flowers and shrubs and trees and vines, each with some overpowering attribute of shape, height, color of bloom, and scent, that it would not be singled out; the sight of this flower would not have inspired in these people a single criminal act.

At what moment is the germ of possession lodged in the heart? When another Spanish marauder, Vasco Núñez de Balboa, was within sight of the Pacific Ocean, he made his army stay behind him, so that he could be the first person like himself (a European person) to see this ocean; it is likely that could this ocean have been taken up and removed to somewhere else (Spain, Portugal, England), the people for whom it had become a spiritual fixture would long for it and at the same time not even know what it was they were missing. And so the dahlia: Who first saw it and longed for it so deeply that it was removed from the place where it had always been, and transformed (hybridized), and renamed? Hernando Cortez would not have noticed it; to him the dahlia would have been one of the details, a small detail, of something large and grim: conquest. The dahlia went to Europe; it was hybridized by the Swedish botanist Andreas Dahl, after whom it was renamed.

I was once in a garden in the mountains way above Kingston (Jamaica), and from a distance I saw a mass of tall stalks of red flames, something in bloom. It looked familiar, but what it resembled, what it reminded me of, was a flower I cannot stand, and these flowers I saw before me I immediately loved, and they made me feel glad for the millionth time that I am from the West Indies. (This worthless feeling, this bestowing special qualities on yourself because of the beauty of the place you are from, is hard to resist — so hard that people who come from the ugliest place deny that it is ugly at all or simply go out and take someone else's beauty for themselves.) These flowering stalks of red flames turned out to be salvia, but I knew it was salvia only because I had seen it grown — a much shorter variety — in North American gardens; and I realized that I cannot stand it when I see it growing in the north because that shade of red can't be borne well by a dwarfish plant.

I do not know the names of the plants in the place I am from (Antigua). I can identify the hibiscus, but I do not know the name of a white lily that blooms in July, opening at night, perfuming the air with a sweetness that is almost sickening, and closing up at dawn. There is a bush called whitehead bush; it was an important ingredient in the potions my mother and her friends made for their abortions, but I do not know its proper name; this same bush I often had to go and cut down and tie in bunches to make a broom for sweeping our yard; both the abortions and the sweeping of the yard, actions deep and shallow, in a place like that (Antigua) would fall into the category called Household Management. I had wanted to see the garden in Kingston so that I could learn the names of some flowers in the West Indies, but along with the salvia the garden had in it only roses and a single anemic-looking yellow lupine (and this surprised me, because lupine is an alpine flower and I had very recently seen it in bloom along the roadside of a town in Finland).

This ignorance of the botany of the place I am from (and am of) really only reflects the fact that when I lived there, I was of the conquered class and living in a conquered place; a principle of this condition is that nothing about you is of any interest unless the conqueror deems it so. For instance, there was a botanical garden not far from where I lived, and in it were plants from various parts of the then British Empire, places that had the same climate as my own; but as I remember, none of the plants were native to Antigua. The rubber tree from Malaysia (or somewhere) is memorable because in the year my father and I were sick at the same time (he with heart disease, I with hookworms), we would go and sit under this tree after we ate our lunch, and under this tree he would tell me about his parents, who had abandoned him and gone off to build the Panama Canal (though of course he disguised the brutality of this). The bamboo grove is memorable because it was there I used to meet people I was in love with. The botanical garden reinforced for me how powerful were the people who had conquered me; they could bring to me the botany of the world they owned. It wouldn't at all surprise me to learn that in Malaysia (or somewhere) was a botanical garden with no plants native to that place.

There was a day not long ago when I realized with a certain amount of bitterness that I was in my garden, a flower garden, a garden planted only because I wished to have such a thing, and that I knew how I wanted it to look and knew the name, proper and common, of each thing growing in it. In the place I am from, I would have been a picture of shame: a woman covered with dirt, smelling of manure, her hair flecked with white dust (powdered lime), her body a cauldron of smells pleasing to her, and her back crooked with pain from bending over. In the place I am from, I would not have allowed a man with the same description as such a woman to kiss me.

It is understandable that a man like Andreas Dahl would not have demurred at his eponymous honor, because this was the eighteenth century and the honor was bestowed on him by a king (a Charles of Spain, who might well have named the flower after himself, or a close relative, or any one of the many henchmen in his service). Andreas Dahl was very familiar with the habit of naming, for he had been a pupil of Carl Linnaeus. This man, Carl Linnaeus, had been a botanist and a doctor, and that made sense, botanist and doctor: they went together because plants were the main source of medicine in that part of the world then, as was true in the other parts of the world then also. From Sweden (his place of origin) he had gone to the Netherlands for his doctor's degree, and it was there, while serving as personal physician to a rich man, that he worked out his system (binomial) of naming plants. The rich man (his name was George Clifford) had four greenhouses filled with plants not native to the Netherlands — not native to Europe at all but native to the places that had been recently conquered. *The Oxford Companion to Gardens* (a book I often want to hurl across the room, it is so full of prejudice) describes Linnaeus as "enraptured" with seeing all these plants from far away, because his native Sweden did not have anything like them, but most likely what happened was that he saw an opportunity, and it was this: These countries in Europe shared the same botany, more or less, but each place called the same thing by a different name; and these people who make up Europe were (are) so contentious anyway, they would not have agreed to one system for all the plants they had in common but these new plants from far away, like the people far away, had no history, no names, and so they could be given names. And who was there to dispute Linnaeus, even if there was someone who would listen?

This naming of things is so crucial to possession — a spiritual padlock with the key thrown irretrievably away — that it is a murder, an erasing, and it is not surprising that when people have felt themselves prey to it (conquest), among their first acts of liberation is to change their names (Rhodesia to Zimbabwe, LeRoi Jones to Amiri Baraka). That the great misery and much smaller joy of existence remain unchanged no matter what anything is called never checks the impulse to reach back and reclaim a loss, to try and make what happened look as if it had not happened at all.

As I started to write this (at the very beginning) I was sitting at a window that looked out over my own garden, a new one (I have just moved to this place), and my eye began in the deep-shade area, where I had planted some astilbe and hosta and *Ranunculus repens*, and I thought how beautifully the leaves of the astilbe went with the leaves of the ranunculus, and I took pleasure in that because in putting things together (plants) you never really know how it will all work until they do something, like bloom. (It will be two or three years before I know whether the clematis really will run up the rosebushes and bloom together with them and whether it will really look the way I have imagined.) Just now the leaves in the shade bed are all complementary (but not in a predictable way — in a way I had not expected, a thrilling way). And I thought how I had crossed a line; but at whose expense? I cannot begin to look, because what if it is someone I know? I have joined the conquering class: Who else could afford this garden — a garden in which I grow things that it would be much cheaper to buy at the store?

My feet are (so to speak) in two worlds, I was thinking as I looked farther   15
into the garden and saw, beyond the pumpkin patch, a fox emerge from
the hedge — the same spot in the hedge where I have seen the rabbits
and a family of malicious woodchucks emerge (the woodchucks to eat not
the lettuce or the beans or the other things I would expect them to eat but
the tender new shoots and tendrils of the squash vines). The fox crossed the
garden and ran behind the shed, and I could see him clearly, his face a set
of sharp angles, his cheeks planed, his body a fabric of tightly woven gray
and silver hair over a taut frame of sinew and bones, his tail a perfect
furpiece. He disappeared into the opposite hedge and field; he, too, had the
look of the marauder, wandering around hedge and field looking for prey.
That night, lying in my bed, I heard from beyond the hedge where he had
emerged sounds of incredible agony; he must have found his prey; but the
fox is in nature, and in nature things work that way.

I am not in nature. I do not find the world furnished like a room, with
cushioned seats and rich-colored rugs. To me, the world is cracked, unwhole,
not pure, accidental; and the idea of moments of joy for no reason is very
strange.

AFTERWORD

*In her fourth paragraph, Jamaica Kincaid asks, "And what is the relationship
between gardening and conquest? Is the conqueror a gardener and the conquered
the person who works in the field?" Every time I read the second question, I think
she will say "and the conquered the earth of the garden?" The notion that there
might be a difference between "the gardener" and "the person who works in the
field" does not occur to the American middle class. For Jamaica Kincaid, born in the
West Indies, imperialism and conquest necessarily form a template through which
the world is observed and measured. This is a gardening column; this is a column
on colonialism and imperialism.*

*Kincaid's prose is full of questions. In the work of a beginning writer, questions
often seem rhetorical or mechanical, even evasive. We want to say, "Make up your
mind. You tell me." But Kincaid writes by setting up and exploring difficult nodes
of thinking, and her questions serve her well. Her style is informal — note how her
dashes qualify or identify, as the rushing mind fills in what it neglected to provide — and includes the reader by its intimacy, while it wanders and leaps, leaps
and wanders. This essay constructs itself to seem random, but by its conclusion
succeeds in picking up loose ends. The tapestry truly and smoothly completes itself.*

BOOKS AVAILABLE IN PAPERBACK

Annie John. New York: Dutton. *Novel.*

At the Bottom of the River. New York: Dutton. *Short Stories.*

Lucy. New York: Dutton. *Novel.*

A Small Place. New York: Dutton. *Nonfiction.*

MAXINE HONG
KINGSTON

*M*AXINE HONG KINGSTON *was born in California in 1940, the eldest of six children in a Chinese immigrant family. English is her second language, and only recently has she begun to dream in it. She grew up in the town of Stockton, in the San Joaquin Valley, where her family ran a laundry. Stockton's small Chinese population, most of whom came from a village called Sun Woi, regularly gathered at the laundry to tell stories. What the young child heard became material for the adult writer.*

Kingston graduated from the University of California at Berkeley in 1962 and taught high school in California and Hawaii, where she has lived for many years. She has published poetry, stories, and articles in a variety of magazines — the New York Times Magazine, New West, Ms., the New Yorker, Iowa Review — and has received extensive honors for her two books of reminiscence. This essay is the first chapter of The Woman Warrior: Memoirs of a Girlhood Among Ghosts *(1975), which won the National Book Critics Circle Award for Nonfiction. She followed it with* China Men *(1980), which received the American Book Award. In 1989, her novel* Tripmaster Monkey: His Fake Book *won the PEN West Award. From stories that an eldest child heard from her mother, and from the nostalgic ambience of a laundry in Stockton, Maxine Hong Kingston assembles narrative and reminiscence that embody the collision and amalgamation of two cultures — the same combination that produced the author herself.*

Writing as a member of a minority, Kingston has encountered a familiar problem: Some Chinese-Americans complain that she is unrepresentative of her cultural sources. She has replied: "When people criticize my work by saying that it does not reflect their experience, I hear an assumption that one of us — in this case, me — is expected to speak for all the rest. I don't think that is a good expectation. Each one

_____ Photo by Jane Scherr

of us has a unique voice, and no one else will see things exactly the way I do, or write about them the way I do." With her eye for particulars, with her intense feeling for family and for her family's alien America, she makes with her unique voice a special human reality.

An interviewer quoted Kingston to herself — "I have no idea how people who don't write endure their lives" — and asked for more. She answered, "When I said that, I was thinking about how words and stories create order. And some of the things that happen to us in life seem to have no meaning, but when you write them down you find the meanings for them; or, as you translate life into words, you force a meaning." One of the anomalies of the writer's life, heaven knows, is never to know whether you have discovered, or invented, the meaning you write down.

Maxine Hong Kingston is tale-teller for her tribe; she is shape-maker for herself and for all of us.

No Name Woman

"You must not tell anyone," my mother said, "what I am about to tell you. In China your father had a sister who killed herself. She jumped into the family well. We say that your father has all brothers because it is as if she had never been born.

"In 1924 just a few days after our village celebrated seventeen hurry-up weddings — to make sure that every young man who went 'out on the road' would responsibly come home — your father and his brothers and your grandfather and his brothers and your aunt's new husband sailed for America, the Gold Mountain. It was your grandfather's last trip. Those lucky enough to get contracts waved good-bye from the decks. They fed and guarded the stowaways and helped them off in Cuba, New York, Bali, Hawaii. 'We'll meet in California next year,' they said. All of them sent money home.

"I remember looking at your aunt one day when she and I were dressing; I had not noticed before that she had such a protruding melon of a stomach. But I did not think, 'She's pregnant,' until she began to look like other pregnant women, her skirt pulling and the white tops of her black pants showing. She could not have been pregnant, you see, because her husband had gone for years. No one said anything. We did not discuss it. In early summer she was ready to have the child, long after the time when it could have been possible.

"The village had also been counting. On the night the baby was to be born the villagers raided our house. Some were crying. Like a great saw, teeth strung with lights, files of people walked zigzag across our land, tearing the rice. Their lanterns doubled in the disturbed black water, which drained away through the broken bunds. As the villagers closed in, we could see that some of them, probably men and women we knew well, wore white masks. The people with long hair hung it over their faces. Women with short hair made it stand up on end. Some had tied white bands around their foreheads, arms, and legs.

"At first they threw mud and rocks at the house. Then they threw eggs 5 and began slaughtering our stock. We could hear the animals scream their deaths — the roosters, the pigs, a last great roar from the ox. Familiar wild heads flared in our night windows; the villagers encircled us. Some of the faces stopped to peer at us, their eyes rushing like searchlights. The hands flattened against the panes, framed heads, and left red prints.

"The villagers broke in the front and the back doors at the same time, even though we had not locked the doors against them. Their knives dripped with the blood of our animals. They smeared blood on the doors and walls. One woman swung a chicken, whose throat she had slit, splattering blood in red arcs about her. We stood together in the middle of our house, in the family hall with the pictures and tables of the ancestors around us, and looked straight ahead.

"At that time the house had only two wings. When the men came back, we would build two more to enclose our courtyard and a third one to begin a second courtyard. The villagers pushed through both wings, even your grandparents' rooms, to find your aunt's, which was also mine until the men returned. From this room a new wing for one of the younger families would grow. They ripped up her clothes and shoes and broke her combs, grinding them underfoot. They tore her work from the loom. They scattered the cooking fire and rolled the new weaving in it. We could hear them in the kitchen breaking our bowls and banging the pots. They overturned the great waist-high earthenware jugs; duck eggs, pickled fruits, vegetables burst out and mixed in acrid torrents. The old woman from the next field swept a broom through the air and loosed the spirits-of-the-broom over our heads. 'Pig.' 'Ghost.' 'Pig,' they sobbed and scolded while they ruined our house.

"When they left, they took sugar and oranges to bless themselves. They cut pieces from the dead animals. Some of them took bowls that were not broken and clothes that were not torn. Afterward we swept up the rice and sewed it back up into sacks. But the smells from the spilled preserves lasted. Your aunt gave birth in the pigsty that night. The next morning when I went for the water, I found her and the baby plugging up the family well.

"Don't let your father know that I told you. He denies her. Now that you have started to menstruate, what happened to her could happen to you. Don't humiliate us. You wouldn't like to be forgotten as if you had never been born. The villagers are watchful."

Whenever she had to warn us about life, my mother told stories that ran 10 like this one, a story to grow up on. She tested our strength to establish realities. Those in the emigrant generations who could not reassert brute survival died young and far from home. <u>Those of us in the first American</u>

generations have had to figure out how the invisible world the emigrants built around our childhoods fit in solid America.

The emigrants confused the gods by diverting their curses, misleading them with crooked streets and false names. They must try to confuse their offspring as well, who, I suppose, threaten them in similar ways — always trying to get things straight, always trying to name the unspeakable. The Chinese I know hide their names; sojourners take new names when their lives change and guard their real names with silence.

Chinese-Americans, when you try to understand what things in you are Chinese, how do you separate what is peculiar to childhood, to poverty, insanities, one family, your mother who marked your growing with stories, from what is Chinese? What is Chinese tradition and what is the movies?

If I want to learn what clothes my aunt wore, whether flashy or ordinary, I would have to begin, "Remember Father's drowned-in-the-well sister?" I cannot ask that. My mother has told me once and for all the useful parts. She will add nothing unless powered by Necessity, a riverbank that guides her life. She plants vegetable gardens rather than lawns; she carries the odd-shaped tomatoes home from the fields and eats food left for the gods.

Whenever we did frivolous things, we used up energy; we flew high kites. We children came up off the ground over the melting cones our parents brought home from work and the American movie on New Year's Day — *Oh, You Beautiful Doll* with Betty Grable one year, and *She Wore A Yellow Ribbon* with John Wayne another year. After the one carnival ride each, we paid in guilt; our tired father counted his change on the dark walk home.

Adultery is extravagance. Could people who hatch their own chicks and   15
eat the embryos and the heads for delicacies and boil the feet in vinegar for party food, leaving only the gravel, eating even the gizzard lining — could such people engender a prodigal aunt? To be a woman, to have a daughter in starvation time was a waste enough. My aunt could not have been the lone romantic who gave up everything for sex. Women in the old China did not choose. Some man had commanded her to lie with him and be his secret evil. I wonder whether he masked himself when he joined the raid on her family.

Perhaps she encountered him in the fields or on the mountain where the daughters-in-law collected fuel. Or perhaps he first noticed her in the marketplace. He was not a stranger because the village housed no strangers. She had to have dealings with him other than sex. Perhaps he worked an adjoining field, or he sold her the cloth for the dress she sewed and wore. His demand must have surprised, then terrified her. She obeyed him; she always did as she was told.

When the family found a young man in the next village to be her husband, she stood tractably beside the best rooster, his proxy, and promised before they met that she would be his forever. She was lucky that he was her age and she would be the first wife, an advantage secure now. The night she first saw him, he had sex with her. Then he left for America. She had almost forgotten what he looked like. When she tried to envision him, she only saw the black and white face in the group photograph the men had had taken before leaving.

The other man was not, after all, much different from her husband. They both gave orders: she followed. "If you tell your family, I'll beat you. I'll kill you. Be here again next week." No one talked sex, ever. And she might have separated the rapes from the rest of living if only she did not have to buy her oil from him or gather wood in the same forest. I want her fear to have lasted just as long as rape lasted so that the fear could have been contained. No drawn-out fear. But women at sex hazarded birth and hence lifetimes. The fear did not stop but permeated everywhere. She told the man, "I think I'm pregnant." He organized the raid against her.

On nights when my mother and father talked about their life back home, sometimes they mentioned an "outcast table" whose business they still seemed to be settling, their voices tight. In a commensal tradition, where food is precious, the powerful older people made wrongdoers eat alone. Instead of letting them start separate new lives like the Japanese, who could become samurais and geishas, the Chinese family, faces averted but eyes glowering sideways, hung on to the offenders and fed them leftovers. My aunt must have lived in the same house as my parents and eaten at an outcast table. My mother spoke about the raid as if she had seen it, when she and my aunt, a daughter-in-law to a different household, should not have been living together at all. Daughters-in-law lived with their husbands' parents, not their own; a synonym for marriage in Chinese is "taking a daughter-in-law." Her husband's parents could have sold her, mortgaged her, stoned her. But they had sent her back to her own mother and father, a mysterious act hinting at disgraces not told me. Perhaps they had thrown her out to deflect the avengers.

She was the only daughter; her four brothers went with her father, husband, and uncles "out on the road" and for some years became Western men. When the goods were divided among the family, three of the brothers took land, and the youngest, my father, chose an education. After my grandparents gave their daughter away to her husband's family, they had dispensed all the adventure and all the property. They expected her alone to keep the traditional ways, which her brothers, now among the barbarians, could fumble without detection. The heavy, deep-rooted women were to maintain the past against the flood, safe for returning. But the rare urge west had fixed upon our family, and so my aunt crossed boundaries not delineated in space.

The work of preservation demands that the feelings playing about in one's guts not be turned into action. Just watch their passing like cherry blossoms. But perhaps my aunt, my forerunner, caught in a slow life, let dreams grow and fade and after some months or years went toward what persisted. Fear at the enormities of the forbidden kept her desires delicate, wire and bone. She looked at a man because she liked the way the hair was tucked behind his ears, or she liked the question-mark line of a long torso curving at the shoulder and straight at the hip. For warm eyes or a soft voice or a slow walk — that's all — a few hairs, a line, a brightness, a sound, a pace, she gave up family. She offered us up for a charm that vanished with tiredness, a pigtail that didn't toss when the wind died. Why, the wrong lighting could erase the dearest thing about him.

It could very well have been, however, that my aunt did not take subtle enjoyment of her friend, but, a wild woman, kept rollicking company. Imagining her free with sex doesn't fit, though. I don't know any women like that, or men either. Unless I see her life branching into mine, she gives me no ancestral help.

To sustain her being in love, she often worked at herself in the mirror, guessing at the colors and shapes that would interest him, changing them frequently in order to hit on the right combination. She wanted him to look back.

On a farm near the sea, a woman who tended her appearance reaped a reputation for eccentricity. All the married women blunt-cut their hair in flaps about their ears or pulled it back in tight buns. No nonsense. Neither style blew easily into heart-catching tangles. And at their weddings they displayed themselves in their long hair for the last time. "It brushed the backs of my knees," my mother tells me. "It was braided, and even so, it brushed the backs of my knees."

At the mirror my aunt combed individuality into her bob. A bun could have been contrived to escape into black streamers blowing in the wind or in quiet wisps about her face, but only the older women in our picture album wear buns. She brushed her hair back from her forehead, tucking the flaps behind her ears. She looped a piece of thread, knotted into a circle between her index fingers and thumbs, and ran the double strand across her forehead. When she closed her fingers as if she were making a pair of shadow geese bite, the string twisted together catching the little hairs. Then she pulled the thread away from her skin, ripping the hairs out neatly, her eyes watering from the needles of pain. Opening her fingers, she cleaned the thread, then rolled it along her hairline and the tops of her eyebrows. My mother did the same to me and my sisters and herself. I used to believe that the expression "caught by the short hairs" meant a captive held with a depilatory string. It especially hurt at the temples, but my mother said we were lucky we didn't have to have our feet bound when we were seven. Sisters used to sit on their beds and cry together, she said, as their mothers or their slave removed the bandages for a few minutes each night and let the blood gush back into their veins. I hope that the man my aunt loved appreciated a smooth brow, that he wasn't just a tits-and-ass man.

Once my aunt found a freckle on her chin, at a spot that the almanac said predestined her for unhappiness. She dug it out with a hot needle and washed the wound with peroxide.

More attention to her looks than these pullings of hairs and pickings at spots would have caused gossip among the villagers. They owned work clothes and good clothes, and they wore good clothes for feasting the new seasons. But since a woman combing her hair hexes beginnings, my aunt rarely found an occasion to look her best. Women looked like great sea snails — the corded wood, babies, and laundry they carried were the whorls on their backs. The Chinese did not admire a bent back; goddesses and warriors stood straight. Still there must have been a marvelous freeing of beauty when a worker laid down her burden and stretched and arched.

Such commonplace loveliness, however, was not enough for my aunt. She dreamed of a lover for the fifteen days of New Year's, the time for families to exchange visits, money, and food. She plied her secret comb. And sure enough she cursed the year, the family, the village, and herself.

Even as her hair lured her imminent lover, many other men looked at her. Uncles, cousins, nephews, brothers would have looked, too, had they been home between journeys. Perhaps they had already been restraining their curiosity, and they left, fearful that their glances, like a field of nesting birds, might be startled and caught. Poverty hurt, and that was their first reason for leaving. But another, final reason for leaving the crowded house was the never-said.

She may have been unusually beloved, the precious only daughter, 30 spoiled and mirror gazing because of the affection the family lavished on her. When her husband left, they welcomed the chance to take her back from the in-laws; she could live like the little daughter for just a while longer. There are stories that my grandfather was different from other people, "crazy ever since the little Jap bayoneted him in the head." He used to put his naked penis on the dinner table, laughing. And one day he brought home a baby girl, wrapped up inside his brown western-style greatcoat. He had traded one of his sons, probably my father, the youngest, for her. My grandmother made him trade back. When he finally got a daughter of his own, he doted on her. They must have all loved her, except perhaps my father, the only brother who never went back to China, having once been traded for a girl.

Brothers and sisters, newly men and women, had to efface their sexual color and present plain miens. Disturbing hair and eyes, a smile like no other, threatened the ideal of five generations living under one roof. To focus blurs, people shouted face to face and yelled from room to room. The immigrants I know have loud voices, unmodulated to American tones even after years away from the village where they called their friendships out across the fields. I have not been able to stop my mother's screams in public libraries or over telephones. Walking erect (knees straight, toes pointed forward, not pigeon-toed, which is Chinese-feminine), and speaking in an inaudible voice, I have tried to turn myself American-feminine. Chinese communication was loud, public. Only sick people had to whisper. But at the dinner table, where the family members came nearest one another, no one could talk, not the outcasts nor any eaters. Every word that falls from the mouth is a coin lost. Silently they gave and accepted food with both hands. A preoccupied child who took his bowl with one hand got a sideways glare. A complete moment of total attention is due everyone alike. Children and lovers have no singularity here, but my aunt used a secret voice, a separate attentiveness.

She kept the man's name to herself throughout her labor and dying; she did not accuse him that he be punished with her. To save her inseminator's name she gave silent birth.

He may have been somebody in her own household, but intercourse with a man outside the family would have been no less abhorrent. All the village were kinsmen, and the titles shouted in loud country voices never let kinship be forgotten. Any man within visiting distance would have been neutralized as a lover — "brother," "younger brother," "older brother" — one hundred and fifteen relationship titles. Parents researched birth charts probably not so much to assure good fortune as to circumvent incest in a population that has but one hundred surnames. Everybody has eight million relatives. How useless then sexual mannerisms, how dangerous.

As if it came from an atavism deeper than fear, I used to add "brother" silently to boys' names. It hexed the boys, who would or would not ask me to dance, and made them less scary and as familiar and deserving of benevolence as girls.

But, of course, I hexed myself also — no dates. I should have stood up, both arms waving, and shouted out across libraries, "Hey you! Love me back." I had no idea, though, how to make attraction selective, how to control its direction and magnitude. If I made myself American-pretty so that the five or six Chinese boys in the class fell in love with me, everyone else — the Caucasian, Negro, and Japanese boys — would too. Sisterliness, dignified and honorable, made much more sense.

Attraction eludes control so stubbornly that whole societies designed to organize relationships among people cannot keep order, not even when they bind people to one another from childhood and raise them together. Among the very poor and the wealthy, brothers married their adopted sisters, like doves. Our family allowed some romance, paying adult brides' prices and providing dowries so that their sons and daughters could marry strangers. Marriage promises to turn strangers into friendly relatives — a nation of siblings.

In the village structure, spirits shimmered among the live creatures, balanced and held in equilibrium by time and land. But one human being flaring up into violence could open up a black hole, a maelstrom that pulled in the sky. The frightened villagers, who depended on one another to maintain the real, went to my aunt to show her a personal, physical representation of the break she had made in the "roundness." Misallying couples snapped off the future, which was to be embodied in true offspring. The villagers punished her for acting as if she could have a private life, secret and apart from them.

If my aunt had betrayed the family at a time of large grain yields and peace, when many boys were born, and wings were being built on many houses, perhaps she might have escaped such severe punishment. But the men — hungry, greedy, tired of planting in dry soil, cuckolded — had had to leave the village in order to send food-money home. There were ghost plagues, bandit plagues, wars with the Japanese, floods. My Chinese brother and sister had died of an unknown sickness. Adultery, perhaps only a mistake during good times, became a crime when the village needed food.

The round moon cakes and round doorways, the round tables of gradu-ated size that fit one roundness into another, round windows and rice bowls — these talismans had lost their power to warn this family of the law: A family must be whole, faithfully keeping the descent line by having sons to feed the old and the dead, who in turn look after the family. The villagers came to show my aunt and her lover-in-hiding a broken house. The villagers were speeding up the circling of events because she was too shortsighted to see that her infidelity had already harmed the village, that waves of conse-quences would return unpredictably, sometimes in disguise, as now, to hurt her. This roundness had to be made coin-sized so that she would see its circumference: Punish her at the birth of her baby. Awaken her to the inexo-rable. People who refused fatalism because they could invest small resources insisted on culpability. Deny accidents and wrest fault from the stars.

After the villagers left, their lanterns now scattering in various directions 40 toward home, the family broke their silence and cursed her. "Aiaa, we're going to die. Death is coming. Death is coming. Look what you've done. You've killed us. Ghost! Dead ghost! Ghost! You've never been born." She ran out into the fields, far enough from the house so that she could no longer hear their voices, and pressed herself against the earth, her own land no more. When she felt the birth coming, she thought that she had been hurt. Her body seized together. "They've hurt me too much," she thought. "This is gall, and it will kill me." With forehead and knees against the earth, her body convulsed and then relaxed. She turned on her back, lay on the ground. The black well of sky and stars went out and out and out forever; her body and her complexity seemed to disappear. She was one of the stars, a bright dot in blackness, without home, without a companion, in eternal cold and silence. An agoraphobia rose in her, speeding higher and higher, bigger and bigger; she would not be able to contain it; there would be no end to fear.

Flayed, unprotected against space, she felt pain return, focusing her body. This pain chilled her — a cold, steady kind of surface pain. Inside, spasmodi-cally, the other pain, the pain of the child, heated her. For hours she lay on the ground, alternately body and space. Sometimes a vision of normal comfort obliterated reality: she saw the family in the evening gambling at the dinner table, the young people massaging their elders' backs. She saw them congratulating one another, high joy on the mornings the rice shoots came up. When these pictures burst, the stars drew yet further apart. Black space opened.

She got to her feet to fight better and remembered that old-fashioned women gave birth in their pigsties to fool the jealous, pain-dealing gods, who do not snatch piglets. Before the next spasms could stop her, she ran to the pigsty, each step a rushing out into emptiness. She climbed over the fence and knelt in the dirt. It was good to have a fence enclosing her, a tribal person alone.

Laboring, this woman who had carried her child as a foreign growth that sickened her every day, expelled it at last. She reached down to touch the hot, wet, moving mass, surely smaller than anything human, and could feel that it was human after all — fingers, toes, nails, nose. She pulled it up on to her belly, and it lay curled there, butt in the air, feet precisely tucked one under the other. She opened her loose shirt and buttoned the child inside. After resting, it squirmed and thrashed and she pushed it up to her breast. It turned its head this way and that until it found her nipple. There, it made little snuffling noises. She clenched her teeth at its preciousness, lovely as a young calf, a piglet, a little dog.

She may have gone to the pigsty as a last act of responsibility: She would protect this child as she had protected its father. It would look after her soul, leaving supplies on her grave. But how would this tiny child without family find her grave when there would be no marker for her anywhere, neither in the earth nor the family hall? No one would give her a family hall name. She had taken the child with her into the wastes. At its birth the two of them had felt the same raw pain of separation, a wound that only the family pressing tight could close. A child with no descent line would not soften her life but only trail after her, ghostlike, begging her to give it purpose. At dawn the villagers on their way to the fields would stand around the fence and look.

Full of milk, the little ghost slept. When it awoke, she hardened her 45 breasts against the milk that crying loosens. Toward morning she picked up the baby and walked to the well.

Carrying the baby to the well shows loving. Otherwise abandon it. Turn its face into the mud. Mothers who love their children take them along. It was probably a girl; there is some hope of forgiveness for boys.

"Don't tell anyone you had an aunt. Your father does not want to hear her name. She has never been born." I have believed that sex was unspeakable and words so strong and fathers so frail that "aunt" would do my father mysterious harm. I have thought that my family, having settled among immigrants who had also been their neighbors in the ancestral land, needed to clean their name, and a wrong word would incite the kinspeople even here. But there is more to this silence: they want me to participate in her punishment. And I have.

In the twenty years since I heard this story I have not asked for details nor said my aunt's name; I do not know it. People who can comfort the dead can also chase after them to hurt them further — a reverse ancestor worship. The real punishment was not the raid swiftly inflicted by the villagers, but the family's deliberately forgetting her. Her betrayal so maddened them, they saw to it that she should suffer forever, even after death. Always hungry, always needing, she would have to beg food from other ghosts, snatch and steal it from those whose living descendants give them gifts. She would have to fight the ghosts massed at crossroads for the buns a few thoughtful citizens leave to decoy her away from village and home so that the ancestral spirits could feast unharassed. At peace, they could act like gods, not ghosts, their descent lines providing them with paper suits and dresses, spirit money, paper houses, paper automobiles, chicken, meat, and rice into eternity — essences delivered up in smoke and flames, steam and incense rising from each rice bowl. In an attempt to make the Chinese care for people outside the family, Chairman Mao encourages us now to give our paper replicas to the spirits of outstanding soldiers and workers, no matter whose ancestors they may be. My aunt remains forever hungry. Goods are not distributed evenly among the dead.

My aunt haunts me — her ghost drawn to me because now, after fifty years of neglect, I alone devote pages of paper to her, though not origamied into houses and clothes. I do not think she always means me well. I am telling on her, and she was a spite suicide, drowning herself in the drinking water. The Chinese are always very frightened of the drowned one, whose weeping ghost, wet hair hanging and skin bloated, waits silently by the water to pull down a substitute.

AFTERWORD

This essay is more narrative than most; it is memoir or reminiscence with a wash of fiction. No one remembers conversations word for word; we are not tempted to believe that the young Maxine switched on a tape recorder whenever her mother spoke. In the act of writing memoir, we feel as if we were transcribing word for word conversations from twenty or forty years back. Upon reflection most of us will admit that phonographic reproduction by memory is most unlikely. We remember characteristic speech and particular plots; our imagination-memory mimics and we transcribe this mimicry. Out of my own memoir writing, I can testify to the conviction with which one writes and to the corroboration of survivors: One can catch the tone of the dead. But also: I have told anecdotes in which I have located a time and place exactly remembered in luminous detail — only to discover, by consulting incontrovertible evidence, that my memory was wrong. None of which expresses skepticism about the truth, or at least the validity, of Kingston's account.

BOOKS AVAILABLE IN PAPERBACK

China Men. New York: Random House–Vintage. *Nonfiction.*

Tripmaster Monkey: His Fake Book. New York: Random House–Vintage. *Novel.*

The Woman Warrior: Memoirs of a Girlhood Among Ghosts. New York: Random House–Vintage. *Nonfiction.*

URSULA K.
LE GUIN

*B*ORN IN CALIFORNIA (1929), graduated from Radcliffe in 1951, Ursula K. Le Guin writes a science fiction unusual in its literary skill and political, often feminist, content. Her work is not limited to the genre of sci-fi; people have put many labels on her fiction: fantasy, realism, magical realism. She has written four books of poems, four books of short stories, and fifteen novels — including The Left Hand of Darkness (1969), The Farthest Shore (1972), which won a National Book Award, The Dispossessed (1974), and Always Coming Home (1985). We take this essay from her second collection of miscellaneous prose, Dancing at the Edge of the World (1989).

Le Guin's mind is energetic, lively, inventive — and often angry, especially about the position of women, both past and present. We represent her by a genre seldom found in essay collections — found twice in The Contemporary Essay — common as it is in the university: the commencement address. Like all the best commencement addresses, it is against commencement addresses.

Bryn Mawr
Commencement Address

Thinking about what I should say to you made me think about what we learn in college; and what we unlearn in college; and then how we learn to unlearn what we learned in college and relearn what we unlearned in college, and so on. And I thought how I have learned, more or less well, three languages, all of them English; and how one of these languages is the one I went to college to learn. I thought I was going to study French and Italian, and I did, but what I learned was the language of power — of social power; I shall call it the father tongue.

This is the public discourse, and one dialect of it is speech-making — by politicians, commencement speakers, or the old man who used to get up early in a village in Central California a couple of hundred years ago and say things very loudly on the order of "People need to be getting up now, there are things we might be doing, the repairs on the sweathouse aren't finished and the tarweed is in seed over on Bald Hill; this is a good time of day for doing things, and there'll be plenty of time for lying around when it gets hot this afternoon." So everybody would get up grumbling slightly, and some of them would go pick tarweed — probably the women. This is the effect, ideally, of the public discourse. It makes something happen, makes somebody — usually somebody else — do something, or at least it gratifies the ego of the speaker. The difference between our politics and that of a native Californian people is clear in the style of the public discourse. The difference wasn't clear to the White invaders, who insisted on calling any Indian who made a speech a "chief," because they couldn't comprehend, they wouldn't admit, an authority without supremacy — a nondominating authority. But it is such an authority that I possess for the brief — we all hope it is decently brief — time I speak to you. I have no right to speak to you. What I have is the responsibility you have given me to speak to you.

The political tongue speaks aloud — and look how radio and television have brought the language of politics right back where it belongs — but the dialect of the father tongue that you and I learned best in college is a written one. It didn't speak itself. It only lectures. It began to develop when printing made written language common rather than rare, five hundred years ago or so, and with electronic processing and copying it continues to develop and proliferate so powerfully, so dominatingly, that many believe this dialect — the expository and particularly the scientific discourse — is the *highest* form of language, the true language, of which all other uses of words are primitive vestiges.

330

And it is indeed an excellent dialect. Newton's *Principia* was written in it in Latin, and Descartes wrote Latin and French in it, establishing some of its basic vocabulary, and Kant wrote German in it, and Marx, Darwin, Freud, Boas, Foucault — all the great scientists and social thinkers wrote it. It is the language of thought that seeks objectivity.

I do not say it is the language of rational thought. Reason is a faculty far larger than mere objective thought. When either the political or the scientific discourse announces itself as the voice of reason, it is playing God, and should be spanked and stood in the corner. The essential gesture of the father tongue is not reasoning but distancing — making a gap, a space, between the subject or self and the object or other. Enormous energy is generated by that rending, that forcing of a gap between Man and World. So the continuous growth of technology and science fuels itself; the Industrial Revolution began with splitting the world-atom, and still by breaking the continuum into unequal parts we keep the imbalance from which our society draws the power that enables it to dominate every other culture, so that everywhere now everybody speaks the same language in laboratories and government buildings and headquarters and offices of business, and those who don't know it or won't speak it are silent, or silenced, or unheard.

You came here to college to learn the language of power — to be empowered. If you want to succeed in business, government, law, engineering, science, education, the media, if you want to succeed, you have to be fluent in the language in which "success" is a meaningful word.

White man speak with forked tongue; White man speak dichotomy. His language expresses the values of the split world, valuing the positive and devaluing the negative in each redivision: subject/object, self/other, mind/body, dominant/submissive, active/passive, Man/Nature, man/woman, and so on. The father tongue is spoken from above. It goes one way. No answer is expected or heard.

In our Constitution and the works of law, philosophy, social thought, and science, in its everyday uses in the service of justice and clarity, what I call the father tongue is immensely noble and indispensably useful. When it claims a privileged relationship to reality, it becomes dangerous and potentially destructive. It describes with exquisite accuracy the continuing destruction of the planet's ecosystem by its speakers. This word from its vocabulary, "ecosystem," is a word unnecessary except in a discourse that excludes its speakers from the ecosystem in a subject/object dichotomy of terminal irresponsibility.

The language of the fathers, of Man Ascending, Man the Conqueror, Civilized Man, is not your native tongue. It isn't anybody's native tongue. You didn't even hear the father tongue your first few years, except on the radio or TV, and then you didn't listen, and neither did your little brother, because it was some old politician with hairs in his nose yammering. And you and your brother had better things to do. You had another kind of power to learn. You were learning your mother tongue.

Using the father tongue, I can speak of the mother tongue only, inevita- 10
bly, to distance it — to exclude it. It is the other, inferior. It is primitive:
inaccurate, unclear, coarse, limited, trivial, banal. It's repetitive, the same
over and over, like the work called women's work; earthbound, house-
bound. It's vulgar, the vulgar tongue, common, common speech, colloquial,
low, ordinary, plebeian, like the work ordinary people do, the lives common
people live. The mother tongue, spoken or written, expects an answer. It is
conversation, a word the root of which means "turning together." The
mother tongue is language not as mere communication but as relation,
relationship. It connects. It goes two ways, many ways, an exchange, a
network. Its power is not in dividing but in binding, not in distancing but
in uniting. It is written, but not by scribes and secretaries for posterity; it
flies from the mouth on the breath that is our life and is gone, like the
outbreath, utterly gone and yet returning, repeated, the breath the same
again always, everywhere, and we all know it by heart. John have you got
your umbrella I think it's going to rain. Can you come play with me? If I
told you once I told you a hundred times. Things here just aren't the same
without Mother, I will now sign your affectionate brother James. Oh what
am I going to do? So I said to her I said if he thinks she's going to stand for
that but then there's his arthritis poor thing and no work. I love you. I hate
you. I hate liver. Joan dear did you feed the sheep, don't just stand around
mooning. Tell me what they said, tell me what you did. Oh how my feet do
hurt. My heart is breaking. Touch me here, touch me again. Once bit twice
shy. You look like what the cat dragged in. What a beautiful night. Good
morning, hello, good-bye, have a nice day, thanks. God damn you to hell
you lying cheat. Pass the soy sauce please. Oh shit. Is it grandma's own
sweet pretty dear? What am I going to tell her? There there don't cry. Go to
sleep now, go to sleep. . . . Don't go to sleep!

It is a language always on the verge of silence and often on the verge of
song. It is the language stories are told in. It is the language spoken by all
children and most women, and so I call it the mother tongue, for we learn
it from our mothers and speak it to our kids. I'm trying to use it here in
public where it isn't appropriate, not suited to the occasion, but I want to
speak it to you because we are women and I can't say what I want to say
about women in the language of capital M Man. If I try to be objective I will
say, "This is higher and that is lower," I'll make a commencement speech
about being successful in the battle of life, I'll lie to you; and I don't want to.

Early this spring I met a musician, the composer Pauline Oliveros, a
beautiful woman like a gray rock in a streambed; and to a group of us,
women, who were beginning to quarrel over theories in abstract, objective
language — and I with my splendid Eastern-women's-college training in the
father tongue was in the thick of the fight and going for the kill — to us,
Pauline, who is sparing with words, said after clearing her throat, "Offer
your experience as your truth." There was a short silence. When we started
talking again, we didn't talk objectively, and we didn't fight. We went back
to feeling our way into ideas, using the whole intellect not half of it, talking

with one another, which involves listening. We tried to offer our experience to one another. Not claiming something: offering something.

How, after all, can one experience deny, negate, disprove, another experience? Even if I've had a lot more of it, *your* experience is your truth. How can one being prove another being wrong? Even if you're a lot younger and smarter than me, *my* being is my truth. I can offer it; you don't have to take it. People can't contradict each other, only words can: words separated from experience for use as weapons, words that make the wound, the split between subject and object, exposing and exploiting the object but disguising and defending the subject.

People crave objectivity because to be subjective is to be embodied, to be a body, vulnerable, violable. Men especially aren't used to that; they're trained not to offer but to attack. It's often easier for women to trust one another, to try to speak our experience in our own language, the language we talk to each other in, the mother tongue; so we empower one another.

But you and I have learned to use the mother tongue only at home or 15 safe among friends, and many men learn not to speak it at all. They're taught that there's no safe place for them. From adolescence on, they talk a kind of degraded version of the father tongue with each other — sports scores, job technicalities, sex technicalities, and TV politics. At home, to women and children talking mother tongue, they respond with a grunt and turn on the ball game. They have let themselves be silenced, and dimly they know it, and so resent speakers of the mother tongue; women babble, gabble all the time. . . . Can't listen to that stuff.

Our schools and colleges, institutions of the patriarchy, generally teach us to listen to people in power, men or women speaking the father tongue; and so they teach us not to listen to the mother tongue, to what the powerless say, poor men, women, children: not to hear that as valid discourse.

I am trying to unlearn these lessons, along with other lessons I was taught by my society, particularly lessons concerning the minds, work, works, and being of women. I am a slow unlearner. But I love my unteachers — the feminist thinkers and writers and talkers and poets and artists and singers and critics and friends, from Wollstonecraft and Woolf through the furies and glories of the seventies and eighties — I celebrate here and now the women who for two centuries have worked for our freedom, the unteachers, the unmasters, the unconquerors, the unwarriors, women who have at risk and at high cost offered their experience as truth. "Let us NOT praise famous women!" Virginia Woolf scribbled in a margin when she was writing *Three Guineas,* and she's right, but still I have to praise these women and thank them for setting me free in my old age to learn my own language.

The third language, my native tongue, which I will never know though I've spent my life learning it: I'll say some words now in this language. First a name, just a person's name, you've heard it before. Sojourner Truth. That name is a language in itself. But Sojourner Truth spoke the unlearned language; about a hundred years ago, talking it in a public place, she said, "I

333

have been forty years a slave and forty years free and would be here forty years more to have equal rights for all." Along at the end of her talk she said, "I wanted to tell you a mite about Woman's Rights, and so I came out and said so. I am sittin' among you to watch; and every once and awhile I will come out and tell you what time of night it is." She said, "Now I will do a little singing. I have not heard any singing since I came here."[1]

Singing is one of the names of the language we never learn, and here for Sojourner Truth is a little singing. It was written by Joy Harjo of the Creek people and is called "The Blanket Around Her."[2]

> maybe it is her birth
> which she holds close to herself
> or her death
> which is just as inseparable
> and the white wind
> that encircles her is a part
> just as
>   the blue sky
> hanging in turquoise from her neck
>
> oh woman
> remember who you are
> woman
> it is the whole earth

So what am I talking about with this "unlearned language" — poetry, literature? Yes, but it can be speeches and science, any use of language when it is spoken, written, read, heard as art, the way dancing is the body moving as art. In Sojourner Truth's words you hear the coming together, the marriage of the public discourse and the private experience, making a power, a beautiful thing, the true discourse of reason. This is a wedding and welding back together of the alienated consciousness that I've been calling the father tongue and the undifferentiated engagement that I've been calling the mother tongue. This is your baby, this baby talk, the language you can spend your life trying to learn.

We learn this tongue first, like the mother tongue, just by hearing it or reading it; and even in our overcrowded, underfunded public high schools they still teach *A Tale of Two Cities* and *Uncle Tom's Cabin;* and in college you can take four solid years of literature, and even creative writing courses. But. It is all taught as if it were a dialect of the father tongue.

Literature takes shape and life in the body, in the womb of the mother tongue: always: And the Fathers of Culture get anxious about paternity. They

---

[1]Sojourner Truth, in *The Norton Anthology of Literature by Women,* ed. Sandra M. Gilbert and Susan Gubar (New York: W. W. Norton & Co., 1985), pp. 255–56. [Le Guin's note.]

[2]Joy Harjo, "The Blanket Around Her," in *That's What She Said: Contemporary Poetry and Fiction by Native American Women,* ed. Rayna Green (Bloomington: Indiana University Press, 1984), p. 127. [Le Guin's note.]

start talking about legitimacy. They steal the baby. They ensure by every means that the artist, the writer, is male. This involves intellectual abortion by centuries of women artists, infanticide of works by women writers, and a whole medical corps of sterilizing critics working to purify the Canon, to reduce the subject matter and style of literature to something Ernest Hemingway could have understood.

But this is our native tongue, this is our language they're stealing: We can read it and we can write it, and what we bring to it is what it needs, the woman's tongue, that earth and savor, that relatedness, which speaks dark in the mother tongue but clear as sunlight in women's poetry, and in our novels and stories, our letters, our journals, our speeches. If Sojourner Truth, forty years a slave, knew she had the right to speak that speech, how about you? Will you let yourself be silenced? Will you listen to what men tell you, or will you listen to what women are saying? I say the Canon has been spiked, and while the Eliots speak only to the Lowells and the Lowells speak only to God, Denise Levertov comes stepping westward quietly, speaking to us.[3]

> There is no savor
> more sweet, more salt
>
> than to be glad to be
> what, woman,
>
> and who, myself,
> I am, a shadow
>
> that grows longer as the sun
> moves, drawn out
>
> on a thread of wonder.
> If I bear burdens
>
> they begin to be remembered
> as gifts, goods, a basket
>
> of bread that hurts
> my shoulders but closes me
>
> in fragrance. I can
> eat as I go.

As I've been using the word "truth" in the sense of "trying hard not to lie," so I use the words "literature," "art," in the sense of "living well, living with skill, grace, energy" — like carrying a basket of bread and smelling it and eating as you go. I don't mean only certain special products made by specially gifted people living in specially privileged garrets, studios, and ivory towers — "High" Art; I mean also all the low arts, the ones men don't want. For instance, the art of making order where people live. In our culture

---

[3]Denise Levertov, "Stepping Westward," in *Norton Anthology*, p. 1951. [Le Guin's note.]

this activity is not considered an art, it is not even considered work. "Do you work?" — and she, having stopped mopping the kitchen and picked up the baby to come answer the door, says, "No, I don't work." People who make order where people live are by doing so stigmatized as unfit for "higher" pursuits; so women mostly do it, and among women, poor, uneducated, or old women more often than rich, educated, and young ones. Even so, many people want very much to keep house but can't, because they're poor and haven't got a house to keep, or the time and money it takes, or even the experience of ever having seen a decent house, a clean room, except on TV. Most men are prevented from housework by intense cultural bias; many women actually hire another woman to do it for them because they're scared of getting trapped in it, ending up like the woman they hire, or like that woman we all know who's been pushed so far over by cultural bias that she can't stand up, and crawls around the house scrubbing and waxing and spraying germ killer on the kids. But even on her kneebones, where you and I will never join her, even she has been practicing as best she knows how a great, ancient, complex, and necessary art. That our society devalues it is evidence of the barbarity, the aesthetic and ethical bankruptcy, of our society.

taking issue w/ Friedan.

As housekeeping is an art, so is cooking and all it involves — it involves, after all, agriculture, hunting, herding. . . . So is the making of clothing and all it involves. . . . And so on; you see how I want to revalue the word "art" so that when I come back as I do now to talking about words it is in the context of the great arts of living, of the woman carrying the basket of bread, bearing gifts, goods. Art not as some ejaculative act of ego but as a way, a skillful and powerful way of being in the world. I come back to words because words are my way of being in the world, but meaning by language as art a matter infinitely larger than the so-called High forms. Here is a poem that tries to translate six words by Hélène Cixous, who wrote *The Laugh of the Medusa*; she said, *"Je suis là où ça parle,"* and I squeezed those six words like a lovely lemon and got out all the juice I could, plus a drop of Oregon vodka.

> I'm there where
> it's talking
> Where that speaks I
> am in that talking place
>   Where
>
> that says
> my being is
>   Where
> my being there
> is speaking
> I am
>   And so
> laughing
> in a stone ear

The stone ear that won't listen, won't hear us, and blames us for its being stone. . . . Women can babble and chatter like monkeys in the wilderness, but the farms and orchards and gardens of language, the wheatfields of art — men have claimed these, fenced them off: No Trespassing, it's a man's world, they say. And I say,

> oh woman
> remember who you are
> woman
> it is the whole earth

We are told, in words and not in words, we are told by their deafness, by their stone ears, that our experience, the life experience of women, is not valuable to men — therefore not valuable to society, to humanity. We are valued by men only as an element of their experience, as things experienced; anything we may say, anything we may do, is recognized only if said or done in their service.

One thing we incontestably do is have babies. So we have babies as the male priests, lawmakers, and doctors tell us to have them, when and where to have them, how often, and how to have them; so that is all under control. But we are *not to talk about* having babies, because that is not part of the experience of men and so nothing to do with reality, with civilization, and no concern of art. — A rending scream in another room. And Prince Andrey comes in and sees his poor little wife dead bearing his son — Or Levin goes out into his fields and thanks his God for the birth of his son — And we know how Prince Andrey feels and how Levin feels and even how God feels, but we don't know what happened. Something happened, something was done, which we know nothing about. But what was it? Even in novels by women we are only just beginning to find out what it is that happens in the other room — what women do.

Freud famously said, "What we shall never know is what a woman wants." Having paused thoughtfully over the syntax of that sentence, in which WE are plural but "a woman" apparently has no plural, no individuality — as we might read that a cow must be milked twice a day or a gerbil is a nice pet — WE might go on then to consider whether WE know anything about, whether WE have ever noticed, whether WE have ever asked a woman what she *does* — what women do.

Many anthropologists, some historians, and others have indeed been asking one another this question for some years now, with pale and affrighted faces — and they are beginning also to answer it. More power to them. The social sciences show us that speakers of the father tongue are capable of understanding and discussing the doings of the mothers, if they will admit the validity of the mother tongue and listen to what women say.

But in society as a whole the patriarchal mythology of what "a woman" does persists almost unexamined, and shapes the lives of women. "What are you going to do when you get out of school?" "Oh, well, just like any other woman, I guess I want a home and family" — and that's fine, but what is this home and family just like other women's? Dad at work, mom home, two kids eating apple pie? This family, which our media and now our government declare to be normal and impose as normative, this nuclear family now accounts for seven percent of the arrangements women live in in America. Ninety-three percent of women don't live that way. They don't do that. Many wouldn't if you gave it to them with bells on. Those who want that, who believe it's their one true destiny — what's their chance of achieving it? They're on the road to Heartbreak House.

But the only alternative offered by the patriarchal mythology is that of the Failed Woman — the old maid, the barren woman, the castrating bitch, the frigid wife, the lezzie, the libber, the Unfeminine, so beloved of misogynists both male and female.

Now indeed there are women who want to be female men; their role model is Margaret Thatcher, and they're ready to dress for success, carry designer briefcases, kill for promotion, and drink the Right Scotch. They want to buy into the man's world, whatever the cost. And if that's true desire, not just compulsion born of fear, OK; if you can't lick 'em join 'em. My problem with that is that I can't see it as a good life even for men, who invented it and make all the rules. There's power in it, but not the kind of power I respect, not the kind of power that sets anybody free. I hate to see an intelligent woman voluntarily double herself up to get under the bottom line. Talk about crawling! And when she talks, what can she talk but father tongue? If she's the mouthpiece for the man's world, what has she got to say for herself?

Some women manage it — they may collude, but they don't sell out as women; and we know that when they speak for those who, in the man's world, are the others: women, children, the poor. . . .

But it is dangerous to put on Daddy's clothes, though not, perhaps, as dangerous as it is to sit on Daddy's knees.

There's no way you can offer your experience as your truth if you deny 35 your experience, if you try to be a mythical creature, the dummy woman who sits there on Big Daddy's lap. Whose voice will come out of her prettily hinged jaw? Who is it says yes all the time? Oh yes, yes, I will. Oh I don't know, you decide. Oh I can't do that. Yes hit me, yes rape me, yes save me, oh yes. That is how A Woman talks, the one in What-we-shall-never-know-is-what-A-Woman-wants.

A Woman's place, need I say, is in the home, plus at her volunteer work or the job where she's glad to get sixty cents for doing what men get paid a dollar for but that's because she's always on pregnancy leave but child care? No! A Woman is home caring for her children! Even if she can't. Trapped in this well-built trap, A Woman blames her mother for luring her into it, while ensuring that her own daughter never gets out; she recoils from the idea of sisterhood and doesn't believe women have friends, because it probably means something unnatural, and anyhow, A Woman is afraid of women. She's a male construct, and she's afraid women will deconstruct her. She's afraid of everything, because she can't change. Thighs forever thin and shining hair and shining teeth and she's my Mom, too, all seven percent of her. And she never grows old.

There are old women — little old ladies, as people always say; little bits, fragments of the great dummy statue goddess A Woman. Nobody hears if old women say yes or no, nobody pays them sixty cents for anything. Old men run things. Old men run the show, press the buttons, make the wars, make the money. In the man's world, the old man's world, the young men run and run and run until they drop, and some of the young women run with them. But old women live in the cracks, between the walls, like roaches, like mice, a rustling sound, a squeaking. Better lock up the cheese, boys. It's terrible, you turn up a corner of civilization and there are all these old women running around on the wrong side —

I say to you, you know, you're going to get old. And you can't hear me. I squeak between the walls. I've walked through the mirror and am on the other side, where things are all backwards. You may look with a good will and a generous heart, but you can't see anything in the mirror but your own face; and I, looking from the dark side and seeing your beautiful young faces, see that that's how it should be.

But when you look at yourself in the mirror, I hope you see yourself. Not one of the myths. Not a failed man — a person who can never succeed because success is basically defined as being male — and not a failed goddess, a person desperately trying to hide herself in the dummy Woman, the image of men's desires and fears. I hope you look away from those myths and into your own eyes, and see your own strength. You're going to need it. I hope you don't try to take your strength from men, or from a man. Secondhand experience breaks down a block from the car lot. I hope you'll take and make your own soul; that you'll feel your life for yourself pain by pain and joy by joy; that you'll feed your life, eat, "eat as you go" — you who nourish, be nourished!

If being a cog in the machine or a puppet manipulated by others isn't what you want, you can find out what you want, your needs, desires, truths, powers, by accepting your own experience as a woman, as this woman, this body, this person, your hungry self. On the maps drawn by men there is an immense white area, terra incognita, where most women live. That country is all yours to explore, to inhabit, to describe.

But none of us lives there alone. Being human isn't something people can bring off alone; we need other people in order to be people. We need one another.

If a woman sees other women as Medusa, fears them, turns a stone ear to them, these days, all her hair may begin to stand up on end hissing, *Listen, listen, listen!* Listen to other women, your sisters, your mothers, your grandmothers — if you don't hear them how will you ever understand what your daughter says to you?

And the men who can talk, converse with you, not trying to talk through the dummy Yes-Woman, the men who can accept your experience as valid — when you find such a man love him, honor him! But don't obey

him. I don't think we have any right to obedience. I think we have a
responsibility to freedom.

And especially to freedom of speech. Obedience is silent. It does not
answer. It is contained. Here is a disobedient woman speaking, Wendy Rose
of the Hopi and Miwok people, saying in a poem called "The Parts of a
Poet,"[4]

> parts of me are pinned
> to earth, parts of me
> undermine song, parts
> of me spread on the water,
> parts of me form a rainbow
> bridge, parts of me follow
> the sandfish, parts of me
> are a woman who judges.

Now this is what I want: I want to hear your judgments. I am sick of the   45
silence of women. I want to hear you speaking all the languages, offering
your experience as your truth, as human truth, talking about working, about
making, about unmaking, about eating, about cooking, about feeding, about
taking in seed and giving out life, about killing, about feeling, about thinking; about what women do; about what men do; about war, about peace;
about who presses the buttons and what buttons get pressed and whether
pressing buttons is in the long run a fit occupation for human beings. There's
a lot of things I want to hear you talk about.

This is what I don't want: I don't want what men have. I'm glad to let
them do their work and talk their talk. But I do not want and will not have
them saying or thinking or telling us that theirs is the only fit work or speech
for human beings. Let them not take our work, our words, from us. If they
can, if they will, let them work with us and talk with us. We can all talk
mother tongue, we can all talk father tongue, and together we can try to
hear and speak that language which may be our truest way of being in the
world, we who speak for a world that has no words but ours.

I know that many men and even women are afraid and angry when
women do speak, because in this barbaric society, when women speak truly
they speak subversively — they can't help it: if you're underneath, if you're
kept down, you break out, you subvert. We are volcanoes. When we women
offer our experience as our truth, as human truth, all the maps change. There
are new mountains.

That's what I want — to hear you erupting. You young Mount St.
Helenses who don't know the power in you — I want to hear you. I want
to listen to you talking to each other and to us all: Whether you're writing
an article or a poem or a letter or teaching a class or talking with friends or
reading a novel or making a speech or proposing a law or giving a judgment
or singing the baby to sleep or discussing the fate of nations, I want to hear

---

[4]Wendy Rose, "The Parts of a Poet," in *That's What She Said,* p. 204. [Le Guin's note.]

you. Speak with a woman's tongue. Come out and tell us what time of night it is! Don't let us sink back into silence. If we don't tell our truth, who will? Who'll speak for my children, and yours?

So I end with the end of a poem by Linda Hogan of the Chickasaw people, called "The Women Speaking."[5]

> Daughters, the women are
> speaking.
> They arrive
> over the wise distances
> on perfect feet.
> Daughters, I love you.

AFTERWORD

Le Guin divides all languages into three parts, as people are wont to divide almost everything. "There are two kinds of people," said the philosopher, "those who divide everything into two parts and those who divide everything into three. The threes are smarter than the twos." The third part makes for a qualitative difference in thought, not just a fifty-percent increase in terms, because two-part thinking necessitates opposition and therefore tends toward stasis or balance. The third option allows for synthesis after thesis and antithesis; it allows thought to turn a corner; it provides new resolutions for conventional oppositions. Look at "native tongue" after "father tongue" and "mother tongue." The sexually opposed phrases can resemble bookends but the third phrase visits another place entirely.

Commencement addresses are normally delivered in the father tongue. Would it be possible to deliver a commencement address entirely in the mother tongue?

Looking at other essayists in this collection, apply Le Guin's distinctions to their language. When you make a determination, consider which parts of the writing led to your conclusion: Structure? Vocabulary or diction? Syntax? Imagery? How many essays mix tongues? Maybe it is reasonable that each of us be trilingual, and know when to use each of our languages. Or maybe we possess the capacity for an infinity of tongues.

---

[5]Linda Hogan, "The Women Speaking," in ibid., p. 172. [Le Guin's note.]

BOOKS AVAILABLE IN PAPERBACK

The Dispossessed: An Ambiguous Utopia. New York: Avon. *Novel.*

The Eye of the Heron and Other Stories. New York: Bantam. *Novella and short stories.*

The Farthest Shore. New York: Bantam. *Novel.*

Going Out with Peacocks and Other Poems. New York: HarperCollins.

The Language of the Night: Essays on Fantasy and Science Fiction. New York: HarperCollins.

The Lathe of Heaven. New York: Avon. *Novel.*

The Left Hand of Darkness. New York: Ace Books. *Novel.*

Orsinian Tales. New York: HarperCollins. *Short Stories.*

Tehanu: The Last Book of Earthsea. New York: Bantam. *Novel.*

The Tombs of Atuan. New York: Bantam. *Novel.*

Very Far Away from Anywhere Else. New York: Bantam. *Novel.*

The Visionary: The Life Story of Flicker of the Serpentine. New York: McGraw. *Novel.*

The Wind's Twelve Quarters. New York: HarperCollins. *Short Stories.*

A Wizard of Earthsea. New York: Bantam. *Novel.*

ALISON
LURIE

*A*LISON LURIE *(b. 1926) grew up in New York City and graduated from Radcliffe College. She has worked as a ghostwriter and librarian, raised three sons, and written six novels, including* The War Between the Tates *(1974),* Only Children *(1979), and* Foreign Affairs *(1984), which won the Pulitzer Prize in fiction. (All these titles are puns.) Her most recent novel is* The Truth About Lorin Jones *(1988). She has lately done a book about children's literature,* Don't Tell the Grown-Ups *(1990). She is a professor of English at Cornell University, and she has been a Fellow of the Guggenheim and Rockefeller Foundations. She teaches part-time and otherwise lives in London and in Key West.*

In the series "The Making of a Writer" in the New York Times Book Review, *Lurie remembered that as a child, certain she would grow up to be an old maid, she took to writing stories. "With a pencil and a paper, I could revise the world." A few years later, instead, she found herself married with small children — and with two novels that publishers would not touch. She tried giving up writing, substituting a family life of tuna fish casseroles and playground excursions. But not writing did not satisfy her. She returned to it by way of the essay, making a memoir of a friend who died young, and then writing her third novel — which publishers touched and readers read.*

Alison Lurie's ironic fiction belongs with the work of modern English novelists like Evelyn Waugh, Nancy Mitford, and Anthony Powell. Her observation has been accused of wickedness; Gore Vidal called her "the Queen Herod of Modern Fiction." When she writes essays — often for the New York Review of Books — *she brings her irony and humor with her. Henry James said that a novelist must be "one of those on whom nothing is lost." In her fiction, and in her observations on the clothes we wear, nothing is lost on Alison Lurie.*

"Clothing as a Sign System" begins her book The Language of Clothes *(1981), which is copiously illustrated. But without illustration, her prose supplies the pictures; and an overriding idea, using analogy as tracks for the train of thought, carries the reader to Alison Lurie's chosen destination.*

Clothing as a Sign System

For thousands of years human beings have communicated with one another first in the language of dress. Long before I am near enough to talk to you on the street, in a meeting, or at a party, you announce your sex, age, and class to me through what you are wearing — and very possibly give me important information (or misinformation) as to your occupation, origin, personality, opinions, tastes, sexual desires, and current mood. I may not be able to put what I observe into words, but I register the information unconsciously; and you simultaneously do the same for me. By the time we meet and converse we have already spoken to each other in an older and more universal tongue.

The statement that clothing is a language, though occasionally made with the air of a man finding a flying saucer in his backyard, is not new. Balzac, in *Daughter of Eve* (1839), observed that for a woman dress is "a continual manifestation of intimate thoughts, a language, a symbol." Today, as semiotics becomes fashionable, sociologists tell us that fashion too is a language of signs, a nonverbal system of communication. The French structuralist Roland Barthes, for instance, in "The Diseases of Costume," speaks of theatrical dress as a kind of writing, of which the basic element is the sign.

None of these theorists, however, have gone on to remark what seems obvious: that if clothing is a language, it must have a vocabulary and a grammar like other languages. Of course, as with human speech, there is not a single language of dress, but many: some (like Dutch and German) closely related and others (like Basque) almost unique. And within every language of clothes there are many different dialects and accents, some almost unintelligible to members of the mainstream culture. Moreover, as with speech, each individual has his own stock of words and employs personal variations of tone and meaning.

The vocabulary of dress includes not only items of clothing, but also hair styles, accessories, jewelry, makeup, and body decoration. Theoretically at least this vocabulary is as large as or larger than that of any spoken tongue, since it includes every garment, hair style, and type of body decoration ever invented. In practice, of course, the sartorial resources of an individual may be very restricted. Those of a sharecropper, for instance, may be limited to five or ten "words" from which it is possible to create only a few "sentences" almost bare of decoration and expressing only the most basic concepts. A so-called fashion leader, on the other hand, may have several hundred "words" at his or her disposal, and thus be able to form thousands of different "sentences" that will express a wide range of meanings. Just as the average English-speaking person knows many more words than he or she will ever use in conversation, so all of us are able to understand the meaning of styles we will never wear.

To choose clothes, either in a store or at home, is to define and describe 5
ourselves. Occasionally, of course, practical considerations enter into these choices: considerations of comfort, durability, availability, and price. Especially in the case of persons of limited wardrobe, an article may be worn because it is warm or rainproof or handy to cover up a wet bathing suit — in the same way that persons of limited vocabulary use the phrase "you know" or adjectives such as "great" or "fantastic." Yet, just as with spoken language, such choices usually give us some information, even if it is only equivalent to the statement "I don't give a damn what I look like today." And there are limits even here. In this culture, like many others, certain garments are taboo for certain persons. Most men, however cold or wet they might be, would not put on a woman's dress, just as they would not use words and phrases such as "simply marvelous," which in this culture are considered specifically feminine.

Besides containing "words" that are taboo, the language of clothes, like speech, also includes modern and ancient words, words of native and foreign origin, dialect words, colloquialisms, slang, and vulgarities. Genuine articles of clothing from the past (or skillful imitations) are used in the same way a writer or speaker might use archaisms: to give an air of culture, erudition, or wit. Just as in educated discourse, such "words" are usually employed sparingly, most often one at a time — a single Victorian cameo or a pair of 1940s platform shoes or an Edwardian velvet waistcoat, never a complete costume. A whole outfit composed of archaic items from a single period, rather than projecting elegance and sophistication, will imply that one is on one's way to a masquerade, acting in a play or film, or putting oneself on display for advertising purposes. Mixing garments from several different periods of the past, on the other hand, suggests a confused but intriguingly "original" theatrical personality. It is therefore often fashionable in those sections of the art and entertainment industry in which instant celebrities are manufactured and sold.

When using archaic words, it is essential to choose ones that are decently old. The sight of a white plastic Courrèges miniraincoat and boots (in 1963 the height of fashion) at a gallery opening or theater today would produce the same shiver of ridicule and revulsion as the use of words such as "groovy," "Negro," or "self-actualizing."

In *Taste and Fashion*, one of the best books ever written on costume, the late James Laver proposed a timetable to explain such reactions; this has come to be known as Laver's Law. According to him, the same costume will be

Indecent	10 years before its time
Shameless	5 years before its time
Daring	1 year before its time
Smart	
Dowdy	1 year after its time
Hideous	10 years after its time
Ridiculous	20 years after its time
Amusing	30 years after its time
Quaint	50 years after its time
Charming	70 years after its time
Romantic	100 years after its time
Beautiful	150 years after its time

Laver possibly overemphasizes the shock value of incoming fashion, which today may be seen merely as weird or ugly. And of course he is speaking of the complete outfit, or "sentence." The speed with which a single "word" passes in and out of fashion can vary, just as in spoken and written languages.

The appearance of foreign garments in an otherwise indigenous costume is similar in function to the use of foreign words or phrases in standard English speech. This phenomenon, which is common in certain circles, may have several different meanings.

First, of course, it can be a deliberate sign of national origin in someone who otherwise, sartorially or linguistically speaking, has no accent. Often this message is expressed through headgear. The Japanese-American lady in Western dress but with an elaborate Oriental hairdo, or the Oxford-educated Arab who tops his Savile Row suit with a turban, are telling us graphically that they have not been psychologically assimilated; that their ideas and opinions remain those of an Asian. As a result we tend to see the non-European in Western dress with native headgear or hairdo as dignified, even formidable; while the reverse outfit — the Oriental lady in a kimono and a plastic rain hat, or the sheik in native robes and a black bowler — appears comic. Such costumes seem to announce that their wearers, though not physically at ease in our country, have their heads full of half-baked Western ideas. It would perhaps be well for Anglo-American tourists to keep this principle in mind when traveling to exotic places. Very possibly the members of a package tour in Mexican sombreros or Russian bearskin hats look equally ridiculous and weak-minded to the natives of the countries they are visiting.

More often the wearing of a single foreign garment, like the dropping of a foreign word or phrase in conversation, is meant not to advertise foreign origin or allegiance but to indicate sophistication. It can also be a means of advertising wealth. When we see a fancy Swiss watch, we know that its owner either bought it at home for three times the price of a good English or American watch, or else he or she spent even more money traveling to Switzerland.

Casual dress, like casual speech, tends to be loose, relaxed, and colorful. It often contains what might be called "slang words": blue jeans, sneakers, baseball caps, aprons, flowered cotton housedresses, and the like. These garments could not be worn on a formal occasion without causing disapproval, but in ordinary circumstances they pass without remark. "Vulgar words" in dress, on the other hand, give emphasis and get immediate attention in almost any circumstances, just as they do in speech. Only the skillful can employ them without some loss of face, and even then they must be used in the right way. A torn, unbuttoned shirt, or wildly uncombed hair, can signify strong emotions: passions, grief, rage, despair. They are most effective if people already think of you as being neatly dressed, just as the curses of well-spoken persons count for more than those of the customarily foul-mouthed.

Items of dress that are the sartorial equivalent of forbidden words have more impact when they appear seldom and as if by accident. The Edwardian lady, lifting her heavy floor-length skirt to board a train, appeared unaware that she was revealing a froth of lacy petticoats and embroidered black stockings. Similarly, today's braless executive woman, leaning over her desk at a conference, may affect not to know that her nipples show through her silk blouse. Perhaps she does not know it consciously; we are here in the ambiguous region of intention vs. interpretation which has given so much trouble to linguists.

In speech, slang terms and vulgarities may eventually become respectable dictionary words; the same thing is true of colloquial and vulgar fashions. Garments or styles that enter the fashionable vocabulary from a colloquial source usually have a longer life span than those that begin as vulgarities. Thigh-high patent leather boots, first worn by the most obvious variety of rentable female as a sign that she was willing to help act out certain male fantasies, shot with relative speed into and out of high fashion; while blue jeans made their way upward much more gradually from work clothes to casual to business and formal wear, and are still engaged in a slow descent.

Though the idea is attractive, it does not seem possible to equate different 15 articles of clothing with the different parts of speech. A case can be made, however, for considering trimmings and accessories as adjectives or adverbs — modifiers in the sentence that is the total outfit — but it must be remembered that one era's trimmings and accessories are another's essential parts of the costume. At one time shoes were actually fastened with buckles, and the buttons on the sleeves of a suit jacket were used to secure turned-up cuffs. Today such buttons, or the linked brass rods on a pair of Gucci shoes, are purely vestigial and have no useful function. If they are missing, however, the jacket or the shoes are felt to be damaged and unfit for wear.

Accessories, too, may be considered essential to an outfit. In the 1940s and 1950s, for instance, a woman was not properly dressed unless she wore gloves. Emily Post, among many others, made this clear:

> Always wear gloves, of course, in church, and also on the street. A really smart woman wears them outdoors always, even in the country. Always wear gloves in a restaurant, in a theatre, when you go to lunch, or to a formal dinner, or to a dance. . . . A lady never takes off her gloves to shake hands, no matter when or where. . . . On formal occasions she should *put gloves on* to shake hands with a hostess or with her own guests.

If we consider only those accessories and trimmings that are currently optional, however, we may reasonably speak of them as modifiers. It then becomes possible to distinguish an elaborately decorated style of dress from a simple and plain one, whatever the period. As in speech, it is harder to communicate well in a highly decorated style, though when this is done successfully the result may be very impressive. A costume loaded with accessories and trimmings can easily appear cluttered, pretentious, or confusing. Very rarely the whole becomes greater than its many parts, and the total effect is luxurious, elegant, and often highly sensual.

As writers on costume have often pointed out, the average individual above the poverty line has many more clothes than he needs to cover his body, even allowing for washing and changes of weather. Moreover, we often discard garments that show little or no wear and purchase new ones. What is the reason for this? Some have claimed that it is all the result of brainwashing by commercial interests. But the conspiracy theory of fashion change — the idea that the adoption of new styles is simply the result of a plot by greedy designers and manufacturers and fashion editors — has, I think, less foundation than is generally believed. Certainly the fashion industry might like us to throw away all our clothes each year and buy a whole new wardrobe, but it has never been able to achieve this goal. For one thing, it is not that the public will wear anything suggested to it, nor has it ever been true. Ever since fashion became big business, designers have proposed a bewildering array of styles every season. A few of these have been selected or adapted by manufacturers for mass production, but only a certain proportion of them have caught on.

As James Laver has remarked, modes are but the reflection of the manners of the time; they are the mirror, not the original. Within the limits imposed by economics, clothes are acquired, used, and discarded just as words are, because they meet our needs and express our ideas and emotions.

All the exhortations of experts on language cannot save outmoded terms of speech or persuade people to use new ones "correctly." In the same way, those garments that reflect what we are or want to be at the moment will be purchased and worn, and those that do not will not, however frantically they may be ballyhooed.

In the past, gifted artists of fashion from Worth to Mary Quant have been   20
able to make inspired guesses about what people will want their clothes to say each year. Today a few designers seem to have retained this ability, but many others have proved to be as hopelessly out of touch as designers in the American auto industry. The classic case is that of the maxiskirt, a style which made women look older and heavier and impeded their movements at a time (1969) when youth, slimness, and energy were at the height of their vogue. The maxiskirt was introduced with tremendous fanfare and not a little deception. Magazines and newspapers printed (sometimes perhaps unknowingly) photos of New York and London street scenes populated with hired models in long skirts disguised as passers-by, to give readers in Podunk and Lesser Puddleton the impression that the capitals had capitulated. But these strenuous efforts were in vain: The maxiskirt failed miserably, producing well-deserved financial disaster for its backers.

The fashion industry is no more able to preserve a style that men and women have decided to abandon than to introduce one they do not choose to accept. In America, for instance, huge advertising budgets and the whole-hearted cooperation of magazines such as *Vogue* and *Esquire* have not been able to save the hat, which for centuries was an essential part of everyone's outdoor (and often of their indoor) costume. It survives now mainly as a utilitarian protection against weather, as part of ritual dress (at formal weddings, for example), or as a sign of age or individual eccentricity.

As with speech, the meaning of any costume depends on circumstances. It is not "spoken" in a vacuum, but at a specific place and time, any change in which may alter its meaning. Like the remark "Let's get on with this damn business," the two-piece tan business suit and boldly striped shirt and tie that signify energy and determination in the office will have quite another resonance at a funeral or picnic.

According to Erving Goffman,° the concept of "proper dress" is totally dependent on situation. To wear the costume considered "proper" for a situation acts as a sign of involvement in it, and the person whose clothes do not conform to these standards is likely to be more or less subtly excluded from participation. When other signs of deep involvement are present, rules about proper dress may be waived. Persons who have just escaped from a fire or flood are not censured for wearing pajamas or having uncombed hair;

Erving Goffman   American sociologist (1922–1982) known for his observation-based theory that humans naturally strive to formulate identities.

someone bursting into a formal social occasion to announce important news is excused for being in jeans and T-shirt.

In language we distinguish between someone who speaks a sentence well — clearly, and with confidence and dignity — and someone who speaks it badly. In dress too, manner is as important as matter, and in judging the meaning of any garment we will automatically consider whether it fits well or is too large or too small; whether it is old or new; and especially whether it is in good condition, slightly rumpled and soiled or crushed and filthy. Cleanliness may not always be next to godliness, but it is usually regarded as a sign of respectability or at least of self-respect. It is also a sign of status, since to be clean and neat always involves the expense of time and money.

In a few circles, of course, disregard for cleanliness has been considered a virtue. Saint Jerome's remark that "the purity of body and its garments means the impurity of the soul" inspired generations of unwashed and smelly hermits. In the sixties some hippies and mystics scorned overly clean and tidy dress as a sign of compromise with the Establishment and too great an attachment to the things of this world. There is also a more widespread rural and small-town dislike of the person whose clothes are too clean, slick, and smooth. He — or, less often, she — is suspected of being untrustworthy, a smoothie or a city slicker.

In general, however, to wear dirty, rumpled, or torn clothing is to invite scorn and condescension. This reaction is ancient; indeed it goes back beyond the dawn of humanity. In most species, a strange animal in poor condition — mangy, or with matted and muddy fur — is more likely to be attacked by other animals. In the same way, shabbily dressed people are more apt to be treated shabbily. A man in a clean, well-pressed suit who falls down in a central London or Manhattan street is likely to be helped up sooner than one in filthy tatters.

At certain times and places — a dark night, a deserted alley — dirt and rags, like mumbled or growled speech, may be alarming. In Dickens's *Great Expectations* they are part of the terror the boy Pip feels when he first sees the convict Magwitch in the graveyard: "A fearful man, all in coarse grey, with a great iron on his leg. A man with no hat, and with broken shoes, and with an old rag tied round his head."

A costume not only appears at a specific place and time, it must be "spoken" — that is, worn — by a specific person. Even a simple statement like "I want a drink" or a simple costume — shorts and T-shirt, for example — will have a very different aspect in association with a sixty-year-old man, a sixteen-year-old girl, and a six-year-old child. But age and sex are not the only variables to be considered. In judging a costume we will also take into account the physical attributes of the person who is wearing it, assessing him or her in terms of height, weight, posture, racial or ethnic type, and facial features and expression. The same outfit will look different on a person whose face and body we consider attractive and on one whom we think ugly. Of course, the idea of "attractiveness" itself is not only subjective, but subject to the historical and geographical vagaries of fashion, as Sir

Kenneth Clark° has demonstrated in *The Nude*. In twentieth-century Britain and America, for instance, weight above the norm has been considered unattractive and felt to detract from dignity and status; as Emily Post put it in 1922, "The tendency of fat is to take away from one's gentility; therefore, any one inclined to be fat must be ultra conservative — in order to counteract the effect." The overweight person who does not follow this rule is in danger of appearing vulgar or even revolting. In Conrad's *Lord Jim* the shame of the corrupt Dutch captain is underlined by the fact that, though grossly fat, he wears orange-and-green-striped pajamas in public.

In dress as in language there is a possible range of expression from the most eccentric statement to the most conventional. At one end of the spectrum is the outfit of which the individual parts or "words" are highly incongruent, marking its wearer (if not on stage or involved in some natural disaster) as very peculiar or possibly deranged. Imagine for instance a transparent sequined evening blouse over a dirty Victorian cotton petticoat and black rubber galoshes. (I have observed this getup in real life; it was worn to a lunch party at a famous Irish country house.) If the same costume were worn by a man, or if the usual grammatical order of the sentence were altered — one of the galoshes placed upside down on the head, for example — the effect of insanity would be even greater.

At the opposite end of the spectrum is that costume that is the equivalent 30 of a cliché; it follows some established style in every particular and instantly establishes its wearer as a doctor, a debutante, a hippie, or a whore. Such outfits are not uncommon, for as two British sociologists have remarked, "Identification with and active participation in a social group always involves the human body and its adornment and clothing." The more significant any social role is for an individual, the more likely he or she is to dress for it. When two roles conflict, the costume will either reflect the more important one or it will combine them, sometimes with incongruous effects, as in the case of the secretary whose sober, efficient-looking dark suit only partly conceals a tight, bright, low-cut blouse.

The cliché outfit may in some cases become so standardized that it is spoken of as a "uniform": the pin-striped suit, bowler, and black umbrella of the London City man, for instance, or the blue jeans and T-shirts of high-school students. Usually, however, these costumes only look like uniforms to outsiders; peers will be aware of significant differences. The London businessman's tie will tell his associates where he went to school; the cut and fabric of his suit will allow them to guess at his income. High-school students, in a single glance, can distinguish new jeans from those that are fashionably worn, functionally or decoratively patched, or carelessly ragged;

Sir Kenneth Clark   British art historian (1903–1983) and author of *Civilisation*, a history of Western civilization made into a television series. *The Nude: A Study in Ideal Form* (1956) is a historical study of the nude form in art.

they grasp the fine distinctions of meaning conveyed by straight-leg, flared, boot-cut, and peg-top. When two pairs of jeans are identical to the naked eye a label handily affixed to the back pocket gives useful information, identifying the garment as expensive (so-called designer jeans) or discount-department-store. And even within the latter category there are distinctions: In our local junior high school, according to a native informant, "freaks always wear Lees, greasers wear Wranglers, and everyone else wears Levis."

Of course, to the careful observer all these students are only identical below the waist; above it they may wear anything from a lumberjack shirt to a lace blouse. Grammatically, this costume seems to be a sign that in their lower or physical natures these persons are alike, however dissimilar they may be socially, intellectually, or aesthetically. If this is so, the opposite statement can be imagined — and was actually made by my own college classmates thirty years ago. During the daytime we wore identical baggy sweaters over a wide variety of slacks, plaid kilts, full cotton or straight tweed or slinky jersey skirts, ski pants, and Bermuda shorts. "We're all nice coeds from the waist up; we think and talk alike," this costume proclaimed, "but as women we are infinitely various."

The extreme form of conventional dress is the costume totally determined by others: the uniform. No matter what sort of uniform it is — military, civil, or religious; the outfit of a general, a postman, a nun, a butler, a football player, or a waitress — to put on such livery is to give up one's right to act as an individual — in terms of speech, to be partially or wholly censored. What one does, as well as what one wears, will be determined by external authorities — to a greater or lesser degree, depending upon whether one is, for example, a Trappist monk, or a boy scout. The uniform acts as a sign that we should not or need not treat someone as a human being, and that they need not and should not treat us as one. It is no accident that people in uniform, rather than speaking to us honestly and straightforwardly, often repeat mechanical lies. "It was a pleasure having you on board," they say; "I cannot give you that information"; or "The doctor will see you shortly."

Constant wearing of official costume can so transform someone that it becomes difficult or impossible for him or her to react normally. Dr. Grantly, the archdeacon in Anthony Trollope's *The Warden* (1855), is pious and solemn even when alone with his wife: "'Tis only when he has exchanged that ever-new shovel hat for a tasselled nightcap, and those shining black habiliments for his accustomed *robe de nuit,* that Dr. Grantly talks, and looks, and thinks like an ordinary man."

To take off a uniform is usually a relief, just as it is a relief to abandon official speech; sometimes it is also a sign of defiance. When the schoolgirls in Flannery O'Connor's story "A Temple of the Holy Ghost" come home on holiday, she writes that "They came in the brown convent uniforms they had to wear at Mount St. Scholastica but as soon as they opened their suitcases, they took off the uniforms and put on red skirts and loud blouses. They put on lipstick and their Sunday shoes and walked around in the high heels all over the house."

In certain circumstances, however, putting on a uniform may be a relief, or even an agreeable experience. It can ease the transition from one role to another, as Anthony Powell points out in *Faces in My Time* when he describes joining the British Army in 1939:

> Complete forgetfulness was needed of all that had constituted one's life only a few weeks before. This condition of mind was helped by the anonymity of uniform, something which has to be experienced to be appreciated; in one sense more noticeable off duty in such environments as railway carriages or bars.

It is also true that both physical and psychological disadvantage can be concealed by a uniform, or even canceled out; the robes of a judge or a surgeon may successfully hide a scrawny physique or fears of incompetence, giving him or her both dignity and confidence.

Unlike most civilian clothing, the uniform is often consciously and deliberately symbolic. It identifies its wearer as a member of some group and often locates him or her within a hierarchy; sometimes it gives information about his or her achievements, as do the merit badges of a scout and the battle ribbons of a general. Even when some details of an official costume are not dictated from above, they may by custom come to have a definite meaning. James Laver remarks that in Britain

> until quite recently it was still possible to deduce a clergyman's religious opinions from his neckwear. If you wore an ordinary collar with a white tie you were probably Low Church and Evangelical. If you wore any version of the Roman collar you displayed your sympathy with the . . . Oxford Movement.

It is likely that when they were first designed all uniforms made symbolic sense and were as easy to "read" as the outfit of a *Playboy* Bunny today. But official costume tends to freeze the styles of the time in which it was invented, and today the sixteenth-century uniforms of the guards at the Tower of London or the late-Edwardian morning dress of the butler may merely seem old-fashioned to us. Military uniforms, as James Laver points out, were originally intended "to impress and even to terrify the enemy" in hand-to-hand combat (just like the war whoops and battle cries that accompanied them), and warriors accordingly disguised themselves as devils, skeletons, and wild beasts. Even after gunpowder made this style of fighting rare, the desire to terrify "survived into modern times in such vestigial forms as the death's head on the hussar's headgear and the bare ribs of the skeleton originally painted on the warrior's body and later transformed into the froggings of his tunic."

The wearing of a uniform by people who are obviously not carrying out the duties it involves has often suggested personal laxity — as in the case of drunken soldiers carousing in the streets. In this century, however, it has been adopted as a form of political protest, and both men and women have appeared at rallies and marches in their Army, Navy, or police uniforms, the implied statement being "I'm a soldier, but I support disarmament/open housing/gay rights," etc. A related development in the 1960s was the American hippie custom of wearing parts of old Army uniforms — Civil War, World War I, and World War II. This military garb puzzled many observers, especially when it appeared in anti-Vietnam demonstrations. Others understood the implicit message, which was that the longhaired kid in the Confederate tunic or the Eisenhower jacket was not some kind of coward or sissy; that he was not against all wars — just against the cruel and unnecessary one he was in danger of being drafted into.

Between cliché and madness in the language of dress are all the known 40 varieties of speech: eloquence, wit, information, irony, propaganda, humor, pathos, and even (though rarely) true poetry. Just as a gifted writer combines unexpected words and images, risking (and sometimes briefly gaining) the reputation of being deranged, so certain gifted persons have been able to combine odd items of clothing, old and new, native and foreign, into a brilliant eloquence of personal statement. While other people merely follow the style of the age in which they live, these men and women transform contemporary fashion into individual expression. Some of their achievements are celebrated in the history of costume, but here, as in all the arts, there must be many unknown geniuses.

Unfortunately, just as there are more no-talent artists than there are geniuses, there are also many persons who do not dress very well, not because of lack of money but because of innate lack of taste. In some cases their clothes are merely monotonous, suggesting an uninteresting but consistent personality. Others seem to have a knack for combining colors, patterns, and styles in a way that — rightly or wrongly — suggests personal awkwardness and disharmony. In Henry James's *The Bostonians* (1886), the bad taste in clothes of the heroine, Verena Tarrant, foreshadows her moral confusion and her bad taste in men. Verena, who has bright-red hair, makes her first public appearance wearing "a light-brown dress, of a shape that struck [Basil Ransom] as fantastic, a yellow petticoat, and a large crimson sash fastened at the side; while round her neck, and falling low upon her flat young chest she had a double chain of amber beads." And, as if this were not enough, Verena also carried "a large red fan, which she kept constantly in movement."

Like any elaborate nonverbal language, costume is sometimes more eloquent than the native speech of its wearers. Indeed, the more inarticulate someone is verbally, the more important are the statements made by his or her clothes. People who are skilled in verbal discourse, on the other hand, can afford to be somewhat careless or dull in their dress, as in the case of certain teachers and politicians. Even they, of course, are telling us something, but they may not be telling us very much.

Men and women in uniform are not the only ones who wear clothes they have not selected themselves. All of us were first dressed in such garments, and often our late childhood and early adolescence were made stormy by our struggles to choose our own wardrobe — in verbal terms, to speak for ourselves. A few of us did not win this battle, or won only temporarily, and became those men (or, more rarely, women) most of whose clothes are selected by their wives, husbands, or mothers.

All of us, however, even as adults, have at some time been the grateful or ungrateful recipients of garments bought by relatives or friends. Such a gift is a mixed blessing, for to wear clothes chosen by someone else is to accept and project their donor's image of you; in a sense, to become a ventriloquist's doll. Sometimes, of course, the gift may be welcome or flattering: the Christmas tie that is just right, the low-cut lace nightgown that encourages a woman of only moderate attractions to think of herself as a glamourpuss. Often, however, the gift is felt as a demand, and one harder to refuse because it comes disguised as a favor. When I was first married I dressed in a style that might be described as Radcliffe Beatnik (black jerseys and bright cotton-print skirts). My mother-in-law, hoping to remodel me into a nice country-club young matron, frequently presented me with tiny-collared, classically styled silk blouses and cashmere sweaters in white, beige, or pale green which I never wore and could not give away because they were monogrammed.

To put on someone else's clothes is symbolically to take on their person- 45 ality. This is true even when one's motives are hostile. In Dickens's *Our Mutual Friend* (1864–65), the teacher Bradley Headstone disguises himself in "rough waterside second-hand clothing" and a "red neckerchief stained black . . . by wear" which are identical with those worn by Rogue Riderhood, so that Riderhood shall be blamed for the murder Headstone is planning to commit. In assuming this costume Headstone literally becomes just such a low, vicious, and guilty man as Riderhood.

In this culture the innocent exchange of clothing is most common among teenage girls, who in this way confirm not only their friendship but their identity, just as they do by using the same slang and expressing the same ideas. The custom may persist into adult life, and also occurs between lovers and between husband and wife, though in the latter case the borrowing is usually one-way. The sharing of clothes is always a strong indication of shared tastes, opinions, and even personality. Next time you are at a large party, meeting, or public event, look around the room and ask yourself if there is anyone present whose clothes you would be willing to wear yourself on that occasion. If so, he or she is apt to be a soul mate.

Perhaps the most difficult aspect of sartorial communication is the fact that any language that is able to convey information can also be used to convey misinformation. You can lie in the language of dress just as you can in English, French, or Latin, and this sort of deception has the advantage that one cannot usually be accused of doing it deliberately. The costume that suggests youth or wealth, unlike the statement that one is twenty-nine years old and has a six-figure income, cannot be directly challenged or disproved.

A sartorial lie may be white, like Cinderella's ball gown; it may be various shades of gray, or it may be downright black, as in the case of the radical-hippie disguise of the FBI informant or the stolen military uniform of the spy. The lie may be voluntary, or it may be involuntary, as when a tomboy is forced into a velvet party dress by her parents. It may even be unconscious, as with the man who innocently wears a leather vest and boots to a bar patronized by homosexuals, or the American lady touring Scotland in a plaid she thought looked awfully pretty in the shop, but to which she has no hereditary right. If a complete grammar of clothing is ever written it will have to deal not only with these forms of dishonesty, but with many others that face linguists and semioticians:° ambiguity, error, self-deception, misinterpretation, irony, and framing.

Theatrical dress, or costume in the colloquial sense, is a special case of sartorial deception, one in which the audience willingly cooperates, recognizing that the clothes the actor wears, like the words he speaks, are not his own. Sometimes, however, what is only a temporary disguise for an actor becomes part of the everyday wardrobe of some members of the public. Popular culture, which has done so much to homogenize our life, has at the same time, almost paradoxically, helped to preserve and even to invent distinctive dress through a kind of feedback process. It is convenient for producers of films, TV programs, and commercials that clothes should instantly and clearly indicate age, class, regional origin, and if possible occupation and personality. Imagine that a certain costume is assigned to an actor representing a tough, handsome young auto mechanic, by a costume designer who has seen something like it in a local bar. Actual auto mechanics, viewing the program and others like it, unconsciously accept this outfit as characteristic; they are imitated by others who have not even seen the program. Finally the outfit becomes standard, and thus genuine.

Somewhere between theatrical costume and the uniform is ritual dress, the special clothing we adopt for the important ceremonies of our life: birth (the christening robe), college graduation, weddings, funerals, and other portentous occasions that also tend to involve ritual speech. 50

A more ambiguous sort of disguise is the costume that is deliberately chosen on the advice of others in order to deceive the beholder. For over a hundred years books and magazines have been busy translating the correct language of fashion, telling men and women what they should wear to seem genteel, rich, sophisticated, and attractive to the other sex. Journals addressed to what used to be called "the career girl" advised her how to dress to attract "the right kind of man" — successful, marriage-minded. Regardless of the current fashion, a discreet femininity was always recommended: soft fabrics and colors, flowers and ruffles in modest profusion, hair slightly

---

semioticians Philosophers who deal with the functions of signs and symbols in language.

longer and curlier than that of the other girls in the office. The costume must be neither too stylish (suggesting expense to the future husband) nor dowdy (suggesting boredom). Above all, a delicate balance must be struck between the prim and the seductive, one tending not to attract men and the other to attract the wrong kind. Times have changed somewhat, and the fashion pages of magazines such as *Cosmopolitan* now seem to specialize in telling the career girl what to wear to charm the particular wrong type of man who reads *Playboy*, while the editorial pages tell her how to cope with the resulting psychic damage.

Two recent paperbacks, *Dress for Success* and *The Woman's Dress for Success Book*, by John T. Molloy, instruct businessmen and women on how to select their clothes so that they will look efficient, authoritative, and reliable even when they are incompetent, weak, and shifty. Molloy, who is by no means unintelligent, claims that his "wardrobe engineering" is based on scientific research and opinion polls. Also, in a departure from tradition, he is interested in telling women how to get promoted, not how to get married. The secret, apparently, is to wear an expensive but conventional "skirted suit" in medium gray or navy wool with a modestly cut blouse. No sweaters, no pants, no very bright colors, no cleavage, no long or excessively curly hair.

Anyone interested in scenic variety must hope that Molloy is mistaken; but my own opinion-polling, unfortunately, backs him up. A fast-rising lady executive in a local bank reports to me — reluctantly — that "Suits do help separate the women from the girls — provided the women can tolerate the separation, which is another question altogether."

We put on clothing for some of the same reasons that we speak: to make living and working easier and more comfortable, to proclaim (or disguise) our identities, and to attract erotic attention. James Laver has designated these motives as the Utility Principle, the Hierarchical Principle, and the Seduction Principle. Anyone who has recently been to a large party or professional meeting will recall that most of the conversation that was not directed to practical ends ("Where are the drinks?" "Here is the agenda for this afternoon.") was principally motivated by the Hierarchical or the Seduction Principle. In the same way, the clothes worn on that occasion, as well as more or less sheltering the nakedness of those present, were chosen to indicate their wearer's place in the world and/or to make him or her look more attractive.

The earliest utilitarian clothing was probably makeshift. Faced with extremes of climate — icy winters, drenching rainstorms, or the baking heat of the sun — men and women slung or tied the skins of animals around themselves; they fastened broad leaves to their heads as simple rain hats and made crude sandals from strips of hide or bark, as primitive tribes do today. Such protective clothing has a long history, but it has never acquired much prestige. The garment with a purely practical function is the glamourless equivalent of the flat, declarative sentence: "It's raining." "I'm working in

55

the garden." But it is difficult, in costume as in speech, to make a truly simple statement. The pair of plain black rubbers which states that it is raining may also remark, "The streets are wet, and I can't afford to damage my shoes." If the streets are not in fact very wet, the rubbers may also declare silently, "This is a dull, timid, fussy person."

Sometimes, regardless of the weather, utility in itself is a minus quality. The more water-repellent a raincoat is, ordinarily, the more it repels admiration — unless it is also fashionably colored or cut, or in some other way evidently expensive. Boots of molded synthetic leather that keep your feet warm and dry are thought to be less aesthetically pleasing than decorated leather ones which soon leak, and thus imply ownership of a car or familiarity with taxis.

Practical clothing usually seems most attractive when it is worn by persons who do not need it and probably never will need it. The spotless starched pinafore that covers a child's party dress or the striped overalls favored by some of today's college students look much more charming than they would on the housemaids and farmers for whom they were first intended.

This transformation of protective clothing into fashionable costume has a long history. As Rachel Kemper points out, the sort of garments that become fashionable most rapidly and most completely are those which were originally designed for warfare, dangerous work, or strenuous sports:

> Garments intended to deflect the point of a lance, flying arrows, or solar radiation possess a strange kind of instant chic and are sure to be modified into fashions for both men and women. Contemporary examples abound: the ubiquitous aviator glasses that line the rails of fashionable singles bars, perforated racing gloves that grip the wheels of sedate family cars, impressively complicated scuba divers' watches that will never be immersed in any body of water more challenging than the country-club pool.

Common sense and most historians of costume have assumed that the demands of either utility, status, or sex must have been responsible for the invention of clothing. However, as sometimes happens in human affairs, both common sense and the historians were apparently wrong: Scholars have recently informed us that the original purpose of clothing was magical. Archaeologists digging up past civilizations and anthropologists studying primitive tribes have come to the conclusion that, as Rachel Kemper puts it, "Paint, ornament, and rudimentary clothing were first employed to attract good animistic powers and to ward off evil." When Charles Darwin visited Tierra del Fuego, a cold, wet, disagreeable land plagued by constant winds, he found the natives naked except for feathers in their hair and symbolic designs painted on their bodies. Modern Australian bushmen, who may spend hours decorating themselves and their relatives with patterns in colored clay, often wear nothing else but an amulet or two.

However skimpy it may be, primitive dress almost everywhere, like 60
primitive speech, is full of magic. A necklace of shark's teeth or a girdle of
cowrie shells or feathers serves the same purpose as a prayer or spell, and
may magically replace — or more often supplement — a spoken charm. In
the first instance a form of *contagious* magic is at work: the shark's teeth are
believed to endow their wearer with the qualities of a fierce and successful
fisherman. The cowrie shells, on the other hand, work through *sympathetic*
magic: since they resemble the female sexual parts, they are thought to
increase or preserve fertility.

In civilized society today belief in the supernatural powers of clothing — like belief in prayers, spells, and charms — remains widespread,
though we denigrate it with the name "superstition." Advertisements announce that improbable and romantic events will follow the application of
a particular sort of grease to our faces, hair, or bodies; they claim that
members of the opposite (or our own) sex will be drawn to us by the smell
of a particular soap. Nobody believes those ads, you may say. Maybe not,
but we behave as though we did: Look in your bathroom cabinet.

The supernatural garments of European folk tales — the seven-league
boots, the cloaks of invisibility, and the magic rings — are not forgotten,
merely transformed, so that today we have the track star who can only win
a race in a particular hat or shoes, the plainclothes cop who feels no one can
see him in his raincoat, and the wife who takes off her wedding ring before
going to a motel with her lover. Amulets also remain very popular: circlets
of elephant hair for strength and long life, copper bracelets as a charm
against arthritis. In both cases what is operating is a form of magical thinking like that of the Australian aborigine: Elephants are strong and long-lived;
if we constantly rub ourselves with their hair we may acquire these qualities.
Copper conducts electricity, therefore it will conduct nerve impulses to
cramped and unresponsive muscles, either by primitive contagious magic
as with the elephant-hair bracelet, or by the modern contagious magic of
pseudoscience: the copper "attracting and concentrating free-floating electrons," as a believer explained it to me.

Sympathethic or symbolic magic is also often employed, as when we
hang crosses, stars, or one of the current symbols of female power and
solidarity around our necks, thus silently involving the protection of Jesus,
Jehovah, or Astarte. Such amulets, of course, may be worn to announce our
allegiance to some faith or cause rather than as a charm. Or they may serve
both purposes simultaneously — or sequentially. The crucifix concealed below the parochial-school uniform speaks only to God until some devilish
human force persuades its wearer to remove his or her clothes; then it acts —
or fails to act — as a warning against sin as well as a protective talisman.

Articles of clothing, too, may be treated as if they had mana, the impersonal supernatural force that tends to concentrate itself in objects. When I
was in college it was common to wear a particular "lucky" sweater, shirt, or
hat to final examinations, and this practice continues today. Here it is usually
contagious magic that is at work: The chosen garment has become lucky by

being worn on the occasion of some earlier success, or has been given to its owner by some favored person. The wearing of such magical garments is especially common in sports, where they are often publicly credited with bringing their owners luck. Their loss or abandonment is thought to cause injury as well as defeat. Actors also believe ardently in the magic of clothes, possibly because they are so familiar with the near-magical transforming power of theatrical costume.

Sometimes the lucky garment is believed to be even more fortunate when it is put on backwards or inside out. There may be different explanations of this belief. A student of my acquaintance, whose faded lucky sweatshirt bears the name of her high-school swimming team, suggests that reversing the garment places the printed side against her body, thus allowing the mana to work on her more directly.

Ordinarily, nonmagical clothes may also be worn inside out or reversed for magical reasons. The custom of turning your apron to change your luck after a series of household mishaps is widely known in both Britain and America; I have seen it done myself in upstate New York. Gamblers today sometimes turn their clothes before commencing play, and the practice was even more common in the past. The eighteenth-century British statesman Charles James Fox often sat at the gaming tables all night long with his coat turned inside out and his face blackened to propitiate the goddess of chance. Or perhaps to disguise himself from her; according to folk tradition, the usual explanation for the turning of garments is that it confuses demons. In blackface and with the elegant trimmings of his dress coat hidden, Fox was invisible to Lady Luck; the evil spirits that haunt housewives fail to recognize their intended victims and fly on to torment someone else.

At the other extreme from clothing which brings good luck and success is the garment of ill-omen. The most common and harmless version of this is the dress, suit, or shirt which (like some children) seems to attract or even to seek out dirt, grease, protruding nails, falling ketchup, and other hazards. Enid Nemy, who has written perceptively about such clothes for the *New York Times,* suggests that they may be lazy: "they'd just as soon rest on a hanger, or in a box — and they revolt when they're hauled into action." Or, she adds, they may be snobs, unwilling to associate with ordinary people. Whatever the cause, such accident-prone garments rarely if ever reform, and once one has been identified it is best to break off relations with it immediately. Otherwise, like accident-prone persons, it is apt to involve you in much inconvenience and possibly actual disaster, turning some important interview or romantic tryst into a scene of farce or humiliation. More sinister, and fortunately more rare, is the garment which seems to attract disasters to you rather than to itself. Ms. Nemy mentions an orange linen dress that apparently took a dislike to its owner, one Margaret Turner of Dover Publications. Orange clothes, as it happens, are likely to arouse hostility in our culture, but this dress seems to have been a special case. "Women friends seemed cattier, men seemed more aloof, and I'd get into bad situations with my boss," Ms. Turner reported. "And that wasn't all. I'd spill coffee, miss train connections, and the car would break down."

Even when our clothes are not invested with this sort of supernatural power, they may have symbolic meanings that tend to increase with age. The man who comes home from work to discover that his wife has thrown out his shabby, stained tweed jacket or his old army pants is often much angrier than the situation seems to call for, and his anger may be mixed with depression and even fear. Not only has he lost a magical garment, he has been forced to see his spouse as in some real sense his enemy — as a person who wishes to deprive him of comfort and protection.

A pleasanter sort of magic occurs in the exchange of garments common among lovers. In the Middle Ages a lady would often give her kerchief or glove to a chosen knight. When he went into battle or fought in a tournament he would place it against his heart or pin it to his helmet. Today, probably because of the taboo against the wearing of female garments by men, the traffic is all one-way. The teenage girl wears her boyfriend's basketball jacket to school; the secretary who has spent the night impulsively and successfully at a friend's apartment goes home next morning with his London Fog raincoat over her disco outfit; and the wife, in a playful and affectionate mood, puts on her husband's red flannel pajama top. Often the woman feels so good and looks so well in the magical borrowed garment that it is never returned.

If the relationship sours, though, the exchange alters its meaning; the good spell becomes a curse. The magical article may be returned, often in poor condition: soiled or wrinkled, or with "accidental" cigarette burns. Or it may be deliberately destroyed: thrown in the trash, or even vindictively cut to shreds. An especially refined form of black magic is to give the garment away to the Salvation Army, in the hope that it will soon be worn by a drunken and incontinent bum — ideally, someplace where your former lover will see and recognize it. 70

As with the spoken language, communication through dress is easiest and least problematic when only one purpose is being served; when we wear a garment solely to keep warm, to attend a graduation ceremony, to announce our political views, to look sexy, or to protect ourselves from bad luck. Unfortunately, just as with speech, our motives in making any statement are apt to be double or multiple. The man who goes to buy a winter coat may simultaneously want it to shelter him from bad weather, look expensive and fashionable, announce that he is sophisticated and rugged, attract a certain sort of sexual partner, and magically infect him with the qualities of Robert Redford.

Naturally it is often impossible to satisfy all these requirements and make all these statements at once. Even if they do not contradict one another, the ideal garment of our fantasy may not be available in any of the stores we can get to, and if it is we may not be able to afford it. Therefore, just as with speech, it often happens that we cannot say what we really mean because we don't have the right "words." The woman who complains formulaically that she hasn't got anything to wear is in just this situation. Like a tourist abroad, she may be able to manage all right in shops and on trains, but she cannot go out to dinner, because her vocabulary is so limited that she would misrepresent herself and perhaps attract ridicule.

At present all these difficulties are compounded by contradictory messages about the value of dress in general. The Protestant ethic stressed modesty and simplicity of dress. Cleanliness was next to godliness, but finery and display were of the Devil, and the serious man or woman had no time for such folly. Even today to declare that one never pays much attention to what he or she is wearing is to claim virtue, and usually to receive respect. At the same time, however, we are told by advertisers and fashion experts that we must dress well and use cosmetics to, as they put it, liberate the "natural" beauty within. If we do not "take care of our looks" and "make the best of ourselves," we are scolded by our relatives and pitied by our friends. To juggle these conflicting demands is difficult and often exhausting.

When two or more wishes or demands conflict, a common psychological result is some disorder of expression. Indeed, one of the earliest theorists of dress, the psychologist J. D. Flügel, saw all human clothing as a neurotic symptom. In his view, the irreconcilable emotions are modesty and the desire for attention:

> Our attitude towards clothes is *ab initio* "ambivalent," to use the invaluable term which has been introduced into psychology by the psychoanalysists; we are trying to satisfy two contradictory tendencies. . . . In this respect the discovery, or at any rate the use, of clothes, seems, in its psychological aspects, to resemble the process whereby a neurotic symptom is developed.

Flügel is considering only a single opposition; he does not even contemplate the neurotic confusion that can result when three or more motives are in conflict — as they often are. Given this state of things, we should not be surprised to find in the language of clothing the equivalent of many of the psychological disorders of speech. We will hear, or rather see, the repetitive stammer of the man who always wears the same jacket or pair of shoes whatever the climate or occasion; the childish lisp of the woman who clings to the frills and ribbons of her early youth; and those embarrassing lapses of the tongue — or rather of the garment — of which the classical examples are the unzipped fly and the slip that becomes a social error. We will also notice the signs of more temporary inner distress: the too-loud or harsh "voice" that exhausts our eye rather than our ear with glaring colors and clashing patterns, and the drab, colorless equivalent of the inability to speak above a whisper.

Dress is an aspect of human life that arouses strong feelings, some intensely pleasant and others very disagreeable. It is no accident that many

75

of our daydreams involve fine raiment; nor that one of the most common and disturbing human nightmares is of finding ourselves in public inappropriately and/or incompletely clothed.

For some people the daily task of choosing a costume is tedious, oppressive, or even frightening. Occasionally such people tell us that fashion is unnecessary; that in the ideal world of the future we will all wear some sort of identical jumpsuit — washable, waterproof, stretchable, temperature-controlled; timeless, ageless, and sexless. What a convenience, what a relief it will be, they say, never to worry about how to dress for a job interview, a romantic tryst, or a funeral!

Convenient perhaps, but not exactly a relief. Such a utopia would give most of us the same kind of chill we feel when a stadium full of Communist-bloc athletes in identical sports outfits, shouting slogans in unison, appears on TV. Most people do not want to be told what to wear any more than they want to be told what to say. In Belfast recently four hundred Irish Republican prisoners "refused to wear any clothes at all, draping themselves day and night in blankets," rather than put on prison uniforms. Even the offer of civilian-style dress did not satisfy them; they insisted on wearing their own clothes brought from home, or nothing. Fashion is free speech, and one of the privileges, if not always one of the pleasures, of a free world.

AFTERWORD

Lurie's title announces the analogy which her essay explores.

Logic tells us that analogy can be dangerous to clear thinking. When Plato wrote The Republic *he told us he constructed not a political system but an analogy to the human mind. This statement has not kept others from taking the analogy for the thing itself — and understanding* The Republic *as a model for republics. Oswald Spengler wrote* The Decline of the West *out of an analogy between political or cultural systems and living organisms. He begins by saying that civilizations are like organisms because each is born, grows mature, becomes old and feeble, and dies. Later he seems to argue in a circle, taking analogy as fact: Civilizations must die because, after all, they are organisms.*

Mostly we use analogy not as structure for a book or an essay but as an illustrative example incidental to exposition or argument. Remove the analogy and the house does not fall down, because analogy was not its foundation. Remove the analogy from Lurie and the house falls down. But who would want to remove the analogy? It works; it provides a continual, varying locus for witty and accurate observation. The secret of the long analogy is a comparison that can be sustained and that continually illuminates while it surprises.

BOOKS AVAILABLE IN PAPERBACK

Don't Tell the Grown-Ups: Why Kids Love the Books They Do. New York: Avon. *Nonfiction.*

Foreign Affairs. New York: Avon. *Novel.*

Imaginary Friends. New York: Avon. *Novel.*

Love and Friendship. New York: Avon. *Novel.*

Nowhere City. New York: Avon. *Novel.*

Only Children. New York: Avon. *Novel.*

The Truth About Lorin Jones. New York: Avon. *Novel.*

The War Between the Tates. New York: Avon. *Novel.*

NANCY
MAIRS

*N*ANCY MAIRS *(b. 1943) came east from California to live in New Hampshire and in Massachusetts, where she attended college. She has worked as an editor and technical writer as well as a teacher. She has published a book of poems,* In All the Rooms of the Yellow House *(1984), and four collections of essays:* Plaintext: Deciphering a Woman's Life *(1986);* Remembering the Bone House: An Erotics of Place and Space *(1989);* Carnal Acts *(1990), from which we take this essay, originally published in* TriQuarterly; *and* Ordinary Time *(1993).*

She has lived with multiple sclerosis for much of her adult life, and calls herself "radical feminist, pacifist, and cripple." An engaging, if daunting, outspokenness is her manner "in defiance of polite discourse." She lives with her husband in Tucson, Arizona.

Carnal Acts

Inviting me to speak at her small liberal-arts college during Women's Week, a young woman set me a task: "We would be pleased," she wrote, "if you could talk on how you cope with your MS disability, and also how you discovered your voice as a writer." Oh, Lord, I thought in dismay, how am I going to pull this one off? How can I yoke two such disparate subjects into a coherent presentation, without doing violence to one, or the other, or both,

_____ Photo by Deidre Hamill

or myself? This is going to take some fancy footwork, and my feet scarcely carry out the basic steps, let alone anything elaborate.

To make matters worse, the assumption underlying each of her questions struck me as suspect. To ask *how* I cope with multiple sclerosis suggests that I *do* cope. Now, "to cope," *Webster's Third* tells me, is "to face or encounter and to find necessary expedients to overcome problems and difficulties." In these terms, I have to confess, I don't feel like much of a coper. I'm likely to deal with my problems and difficulties by squawking and flapping around like that hysterical chicken who was convinced the sky was falling. Never mind that in my case the sky really *is* falling. In response to a clonk on the head, regardless of its origin, one might comport oneself with a grace and courtesy I generally lack.

As for "finding" my voice, the implication is that it was at one time lost or missing. But I don't think it ever was. Ask my mother, who will tell you a little wearily that I was speaking full sentences by the time I was a year old and could never be silenced again. As for its being a writer's voice, it seems to have become one early on. Ask Mother again. At the age of eight I rewrote the Trojan War, she will say, and what Nestor was about to do to Helen at the end doesn't bear discussion in polite company.

Faced with these uncertainties, I took my own teacherly advice, something, I must confess, I don't always do. "If an idea is giving you trouble," I tell my writing students, "put it on the back burner and let it simmer while you do something else. Go to the movies. Reread a stack of old love letters. Sit in your history class and take detailed notes on the Teapot Dome scandal. If you've got your idea in mind, it will go on cooking at some level no matter what else you're doing." "I've had an idea for my documented essay on the back burner," one of my students once scribbled in her journal, "and I think it's just boiled over!"

I can't claim to have reached such a flash point. But in the weeks I've had the themes "disability" and "voice" sitting around in my head, they seem to have converged on their own, without my having to wrench them together and bind them with hoops of tough rhetoric. They *are* related, indeed interdependent, with an intimacy that has for some reason remained, until now, submerged below the surface of my attention. Forced to juxtapose them, I yank them out of the depths, a little startled to discover how they were intertwined down there out of sight. This kind of discovery can unnerve you at first. You feel like a giant hand that, pulling two swimmers out of the water, two separate heads bobbling on the iridescent swells, finds the two bodies below, legs coiled around each other, in an ecstasy of copulation. You don't quite know where to turn your eyes.

Perhaps the place to start illuminating this erotic connection between who I am and how I speak lies in history. I have known that I have multiple sclerosis for about seventeen years now, though the disease probably started long before. The hypothesis is that the disease process, in which the protective covering of the nerves in the brain and spinal cord is eaten away and replaced by scar tissue, "hard patches," is caused by an autoimmune reaction to a slow-acting virus. Research suggests that I was infected by this virus, which no one has ever seen and which therefore, technically, doesn't even "exist," between the ages of four and fifteen. In effect, living with this mysterious mechanism feels like having your present self, and the past selves it embodies, haunted by a capricious and meanspirited ghost, unseen except for its footprints, which trips you even when you're watching where you're going, knocks glassware out of your hand, squeezes the urine out of your bladder before you reach the bathroom, and weights your whole body with a weariness no amount of rest can relieve. An alien invader must be at work. But of course it's not. It's your own body. That is, it's you.

This, for me, has been the most difficult aspect of adjusting to a chronic incurable degenerative disease: the fact that it has rammed my "self" straight back into the body I had been trained to believe it could, through high-minded acts and aspirations, rise above. The Western tradition of distinguishing the body from the mind and/or the soul is so ancient as to have become part of our collective unconscious, if one is inclined to believe in such a noumenon, or at least to have become an unquestioned element in the social instruction we impose upon infants from birth, in much the same way we inculcate, without reflection, the gender distinctions "female" and "male." I *have* a body, you are likely to say if you talk about embodiment at all; you don't say, I *am* a body. A body is a separate entity possessable by the "I"; the "I" and the body aren't, as the copula would make them, grammatically indistinguishable.

To widen the rift between the self and the body, we treat our bodies as subordinates, inferior in moral status. Open association with them shames us. In fact, we treat our bodies with very much the same distance and ambivalence women have traditionally received from men in our culture. Sometimes this treatment is benevolent, even respectful, but all too often it is tainted by outright sadism. I think of the bodybuilding regimens that have become popular in the last decade or so, with the complicated vacillations they reflect between self-worship and self-degradation: joggers and aerobic dancers and weightlifters all beating their bodies into shape. "No pain, no gain," the saying goes. "Feel the burn." Bodies get treated like wayward women who have to be shown who's boss, even if it means slapping them around a little. I'm not for a moment opposing rugged exercise here. I'm simply questioning the spirit in which it is often undertaken.

Since, as Hélène Cixous points out in her essay on women and writing, "Sorties,"[1] thought has always worked "through dual, hierarchical opposi-tions" (p. 64), the mind/body split cannot possibly be innocent. The utter-ance of an "I" immediately calls into being its opposite, the "not-I," Western discourse being unequipped to conceive "that which is neither 'I' nor 'not-I,'" "that which is both 'I' and 'not-I,'" or some other permutation which

---

[1] In *The Newly Born Woman,* translated by Betsy Wing (Minneapolis: University of Minnesota Press, 1986). [Mairs's note.]

language doesn't permit me to speak. The "not-I" is, by definition, other. And we've never been too fond of the other. We prefer the same. We tend to ascribe to the other those qualities we prefer not to associate with our selves: It is the hidden, the dark, the secret, the shameful. Thus, when the "I" takes possession of the body, it makes the body into an other, direct object of a transitive verb, with all the other's repudiated and potentially dangerous qualities.

At the least, then, the body had best be viewed with suspicion. And a woman's body is particularly suspect, since so much of it is in fact hidden, dark, secret, carried about on the inside where, even with the aid of a speculum, one can never perceive all of it in the plain light of day, a graspable whole. I, for one, have never understood why anyone would want to carry all that delicate stuff around on the outside. It would make you awfully anxious, I should think, put you constantly on the defensive, create a kind of siege mentality that viewed all other beings, even your own kind, as threats to be warded off with spears and guns and atomic missiles. And you'd never get to experience that inward dreaming that comes when your flesh surrounds all your treasures, holding them close, like a sturdy shuttered house. Be my personal skepticism as it may, however, as a cultural woman I bear just as much shame as any woman for my dark, enfolded secrets. Let the word for my external genitals tell the tale: my pudendum, from the Latin infinitive meaning "to be ashamed."

It's bad enough to carry your genitals like a sealed envelope bearing the cipher that, once unlocked, might loose the chaotic flood of female pleasure — *jouissance*, the French call it — upon the world-of-the-same. But I have an additional reason to feel shame for my body, less explicitly connected with its sexuality: It is a crippled body. Thus it is doubly other, not merely by the homo-sexual standards of patriarchal culture but by the standards of physical desirability erected for every body in our world. Men, who are by definition exonerated from shame in sexual terms (this doesn't mean that an individual man might not experience sexual shame, of course; remember that I'm talking in general about discourse, not folks), may — more likely must — experience bodily shame if they are crippled. I won't presume to speak about the details of their experience, however. I don't know enough. I'll just go on telling what it's like to be a crippled woman, trusting that, since we're fellow creatures who've been living together for some thousands of years now, much of my experience will resonate with theirs.

I was never a beautiful woman, and for that reason I've spent most of my life (together with probably at least 95 percent of the female population of the United States) suffering from the shame of falling short of an unattainable standard. The ideal woman of my generation was . . . perky, I think you'd say, rather than gorgeous. Blond hair pulled into a bouncing ponytail. Wide blue eyes, a turned-up nose with maybe a scattering of golden freckles across it, a small mouth with full lips over straight white teeth. Her breasts were large but well harnessed high on her chest; her tiny waist flared to hips just wide enough to give the crinolines under her circle skirt a starting outward push. In terms of personality, she was outgoing, even bubbly, not pensive or mysterious. Her milieu was the front fender of a white Corvette convertible, surrounded by teasing crewcuts, dressed in black flats, a sissy blouse, and the letter sweater of the Corvette owner. Needless to say, she never missed a prom.

Ten years or so later, when I first noticed the symptoms that would be diagnosed as MS, I was probably looking my best. Not beautiful still, but the ideal had shifted enough so that my flat chest and narrow hips gave me an elegantly attenuated shape, set off by a thick mass of long, straight, shining hair. I had terrific legs, long and shapely, revealed nearly to the pudendum by the fashionable miniskirts and hot pants I adopted with more enthusiasm than delicacy of taste. Not surprisingly, I suppose, during this time I involved myself in several pretty torrid love affairs.

The beginning of MS wasn't too bad. The first symptom, besides the pernicious fatigue that had begun to devour me, was "foot drop," the inability to raise my left foot at the ankle. As a consequence, I'd started to limp, but I could still wear high heels, and a bit of a limp might seem more intriguing than repulsive. After a few months, when the doctor suggested a cane, a crippled friend gave me quite an elegant wood-and-silver one, which I carried with a fair amount of panache. The real blow to my self-image came when I had to get a brace. As braces go, it's not bad: lightweight plastic molded to my foot and leg, fitting down into an ordinary shoe and secured around my calf by a Velcro strap. It reduces my limp and, more important, the danger of tripping and falling. But it meant the end of high heels. And it's ugly. Not as ugly as I think it is, I gather, but still pretty ugly. It signified for me, and perhaps still does, the permanence and irreversibility of my condition. The brace makes my MS concrete and forces me to wear it on the outside. As soon as I strapped the brace on, I climbed into trousers and stayed there (though not in the same trousers, of course). The idea of going around with my bare brace hanging out seemed almost as indecent as exposing my breasts. Not until 1984, soon after I won the Western States Book Award for poetry, did I put on a skirt short enough to reveal my plasticized leg. The connection between winning a writing award and baring my brace is not merely fortuitous; being affirmed as a writer really did embolden me. Since then, I've grown so accustomed to wearing skirts that I don't think about my brace any more than I think about my cane. I've incorporated them, I suppose: made them, in their necessity, insensate but fundamental parts of my body.

Meanwhile, I had to adjust to the most outward and visible sign of all, 15 a three-wheeled electric scooter called an Amigo. This lessens my fatigue and increases my range terrifically, but it also shouts out to the world, "Here is a woman who can't stand on her own two feet." At the same time, paradoxically, it renders me invisible, reducing me to the height of a seven-year-old, with a child's attendant low status. "Would she like smoking or nonsmoking?" the gate agent assigning me a seat asks the friend traveling with me. In crowds I see nothing but buttocks. I can tell you the names of every type of designer jeans ever sold. The wearers, eyes front, trip over me and fall across my handlebars into my lap. "Hey!" I want to shout to the lofty world. "Down here! There's a person down here!" But I'm not, by their standards, quite a person anymore.

My self-esteem diminishes further as age and illness strip away from me the features that made me, for a brief while anyway, a good-looking, even sexy, young woman. No more long, bounding strides: I shuffle along with the timid gait I remember observing, with pity and impatience, in the little old ladies at Boston's Symphony Hall on Friday afternoons. No more lithe, girlish figure: My belly sags from the loss of muscle tone, which also creates all kinds of intestinal disruptions, hopelessly humiliating in a society in which excretory functions remain strictly unspeakable. No more sex, either, if society had its way. The sexuality of the disabled so repulses most people that you can hardly get a doctor, let alone a member of the general population, to consider the issues it raises. Cripples simply aren't supposed to Want It, much less Do It. Fortunately, I've got a husband with a strong libido and a weak sense of social propriety, or else I'd find myself perforce practicing a vow of chastity I never cared to take.

Afflicted by the general shame of having a body at all, and the specific shame of having one weakened and misshapen by disease, I ought not to be able to hold my head up in public. And yet I've gotten into the habit of holding my head up in public, sometimes under excruciating circumstances. Recently, for instance, I had to give a reading at the University of Arizona. Having smashed three of my front teeth in a fall onto the concrete floor of my screened porch, I was in the process of getting them crowned, and the temporary crowns flew out during dinner right before the reading. What to do? I wanted, of course, to rush home and hide till the dental office opened the next morning. But I couldn't very well break my word at this last moment. So, looking like Hansel and Gretel's witch, and lisping worse than the Wife of Bath, I got up on stage and read. Somehow, over the years, I've learned how to set shame aside and do what I have to do.

Here, I think, is where my "voice" comes in. Because, in spite of my demurral at the beginning, I do in fact cope with my disability at least some of the time. And I do so, I think, by speaking about it, and about the whole experience of being a body, specifically a female body, out loud, in a clear, level tone that drowns out the frantic whispers of my mother, my grandmothers, all the other trainers of wayward childish tongues: "Sssh! Sssh! Nice girls don't talk like that. Don't mention sweat. Don't mention menstrual blood. Don't ask what your grandfather does on his business trips. Don't laugh so loud. You sound like a loon. Keep your voice down. Don't tell. Don't tell. Don't tell." Speaking out loud is an antidote to shame. I want to distinguish clearly here between "shame," as I'm using the word, and "guilt" and "embarrassment," which, though equally painful, are not similarly poisonous. Guilt arises from performing a forbidden act or failing to perform a required one. In either case, the guilty person can, through reparation, erase the offense and start fresh. Embarrassment, less opprobrious though not necessarily less distressing, is generally caused by acting in a socially stupid or awkward way. When I trip and sprawl in public, when I wet myself, when my front teeth fly out, I feel horribly embarrassed, but, like the pain of childbirth, the sensation blurs and dissolves in time. If it didn't, every child would be an only child, and no one would set foot in public after the onset of puberty, when embarrassment erupts like a geyser and bathes one's whole life in its bitter stream. Shame may attach itself to guilt or embarrassment, complicating their resolution, but it is not the same emotion. I feel guilt or embarrassment for something I've done; shame, for who I am. I may stop doing bad or stupid things, but I can't stop being. How then can I help but be ashamed? Of the three conditions, this is the one that cracks and stifles my voice.

I can subvert its power, I've found, by acknowledging who I am, shame and all, and, in doing so, raising what was hidden, dark, secret about my life into the plain light of shared human experience. What we aren't permitted to utter holds us, each isolated from every other, in a kind of solipsistic thrall. Without any way to check our reality against anyone else's, we assume that our fears and shortcomings are ours alone. One of the strangest consequences of publishing a collection of personal essays called *Plaintext* has been the steady trickle of letters and telephone calls saying essentially, in a tone of unmistakable relief, "Oh, me too! Me too!" It's as though the part I thought was solo has turned out to be a chorus. But none of us was singing loud enough for the others to hear.

Singing loud enough demands a particular kind of voice, I think. And I 20 was wrong to suggest, at the beginning, that I've always had my voice. I have indeed always had *a* voice, but it wasn't *this* voice, the one with which I could call up and transform my hidden self from a naughty girl into a woman talking directly to others like herself. Recently, in the process of writing a new book, a memoir entitled *Remembering the Bone House,* I've had occasion to read some of my early writing, from college, high school, even junior high. It's not an experience I recommend to anyone susceptible to shame. Not that the writing was all that bad. I was surprised at how competent a lot of it was. Here was a writer who already knew precisely how the language worked. But the voice . . . oh, the voice was all wrong: maudlin, rhapsodic, breaking here and there into little shrieks, almost, you might say, hysterical. It was a voice that had shucked off its own body, its own homely life of Cheerios for breakfast and seventy pages of Chaucer to read before the exam on Tuesday and a planter's wart growing painfully on the ball of its foot, and reeled now wraithlike through the air, seeking incarnation only as the heroine who enacts her doomed love for the tall, dark, mysterious stranger. If it didn't get that part, it wouldn't play at all.

Among all these overheated and vaporous imaginings, I must have retained some shred of sense, because I stopped writing prose entirely, except for scholarly papers, for nearly twenty years. I even forgot, not exactly that I had written prose, but at least what kind of prose it was. So when I needed to take up the process again, I could start almost fresh, using the vocal range

I'd gotten used to in years of asking the waiter in the Greek restaurant for an extra anchovy on my salad, congratulating the puppy on making a puddle outside rather than inside the patio door, pondering with my daughter the vagaries of female orgasm, saying good-bye to my husband, and hello, and good-bye, and hello. This new voice — thoughtful, affectionate, often amused — was essential because what I needed to write about when I returned to prose was an attempt I'd made not long before to kill myself, and suicide simply refuses to be spoken of authentically in high-flown romantic language. It's too ugly. Too shameful. Too strictly a bodily event. And, yes, too funny as well, though people are sometimes shocked to find humor shoved up against suicide. They don't like the incongruity. But let's face it, life (real life, I mean, not the edited-for-television version) is a cacophonous affair from start to finish. I might have wanted to portray my suicidal self as a languishing maiden, too exquisitely sensitive to sustain life's wounding pressures on her soul. (I didn't want to, as a matter of fact, but I might have.) The truth remained, regardless of my desires, that when my husband lugged me into the emergency room, my hair matted, my face swollen and gray, my nightgown streaked with blood and urine, I was no frail and tender spirit. I was a body, and one in a hell of a mess.

I "should" have kept quiet about that experience. I know the rules of polite discourse. I should have kept my shame, and the nearly lethal sense of isolation and alienation it brought, to myself. And I might have, except for something the psychiatrist in the emergency room had told my husband. "You might as well take her home," he said. "If she wants to kill herself, she'll do it no matter how many precautions we take. They always do." *They* always do. I was one of "them," whoever they were. I was, in this context anyway, not singular, not aberrant, but typical. I think it was this sense of commonality with others I didn't even know, a sense of being returned somehow, in spite of my appalling act, to the human family, that urged me to write that first essay, not merely speaking out but calling out, perhaps. "Here's the way I am," it said. "How about you?" And the answer came, as I've said: "Me too! Me too!"

This has been the kind of work I've continued to do: to scrutinize the details of my own experience and to report what I see, and what I think about what I see, as lucidly and accurately as possible. But because feminine experience has been immemorially devalued and repressed, I continue to find this task terrifying. "Every woman has known the torture of beginning to speak aloud," Cixous writes, "heart beating as if to break, occasionally falling into loss of language, ground and language slipping out from under her, because for woman speaking — even just opening her mouth — in public is something rash, a transgression" (p. 92).

The voice I summon up wants to crack, to whisper, to trail back into silence. "I'm sorry to have nothing more than this to say," it wants to apologize. "I shouldn't be taking up your time. I've never fought in a war, or even in a schoolyard free-for-all. I've never tried to see who could piss farthest up the barn wall. I've never even been to a whorehouse. All the important formative experiences have passed me by. I was raped once. I've borne two children. Milk trickling out of my breasts, blood trickling from between my legs. You don't want to hear about it. Sometimes I'm too scared to leave my house. Not scared *of* anything, just scared: mouth dry, bowels writhing. When the fear got really bad, they locked me up for six months, but that was years ago. I'm getting old now. Misshapen, too. I don't blame you if you can't get it up. No one could possibly desire a body like this. It's not your fault. It's mine. Forgive me. I didn't mean to start crying. I'm sorry . . . sorry . . . sorry. . . ."

An easy solace to the anxiety of speaking aloud: this slow subsidence   25
beneath the waves of shame, back into what Cixous calls "this body that has been worse than confiscated, a body replaced with a disturbing stranger, sick or dead, who so often is a bad influence, the cause and place of inhibitions. By censuring the body," she goes on, "breath and speech are censored at the same time" (p. 97). But I am not going back, not going under one more time. To do so would demonstrate a failure of nerve far worse than the depredations of MS have caused. Paradoxically, losing one sort of nerve has given me another. No one is going to take my breath away. No one is going to leave me speechless. To be silent is to comply with the standard of feminine grace. But my crippled body already violates all notions of feminine grace. What more have I got to lose? I've gone beyond shame. I'm shameless, you might say. You know, as in "shameless hussy"? A woman with her bare brace and her tongue hanging out.

I've "found" my voice, then, just where it ought to have been, in the body-warmed breath escaping my lungs and throat. Forced by the exigencies of physical disease to embrace my self in the flesh, I couldn't write bodiless prose. The voice is the creature of the body that produces it. I speak as a crippled woman. At the same time, in the utterance I redeem both "cripple" and "woman" from the shameful silences by which I have often felt surrounded, contained, set apart; I give myself permission to live openly among others, to reach out for them, stroke them with fingers and sighs. No body, no voice; no voice, no body. That's what I know in my bones.

AFTERWORD

It is a journalistic commonplace that an essay narrate the story of its own composition. Journalists doing interviews begin their articles by telling us that it was raining so they had a hard time getting a taxi to see the Queen; the Queen turns up in a later paragraph. In this wonderful essay, Nancy Mairs tells us about an invitation to lecture at Colby College; talk-subject becomes essay topic. This device can become a tic, lazy or automatic; it can be narcissistic — "Now let me tell you about the Queen. She said my last book was superb." — but if used well it can provide intimate entry to a subject.

This essay is partly about the act of writing. An essay good enough for a model that also contains ideas about the writing process is a two-for-one bargain.

When we use the first person, describing successes or disasters, we must avoid the sounds of bragging or complaining. (To avoid the tone may help the writer avoid the fault; writing can be therapeutic.) When Mairs talks about her multiple sclerosis, she admits fear and sorrow, but never asks the reader to admire or pity her because she suffers. This essay's intelligence, as well as its willingness to undertake difficult matters, underlies the success of its tone. Even the author's erotic history is relevant to her developing notions of mind and body. It is also, of course, a point when the reader's attention is caught as upon a hook.

"No body, no voice; no voice, no body."

BOOKS AVAILABLE IN PAPERBACK

Carnal Acts: Essays. New York: HarperCollins.

In All the Rooms of the Yellow House. New York: Blue Moon Books. *Poetry.*

Plaintext: Deciphering a Woman's Life. Tucson: University of Arizona Press. *Essays.*

Remembering the Bone House: An Erotics of Place and Space. New York: Harper-Collins. *Essays.*

JOHN
McPHEE

*J*OHN McPHEE *was born in Princeton, New Jersey (1931), where he took his
*B.A. at the University and where he lives. He attended Cambridge University
in England, wrote for television, worked on the staff of* Time, *and now writes
regularly for the* New Yorker *magazine. His first book was a profile of the Princeton
University basketball player Bill Bradley, later a Rhodes scholar at Oxford, then a
forward for the New York Knickerbockers, and now a U.S. senator from New Jersey.
McPhee has written about the headmaster of a prep school, a desolate section of New
Jersey, tennis, geology, Alaska, the Scottish Highlands, physics, and whitewater
canoeing. His wide-ranging nonfiction books begin with* A Sense of Where You
Are *(1965) and continue through many titles to his profile of the state of Alaska,*
Coming into the Country *(1977), and include a collection of miscellaneous pieces
called* Table of Contents *(1985), which tells about bears, about doctors in rural
family practice, about another John McPhee who is a bush pilot in Maine, about
small hydroelectric plants, and about riding the boom extension.*

Some recent titles are The Control of Nature *(1989),* Looking for a Ship
(1990), and Assembling California *(1993). His best work is longish, and hard to
excerpt. If McPhee makes music out of facts, it is useless to take twelve bars from a
symphony and call it a song. "The Search for Marvin Gardens" comes from a
collection of shorter essays,* Pieces of the Frame *(1975). It describes a game that
remains timeless and a city that changes; Atlantic City earlier in this century was
a genteel and elegant ocean resort; it is now a gambling mecca, Trump Town, Las
Vegas East. Between these eras, and in "The Search for Marvin Gardens," the city
turned seedy, a run-down resort town.*

*His work appeals to readers not because of his authority about a subject — like
Lewis Thomas's in medicine and biology or Stephen Hawking's in cosmology — but*

because readers trust him to collect ten thousand items of detail and to assemble this information into shapely paragraphs and impeccable sentences. Give him the materials of an improbable subject — oranges, pinball, birch bark canoes — and McPhee's carpentry will fashion a palace of pleasurable prose.

Headnotes about John McPhee are notoriously brief. Unlike most essayists (not only Dillard and Hoagland but Montaigne), McPhee enjoys remaining invisible and with few exceptions keeps his opinions to himself. There is not much to say about John McPhee; there is much to say about the books he signs with his name.

The Search for
Marvin Gardens

Go. I roll the dice — a six and a two. Through the air I move my token, the flatiron, to Vermont Avenue, where dog packs range.

•

The dogs are moving (some are limping) through ruins, rubble, fire damage, open garbage. Doorways are gone. Lath is visible in the crumbling walls of the buildings. The street sparkles with shattered glass. I have never seen, anywhere, so many broken windows. A sign — "SLOW, CHILDREN AT PLAY" — has been bent backward by an automobile. At the lighthouse, the dogs turn up Pacific and disappear. George Meade, Army engineer, built the lighthouse — brick upon brick, six hundred thousand bricks, to reach up high enough to throw a beam twenty miles over the sea. Meade, seven years later, saved the Union at Gettysburg.

•

I buy Vermont Avenue for $100. My opponent is a tall, shadowy figure, across from me, but I know him well, and I know his game like a favorite tune. If he can, he will always go for the quick kill. And when it is foolish to go for the quick kill he will be foolish. On the whole, though, he is a master assessor of percentages. It is a mistake to underestimate him. His eleven carries his top hat to St. Charles Place, which he buys for $140.

•

The sidewalks of St. Charles Place have been cracked to shards by through-growing weeds. There are no buildings. Mansions, hotels once stood here. A few street lamps now drop cones of light on broken glass and vacant spaces behind a chain-link fence that some great machine has in places bent to the ground. Five plane trees — in full summer leave, flecking the light — are all that live on St. Charles Place.

•

Block upon block gradually, we are cancelling each other out — in the blues, the lavenders, the oranges, the greens. My opponent follows a plan of his own devising. I use the Hornblower & Weeks opening and the Zuricher defense. The first game draws tight, will soon finish. In 1971, a group of people in Racine, Wisconsin, played for seven hundred and sixty-eight hours. A game begun a month later in Danville, California, lasted eight hundred and twenty hours. These are official records, and they stun us. We have been playing for eight minutes. It amazes us that Monopoly is thought of as a long game. It is possible to play to a complete, absolute, and final conclusion in less than fifteen minutes, all within the rules as written. My opponent and I have done so thousands of times. No wonder we are sitting across from each other now in this best-of-seven series for the international singles championship of the world.

•

On Illinois Avenue, three men lean out from second-story windows. A girl is coming down the street. She wears dungarees and a bright-red shirt, has ample breasts and a Hadendoan Afro, a black halo, two feet in diameter. Ice rattles in the glasses in the hands of the men.

"Hey, sister!"

"Come on up!"

She looks up, looks from one to another to the other, looks them flat in the eye.

"What for?" she says, and she walks on.

•

I buy Illinois for $240. It solidifies my chances, for I already own Kentucky and Indiana. My opponent pales. If he had landed first on Illinois, the game would have been over then and there, for he has houses built on Boardwalk and Park Place, we share the railroads equally, and we have cancelled each other everywhere else. We never trade.

•

In 1852, R. B. Osborne, an immigrant Englishman, civil engineer, surveyed the route of a railroad line that would run from Camden to Absecon Island, in New Jersey, traversing the state from the Delaware River to the barrier beaches of the sea. He then sketched in the plan of a "bathing village" that would surround the eastern terminus of the line. His pen flew glibly, framing and naming spacious avenues parallel to the shore — Mediterranean, Baltic, Oriental, Ventnor — and narrower transsecting avenues: North Carolina, Pennsylvania, Vermont, Connecticut, States, Virginia, Tennessee, New York, Kentucky, Indiana, Illinois. The place as a whole had no name, so when he had completed the plan Osborne wrote in large letters over the ocean, "Atlantic City." No one ever challenged the name, or the names of Osborne's streets. Monopoly was invented in the early 1930s by Charles B. Darrow, but Darrow was only transliterating what Osborne had created. The railroads, crucial to any player, were the making of Atlantic City. After the rails were down, houses and hotels burgeoned from Mediterranean and Baltic to New York and Kentucky. Properties — building lots — sold for as little as six dollars apiece and as much as a thousand dollars. The original investors in the railroads and the real estate called themselves the Camden & Atlantic Land Company. Reverently, I repeat their names: Dwight Bell, William Coffin, John DaCosta, Daniel Deal, William Fleming, Andrew Hay, Joseph Proter, Jonathan Pitney, Samuel Richards — founders, fathers, forerunners, archetypical masters of the quick kill.

•

My opponent and I are now in a deep situation of classical Monopoly. The torsion is almost perfect — Boardwalk and Park Place versus the brilliant reds. His cash position is weak, though, and if I escape him now he may fade. I land on Luxury Tax, contiguous to but in sanctuary from his power. I have four houses on Indiana. He lands there. He concedes.

•

Indiana Avenue was the address of the Brighton Hotel, gone now. The Brighton was exclusive — a word that no longer has retail value in the city. If you arrived by automobile and tried to register at the Brighton, you were sent away. Brighton-class people came in private railroad cars. Brighton-class people had other private railroad cars for their horses — dawn rides on the firm sand at water's edge, skirts flying. Colonel Anthony J. Drexel Biddle — the sort of name that would constrict throats in Philadelphia — lived, much of the year, in the Brighton.

•

Colonel Sanders' fried chicken is on Kentucky Avenue. So is Clifton's 15 Club Harlem, with the Sepia Revue and the Sepia Follies, featuring the Honey Bees, the Fashions, and the Lords.

•

My opponent and I, many years ago, played 2,428 games of Monopoly in a single season. He was then a recent graduate of the Harvard Law School, and he was working for a downtown firm, looking up law. Two people we knew — one from Chase Manhattan, the other from Morgan, Stanley — tried to get into the game, but after a few rounds we found that they were not in the conversation and we sent them home. Monopoly should always be *mano a mano* anyway. My opponent won 1,199 games, and so did I. Thirty were ties. He was called into the Army, and we stopped just there. Now, in Game

2 of the series, I go immediately to jail, and again to jail while my opponent seines property. He is dumbfoundingly lucky. He wins in twelve minutes.

•

Visiting hours are daily, eleven to two; Sunday, eleven to one: evenings, six to nine. "NO MINORS, NO FOOD, IMMEDIATE FAMILY ONLY ALLOWED IN JAIL." All this above a blue steel door in a blue cement wall in the windowless interior of the basement of the city hall. The desk sergeant sits opposite the door in the jail. In a cigar box in front of him are pills in every color, a banquet of fruit salad an inch and a half deep — leapers, copilots, footballs, truck drivers, peanuts, blue angels, yellow jackets, redbirds, rainbows. Near the desk are two soldiers, waiting to go through the blue door. They are about eighteen years old. One of them is trying hard to light a cigarette. His wrists are in steel cuffs. A military policeman waits, too. He is a year or so older than the soldiers, taller, studious in appearance, gentle, fat. On a bench against a wall sits a good-looking girl in slacks. The blue door rattles, swings heavily open. A turnkey stands in the doorway. "Don't you guys kill yourselves back there now," says the sergeant to the soldiers.

"One kid, he overdosed himself about ten and a half hours ago," says the M.P.

The M.P., the soldiers, the turnkey, and the girl on the bench are white. The sergeant is black. "If you take off the handcuffs, take off the belts," says the sergeant to the M.P. "I don't want them hanging themselves back there." The door shuts and its tumblers move. When it opens again, five minutes later, a young white man in sandals and dungarees and a blue polo shirt emerges. His hair is in a ponytail. He has no beard. He grins at the good-looking girl. She rises, joins him. The sergeant hands him a manila envelope. From it he removes his belt and a small notebook. He is out of jail, free. What did he do? He offended Atlantic City in some way. He spent a night in the jail. In the 1930s, men visiting Atlantic City went to jail, directly to jail, did not pass Go, for appearing in topless bathing suits on the beach. A city statute requiring all men to wear full-length bathing suits was not seriously challenged until 1937, and the first year in which a man could legally go bare-chested on the beach was 1940.

•

Game 3. After seventeen minutes, I am ready to begin construction on overpriced and sluggish Pacific, North Carolina, and Pennsylvania. Nothing else being open, opponent concedes.

•

The physical profile of streets perpendicular to the shore is something like a playground slide. It begins in the high skyline of Boardwalk hotels, plummets into warrens of "side-avenue" motels, crosses Pacific, slopes through church missions, convalescent homes, burlesque houses, rooming houses, and liquor stores, crosses Atlantic, and runs level through the bombed-out ghetto as far — Baltic, Mediterranean — as the eye can see. North Carolina Avenue, for example, is flanked at its beach end by the Chalfonte and the Haddon Hall (908 rooms, air-conditioned), where, according to one biographer, John Philip Sousa (1854–1932) first played when he was twenty-two, insisting, even then, that everyone call him by his entire name. Behind these big hotels, motels — Barbizon, Catalina — crouch. Between Pacific and Atlantic is an occasional house from 1910 — wooden porch, wooden mullions, old yellow paint — and two churches, a package store, a strip show, a dealer in fruits and vegetables. Then, beyond Atlantic Avenue, North Carolina moves on into the vast ghetto, the bulk of the city, and it looks like Metz in 1919, Cologne in 1944. Nothing has actually exploded. It is not bomb damage. It is deep and complex decay. Roofs are off. Bricks are scattered in the street. People sit on porches, six deep, at nine on a Monday morning. When they go off to wait in unemployment lines, they wait sometimes two hours. Between Mediterranean and Baltic runs a chain-link fence, enclosing rubble. A patrol car sits idling by the curb. In the back seat is a German shepherd. A sign on the fence says, "BEWARE OF BAD DOGS."

Mediterranean and Baltic are the principal avenues of the ghetto. Dogs are everywhere. A pack of seven passes me. Block after block, there are three-story brick row houses. Whole segments of them are abandoned, a thousand broken windows. Some parts are intact, occupied. A mattress lies in the street, soaking in a pool of water. Wet stuffing is coming out of the mattress. A postman is having a rye and a beer in the Plantation Bar at 9:15 in the morning. I ask him idly if he knows where Marvin Gardens is. He does not. "HOOKED AND NEED HELP? CONTACT N.A.R.C.O." "REVIVAL NOW GOING ON, CONDUCTED BY REVEREND H. HENDERSON OF TEXAS." These are signboards on Mediterranean and Baltic. The second one is upside down and leans against a boarded-up window of the Faith Temple Church of God in Christ. There is an old peeling poster on a warehouse wall showing a figure in an electric chair. "The Black Panther Manifesto" is the title of the poster, and its message is, or was, that "the fascists have already decided in advance to murder Chairman Bobby Seale in the electric chair." I pass an old woman who carries a bucket. She wears blue sneakers, worn through. Her feet spill out. She wears red socks, rolled at the knees. A white handkerchief, spread over her head, is knotted at the corners. Does she know where Marvin Gardens is? "I sure don't know," she says, setting down the bucket. "I sure don't know. I've heard of it somewhere, but I just can't say where." I walk on, through a block of shattered glass. The glass crunches underfoot like coarse sand. I remember when I first came here — a long train ride from Trenton, long ago, games of poker in the train — to play basketball against Atlantic City. We were half black, they were all black. We scored forty points, they scored eighty, or something like it. What I remember most is that they had glass blackboards — glittering, pendent, expensive glass backboards, a rarity then in high schools, even in colleges, the only ones we played on all year.

I turn on Pennsylvania, and start back toward the sea. The windows of the Hotel Astoria, on Pennsylvania near Baltic, are boarded up. A sheet of unpainted plywood is the door, and in it is a triangular peephole that now frames an eye. The plywood door opens. A man answers my question. Rooms there are six, seven, and ten dollars a week. I thank him for the information and move on, emerging from the ghetto at the Catholic Daughters of America Women's Guest House, between Atlantic and Pacific. Between Pacific and the Boardwalk are the blinking vacancy signs of the Aristocrat and Colton Manor motels. Pennsylvania terminates at the Sheraton-Seaside — thirty-two dollars a day, ocean corner. I take a walk on the Boardwalk and into the Holiday Inn (twenty-three stories). A guest is registering. "You reserved for Wednesday, and this is Monday," the clerk tells him. "But that's all right. We have *plenty* of rooms." The clerk is very young, female, and has soft brown hair that hangs below her waist. Her superior kicks her.

He is a middle-aged man with red spiderwebs in his face. He is jacketed and tied. He takes her aside. "Don't say 'plenty,'" he says. "Say 'You are fortunate, sir. We have rooms available.'"

The face of the young woman turns sour. "We have all the rooms you 25 need," she says to the customer, and, to her superior, "How's that?"

•

Game 4. My opponent's luck has become abrasive. He has Boardwalk and Park Place, and has sealed the board.

•

Darrow was a plumber. He was, specifically, a radiator repairman who lived in Germantown, Pennsylvania. His first Monopoly board was a sheet of linoleum. On it he placed houses and hotels that he had carved from blocks of wood. The game he thus invented was brilliantly conceived, for it was an uncannily exact reflection of the business milieu at large. In its depth, range, and subtlety, in its luck-skill ratio, in its sense of infrastructure and socioeconomic parameters, in its philosophical characteristics, it reached to the profundity of the financial community. It was as scientific as the stock market. It suggested the manner and means through which an underdeveloped world had been developed. It was chess at Wall Street level. "Advance token to the nearest Railroad and pay owner twice the rental to which he is otherwise entitled. If Railroad is unowned, you may buy it from the Bank. Get out of Jail, free. Advance token to nearest Utility. If unowned, you may buy it from the Bank. If owned, throw dice and pay owner a total ten times the amount thrown. You are assessed for street repairs: $40 per house, $115 per hotel. Pay poor tax of $15. Go to Jail. Go directly to Jail. Do not pass Go. Do not collect $200."

•

The turnkey opens the blue door. The turnkey is known to the inmates as Sidney K. Above his desk are ten closed-circuit TV screens — assorted viewpoints of the jail. There are three cellblocks — men, women, juvenile boys. Six days is the average stay. Showers twice a week. The steel doors and the equipment that operates them were made in San Antonio. The prisoners sleep on bunks of butcher block. There are no mattresses. There are three prisoners to a cell. In winter, it is cold in here. Prisoners burn newspapers to keep warm. Cell corners are black with smudge. The jail is three years old. The men's block echoes with chatter. The man in the cell nearest Sidney K. is pacing. His shirt is covered with broad stains of blood. The block for juvenile boys is, by contrast, utterly silent — empty corridor, empty cells. There is only one prisoner. He is small and black and appears to be thirteen. He says he is sixteen and that he has been alone in here for three days.

"Why are you here? What did you do?"

"I hit a jitney driver."

30

•

The series stands at three all. We have split the fifth and sixth games. We are scrambling for property. Around the board we fairly fly. We move so fast because we do our own banking and search our own deeds. My opponent grows tense.

•

Ventnor Avenue, a street of delicatessens and doctors' offices, is leafy with plane trees and hydrangeas, the city flower. Water Works is on the mainland. The water comes over in submarine pipes. Electric Company gets power from across the state, on the Delaware River, in Deepwater. States Avenue, now a wasteland like St. Charles, once had gardens running down the middle of the street, a horse-drawn trolley, private homes. States Avenue was as exclusive as the Brighton. Only an apartment house, a small motel, and the All Wars Memorial Building — monadnocks spaced widely apart — stand along States Avenue now. Pawnshops, convalescent homes, and the Paradise Soul-Saving Station are on Virginia Avenue. The soul-saving station is pink, orange, and yellow. In the windows flanking the door of the Virginia Money Loan Office are Nikons, Polaroids, Yashicas, Sony TVs, Underwood typewriters, Singer sewing machines, and pictures of Christ. On the far side of town, beside a single track and locked up most of the time, is the new railroad station, a small hut made of glazed firebrick, all that is left of the lines that built the city. An authentic phrenologist works on New York Avenue close to Frank's Extra Dry Bar and a church where the sermon today is "Death in the Pot." The church is of pink brick, has blue and amber windows and two red doors. St. James Place, narrow and twisting, is lined with boarding houses that have wooden porches on each of three stories, suggesting a New Orleans made of salt-bleached pine. In a vacant lot on Tennessee is a white Ford station wagon stripped to the chassis. The windows are smashed. A plastic Clorox bottle sits on the driver's seat. The wind has pressed newspaper against the chain-link fence around the lot. Atlantic Avenue, the city's principal thoroughfare, could be seventeen American Main Streets placed end to end — discount vitamins and Vienna Corset shops, movie theatres, shoe stores, and funeral homes. The Boardwalk is made of yellow pine and Douglas fir, soaked in pentachlorophenol. Down-beach, it reaches far beyond the city. Signs everywhere — on windows, lampposts, trash baskets — proclaim "BIENVENUE CANADIENS!" The salt air is full of Canadian French. In the Claridge Hotel, on Park Place, I ask a clerk if she knows where Marvin Gardens is. She says, "Is it a floral shop?" I ask a cabdriver, parked outside. He says, "Never heard of it." Park Place is one block long, Pacific to Boardwalk. On the roof of the Claridge is the Solarium, the highest point in town — panoramic view of the ocean, the bay, the salt-water ghetto. I look down at the rooftops of the side-avenue motels and into swimming pools. There are hundreds of people around the rooftop pools, sunbathing, reading — many more people than are on the beach. Walls, windows, and a block of sky are all that is visible from these pools — no sand, no sea. The pools are craters, and with the people around them they are countersunk into the motels.

•

The seventh, and final, game is ten minutes old and I have hotels on Oriental, Vermont, and Connecticut. I have Tennessee and St. James. I have North Carolina and Pacific. I have Boardwalk, Atlantic, Ventnor, Illinois, Indiana. My fingers are forming a "V." I have mortgaged most of these properties in order to pay for others, and I have mortgaged the others to pay for the hotels. I have seven dollars. I will pay off the mortgages and build my reserves with income from the three hotels. My cash position may be low, but I feel like a rocket in an underground silo. Meanwhile, if I could go to jail for a time I could pause there, wait there, until my opponent, in his inescapable rounds, pays the rates of my hotels. Jail, at times, is the strategic place to be. I roll boxcars from the Reading and move the flatiron to Community Chest. "Go to Jail. Go directly to Jail."

•

The prisoners, of course, have no pens and no pencils. They take paper napkins, roll them tight as crayons, char the ends with matches, and write on the walls. The things they write are not entirely idiomatic; for example, "In God We Trust." All is in carbon. Time is required in the writing. "Only humanity could know of such pain." "God So Loved the World." "There is no greater pain than life itself." In the women's block now there are six blacks, giggling, and a white asleep in red shoes. She is drunk. The others are pushers, prostitutes, an auto thief, a burglar caught with pistol in purse. A sixteen-year-old accused of murder was in here last week. These words are written on the wall of a now empty cell: "Laying here I see two bunks about six inches thick, not counting the one I'm laying on, which is hard as brick. No cushion for my back. No pillow for my head. Just a couple scratchy blankets which is best to use it's said. I wake up in the morning so shivery and cold, waiting and waiting till I am told the food is coming. It's on its way. It's not worth waiting for, but I eat it anyway. I know one thing when they set me free I'm gonna be good if it kills me."

•

How many years must a game be played to produce an Anthony J. Drexel Biddle and chestnut geldings on the beach? About half a century was the original answer, from the first railroad to Biddle at his peak. Biddle, at his peak, hit an Atlantic City streetcar conductor with his fist, laid him out with one punch. This increased Biddle's legend. He did not go to jail. While John Philip Sousa led his band along the Boardwalk playing "The Stars and Stripes Forever" and Jack Dempsey ran up and down in training for his fight with Gene Tunney, the city crossed the high curve of its parabola. Al Capone held conventions here — upstairs with his sleeves rolled, apportioning among his lieutenant governors the states of the Eastern seaboard. The natural history of an American resort proceeds from Indians to French Canadians via Biddles and Capones. French Canadians, whatever they may be at home, are Visigoths here. Bienvenue Visigoths!

•

My opponent plods along incredibly well. He has got his fourth railroad, and patiently, unbelievably, he has picked up my potential winners until he has blocked me everywhere but Marvin Gardens. He has avoided, in the fifty-dollar zoning, my increasingly petty hotels. His cash flow swells. His railroads are costing me two hundred dollars a minute. He is building hotels on States, Virginia, and St. Charles. He has temporarily reversed the current. With the yellow monopolies and my blue monopolies, I could probably defeat his lavenders and his railroads. I have Atlantic and Ventnor. I need Marvin Gardens. My only hope is Marvin Gardens.

•

There is a plaque at Boardwalk and Park Place, and on it in relief is the leonine profile of a man who looks like an officer in a metropolitan bank — "CHARLES B. DARROW, 1889–1967, INVENTOR OF THE GAME OF MONOPOLY." "Darrow," I address him aloud. "Where is Marvin Gardens?" There is, of course, no answer. Bronze, impassive, Darrow looks south down the Board-walk. "Mr. Darrow, please, where is Marvin Gardens?" Nothing. Not a sign. He just looks south down the Boardwalk.

•

My opponent accepts the trophy with his natural ease, and I make, from notes, remarks that are even less graceful than his.

•

Marvin Gardens is the one color-block Monopoly property that is not in Atlantic City. It is a suburb within a suburb secluded. It is a planned compound of seventy-two handsome houses set on curvilinear private streets under yews and cedars, poplars and willows. The compound was built around 1920, in Margate, New Jersey, and consists of solid buildings of stucco, brick, and wood, with slate roofs, tile roofs, multi-mullioned porches, Giraldic° towers, and Spanish grilles. Marvin Gardens, the ultimate outwash of Monopoly, is a citadel and sanctuary of the middle class. "We're heavily patrolled by police here. We don't take no chances. Me? I'm living here nine years. I paid seventeen thousand dollars and I've been offered thirty. Number one, I don't want to move. Number two, I don't need the money. I have four bedrooms, two and a half baths, front den, back den. No basement. The Atlantic is down there. Six feet down and you float. A lot of people have a hard time finding this place. People that lived in Atlantic City all their life don't know how to find it. They don't know where the hell they're going. They just know it's south, down the Boardwalk."

AFTERWORD

The trick is clear from the start, and ten pages later it is still tricky. The idea or gimmick sets the board game and the city against each other. Segueing without pause from the one to the other, McPhee juxtaposes without transition, shrewdly supplying connections almost subliminally. The broken-up prose reads almost as continuously as — in other pieces — a famous McPhee three-page paragraph.

Look at how a word in paragraph 1 makes a transition to paragraph 2. Look at the word on which paragraph 14 twists to become paragraph 15.

BOOKS AVAILABLE IN PAPERBACK

Basin and Range. New York: Farrar, Straus & Giroux. *Nonfiction.*

Coming into the Country. New York: Bantam. *Nonfiction.*

The Control of Nature. New York: Farrar, Straus & Giroux. *Essays.*

The Crofter and the Laird. New York: Farrar, Straus & Giroux. *Nonfiction.*

The Curve of Binding Energy: A Journey into the Awesome and Alarming World of Theodore B. Taylor. New York: Ballantine. *Nonfiction.*

The Deltoid Pumpkin Seed. New York: Farrar, Straus & Giroux. *Nonfiction.*

Giraldic Resembling the three-hundred-foot Giralda Tower adjoining the Cathedral of Seville, Spain. The original tower was completed in 1184; in 1568 it was converted to a bell tower with an ornate Renaissance superstructure.

Encounters with the Archdruid. New York: Farrar, Straus & Giroux. *Nonfiction.*

Giving Good Weight. New York: Farrar, Straus & Giroux. *Essays.*

The Headmaster: Frank L. Boyden of Deerfield. New York: Farrar, Straus & Giroux. *Nonfiction.*

Heirs of General Practice. New York: Farrar, Straus & Giroux. *Nonfiction.*

In Suspect Terrain. New York: Farrar, Straus & Giroux. *Nonfiction.*

The John McPhee Reader. New York: Farrar, Straus & Giroux. *Essays.*

Levels of the Game. New York: Farrar, Straus & Giroux. *Nonfiction.*

Looking for a Ship. New York: Farrar, Straus & Giroux. *Essays.*

Oranges. New York: Farrar, Straus & Giroux. *Nonfiction.*

Pieces of the Frame. New York: Farrar, Straus & Giroux. *Nonfiction.*

The Pine Barrens. New York: Farrar, Straus & Giroux. *Nonfiction.*

La Place de la Concorde Suisse. New York: Farrar, Straus & Giroux. *Nonfiction.*

Riding the Boom Extension. Worcester, Mass.: Metacom Press. *Nonfiction.*

Rising from the Plains. New York: Farrar, Straus & Giroux. *Nonfiction.*

A Roomful of Hovings and Other Profiles. New York: Farrar, Straus & Giroux. *Nonfiction.*

A Sense of Where You Are: A Profile of William Warren Bradley, 2nd ed. New York: Farrar, Straus & Giroux. *Nonfiction.*

The Survival of the Bark Canoe. New York: Farrar, Straus & Giroux. *Nonfiction.*

Table of Contents. New York: Farrar, Straus and Giroux. *Essays.*

NAOMI
SHIHAB NYE

*N*AOMI SHIHAB NYE *(b. 1952) grew up in St. Louis and lives in San Antonio. She is a poet* — Different Ways to Pray *(1980),* Hugging the Jukebox *(National Poetry Series, 1982),* Yellow Glove *(1986) — who has been publishing stories and essays in quarterlies like the* Georgia Review *and the* Southwest Review, *where we found this one. Another essay appeared in* Best American Essays 1991, *edited by Joyce Carol Oates and Robert Atwan.*

When people ask Naomi Shihab Nye where she gets ideas for things to write about, she answers, "Where do you not?" Ezra Pound said that the most important quality of a writer's mind was curiosity. Nye and her family live in an old house "one block from the quiet San Antonio River, downtown. I want to dig under our house."

Newcomers
in a Troubled Land

Our four-year-old son is printing his name on a piece of yellow construction paper. I bend to see which name it is today. For awhile he wanted to be *called* Paper. Today he's gone back to the real one. Each blocky letter a house, a mountain, a caboose . . . then he prints my name underneath his.

He draws squiggly lines from the letters in my name to the same letters in his own. "Naomi, look, we're inside one another, did you know that? Your name is here, inside mine!"

Every letter of *Naomi* contained in his name *Madison* — we pause together mouths open. I did not know that. Although we have been mouthing one another's names for years, and already as mother and son we contain one another in so many ways it would be hard to name them all.

For a long time he sits staring, smiling at the paper, turning it around on the table. "Do I have any friends," he asks, "who have *their* mother's names inside their names?" We try a few — none does. And the soft afternoon light falling into the kitchen where we sit says, *this is a gift.*

When I was small, the name *Naomi*, which means *pleasant*, seemed hard to live up to. And *Shihab*, shooting star or meteor in Arabic, harder yet. I never met another of either in those days. My mother, whose name meant *bitter*, said I didn't know how lucky I was.

Hiking the tree-lined streets of our St. Louis borough en route to school,   5 I felt common names spring up inside my mouth, waving their leafy syllables. I'd tongue them for blocks, trying them on. Susie. Karen. Debbie. Who would I be if I'd had a different name? I turned right on a street called Louise. Did all Karens have some region of being in which they were related? I called my brother *Alan* for a week without letting our parents hear. He was really Adlai, for Adlai Stevenson, a name that also means *justice* in Arabic, if pronounced with enough flourish.

Neither of us had middle names.

I admired our parents for that. They hadn't tried to pad us or glue us together with any little wad of name stuck in the middle.

Not until I was sixteen, riding slouched and sleepy in the back seat of my best friend's sister's car, did I fall in love with my own name. It had something to do with neon on a shopping center sign, that steady color holding firm as the nervous December traffic swarmed past. Holding my eyes to the radiant green bars of light as the engine idled, I felt the soft glow of my own name stretch warmly awake inside me. It balanced on my tongue. It seemed pleasurable, at long last, to feel recognizable to oneself. Was this a secret everyone knew?

Names of old countries and towns had always seemed exquisitely arbitrary, odd. The tags in the backs of garments, the plump bodies of words. We had moved from the city of one saint to the city of another, San Antonio, whose oldest inner-city streets had names like *Eager* and *Riddle*. We had left the river of many syllables, with a name long enough to be used as a timing device, Mississippi, for a river so small you could call it Creek or Stream and not be too far off. We ate *kousa, tabooleh, baba ghannouj* — Arabic food — on a street called Arroya Vista.

Earlier, I'd stood with my St. Louis schoolmates as the last gleaming   10 silver segment of the Gateway Arch was swung into place by a giant crane.

We held our breaths, imagining a crash as the parts clanged together, or a terrible disaster if the piece were to slip loose. Worse yet, what if the section didn't fit? Each of us had been keeping close watch on the massive legs as they grew and grew in what used to be a weedy skid-row riverfront lot, a few blocks from the licorice factory. Each of us had our own ideas about whether we'd really trust the elevator inside that thing. But I doubt if anybody questioned the slogan accompanying its name — Gateway to the West. In those days we probably accepted winning the West as something that had really happened.

Studying history in grade school, we learned that everything our country had ever done was good, good, good. Nothing smoldered with dubious implications. Occasionally my father offered different views on foreign policies, but no one ever suggested a pilgrim or pioneer might have been less than honorable. I recall preferring Indian headdresses to Pilgrim hats. The Indians had a more powerful mystique. I recall feeling profound indignation over missionaries. Somehow they seemed so insulting — like coming into someone else's neighborhood and telling them how to do things. My father, sent to Kansas as an immigrant student because he wanted to go "to the middle" of the country, left his first university town because local evangelists wouldn't leave him alone.

Long later, I'd read the Chilean poet Pablo Neruda, who wrote, "Why wasn't Christopher Columbus able to discover Spain?"

Long later, after our country was able to "celebrate victory" in a war that massacred scores of people no more criminal than you or I, our son sat quietly reading a book called *Stanley,* in which cavemen come out of their caves and build houses for the first time. The animals speak in human tongues. They say, "Don't eat my grass and I'll let you live by me." The cavemen plant flowers around their doorways. They learn how to be nice to one another. They put down their clubs. "Isn't it strange," my son said, "that a caveman would be called Stanley?" He had an older man friend named Stanley. It just didn't seem like a caveman kind of name.

I passed under the Gateway to the West into the land of many questions. On a Christmas Eve as far west as we could go in "our own country," we sat in downtown Honolulu in the back pew of the historic Kawaiho Church, the "Westminster Abbey of the Pacific." We each held a candle wearing a little white collar as short-sleeved men and women filed into the pews, wearing leis, wearing Christmas-patterned Aloha shirts. I grew quietly aware that a group of people had entered and were now sitting in the carved wooden box behind us, the space once reserved for royalty, still set aside by a velvet rope. The matriarch of the group wore black, and a distinguished hat, unusual for Honolulu. She stared straight ahead with handsome queenly elegance. The rest of her family, while attractive, could have blended easily into the crowd.

I don't know why I grew so obsessed with her presence behind us, as we rose for "Joy to the World!" or took seats again for the handbell choir. Maybe it was that row of royal portraits on the second-floor balcony visible

15

over the rail, or my growing curiosity over the ways our fiftieth state had been acquired. I just kept wondering what she thought about it all. Once her family had ruled this little land most remote from all other lands on the globe — a favorite Hawaiian statistic. And now? She was served her wafer and tiny cup of grape juice first, before the rest of the packed congregation. And she walked out into the warm streets, this daughter of Hawaii's last king, on her own two feet when it was over.

My husband first appeared to me in a now-vanished downtown San Antonio eatery with a pleasantly understated name, Quinney's Just Good Food. Businessmen in white shirts and ties swarmed around us, woven together by steaming plates of fried fish and mashed potatoes. I knew, from the first moment of our chance encounter, that he was "the one" — it felt like a concussion to know this.

Walking up South Presa Street later with my friend Sue, who'd introduced us, I asked dizzily, "What *was* his last name?" She said, "Nye, like eye," and the rhymes began popping into my head. They matched our steps. Like *hi*, like *why*, like *bye* — suddenly like every word that seemed to matter. She waved good-bye at her corner and I stood there a long time, staring as the cross-signal changed back and forth from a red raised hand to a little man walking. And I knew that every street I crossed from that moment on would be a different street.

Because I am merely a tenant of this name Nye — it is not the house I always occupied — it inspires a traveler's warm affection to me. I appreciate its brevity. Reading about the thirteenth-century Swedes who fled internal uprisings in their own country to resettle in Denmark in settlements prefixed by *Ny* — meaning new, or newcomer — deserves a border-crosser's nod.

Hundreds of families listed in the *Nye Family of America Association* volumes gather regularly at Sandwich, Massachusetts, to shake hands and share each other's lives. I would like to join them, which surprises me. They started their tradition of gathering in 1903. R. Glen Nye writes, "How can we reach you to tell you how important it is for you to know your origins. . . . Those who read this are the oldsters of tomorrow . . . a hundred years hence, we will be the very ones someone will yearn to know about. Who will they turn to then, if we do not help them now?"

Because my own father came to New York on the boat from his old 20 country of Palestine in 1950, I am curious about these Nyes who came on the boat just following the *Mayflower*, who stayed and stayed and stayed, who built the Nye Homestead on Cape Cod, now a museum pictured on postcards and stationery notes. They have kept such good track of one another. Thick volumes list them, family by family, birthdates, children, occupations.

On a driving trip east, my husband and I paused one blustery day to walk around the cemetery at Sandwich. It felt eerie to sidestep so many imposing granite markers engraved with our own name. Oh Benjamin, oh Katherine and Reuben, you who had no burglar alarms, what did you see that we will never see? And the rest of you Nyes, wandering out across America even as far as Alaska where cars and trucks and jeeps all have their license plates set into little metal frames proclaiming NYE in honor of some enterprising car dealer who claimed the Land of the Midnight Sun as his territory, where did you get your energy? What told you to go?

Once my husband and I invited every "Nye" in the San Antonio telephone book to dinner. Such reckless festivity would have been more difficult had our name been Sanchez or Smith; as it stood, the eleven entries for "Nye" seemed too provocative to pass up. Eleven groups of people sharing a name within one city — and we didn't know any of them.

Handwritten invitation — "If you're named Nye, you're invited." Would they *get it?* I was brazen enough to style it a "potluck" — a gathering where the parties themselves would be a potluck — and asked all to RSVP. A week later each family had responded positively, with glinting curiosity, except one humorless fireman, whom I telephoned at the last minute. He was too busy for such frivolous pursuit.

They came in a wild assortment of vehicles, a pickup truck and a white Cadillac pulled sleekly into the driveway. They came, all thirty-two of them, children and wives, in overalls and neckties. One gracious couple, both ninety-two years old, amazed us with their spunk, traveling out in the evening to some inner-city house they didn't even know. Only three groups of the ten present were related or acquainted.

Later I would remember how the picnic table in our backyard spilled a rich offering of pies and green beans and potato salads, how the talk seemed infinite in its variety, how the laughter — "What a wacky idea, Babe!" — some Nye slapping me on the back with sudden gusto — rolled and rolled.

The experience I'd had at a Women's Writing Weekend in Austin where a visiting poet singled me out with displeasure — "What are these three names of yours? So, you've compromised yourself to marriage? I suppose you'd let a *man* publish your work?" — seemed nullified, erased. I'd walked out of that place, throat burning. It probably wouldn't have made any difference had I told her that I happened to *like* the name, or that sometimes it's a pleasure to become someone else midstream in your life. Had the name in question been Smithers or Lumpkin, I might have passed. But this little syllable, this glittering eye, held mine. I could almost have made it up.

No one encouraged us much when we set out one July to drive across the wide western expanse of the United States with a two-year-old. I had a job lined up through rural libraries of the state of Oregon, to be a visiting writer town-to-town for three months. It sounded delicious. It bore the aroma of blackberry jam and grilled salmon. For years I'd said I hoped to live in Oregon someday, if I was lucky enough to get old.

"You'll get old all right, before your time," said our dubious friends. "A two-year-old? Strapped in a car seat for hours on end? You'll be pulling your hair out. *He'll* be pulling your hair out. How will he stand it? How will he be able to sleep in so many strange places?"

One friend asked if we were going to haul his crib on the roof of the car.

I lay awake nights and worried. I rolled his socks into tight balls. Our 30
son, on the other hand, seemed anxious to depart. He'd been throwing
things into his little suitcase for weeks. I'd find the salt box in there. Or a
wad of dried clay. "I'm ready for Oregon," he kept repeating. "When do we
go? I won't stand up in my car seat!"

The moment we rolled onto the highway, exhausted by the tedium of
departure, a familiar flood of relief washed over us. We found ourselves
driving slowly, casually, absorbing the countryside. Home again! Hadn't
Americans become too destination-oriented, leaving toward places when we
barely had time enough to get there, driving fast all the way? We didn't
want to do that. We wanted to fall back into waltz rhythm. To pull into the
long driveway that said FRESH CORN MEAL GROUND TODAY even though we
didn't know when we'd have an oven again.

It worked out. We stopped at every playground between San Antonio
and Portland. (The best one, for anyone following our circuitous route, is at
Baker, Oregon — an old-fashioned paradise of high slides and well-oiled
merry-go-rounds.) We ate Japanese food in Santa Fe. We unrolled our moldy-
smelling tent on a spot of ground in Utah and by morning it was encircled
by clamoring chipmunks, who had found a wealthy source of cracker
crumbs. They were calling for more.

We camped high up in Idaho's Sawtooth Forest near the Sublette junction, where pioneers on the Oregon Trail split off south toward California
or continued west toward the Columbia River. Some legends say the signs
toward Oregon were written in fancy handwriting (Oregon favored literate
settlers) while the signs toward California bore only a painted gold chunk.
We had been reading aloud in a series of *National Geographics* about these
early vagabonds, how the trail was littered with furniture they pitched from
their wagons. How many people died, how many got all the way there,
paused awhile, and turned back? What was it they didn't find? Some places
in Wyoming, Idaho, Oregon, the deep ruts of their wheels are still engraved
in the earth.

Inside our zippered tent I finished reading the essays about the Oregon
Trail by flashlight, one of those fancy flashlights that do three different
things. I felt scared to walk to the car for something I had forgotten. It was
so *big* out there. Where had everyone gone? That night I would dream a
bear grabbed my toe through the tent's opening and shook it, hard. Long
wild voices pulled at us out of the air.

To consider our evolution into good-gas-mileage sedans, with well- 35
fingered atlases tucked between the seats, seemed critical. Long trip? You
call this a long trip?

On one of those Idaho back roads, I contemplated deeply the sweet
emblem of a stranger's hand raised in passing, a car or truck traveling the
other way whose driver wanted somehow to say, "Good journey, I've been
where you're going, travel well." I wanted to tell my friends back home who

were teaching their children not to talk to strangers that they had it all wrong. Do talk to strangers. Raise your hand to them in strange places, on back roads where leaning fields of tasseled grass have more identity than you do. Ask strangers anything you want. Maybe they'll have an answer. Don't go home with them, don't take your pants off with them, but talk, talk, talk. Anyway, in this mobile twentieth century, who among us is *not* strange?

I remember thinking, that night, that talking to strangers has been the most important thing I do in my life. It seemed doubtful two wagons on the Oregon Trail would have overtaken one another without a word or message being exchanged.

How much have we lost in this cornucopia land?

When my eye picked out a town name Nye on the map near Pendleton, the town famous for woolens in eastern Oregon, it became suddenly imperative to visit it. Only twenty-eight miles off the interstate — I didn't care how far it was. At our stop for lunch I wrote quick, wild messages to every Nye I could think of, planning to mail them there. Like Thoreau, New Mexico, or Valentine, Texas — a luminous postmark. This would be better than the tucked-away alley called Nye in El Paso, which no house even faces. Better than the old schoolhouse called Nye in Laredo, named for a beloved teacher.

The road south from Pendleton loomed rolling and golden as the road 40 to Oz. It held its breath — no signs, structures, other cars. The men slept in the back seat.

I couldn't stop imagining it. Maybe there would be a Nye Café. We could swivel on stools at the gleaming counter, ordering cocoa in thick white cups, or vanilla milkshakes. When people looked at us curiously — you here to visit someone? — we'd say the best thing possible to a little lost place in America: "No, we just came here to see the town." Maybe they'd take us around.

The first thing my husband and I ever did together, after that initial meeting at Quinney's, was stare at a map of Texas and pick out a little village called Sweet Home. We drove there in the first excited flush of our togetherness, simply to see what could *be* at a place called that. All day we sat in a pool hall with the regulars, at a metal-topped table inscribed with the name of some beer. An older woman with a gravelly voice showed us her gold wedding band. "Lemme tell ya, I waited," she proclaimed. Waited?

"Met Randolph back high school days, but wasn't no way he was going to stick around this little old place after we was through. He took off, *off*, and I stayed here ta Sweet Home, with my mama and daddy, all my relatives was here, did farming, my daddy fixed those old kinda tractors nobody uses anymore. I was just a small-town girl, ya know? But I don't marry no one else, no matter who comes along, I keep thinkin' a Randolph and I say to myself, Randolph's the one fer me. Well he marry somebody else, up some bigger town by Houston, and they stay married all her life but God bless

her she died. And one day last year Randolph come through here just to see
how we all turned into nothin'."

She grinned.

"Nothin'"? 45

"Sure. Like small-town people do. They happy just to stay home and
turn into nothin' else than what they started out to be. Yeah? It's not a bad
nothin'. So he come through and here I am, not married yet, age sixty-nine
and still waitin'! He sweep me off my feet." Her face grew rosy. "I'm here
to say some things can happen good. Ain't it pretty?" She turned the shiny
band over and over in the soft afternoon light.

Where was Randolph today? "Up ta Shiner buyin' seed." Had Sweet
Home changed much in fifty years? "Oh yeah. Went downhill completely.
But we still love it."

After dark we drove back to San Antonio on one of those old two-lanes
without much shoulder on either side. I grew sleepy and curled up on the
front seat with my head in my husband-to-be's lap. And dreamed, and
dreamed. Some things can happen good.

At the junction where Nye, Oregon, was supposed to be, a single ragged
spoke spun on a crooked windmill over a leaning, empty shack of a barn.
Purely desolate. No human, no house, nothing to indicate this was the place.

We drove one leg of the junction, looking. Fields of lush range grass. The 50
long, lonely land. We tried the other leg — emptier yet. Back at the battered
windmill, I turned off the engine. Our boy chanted for juice. While he sucked
at the tiny straw and the wind blew through our open doors, a deer bolted,
bright-eyed, from a ditch.

It approached our car instead of heading the other way. The deer stared
and stared and did not run, examining us with no evident sense of danger.
More petite than Texas deer, it sidestepped gracefully around our car, then
tiptoed into the brush.

"I think we're here," my husband said, looking down at the map and up
again at the small black number that indicated the junction. There was no
other sign.

I felt suddenly panicky, my voice shrill in the giant silence. "But where
is it? We must be turned around! Wouldn't there be some indication?"

We compared the size of the Nye on the map with a few Oregon towns
we'd already been through. "Look, this Nye is bigger than the name of that
town we passed through that had a thousand people. This is the size of a
three-thousand-person town. Weird! It's got to be here!"

My husband gazed. "I've seen ghost towns better looking than this." 55

Heaving my stiff legs out the door, I walked around. A tumbled chimney
whistled *Home*. Wishing for some scrap of women, or love — lace, a wad of
pinned hair — I caught instead the wisp of a woman's gaze staring far off,
the sweet hinges of cloud that held it. That long look that said *something else*.

If this were indeed it, where had the toughened settlers gone? Perhaps
they wished neighbors to lay down wheels, saying, "I'll build here too" —

the slim-sided seed of a town, awakening. Perhaps they wished, and everybody passed them by. Among thistles, broken trough, I poked for a sign.
And the ache in the throat of that long wind kept hurting.

Finally a red pickup truck appeared on the highway, and we flagged it.
A blonde woman squinted at us, scratched her head. "Yep, that's Nye. Not
much to look at, is there? When I was little, someone still lived in that
beat-up house, but we never knew him. I have a memory of an old guy
bending down in the weeds. It didn't look much better then, that's for sure.
Actually, none of us around here ever thought of Nye as anything more than
a turnoff, you know? I mean, it seems strange that the map makes it look
like a town."

Before she drove off, she apologized. We stood around a while longer, as
you would at a grave, before driving off toward Portland quietly. I don't
think anyone spoke for a hundred miles.

Later the *Oregon Directory of Geographical Names* would say this point on   60
the highway once boasted a post office named Nye, service discontinued
1917. It had probably been named for A. W. Nye, a well-known early resident, though why he was well known, or anything else about him, had
filtered into the wind above Umatilla County and disappeared, perhaps
toward the town of Echo, relatively nearby on the road back toward men.

"Go to Newport," people in Portland told us later. "There's a street called
Nye in Newport. There's a beach called Nye, and an art center." We saved
it for another time.

Sometimes the calls come late at night. "I'm looking for a Nye who was
a well-known country-and-western singer in the 1950s. He wore these pants
printed with rainbow-colored spurs. That wouldn't happen to be your husband, would it?"

Or, "I'm looking for my great-aunt's friends named Nye — she had a real
bad dream, few nights ago, that they drove off a cliff, and she keeps begging
us to call them. She can't remember the man's first name. Do you happen
to know Celia Withers of Weatherford?"

One evening a rich, musical voice phones in from small-town east Texas.
She's seen my husband's name in the Corsicana newspaper, and says she's
been looking for him for seventeen years. Her name is Peachy Gardner.
"Honey! I took care of babies all my life and no baby ever got into my heart
like that little Nye did. He'd tweak my ear and kiss me. HONEY! I loved
him so much. I just want to see what he grew into. When his parents moved
away I nearly died. They sent me Christmas cards for a while but then —
you know what happens. People just get lost."

Then she says they lived in Dallas. My husband never did. And when   65
was the loving baby born? Four years after my husband. I hate to tell her
this.

"Are you positive? Are you sure his daddy's name isn't James?"

We talk a while longer. She wrote to the place they had moved and her
letter came back. America, she says, eats people up. They get too busy. I

promise to start looking for the man with my husband's name, taking her number, in case he appears. We talk about the trees in her part of Texas; she lives in a thicket so dense the light barely shines through. She says, "I guess it's strange to want to see someone so bad this long after. I mean, he wouldn't look twice at me now. I know that. But I can't forget how he said — Peachy. I can't forget — his little hand."

AFTERWORD

All people, at some point in childhood or adolescence, loathe their own names. ("Donald" struck me as offensively mild; "Don" was a dog's name.) An essay that touches upon a universal tic may seem too obvious; on the other hand, it may lure readers into themselves. The writer, talking about something common, colors it with the particular. In the case of Naomi Shihab Nye, as for so many Americans, her three-part name raises issues of ethnicity, of belonging and alienation. The child's point of view, challenging received history, allows Nye to make use of naiveté's telling innocent eye. The generosity, charm, energy, and engagingness of the speaker — writing all the Nyes of San Antonio; crossing the country with a two-year-old — leaves us vulnerable to her import.

If you question the subject of Nye's essay, look at the title. (When in doubt, always look at the title. It is the author's latest thought, and a clue to intention. When you make your own titles, think of the reader.) This essay is about the challenge of feeling new in a new land, the scary loneliness, the loss or failure possible, and the pleasures of unrehearsed good feeling among strangers.

BOOK AVAILABLE IN PAPERBACK

Yellow Glove. Portland, Oreg.: Breitenbush Books. *Poetry.*

JOYCE
CAROL
OATES

*I*N THE 1993 Who's Who, *Joyce Carol Oates at the age of forty-five listed
thirteen books of short stories, twenty-eight novels, eight books of poetry, four
plays, and five books of nonfiction. In 1993 she added a new novel called* Foxfire:
Confessions of a Girl Gang, *and in 1994 another collection of short stories,* Where
Is Here? *"Her idea of taking a break from the tension of writing novels," said one
statistician, "is to write poetry and short stories." She also enjoys cooking, jogging,
bicycling, playing the piano, and visiting New York City. She teaches at Princeton
University and with her husband edits a press and a magazine, and yet she publishes
more than a book a year.*

*This prodigy was born in small-town upstate New York (1938) and published
her first story in* Mademoiselle *when she was still an undergraduate at Syracuse
University. She took her M.A. at the University of Wisconsin and taught at the
universities of Detroit and Windsor (Ontario) while she began to write and publish
in earnest. Her third novel, called* them *(which is not a typographical error), won
the National Book Award in 1970.*

Almost from the start she has been criticized for writing too much. An Esquire
*critic titled his trashing "Stop Me Before I Write Again." The charge is illogical: If
you like what she writes, the more the better; if you don't like it, then you must have
intrinsic reasons for disliking it. When I hear critics crying about quantity, I hear
two things: They are lazy and they are envious.*

In an interview published by the Paris Review, *Oates speaks about suffering
from periods of "inertia and depression" and about other times when she starts
writing early, before breakfast, and delays breakfast until three in the afternoon. All
writers, it has been suggested, are manic-depressive — which of course does not
mean psychotic; many people with unusual volatility suffer not from delusions,*

Photo by Norman Seef

which would be a thought disorder, but from a mood disorder. Balzac wrote long novels in twenty-hour days virtually without sleep, then sank into sloth and despair. Mania gives high energy; mania makes for clear seeing and for hard work. Someone has suggested that writers create while manic and while remembering depression. Surely the world of much fiction and poetry is dark enough.

Oates's fiction describes a fallen world, and critics have found in it a Calvinist sense of total depravity. In The Contemporary Essay *many of our best writers, turning like Edward Abbey from a despised culture, find solace in the open spaces of the natural world. Not this writer. For Oates, the natural world is as fallen as anything; when Adam fell, and Eve, the garden also fell. "Against Nature" originally appeared in* Antaeus.

Against Nature

We soon get through with Nature. She excites an expectation which she cannot satisfy.

— THOREAU, *Journal,* 1854

Sir, if a man has experienced the inexpressible, he is under no obligation to attempt to express it.

— SAMUEL JOHNSON

The writer's resistance to Nature.

It has no sense of humor: In its beauty, as in its ugliness, or its neutrality, there is no laughter.

It lacks a moral purpose.

It lacks a satiric dimension, registers no irony.

Its pleasures lack resonance, being accidental; its horrors, even when   5
premeditated, are equally perfunctory, "red in tooth and claw" et cetera.

It lacks a symbolic subtext — excepting that provided by man.

It has no (verbal) language.

It has no interest in ours.

It inspires a painfully limited set of responses in "nature-writers" — REVERENCE, AWE, PIETY, MYSTICAL ONENESS.

It eludes us even as it prepares to swallow us up, books and all.   10

* * *

I was lying on my back in the dirt-gravel of the towpath beside the Delaware-Raritan Canal, Titusville, New Jersey, staring up at the sky and trying, with no success, to overcome a sudden attack of tachycardia that had come upon me out of nowhere — such attacks are always "out of nowhere," that's their charm — and all around me Nature thrummed with life, the air smelling of moisture and sunlight, the canal reflecting the sky, red-winged blackbirds testing their spring calls — the usual. I'd become the jar in Tennessee,° a fictitous center, or parenthesis, aware beyond my erratic heartbeat of the numberless heartbeats of the earth, its pulsing pumping life, sheer life, incalculable. Struck down in the midst of motion — I'd been jogging a minute before — I was "out of time" like a fallen, stunned boxer, privileged (in an abstract manner of speaking) to be an involuntary witness to the random, wayward, nameless motion on all sides of me.

Paroxysmal tachycardia is rarely fatal, but if the heartbeat accelerates to 250–270 beats a minute you're in trouble. The average attack is about 100–150 beats and mine seemed so far to be about average; the trick now was to prevent it from getting worse. Brainy people try brainy strategies, such as thinking calming thoughts, pseudo-mystic thoughts, *If I die now it's a good death,* that sort of thing, *if I die this is a good place and a good time,* the idea is to deceive the frenzied heartbeat that, really, you don't care: You hadn't any other plans for the afternoon. The important thing with tachycardia is to prevent panic! you must prevent panic! otherwise you'll have to be taken by ambulance to the closest emergency room, which is not so very nice a way to spend the afternoon, really. So I contemplated the blue sky overhead. The earth beneath my head. Nature surrounding me on all sides, I couldn't quite see it but I could hear it, smell it, sense it — there is something *there,* no mistake about it. Completely oblivious to the predicament of the individual but that's only "natural" after all, one hardly expects otherwise.

When you discover yourself lying on the ground, limp and unresisting, head in the dirt, and helpless, the earth seems to shift forward as a presence; hard, emphatic, not mere surface but a genuine force — there is no other word for it but *presence.* To keep in motion is to keep in time and to be stopped, stilled, is to be abruptly out of time, in another time-dimension perhaps, an alien one, where human language has no resonance. Nothing to be said about it expresses it, nothing touches it, it's an absolute against which nothing human can be measured. . . . Moving through space and time by way of your own volition you inhabit an interior consciousness, a hallucinatory consciousness, it might be said, so long as breath, heartbeat, the body's autonomy hold; when motion is stopped you are jarred out of it. The interior is invaded by the exterior. The outside wants to come in, and only the self's fragile membrane prevents it.

The fly buzzing at Emily's death.°

Still, the earth *is* your place. A tidy grave-site measured to your size. Or, from another angle of vision, one vast democratic grave. 15

---

jar in Tennessee   A reference to Wallace Stevens's poem "Anecdote of the Jar."
fly buzzing at Emily's death   Reference to poem by Emily Dickinson, "I heard a Fly buzz — when I died —."

Let's contemplate the sky. Forget the crazy hammering heartbeat, don't listen to it, don't start counting, remember that there is a clever way of breathing that conserves oxygen as if you're lying below the surface of a body of water breathing through a very thin straw but you *can* breathe through it if you're careful, if you don't panic, one breath and then another and then another, isn't that the story of all lives? careers? Just a matter of breathing. Of course it is. But contemplate the sky, it's there to be contemplated. A mild shock to see it so blank, blue, a thin airy ghostly blue, no clouds to disguise its emptiness. You are beginning to feel not only weightless but near-bodiless, lying on the earth like a scrap of paper about to be blown off. Two dimensions and you'd imagined you were three! And there's the sky rolling away forever, into infinity — if "infinity" can be "rolled into" — and the forlorn truth is, that's where you're going too. And the lovely blue isn't even blue, is it? isn't even there, is it? a mere optical illusion, isn't it? no matter what art has urged you to believe.

* * *

Early Nature memories. Which it's best not to suppress.

. . . Wading, as a small child, in Tonawanda Creek near our house, and afterward trying to tear off, in a frenzy of terror and revulsion, the sticky fat black bloodsuckers that had attached themselves to my feet, particularly between my toes.

. . . Coming upon a friend's dog in a drainage ditch, dead for several days, evidently the poor creature had been shot by a hunter and left to die, bleeding to death, and we're stupefied with grief and horror but can't resist sliding down to where he's lying on his belly, and we can't resist squatting over him, turning the body over . . .

. . . The raccoon, mad with rabies, frothing at the mouth and tearing at his own belly with his teeth, so that his intestines spilled out onto the ground . . . a sight I seem to remember though in fact I did not see. I've been told I did not see.

* * *

Consequently, my chronic uneasiness with Nature-mysticism; Nature-adoration; Nature-as-(moral)-instruction-for-mankind. My doubt that one can, with philosophical validity, address "Nature" as a single coherent noun, anything other than a Platonic, hence discredited, isness. My resistance to "Nature-writing" as a genre, except when it is brilliantly fictionalized in the service of a writer's individual vision — Thoreau's books and *Journal,* of course — but also, less known in this country, the miniaturist prose-poems of Colette (*Flowers and Fruit*) and Ponge (*Taking the Side of Things*) — in which case it becomes yet another, and ingenious, form of storytelling. The subject is *there* only by the grace of the author's language.

Nature has no instructions for mankind except that our poor beleaguered humanist-democratic way of life, our fantasies of the individual's high worth, our sense that the weak, no less than the strong, have a right to survive, are absurd.

In any case, where *is* Nature? one might (skeptically) inquire. Who has looked upon her/its face and survived?

* * *

But isn't this all exaggeration, in the spirit of rhetorical contentiousness? Surely Nature is, for you, as for most reasonably intelligent people, a "perennial" source of beauty, comfort, peace, escape from the delirium of civilized life; a respite from the ego's ever-frantic strategies of self-promotion, as a way of insuring (at least in fantasy) some small measure of immortality? Surely Nature, as it is understood in the usual slapdash way, as human, if not dilettante, *experience* (hiking in a national park, jogging on the beach at dawn, even tending, with the usual comical frustrations, a suburban garden), is wonderfully consoling; a place where, when you go there, it has to take you in? — a palimpsest of sorts you choose to read, layer by layer, always with care, always cautiously, in proportion to your psychological strength?

Nature: as in Thoreau's upbeat transcendentalist mode ("The indescribable innocence and beneficence of Nature, — such health, such cheer, they afford forever! and such sympathy have they ever with our race, that all Nature would be affected . . . if any man should ever for a just cause grieve"), and not in Thoreau's grim mode ("Nature is hard to be overcome but she must be overcome"). 25

Another way of saying, not *Nature-in-itself* but *Nature-as-experience.*

The former, Nature-in-itself, is, to allude slantwise to Melville, a blankness ten times blank; the latter is what we commonly, or perhaps always, mean when we speak of Nature as a noun, a single entity — something of ours. Most of the time it's just an activity, a sort of hobby, a weekend, a few days, perhaps a few hours, staring out of the window at the mind-dazzling autumn foliage of, say, Northern Michigan, being rendered speechless — temporarily — at the sight of Mt. Shasta, the Grand Canyon, Ansel Adams's West. Or Nature writ small, contained in the back yard. Nature filtered through our optical nerves, our "senses," our fiercely romantic expectations. Nature that pleases us because it mirrors our souls, or gives the comforting illusion of doing so. As in our first mother's awakening to the self's fatal beauty —

> I thither went
> With unexperienc't thought, and laid me down
> On the green bank, to look into the clear
> Smooth Lake, that to me seem'd another Sky.
> As I bent down to look, just opposite,
> A Shape within the watr'y gleam appear'd
> Bending to look on me, I started back,
> It started back, but pleas'd I soon return'd,
> Pleas'd it return'd as soon with answering looks
> Of sympathy and love; there I had fixt
> Mine eyes till now, and pin'd with vain desire.

— in these surpassingly beautiful lines from the Book IV of Milton's *Paradise Lost.*

Nature as the self's (flattering) mirror, but not ever, no never, Nature-in-itself.

* * *

Nature is mouths, or maybe a single mouth. Why glamorize it, romanticize it, well yes but we must, we're writers, poets, mystics (of a sort) aren't we, precisely what else are we to do but glamorize and romanticize and generally exaggerate the significance of anything we focus the white heat of our "creativity" upon . . . ? And why not Nature, since it's there, common property, mute, can't talk back, allows us the possibility of transcending the human condition for a while, writing prettily of mountain ranges, white-tailed deer, the purple crocuses outside this very window, the thrumming dazzling "life-force" we imagine we all support. Why not.

Nature *is* more than a mouth — it's a dazzling variety of mouths. And it pleases the senses, in any case, as the physicists' chill universe of numbers certainly does not.

* * *

Oscar Wilde, on our subject: "Nature is no great mother who has borne us. She is our creation. It is in our brain that she quickens to life. Things are because we see them, and what we see, and how we see it, depends on the Arts that have influenced us. To look at a thing is very different from seeing a thing. . . . At present, people see fogs, not because there are fogs, but because poets and painters have taught them the mysterious loveliness of such effects. There may have been fogs for centuries in London. I dare say there were. But no one saw them. They did not exist until Art had invented them. . . . Yesterday evening Mrs. Arundel insisted on my going to the window and looking at the glorious sky, as she called it. And so I had to look at it. . . . And what was it? It was simply a very second-rate Turner, a Turner of a bad period, with all the painter's worst faults exaggerated and over-emphasized."

(If we were to put it to Oscar Wilde that he exaggerates, his reply might well be: "Exaggeration? I don't know the meaning of the word.")

* * *

Walden, that most artfully composed of prose fictions, concludes, in the rhapsodic chapter "Spring," with Henry David Thoreau's comtemplation of death, decay, and regeneration as it is suggested to him, or to his protagonist, by the spectacle of vultures feeding off carrion. There is a dead horse close by his cabin and the stench of its decomposition, in certain winds, is daunting. Yet: ". . . the assurance it gave me of the strong appetite and inviolable health of Nature was my compensation. I love to see that Nature is so rife with life that myriads can be afforded to be sacrificed and suffered to prey upon one another; that tender organizations can be so serenely squashed out of existence like pulp, — tadpoles which herons gobble up, and tortoises and toads run over in the road; and that sometimes it has rained flesh and blood! . . . The impression made on a wise man is that of universal innocence."

Come off it, Henry David. You've grieved these many years for your elder brother John, who died a ghastly death of lockjaw, you've never wholly recovered from the experience of watching him die. And you know, or must know, that you're fated too to die young of consumption. . . . But this doctrinaire transcendentalist passage ends *Walden* on just the right note. It's as impersonal, as coolly detached, as the Oversoul itself: a "wise man" filters his emotions through his brain.

Or through his prose. 35

* * *

Nietzsche: "We all pretend to ourselves that we are more simple-minded than we are: that is how we get a rest from our fellow men."

> Once out of nature I shall never take
> My bodily form from any natural thing,
> But such a form as Grecian goldsmiths make
> Of hammered gold and gold enamelling
> To keep a drowsy Emperor awake;
> Or set upon a golden bough to sing
> To lords and ladies of Byzantium
> Of what is past, or passing, or to come.
> – WILLIAM BUTLER YEATS, "Sailing to Byzantium"

Yet even the golden bird is a "bodily form taken from (a) natural thing." No, it's impossible to escape!

* * *

The writer's resistance to Nature.

Wallace Stevens: "In the presence of extraordinary actuality, consciousness takes the place of imagination."

* * *

Once, years ago, in 1972 to be precise, when I seemed to have been another person, related to the person I am now as one is related, tangentially, sometimes embarrassingly, to cousins not seen for decades, — once, when we were living in London, and I was very sick, I had a mystical vision. That is, I "had" a "mystical vision" — the heart sinks: such pretension — or something resembling one. A fever-dream, let's call it. It impressed me enormously and impresses me still, though I've long since lost the capacity to see it with my mind's eye, or even, I suppose, to believe in it. There is a statute of limitations on "mystical visions" as on romantic love.

I was very sick, and I imagined my life as a thread, a thread of breath, 40 or heartbeat, or pulse, or light, yes it was light, radiant light, I was burning with fever and I ascended to that plane of serenity that might be mistaken for (or *is*, in fact) Nirvana, where I had a waking dream of uncanny lucidity —

My body is a tall column of light and heat.

My body is not "I" but "it."

My body is not one but many.

My body, which "I" inhabit, is inhabited as well by other creatures, unknown to me, imperceptible — the smallest of them mere sparks of light.

My body, which I perceive as substance, is in fact an organization of 45 infinitely complex, overlapping, imbricated structures, radiant light their manifestation, the "body" a tall column of light and blood-heat, a temporary agreement among atoms, like a high-rise building with numberless rooms, corridors, corners, elevator shafts, windows. . . . In this fantastical structure the "I" is deluded as to its sovereignty, let alone its autonomy in the (outside) world; the most astonishing secret is that the "I" doesn't exist! — but it behaves as if it does, as if it were one and not many.

In any case, without the "I" the tall column of light and heat would die, and the microscopic life-particles would die with it . . . will die with it. The "I," which doesn't exist, is everything.

But Dr. Johnson is right, the inexpressible need not be expressed. And what resistance, finally? There is none.

* * *

This morning, an invasion of tiny black ants. One by one they appear, out of nowhere — that's their charm too! — moving single file across the white Parsons table where I am sitting, trying without much success to write a poem. A poem of only three or four lines is what I want, something short, tight, mean. I want it to hurt like a white-hot wire up the nostrils, small and compact and turned in upon itself with the density of a hunk of rock from the planet Jupiter. . . .

But here come the black ants: harbingers, you might say, of spring. One by one by one they appear on the dazzling white table and one by one I kill them with a forefinger, my deft right forefinger, mashing each against the surface of the table and then dropping it into a wastebasket at my side. Idle labor, mesmerizing, effortless, and I'm curious as to how long I can do it, sit here in the brilliant March sunshine killing ants with my right forefinger, how long I, and the ants, can keep it up.

After a while I realize that I can do it a long time. And that I've written 50 my poem.

AFTERWORD

This is the essay as notes toward a subject, discrete entries on a subject, paragraphs that could have been culled from a journal. It is fine to space your essay by a row of three asterisks when you are Joyce Carol Oates and when the essay coheres—but a student should consult the instructor before using typographical devices to replace transitions.

Note how the beginnings of each separate passage, or summaries of each beginning, lay out the essay's structure: "The writer's [meaning My] resistance to Nature." | Anecdote of tachycardia | "Early Nature memories." | ". . . uneasiness with Nature-mysticism." | Imagined counterargument | Counter-counter number one | Counter-counter number two, Wilde | Walden | Nietzsche |Yeats | Stevens | Anecdote two, fever-dream | Antinatural climactic vision of ants.

Note that, despite its episodic structure, this essay fulfills most of the expectations that the classic essay raises. It explores by reminiscence and allusion a single, general topic. At moments it includes narrative, like fiction; at others it includes the imagistic, or the apothegmatic, like poetry. Note also Oates's intellectual skepticism over the romantic inflation of nature. She manages to suggest, with a delicate stab of irony, that Thoreau's bad thinking comes not from deficiency of mind but from devotion to his own prose style.

BOOKS AVAILABLE IN PAPERBACK

American Appetites. New York: HarperCollins. *Novel.*

The Assignation. New York: HarperCollins. *Short stories.*

Because It Is Bitter and Because It Is My Heart. New York: Dutton. *Novel.*

Bellefleur. New York: Dutton. *Novel.*

Black Water. New York: Dutton. *Novel.*

Childwold. New York: Fawcett Books. *Novel.*

Crossing the Border. New York: Fawcett Books. *Short stories.*

Expensive People. New York: Fawcett Books. *Novel.*

The Fabulous Beasts: Poems. Baton Rouge: Louisiana State University Press.

Heat, and Other Stories. New York: Dutton. *Short stories.*

New Heaven, New Earth: The Visionary Experience in Literature. New York: Fawcett Books. *Nonfiction.*

Night-Side. New York: Fawcett Books. *Short stories.*

On Boxing. New York: Zebra Books. *Nonfiction.*

The Profane Art: Essays and Reviews. New York: Persea Books.

Raven's Wing. New York: Dutton. *Novel.*

The Rise of Life on Earth. New York: New Directions Books. *Novel.*

Son of the Morning. New York: Fawcett Books. *Novel.*

them. New York: Fawcett Books. *Novel.*

Three Plays. Princeton: Ontario Review.

The Time Traveler. New York: Dutton. *Poetry.*

The Triumph of the Spider Monkey. New York: Fawcett Books. *Novel.*

Twelve Plays. New York: Dutton.

Where Are You Going, Where Have You Been? Selected Early Stories. Princeton: Ontario Review. *Short stories.*

Where Is Here? Stories. New York: Ecco Press. *Short stories.*

Woman Writer: Occasions and Opportunities. New York: Dutton. *Essays.*

Wonderland. Princeton: Ontario Review. *Novel.*

You Must Remember This. New York: HarperCollins. *Novel.*

CYNTHIA
OZICK

*R*AISED IN THE BRONX, *Cynthia Ozick (b. 1928) took her B.A. at New York University, went out to Ohio State University for her M.A., married a lawyer, bore a daughter, and returned to live in New Rochelle. She is a novelist and short-story writer, with a strong second calling in the essay. Her first novel was* Trust *in 1966. More recently she published a book of short stories,* Levitation *(1982); an essay collection,* Art and Ardor *(1983); and in the same year another novel,* The Cannibal Galaxy. *Also in 1983 she was presented with one of the Harold and Mildred Strauss Living Awards, thirty-five thousand dollars a year for five years in support of her work. In 1987 she published* The Messiah of Stockholm, *only four years after her previous novel, which had come sixteen years after her first. "The First Day of School" appeared in* Harper's *in 1989 when she also published* Metaphor and Memory, *a collection of essays. In the same year she published* The Shawl, *a novella and a short story about the Holocaust.*

In an interview in Publishers Weekly, *Ozick discloses unusual habits. Most writers as they get older tend to write early in the morning, when they feel their energy highest. Cynthia Ozick writes late at night. She finishes when dawn arrives with "the racket of those damn birds. . . . The depth of the night is guilt free, responsibility free; nobody will telephone you, importune you, make any claims on you. You own the world." She also acknowledges that "my first draft is the last." But she defines "first draft" so that we understand her: A first draft can be the product of much scratching around. "I must perfect each sentence madly before I go on to the next," she says, because "at the end I want to be finished."*

The First Day of School:
Washington Square, 1946

> This portion of New York appears to many persons the most delectable.
> It has a kind of established repose which is not of frequent occurrence
> in other quarters of the long, shrill city; it has a riper, richer, more
> honorable look than any of the upper ramifications of the great longi-
> tudinal thoroughfare — the look of having had something of a social
> history.
>
> — HENRY JAMES, *Washington Square*

I first came down to Washington Square on a colorless February morning
in 1946. I was seventeen and a half years old and was carrying my lunch in
a brown paper bag, just as I had carried it to high school only a month
before. It was — I thought it was — the opening day of spring term at
Washington Square College, my initiation into my freshman year at New
York University. All I knew of NYU then was that my science-minded
brother had gone there; he had written from the army that I ought to go
there too. With master-of-ceremonies zest he described the Browsing Room
on the second floor of the Main Building as a paradisal chamber whose
bookish loungers leafed languidly through magazines and exchanged high-
principled witticisms between classes. It had the sound of a carpeted Olym-
pian club in Oliver Wendell Holmes's Boston, Hub of the Universe, strewn
with leather chairs and delectable old copies of *The Yellow Book*.

On that day I had never heard of Oliver Wendell Holmes or *The Yellow
Book*, and Washington Square was a faraway bower where wounded birds
fell out of trees. My brother had once brought home from Washington Square
Park a baby sparrow with a broken leg, to be nurtured back to flight. It died
instead, emitting in its last hours melancholy faint cheeps, and leaving
behind a dense recognition of the minute explicitness of morality. All the
same, in the February grayness Washington Square had the allure of the
celestial unknown. A sparrow might die, but my own life was luminously
new: I felt my youth like a nimbus.

Which dissolves into the dun gauze of a low and sullen city sky. And
here I am flying out of the Lexington Avenue subway at Astor Place, just a
few yards from Wanamaker's, here I am turning a corner past a secondhand
bookstore and a union hall; already late, I begin walking very fast toward
the park. The air is smoky with New York winter grit, and on clogged
Broadway a mob of trucks shifts squawking gears. But there, just ahead,
crisscrossed by paths under high branches, is Washington Square; and on a
single sidewalk, three clear omens — or call them riddles, intricate and

Addresses
Reader

redolent. These I will disclose in a moment, but before that you must push
open the heavy brass-and-glass doors of the Main Building and come with
me, at a hard and panting pace, into the lobby of Washington Square College
on the earliest morning of my freshman year.

On the left, a bank of elevators. Straight ahead, a long burnished corridor,
spooky as a lit tunnel. And empty, all empty. I can hear my solitary footsteps
reverberate, as in a radio mystery drama: They lead me up a short staircase
into a big dark ghost-town cafeteria. My brother's letter, along with his
account of the physics and chemistry laboratories (I will never see them),
has already explained that this place is called Commons — and here my
heart will learn to shake with the merciless newness of life. But not today;
today there is nothing. Tables and chairs squat in dead silhouette. I race back
through a silent maze of halls and stairways to the brass-and-glass doors —
there stands a lonely guard. From the pocket of my coat I retrieve a scrap
with a classroom number on it and ask the way. The guard announces in a
sly croak that the first day of school is not yet; come back tomorrow, he says.

A dumb bad joke: I'm humiliated. I've journeyed the whole way down   5
from the end of the line — Pelham Bay, in the northeast Bronx — to find
myself in desolation, all because of a muddle: Tuesday isn't Wednesday. The
nimbus of expectation fades. The lunch bag in my fist takes on a greasy
sadness. I'm not ready to dive back into the subway — I'll have a look
around.

Across the street from the Main Building, the three omens. First, a pretzel
man with a cart. He's wearing a sweater, a cap that keeps him faceless —
he's nothing but the shadows of his creases — and wool gloves with the
fingertips cut off. He never moves; he might as well be made of papier-
mâché, set up and left out in the open since spring. There are now almost
no pretzels for sale, and this gives me a chance to inspect the construction
of his bare pretzel-poles. The pretzels are hooked over a column of gray
cardboard cylinders, themselves looped around a stick, the way horseshoes
drop around a post. The cardboard cylinders are the insides of toilet paper
rolls.

The pretzel man is rooted between a Chock Full O' Nuts (that's the
second omen) and a newsstand (that's the third).

The Chock Full: The doors are like fans, whirling remnants of conversation. *She will marry him. She will not marry him.* Fragrance of coffee and hot
chocolate. *We can prove that the senses are partial and unreliable vehicles of
information, but who is to say that reason is not equally a product of human
limitation?* Powdered doughnut sugar on their lips.

Attached to a candy store, the newsstand. Copies of *Partisan Review:* the
table of the gods. Jean Stafford, Mary McCarthy, Elizabeth Hardwick, Irving
Howe, Delmore Schwartz, Alfred Kazin, Clement Greenberg, Stephen
Spender, William Phillips, John Berryman, Saul Bellow, Philip Rahv, Richard
Chase, Randall Jarrell, Simone de Beauvoir, Karl Shapiro, George Orwell! I
don't know a single one of these names, but I feel their small conflagration

flaming in the gray street: the succulent hotness of their promise. I mean to penetrate every one of them. Since all the money I have is my subway fare — a nickel — I don't buy a copy (the price of *Partisan* in 1946 is fifty cents); I pass on.

I pass on to the row of houses on the north side of the square. Henry 10 James was born in one of these, but I don't know that either. Still, they are plainly old, though no longer aristocratic: haughty last-century shabbies with shut eyelids, built of rosy-ripe respectable brick, down on their luck. Across the park bulks Judson Church, with its squat squarish bell tower; by the end of the week I will be languishing at the margins of a basketball game in its basement, forlorn in my blue left-over-from-high-school gym suit and mooning over Emily Dickinson:

> There's a certain Slant of light,
> Winter Afternoons —
> That oppresses, like the Heft
> Of Cathedral Tunes —

There is more I don't know. I don't know that W. H. Auden lives just down *there*, and might at any moment be seen striding toward home under his tall rumpled hunch; I don't know that Marianne Moore is only up the block, her doffed tricorn resting on her bedroom dresser. It's Greenwich Village — I know *that* — no more than twenty years after Edna St. Vincent Millay has sent the music of her name (her best, perhaps her only, poem) into these bohemian streets: bohemia, the honeypot of poets.

On that first day in the tea-leafed cup of the town I am ignorant, ignorant! But the three riddle-omens are soon to erupt, and all of them together will illumine Washington Square.

Begin with the benches in the park. Here, side by side with students and their looseleafs, lean or lie the shadows of the pretzel man, his creased ghosts or doubles: all those pitiables, half-women and half-men, neither awake nor asleep; the discountable, the repudiated, the unseen. No more notice is taken of any of them than of a scudding fragment of newspaper in the path. Even then, even so long ago, the benches of Washington Square are pimpled with this hell-tossed crew, these Mad Margarets and Cokey Joes, these volcanic coughers, shakers, groaners, tremblers, droolers, blasphemers, these public urinators with vomitous breath and rusted teeth stumps, dead-eyed and self-abandoned, dragging their makeshift junkyard shoes, their buttonless layers of raggedy ratfur. The pretzel man with his toilet paper rolls conjures and spews them all — he is a loftier brother to these citizens of the lower pox, he is guardian of the garden of the jettisoned. They rattle along all the seams of Washington Square. They are the pickled city, the true and universal City-Below-Cities, the wolfish vinegar-Babylon that dogs the spittled skirts of bohemia. The toilet paper rolls are the temple columns of this sacred grove.

The First Day of School: Washington Square, 1946

Next, the whirling doors of Chock Full O' Nuts. Here is the marketplace of Washington Square, its bazaar, its roiling gossip-parlor, its matchmaker's office and arena — the outermost wing, so to speak, evolved from the Commons. On a day like today, when the Commons is closed, the Chock Full is thronged with extra power, a cello making up for a missing viola. Until now, the fire of my vitals has been for the imperious tragedians of the *Aeneid;* I have lived in the narrow throat of poetry. Another year or so of this oblivion, until at last I am hammerstruck with the shock of Europe's skull, the bled planet of death camp and war. Eleanor Roosevelt has not yet written her famous column announcing the discovery of Anne Frank's diary. The term *cold war* is new. The Commons, like the college itself, is overcrowded, veterans in their pragmatic thirties mingling with the reluctant dreamy young. And the Commons is convulsed with politics: A march to the docks is organized, no one knows by whom, to protest the arrival of Walter Gieseking, the German musician who flourished among Nazis. The Communists — two or three readily recognizable cantankerous zealots — stomp through with their daily leaflets and sneers. There is even a Monarchist, a small poker-faced rectangle of a man with secretive tireless eyes who, when approached for his views, always demands, in perfect Bronx tones, the restoration of his king. The engaged girls — how many of them there seem to be! — flash their rings and tangle their ankles in their long New Look skirts. There is no feminism and no feminists: I am, I think, the only one. The Commons is a tide: It washes up the cold war, it washes up the engaged girls' rings, it washes up the several philosophers and the numerous poets. The philosophers are all existentialists; the poets are all influenced by *The Waste Land.* When the Commons overflows, the engaged girls cross the street to show their rings at the Chock Full.

Call it density, call it intensity, call it continuity: Call it, finally, society. The Commons belongs to the satirists. Here, one afternoon, is Alfred Chester, holding up a hair, a single strand, before a crowd. (He will one day write stories and novels. He will die young.) "What is that hair?" I innocently ask, having come late on the scene. "A pubic hair," he replies, and I feel as Virginia Woolf did when she declared human nature to have "changed in or about December 1910" — soon after her sister Vanessa explained away a spot on her dress as "semen."

In or about February 1946 human nature does not change; it keeps on. On my bedroom wall I tack — cut out from *Life* magazine — the wildest Picasso I can find: a face that is also a belly. Mr. George E. Mutch, a lyrical young English teacher still in his twenties, writes on the blackboard: "When lilacs last in the dooryard bloom'd," and "Bare, ruined choirs, where late the sweet birds sang," and "A green thought in a green shade"; he tells us to burn, like Pater, with a hard, gemlike flame. Another English teacher — older and crustier — compares Walt Whitman to a plumber; the next year he is rumored to have shot himself in a wood. The initial letters of Wash-

15

ington Square College are a device to recall three of the seven deadly sins: Wantonness, Sloth, Covetousness. In the Commons they argue the efficacy of the orgone box.° Eda Lou Walton, sprightly as a bird, knows all the Village bards, and is a Village bard herself. Sidney Hook is an intellectual rumble in the logical middle distance. Homer Watt, chairman of the English department, is the very soul who, in a far-off time of bewitchment, hired Thomas Wolfe.

And so, in February 1946, I make my first purchase of a "real" book — which is to say, not for the classroom. It is displayed in the window of the secondhand bookstore between the Astor Place subway station and the union hall, and for weeks I have been coveting it: *Of Time and the River.* I am transfigured; I am pierced through with rapture; skipping gym, I sit among morning mists on a windy bench a foot from the stench of Mad Margaret, sinking into that cascading syrup:

> Man's youth is a wonderful thing: It is so full of anguish and of magic and he never comes to know it as it is, until it is gone from him forever. . . . And what is the essence of that strange and bitter miracle of life which we feel so poignantly, so unutterably, with such a bitter pain and joy, when we are young?

Thomas Wolfe, lost, and by the wind grieved, ghost, come back again! In Washington Square I am appareled in the "numb exultant secrecies of fog, fog-numb air filled with solemn joy of nameless and impending prophecy, an ancient yellow light, the old smoke-ochre of the morning. . . ."

The smoke-ochre of the morning. Ah, you who have flung Thomas Wolfe, along with your strange and magical youth, onto the ash-heap of juvenilia and excess, myself among you, isn't this a lovely phrase still? It rises out of the old pavements of Washington Square as delicately colored as an eggshell.

The veterans in their pragmatic thirties are nailed to Need; they have families and futures to attend to. When Mr. George E. Mutch exhorts them to burn with a hard, gemlike flame, and writes across the blackboard the line that reveals his own name,

> The world is too much with us; late and soon,
> Getting and spending, we lay waste our
> powers,

one of the veterans heckles, "What about getting a Buick, what about spending a buck?" Chester, at sixteen, is a whole year younger than I; he has transparent eyes and a rosebud mouth, and is in love with a poet named Diana. He has already found his way to the Village bars, and keeps in his wallet Truman Capote's secret telephone number. We tie our scarves tight against the cold and walk up and down Fourth Avenue, winding in and out of the rows of secondhand bookshops crammed one against the other. The

---

orgone box Invented by the Austrian psychiatrist and biophysicist Wilhelm Reich (1897–1957), the orgone box was supposed to restore human energy; it was declared a fraud.

proprietors sit reading their wares and never look up. The books in all their thousands smell sleepily of cellar. Our envy of them is speckled with longing; our longing is sick with envy. We are the sorrowful literary young.

Every day, month after month, I hang around the newsstand near the candy store, drilling through the enigmatic pages of *Partisan Review.* I still haven't bought a copy; I still can't understand a word. I don't know what cold war means. Who is Trotsky? I haven't read *Ulysses;* my adolescent phantoms are rowing in the ablative absolute with *pius* Aeneas. I'm in my mind's cradle, veiled by the exultant secrecies of fog.

Washington Square will wake me. In a lecture room in the Main Building, Dylan Thomas will cry his webwork syllables. Afterward he'll warm himself at the White Horse Tavern. Across the corridor I will see Sidney Hook plain. I will read the Bhagavad-Gita and Catullus and Lessing, and, in Hebrew, a novel eerily called *Whither?* It will be years and years before I am smart enough, worldly enough, to read Alfred Kazin and Mary McCarthy.

In the spring, all of worldly Washington Square will wake up to the luster of little green leaves.

AFTERWORD

The first day at college is a universal subject, though the particulars of Washington Square will clash with the particulars of Ann Arbor, Eugene, Tuscaloosa, and College Station — any college station.

Many of Ozick's essays are moral and even religious. This reminiscent piece is colored with a remembered past redolent of what's to come, the future nascent in the moment. In Art and Ardor *Ozick had written: "The secrets that engage me — that sweep me away — are generally secrets of an inheritance: how the pear seed becomes a pear tree, for instance, rather than a polar bear. Ideas are emotions that penetrate the future of coherence — " This essay performs an odd trick. It tells of the future, of life after the first day, in a persistent series of negatives: "I did not know," "I had not read," "Later this or that will happen." The device collapses the years into the box of a narrow moment.*

BOOKS AVAILABLE IN PAPERBACK

The Cannibal Galaxy. New York: Dutton. *Novel.*

The Messiah of Stockholm. New York: Random House–Vintage. *Novel.*

The Pagan Rabbi and Other Stories. New York: Penguin Books. *Short stories.*

The Shawl. New York: Random House–Vintage. *Novella and short story.*

WALKER
PERCY

*W*ALKER PERCY (1916–1990) was educated as a physician and completed
his internship but became a novelist. (Maybe medical training is more useful
than writers' workshops; the playwright and story writer Anton Chekhov studied to
be a doctor; John Keats and William Carlos Williams were two doctors turned poets.)
Born in Alabama, Percy took his B.A. at the University of North Carolina, then
attended medical school at Columbia University, in New York City, where he also
interned. He returned to reside in the South, where he lived in Covington, Louisiana,
near New Orleans, the site of much of his fiction. ("I choose to live in a small town.
One reason is that people here don't take writers very seriously and accordingly I
don't either.") The most important biographical information about Walker Percy is
his religion: He was a convert to Roman Catholicism, and his religious sensibility
informed his imagination and his thought.

While interning after medical school he contracted tuberculosis. For two years
he stayed in bed reading. Trying to return to medicine he suffered a relapse, and after
a further period for recovery, he retired from medicine and began writing. He was
middle-aged before he published his first novel, The Moviegoer, in 1961; it won the
National Book Award, and Percy was immediately recognized as a major contemporary novelist. Subsequent novels include The Last Gentleman (1966), The Second
Coming (1980), and The Thanatos Syndrome (1987). In 1975 he published a book
of essays, The Message in the Bottle, from which "The Loss of the Creature" is
taken. The articles in that book appeared over twenty years, in literary quarterlies
(The Southern Review, Sewanee Review, Partisan Review) and in philosophical
journals (Thought, The Journal of Philosophy, Philosophy and Pheno-
menological Research). Few philosophers publish in literary quarterlies; few nov-

elists publish in philosophical quarterlies. In 1983 Percy published Lost in the Cosmos, *a collection of parodies and essays critical of contemporary society.*

In his author's note to The Message in the Bottle, *Percy refers to his "recurring interest" in "the nature of human communication." "The Loss of the Creature" begins with people naming something and continues by examining the relation of experience to the language by which we communicate experience. The loss that Percy describes is a psychic distance that civilization, or its development in our time, puts between reality and our mind's connection to reality. Before you read it, tuck away in your mind the author's subtitle for* The Message in the Bottle: How Queer Man Is, How Queer Language Is, and What One Has to Do with the Other.

The Loss of
the Creature

I

Every explorer names his island Formosa, beautiful. To him it is beautiful because, being first, he has access to it and can see it for what it is. But to no one else is it ever as beautiful — except the rare man who manages to recover it, who knows that it has to be recovered.

Garcia López de Cárdenas discovered the Grand Canyon and was amazed at the sight. It can be imagined. One crosses miles of desert, breaks through the mesquite, and there it is at one's feet. Later the government set the place aside as a national park, hoping to pass along to millions the experience of Cárdenas. Does not one see the same sight from the Bright Angel Lodge that Cárdenas saw?

The assumption is that the Grand Canyon is a remarkably interesting and beautiful place and that if it had a certain value P for Cárdenas, the same value P may be transmitted to any number of sightseers — just as Banting's discovery of insulin can be transmitted to any number of diabetics. A counterinfluence is at work, however, and it would be nearer the truth to say that if the place is seen by a million sightseers, a single sightseer does not receive value P but a millionth part of value P.

It is assumed that since the Grand Canyon has the fixed interest value P, tours can be organized for any number of people. A man in Boston decides to spend his vacation at the Grand Canyon. He visits his travel bureau, looks at the folder, signs up for a two-week tour. He and his family take the tour, see the Grand Canyon, and return to Boston. May we say that this man has seen the Grand Canyon? Possibly he has. But it is more likely that what he has done is the one sure way not to see the canyon.

Why is it almost impossible to gaze directly at the Grand Canyon under   5
these circumstances and see it for what it is — as one picks up a strange
object from one's backyard and gazes directly at it? It is almost impossible
because the Grand Canyon, the thing as it is, has been appropriated by the
symbolic complex which has already been formed in the sightseer's mind.
Seeing the canyon under approved circumstances is seeing the symbolic
complex head on. The thing is no longer the thing as it confronted the
Spaniard; it is rather that which has already been formulated — by picture
postcard, geography book, tourist folders, and the words *Grand Canyon*. As
a result of this preformulation, the source of the sightseer's pleasure undergoes a shift. Where the wonder and delight of the Spaniard arose from his
penetration of the thing itself, from a progressive discovery of depths, patterns, colors, shadows, etc., now the sightseer measures his satisfaction *by
the degree to which the canyon conforms to the preformed complex*. If it does so,
if it looks just like the postcard, he is pleased; he might even say, "Why it
is every bit as beautiful as a picture postcard!" He feels he has not been
cheated. But if it does not conform, if the colors are somber, he will not be
able to see it directly; he will only be conscious of the disparity between
what it is and what it is supposed to be. He will say later that he was
unlucky in not being there at the right time. The highest point, the term of
the sightseer's satisfaction, is not the sovereign discovery of the thing before
him; it is rather the measuring up of the thing to the criterion of the
preformed symbolic complex.

Seeing the canyon is made even more difficult by what the sightseer does
when the moment arrives, when sovereign knower confronts the thing to be
known. Instead of looking at it, he photographs it. There is no confrontation
at all. At the end of forty years of preformulation and with the Grand
Canyon yawning at his feet, what does he do? He waives his right of seeing
and knowing and records symbols for the next forty years. For him there is
no present; there is only the past of what has been formulated and seen and
the future of what has been formulated and not seen. The present is surrendered to the past and the future.

The sightseer may be aware that something is wrong. He may simply be
bored; or he may be conscious of the difficulty: that the great thing yawning
at his feet somehow eludes him. The harder he looks at it, the less he can
see. It eludes everybody. The tourist cannot see it; the bellboy at the Angel
Lodge cannot see it: for him it is only one side of the space he lives in, like
one wall of a room; to the ranger it is a tissue of everyday signs relevant to
his own prospects — the blue haze down there means that he will probably
get rained on during the donkey ride.

How can the sightseer recover the Grand Canyon? He can recover it in
any number of ways, all sharing in common the stratagem of avoiding the
approved confrontation of the tour and the Park Service.

It may be recovered by leaving the beaten track. The tourist leaves the
tour, camps in the back country. He arises before dawn and approaches the
South Rim through a wild terrain where there are no trails and no railed-in

lookout points. In other words, he sees the canyon by avoiding all the facilities for seeing the canyon. If the benevolent Park Service hears about this fellow and thinks he has a good idea and places the following notice in the Bright Angel Lodge: *Consult ranger for information on getting off the beaten track* — the end result will only be the closing of another access to the canyon.

It may be recovered by a dialectical movement which brings one back to the beaten track but at a level above it. For example, after a lifetime of avoiding the beaten track and guided tours, a man may deliberately seek out the most beaten track of all, the most commonplace tour imaginable: he may visit the canyon by a Greyhound tour in the company of a party from Terre Haute — just as a man who has lived in New York all his life may visit the Statue of Liberty. (Such dialectical savorings of the familiar as the familiar are, of course, a favorite stratagem of the *New Yorker* magazine.) The thing is recovered from familiarity by means of an exercise in familiarity. Our complex friend stands behind the fellow tourists at the Bright Angel Lodge and sees the canyon through them and their predicament, their picture taking and busy disregard. In a sense, he exploits his fellow tourists; he stands on their shoulders to see the canyon.

Such a man is far more advanced in the dialectic than the sightseer who is trying to get off the beaten track — getting up at dawn and approaching the canyon through the mesquite. This strategem is, in fact, for our complex man the weariest, most beaten track of all.

It may be recovered as a consequence of a breakdown of the symbolic machinery by which the experts present the experience to the consumer. A family visits the canyon in the usual way. But shortly after their arrival, the park is closed by an outbreak of typhus in the south. They have the canyon to themselves. What do they mean when they tell the home folks of their good luck: "We had the whole place to ourselves"? How does one see the thing better when the others are absent? Is looking like sucking: The more lookers, the less there is to see? They could hardly answer, but by saying this they testify to a state of affairs which is considerably more complex than the simple statement of the schoolbook about the Spaniard and the millions who followed him. It is a state in which there is a complex distribution of sovereignty, of zoning.

It may be recovered in a time of national disaster. The Bright Angel Lodge is converted into a rest home, a function that has nothing to do with the canyon a few yards away. A wounded man is brought in. He regains consciousness; there outside his window is the canyon.

The most extreme case of access by privilege conferred by disaster is the Huxleyan° novel of the adventures of the surviving remnant after the great wars of the twentieth century. An expedition from Australia lands in Southern California and heads east. They stumble across the Bright Angel Lodge,

---

Huxleyan   Referring to Aldous Huxley (1894–1963), an English writer best known for his novel *Brave New World* (1932), which depicts a scientific, mechanized utopia.

now fallen into ruins. The trails are grown over, the guard rails fallen away, the dime telescope at Battleship Point rusted. But there is the canyon, exposed at last. Exposed by what? By the decay of those facilities which were designed to help the sightseer.

This dialectic of sightseeing cannot be taken into account by planners, 15 for the object of the dialectic is nothing other than the subversion of the efforts of the planners.

The dialectic is not known to objective theorists, psychologists, and the like. Yet it is quite well known in the fantasy-consciousness of the popular arts. The devices by which the museum exhibit, the Grand Canyon, the ordinary thing, is recovered have long since been stumbled upon. A movie shows a man visiting the Grand Canyon. But the moviemaker knows something the planner does not know. He knows that one cannot take the sight frontally. The canyon must be approached by the stratagems we have mentioned: the Inside Track, the Familiar Revisited, the Accidental Encounter. Who is the stranger at the Bright Angel Lodge? Is he the ordinary tourist from Terre Haute that he makes himself out to be? He is not. He has another objective in mind, to revenge his wronged brother, counterespionage, etc. By virtue of the fact that he has other fish to fry, he may take a stroll along the rim after supper and then we can see the canyon through him. The movie accomplishes its purpose by concealing it. Overtly the characters (the American family marooned by typhus) and we the onlookers experience pity for the sufferers, and the family experience anxiety for themselves; covertly and in truth they are the happiest of people and we are happy through them, for we have the canyon to ourselves. The movie cashes in on the recovery of sovereignty through disaster. Not only is the canyon now accessible to the remnant: The members of the remnant are now accessible to each other; a whole new ensemble of relations becomes possible — friendship, love, hatred, clandestine sexual adventures. In a movie when a man sits next to a woman on a bus, it is necessary either that the bus break down or that the woman lose her memory. (The question occurs to one: Do you imagine there are sightseers who see sights just as they are supposed to? A family who live in Terre Haute, who decide to take the canyon tour, who go there, see it, enjoy it immensely, and go home content? A family who are entirely innocent of all the barriers, zones, losses of sovereignty I have been talking about? Wouldn't most people be sorry if Battleship Point fell into the canyon, carrying all one's fellow passengers to their death, leaving one alone on the South Rim? I cannot answer this. Perhaps there are such people. Certainly a great many American families would swear they had no such problems, that they came, saw, and went away happy. Yet it is just these families who would be happiest if they had gotten the Inside Track and been among the surviving remnant.)

It is now apparent that as between the many measures which may be taken to overcome the opacity, the boredom, of the direct confrontation of the thing or creature in its citadel of symbolic investiture, some are less authentic than others. That is to say, some stratagems obviously serve other purposes than that of providing access to being — for example, various unconscious motivations which it is not necessary to go into here.

Let us take an example in which the recovery of being is ambiguous, where it may under the same circumstances contain both authentic and unauthentic components. An American couple, we will say, drives down into Mexico. They see the usual sights and have a fair time of it. Yet they are never without the sense of missing something. Although Taxco and Cuernavaca are interesting and picturesque as advertised, they fall short of "it." What do the couple have in mind by "it"? What do they really hope for? What sort of experience could they have in Mexico so that upon their return, they would feel that "it" had happened? We have a clue: Their hope has something to do with their own role as tourists in a foreign country and the way in which they conceive this role. It has something to do with other American tourists. Certainly they feel that they are very far from "it" when, after traveling five thousand miles, they arrive at the plaza in Guanajuato only to find themselves surrounded by a dozen other couples from the Midwest.

Already we may distinguish authentic and unauthentic elements. First, we see the problem the couple faces and we understand their efforts to surmount it. The problem is to find an "unspoiled" place. "Unspoiled" does not mean only that a place is left physically intact; it means also that it is not encrusted by renown and by the familiar (as in Taxco), that it has not been discovered by others. We understand that the couple really want to get at the place and enjoy it. Yet at the same time we wonder if there is not something wrong in their dislike of their compatriots. Does access to the place require the exclusion of others?

Let us see what happens. 20

The couple decide to drive from Guanajuato to Mexico City. On the way they get lost. After hours on a rocky mountain road, they find themselves in a tiny valley not even marked on the map. There they discover an Indian village. Some sort of religious festival is going on. It is apparently a corn dance in supplication of the rain god.

The couple know at once that this is "it." They are entranced. They spend several days in the village, observing the Indians and being themselves observed with friendly curiosity.

Now may we not say that the sightseers have at last come face to face with an authentic sight, a sight which is charming, quaint, picturesque, unspoiled, and that they see the sight and come away rewarded? Possibly this may occur. Yet it is more likely that what happens is a far cry indeed from an immediate encounter with being, that the experience, while masquerading as such, is in truth a rather desperate impersonation. I use the word *desperate* advisedly to signify an actual loss of hope.

The clue to the spuriousness of their enjoyment of the village and the festival is a certain restiveness in the sightseers themselves. It is given expression by their repeated exclamations that "this is too good to be true," and by their anxiety that it may not prove to be so perfect, and finally by their downright relief at leaving the valley and having the experience in the bag, so to speak — that is, safely embalmed in memory and movie film.

What is the source of their anixety during the visit? Does it not mean 25 that the couple are looking at the place with a certain standard of performance in mind? Are they like Fabre,° who gazed at the world about him with wonder, letting it be what it is; or are they not like the overanxious mother who sees her child as one performing, now doing badly, now doing well? The village is their child and their love for it is an anxious love because they are afraid that at any moment it might fail them.

We have another clue in their subsequent remark to an ethnologist friend. "How we wished you had been there with us! What a perfect goldmine of folkways! Every minute we would say to each other, if only you were here! You must return with us." This surely testifies to a generosity of spirit, a willingness to share their experience with others, not at all like their feelings toward their fellow Iowans on the plaza at Guanajuato!

I am afraid this is not the case at all. It is true that they longed for their ethnologist friend, but it was for an entirely different reason. They wanted him, not to share their experience, but to certify their experience as genuine.

"This is it" and "Now we are really living" do not necessarily refer to the sovereign encounter of the person with the sight that enlivens the mind and gladdens the heart. It means that now at last we are having the acceptable experience. The present experience is always measured by a prototype, the "it" of their dreams. "Now I am really living" means that now I am filling the role of sightseer and the sight is living up to the prototype of sights. This quaint and picturesque village is measured by a Platonic ideal of the Quaint and the Picturesque.

Hence their anxiety during the encounter. For at any minute something could go wrong. A fellow Iowan might emerge from a 'dobe hut; the chief might show them his Sears catalogue. (If the failures are "wrong" enough, as these are, they might still be turned to account as rueful conversation pieces: "There we were expecting the chief to bring us a churinga and he shows up with a Sears catalogue!") They have snatched victory from disaster, but their experience always runs the danger of failure.

They need the ethnologist to certify their experience as genuine. This is 30 borne out by their behavior when the three of them return for the next corn dance. During the dance, the couple do not watch the goings-on; instead they watch the ethnologist! Their highest hope is that their friend should find the dance interesting. And if he should show signs of true absorption, an interest in the goings-on so powerful that he becomes oblivious of his friends — then their cup is full. "Didn't we tell you?" they say at last. What they want from him is not ethnological explanations; all they want is his approval.

What has taken place is a radical loss of sovereignty over that which is as much theirs as it is the ethnologist's. The fault does not lie with the ethnologist. He has no wish to stake a claim to the village; in fact, he desires the opposite: He will bore his friends to death by telling them about the

---

Fabre Jean-Henri Fabre (1823–1915), French entomologist (a scientist who studies insects).

village and the meaning of the folkways. A degree of sovereignty has been surrendered by the couple. It is the nature of the loss, moreover, that they are not aware of the loss, beyond a certain uneasiness. (Even if they read this and admitted it, it would be very difficult for them to bridge the gap in their confrontation of the world. Their consciousness of the corn dance cannot escape their consciousness of their consciousness, so that with the onset of the first direct enjoyment, their higher consciousness pounces and certifies: "Now you are doing it! Now you are really living!" and, in certifying the experience, sets it at nought.)

Their basic placement in the world is such that they recognize a priority of title of the expert over his particular department of being. The whole horizon of being is staked out by "them," the experts. The highest satisfaction of the sightseer (not merely the tourist but any layman seer of sights) is that his sight should be certified as genuine. The worst of this impoverishment is that there is no sense of impoverishment. The surrender of title is so complete that it never even occurs to one to reassert title. A poor man may envy the rich man, but the sightseer does not envy the expert. When a caste system becomes absolute, envy disappears. Yet the caste of layman-expert is not the fault of the expert. It is due altogether to the eager surrender of sovereignty by the layman so that he may take up the role not of the person but of the consumer.

I do not refer only to the special relation of layman to theorist. I refer to the general situation in which sovereignty is surrendered to a class of privileged knowers, whether these be theorists or artists. A reader may surrender sovereignty over that which has been written about, just as a consumer may surrender sovereignty over a thing which has been theorized about. The consumer is content to receive an experience just as it has been presented to him by theorists and planners. The reader may also be content to judge life by whether it has or has not been formulated by those who know and write about life. A young man goes to France. He too has a fair time of it, sees the sights, enjoys the food. On his last day, in fact as he sits in a restaurant in Le Havre waiting for his boat, something happens. A group of French students in the restaurant get into an impassioned argument over a recent play. A riot takes place. Madame la concierge joins in, swinging her mop at the rioters. Our young American is transported. This is "it." And he had almost left France without seeing "it"!

But the young man's delight is ambiguous. On the one hand, it is a pleasure for him to encounter the same Gallic temperament he had heard about from Puccini° and Rolland.° But on the other hand, the source of his pleasure testifies to a certain alienation. For the young man is actually barred from a direct encounter with anything French excepting only that which has

---

Puccini   Giacomo Puccini (1853–1924), Italian composer of emotional, somewhat melancholic operas.

Rolland   Romain Rolland (1866–1944), French author and playwright whose works depicted the contemporary French character.

been set forth, authenticated by Puccini and Rolland — those who know. If he had encountered the restaurant scene without reading Hemingway, without knowing that the performance was so typically, charmingly French, he would not have been delighted. He would only have been anxious at seeing things get so out of hand. The source of his delight is the sanction of those who know.

This loss of sovereignty is not a marginal process, as might appear from   35
my example of estranged sightseers. It is a generalized surrender of the horizon to those experts within whose competence a particular segment of the horizon is thought to lie. Kwakiutls are surrendered to Franz Boas;° decaying Southern mansions are surrendered to Faulkner and Tennessee Williams. So that, although it is by no means the intention of the expert to expropriate sovereignty — in fact he would not even know what sovereignty meant in this context — the danger of theory and consumption is a seduction and deprivation of the consumer.

In the New Mexican desert, natives occasionally come across strange-looking artifacts which have fallen from the skies and which are stenciled: *Return to U.S. Experimental Project, Alamogordo. Reward.* The finder returns the object and is rewarded. He knows nothing of the nature of the object he has found and does not care to know. The sole role of the native, the highest role he can play, is that of finder and returner of the mysterious equipment.

The same is true of the layman's relation to *natural* objects in a modern technical society. No matter what the object or event is, whether it is a star, a swallow, a Kwakiutl, a "psychological phenomenon," the layman who confronts it does not confront it as a sovereign person, as Crusoe confronts a seashell he finds on the beach. The highest role he can conceive himself as playing is to be able to recognize the title of the object, to return it to the appropriate expert and have it certified as a genuine find. He does not even permit himself to see the thing — as Gerard Hopkins° could see a rock or a cloud or a field. If anyone asks him why he doesn't look, he may reply that he didn't take that subject in college (or he hasn't read Faulkner).

This loss of sovereignty extends even to oneself. There is the neurotic who asks nothing more of his doctor than that his symptoms should prove interesting. When all else fails, the poor fellow has nothing to offer but his own neurosis. But even this is sufficient if only the doctor will show interest when he says, "Last night I had a curious sort of dream; perhaps it will be significant to one who knows about such things. It seems I was standing in a sort of alley — " (I have nothing else to offer you but my own unhappiness. Please say that it, at least, measures up, that it is a *proper* sort of unhappiness.)

Franz Boas German-born American anthropologist and ethnologist (1858–1942) whose fieldwork took place primarily in North America, Mexico, and Puerto Rico.

Gerard Hopkins Gerard Manley Hopkins (1844–1889), English poet noted for his innovative rhythms and his keen observation of the details of nature.

II

A young Falkland Islander walking along a beach and spying a dead dogfish and going to work on it with his jackknife has, in a fashion wholly unprovided in modern educational theory, a great advantage over the Scarsdale high-school pupil who finds the dogfish on his laboratory desk. Similarly the citizen of Huxley's *Brave New World* who stumbles across a volume of Shakespeare in some vine-grown ruins and squats on a potsherd to read it is in a fairer way of getting at a sonnet than the Harvard sophomore taking English Poetry II.

The educator whose business it is to teach students biology or poetry is 40 unaware of a whole ensemble of relations which exist between the student and the dogfish and between the student and the Shakespeare sonnet. To put it bluntly: A student who has the desire to get at a dogfish or a Shakespeare sonnet may have the greatest difficulty in salvaging the creature itself from the educational package in which it is presented. The great difficulty is that he is not aware that there is a difficulty; surely, he thinks, in such a fine classroom, with such a fine textbook, the sonnet must come across! What's wrong with me?

The sonnet and the dogfish are obscured by two different processes. The sonnet is obscured by the symbolic package which is formulated not by the sonnet itself but by the *media* through which the sonnet is transmitted, the media which the educators believe for some reason to be transparent. The new textbook, the type, the smell of the page, the classroom, the aluminum windows and the winter sky, the personality of Miss Hawkins — these media which are supposed to transmit the sonnet may only succeed in transmitting themselves. It is only the hardiest and cleverest of students who can salvage the sonnet from this many-tissued package. It is only the rarest student who knows that the sonnet must be salvaged from the package. (The educator is well aware that something is wrong, that there is a fatal gap between the student's learning and the student's life: The student reads the poem, appears to understand it, and gives all the answers. But what does he recall if he should happen to read a Shakespeare sonnet twenty years later? Does he recall the poem or does he recall the smell of the page and the smell of Miss Hawkins?)

One might object, pointing out that Huxley's citizen reading his sonnet in the ruins and the Falkland Islander looking at his dogfish on the beach also receive them in a certain package. Yes, but the difference lies in the fundamental placement of the student in the world, a placement which makes it possible to extract the thing from the package. The pupil at Scarsdale High sees himself placed as a consumer receiving an experience-package; but the Falkland Islander exploring his dogfish is a person exercising the sovereign right of a person in his lordship and mastery of creation. He too could use an instructor and a book and a technique, but he would use them as his subordinates, just as he uses his jackknife. The biology student does not use his scalpel as an instrument; he uses it as a magic wand! Since it is a "scientific instrument," it should do "scientific things."

The dogfish is concealed in the same symbolic package as the sonnet. But the dogfish suffers an additional loss. As a consequence of this double deprivation, the Sarah Lawrence student who scores A in zoology is apt to know very little about a dogfish. She is twice removed from the dogfish, once by the symbolic complex by which the dogfish is concealed, once again by the spoliation of the dogfish by theory which renders it invisible. Through no fault of zoology instructors, it is nevertheless a fact that the zoology laboratory at Sarah Lawrence College is one of the few places in the world where it is all but impossible to see a dogfish.

The dogfish, the tree, the seashell, the American Negro, the dream, are rendered invisible by a shift of reality from concrete thing to theory which Whitehead° has called the fallacy of misplaced concreteness. It is the mistaking of an idea, a principle, an abstraction, for the real. As a consequence of the shift, the "specimen" is seen as less real than the theory of the specimen. As Kierkegaard° said, once a person is seen as a specimen of a race or a species, at that very moment he ceases to be an individual. Then there are no more individuals but only specimens.

To illustrate: A student enters a laboratory which, in the pragmatic view, 45 offers the student the optimum conditions under which an educational experience may be had. In the existential view, however — the view of the student in which he is regarded not as a receptacle of experience but as a knowing being whose peculiar property it is to see himself as being in a certain situation — the modern laboratory could not have been more effectively designed to conceal the dogfish forever.

The student comes to his desk. On it, neatly arranged by his instructor, he finds his laboratory manual, a dissecting board, instruments, and a mimeographed list:

Exercise 22: Materials

1 dissecting board
1 scalpel
1 forceps
1 probe
1 bottle india ink and syringe
1 specimen of *Squalus acanthias*

The clue to the situation in which the student finds himself is to be found in the last item: one specimen of *Squalus acanthias*.

The phrase *specimen of* expresses in the most succinct way imaginable the radical character of the loss of being which has occurred under his very nose. To refer to the dogfish, the unique concrete existent before him, as a "speci-

---

Whitehead   Alfred North Whitehead (1861–1947), English mathematician and philosopher.

Kierkegaard   Sören Aabye Kierkegaard (1813–1855), Danish philosopher and theologian whose philosophy was based on faith and knowledge, thought and reality.

men of *Squalus acanthias"* reveals by its grammar the spoliation of the dogfish by the theoretical method. This phase, *specimen of,* example of, instance of, indicates the ontological status of the individual creature in the eyes of the theorist. The dogfish itself is seen as a rather shabby expression of an ideal reality, the species *Squalus acanthias.* The result is the radical devaluation of the individual dogfish. (The *reductio ad absurdum°* of White-head's shift is Toynbee's° employment of it in his historical method. If a gram of NaCl is referred to by the chemist as a "sample of" NaCl, one may think of it as such and not much is missed by the oversight of the act of being of this particular pinch of salt, but when the Jews and the Jewish religion are understood as — in Toynbee's favorite phrase — a "classical example of" such and such a kind of *Voelkerwanderung,°* we begin to suspect that something is being left out.)

If we look into the ways in which the student can recover the dogfish (or the sonnet), we will see that they have in common the stratagem of avoiding the educator's direct presentation of the object as a lesson to be learned and restoring access to sonnet and dogfish as beings to be known, reasserting the sovereignty of knower over known.

In truth, the biography of scientists and poets is usually the story of the discovery of the indirect approach, the circumvention of the educator's presentation — the young man who was sent to the *Technikum°* and on his way fell into the habit of loitering in book stores and reading poetry; or the young man dutifully attending law school who on the way became curious about the comings and goings of ants. One remembers the scene in *The Heart Is a Lonely Hunter°* where the girl hides in the bushes to hear the Capehart in the big house play Beethoven. Perhaps she was the lucky one after all. Think of the unhappy souls inside, who see the record, worry about scratches, and most of all worry about whether they are *getting it,* whether they are bona fide music lovers. What is the best way to hear Beethoven: sitting in a proper silence around the Capehart or eavesdropping from an azalea bush?

However it may come about, we notice two traits of the second situation: (1) an openness of the thing before one — instead of being an exercise to be learned according to an approved mode, it is a garden of delights which beckons to one; (2) a sovereignty of the knower — instead of being a consumer of a prepared experience, I am a sovereign wayfarer, a wanderer in the neighborhood of being who stumbles into the garden.

One can think of two sorts of circumstances through which the thing may be restored to the person. (There is always, of course, the direct recovery: A

---

reductio ad absurdum   A method of disproving a proposition by showing that it leads to an absurdity when carried to its logical conclusion.

Toynbee   Arnold Toynbee (1889–1975), English historian, believed that history is shaped by spiritual rather than economic forces.

Voelkerwanderung   Barbarian invasion.

Technikum   Technical school.

The Heart Is a Lonely Hunter   Novel (1940) by Carson McCullers (1917–1967).

student may simply be strong enough, brave enough, clever enough to take the dogfish and the sonnet by storm, to wrest control of it from the educators and the educational package.) First by ordeal: The Bomb falls; when the young man recovers consciousness in the shambles of the biology laboratory, there not ten inches from his nose lies the dogfish. Now all at once he can see it, directly and without let, just as the exile or the prisoner or the sick man sees the sparrow at his window in all its inexhaustibility; just as the commuter who has had a heart attack sees his own hand for the first time. In these cases, the simulacrum of everydayness and of consumption has been destroyed by disaster; in the case of the bomb, literally destroyed. Secondly, by apprenticeship to a great man: One day a great biologist walks into the laboratory; he stops in front of our student's desk; he leans over, picks up the dogfish, and, ignoring instruments and procedure, probes with a broken fingernail into the little carcass. "Now here is a curious business," he says, ignoring also the proper jargon of the specialty. "Look here how this little duct reverses its direction and drops into the pelvis. Now if you would look into a coelacanth, you would see that it — " And all at once the student can see. The technician and the sophomore who loves his textbooks are always offended by the genuine research man because the latter is usually a little vague and always humble before the thing; he doesn't have much use for equipment or the jargon. Whereas the technician is never vague and never humble before the thing; he holds the thing disposed of by the principle, the formula, the textbook outline; and he thinks a great deal of equipment and jargon.

But since neither of these methods of recovering the dogfish is pedagogically feasible — perhaps the great man even less so than the Bomb — I wish to propose the following educational technique which should prove equally effective for Harvard and Shreveport High School. I propose that English poetry and biology should be taught as usual, but that at irregular intervals, poetry students should find dogfishes on their desks and biology students should find Shakespeare sonnets on their dissecting boards. I am serious in declaring that a Sarah Lawrence English major who began poking about in a dogfish with a bobby pin would learn more in thirty minutes than a biology major in a whole semester; and that the latter upon reading on her dissecting board

> That time of year Thou may'st in me behold
> When yellow leaves, or none, or few, do hang
> Upon those boughs which shake against the cold —
> Bare ruin'd choirs where late the sweet birds sang.

might catch fire at the beauty of it.

The situation of the tourist at the Grand Canyon and the biology student are special cases of a predicament in which everyone finds himself in a modern technical society — a society, that is, in which there is a division between expert and layman, planner and consumer, in which experts and planners take special measures to teach and edify the consumer. The measures taken are measures appropriate to the consumer: The expert and the planner *know* and *plan*, but the consumer *needs* and *experiences*.

There is a double deprivation. First, the thing is lost through its packaging. The very means by which the thing is presented for consumption, the very techniques by which the thing is made available as an item of need-satisfaction, these very means operate to remove the thing from the sovereignty of the knower. A loss of title occurs. The measures which the museum curator takes to present the thing to the public are self-liquidating. The upshot of the curator's efforts are not that everyone can see the exhibit but that no one can see it. The curator protests: Why are they so indifferent? Why do they even deface the exhibit? Don't they know it is theirs? But it is not theirs. It is his, the curator's. By the most exclusive sort of zoning, the museum exhibit, the park oak tree, is part of an ensemble, a package, which is almost impenetrable to them. The archaeologist who puts his find in a museum so that everyone can see it accomplished the reverse of his expectations. The result of his action is that no one can see it now but the archaeologist. He would have done better to keep it in his pocket and show it now and then to strangers.

The tourist who carves his initials in a public place, which is theoretically "his" in the first place, has good reasons for doing so, reasons which the exhibitor and planner know nothing about. He does so because in his role of consumer of an experience (a "recreational experience" to satisfy a "recreational need") he knows that he is disinherited. He is deprived of his title over being. He knows very well that he is in a very special sort of zone in which his only rights are the rights of a consumer. He moves like a ghost through schoolroom, city streets, trains, parks, movies. He carves his initials as a last desperate measure to escape his ghostly role of consumer. He is saying in effect: I am not a ghost after all; I am a sovereign person. And he establishes title the only way remaining to him, by staking his claim over one square inch of wood or stone.

Does this mean that we should get rid of museums? No, but it means that the sightseer should be prepared to enter into a struggle to recover a sight from a museum.

The second loss is the spoliation of the thing, the tree, the rock, the swallow, by the layman's misunderstanding of scientific theory. He believes that the thing is *disposed of* by theory, that it stands in the Platonic relation of being a *specimen of* such and such an underlying principle. In the transmission of scientific theory from theorist to layman, the expectation of the theorist is reversed. Instead of the marvels of the universe being made available to the public, the universe is disposed of by theory. The loss of sovereignty takes this form: As a result of the science of botany, trees are not made available to every man. On the contrary. The tree loses its proper density and mystery as a concrete existent and, as merely another *specimen of* a species, becomes itself nugatory.

Does this mean that there is no use taking biology at Harvard and Shreveport High? No, but it means that the student should know what a fight he has on his hands to rescue the specimen from the educational package. The educator is only partly to blame. For there is nothing the educator can do to provide for this need of the student. Everything the educator does only succeeds in becoming, for the student, part of the educational package. The highest role of the educator is the maieutic role of Socrates: to help the student come to himself not as a consumer of experience but as a sovereign individual.

The thing is twice lost to the consumer. First, sovereignty is lost: It is theirs, not his. Second, it is radically devalued by theory. This is a loss which has been brought about by science but through no fault of the scientist and through no fault of scientific theory. The loss has come about as a consequence of the seduction of the layman by science. The layman will be seduced as long as he regards beings as consumer items to be experienced rather than prizes to be won, and as long as he waives his sovereign rights as a person and accepts his role of consumer as the highest estate to which the layman can aspire. 60

As Mounier said, the person is not something one can study and provide for; he is something one struggles for. But unless he also struggles for himself, unless he knows that there is a struggle, he is going to be just what the planners think he is.

AFTERWORD

When Walker Percy wrote novels he pursued thought by means of narrative and character that embody ideas and even a thesis, though the reader never sees these fictions as allegorical — ideas talking and wearing clothes — for Percy had the novelist's gift of bestowing life. Similarly his essays use fiction: all these imagined tourists, the imagined real Spanish discoverer, for that matter. If we know his novels, we can imagine a scene where a Percy protagonist visits the Grand Canyon, a chapter which would include the concepts of "The Loss of the Creature."

Although Percy like a modern philosopher resorts to mathematical technique — P for pleasure, or perhaps place — his thought is anecdotal and his philosophy reveals itself through imagined situations. For readers who prefer fiction to algebra, Percy's language makes its point. This essay should touch most immediately upon the college student, who has been trained in abstraction for at least six years and who undergoes during college a quantum leap in abstraction. As Percy says, the student has "a fight . . . on his hands to rescue the specimen from the educational package."

BOOKS AVAILABLE IN PAPERBACK

Lancelot. New York: Avon. *Novel*.

The Last Gentleman. New York: Avon. *Novel*.

Lost in the Cosmos: The Last Self-Help Book. New York: Farrar, Straus & Giroux. *Nonfiction*.

The Message in the Bottle: How Queer Man Is, How Queer Language Is, and What One Has to Do with the Other. New York: Farrar, Straus & Giroux. *Essays*.

The Moviegoer. New York: Ivy Books. *Novel*.

The Second Coming. New York: Ivy Books. *Novel*.

Signposts in a Strange Land. New York: Farrar, Straus & Giroux. *Nonfiction*.

The Thanatos Syndrome. New York: Ivy Books. *Novel*.

ADRIENNE RICH

*W*HEN ADRIENNE RICH *(b. 1929) was a junior in college, the poet W. H. Auden selected her first book of poems,* A Change of World, *for the Yale Series of Younger Poets Award. It was published in 1951 as she graduated from Radcliffe College, and a year later she became a Guggenheim Fellow. After six further books of poems, including* Diving into the Wreck, *which won the National Book Award in 1974, she published* The Fact of a Doorframe: Poems Selected and New, 1950–1984; *more recently she collected new poems in* An Atlas of the Difficult World: Poems 1988–1991 *(1991), and brought out* Collected Early Poems, 1950–1970 *(1993). In* What Is Found There *(1993), from which we take "A Leak in History," she has gathered recent essays.*

Rich's first prose book *was* Of Woman Born: Motherhood as Experience and Institution *(1976), which she followed with an essay collection,* On Lies, Secrets, and Silence *(1979). In 1986 she collected* Blood, Bread, and Poetry: Selected Prose, 1979–1985. *At the time of her remarkable early success, she was widely praised as a talented young writer and sometimes criticized as conventional or even complacent. In a long and gradual change, she has become a spokeswoman for the principled anger of feminist outrage. No one of her talented generation of American writers has taken so decisively radical a direction.*

When she was still in her early twenties, she developed arthritis which, with some periods of remission, has afflicted her ever since and required many operations. She has three sons and was widowed in 1970. She has taught widely: Brandeis University, Douglass College of Rutgers University, and most recently Stanford University, where she is a professor of English and feminist studies. In 1994 she was awarded a five-year grant from the MacArthur Foundation.

A Leak in History

I'm staying in a house in the Vermont countryside, shaded in front by three big sugar maples. Behind it lies a grove of the same trees, and on a hillside far away I can see another grove, glowing green in rich late-afternoon light. In autumn the leaves turn scarlet; in late winter thaw the pale aqueous sap starts rising and is gathered and laboriously evaporated, in little steamy shacks and cabins, down to its essence, a syrup fine as honey. The Abnaki Indians knew this process before the Yankees came to clear scattered pools of land for grazing, leaving old forest lands in between. Taught by the Abnaki, the first white men made maple sugar in Vermont in 1752.

Under snow, the sap shrinks back. In early thaw, farmers trudge and horse-sledge through the woods to drill little taps into the rough-barked trunks. The sap used to be collected in wooden firkins, then in tin pails hung over the taps; more recently, where terrain and weather allow, plastic tubing is used. A culture formed around this labor-intensive harvesting, first ritual of the northern spring, the culture of the sugarhouse with its ancient sprung castoff chairs, steaming evaporation trays, wet snow and mud trodden inside on heavy boots, doughnuts and coffee, pickles, frankfurters, and beer brought down by women from farm kitchens, eaten and drunk by men lugging and pouring sap and stoking the wood fires. Hard manual labor — about forty gallons of sap being collected and boiled down to obtain one gallon of syrup — and adept, sensitive calculation of the cycles of thaw and freeze that make for the best sugaring-off; testing for the moment when the thin, faintly sweet sap has reached the density of amber syrup. The sour crispness of pickle on the tongue amid all that sweaty sweetness. There is a summer culture too, at church suppers and county fairs, where "sugar on snow" still competes with cotton-candy machines and barbecue — pans of last winter's snow from icehouse, cemetery vault, or freezer, sticky arabesques of hot syrup poured on, served on paper plates with the necessary pickle and doughnut on the side.

Maple trees reproduce with energy: Under any big tree you will find dozens of seedlings crowding each other; in spring the seeds, or keys, blow far afield on little brown wings soon after the new leaves uncurl. The root system of a full-grown maple is many times the circumference of the great crown. In their early-summer-evening green, in the hectic flare of their October changing, in the strong, stripped upreaching of their winter bareness, they are presences of enormous vitality and generosity, trees that yield much to the eye, to the tongue, to the modest cash assets of farm families.

It's said that acid rain and road salt are slowly dooming the sugar maples. Studying and testing the rings of mature trees, scientists have found that up until 1955 they show no evidence of chemical stress; since 1955 acidity has been wearing into the trees and will eventually destroy them. I look out at the grove on the hill, the old trees just outside the window; all seems as it has always been, without smirch or taint.

I remember other trees that stood in this landscape when I first knew it: 5 the wineglass elms. Every village common, every roadside, had them. *Ulmus americanus,* outspreading limbs sweeping up from a straight and slender trunk in the form of a true wineglass, green in summer, golden in autumn, architecturally elegant in nakedness. An old pamphlet from the State Agricultural Service, found in a drawer, implores cooperation in destroying infested bark and wood and protecting still-healthy trees. But the fungus-carrying elm bark beetle won out. Throughout New England, elms fell barren in summer, sick to death, easily splintered by winds. Soon a living elm in leaf was something rare and precious. Now it's hard to remember where they stood.

The poorer we become, the less we remember what we had. Whenever I walk into this house after an absence, I drink, slowly and deliberately, a glass of pure cold water from the spring-fed tap. I don't drink from most taps because I don't like their ill flavor. And the taste of bottled water from the supermarket has no savor; it reminds me of nothing. The spring water flowing into this house does — in its transparency, its lucidity, its original cold. Of course it tastes of this place, sharp with memories, but also of water I drank as a child in the 1930s, from an iron pipe set in the side of a ravine where I used to play. It seemed like the saving, merciful drink of water in legends or poetry; through it I sensuously understood the beautiful, lip-smacking words "to quench a thirst." This was not in the country, but in a wooded park in Baltimore. There was a stream there too, where we waded, and plunged our hands in to the wrists, and never got sick.

Three thousand miles to the west, where I live now, on a much-traveled hill road winding eastward from the coast, there is a standing pipe called the Lombardi Spring. A few cars and trucks are almost always parked on the shoulder, people lined up with jugs and bottles, because that water is held to be particularly delicious and good. And it is free.

Sensual vitality is essential to the struggle for life. It's as simple — and as threatened — as that. To have no love for the taste of the water you drink is a loss of vitality. If your appetite is embalmed in prescriptives, you are weakened for the struggle. Under the most crushing conditions of deprivation, people have to fill their stomachs, eat earth, eat plain starch, force down watery and rancid soup, drink urine for survival. Yet there's another story. In the newsletter produced by inmates in a women's facility, among columns on law, religion, politics, current prison issues, there is the "Konvict Kitchen," with recipes for special microwaved dishes to be created by combining items from the prison store:

1 can Mixin' Chicken
1 Shrimp Noodle Cup
jalapeño peppers (optional)

onions (optional)
bell peppers (optional)
2 packages margarine

Crush noodles and put in large microwave bowl with enough
water to cover them. Let sit for three minutes. Take bell peppers, onions, and hot peppers and saute in microwave for two
minutes. Take mixture out, add noodles, stir thoroughly and
cook in microwave for approximately 20–25 minutes, until
noodles are crisp. Stir every five minutes. Keep lid lightly on
mixture but not tightly closed. Serves 2.

– GLORIA BOLDEN

Poetry being a major form of prison literature, it goes without saying that
there are poems in the newsletter. Like the recipe above, they work within
the prison context but refuse to be subdued:

This is prison not the Hilton
Heard we got it made in here?
This is livin' at its finest?
Country clubs with kegs of beer?
Say — listen up my friend
let me tell you what it's like
to be livin' in the sewer
flushed further down the pipe . . .

This is prison not the Hilton
Election time is on its way
you'll hear it on the TV
we should suffer every day
days of torture
nights of terror —
feel your heart's been torn in shreds?
Say you're showered with asbestos,
drinking nitrate in your bed? . . .

This is prison not the Hilton
care to change your place for mine?
Think that 20 out of 60
isn't doing enough time?
Care to try this life of leisure?
Care to leave your folks behind?
This is prison not the Hilton
and its hell here all the time.[1]

Sensual vitality is essential to the struggle for life. Many people drink as 10
if filling themselves with dirt or starch: the filling of an emptiness. But what

---

[1]Composed by Jacqueline Dixon-Bey and Mary Glover, inside Florence Crane Women's
Prison, Coldwater, Michigan, Spring 1990; recipe and poem from *Insight: Serving the Women
of Florence Crane Women's Facility*, 2d quarter ed. (1990). [Rich's note.]

comes after is a greater emptiness. In the reputations of poets like Hart Crane, Dylan Thomas, Kenneth Rexroth, James Wright, Richard Hugo, Delmore Schwartz, Robert Lowell, Elizabeth Bishop, John Berryman, Anne Sexton, drinking has been romanticized as part of the "poetic fate," the "despondency and madness" of the poet — as if bricklayers, surgeons, housewives, miners, generals, salesmen haven't also poured down liquids to fire up or numb interior spaces of dread. A politician's wife confesses to having drunk aftershave, nail-polish remover, in desperate substitute for confiscated bottles. Whether done with nail-polish remover or antique liqueur of pear, this is self-poisoning.

But there's a sensual vitality in drinking wine and "spirits" as in drinking pure water. Both belong to ancient human rites and memories. People have fermented the apple, the grape, the palm, hops and barley, rice, berries, the potato, the dandelion, the plum. Along with the rising of the yeast in bread was the fermentation of the grain, the fruit. Blessed be the Spirit of the Universe, who created the fruit of the vine. For us to use it as we may.

That so many of us use, or have used, the fruit of the vine in an attempt to fill our terrifying voids may point to the failure of a general communal vitality more than to some inherent poisoning in the fermentation process. I don't minimize the ultimate transaction between the individual and the bottle. But the individual's sense of emptiness reflects — and helps perpetuate — a public emptiness.

When a vast, stifling denial in the public realm is felt by every individual yet there is no language, no depiction, of what is being denied, it becomes for each his or her own anxious predicament, a daily struggle to act "as if" everything were normal. Alcohol, drugs offer a reprieve — not ceremony or celebration, but a substitute for vital bonds of community and friendship, for collective memory and responsibility. Where there is no public face of interdependence, of justice and mercy, where there is no social language for "picking up the pieces when we don't know what/where they are," anomie and amnesia, alcohol and drug abuse can work as social controls and, because they appear "normal," can be more effective — in a very large country — than terrorization by a secret police.

The danger lies in forgetting what we had. The flow between generations becomes a trickle, grandchildren tape-recording grandparents' memories on special occasions perhaps — no casual storytelling jogged by daily life, there being no shared daily life what with migrations, exiles, diasporas, rendings, the search for work. Or there is a shared daily life riddled with holes of silence. In 1979 Helen Epstein published her book of interviews, *Children of the Holocaust*. In 1985 Judy Kaplan and Linn Shapiro edited *Red Diaper Babies: Children of the Left*, a compilation of transcripts of taped sessions at two conferences held in 1982 and 1983 by children of leftist and Communist families, then in their thirties and forties. There are haunting resonances between the two groups of testimony: the children's experience of knowing that there was something of major weight at the center of their parents' lives, something secret, unspoken, unspeakable. (Epstein refers to "that quiet, invisible community, that peer group without a sign.") Both groups of children knowing about things that could not be discussed on the playground or with "strangers," that were to a greater or lesser degree unmentionable even at home. A tattoo on an aunt's wrist. A neighbor's withdrawal. A mother's nightmares; a parent's terror when a child left the house or came home late. A father in jail or underground. Close friends who suddenly could not be mentioned. Certain newspapers having to be hidden; jobs inexplicably lost; children trained that "the walls have ears"; a car parked across the street for hours, one day every week, two men sitting inside. There can be no question of equalizing the events that catalyzed these two silences. Yet the passing on of living history is an essential ingredient of individual and communal self-knowledge, and in both cases that continuity was breached. Forty years is a wilderness of silence.

The loss can be a leak in history or a shrinking in the vitality of everyday life. Fewer and fewer people in this country entertain each other with verbal games, recitations, charades, singing, playing on instruments, doing anything as amateurs — people who are good at something because they enjoy it. To be good at talk, not pompously eloquent or didactic, but having a vivid tongue, savoring turns of phrase — to sing on key and know many songs by heart — to play fiddle, banjo, mandolin, flute, accordion, harmonica — to write long letters — to draw pictures or whittle wood with some amount of skill — to do moderately and pleasingly well, in short, a variety of things without solemn investment or disenabling awe — these were common talents till recently, crossing class and racial lines. People used their human equipment — memory, image making, narrative, voice, hand, eye — unselfconsciously, to engage with other people, and not as specialists or "artistes." My father and his mother both loved to recite poetry learned long ago in school. He had Poe's "The Raven" and "Annabel Lee" from memory, and he had won a school medal for his recitation of a long narrative poem called "Lasca," which began:

> I want free life and I want fresh air,
> And I sigh for the canter after the cattle,
> The crack of whips like shots in a battle,
> The green below, and the blue above,
> And dash, and danger, and life, and love —
> And Lasca.

And my grandmother still remembered a poem she'd learned in Vicksburg, Mississippi — Jewish girl sent to a convent school where there were no secular schools. In her seventies she could recite, black eyes glowing, "Asleep at the Switch":

> It was down in the Lehigh Valley,
> At the bottom of the bottomless ditch,
> I lived alone in a cabin,
> And attended the railway switch.

The reciters of these two poems could not have been in person more unlike the "speaker" of each poem, and that was part of the excitement: to see a known person become someone new and different, change his or her identity but within a framework that allowed each to change back at the end — from Texan desperado to my sedentary, scholarly father; from negligent, solitary switchman to my sheltered, precise grandmother. And such recitations let a child feel that poetry (verse, really, with its structured rhymes, meters, and ringingly fulfilled aural expectations) was not just words on the page, but could live in people's minds for decades, to be summoned up with relish and verve, and that poetry was not just literature, but embodied in voices.

For ordinary people to sing or whistle used to be as common as breathing. I remember men whistling, briskly or hauntingly, women humming with deep-enclosed chest tones. Where did it go? A technology of "canned" music available through car radios, portable "boom boxes," and cassette players, programmed music piped into the workplace, has left people born in the 1950s and later largely alien to the experience of hearing or joining in casual music making. Knowing how to pitch your voice isn't the privilege of the conservatory; people used to learn it from hearing others casually, unself-consciously sing, as they learned language, accent, inflection in speech. Now singing belongs to professionals, is preserved in churches; rap, a spontaneous and sophisticated expression of black street youth at first, quickly became a commodity on videotape, adapted as a new style for television commercials. (Yet rap goes on around the world, picking up on local griefs, local insurgencies.)

Part of the experience of casual singing was the undeliberate soaking up of many songs, many verses. Ballads, hymns, work songs, opera arias, folk songs, popular songs, labor songs, schoolchildren's playground songs. And, of course, with the older songs words changed over time, new generations of singers misremembering or modifying. Tunes changed, too, as songs traveled: from England or Wales to Appalachia, from Africa to the Sea Islands, France to Québec, and across the continent.

To ears accustomed to high-technology amplification and recording processes, the unamplified human voice, the voice not professionally trained, may sound acoustically lacking, even perhaps embarrassing. And so we're severed from a physical release and pleasure, whether in solitude or community — the use of breath to produce song. But breath is also *Ruach*, spirit, the human connection to the universe.

AFTERWORD

"*The danger lies in forgetting what we had.*" *Adrienne Rich is a poet well known as a political figure, an angry and intelligent progressive feminist. She writes essays that combine historical learning — and anger at sexism and racism — with the life and language of poetry. In this essay, she argues a radical cause by reference to values often called traditional; she appeals to standards usually proposed by conservatives. This association — pure water and a rural culture, on the one hand; anecdotes of prison inmates on the other — is uncommonly made. By suggesting an unusual combination, Rich abets the mind's necessary and unceasing battle with its tendency toward stereotype, toward the sterility of received ideas.*

"*Sensual vitality is essential to the struggle for life.*" *Adrienne Rich uses this sentence like a refrain in a poem. Like some refrains, it becomes increasingly powerful. This radical thinker looks for the repair of broken community by remembering "what we had," searching to reconstitute the best of the past to create a usable present.*

BOOKS AVAILABLE IN PAPERBACK

Adrienne Rich's Poetry. New York: Norton.

An Atlas of the Difficult World: Poems 1988–1991. New York: Norton.

Blood, Bread, and Poetry: Selected Prose, 1979–1985. New York: Norton. *Essays.*

Diving into the Wreck: Poems 1971–72. New York: Norton.

The Dream of a Common Language: Poems 1974–1977. New York: Norton.

The Fact of a Doorframe: Poems Selected and New, 1950–1984. New York: Norton.

Of Woman Born: Motherhood as Experience and Institution. New York: Norton. *Nonfiction.*

On Lies, Secrets, and Silence: Selected Prose, 1966–1978. New York: Norton. *Essays.*

Time's Power: Poems 1985–1988. New York: Norton. *Poetry.*

A Wild Patience Has Taken Me This Far: Poems, 1978–1981. New York: Norton.

Will to Change: Poems. New York: Norton.

Your Native Land, Your Life: Poems. New York: Norton.

RICHARD
RODRIGUEZ

*R*ICHARD RODRIGUEZ *was born in San Francisco (1944), the son of Mexican immigrants. The family moved to Sacramento, where Rodriguez grew up speaking Spanish until he attended a Catholic school at the age of six. He delivered newspapers as a boy and worked as a gardener in the summer. He attended a Christian Brothers high school on a scholarship, then Stanford University for his B.A., and he did graduate work at Columbia University, the Warburg Institute in London, and the University of California at Berkeley. He took his Ph.D. in English Renaissance literature. He now works as a lecturer and educational consultant as well as a freelance writer.*

As an assimilated second-generation American, Rodriguez in his reminiscences — Hunger of Memory *(1982) — argues against affirmative action and bilingual education. "The Achievement of Desire" is a chapter from* Hunger of Memory, *a personal narrative of Rodriguez's education away from his heritage, "separating me from the life I enjoyed before becoming a student." Unlike many members of American ethnic minorities, Rodriguez largely celebrates this separation. His work has been admired and denounced. While he tells his experiences of schooling, in a lucid progress of autobiographical exposition, he continually comments on his own story and reaches out for understanding by cross-cultural analogy to a book by an Englishman, separated as a "scholarship boy" from his working-class origins.*

In 1993 Rodriguez published Days of Obligation, *a new book of reminiscence centering on his father, and on generational problems of ethnicity. He appears frequently as an essayist on the PBS program* The MacNeil-Lehrer News Hour.

The Achievement
of Desire

I stand in the ghetto classroom — "the guest speaker" — attempting to lecture on the mystery of the sounds of our words to rows of diffident students. "Don't you hear it? Listen! The music of our words. '*Sumer is i-cumen in. . . .*' And songs on the car radio. We need Aretha Franklin's voice to fill plain words with music — her life." In the face of their empty stares, I try to create an enthusiasm. But the girls in the back row turn to watch some boy passing outside. There are flutters of smiles, waves. And someone's mouth elongates heavy, silent words through the barrier of glass. Silent words — the lips straining to shape each voiceless syllable: "*Meet meee late errr.*" By the door, the instructor smiles at me, apparently hoping that I will be able to spark some enthusiasm in the class. But only one student seems to be listening. A girl, maybe fourteen. In this gray room her eyes shine with ambition. She keeps nodding and nodding at all that I say; she even takes notes. And each time I ask a question, she jerks up and down in her desk like a marionette, while her hand waves over the bowed heads of her classmates. It is myself (as a boy) I see as she faces me now (a man in my thirties).

The boy who first entered a classroom barely able to speak English, twenty years later concluded his studies in the stately quiet of the reading room in the British Museum. Thus with one sentence I can summarize my academic career. It will be harder to summarize what sort of life connects the boy to the man.

With every award, each graduation from one level of education to the next, people I'd meet would congratulate me. Their refrain always the same: "Your parents must be very proud." Sometimes then they'd ask me how I managed it — my "success." (How?) After a while, I had several quick answers to give in reply. I'd admit, for one thing, that I went to an excellent grammar school. (My earliest teachers, the nuns, made my success their ambition.) And my brother and both my sisters were very good students. (They often brought home the shiny school tropies I came to want.) And my mother and father always encouraged me. (At every graduation they were behind the stunning flash of the camera when I turned to look at the crowd.)

As important as these factors were, however, they account inadequately for my academic advance. Nor do they suggest what an odd success I managed. For although I was a very good student, I was also a very bad student. I was a "scholarship boy," a certain kind of scholarship boy. Always successful, I was always unconfident. Exhilarated by my progress. Sad. I became the prized student — anxious and eager to learn. Too eager, too anxious — an imitative and unoriginal pupil. My brother and two sisters enjoyed the advantages I did, and they grew to be as successful as I, but none of them ever seemed so anxious about their schooling. A second-grade student, I was the one who came home and corrected the "simple" grammatical mistakes of our parents. ("Two negatives make a positive.") Proudly I announced — to my family's startled silence — that a teacher had said I was losing all trace of a Spanish accent. I was oddly annoyed when I was unable to get parental help with a homework assignment. The night my father tried to help me with an arithmetic exercise, he kept reading the instructions, each time more deliberately, until I pried the textbook out of his hands, saying, "I'll try to figure it out some more by myself."

When I reached the third grade, I outgrew such behavior. I became more tactful, careful to keep separate the two very different worlds of my day. But then, with ever-increasing intensity, I devoted myself to my studies. I became bookish, puzzling to all my family. Ambition set me apart. When my brother saw me struggling home with stacks of library books, he would laugh, shouting: "Hey, Four Eyes!" My father opened a closet one day and was startled to find me inside, reading a novel. My mother would find me reading when I was supposed to be asleep or helping around the house or playing outside. In a voice angry or worried or just curious, she'd ask: "What do you see in your books?" It became the family's joke. When I was called and wouldn't reply, someone would say I must be hiding under my bed with a book.

(How did I manage my success?)

What I am about to say to you has taken me more than twenty years to admit: *A primary reason for my success in the classroom was that I couldn't forget that schooling was changing me and separating me from the life I enjoyed before becoming a student.* That simple realization! For years I never spoke to anyone about it. Never mentioned a thing to my family or my teachers or classmates. From a very early age, I understood enough, just enough about my classroom experiences to keep what I knew repressed, hidden beneath layers of embarrassment. Not until my last months as a graduate student, nearly thirty years old, was it possible for me to think much about the reasons for my academic success. Only then. At the end of my schooling, I needed to determine how far I had moved from my past. The adult finally confronted, and now must publicly say, what the child shuddered from knowing and could never admit to himself or to those many faces that smiled at his every success. ("Your parents must be very proud. . . .")

I

At the end, in the British Museum (too distracted to finish my dissertation) for weeks I read, speed-read, books by modern educational theorists, only to find infrequent and slight mention of students like me. (Much more is written about the more typical case, the lower-class student who barely is helped by his schooling.) Then one day, leafing through Richard Hoggart's *The Uses of Literacy,* I found, in his description of the scholarship boy, myself. For the first time I realized that there were other students like me, and so I was able to frame the meaning of my academic success, its consequent price — the loss.

Hoggart's description is distinguished, at least initially, by deep understanding. What he grasps very well is that the scholarship boy must move between environments, his home and the classroom, which are at cultural extremes, opposed. With his family, the boy has the intense pleasure of intimacy, the family's consolation in feeling public alienation. Lavish emotions texture home life. *Then,* at school, the instruction bids him to trust lonely reason primarily. Immediate needs set the pace of his parents' lives. From his mother and father the boy learns to trust spontaneity and nonrational ways of knowing. *Then,* at school, there is mental calm. Teachers emphasize the value of a reflectiveness that opens a space between thinking and immediate action.

Years of schooling must pass before the boy will be able to sketch the   10
cultural differences in his day as abstractly as this. But he senses those differences early. Perhaps as early as the night he brings home an assignment from school and finds the house too noisy for study.

> He has to be more and more alone, if he is going to "get on." He will have, probably unconsciously, to oppose the ethos of the hearth, the intense gregariousness of the working-class family group. Since everything centers upon the living-room, there is unlikely to be a room of his own; the bedrooms are cold and inhospitable, and to warm them or the front room, if there is one, would not only be expensive but would require an imaginative leap — out of the tradition — which most families are not capable of making. There is a corner of the living-room table. On the other side Mother is ironing, the wireless is on, someone is singing a snatch of song or Father says intermittently whatever comes into his head. The boy has to cut himself off mentally, so as to do his homework, as well as he can.[1]

The next day, the lesson is as apparent at school. There are even rows of desks. Discussion is ordered. The boy must rehearse his thoughts and raise his hand before speaking out in a loud voice to an audience of classmates. And there is time enough, and silence, to think about ideas (big ideas) never considered at home by his parents.

Not for the working-class child alone is adjustment to the classroom difficult. Good schooling requires that any student alter early childhood

---

[1]All quotations in this [selection] are from Richard Hoggart, *The Uses of Literacy* (London: Chatto and Windus, 1957), chapter 10. [Rodriguez's note.]

habits. But the working-class child is usually least prepared for the change. And, unlike many middle-class children, he goes home and sees in his parents a way of life not only different but starkly opposed to that of the classroom. (He enters the house and hears his parents talking in ways his teachers discourage.)

Without extraordinary determination and the great assistance of others — at home and at school — there is little chance for success. Typically most working-class children are barely changed by the classroom. The exception succeeds. The relative few become scholarship students. Of these, Richard Hoggart estimates, most manage a fairly graceful transition. Somehow they learn to live in the two very different worlds of their day. There are some others, however, those Hoggart pejoratively terms "scholarship boys," for whom success comes with special anxiety. Scholarship boy: good student, troubled son. The child is "moderately endowed," intellectually mediocre, Hoggart supposes — though it may be more pertinent to note the special qualities of temperament in the child. High-strung child. Brooding. Sensitive. Haunted by the knowledge that one *chooses* to become a student. (Education is not an inevitable or natural step in growing up.) Here is a child who cannot forget that his academic success distances him from a life he loved, even from his own memory of himself.

Initially, he wavers, balances allegiance. ("The boy is himself [until he reaches, say, the upper forms] very much of *both* the worlds of home and school. He is enormously obedient to the dictates of the world of school, but emotionally still strongly wants to continue as part of the family circle.") Gradually, necessarily, the balance is lost. The boy needs to spend more and more time studying, each night enclosing himself in the silence permitted and required by intense concentration. He takes his first step toward academic success, away from his family.

From the very first days, through the years following, it will be with his parents — the figures of lost authority, the persons toward whom he feels deepest love — that the change will be most powerfully measured. A separation will unravel between them. Advancing in his studies, the boy notices that his mother and father have not changed as much as he. Rather, when he sees them, they often remind him of the person he once was and the life he earlier shared with them. He realizes what some Romantics also know when they praise the working class for the capacity for human closeness, qualities of passion and spontaneity, that the rest of us experience in like measure only in the earliest part of our youth. For the Romantic, this doesn't make working-class life childish. Working-class life challenges precisely because it is an *adult* way of life.

The scholarship boy reaches a different conclusion. He cannot afford to admire his parents. (How could he and still pursue such a contrary life?) He permits himself embarrassment at their lack of education. And to evade nostalgia for the life he has lost, he concentrates on the benefits education will bestow upon him. He becomes especially ambitious. Without the support of old certainties and consolations, almost mechanically, he assumes the

15

procedures and doctrines of the classroom. The kind of allegiance the young student might have given his mother and father only days earlier, he transfers to the teacher, the new figure of authority. "[The scholarship boy] tends to make a father-figure of his form-master," Hoggart observes.

But Hoggart's calm prose only makes me recall the urgency with which I came to idolize my grammar school teachers. I began by imitating their accents, using their diction, trusting their every direction. The very first facts they dispensed, I grasped with awe. Any book they told me to read, I read — then waited for them to tell me which books I enjoyed. Their every casual opinion I came to adopt and to trumpet when I returned home. I stayed after school "to help" — to get my teacher's undivided attention. It was the nun's encouragement that mattered most to me. (She understood exactly what — my parents never seemed to appraise so well — all my achievements entailed.) Memory gently caressed each word of praise bestowed in the classroom so that compliments teachers paid me years ago come quickly to mind even today.

The enthusiasm I felt in second-grade classes I flaunted before both my parents. The docile, obedient student came home a shrill and precocious son who insisted on correcting and teaching his parents with the remark: "My teacher told us . . ."

I intended to hurt my mother and father. I was still angry at them for having encouraged me toward classroom English. But gradually this anger was exhausted, replaced by guilt as school grew more and more attractive to me. I grew increasingly successful, a talkative student. My hand was raised in the classroom; I yearned to answer any question. At home, life was less noisy than it had been. (I spoke to classmates and teachers more often each day than to family members.) Quiet at home, I sat with my papers for hours each night. I never forgot that schooling had irretrievably changed my family's life. That knowledge, however, did not weaken ambition. Instead, it strengthened resolve. Those times I remembered the loss of my past with regret, I quickly reminded myself of all the things my teachers could give me. (They could make me an educated man.) I tightened my grip on pencil and books. I evaded nostalgia. Tried hard to forget. But one does not forget by trying to forget. One only remembers. I remembered too well that education had changed my family's life. I would not have become a scholarship boy had I not so often remembered.

Once she was sure that her children knew English, my mother would tell us, "You should keep up your Spanish." Voices playfully groaned in response. "*Pochos!*"° my mother would tease. I listened silently.

After a while, I grew more calm at home. I developed tact. A fourth-grade student, I was no longer the show-off in front of my parents. I became a conventionally dutiful son, politely affectionate, cheerful enough, even — for reasons beyond choosing — my father's favorite. And much about my fam-

---

pochos   Mexican slang meaning "outsiders."

ily life was easy then, comfortable, happy in the rhythm of our living together: hearing my father getting ready for work; eating the breakfast my mother had made me; looking up from a novel to hear my brother or one of my sisters playing with friends in the backyard; in winter, coming upon the house all lighted up after dark.

But withheld from my mother and father was any mention of what most mattered to me: the extraordinary experience of first-learning. Late afternoon: In the midst of preparing dinner, my mother would come up behind me while I was trying to read. Her head just over mine, her breath warmly scented with food. "What are you reading?" Or, "Tell me all about your new courses." I would barely respond, "Just the usual things, nothing special." (A half smile, then silence. Her head moving back in the silence. Silence! Instead of the flood of intimate sounds that had once flowed smoothly between us, there was this silence.) After dinner, I would rush to a bedroom with papers and books. As often as possible, I resisted parental pleas to "save lights" by coming to the kitchen to work. I kept so much, so often, to myself. Sad. Enthusiastic. Troubled by the excitement of coming upon new ideas. Eager. Fascinated by the promising texture of a brand-new book. I hoarded the pleasures of learning. Alone for hours. Enthralled. Nervous. I rarely looked away from my books — or back on my memories. Nights when relatives visited and the front rooms were warmed by Spanish sounds, I slipped quietly out of the house.

It mattered that education was changing me. It never ceased to matter. My brother and sisters would giggle at our mother's mispronounced words. They'd correct her gently. My mother laughed girlishly one night, trying not to pronounce *sheep* as *ship*. From a distance I listened sullenly. From that distance, pretending not to notice on another occasion, I saw my father looking at the title pages of my library books. That was the scene on my mind when I walked home with a fourth-grade companion and heard him say that his parents read to him every night. (A strange-sounding book — *Winnie the Pooh*.) Immediately, I wanted to know, "What is it like?" My companion, however, thought I wanted to know about the plot of the book. Another day, my mother surprised me by asking for a "nice" book to read. "Something not too hard you think I might like." Carefully I chose one, Willa Cather's *My Ántonia*. But when, several weeks later, I happened to see it next to her bed unread except for the first few pages, I was furious and suddenly wanted to cry. I grabbed up the book and took it back to my room and placed it in its place, alphabetically on my shelf.

"Your parents must be very proud of you." People began to say that to me about the time I was in sixth grade. To answer affirmatively, I'd smile. Shyly I'd smile, never betraying my sense of the irony: I was not proud of my mother and father. I was embarrassed by their lack of education. It was not that I ever thought they were stupid, though stupidly I took for granted their enormous native intelligence. Simply, what mattered to me was that they were not like my teachers.

But, "Why didn't you tell us about the award?" my mother demanded, her frown weakened by pride. At the grammar school ceremony several weeks after, her eyes were brighter than the trophy I'd won. Pushing back the hair from my forehead, she whispered that I had "shown" the *gringos*. A few minutes later, I heard my father speak to my teacher and felt ashamed of his labored, accented words. Then guilty for the shame. I felt such contrary feelings. (There is no simple road-map through the heart of the scholarship boy.) My teacher was so soft-spoken and her words were edged sharp and clean. I admired her until it seemed to me that she spoke too carefully. Sensing that she was condescending to them, I became nervous. Resentful. Protective. I tried to move my parents away. "You both must be very proud of Richard," the nun said. They responded quickly. (They were proud.) "We are proud of all our children." Then this afterthought: "They sure didn't get their brains from us." They all laughed. I smiled.

Tightening the irony into a knot was the knowledge that my parents were   25
always behind me. They made success possible. They evened the path. They sent their children to parochial schools because the nuns "teach better." They paid a tuition they couldn't afford. They spoke English to us.

For their children my parents wanted chances they never had — an easier way. It saddened my mother to learn that some relatives forced their children to start working right after high school. To *her* children she would say, "Get all the education you can." In schooling she recognized the key to job advancement. And with the remark she remembered her past.

As a girl new to America my mother had been awarded a high school diploma by teachers too careless or busy to notice that she hardly spoke English. On her own, she determined to learn how to type. That skill got her jobs typing envelopes in letter shops, and it encouraged in her an optimism about the possibility of advancement. (Each morning when her sisters put on uniforms, she chose a bright-colored dress.) The years of young womanhood passed, and her typing speed increased. She also became an excellent speller of words she mispronounced. "And I've never been to college," she'd say, smiling, when her children asked her to spell words they were too lazy to look up in a dictionary.

Typing, however, was dead-end work. Finally frustrating. When her youngest child started high school, my mother got a full-time office job once again. (Her paycheck combined with my father's to make us — in fact — what we had already become in our imagination of ourselves — middle class.) She worked then for the (California) state government in numbered civil service positions secured by examinations. The old ambition of her youth was rekindled. During the lunch hour, she consulted bulletin boards for announcements of openings. One day she saw mention of something called an "antipoverty agency." A typing job. A glamorous job, part of the governor's staff. "A knowledge of Spanish required." Without hesitation she applied and became nervous only when the job was suddenly hers.

"Everyone comes to work all dressed up," she reported at night. And didn't need to say more than that her coworkers wouldn't let her answer the phones. She was only a typist, after all, albeit a very fast typist. And an excellent speller. One morning there was a letter to be sent to a Washington cabinet officer. On the dictating tape, a voice referred to urban guerrillas. My mother typed (the wrong word, correctly): "gorillas." The mistake horrified the antipoverty bureaucrats who shortly after arranged to have her returned to her previous position. She would go no further. So she willed her ambition to her children. "Get all the education you can; with an education you can do anything." (With a good education *she* could have done anything.)

When I was in high school, I admitted to my mother that I planned to become a teacher someday. That seemed to please her. But I never tried to explain that it was not the occupation of teaching I yearned for as much as it was something more elusive: I wanted to *be* like my teachers, to possess their knowledge, to assume their authority, their confidence, even to assume a teacher's persona. *destructive*

In contrast to my mother, my father never verbally encouraged his children's academic success. Nor did he often praise us. My mother had to remind him to "say something" to one of his children who scored some academic success. But whereas my mother saw in education the opportunity for job advancement, my father recognized that education provided an even more startling possibility: It could enable a person to escape from a life of mere labor.

In Mexico, orphaned when he was eight, my father left school to work as an "apprentice" for an uncle. Twelve years later, he left Mexico in frustration and arrived in America. He had great expectations then of becoming an engineer. ("Work for my hands and my head.") He knew a Catholic priest who promised to get him money enough to study full time for a high school diploma. But the promises came to nothing. Instead there was a dark succession of warehouse, cannery, and factory jobs. After work he went to night school along with my mother. A year, two passed. Nothing much changed, except that fatigue worked its way into the bone; then everything changed. He didn't talk anymore of becoming an engineer. He stayed outside on the steps of the school while my mother went inside to learn typing and shorthand.

By the time I was born, my father worked at "clean" jobs. For a time he was a janitor at a fancy department store. ("Easy work; the machines do it all.") Later he became a dental technician. ("Simple.") But by then he was pessimistic about the ultimate meaning of work and the possibility of ever escaping its claims. In some of my earliest memories of him, my father already seems aged by fatigue. (He has never really grown old like my mother.) From boyhood to manhood, I have remembered him in a single image: seated, asleep on the sofa, his head thrown back in a hideous corpse-like grin, the evening newspaper spread out before him. "But look at all you've accomplished," his best friend said to him once. My father said nothing. Only smiled.

It was my father who laughed when I claimed to be tired by reading and writing. It was he who teased me for having soft hands. (He seemed to sense that some great achievement of leisure was implied by my papers and books.) It was my father who became angry while watching on television some woman at the Miss America contest tell the announcer that she was going to college. ("Majoring in fine arts.") "College!" he snarled. He despised the trivialization of higher education, the inflated grades and cheapened diplomas, the half education that so often passed as mass education in my generation.

It was my father again who wondered why I didn't display my awards 35 on the wall of my bedroom. He said he liked to go to doctors' offices and see their certificates and degrees on the wall. ("Nice.") My citations from school got left in closets at home. The gleaming figure astride one of my trophies was broken, wingless, after hitting the ground. My medals were placed in a jar of loose change. And when I lost my high school diploma, my father found it as it was about to be thrown out with the trash. Without telling me, he put it away with his own things for safekeeping.

These memories slammed together at the instant of hearing that refrain familiar to all scholarship students: "Your parents must be very proud. . . ." Yes, my parents were proud. I knew it. But my parents regarded my progress with more than mere pride. They endured my early precocious behavior — both with what private anger and humiliation? As their children got older and would come home to challenge ideas both of them held, they argued before submitting to the force of logic or superior factual evidence with the disclaimer "It's what we were taught in our time to believe." These discussions ended abruptly, though my mother remembered them on other occasions when she complained that our "big ideas" were going to our heads. More acute was her complaint that the family wasn't close anymore, like some others she knew. Why weren't we close, "more in the Mexican style"? Everyone is so private, she added. And she mimicked the yes and no answers she got in reply to her questions. Why didn't we talk more? (My father never asked.) I never said.

I was the first in my family who asked to leave home when it came time to go to college. I had been admitted to Stanford, one hundred miles away. My departure would only make physically apparent the separation that had occurred long before. But it was going too far. In the months preceding my leaving, I heard the question my mother never asked except indirectly. In the hot kitchen, tired at the end of her workday, she demanded to know, "Why aren't the colleges here in Sacramento good enough for you? They are for your brother and sister." In the middle of a car ride, not turning to face me, she wondered, "Why do you need to go so far away?" Late at night, ironing, she said with disgust, "Why do you have to put us through this big expense? You know your scholarship will never cover it all." But when September came there was a rush to get everything ready. In a bedroom that last night I packed the big brown valise, and my mother sat nearby sewing initials onto the clothes I would take. And she said no more about my leaving.

Months later, two weeks of Christmas vacation: The first hours home were the hardest. ("What's new?") My parents and I sat in the kitchen for a conversation. (But, lacking the same words to develop our sentences and to shape our interests, what was there to say? What could I tell them of the term paper I had just finished on the "universality of Shakespeare's appeal"?) I mentioned only small, obvious things: my dormitory life; weekend trips I had taken; random events. They responded with news of their own. (One was almost grateful for a family crisis about which there was much to discuss.) We tried to make our conversation seem like more than an interview.

I I

From an early age I knew that my mother and father could read and write both Spanish and English. I had observed my father making his way through what, I now suppose, must have been income tax forms. On other occasions I waited apprehensively while my mother read onion-paper letters airmailed from Mexico with news of a relative's illness or death. For both my parents, however, reading was something done out of necessity and as quickly as possible. Never did I see either of them read an entire book. Nor did I see them read for pleasure. Their reading consisted of work manuals, prayer books, newspapers, recipes.

Richard Hoggart imagines how, at home,   40

> [The scholarship boy] sees strewn around, and reads regularly himself, magazines which are never mentioned at school, which seem not to belong to the world to which the school introduces him; at school he hears about and reads books never mentioned at home. When he brings those books into the house they do not take their place with other books which the family are reading, for often there are none or almost none; his books look, rather, like strange tools.

In our house each school year would begin with my mother's careful instruction: "Don't write in your books so we can sell them at the end of the year." The remark was echoed in public by my teachers, but only in part: "Boys and girls, don't write in your books. You must learn to treat them with great care and respect."

OPEN THE DOORS OF YOUR MIND WITH BOOKS, read the red and white poster over the nun's desk in early September. It soon was apparent to me that reading was the classroom's central activity. Each course had its own book. And the information gathered from a book was unquestioned. READ TO LEARN, the sign on the wall advised in December. I privately wondered: What was the connection between reading and learning? Did one learn something only by reading it? Was an idea only an idea if it could be written

465

down? In June, CONSIDER BOOKS YOUR BEST FRIENDS. Friends? Reading was, at best, only a chore. I needed to look up whole paragraphs of words in a dictionary. Lines of type were dizzying, the eye having to move slowly across the page, then down, and across. . . . The sentences of the first books I read were coolly impersonal. Toned hard. What most bothered me, however, was the isolation reading required. To console myself for the loneliness I'd feel when I read, I tried reading in a very soft voice. Until: "Who is doing all that talking to his neighbor?" Shortly after, remedial reading classes were arranged for me with a very old nun.

At the end of each school day, for nearly six months, I would meet with her in the tiny room that served as the school's library but was actually only a storeroom for used textbooks and a vast collection of *National Geographics*. Everything about our sessions pleased me: the smallness of the room; the noise of the janitor's broom hitting the edge of the long hallway outside the door; the green of the sun, lighting the wall; and the old woman's face blurred white with a beard. Most of the time we took turns. I began with my elementary text. Sentences of astonishing simplicity seemed to me lifeless and drab: "The boys ran from the rain . . . She wanted to sing . . . The kite rose in the blue." Then the old nun would read from her favorite books, usually biographies of early American presidents. Playfully she ran through complex sentences, calling the words alive with her voice, making it seem that the author somehow was speaking directly to me. I smiled just to listen to her. I sat there and sensed for the very first time some possibility of fellowship between a reader and a writer, a communication, never *intimate* like that I heard spoken words at home convey, but one nonetheless *personal*.

One day the nun concluded a session by asking me why I was so reluctant to read by myself. I tried to explain; said something about the way written words made me feel all alone — almost, I wanted to add but didn't, as when I spoke to myself in a room just emptied of furniture. She studied my face as I spoke; she seemed to be watching more than listening. In an uneventful voice she replied that I had nothing to fear. Didn't I realize that reading would open up whole new worlds? A book could open doors for me. It could introduce me to people and show me places I never imagined existed. She gestured toward the bookshelves. (Bare-breasted African women danced, and the shiny hubcaps of automobiles on the back covers of the *Geographic* gleamed in my mind.) I listened with respect. But her words were not very influential. I was thinking then of another consequence of literacy, one I was too shy to admit but nonetheless trusted. Books were going to make me "educated." *That* confidence enabled me, several months later, to overcome my fear of the silence.

In fourth grade I embarked upon a grandiose reading program. "Give me the names of important books," I would say to startled teachers. They soon found out that I had in mind "adult books." I ignored their suggestion of anything I suspected was written for children. (Not until I was in college, as a result, did I read *Huckleberry Finn* or *Alice's Adventures in Wonderland*.)

Instead, I read *The Scarlet Letter* and Franklin's *Autobiography*. And whatever I read I read for extra credit. Each time I finished a book, I reported the achievement to a teacher and basked in the praise my effort earned. Despite my best efforts, however, there seemed to be more and more books I needed to read. At the library I would literally tremble as I came upon whole shelves of books I hadn't read. So I read and I read and I read: *Great Expectations*; all the short stories of Kipling; *The Babe Ruth Story*; the entire first volume of the *Encyclopaedia Britannica* (A–ANSTEY); the *Iliad*; *Moby Dick*; *Gone with the Wind*; *The Good Earth*; *Ramona*; *Forever Amber*; *The Lives of the Saints*; *Crime and Punishment*; *The Pearl*. . . . Librarians who initially frowned when I checked out the maximum ten books at a time started saving books they thought I might like. Teachers would say to the rest of the class, "I only wish the rest of you took reading as seriously as Richard obviously does."

But at home I would hear my mother wondering, "What do you see in your books?" (Was reading a hobby like her knitting? Was so much reading even healthy for a boy? Was it the sign of "brains"? Or was it just a convenient excuse for not helping about the house on Saturday mornings?) Always, "What do you see . . . ?" —45

What *did* I see in my books? I had the idea that they were crucial for my academic success, though I couldn't have said exactly how or why. In the sixth grade I simply concluded that what gave a book its value was some major idea or theme it contained. If that core essence could be mined and memorized, I would become learned like my teachers. I decided to record in a notebook the themes of the books that I read. After reading *Robinson Crusoe*, I wrote that its theme was "the value of learning to live by oneself." When I completed *Wuthering Heights*, I noted the danger of "letting emotions get out of control." Rereading these brief moralistic appraisals usually left me disheartened. I couldn't believe that they were really the source of reading's value. But for many more years, they constituted the only means I had of describing to myself the educational value of books.

In spite of my earnestness, I found reading a pleasurable activity. I came to enjoy the lonely good company of books. Early on weekday mornings, I'd read in my bed. I'd feel a mysterious comfort then, reading in the dawn quiet — the blue-gray silence interrupted by the occasional churning of the refrigerator motor a few rooms away or the more distant sounds of a city bus beginning its run. On weekends I'd go to the public library to read, surrounded by old men and women. Or, if the weather was fine, I would take my books to the park and read in the shade of a tree. A warm summer evening was my favorite reading time. Neighbors would leave for vacation and I would water their lawns. I would sit through the twilight on the front porches or in backyards, reading to the cool, whirling sounds of the sprinklers.

I also had favorite writers. But often those writers I enjoyed most I was least able to value. When I read William Saroyan's *The Human Comedy*, I was immediately pleased by the narrator's warmth and the charm of his story.

But as quickly I became suspicious. A book so enjoyable to read couldn't be very "important." Another summer I determined to read all the novels of Dickens. Reading his fat novels, I loved the feeling I got — after the first hundred pages — of being at home in a fictional world where I knew the names of the characters and cared about what was going to happen to them. And it bothered me that I was forced away at the conclusion, when the fiction closed tight, like a fortune-teller's fist — the futures of all the major characters neatly resolved. I never knew how to take such feelings seriously, however. Nor did I suspect that these experiences could be part of a novel's meaning. Still, there were pleasures to sustain me after I'd finish my books. Carrying a volume back to the library, I would be pleased by its weight. I'd run my fingers along the edge of the pages and marvel at the breadth of my achievement. Around my room, growing stacks of paperback books reenforced my assurance.

I entered high school having read hundreds of books. My habit of reading made me a confident speaker and writer of English. Reading also enabled me to sense something of the shape, the major concerns, of Western thought. (I was able to say something about Dante and Descartes and Engels and James Baldwin in my high school term papers.) In these various ways, books brought me academic success as I hoped that they would. But I was not a good reader. Merely bookish, I lacked a point of view when I read. Rather, I read in order to acquire a point of view. I vacuumed books for epigrams, scraps of information, ideas, themes — anything to fill the hollow within me and make me feel educated. When one of my teachers suggested to his drowsy tenth-grade English class that a person could not have a "complicated idea" until he had read at least two thousand books, I heard the remark without detecting either its irony or its very complicated truth. I merely determined to compile a list of all the books I had ever read. Harsh with myself, I included only once a title I might have read several times. (How, after all, could one read a book more than once?) And I included only those books over a hundred pages in length. (Could anything shorter be a book?)

There was yet another high school list I compiled. One day I came across 50 a newspaper article about the retirement of an English professor at a nearby state college. The article was accompanied by a list of the "hundred most important books of Western Civilization." "More than anything else in my life," the professor told the reporter with finality, "these books have made me all that I am." That was the kind of remark I couldn't ignore. I clipped out the list and kept it for the several months it took me to read all of the titles. Most books, of course, I barely understood. While reading Plato's *Republic,* for instance, I needed to keep looking at the book jacket comments to remind myself what the text was about. Nevertheless, with the special patience and superstition of a scholarship boy, I looked at every word of the text. And by the time I reached the last word, relieved, I convinced myself that I had read *The Republic.* In a ceremony of great pride, I solemnly crossed Plato off my list.

III

The scholarship boy pleases most when he is young — the working-class child struggling for academic success. To his teachers, he offers great satisfaction; his success is their proudest achievement. Many other persons offer to help him. A businessman learns the boy's story and promises to underwrite part of the cost of his college education. A woman leaves him her entire library of several hundred books when she moves. His progress is featured in a newspaper article. Many people seem happy for him. They marvel. "How did you manage so fast?" From all sides, there is lavish praise and encouragement.

In his grammar school classroom, however, the boy already makes students around him uneasy. They scorn his desire to succeed. They scorn him for constantly wanting the teacher's attention and praise. "Kiss Ass," they call him when his hand swings up in response to every question he hears. Later, when he makes it to college, no one will mock him aloud. But he detects annoyance on the faces of some students and even some teachers who watch him. It puzzles him often. In college, then in graduate school, he behaves much as he always has. If anything is different about him it is that he dares to anticipate the successful conclusion of his studies. At last he feels that he belongs in the classroom, and this is exactly the source of the dissatisfaction he causes. To many persons around him, he appears too much the academic. There may be some things about him that recall his beginnings — his shabby clothes; his persistent poverty; or his dark skin (in those cases when it symbolizes his parents' disadvantaged condition) — but they only make clear how far he has moved from his past. He has used education to remake himself.

It bothers his fellow academics to face this. They will not say why exactly. (They sneer.) But their expectations become obvious when they are disappointed. They expect — they want — a student less changed by his schooling. If the scholarship boy, from a past so distant from the classroom, could remain in some basic way unchanged, he would be able to prove that it is possible for anyone to become educated without basically changing from the person one was.

Here is no fabulous hero, no idealized scholar-worker. The scholarship boy does not straddle, cannot reconcile, the two great opposing cultures of his life. His success is unromantic and plain. He sits in the classroom and offers those sitting beside him no calming reassurance about their own lives. He sits in the seminar room — a man with brown skin, the son of working-class Mexican immigrant parents. (Addressing the professor at the head of the table, his voice catches with nervousness.) There is no trace of his parents' accent in his speech. Instead he approximates the accents of teachers and classmates. Coming from *him* those sounds seem suddenly odd. Odd too is the effect produced when *he* uses academic jargon — bubbles at the tip of his tongue: "*Topos* . . . negative capability . . . vegetation imagery in Shakespearean comedy." He lifts an opinion from Coleridge, takes something else from Frye or Empsom or Leavis. He even repeats exactly his professor's earlier comment. All his ideas are clearly borrowed. He seems to have no thought of his own. He chatters while his listeners smile — their look one of disdain.

When he is older and thus when so little of the person he was survives, 55 the scholarship boy makes only too apparent his profound lack of *self-confidence*. This is the conventional assessment that even Richard Hoggart repeats:

> [The scholarship boy] tends to overstress the importance of examinations, of the piling-up of knowledge and of received opinions. He discovers a technique of apparent learning, of the acquiring of facts rather than of the handling and use of facts. He learns how to receive a purely literate education, one using only a small part of the personality and challenging only a limited area of his being. He begins to see life as a ladder, as a permanent examination with some praise and some further exhortation at each stage. He becomes an expert imbiber and doler-out; his competence will vary, but will rarely be accompanied by genuine enthusiasms. He rarely feels the reality of knowledge, of other men's thoughts and imaginings, on his own pulses. . . . He has something of the blinkered pony about him.

But this is criticism more accurate than fair. The scholarship boy is a very bad student. He is the great mimic; a collector of thoughts, not a thinker; the very last person in class who ever feels obliged to have an opinion of his own. In large part, however, the reason he is such a bad student is because he realizes more often and more acutely than most other students — than Hoggart himself — that education requires radical self-reformation. As a very young boy, regarding his parents, as he struggles with an early homework assignment, he knows this too well. That is why he lacks self-assurance. He does not forget that the classroom is responsible for remaking him. He relies on his teacher, depends on all that he hears in the classroom and reads in his books. He becomes in every obvious way the worst student, a dummy mouthing the opinions of others. But he would not be so bad — nor would he become so successful, a *scholarship* boy — if he did not accurately perceive that the best synonym for primary "education" is "imitation."

Those who would take seriously the boy's success — and his failure — would be forced to realize how great is the change any academic undergoes, how far one must move from one's past. It is easiest to ignore such considerations. So little is said about the scholarship boy in pages and pages of educational literature. Nothing is said of the silence that comes to separate the boy from his parents. Instead, one hears proposals for increasing the self-esteem of students and encouraging early intellectual independence. Paragraphs glitter with a constellation of terms like *creativity* and *originality*. (Ignored altogether is the function of imitation in a student's life.) Radical educationalists meanwhile complain that ghetto schools "oppress" students by trying to mold them, stifling native characteristics. The truer critique would be just the reverse: not that schools change ghetto students too much, but that while they might promote the occasional scholarship student, they change most students barely at all.

From the story of the scholarship boy there is no specific pedagogy to glean. There is, however, a much larger lesson. His story makes clear that education is a long, unglamorous, even demeaning process — *a nurturing never natural to the person one was before one entered a classroom.* At once different from most other students, the scholarship boy is also the archetypal "good student." He exaggerates the difficulty of being a student, but his exaggeration reveals a general predicament. Others are changed by their schooling as much as he. They too must re-form themselves. They must develop the skill of memory long before they become truly critical thinkers. And when they read Plato for the first several times, it will be with awe more than deep comprehension.

The impact of schooling on the scholarship boy is only more apparent to the boy himself and to others. Finally, although he may be laughable — a blinkered pony — the boy will not let his critics forget their own change. He ends up too much like them. When he speaks, they hear themselves echoed. In his pedantry, they trace their own. His ambitions are theirs. If his failure were singular, they might readily pity him. But he is more troubling than that. They would not scorn him if this were not so.

I V

Like me, Hoggart's imagined scholarship boy spends most of his years in the classroom afraid to long for his past. Only at the very end of his schooling does the boy-man become nostalgic. In this sudden change of heart, Richard Hoggart notes:

> He longs for the membership he lost, "he pines for some Nameless Eden where he never was." The nostalgia is the stronger and the more ambiguous because he is really "in quest of his own absconded self yet scared to find it." He both wants to go back and yet thinks he has gone beyond his class, feels himself weighted with knowledge of his own and their situation, which hereafter forbids him the simpler pleasures of his father and mother.

According to Hoggart, the scholarship boy grows nostalgic because he remains the uncertain scholar, bright enough to have moved from his past, yet unable to feel easy, a part of a community of academics.

This analysis, however, only partially suggests what happened to me in 60 my last year as a graduate student. When I traveled to London to write a dissertation on English Renaissance literature, I was finally confident of membership in a "community of scholars." But the pleasure that confidence gave me faded rapidly. After only two or three months in the reading room of the British Museum, it became clear that I had joined a lonely community. Around me each day were dour faces eclipsed by large piles of books. There were the regulars, like the old couple who arrived every morning, each holding a loop of the shopping bag which contained all their notes. And there was the historian who chattered madly to herself. ("Oh dear! Oh! Now, what's this? What? Oh, my!") There were also the faces of young men and women worn by long study. And everywhere eyes turned away the moment our glance accidentally met. Some persons I sat beside day after day, yet we passed silently at the end of the day, strangers. Still, we were united by a common respect for the written word and for scholarship. We did form a union, though one in which we remained distant from one another.

More profound and unsettling was the bond I recognized with those writers whose books I consulted. Whenever I opened a text that hadn't been used for years, I realized that my special interests and skills united me to a mere handful of academics. We formed an exclusive — eccentric! — society, separated from others who would never care or be able to share our concerns. (The pages I turned were stiff like layers of dead skin.) I began to wonder: Who, besides my dissertation director and a few faculty members, would ever read what I wrote? And: Was my dissertation much more than an act of social withdrawal? These questions went unanswered in the silence of the Museum reading room. They remained to trouble me after I'd leave the library each afternoon and feel myself shy — unsteady, speaking simple sentences at the grocer's or the butcher's on my way back to my bed-sitter.

Meanwhile my file cards accumulated. A professional, I knew exactly how to search a book for pertinent information. I could quickly assess and summarize the usability of the many books I consulted. But whenever I started to write, I knew too much (and not enough) to be able to write anything but sentences that were overly cautious, timid, strained brittle under the heavy weight of footnotes and qualifications. I seemed unable to dare a passionate statement. I felt drawn by professionalism to the edge of sterility, capable of no more than pedantic, lifeless, unassailable prose.

Then nostalgia began.

After years spent unwilling to admit its attractions, I gestured nostalgically toward the past. I yearned for that time when I had not been so alone. I became impatient with books. I wanted experience more immediate. I feared the library's silence. I silently scorned the gray, timid faces around me. I grew to hate the growing pages of my dissertation on genre and Renaissance literature. (In my mind I heard relatives laughing as they tried to make sense of its title.) I wanted something — I couldn't say exactly what. I told myself that I wanted a more passionate life. And a life less thoughtful. And above all, I wanted to be less alone. One day I heard some Spanish academics whispering back and forth to each other, and their sounds seemed ghostly voices recalling my life. Yearning became preoccupation then. Boyhood memories beckoned, flooded my mind. (Laughing intimate voices. Bounding up the front steps of the porch. A sudden embrace inside the door.)

For weeks after, I turned to books by educational experts. I needed to 65 learn how far I had moved from my past — to determine how fast I would be able to recover something of it once again. But I found little. Only a chapter in a book by Richard Hoggart. . . . I left the reading room and the circle of faces.

I came home. After the year in England, I spent three summer months living with my mother and father, relieved by how easy it was to be home. It no longer seemed very important to me that we had little to say. I felt easy sitting and eating and walking with them. I watched them, nevertheless, looking for evidence of those elastic, sturdy strands that bind generations in a web of inheritance. I thought as I watched my mother one night: Of course a friend had been right when she told me that I gestured and laughed just like my mother. Another time I saw for myself: My father's eyes were much like my own, constantly watchful.

But after the early relief, this return, came suspicion, nagging until I realized that I had not neatly sidestepped the impact of schooling. My desire to do so was precisely the measure of how much I remained an academic. *Negatively* (for that is how this idea first occurred to me): My need to think so much and so abstractly about my parents and our relationship was in itself an indication of my long education. My father and mother did not pass their time thinking about the cultural meanings of their experience. It was I who described their daily lives with airy ideas. And yet, *positively:* The ability to consider experience so abstractly allowed me to shape into desire what would otherwise have remained indefinite, meaningless longing in the British Museum. If, because of my schooling, I had grown culturally separated from my parents, my education finally had given me ways of speaking and caring about the fact.

My best teachers in college and graduate school, years before, had tried to prepare me for this conclusion, I think, when they discussed texts of aristocratic pastoral literature. Faithfully, I wrote down all that they said. I memorized it: "The praise of the unlettered by the highly educated is one of the primary themes of 'elitist' literature." But, "the importance of the praise given the unsolitary, richly passionate and spontaneous life is that it simultaneously reflects the value of a reflective life." I heard it all. But there was no way for any of it to mean very much to me. I was a scholarship boy at the time, busily laddering my way up the rungs of education. To pass an examination, I copied down exactly what my teachers told me. It would require many more years of schooling (an inevitable miseducation) in which I came to trust the silence of reading and the habit of abstracting from immediate experience — moving away from a life of closeness and immediacy I remembered with my parents, growing older — before I turned unafraid to desire the past, and thereby achieved what had eluded me for so long — the end of education.

AFTERWORD

Rodriguez's essay is memoir and it is argument, addressing issues of education by means of personal experience. The writer who speaks on public issues from private or personal experience projects an authority that separates him from the theorist. Anecdote and detail, remembered, not invented or found in library research, give argument the edges of reality and candor.

When we argue from our lives our authority is real but it is narrow. We run the risk of special pleading, of generalizing from the particular. Aware of this potential limitation, Rodriguez adds the library to the autobiography. When we find by research the testimony of others, to support the testimony of reminiscence, we are luckiest and most effective if the supporting material is unlike our own; as in metaphor or analogy, the best comparison combines least likely with most apt.

The English scholarship boy does not at first sight resemble the Mexican-American. At second sight, or rather with the careful parallelism (and scrupulous avowal of difference) shown by the essayist, the likeness of the unlike compels the reader's acquiescence.

Rodriguez uses Hoggart structurally, leaving him and coming back to him. The essay's power comes from memory's anecdote and detail — with the support of historical background supplied from reading.

BOOKS AVAILABLE IN PAPERBACK

Days of Obligation: An Argument with My Mexican Father. New York: Penguin. *Essays.*

Hunger of Memory: The Education of Richard Rodriguez. New York: Bantam. *Essays.*

SCOTT
RUSSELL
SANDERS

S*COTT RUSSELL SANDERS teaches English at Indiana University and writes science fiction, literary criticism, short stories, folklore, and essays; therefore he publishes in the* Georgia Review, Omni, North American Review, *and* Isaac Asimov's Science Fiction Magazine. *Born in Tennessee (1945) he did his undergraduate work at Brown University, then took a Ph.D. at Cambridge University where he was a Woodrow Wilson and a Danforth Fellow. Some of his books are* Fetching the Dead: Stories *(1984),* Wonders Hidden: Audubon's Early Years *(1984),* Hear the Wind Blow: American Folksongs Retold *(1985), and* Staying Put: Making a Home in a Restless World *(1993). This essay comes from* The Paradise of Bombs *(1987), which he describes as "a collection of personal narratives about the culture of violence in America."*

In a note that he wrote for Contemporary Authors, *Sanders spoke of the division, in his life and work, between the sciences and the arts. Clearly his science fiction is one result; he has written a book about Audubon and plans to write another. "In all of my work, regardless of period or style, I am concerned with the ways in which human beings come to terms with the practical problems of living on a small planet, in nature and in communities."*

Photo by Eva Sanders

477

Doing Time in the
Thirteenth Chair

The courtroom is filled with the ticking of a clock and the smell of mold. Listening to the minutes click away, I imagine bombs or mechanical hearts sealed behind the limestone walls. Forty of us have been yanked out of our usual orbits and called to appear for jury duty in this ominous room, beneath the stained-glass dome of the county courthouse. We sit in rows like strangers in a theater, coats rumpled in our laps, crossing and uncrossing our legs, waiting for the show to start.

I feel sulky and rebellious, the way I used to feel when a grade-school teacher made me stay inside during recess. This was supposed to have been the first day of my Christmas vacation, and the plain, uncitizenly fact is that I don't want to be here. I want to be home hammering together some bookshelves for my wife. I want to be out tromping the shores of Lake Monroe with my eye cocked skyward for bald eagles and sharp-shinned hawks.

But the computer-printed letter said to report today for jury duty, and so here I sit. The judge beams down at us from his bench. Tortoise-shell glasses, twenty-dollar haircut, square boyish face: Although probably in his early forties, he could pass for a student-body president. He reminds me of an owlish television know-it-all named Mr. Wizard who used to conduct scientific experiments (Magnetism! Litmus tests! Sulphur dioxide!) on a kids' show in the 1950s. Like Mr. Wizard, he lectures us in slow, pedantic speech: trial by one's peers, tradition stretching back centuries to England, defendant innocent until proven guilty beyond a reasonable doubt, and so abundantly on. I spy around for the clock. It must be overhead, I figure, up in the cupola above the dome, raining its ticktocks down on us.

When the lecture is finished, the judge orders us to rise, lift our hands, and swear to uphold the truth. There is a cracking of winter-stiff knees as we stand and again as we sit down. Then he introduces the principal actors: the sleek young prosecutor, who peacocks around like a politician on the hustings; the married pair of brooding, elegantly dressed defense lawyers; and the defendant. I don't want to look at this man who is charged with crimes against the "peace and dignity" of the State of Indiana. I don't want anything to do with his troubles. But I grab an image anyway, of a squat, slit-eyed man about my age, mid-thirties, stringy black hair parted in the middle and dangling like curtains across his face, sparse black beard. The chin whiskers and squinted-up eyes make him look faintly Chinese, and faintly grimacing.

Next the judge reads a list of twelve names, none of them mine, and twelve sworn citizens shuffle into the jury box. The lawyers have at them,

478

darting questions. How do you feel about drugs? Would you say the defendant there looks guilty because he has a beard? Are you related to any police officers? Are you pregnant? When these twelve have finished answering, the attorneys scribble names on sheets of paper which they hand to the judge, and eight of the first bunch are sent packing. The judge reads eight more names, the jury box fills up with fresh bodies, the questioning resumes. Six of these get the heave-ho. And so the lawyers cull through the potential jurors, testing and chucking them like two men picking over apples in the supermarket. At length they agree on a dozen, and still my name has not been called. Hooray, I think. I can build those bookshelves after all, can watch those hawks.

Before setting the rest of us free, however, the judge consults his list. "I am calling alternate juror number one," he says, and then he pronounces my name.

Groans echo down my inmost corridors. For the first time I notice a thirteenth chair beside the jury box, and that is where the judge orders me to go.

"Yours is the most frustrating job," the judge advises me soothingly. "Unless someone else falls ill or gets called away, you will have to listen to all the proceedings without taking part in the jury's final deliberations or decisions."

I feel as though I have been invited to watch the first four acts of a five-act play. Never mind, I console myself: The lawyers will throw me out. I'm the only one in the courtroom besides the defendant who sports a beard or long hair. A backpack decorated with NO NUKES and PEACE NOW and SAVE THE WHALES buttons leans against my boots. How can they expect me, a fiction writer, to confine myself to facts? I am unreliable, a confessed fabulist, a marginal Quaker and Wobbly socialist, a man so out of phase with my community that I am thrown into fits of rage by the local newspaper. The lawyers will take a good look at me and race one another to the bench for the privilege of having the judge boot me out.

But neither Mr. Defense nor Mr. Prosecution quite brings himself to focus 10 on my shady features. Each asks me a perfunctory question, the way vacationers will press a casual thumb against the spare tire before hopping into the car for a trip. If there's air in the tire, you don't bother about blemishes. And that is all I am, a spare juror stashed away in the trunk of the court, in case one of the twelve originals gives out during the trial.

Ticktock. The judge assures us that we should be finished in five days, just in time for Christmas. The real jurors exchange forlorn glances. Here I sit, number thirteen, and nobody looks my way. Knowing I am stuck here for the duration, I perk up, blink my eyes. Like the bear going over the mountain, I might as well see what I can see.

What I see is a parade of mangled souls. Some of them sit on the witness stand and reveal their wounds; some of them remain offstage, summoned up only by the words of those who testify. The case has to do with the alleged sale, earlier this year, of hashish and cocaine to a confidential informer. First the prosecutor stands at a podium in front of the jury and tells us how it all happened, detail by criminal detail, and promises to prove every fact to our utter satisfaction. Next, one of the defense attorneys has a fling at us. It is the husband of the Mr.-and-Mrs. team, a melancholy-looking man with bald pate and mutton-chop sideburns, deep creases in the chocolate skin of his forehead. Leaning on the podium, he vows that he will raise a flock of doubts in our minds — grave doubts, reasonable doubts — particularly regarding the seedy character of the confidential informer. They both speak well, without hemming and hawing, without stumbling over syntactic cliffs, better than senators at a press conference. Thus, like rival suitors, they begin to woo the jury.

At midmorning, before hearing from the first witness, we take a recess. (It sounds more and more like school.) Thirteen of us with peel-away JUROR tags stuck to our shirts and sweaters retreat to the jury room. We drink coffee and make polite chat. Since the only thing we have in common is this trial, and since the judge has just forbidden us to talk about that, we grind our gears trying to get a conversation started. I find out what everybody does in the way of work: a bar waitress, a TV repairman (losing customers while he sits here), a department store security guard, a dentist's assistant, an accountant, a nursing home nurse, a cleaning woman, a caterer, a mason, a boisterous old lady retired from rearing children (and married, she tells us, to a school-crossing guard), a meek college student with the demeanor of a groundhog, a teacher. Three of them right now are unemployed. Six men, six women, with ages ranging from twenty-one to somewhere above seventy. Chaucer could gather this bunch together for a literary pilgrimage, and he would not have a bad sampling of small-town America.

Presently the bailiff looks in to see what we're up to. She is a jowly woman, fiftyish, with short hair the color and texture of buffed aluminum. She wears silvery half-glasses of the sort favored by librarians; in the courtroom she peers at us above the frames with a librarian's skeptical glance, as if to make sure we are awake. To each of us she now gives a small yellow pad and a ballpoint pen. We are to write our names on the back, take notes on them during the trial, and surrender them to her whenever we leave the courtroom. (School again.) Without saying so directly, she lets us know that we are her flock and she is our shepherd. Anything we need, any yen we get for traveling, we should let her know.

I ask her whether I can go downstairs for a breath of air, and the bailiff 15 answers "sure." On the stairway I pass a teenage boy who is listlessly polishing with a rag the wrought-iron filigree that supports the banister. Old men sheltering from December slouch on benches just inside the ground-floor entrance of the courthouse. Their faces have been caved in by disappointment and the loss of teeth. Two-dollar cotton work gloves, the cheapest winter hand-covers, stick out of their back pockets. They are veterans of this place; so when they see me coming with the blue JUROR label pasted on my chest, they look away. Don't tamper with jurors, especially under the very nose of the law. I want to tell them I'm not a real juror, only a spare, number thirteen. I want to pry old stories out of them, gossip about hunting and dogs, about their favorite pickup trucks, their worst jobs. I want to ask them when and how it all started to go wrong for them. Did they hear a snap when the seams of their life began to come apart? But they will not be fooled into looking at me, not these wily old men with the crumpled faces. They believe the label on my chest and stare down at their unlaced shoes.

I stick my head out the door and swallow some air. The lighted thermometer on the bank reads twenty-eight degrees. Schmaltzy Christmas organ music rebounds from the brick-and-limestone shopfronts of the town square. The Salvation Army bell rings and rings. Delivery trucks hustling through yellow lights blare their horns at jaywalkers.

The bailiff must finally come fetch me, and I feel like a wayward sheep. On my way back upstairs, I notice the boy dusting the same square foot of iron filigree, and realize that he is doing this as a penance. Some judge ordered him to clean the metalwork. I'd like to ask the kid what mischief he's done, but the bailiff, looking very dour, is at my heels.

In the hallway she lines us up in our proper order, me last. Everybody stands up when we enter the courtroom, and then, as if we have rehearsed these routines, we all sit down at once. Now come the facts.

The facts are a mess. They are full of gaps, chuckholes, switchbacks, and dead ends — just like life.

At the outset we are shown three small plastic bags. Inside the first is a 20 wad of aluminum foil about the size of an earlobe; the second contains two white pills; the third holds a pair of stamp-sized, squarish packets of folded brown paper. A chemist from the state police lab testifies that he examined these items and found cocaine inside the brown packets, hashish inside the wad of aluminum foil. As for the white pills, they are counterfeits of a popular barbiturate, one favored by politicians and movie stars. They're depressants — downers — but they contain no "controlled substances."

There follows half a day's worth of testimony about how the bags were sealed, who locked them in the narcotics safe at the Bloomington police station, which officer drove them up to the lab in Indianapolis and which drove them back again, who carried them in his coat pocket and who carried them in his briefcase. Even the judge grows bored during this tedious business. He yawns, tips back in his chair, sips coffee from a mug, folds and unfolds with deft thumbs a square of paper about the size of the cocaine packets. The wheels of justice grind slowly. We hear from police officers in uniform, their handcuffs clanking, and from mustachioed officers in civvies, revolvers bulging under their suitcoats. From across the courtroom, the bailiff glares at us above her librarian's glasses, alert to catch us napping. She must be an expert at judging the degrees of tedium.

"Do you have to go back and be in the jail again tomorrow?" my little boy asks me at supper.

"Not jail," I correct him. *"Jury.* I'm in the jury."
"With real police?"
"Yes."
"And guns?"
"Yes, real guns."

On the second day there is much shifting of limbs in the jury box when the confidential informer, whom the police call I90, takes the stand. Curly-haired, thirty-three years old, bear-built and muscular like a middle-range wrestler, slow of eye, calm under the crossfire of questions, I90 works — when he works — as a drywall finisher. (In other words, he gets plasterboard ready for painting. It's a dusty, blinding job; you go home powdered white as a ghost, and you taste the joint filler all night.) Like roughly one-quarter of the construction workers in the county, right now he's unemployed.

The story he tells is essentially this: Just under a year ago, two cops showed up at his house. They'd been tipped off that he had a mess of stolen goods in his basement, stuff he'd swiped from over in a neighboring county. "Now look here," the cops said to him, "you help us out with some cases we've got going, and we'll see what we can do to help you when this here burglary business comes to court." "Like how?" he said. "Like tell us what you know about hot property, and maybe finger a drug dealer or so." He said yes to that, with the two cops sitting at his kitchen table, and — zap! — he was transformed into I90. (Hearing of this miraculous conversion, I am reminded of Saul on the road to Damascus, the devil's agent suddenly seeing the light and joining the angels.) In this new guise he gave information that led to several arrests and some prison terms, including one for his cousin and two or three for other buddies.

In this particular case, his story goes on, he asked a good friend of his where a guy could buy some, you know, drugs. The friend's brother led him to Bennie's trailer, where Bennie offered to sell I90 about any kind of drug a man's heart could desire. "All I want's some hash," I90 told him, "but I got to go get some money off my old lady first." "Then go get it," said Bennie.

Where I90 went was to the police station. There they fixed him up to make a "controlled buy": searched him, searched his car; strapped a radio transmitter around his waist; took his money and gave him twenty police dollars to make the deal. Back I90 drove to Bennie's place, and on his tail in an unmarked police car drove Officer B., listening over the radio to every burp and glitch sent out by I90's secret transmitter. On the way, I90 picked up a six-pack of Budweiser. ("If you walk into a suspect's house drinking a can of beer," Officer B. later tells us, "usually nobody'll guess you're working for the police.") Inside the trailer, the woman Bennie lives with was now fixing supper, and her three young daughters were playing cards on the linoleum floor. I90 bought a gram of blond Lebanese hashish from Bennie for six dollars. Then I90 said that his old lady was on him bad to get her some downers, and Bennie obliged by selling him a couple of 714s (the white pills favored by movie stars and politicians) at seven dollars for the pair. They shot the bull awhile, Bennie bragging about how big a dealer he used to be (ten pounds of hash and five hundred hits of acid a week), I90 jawing along like an old customer. After about twenty minutes in the trailer, I90 drove to a secluded spot near the L & N railroad depot, and there he handed over the hash and pills to Officer B., who milked the details out of him.

Four days later, I90 went through the same routine, this time buying two packets of cocaine — two "dimes'" worth — from Bennie for twenty dollars. Inside the trailer were half a dozen or so of Bennie's friends, drinking whiskey and smoking pot and watching TV and playing backgammon and generally getting the most out of a Friday night. Again Officer B. tailed I90, listened to the secret radio transmission, and took it all down in a debriefing afterwards behind the Colonial Bakery.

The lawyers burn up a full day leading I90 through this story, dropping questions like breadcrumbs to lure him on, Mr. Prosecutor trying to guide him out of the labyrinth of memory and Mr. Defense trying to get him lost. I90 refuses to get lost. He tells and retells his story without stumbling, intent as a wrestler on a dangerous hold.

On the radio news I hear that U.S. ships have intercepted freighters bound out from Beirut carrying tons and tons of Lebanese hashish, the very same prize strain of hash that I90 claims he bought from Bennie. Not wanting to irk the Lebanese government, the radio says, our ships let the freighters through. Tons and tons sailing across the Mediterranean — into how many one-gram slugs could that cargo be divided?

Out of jail the defense lawyers subpoena one of I90's brothers, who is awaiting his own trial on felony charges. He has a rabbity look about him, face pinched with fear, ready to bolt for the nearest exit. His canary yellow T-shirt is emblazoned with a scarlet silhouette of the Golden Gate Bridge. The shirt and the fear make looking at him painful. He is one of seven brothers and four sisters. Hearing that total of eleven children — the same number as in my father's family — I wonder if the parents were ever booked for burglary or other gestures of despair.

This skittish gent tells us that he always buys his drugs from his brother, good old I90. And good old I90, he tells us further, has a special fondness for snorting cocaine. Glowing there on the witness stand in his yellow shirt, dear brother gives the lie to one after another of I90's claims. But just when I'm about ready, hearing all of this fraternal gossip, to consign I90 to the level of hell reserved by Dante for liars, the prosecutor takes over the questioning. He soon draws out a confession that there has been a bitter feud recently between the two brothers. "And haven't you been found on three occasions to be mentally incompetent to stand trial?" the prosecutor demands.

"Yessir," mutters the brother.

"And haven't you spent most of the past year in and out of mental institutions?"

"Yessir."

This second admission is so faint, like a wheeze, that I must lean forward 40 to hear it, even though I am less than two yards away. While the prosecutor lets this damning confession sink into the jury, the rabbity brother just sits there, as if exposed on a rock while the hawks dive, his eyes pinched closed.

By day three of the trial, we jurors are no longer strangers to one another. Awaiting our entry into court, we exhibit wallet photos of our children, of nieces and nephews. We moan in chorus about our Christmas shopping lists. The caterer tells about serving three thousand people at a basketball banquet. The boisterous old lady, to whom we have all taken a liking, explains how the long hairs on her white cats used to get on her husband's black suit pants until she put the cats out in the garage with heating pads in their boxes.

"Where do you leave your car?" the accountant asks.

"On the street," explains the lady. "I don't want to crowd those cats. They're particular as all get-out."

People compare their bowling scores, their insurance rates, their diets. The mason, who now weighs about 300 pounds, recounts how he once lost 129 pounds in nine months. His blood pressure got so bad he had to give up dieting, and inside of a year he'd gained all his weight back and then some. The nurse, who wrestles the bloated or shriveled bodies of elderly paupers at the city's old folks' home, complains about her leg joints, and we all sympathize. The security guard entertains us with sagas about shoplifters. We compare notes on car wrecks, on where to get a transmission overhauled, on the outgoing college football coach and the incoming city mayor. We talk, in fact, about everything under the sun except the trial.

In the hall, where we line up for our reentry into the courtroom, a sullen 45 boy sits at a table scrawling on a legal pad. Line after line he copies the same sentence: "I never will steal anything ever again." More penance. He's balancing on the first rung of a ladder that leads up — or down — to the electric chair. Somewhere in the middle of the ladder is a good long prison sentence, and that, I calculate, is what is at stake in our little drug-dealing case.

On the third day of testimony, we learn that I90 has been hidden away overnight by police. After he stepped down from the witness stand yesterday, Bennie's mate, Rebecca, greeted the informant outside in the lobby and threatened to pull a bread knife out of her purse and carve him into mincemeat. I look with new interest at the stolid, bulky, black-haired woman who has been sitting since the beginning of the trial right behind the defendant. From time to time she has leaned forward, touched Bennie on the shoulder, and bent close to whisper something in his good ear. She reminds me of the Amish farm wives of my Ohio childhood — stern, unpainted, built stoutly for heavy chores, her face a fortress against outsiders.

When Rebecca takes the stand, just half a dozen feet from where I sit in chair thirteen, I sense a tigerish fierceness beneath her numb surface. She plods along behind the prosecutor's questions until he asks her, rhetorically, whether she would like to see Bennie X put in jail; then she lashes out. God no, she doesn't want him locked away. Didn't he take her in when she had two kids already and a third in the oven, and her first husband run off, and the cupboards empty? And haven't they been living together just as good as married for eight years, except while he was in jail, and don't her three little girls call him Daddy? And hasn't he been working on the city garbage trucks, getting up at four in the morning, coming home smelling like other people's trash, and hasn't she been bagging groceries at the supermarket, her hands slashed with paper cuts, and her mother looking after the girls, all so they can keep off the welfare? Damn right she doesn't want him going to any prison.

What's more, Rebecca declares, Bennie don't deserve prison because he's clean. Ever since he got out of the slammer a year ago, he's quit dealing. He's done his time and he's mended his ways and he's gone straight. What about that sale of cocaine? the prosecutor wants to know. It never happened, Rebecca vows. She was there in the trailer the whole blessed night, and she never saw Bennie sell nobody nothing, least of all cocaine, which he never used because it's too expensive — it'll run you seventy-five dollars a day — and which he never sold even when he was dealing. The prosecutor needles her: How can she remember that particular night so confidently? She can remember, she flares at him, because early that evening she got a call saying her sister's ten-year-old crippled boy was fixing to die, and all the family was going to the children's hospital in Indianapolis to watch him pass away. That was a night she'll never forget as long as she lives.

When I was a boy, my friends and I believed that if you killed a snake, the mate would hunt you out in your very bed and strangle or gnaw or smother you. We held a similar belief regarding bears, wolves, and mountain lions, although we were much less likely to run into any of those particular beasts. I have gone years without remembering that bit of child's lore, until today, when Rebecca's tigerish turn on the witness stand revives it. I can well imagine her stashing a bread knife in her purse. And if she loses her man for years and stony years, and has to rear those three girls alone, the cupboards empty again, she might well jerk that knife out of her purse one night and use it on something other than bread.

During recess, we thirteen sit in the jury room and pointedly avoid talking about the bread knife. The mason tells how a neighbor kid's Ford Pinto skidded across his lawn and onto his front porch, blocking the door and nosing against the picture window. "I took the wheels off and chained the bumper to my maple tree until his daddy paid for fixing my porch."

Everyone, it seems, has been assaulted by a car or truck. Our vehicular yarns wind closer and closer about the courthouse. Finally, two of the women jurors — the cigarillo-smoking caterer and the elderly cat lady — laugh nervously. The two of them were standing just inside the plate-glass

50

door of the courthouse last night, the caterer says, when along came a pickup truck, out poked an arm from the window, up flew a smoking beer can, and then BAM! the can exploded. "We jumped a yard in the air!" cries the old woman. "We thought it was some of Bennie's mean-looking friends," the caterer admits. Everybody laughs at the tableau of speeding truck, smoking can, exploding cherry bomb, leaping jurors. Then we choke into sudden silence, as if someone has grabbed each of us by the throat.

Four of Bennie's friends — looking not so much mean as broken, like shell-shocked refugees — testify on his behalf during the afternoon of day three. Two of them are out-of-work men in their twenties, with greasy hair to their shoulders, fatigue jackets, and clodhopper boots: their outfits and world-weary expressions are borrowed from record jackets. They are younger versions of the old men with caved-in faces who crouch on benches downstairs, sheltering from December. The other two witnesses are young women with reputations to keep up, neater than the scruffy men; gold crosses dangle over their sweaters, and gum cracks between crooked teeth. All four speak in muttered monosyllables and orphaned phrases, as if they are breaking a long vow of silence and must fetch bits and pieces of language from the archives of memory. They were all at Bennie's place on the night of the alleged cocaine sale, and they swear in unison that no such sale took place.

Officer B., the puppetmaster who pulled the strings on I90, swears just as adamantly that both the sales, of cocaine and of hash, *did* take place, for he listened to the proceedings over the radio in his unmarked blue Buick. He is a sleepy-eyed man in his midthirties, about the age of the informant and the defendant, a law-upholding alter ego for those skewed souls.

Double-chinned, padded with the considerable paunch that seems to be issued along with the police badge, Officer B. answers Mr. Prosecutor and Mr. Defense in a flat, walkie-talkie drawl, consulting a sheaf of notes in his lap, never contradicting himself. Yes, he neglected to tape the opening few minutes of the first buy, the minutes when the exchange of hashish and money actually took place. Why? "I had a suspicion my batteries were weak, and I wanted to hold off." And, yes, he did erase the tape of the debriefing that followed buy number one. Why? "It's policy to reuse the old cassettes. Saves the taxpayers' money." And, yes, the tape of the second buy is raw, indecipherable noise, because a blaring TV in the background drowns out all human voices. (Listening to the tape, we can understand nothing in the scrawking except an ad for the American Express Card.) The tapes, in other words, don't prove a thing. What it all boils down to is the word of the law and of the unsavory informer versus the word of the many-times-convicted defendant, his mate, and his friends.

Toward the end of Officer B.'s testimony, there is a resounding clunk, like a muffled explosion, at the base of the witness stand. We all jump — witness, judge, jury, onlookers — and only relax when the prosecutor squats down and discovers that a pair of handcuffs has fallen out of Officer B.'s belt. Just

55

a little reminder of the law's muscle. All of us were envisioning bombs. When Officer B. steps down, the tail of his sportcoat is hitched up over the butt of his gun.

The arrest: A squad car pulls up to the front of the trailer, and out the trailer's back door jumps Bennie, barefooted, wearing T-shirt and cut-off jeans. He dashes away between tarpaper shacks, through dog yards, over a stubbled field (his bare feet bleeding), through a patch of woods to a railroad cut. Behind him puffs a skinny cop (who recounts this scene in court), shouting, "Halt! Police!" But Bennie never slows down until he reaches that railroad cut, where he stumbles, falls, rolls down to the tracks like the sorriest hobo. The officer draws his gun. Bennie lifts his hands for the familiar steel cuffs. The two of them trudge back to the squad car, where Officer B. reads the arrest warrant and Bennie blisters everybody with curses.

The judge later instructs us that flight from arrest may be regarded as evidence, not of guilt but of *consciousness* of guilt. Oh ho! A fine distinction! Guilt for what! Selling drugs? Playing hooky? Original sin? Losing his job at Coca-Cola? I think of those bleeding feet, the sad chase. I remember a drunken uncle who stumbled down a railroad cut, fell asleep between the tracks, and died of fear when a train passed over.

On day four of the trial, Bennie himself takes the stand. He is shorter than I thought, and fatter — too many months of starchy jail food and no exercise. With exceedingly long thumbnails he scratches his jaw. When asked a question, he rolls his eyes, stares at the ceiling, then answers in a gravelly country voice, the voice of a late-night disk jockey. At first he is gruffly polite, brief in his replies, but soon he gets cranked up and rants in a grating monologue about his painful history.

He graduated from high school in 1968, worked eight months at RCA and Coca-Cola, had a good start, had a sweetheart, then the Army got him, made him a cook, shipped him to Vietnam. After a few weeks in the kitchen, he was transferred to the infantry because the fodder-machine was short of foot soldiers. "Hey, listen, man, I ain't nothing but a cook," he told them. "I ain't been trained for combat." And they said, "Don't you worry; you'll get on-the-job training. Learn or die." The artillery ruined his hearing. (Throughout the trial he has held a hand cupped behind one ear, and has followed the proceedings like a grandfather.) Some of his buddies got shot up. He learned to kill people. "We didn't even know what we was there for." To relieve his constant terror, he started doing drugs: marijuana, opium, just about anything that would ease a man's mind. Came home from Vietnam in 1971 a wreck, got treated like dirt, like a baby-killer, like a murdering scumbag, and found no jobs. His sweetheart married an insurance salesman.

Within a year after his return he was convicted of shoplifting and bur- 60 glary. He was framed on the second charge by a friend, but couldn't use his only alibi because he had spent the day of the robbery in bed with a sixteen-year-old girl, whose father would have put him away for statutory rape. As it was, he paid out two years in the pen, where he sank deeper into drugs than ever before. "If you got anything to buy or trade with, you can score more stuff in the state prisons than on the streets of Indianapolis." After prison, he still couldn't find work, couldn't get any help for his drug thing from the Veterans' Administration, moved in with Rebecca and her three girls, eventually started selling marijuana and LSD. "Everytime I went to somebody for drugs, I got ripped off. That's how I got into dealing. If you're a user, you're always looking for a better deal."

In 1979 he was busted for selling hash, in 1980 for possessing acid, betrayed in both cases by the man from whom he had bought his stock. "He's a snitch, just a filthy snitch. You can't trust nobody." Back to prison for a year, back out again in December 1981. No jobs, no jobs, no damn jobs; then part-time on the city garbage truck, up at four in the morning, minus five degrees and the wind blowing and the streets so cold his gloves stuck to the trash cans. Then March came, and this I90 guy showed up, wanted to buy some drugs, and "I told him I wasn't dealing any more. I done my time and gone straight. I told him he didn't have enough money to pay me for no thirty years in the can." (The prosecutor bristles, the judge leans meaningfully forward: We jurors are not supposed to have any notion of the sentence that might follow a conviction on this drug charge.)

In his disk-jockey voice, Bennie denies ever selling anything to this I90 snitch. (He keeps using the word "snitch": I think of tattle-tales, not this adult betrayal.) It was I90, he swears, who tried to sell *him* the hash. Now the pills, why, those he had lying around for a friend who never picked them up, and so he just gave them to I90. "They was give to me, and so I couldn't charge him nothing. They wasn't for me anyway. Downers I do not use. To me, life is a downer. Just to cope with every day, that is way down low enough for me."And as for the cocaine, he never laid eyes on it until the man produced that little plastic bag in court. "I don't use coke. It's too expensive. That's for the bigwigs and the upstanding citizens, as got the money."

Sure, he admits, he ran when the police showed up at his trailer. "I'm flat scared of cops. I don't like talking to them about anything. Since I got back from Vietnam, every time they cross my path they put bracelets on me." (He holds up his wrists. They are bare now, but earlier this morning, when I saw a deputy escorting him into the courthouse, they were handcuffed.) He refuses to concede that he is a drug addict, but agrees he has a terrible habit, "a gift from my country in exchange for me going overseas and killing a bunch of strangers."

After the arrest, forced to go cold turkey on his dope, he begged the jail doctor — "He's no kind of doctor, just one of them that fixes babies" — to zonk him out on something. And so, until the trial, he has spent eight months drowsing under Valium and Thorazine. "You can look down your nose at me for that if you want, but last month another vet hung himself two cells down from me." (The other guy was a scoutmaster, awaiting trial for sexually molesting one of his boys. He had a record of severe depression dating from the war, and used his belt for the suicide.)

"The problem with my life," says Bennie, "is Vietnam." For a while after coming home, he slept with a knife under his pillow. Once, wakened suddenly, thinking he was still in Vietnam, he nearly killed his best friend. During the week of our trial, another Vietnam vet up in Indianapolis shot his wife in the head, imagining she was a gook. Neighbors got to him before he could pull out her teeth, as he used to pull out the teeth of the enemies he bagged over in Vietnam.

When I look at Bennie, I see a double image. He was drafted during the same month in which I, studying in England, gave Uncle Sam the slip. I hated that war, and feared it, for exactly the reasons he describes — because it was foul slaughter, shameful, sinful, pointless butchery. While he was over there killing and dodging, sinking into the quicksand of drugs, losing his hearing, storing up a lifetime's worth of nightmares, I was snug in England, filling my head with words. We both came home to America in the same year, I to job and family, he to nothing. Ten years after that homecoming, we stare across the courtroom at one another as into a funhouse mirror.

As the twelve jurors file past me into the room where they will decide on Bennie's guilt or innocence, three of them pat my arm in a comradely way. They withdraw beyond a brass-barred gate; I sit down to wait on a deacon's bench in the hallway outside the courtroom. I feel stymied, as if I have rocketed to the moon only to be left riding the ship round and round in idle orbit while my fellow astronauts descend to the moon's surface. At the same time I feel profoundly relieved, because, after the four days of testimony, I still cannot decide whether Bennie truly sold those drugs, or whether I90, to cut down on his own prison time, set up this ill-starred Bennie for yet another fall. Time, time — it always comes down to time: in jail, job, and jury box we are spending and hoarding our only wealth, the currency of days.

Even through the closed doors of the courtroom, I still hear the ticking of the clock. The sound reminds me of listening to my daughter's pulse through a stethoscope when she was still riding, curled up like a stowaway, in my wife's womb. Ask not for whom this heart ticks, whispered my unborn daughter through the stethoscope: It ticks for thee. So does the courtroom clock. It grabs me by the ear and makes me fret about time — about how little there is of it, about how we are forever bumming it from one another as if it were cups of sugar or pints of blood ("You got a minute?" "Sorry, have to run, not a second to spare"). Seize the day, we shout, to cheer ourselves; but the day has seized us and flings us forward pell-mell toward the end of all days.

Now and again there is a burst of laughter from the jury room, but it is always squelched in a hurry. They are tense, and laugh to relieve the tension, and then feel ashamed of their giddiness. Lawyers traipse past me — the men smoking, striking poses, their faces like lollipops atop their ties; the women teetering on high heels. The bailiff walks into our judge's office carrying a bread knife. To slice her lunch? As evidence against Rebecca? A moment later she emerges bearing a piece of cake and licking her fingers. Christmas parties are breaking out all over the courthouse.

Rebecca herself paces back and forth at the far end of my hallway, her   70 steps as regular as the clock's tick, killing time. Her bearded and cross-wearing friends sidle up to comfort her, but she shrugs them away. Once she paces down my way, glances at the barred door of the jury room, hears muffled shouts. This she must take for good news, because she throws me a rueful smile before turning back.

Evidently the other twelve are as muddled by the blurred and contradictory "facts" of the case as I am, for they spend from noon until five reaching their decision. They ask for lunch. They ask for a dictionary. They listen again to the tapes. Sullen teenagers, following in the footsteps of Bennie and I90, slouch into the misdemeanor office across the hall from me; by and by they slouch back out again, looking unrepentant. At length the three-hundred-pound mason lumbers up to the gate of the jury room and calls the bailiff. "We're ready as we're going to be." He looks bone-weary, unhappy, and dignified. Raising his eyebrows at me, he shrugs. Comrades in uncertainty.

The cast reassembles in the courtroom, the judge asks the jury for its decision, and the mason stands up to pronounce Bennie guilty. I stare at my boots. Finally I glance up, not at Bennie or Rebecca or the lawyers, but at my fellow jurors. They look distraught, wrung out and despairing, as if they have just crawled out of a mine after an explosion and have left some of their buddies behind. Before quitting the jury room, they composed and signed a letter to the judge pleading with him to get some help — drug help, mind help, any help — for Bennie.

The ticking of the clock sounds louder in my ears than the judge's closing recital. But I do, with astonishment, hear him say that we must all come back tomorrow for one last piece of business. He is sorry, he knows we are worn out, but the law has prevented him from warning us ahead of time that we might have to decide on one more question of guilt.

The legal question posed for us on the morning of day five is simple: Has Bennie been convicted, prior to this case, of two or more unrelated felonies? If so, then he is defined by Indiana state law as a "habitual offender," and we must declare him to be such. We are shown affidavits for those earlier convictions — burglary, sale of marijuana, possession of LSD — and so the answer to the legal question is clear.

But the moral and psychological questions are tangled, and they occupy   75 the jury for nearly five more hours on this last day of the trial. Is it fair to sentence a person again, after he has already served time for his earlier offenses? How does the prosecutor decide when to apply the habitual offender statute, and does its use in this case have anything to do with the political ambitions of the sleek young attorney? Did Bennie really steal that

$150 stereo, for which he was convicted a decade ago, or did he really spend the day in bed with his sixteen-year-old girlfriend? Did Vietnam poison his mind and blight his life?

Two sheriff's deputies guard the jury today; another guards me in my own little cell. The bailiff would not let me stay out on the deacon's bench in the hall, and so, while a plainclothes detective occupies my old seat, I sit in a room lined with file cabinets and stare out like a prisoner through the glass door. "I have concluded," wrote Pascal, "that the whole misfortune of men comes from a single thing, and that is their inability to remain at rest in a room." I agree with him; nothing but that cruising deputy would keep me here.

This time, when the verdict is announced, Rebecca has her daughters with her, three little girls frightened into unchildlike stillness by the courtroom. Their lank hair and washed-out eyes remind me of my childhood playmates, the children of dead-end, used-up West Virginia coal miners who'd moved to Ohio in search of work. The mother and daughter are surrounded by half a dozen rough customers, guys my age with hair down over their shoulders and rings in their ears, with flannel shirts, unfocused eyes. Doubtless they are the reason so many holstered deputies and upholstered detectives are patrolling the courthouse, and the reason I was locked safely away in a cell while the jury deliberated.

When the mason stands to pronounce another verdict of guilty, I glimpse what I do not want to glimpse: Bennie flinging his head back, Rebecca snapping hers forward into her palms, the girls wailing.

The judge accompanies all thirteen of us into the jury room, where he keeps us for an hour while the deputies clear the rough customers from the courthouse. We are not to be alarmed, he reassures us; he is simply being cautious, since so much was at stake for the defendant. "How much?" the mason asks. "Up to twenty-four years for the drug convictions, plus a mandatory thirty years for the habitual offender charges," the judge replies. The cleaning woman, the nurse, and the TV repairman begin crying. I swallow carefully. For whatever it's worth, the judge declares comfortingly, he agrees with our decisions. If we knew as much about this Bennie as he knows, we would not be troubled. And that is just the splinter in the brain, the fact that we know so little — about Bennie, about Vietnam, about drugs, about ourselves — and yet we must grope along in our ignorance, pronouncing people guilty or innocent, squeezing out of one another that precious fluid, time.

And so I do my five days in the thirteenth chair. Bennie may do as many as fifty-four years in prison, buying his drugs from meaner dealers, dreaming of land mines and of his adopted girls, checking the date on his watch, wondering at what precise moment the hinges of his future slammed shut. 80

AFTERWORD

Use of the present tense is common, these days, both in essay and fiction. Many times it seems only an affectation, not integral to the telling of a particular tale but merely the fashion. The present tense can provide an artificial heightening of effect, a technical urgency, playing the moment's tape. I suppose it comes from television, as our brains turn into small Sonys: There is no past tense on the screen that alters so rapidly before us, on which advertisers with fifty cuts in thirty seconds speed epics into telegrams.

There are legitimate uses for the present tense. Scott Russell Sanders's "Doing Time in the Thirteenth Chair," his essay on jury duty, is indeed a "personal narrative about the culture of violence in America" — and it is narrative first of all. We follow the story as it unfolds, gradually and finally arriving at the moral of the story. The present tense allows us to understand events as they happen, not from the perspective of a digested experience. The result is not only a greater immediacy, which could be merely technical, but more intimacy with the author's voice — as we learn with him and not just from him.

BOOKS AVAILABLE IN PAPERBACK

In Limestone Country. Boston: Beacon Press. *Nonfiction.*

The Paradise of Bombs. Boston: Beacon Press. *Essays.*

Secrets of the Universe: Scenes from the Journey Home. Boston: Beacon Press. *Essays.*

Wilderness Plots: Tales About the Settlement of the American Land. Ohio State University Press. *Short stories.*

RANDY
SHILTS

R ANDY SHILTS (1951–1994) *died of AIDS at forty-two. He was a journalist, a reporter for the* San Francisco Chronicle *for the last thirteen years of his life, and a writer whose books, one commentator remarked, "singlehandedly probably did more to educate this world about AIDS" than anyone else's. "He demonstrated," said another editor, "that you could be gay and still write one hell of a story and play it down the middle and be balanced." In 1982 he wrote* The Mayor of Castro Street: The Life and Times of Harvey Milk, *about the rise of gay political power in San Francisco. His best-known work is* And the Band Played On: Politics, People, and the AIDS Epidemic, *the topic of the following essay. Shortly before he died he published* Conduct Unbecoming: Gays and Lesbians in the U.S. Military *(1993).*

Talking AIDS to Death

I'm talking to my friend Kit Herman when I notice a barely perceptible spot on the left side of his face. Slowly, it grows up his cheekbone, down to his chin, and forward to his mouth. He talks on cheerfully, as if nothing is wrong, and I'm amazed that I'm able to smile and chat on, too, as if nothing were there. His eyes become sunken; his hair turns gray; his ear is turning purple now, swelling into a carci-

---

Photo by James D. Wilson

nomatous cauliflower, and still we talk on. He's dying in front of me. He'll be dead soon if nothing is done.

Dead soon if nothing is done.

"Excuse me, Mr. Shilts, I asked if you are absolutely sure, if you can categorically state that you definitely can*not* get AIDS from a mosquito."

I forget the early-morning nightmare and shift into my canned response. All my responses are canned now. I'm an AIDS talk-show jukebox. Press the button, any button on the AIDS question list, and I have my canned answer ready. Is this Chicago or Detroit?

"Of course you can get AIDS from a mosquito," I begin.   5

Here I pause for dramatic effect. In that brief moment, I can almost hear the caller murmur, "I *knew* it."

"If you have unprotected anal intercourse with an infected mosquito, you'll get AIDS," I continue. "Anything short of that and you won't."

The talk-show host likes the answer. All the talk-show hosts like my answers because they're short, punchy, and to the point. Not like those boring doctors with long recitations of scientific studies so overwritten with maybes and qualifiers that they frighten more than they reassure an AIDS-hysteric public. I give good interview, talk-show producers agree. It's amazing, they say, how I always stay so cool and never lose my temper.

"Mr. Shilts, has there ever been a case of anyone getting AIDS from a gay waiter?"

"In San Francisco, I don't think they allow heterosexuals to be waiters.   10 This fact proves absolutely that if you could get AIDS from a gay waiter, all northern California would be dead by now."

I gave that same answer once on a Bay Area talk show, and my caller, by the sound of her a little old lady, quickly rejoined, "What if that gay waiter took my salad back into the kitchen and ejaculated into my salad dressing? Couldn't I get AIDS then?"

I didn't have a pat answer for that one, and I still wonder at what this elderly caller thought went on in the kitchens of San Francisco restaurants. Fortunately, this morning's phone-in — in Chicago, it turned out — is not as imaginative.

"You know, your question reminds me of a joke we had in California a couple of years back," I told the caller. "How many heterosexual waiters in San Francisco does it take to screw in a light bulb? The answer is both of them."

The host laughs, the caller is silent. Next comes the obligatory question about whether AIDS can be spread through coughing.

I had written a book to change the world, and here I was on talk shows   15 throughout America, answering questions about mosquitoes and gay waiters.

This wasn't exactly what I had envisioned when I began writing *And the Band Played On*. I had hoped to effect some fundamental changes. I really believed I could alter the performance of the institutions that had allowed AIDS to sweep through America unchecked.

AIDS had spread, my book attested, because politicians, particularly those in charge of federal-level response, had viewed the disease as a political issue, not an issue of public health — they deprived researchers of anything near the resources that were needed to fight it. AIDS had spread because government health officials consistently lied to the American people about the need for more funds, being more concerned with satisfying their political bosses and protecting their own jobs than with telling the truth and protecting the public health. And AIDS had spread because indolent news organizations shunned their responsibility to provide tough, adversarial reportage, instead basing stories largely on the Official Truth of government press releases. The response to AIDS was never even remotely commensurate with the scope of the problem.

I figured the federal government, finally exposed, would stumble over itself to accelerate the pace of AIDS research and put AIDS prevention programs on an emergency footing. Once publicly embarrassed by the revelations of its years of shameful neglect, the media would launch serious investigative reporting on the epidemic. Health officials would step forward and finally lay bare the truth about how official disregard had cost this country hundreds of thousands of lives. And it would never happen again.

I was stunned by the "success" of my book. I quickly acquired all the trappings of bestsellerdom: *60 Minutes* coverage of my "startling" revelations, a Book-of-the-Month Club contract, a miniseries deal with NBC, translation into six languages, book tours on three continents, featured roles in movie-star-studded AIDS fund raisers, regular appearances on network news shows, and hefty fees on the college lecture circuit. A central figure in my book became one of *People* magazine's "25 Most Intriguing People of 1987," even though he had been dead for nearly four years, and the *Los Angeles Herald Examiner* pronounced me one of the "in" authors of 1988. The mayor of San Francisco even proclaimed my birthday last year "Randy Shilts Day."

And one warm summer day as I was sunning at a gay resort in the redwoods north of San Francisco, a well-toned, perfectly tanned young man slid into a chaise next to me and offered the ultimate testimony to my fifteen minutes of fame. His dark eyelashes rising and falling shyly, he whispered, "When I saw you on *Good Morning America* a couple weeks ago, I wondered what it would be like to go to bed with you."

"You're the world's first AIDS celebrity," enthused a friend at the World Health Organization, after hearing one of WHO's most eminent AIDS authorities say he would grant me an interview on one condition — that I autograph his copy of my book. "It must be great," he said.

It's not so great.

The bitter irony is, my role as an AIDS celebrity just gives me a more elevated promontory from which to watch the world make the same mistakes in the handling of the AIDS epidemic that I had hoped my work would help to change. When I return from network tapings and celebrity glad-handing, I come back to my home in San Francisco's gay community and see friends dying. The lesions spread from their cheeks to cover their faces, their hair falls out, they die slowly, horribly, and sometimes suddenly, before anybody has a chance to know they're sick. They die in my arms and in my dreams, and nothing at all has changed.

Never before have I succeeded so well; never before have I failed so miserably.

I gave my first speech on the college lecture circuit at the University of 25 California at Los Angeles in January 1988. I told the audience that there were 50,000 diagnosed AIDS cases in the United States as of that week and that within a few months there would be more people suffering from this deadly disease in the United States than there were Americans killed during the Vietnam War. There were audible gasps. During the question-and-answer session, several students explained that they had heard that the number of AIDS cases in America was leveling off.

In the next speech, at the University of Tennessee, I decided to correct such misapprehension by adding the federal government's projections — the 270,000 expected to be dead or dying from AIDS in 1991, when the disease would kill more people than any single form of cancer, more than car accidents. When I spoke at St. Cloud State University in Minnesota three months later, I noted that the number of American AIDS cases had that week surpassed the Vietnam benchmark. The reaction was more a troubled murmur than a gasp.

By the time I spoke at New York City's New School for Social Research in June and there were 65,000 AIDS cases nationally, the numbers were changing so fast that the constant editing made my notes difficult to read. By then as many as 1,000 Americans a week were learning that they, too, had AIDS, or on the average, about one every fourteen minutes. There were new government projections to report, too: By 1993, some 450,000 Americans would be diagnosed with AIDS. In that year, one American will be diagnosed with the disease every thirty-six seconds. Again, I heard the gasps.

For my talk at a hospital administrators' conference in Washington in August, I started using little yellow stick-ons to update the numbers on my outline. That made it easier to read; there were now 72,000 AIDS cases. Probably this month, or next, I'll tell another college audience that the nation's AIDS case load has topped 100,000, and there will be gasps again.

The gasps always amaze me. Why are they surprised? In epidemics, people get sick and die. That's what epidemics do to people and that's why epidemics are bad.

When Kit Herman was diagnosed with AIDS on May 13, 1986, his doctor 30 leaned over his hospital bed, took his hand, and assured him, "Don't worry, you're in time for AZT." The drug worked so well that all Kit's friends let themselves think he might make it. And we were bolstered by the National Institutes of Health's assurance that AZT was only the first generation of

AIDS drugs, and that the hundreds of millions of federal dollars going into AIDS treatment research meant there would soon be a second and third generation of treatments to sustain life beyond AZT's effectiveness. Surely nothing was more important, considering the federal government's own estimates that between 1 and 1.5 million Americans were infected with the Human Immunodeficiency Virus (HIV), and virtually all would die within the next decade if nothing was done. The new drugs, the NIH assured everyone, were "in the pipeline," and government scientists were working as fast as they possibly could.

Despite my nagging, not one of dozens of public-affairs-show producers chose to look seriously into the development of those long-sought second and third generations of AIDS drugs. In fact, clinical trials of AIDS drugs were hopelessly stalled in the morass of bureaucracy at the NIH, but this story tip never seemed to cut it with producers. Clinical trials were not sexy. Clinical trials were boring.

I made my third *Nightline* appearance in January 1988 because new estimates had been released revealing that one in sixty-one babies born in New York City carried antibodies to the AIDS virus. And the link between those babies and the disease was intravenous drug use by one or both parents. Suddenly, junkies had become the group most likely to catch and spread AIDS through the heterosexual community. Free needles to junkies — now there was a sizzling television topic. I told the show's producers I'd talk about that, but that I was much more interested in the issue of AIDS treatments — which seemed most relevant to the night's program, since Ted Koppel's other guest was Dr. Anthony Fauci, associate NIH director for AIDS, and the Reagan administration's most visible AIDS official.

After fifteen minutes of talk on the ins and outs and pros and cons of free needles for intravenous drug users, I raised the subject of the pressing need for AIDS treatments. Koppel asked Fauci what was happening. The doctor launched into a discussion of treatments "in the pipeline" and how government scientists were working as fast as they possibly could.

I'd heard the same words from NIH officials for three years: Drugs were in the pipeline. Maybe it was true, but when were they going to come out of their goddamn pipeline? Before I could formulate a polite retort to Fauci's stall, however, the segment was over, Ted was thanking us, and the red light on the camera had blipped off. Everyone seemed satisfied that the government was doing everything it possibly could to develop AIDS treatments.

Three months later, I was reading a week-old *New York Times* in Kit's 35 room in the AIDS ward at San Francisco General Hospital. It was April, nearly two years after my friend's AIDS diagnosis. AZT had given him two years of nearly perfect health, but now its effect was wearing off, and Kit had suffered his first major AIDS-related infection since his original bout with pneumonia — cryptococcal meningitis. The meningitis could be treated, we all knew, but the discovery of this insidious brain infection meant more diseases were likely to follow. And the long-promised second and third generations of AIDS drugs were still nowhere on the horizon.

While perusing the worn copy of the *Times*, I saw a story about Dr. Fauci's testimony at a congressional hearing. After making Fauci swear an oath to tell the truth, a subcommittee headed by Congressman Ted Weiss of New York City asked why it was taking so long to get new AIDS treatments into testing at a time when Congress was putting hundreds of millions of dollars into NIH budgets for just such purposes. At first Fauci talked about unavoidable delays. He claimed government scientists were working as fast as they could. Pressed harder, he finally admitted that the problem stemmed "almost exclusively" from the lack of staffing in his agency. Congress had allocated funds, it was true, but the Reagan administration had gotten around spending the money by stingily refusing to let Fauci hire anybody. Fauci had requested 127 positions to speed the development of AIDS treatments; the administration had granted him eleven. And for a year, he had not told anyone. For a year, this spokesman for the public health answered reporters that AIDS drugs were in the pipeline and that government scientists had all the money they needed. It seemed that only when faced with the penalty of perjury would one of the administration's top AIDS officials tell the truth. That was the real story, I thought, but for some reason nobody else had picked up on it.

At the international AIDS conference in Stockholm two months later, the other reporters in "the AIDS pack" congratulated me on my success and asked what I was working on now. I admitted that I was too busy promoting the British and German release of my book to do much writing myself, and next month I had the Australian tour. But if I *were* reporting, I added with a vaguely conspiratorial tone, *I'd* look at the *scandal* in the NIH. Nobody had picked up that *New York Times* story from a few months ago about staffing shortages on AIDS clinical trials. The lives of 1.5 million HIV-infected Americans hung in the balance, and the only way you could get a straight answer out of an administration AIDS official was to put him under oath and make him face the charge of perjury. Where I went to journalism school, *that* was a news story.

One reporter responded to my tip with the question "But who's going to play *you* in the miniseries?"

A few minutes later, when Dr. Fauci came into the press room, the world's leading AIDS journalists got back to the serious business of transcribing his remarks. Nobody asked him if he was actually telling the truth, or whether they should put him under oath to ensure a candid response to the questions about when we'd get AIDS treatments. Most of the subsequent news accounts of Dr. Fauci's comments faithfully reported that many AIDS treatments were in the pipeline. Government scientists, he said once more, were doing all they possibly could.

The producer assured my publisher that Morton Downey, Jr., would be "serious" about AIDS. "He's not going to play games on this issue," the producer said, adding solemnly, "His brother has AIDS. He understands the need for compassion." The abundance of Mr. Downey's compassion was implicit in the night's call-in poll question: "Should all people with AIDS be quarantined?"

Downey's first question to me was, "You *are* a homosexual, aren't you?"

He wasn't ready for my canned answer: "Why do you ask? Do you want a date or something?"

The show shifted into an earnest discussion of quarantine. In his television studio, Clearasil-addled high school students from suburban New Jersey held up MORTON DOWNEY FAN CLUB signs and cheered aggressively when the truculent, chain-smoking host appeared to favor a kind of homespun AIDS Auschwitz. The youths shouted down any audience member who stepped forward to defend the rights of AIDS sufferers, their howls growing particularly vitriolic if the speakers were gay. These kids were the ilk from which Hitler drew his Nazi youth. In the first commercial break, the other guest, an AIDS activist, and I told Downey we would walk off the show if he didn't tone down his gay-baiting rhetoric. Smiling amiably, Downey took a long drag on his cigarette and assured us, "Don't worry, I have a fallback position."

That comment provided one of the most lucid moments in my year as an AIDS celebrity. Downey's "fallback position," it was clear, was the opposite of what he was promoting on the air. Of course, he didn't *really* believe that people with AIDS, people like his brother, should all be locked up. This was merely a deliciously provocative posture to exploit the working-class resentments of people who needed someone to hate. AIDS sufferers and gays would do for this week. Next week, if viewership dropped and Downey needed a new whipping boy, maybe he'd move on to Arabs, maybe Jews. It didn't seem to matter much to him, since he didn't believe what he was saying anyway. For Morton Downey, Jr., talking about AIDS was not an act of conscience; it was a ratings ploy. He knew it, he let his guests know it, his producers certainly knew it, and his television station knew it. The only people left out of the joke were his audience.

The organizers of the Desert AIDS Project had enlisted actor Kirk 45 Douglas and CBS morning anchor Kathleen Sullivan to be honorary co-chairs of the Palm Springs fund-raiser. The main events would include a celebrity tennis match pitting Douglas against Mayor Sonny Bono, and a $1,500-a-head dinner at which I would receive a Lucite plaque for my contributions to the fight against AIDS. The next morning I would fly to Los Angeles to speak at still another event, this one with Shirley MacLaine, Valerie Harper, and Susan Dey of *L.A. Law*.

The desert night was exquisite. There were 130 dinner guests, the personification of elegance and confidence, who gathered on a magnificent patio of chocolate-brown Arizona flagstone at the home of one of Palm Springs's most celebrated interior designers. A lot of people had come simply to see what was regarded as one of the most sumptuous dwellings in this sumptuous town.

When I was called to accept my reward, I began with the same lineup of jokes I use on talk shows and on the college lecture circuit. They work every time.

I told the crowd about how you get AIDS from a mosquito.

Kirk Douglas laughed; everybody laughed.

Next, I did the how-many-gay-waiters joke. 50

Kirk Douglas laughed; everybody laughed.

Then I mentioned the woman who asked whether she could get AIDS from a waiter ejaculating in her salad dressing.

That one always has my college audiences rolling in the aisles, so I paused for the expected hilarity.

But in the utter stillness of the desert night air, all that could be heard was the sound of Kirk Douglas's steel jaw dropping to the magnificent patio of chocolate-brown Arizona flagstone. The rest was silence.

"You've got to remember that most of these people came because they're 55 my clients," the host confided later. "You said that, and all I could think was how I'd have to go back to stitching slipcovers when this was done."

It turned out that there was more to my lead-balloon remark than a misjudged audience. Local AIDS organizers told me that a year earlier, a rumor that one of Palm Springs's most popular restaurants was owned by a homosexual, and that most of its waiters were gay, had terrified the elite community. Patronage at the eatery quickly plummeted, and it had nearly gone out of business. Fears that I dismissed as laughable were the genuine concerns of my audience, I realized. My San Francisco joke was a Palm Springs fable.

As I watched the busboys clear the tables later that night, I made a mental note not to tell that joke before dinner again. Never had I seen so many uneaten salads, so much wasted iceberg lettuce.

A friend had just tested antibody positive, and I was doing my best to cheer him up as we ambled down the sidewalk toward a Castro Street restaurant a few blocks from where I live in San Francisco. It seems most of my conversations now have to do with who has tested positive or lucked out and turned up negative, or who is too afraid to be tested. We had parked our car near Coming Home, the local hospice for AIDS patients and others suffering from terminal illnesses, and as we stepped around a nondescript, powder-blue van that blocked our path, two men in white uniforms emerged from the hospice's side door. They carried a stretcher, and on the stretcher was a corpse, neatly wrapped in a royal-blue blanket and secured with navy-blue straps. My friend and I stopped walking. The men quickly guided the stretcher into the back of the van, climbed in the front doors, and drove away. We continued our walk but didn't say anything.

I wondered if the corpse was someone I had known. I'd find out Thursday when the weekly gay paper came out. Every week there are at least two pages filled with obituaries of the previous week's departed. Each week, when I turn to those pages, I hold my breath, wondering whose picture I'll see. It's the only way to keep track, what with so many people dying.

Sometimes I wonder if an aberrant mother or two going to mass at the 60
Most Holy Redeemer Church across the street from Coming Home Hospice
has ever warned a child, "That's where you'll end up if you don't obey
God's law." Or whether some youngster, feeling that first awareness of a
different sexuality, has looked at the doorway of this modern charnel house
with an awesome, gnawing dread of annihilation.

"Is the limousine here? Where are the dancers?"

The room fell silent. Blake Rothaus had sounded coherent until that
moment, but he was near death now and his brain was going. We were
gathered around his bed in a small frame house on a dusty street in Oklahoma City. The twenty-four-year-old was frail and connected to life through
a web of clear plastic tubing. He stared up at us and seemed to recognize
from our looks that he had lapsed into dementia. A friend broke the uncom-
fortable silence.

"Of course, we all brought our dancing shoes," he said. "Nice fashionable
pumps at that. I wouldn't go out without them."

Everyone laughed and Blake Rothaus was lucid again.

Blake had gone to high school in a San Francisco suburb. When he was 65
a sophomore, he told us, he and his best friend sometimes skipped school,
sneaking to the city to spend their afternoons in the gay neighborhood
around Castro Street.

It's a common sight, suburban teenagers playing hooky on Castro Street.
I could easily imagine him standing on a corner not far from my house. But
back in 1982, when he was eighteen, I was already writing about a mysterious, unnamed disease that had claimed 330 victims in the United States.

Blake moved back to Oklahoma City with his family after he graduated
from high school. When he fell ill with AIDS, he didn't mope. Instead, he
started pestering Oklahoma health officials with demands to educate people
about this disease and to provide services for the sick. The state health
department didn't recoil. At the age of twenty-two, Blake Rothaus had
become the one-man nucleus for Oklahoma's first AIDS patient services. He
was the hero of the Sooner State's AIDS movement and something of a local
legend.

Though the state had reported only 250 AIDS cases, Oklahoma City had
a well-coordinated network of religious leaders, social workers, health-care
providers, gay-rights advocates, state legislators, and businessmen, all committed to providing a sane and humane response to this frightening new
disease.

"I think it's the old Dust Bowl mentality," suggested one AIDS organizer.
"When the hard times come, people pull together."

My past year's travels to twenty-nine states and talks with literally 70
thousands of people have convinced me of one thing about this country and
AIDS: Most Americans want to do the right thing about this epidemic. Some

might worry about mosquitoes and a few may be suspicious of their salad dressing. But beyond these fears is a reservoir of compassion and concern that goes vastly underreported by a media that needs conflict and heartlessness to fashion a good news hook.

In Kalamazoo, Michigan, when I visited my stepmother, I was buttonholed by a dozen middle-aged women who wondered anxiously whether we were any closer to a vaccine or a long-term treatment. One mentioned a hemophiliac nephew. Another had a gay brother in Chicago. A third went to a gay hairdresser who, she quickly added, was one of the finest people you'd ever meet. When I returned to my conservative hometown of Aurora, Illinois, nestled among endless fields of corn and soy, the local health department told me they receive more calls than they know what to do with from women's groups, parishes, and community organizations that want to do something to help. In New Orleans, the archconservative, pro-nuke, antigay bishop had taken up the founding of an AIDS hospice as a personal mission because, he said, when people are sick, you've got to help them out.

Scientists, reporters, and politicians privately tell me that of course *they* want to do more about AIDS, but they have to think about the Morton Downeys of the world, who argue that too much research or too much news space or too much official sympathy is being meted out to a bunch of miscreants. They do as much as they can, they insist; more would rile the resentments of the masses. So the institutions fumble along, convinced they must pander to the lowest common denominator, while the women and men of America's heartland pull me aside to fret about a dying cousin or co-worker and to plead, "When will there be a cure? When will this be over?"

"I think I'll make it through this time," Kit said to me, "but I don't have it in me to go through it again."

We were in room 3 in San Francisco General Hospital's ward 5A, the AIDS ward. The poplar trees outside Kit's window were losing their leaves, and the first winter's chill was settling over the city. I was preparing to leave for my fourth and, I hoped, final media tour, this time for release of the book in paperback and on audiocassette; Kit was preparing to die.

The seizures had started a week earlier, indicating he was suffering either from toxoplasmosis, caused by a gluttonous protozoa that sets up housekeeping in the brain; or perhaps it was a relapse of cryptococcal meningitis; or, another specialist guessed, it could be one of those other nasty brain infections that nobody had seen much of until the past year. Now that AIDS patients were living longer, they fell victim to even more exotic infections than in the early days. But the seizures were only part of it. Kit had slowly been losing the sight in his left eye to a herpes infection. And the Kaposi's sarcoma lesions that had scarred his face were beginning to coat the inside of his lungs. When Kit mentioned he'd like to live until Christmas, the doctors said he might want to consider having an early celebration this year, because he wasn't going to be alive in December.

"I can't take another infection," Kit said.

"What does that mean?"

"Morphine," Kit answered, adding mischievously, "lots of it."

We talked briefly about the mechanics of suicide. We both knew people who'd made a mess of it, and people who had done it right. It was hardly the first time the subject had come up in conversation for either of us. Gay men facing AIDS now exchange formulas for suicide as casually as housewives swap recipes for chocolate-chip cookies.

Kit was released from the hospital a few days later. He had decided to take his life on a Tuesday morning. I had to give my first round of interviews in Los Angeles that day, so I stopped on the way to the airport to say good-bye on Monday. All day Tuesday, while I gave my perfectly formed sound bites in a round of network radio appearances, I wondered: Is this the moment he's slipping out of consciousness and into that perfect darkness? When I called that night, it turned out he'd delayed his suicide until Thursday to talk to a few more relatives. I had to give a speech in Portland that day, so on the way to the airport I stopped again. He showed me the amber-brown bottle with the bubble-gum-pink morphine syrup, and we said another good-bye.

The next morning, Kit drank his morphine and fell into a deep sleep. That afternoon, he awoke and drowsily asked what time it was. When told it was five hours later, he murmured, "That's amazing. I should have been dead hours ago."

And then he went back to sleep.

That night, Kit woke up again.

"You know what they say about near-death experiences? he asked. "Going toward the light?"

Shaking his head, he sighed. "No light. Nothing."

His suicide attempt a failure, Kit decided the timing of his death would now be up to God. I kept up on the bizarre sequence of events by phone and called as soon as I got back to San Francisco. I was going to tell Kit that his theme song should be "Never Can Say Good-bye," but then the person on the other end of the phone told me that Kit had lapsed into a coma.

The next morning, he died.

Kit's death was like everything about AIDS — anticlimactic. By the time he actually did die, I was almost beyond feeling.

The next day, I flew to Boston for the start of the paperback tour, my heart torn between rage and sorrow. All week, as I was chauffeured to my appearances on *Good Morning America*, *Larry King Live*, and various CNN shows, I kept thinking, It's all going to break. I'm going to be on a TV show with some officious government health spokesman lying to protect his job, and I'm going to start shouting, "You lying son of a bitch. Don't you know there are people, real people, people I love out there dying?" Or I'll be on a call-in show and another mother will phone about her thirty-seven-year-old son who just died and it will hit me all at once, and I'll start weeping.

But day after day as the tour went on, no matter how many official lies I heard and how many grieving mothers I talked to, the crack-up never occurred. All my answers came out rationally in tight little sound bites about institutional barriers to AIDS treatments and projections about 1993 case loads.

By the last day of the tour, when a limousine picked me up at my Beverly Hills hotel for my last round of satellite TV interviews, I knew I had to stop. In a few weeks I'd return to being national correspondent for the *Chronicle,* and it was time to get off the AIDS celebrity circuit, end the interviews and decline the invitations to the star-studded fund raisers, and get back to work as a newspaper reporter. That afternoon, there was just one last radio interview to a call-in show in the San Fernando Valley, and then it would be over.

The first caller asked why his tax money should go toward funding an AIDS cure when people got the disease through their own misdeeds.

I used my standard jukebox answer about how most cancer cases are linked to people's behavior but that nobody ever suggested we stop trying to find a cure for cancer.

A second caller phoned to ask why her tax money should go to finding an AIDS cure when these people clearly deserved what they got.

I calmly put a new spin on the same answer, saying in America you 95 usually don't sentence people to die for having a different lifestyle from yours.

Then a third caller phoned in to say that he didn't care if all those queers and junkies died, as did a fourth and fifth and sixth caller. By then I was shouting, "You stupid bigot. You just want to kill off everybody you don't like. You goddamn Nazi."

The talk-show host sat in stunned silence. She'd heard I was so *reasonable.* My anger baited the audience further, and the seventh and eighth callers began talking about "you guys," as if only a faggot like myself could give a shit about whether AIDS patients all dropped dead tomorrow.

In their voices, I heard the reporters asking polite questions of NIH officials. Of course, they had to be polite to the government doctors; dying queers weren't anything to lose your temper over. I heard the dissembling NIH researchers go home to their wives at night, complain about the lack of personnel, and shrug; this was just how it was going to have to be for a while. They'd excuse their inaction by telling themselves that if they went public and lost their jobs, worse people would replace them. It was best to go along. But how would they feel if *their* friends, *their* daughters, were dying of this disease? Would they be silent — or would they shout? Maybe they'll forgive me for suspecting they believed that ultimately a bunch of fags weren't worth losing a job over. And when I got home, I was going to have to watch my friends get shoved into powder-blue vans, and it wasn't going to change.

The history of the AIDS epidemic, of yesterday and of today, was echoing in the voices of those callers. And I was screaming at them, and the show host just sat there stunned, and I realized I had rendered myself utterly and completely inarticulate.

I stopped, took a deep breath, and returned to compound-complex sen- 100
tences about the American tradition of compassion and the overriding need
to overcome institutional barriers to AIDS treatments.

When I got home to San Francisco that night, I looked over some notes
I had taken from a conversation I'd had with Kit during his last stay in the
hospital. I was carping about how frustrated I was at the prospect of returning to my reporting job. If an internationally acclaimed best seller hadn't
done shit to change the world, what good would mere newspaper stories do?

"The limits of information," Kit said. "There's been a lot written on it."

"Oh," I said.

Kit closed his eyes briefly and faded into sleep while plastic tubes fed
him a cornucopia of antibiotics. After five minutes, he stirred, looked up,
and added, as if we had never stopped talking, "But you don't really have
a choice. You've got to keep on doing it. What else are you going to do?"

AFTERWORD

*When you develop a mortal disease, you start to hear the Aunt Bertha stories.
Say you develop heart cancer. Two-thirds of your friends, it turns out, have an Aunt
Bertha still plugging along at ninety-seven, eighty years after she first developed the
disease. The other third, possibly not your best friends, had an Aunt Bertha who
died thirty minutes after diagnosis and passed the disease to her relatives.*

*The health industry's harshest description of medical talk is "anecdotal." Stories
of remissions caused by peach pits, or by diets of honey and celery juice, are
anecdotal. They are not medical studies with scrupulous monitoring, exact records,
and control groups.*

An essay is not medical research, and Esquire, *where this essay appeared, is not
the* New England Journal of Medicine. *In "Talking AIDS to Death," the author
tells stories out of his book tour, and out of his continuing experience of the disease
among his friends. Shilts uses a popular publication to promote his purposes: to raise
concern, to stimulate action.*

*With skill he mixes horror and humor. Starting in italics with a nightmare (note
how gently he identifies the paragraph's source, three paragraphs later), he uses the
narrative of his tour to tell amusing stories that dispel ignorance. He weaves together
anecdotes of public ignorance with descriptions of the plague and its misery in the
daily life of his city and his friends.*

*As a laboratory defines proof, anecdotes prove nothing. For the truth of observa-
tion, for compassion's emotional truth, assemble a clutch of well-told stories.*

BOOKS AVAILABLE IN PAPERBACK

And the Band Played On: Politics, People, and the AIDS Epidemic. New York: Penguin. *Nonfiction.*

Conduct Unbecoming: Gays and Lesbians in the U.S. Military. New York: Fawcett. *Nonfiction.*

The Mayor of Castro Street: The Life and Times of Harvey Milk. New York: St. Martin's Press. *Nonfiction.*

CHARLES
SIMIC

*C*HARLES SIMIC (b. 1938) left Yugoslavia when he was fifteen years old and has become a leading American poet. He has written three books of essays — The Uncertain Certainty (1985), Wonderful Words, Silent Truth (1990), and The Unemployed Fortune Teller (1994). Simic wrote "The Spider's Web" in 1993, when the tripartite (Serb, Croat, Muslim) conflict in Yugoslavia had already raged for two years. His book on Joseph Cornell's art is Dime-Store Alchemy (1992). A book of poems, The World Doesn't End, won the 1990 Pulitzer Prize, and he has received fellowships from the Guggenheim Foundation, the National Endowment for the Arts, and the MacArthur Foundation. A Wedding in Hell (1994) is his seventeenth book of poems. He lives in New Hampshire, fleeing from time to time to Paris and other European cities.

The Spider's Web

Mistaken ideas always end in bloodshed, but in every case it is someone else's blood. This is why our thinkers feel free to say just about
everything.

— ALBERT CAMUS

In a letter to Hannah Arendt,° Karl Jaspers° describes how the philosopher Spinoza used to amuse himself by placing flies in a spider's web, then
adding two spiders so he could watch them fight over the flies. "Very strange
and difficult to interpret," concludes Jaspers. As it turns out, this was the
only time the otherwise somber philosopher was known to laugh.

A friend from Yugoslavia called me about a year ago and said: "Charlie,
why don't you come home and hate with your own people?" I knew he was
pulling my leg, but I was shocked nevertheless. I told him that I was never
very good at hating, that I've managed to loathe a few individuals here and
there, but have never managed to progress to hating whole peoples.

"In that case," he replied, "you're missing out on the greatest happiness
one can have in life."

I'm surprised that there is no History of Stupidity. I envision a work of
many volumes, encyclopedic, cumulative, with an index listing millions of
names. I only have to think about history for a moment or two before I
realize the absolute necessity of such a book. I do not underestimate the
influence of religion, nationalism, economics, personal ambition and even
chance on events, but the historian who does not admit that men are also
fools has not really understood his subject.

Watching Yugoslavia dismember itself, for instance, is like watching a   5
man mutilate himself in public. He has already managed to make himself
legless, armless and blind, and now in his frenzy he's struggling to tear his
heart out with his teeth. Between bites, he shouts to us that he is a martyr
for a holy cause, but we know that he is mad, that he is monstrously stupid.

It required no extraordinary wisdom to predict this tragedy. If our own
specialists in ethnic pride in the United States ever start shouting that they
can't live with each other, we can expect the same bloodshed to follow. For
that reason, what amazed me in the case of Yugoslavia was the readiness
with which American intellectuals accepted as legitimate the claim of every

---

Hannah Arendt German-American political scientist and philosopher (1906–1975)
known for her study of totalitarianism.

Karl Jaspers German philosopher (1883–1969) considered to be a prominent existen-
tialist thinker.

nationalist there. The desirability of breaking up into ethnic and religious states a country that had existed since 1918 and that had complicated internal and outside agreements was welcomed with unreserved enthusiasm by everybody from the *New York Times* to the German government. It probably takes much longer to get a Kentucky Fried Chicken franchise than it took to convince the world that Yugoslavia should be replaced by as many little states as the natives desire.

What are you? Americans ask me. I explain that I was born in Belgrade, that I left when I was fifteen, that we always thought of ourselves as Yugoslavs, that for the last thirty years I have been translating Serbian, Croatian, Slovenian, and Macedonian poets into English, that whatever differences I found among these people delighted me and that I couldn't care less about any of these nationalist leaders and their programs.

"Oh, so you're a Serb!" they exclaim triumphantly.

Over the last forty years I've known Russians, Yugoslavs, Hungarians, Poles, Argentinians, Chinese, Iranians, and a dozen other nationalities, all refugees from murderous regimes. The only people of honor on the whole planet. This summer in Paris and Amsterdam I met more "traitors," men and women who refused to identify themselves with various nationalist groups in Yugoslavia. They wanted to remain free of tribal pieties and that was their heresy. They are the other orphans of that civil war. (Five of us were sitting in the Brasserie Cluny in Paris writing a protest letter to Milošević and arguing about the wording when one member of our group remembered that Tito had conducted his illegal business for the Comintern in the same brasserie before the war. Does this crap ever end? someone wondered aloud.)

The destruction of Vukovar and Sarajevo will not be forgiven the Serbs. 10 Whatever moral credit they had as the result of their history they squandered by these two acts. The suicidal and abysmal idiocy of nationalism is revealed here better than anywhere else. No human being or group of people has the right to pass a death sentence on a city. "Defend your own, but respect what others have," my grandfather used to say, and he was a highly decorated officer in the First World War and certainly a Serbian patriot. I imagine he would have agreed with me. There will be no happy future for people who have made the innocent suffer.

Here is something we can all count on. Sooner or later our tribe always comes to ask us to agree to murder.

"In the hour of need you walked away from your own people," a fellow I know said to me when I turned down the invitation. True. I refused to turn my conscience over to the leader of the pack. I continued stubbornly to believe in more than one truth. Only the individual is real, I kept saying over and over again. I praised the outcast, the pariah, while my people were offering me an opportunity to become a part of a mystic whole. I insisted on remaining aloof, self-absorbed, lovingly nursing my suspicions.

"For whom does your poetry speak when you have no tribe anywhere you can call your own?" my interlocutor wanted to know.

"The true poet is never a member of any tribe," I shouted back. "It is his refusal of his birthright that makes him a poet and an individual worth respecting." I explained.

This wasn't true, of course. Many of the greatest poets in the history of the world have been fierce nationalists. The sole function of the epic poet is to find excuses for the butcheries of the innocent. In our big and comfy family bed today's murderers will sleep like little babies is what they are always saying.

On the other side are the poets who trust only the solitary human voice. The lyric poet is almost by definition a traitor to his own people. He is the stranger who speaks that harsh truth that only individual lives are unique and therefore sacred. He may be loved by his people, but his example is also the one to be warned against. The tribe must pull together to face the invading enemy while the lyric poet sits talking to the skull in the graveyard. For that reason he deserves to be exiled, put to death, and remembered.

The terrifying thing about modern intellectuals everywhere is that they are always changing idols. At least religious fanatics stick mostly to what they believe in. All the rabid nationalists in Eastern Europe were Marxists yesterday and Stalinists last week. The freedom of the individual has never been their concern. They were after bigger fish. The sufferings of the world are an ideal chance for all intellectuals to have an experience of tragedy and to fulfill their utopian longings. If, in the meantime, one comes to share the views of some mass murderer, the ends justify the means. Modern tyrants have had some of the most illustrious literary salons.

Nationalism, as much as communism, provides an opportunity to rewrite history. The problem with true history and great literature is that they wallow in ambiguities, unresolved issues, nuances, and baffling contradictions. Let's not kid ourselves, the Manichean view of the world is much more satisfying. Any revision of history is acceptable provided it gives us some version of the struggle between angels and devils. If, in reality, this means dividing murderers in Yugoslavia into good and bad, so be it. If it means weeping from one eye at the death of a Muslim woman and winking from the other at the death of her Orthodox husband, that's the secret attraction of simple plots.

American media, too, treat complexity the way Victorians treated sexuality — as something from which the viewer and the reader need to be protected. In the case of Yugoslavia, where nothing is simple, the consequences are more evil. Our columnists and intellectuals often have views identical to those of their nationalist counterparts in various regions of that country. It's as if in an age of P.C., they miss having someone to hate. The democratic forces in Yugoslavia can expect nothing from our side. At home they'll be treated as traitors, and abroad their version of events will be greeted with silence for making the plot too complicated.

So what's to be done? people rightly ask. I've no idea. As an elegist I 20
mourn and expect the worst. Vileness and stupidity always have a rosy
future. The world is still a few evils short, but they'll come. Dark despair is
the only healthy outlook if you identify yourself with the flies, as I do. If,
however, you secretly think of yourself as one of the spiders, or, God forbid,
as the laughing philosopher himself, you have much less to worry about.
Since you'll be on the winning side, you can always rewrite history and
claim you were flies. Elegies in a spider's web is all we bona fide flies get.
That and the beauty of sunrise, like some unexpected touch of the execu-
tioner's final courtesy the day they take us out to be slaughtered. In the
meantime, my hope is very modest. Let's have a true cease-fire for once, so
the old lady can walk out into the rubble and find her cat.

AFTERWORD

*Living in New Hampshire, watching the news, in touch with old friends in the
former Yugoslavia, Simic had to write about warfare among the tribes of his old
country. He published the essay first in a Polish newspaper, and the* New Republic
reprinted it.

*How does one speak, or write, about the monstrosity of events in Bosnia?
Murderous partisanship, alas, never lacks for words, however much it lacks for sense.
Simic's impartial outrage finds its theme in contempt for human history. "The
historian who does not admit that men are . . . fools has not really understood his
subject." Contempt is not indifference; Simic's outrage is passion on behalf of human
intelligence. The only people of honor on this planet, he tells us, are the traitors —
whose treachery has denied "the suicidal and abysmal idiocy of nationalism." Many
of his sentences might be carved into stone in public places: "I refused to turn my
conscience over to the leader of the pack." "Only the individual is real." "The true
poet is never a member of any tribe."*

*But then Simic says, "This wasn't true, of course." His honesty will not allow
him to stand by his own ringing words; he refuses to become fanatic even in his
denunciation of fanaticism. In this essay of outrage, Simic's humor — as black as it
is funny, the same as his poems — allows him to speak with decision and clarity
while keeping the voice of a human being.*

*If "vileness and stupidity always have a rosy future," the solitary thinker may
ask only for modest resolutions: "A true cease-fire for once" may allow an old lady
to "walk out into the rubble and find her cat."*

BOOKS AVAILABLE IN PAPERBACK

Austerities. New York: George Braziller. *Poetry.*

The Book of Gods and Devils. San Diego: Harcourt Brace Jovanovich. *Poetry.*

The Chicken Without a Head: A New Version. Portland, Oreg.: Trace. *Poetry.*

Classic Ballroom Dances. New York: George Braziller. *Poetry.*

Dime-Store Alchemy: The Art of Joseph Cornell. Hopewell, N.J.: Ecco Press. *Nonfiction.*

Dismantling the Silence. New York: George Braziller. *Poetry.*

Nine Poems: A Childhood Story. Cambridge, Mass.: Exact Change.

Selected Poems, 1963–1983. New York: George Braziller.

The Uncertain Certainty: Interviews, Essays and Notes on Poetry. Ann Arbor: University of Michigan Press.

Unending Blues: Poems. San Diego: Harcourt Brace Jovanovich.

Weather Forecast for Utopia & Vicinity: 1967–1982. Barrytown, N.Y.: Station Hill Press. *Poetry.*

Wonderful Words, Silent Truth: Essays on Poetry and Memoir. Ann Arbor: University of Michigan Press.

The World Doesn't End: Prose Poems. San Diego: Harcourt Brace Jovanovich.

GARY SOTO

GARY SOTO was born in Fresno (1952) and teaches at the University of California in Berkeley. He has published many books of poems, including The Elements of San Joaquin *(1977),* Black Hair *(1985), and* Home Course in Religion: New Poems *(1991). More recently Soto has written essays, usually reminiscent, out of his Chicano childhood:* Living Up the Street *(1985),* Small Faces *(1986), and* A Summer Life *(1990).*

what about mental aspect of physical labor —

*mental discipline to go every morning
learning the job — differentiating between tires —*

Black Hair
But within weeks. . . . (522)

*1st sentence leads reader to believe that writer is going to make
some kind of commentary on the 2 forms of "work" going to make
only discusses the latter, why bring up the first*

There are two kinds of work: One uses the mind and the other uses muscle. As a kid I found out about the latter. I'm thinking of the summer of 1969 when I was a seventeen-year-old runaway who ended up in Glendale, California, working for Valley Tire Factory. To answer an ad in the newspaper I walked miles in the afternoon sun, my stomach slowly knotting on a doughnut that was breakfast, my teeth like bright candles gone yellow.

I walked in the door sweating and feeling ugly because my hair was still stiff from a swim at the Santa Monica beach the day before. Jules, the accountant and part owner, looked droopily through his bifocals at my application and then at me. He tipped his cigar in the ashtray, asked my age

*— perhaps alludes to a division in his own life — thinks
of youth as physically laborious and then moved into
mental work*

Photo by Carolyn Soto

— last sentence captures reader's attention — misery

as if he didn't believe I was seventeen, but finally, after a moment of silence, said, "Come back tomorrow. Eight-thirty."

I thanked him, left the office, and went around to the chain-link fence to watch the workers heave tires into a bin; others carted uneven stacks of tires on hand trucks. Their faces were black from tire dust, and when they talked — or cussed — their mouths showed a bright pink.

From there I walked up a commercial street, past a cleaners, a motorcycle shop, and a gas station where I washed my face and hands; before leaving I took a bottle that hung on the side of the Coke machine, filled it with water, and stopped it with a scrap of paper and a rubber band.

The next morning I arrived early at work. The assistant foreman, a 5 potbellied Hungarian, showed me a time card and how to punch in. He showed me the Coke machine and the locker room with its slimy shower, and also pointed out the places where I shouldn't go: the ovens where the tires were recapped and the customer service area, which had a slashed couch, a coffee table with greasy magazines, and an ashtray. He introduced me to Tully, a fat man with one ear who worked the buffers that resurfaced the whitewalls. I was handed an apron and a face mask and shown how to use the buffer: Lift the tire and center it, inflate it with a foot pedal, press the buffer against the white band until cleaned, and then deflate and blow off the tire with an air hose.

With a paintbrush he stirred a can of industrial preserver. "Then slap this blue stuff on." While he was talking a coworker came up quietly behind him and goosed him with the air hose. Tully jumped as if he had been struck by a bullet and then turned around cussing and cupping his genitals in his hands as the other worker walked away calling out foul names. When Tully turned to me, smiling his gray teeth, I lifted my mouth into a smile because I wanted to get along. He has to be on my side, I thought. He's the one who'll tell the foreman how I'm doing.

I worked carefully that day, setting the tires on the machine as if they were babies, because it was easy to catch a finger in the rim that expanded to inflate the tire. At the day's end we swept up the tire dust and emptied the trash into bins.

At five the workers scattered for their cars and motorcycles while I crossed the street to wash at a burger stand. My hair was stiff with dust and my mouth showed pink against the backdrop of my dirty face. I ordered a hotdog and walked slowly in the direction of the abandoned house where I had stayed the night before. I lay under the trees and within minutes was asleep. When I woke my shoulders were sore, and my eyes burned when I squeezed the lids together.

From the backyard I walked dully through a residential street, and as evening came on, the TV glare in the living rooms and the headlights of passing cars showed against the blue drift of dusk. I saw two children coming up the street with snow cones, their tongues darting at the packed ice. I saw a boy with a peach and wanted to stop him but felt embarrassed by my hunger. I walked for an hour, only to return and discover the house lit brightly. Behind the fence I heard voices and saw a flashlight poking at the garage door. A man on the back steps mumbled something about the refrigerator to the one with the flashlight.

I waited for them to leave but had the feeling they wouldn't because there was a commotion of furniture being moved. Tired, even more desperate, I started walking again with a great urge to kick things and tear the day from my life. I felt weak and my mind kept drifting because of hunger. I crossed the street to a gas station where I sipped at the water fountain and searched the Coke machine for change. I started walking again, first up a commercial street, then into a residential area where I lay down on someone's lawn and replayed a scene at home — my mother crying at the kitchen table, my stepfather yelling with food in his mouth. They're cruel, I thought, and warned myself that I should never forgive them. How could they do this to me?

When I got up from the lawn it was late. I searched out a place to sleep and found an unlocked car that seemed safe. In the backseat, with my shoes off, I fell asleep but woke up startled about four in the morning when the owner, a nurse on her way to work, opened the door. She got in and was about to start the engine when I raised my head to explain my presence. She screamed so loudly when I said "I'm sorry" that I sprinted from the car with my shoes in hand. Her screams faded, then stopped altogether, as I ran down the block, hid behind a trash bin, and waited for a police siren to sound. Nothing. I crossed the street to a church where I slept stiffly on cardboard in the balcony.

I woke up feeling tired and greasy. It was early and a few streetlights were still lit, the east growing pink with dawn. I washed myself from a garden hose and returned to the church to break into what looked like a kitchen. Paper cups, plastic spoons, a coffee pot littered on a table. I found a box of Nabisco crackers and ate until I was full.

At work I spent the morning at the buffer, but was then told to help Iggy, an old Mexican who was responsible for choosing tires that could be recapped without the risk of exploding at high speeds. Every morning a truck would deliver used tires, and after I unloaded them Iggy would step among the tires to inspect them for punctures and rips on the sidewalls.

With yellow chalk he marked circles and Xs to indicate damage and called out "junk." Tires that could be recapped got a "goody" from Iggy, and I placed them on my hand truck. When I had a stack of eight I kicked the truck at an angle and balanced off to another work area, where Iggy again inspected the tires, scratching Xs and calling out "junk."

Iggy worked only until three in the afternoon, at which time he went to the locker room to wash and shave and to dress in a two-piece suit. When he came out he glowed with a bracelet, watch, rings, and a shiny fountain pen in his breast pocket. His shoes sounded against the asphalt. He was the image of a banker stepping into sunlight with millions on his mind. He said a few low words to workers with whom he was friendly and none to people like me.

I was seventeen, stupid because I couldn't figure out the difference between an F78 14 and a 750 14 at sight. Iggy shook his head when I brought him the wrong tires, especially since I had expressed interest in being his understudy. "Mexican, how can you be so stupid?" he would yell at me, slapping a tire from my hands. But within weeks I learned a lot about tires, from sizes and makes to how they are molded in iron forms to how Valley stole from other companies. Now and then we received a truckload of tires, most of them new or nearly new, and they were taken to our warehouse in the back, where the serial numbers were ground off with a sander. On those days the foreman handed out Cokes and joked with us as we worked to get the numbers off.

Most of the workers were Mexican or black, though a few redneck whites worked there. The base pay was a dollar sixty-five but the average was three dollars. Of the black workers, I knew Sugar Daddy the best. His body carried 250 pounds and armfuls of scars, and he had a long knife that made me jump when he brought it out from his boot without warning. At one time he had been a singer and had cut a record in 1967 called *Love's Chance*, which broke into the R & B charts. But nothing came of it. No big contract, no club dates, no tours. He made very little from record sales, only enough for an operation to pull a steering wheel from his gut when, drunk and mad at a lady friend, he slammed his Mustang into a row of parked cars.

"Touch it," he smiled at me one afternoon as he raised his shirt, his black belly kinked with hair. Scared, I traced the scar that ran from his chest to the left of his belly button, and I was repelled but hid my disgust.

Among the Mexicans I had few friends because I was different, a *pocho*° who spoke bad Spanish. At lunch they sat in tires and laughed over burritos, looking up at me to laugh even harder. I also sat in tires while nursing a Coke and felt dirty and sticky because I was still living on the street and had not had a real bath in over a week. Nevertheless, when the border patrol came to round up the nationals, I ran with them as they scrambled for the fence or hid among the tires behind the warehouse. The foreman, who thought I was an undocumented worker, yelled at me to run, to get away. I did just that. At the time it seemed fun because there was no risk, only a good-hearted feeling of hide-and-seek, and besides, it meant an hour away from work on company time. When the police left we came back, and some of the nationals made up stories of how they were almost caught — how they outraced the police. Some of the stories were so convoluted and unconvincing that everyone laughed and shouted *"mentiras,"*° especially when one described how he overpowered a policeman, took his gun away, and sold the patrol car. We laughed and he laughed, happy to be there to make up such a story.

---

pocho Mexican slang meaning "outsider."
mentiras Spanish: "lies."

If work was difficult, so were the nights. I still had not gathered enough 20 money to rent a room, so I spent the nights sleeping in parked cars or in the church balcony. After a week I found a newspaper ad for a room for rent, phoned, and was given directions. Finished with work, I walked the five miles down Mission Road looking back into the traffic with my thumb out. No rides. After eight hours of handling tires I was frightening to drivers, I suppose, since they seldom looked at me; if they did, it was a quick glance. For the next six weeks I would try to hitchhike, but the only person to stop was a Mexican woman who gave me two dollars to take the bus. I told her it was too much and that no bus ran from Mission Road to where I lived, but she insisted that I keep the money and trotted back to her idling car. It must have hurt her to see me day after day walking in the heat and looking very much the dirty Mexican to the many minds that didn't know what it meant to work at hard labor. That woman knew. Her eyes met mine as she opened the car door, and there was a tenderness that was surprisingly true — one for which you wait for years but when it comes it doesn't help. Nothing changes. You continue on in rags, with the sun still above you.

I rented a room from a middle-aged couple whose lives were a mess. She was a schoolteacher and he was a fireman. A perfect setup, I thought. But during my stay there they would argue for hours in their bedroom.

When I rang at the front door both Mr. and Mrs. Van Deusen answered and didn't bother to disguise their shock at how awful I looked. But they let me in all the same. Mrs. Van Deusen showed me around the house, from the kitchen and bathroom to the living room with its grand piano. On her fingers she counted out the house rules as she walked me to my room. It was a girl's room with lace curtains, scenic wallpaper of a Victorian couple enjoying a stroll, a canopied bed, and stuffed animals in a corner. Leaving, she turned and asked if she could do laundry for me. Feeling shy and hurt, I told her no; perhaps the next day. She left and I undressed to take a bath, exhausted as I sat on the edge of the bed probing my aches and my bruised places. With a towel around my waist I hurried down the hallway to the bathroom where Mrs. Van Deusen had set out an additional towel with a tube of shampoo. I ran water into the tub and sat on the closed toilet, watching the steam curl toward the ceiling. When I lowered myself into the tub I felt my body sting. I soaped a washcloth and scrubbed my arms until they lightened, even glowed pink, but I still looked unwashed around my neck and face no matter how hard I rubbed. Back in the room I sat in bed reading a magazine, happy and thinking of no better luxury than a girl's sheets, especially after nearly two weeks of sleeping on cardboard at the church.

I was too tired to sleep, so I sat at the window watching the neighbors move about in pajamas, and, curious about the room, looked through the bureau drawers to search out personal things — snapshots, a messy diary, and high-school yearbook. I looked up the Van Deusen's daughter, Barbara, and studied her face as if I recognized her from my own school — a face that said "promise," "college," "nice clothes in the closet." She was a skater and a member of the German Club; her greatest ambition was to sing at the Hollywood Bowl.

After a while I got into bed, and as I drifted toward sleep I thought about her. In my mind I played a love scene again and again and altered it slightly each time. She comes home from college and at first is indifferent to my presence in her home, but finally I overwhelm her with deep pity when I come home hurt from work, with blood on my shirt. Then there was another version: Home from college she is immediately taken with me, in spite of my work-darkened face, and invites me into the family car for a milkshake across town. Later, back at the house, we sit in the living room talking about school until we're so close I'm holding her hand. The truth of the matter was that Barbara did come home for a week but was bitter toward her parents for taking in boarders (two others besides me). During that time she spoke to me only twice: Once, while searching the refrigerator, she asked if we had any mustard; the other time she asked if I had seen her car keys.

But it was a place to stay. Work had become more and more difficult. I   25
worked not only with Iggy but also with the assistant foreman, who was in charge of unloading trucks. After they backed in I hopped on top to pass the tires down, bouncing them on the tailgate to give them an extra spring so they would be less difficult to handle on the other end. Each truck was weighted down with more than two hundred tires, each averaging twenty pounds, so that by the time the truck was emptied and swept clean I glistened with sweat and my T-shirt stuck to my body. I blew snot threaded with tire dust onto the asphalt, indifferent to the customers who watched from the waiting room.

The days were dull. I did what there was to do from morning until the bell sounded at five; I tugged, pulled, and cussed at tires until I was listless and my mind drifted and caught on small things, from cold sodas to shoes to stupid talk about what we would do with a million dollars. I remember unloading a truck with Hamp, a black man.

"What's better than a sharp lady?" he asked me as I stood sweaty on a pile of junked tires. "Water. With ice," I said.

He laughed with his mouth open wide. With his fingers he pinched the sweat from his chin and flicked at me. "You be too young, boy. A woman can make you a god."

As a kid I had chopped cotton and picked grapes, so I knew work. I knew the fatigue and the boredom and the feeling that there was a good possibility that you might have to do such work for years, if not for a lifetime. In fact, as a kid I had imagined a dark fate: to marry Mexican poor, work Mexican hours, and in the end die a Mexican death, broke and in despair.

But this job at Valley Tire Company confirmed that there was something   30
worse than fieldwork, and I was doing it. We were all doing it, from the foreman to the newcomers like me, and what I felt heaving tires for eight hours a day was felt by everyone — black, Mexican, redneck. We all de-

spised those hours but didn't know what else to do. The workers were unskilled, some undocumented and fearful of deportation, and all struck with uncertainty at what to do with their lives. Although everyone bitched about work, no one left. Some had worked there for twelve years; some had sons working there. Few quit; no one was ever fired. It amazed me that no one gave up when the border patrol jumped from their vans, batons in hand, because I couldn't imagine any work that could be worse — or any life. What was out there, in the world, that made men run for the fence in fear?

Iggy was the only worker who seemed sure of himself. After five hours of "junking," he brushed himself off, cleaned up in the washroom, and came out gleaming with an elegance that humbled the rest of us. Few would look him straight in the eye or talk to him in our usual stupid way because he was so much better. He carried himself as a man should — with Old World "dignity" — while the rest of us muffed our jobs and talked dully about dull things as we worked. From where he worked in his open shed he would now and then watch us with his hands on his hips. He would shake his head and click his tongue in disgust.

The rest of us lived dismally. I often wondered what the others' homes were like; I couldn't imagine that they were much better than our workplace. No one indicated that his outside life was interesting or intriguing. We all looked defeated and contemptible in our filth at the day's end. I imagined the average welcome at home: Rafael, a Mexican national who had worked at Valley for five years, returned to a beaten house full of kids dressed in mismatched clothes and playing kick the can. As for Sugar Daddy, he returned home to a stuffy room where he would read and reread old magazines. He ate potato chips, drank beer, and watched TV. There was no grace in dipping socks into a washbasin where later he would wash his cup and plate.

There was no grace at work. It was all ridicule. The assistant foreman drank Cokes in front of the newcomers as they laced tires in the afternoon sun. Knowing that I had a long walk home, Rudy, the college student, passed me waving and yelling "Hello" as I started down Mission Road on the way home to eat out of cans. Even our plump secretary got into the act by wearing short skirts and flaunting her milky legs. If there was love, it was ugly. I'm thinking of Tully and an older man whose name I can no longer recall fondling one another in the washroom. I had come in cradling a smashed finger to find them pressed together in the shower, their pants undone and partly pulled down. When they saw me they smiled with their pink mouths but didn't bother to push away.

How we arrived at such a place is a mystery to me. Why anyone would stay for years is an even deeper concern. You showed up, but from where? What broken life? What ugly past? The foreman showed you the Coke machine, the washroom, and the yard where you'd work. When you picked up a tire, you were amazed at the black it could give off.

[handwritten annotations:]
- addresses the reader — you — for the first time
- anyone could find themself in this situation
- last sentence is mysterious — meaning?
- whole ¶ seems like it would be better as part of the body — "black" equated w/ the dismal nature of the job
- not a good summary

AFTERWORD

A professor at the University of California at Berkeley remembers life as a seventeen-year-old runaway. Reading the essay, "Black Hair," the reader catches no glimpse of the author as English professor, neither in stereotypes of tweed and pedantic language nor in realities of term papers, office hours, and committee meetings. Reading Gary Soto, we remain locked into the world of the seventeen-year-old Chicano boy with black hair, in the smell, heat, and noise of a lowly job. Images and details bring the reader intensely inside a remembered present, into the sweaty exhausted body of the tale's teller. We undergo the experience, and because we do, we are persuaded into a compassion that has political or social consequence. We might have resisted argument and rhetoric but we may not resist our senses.

BOOKS AVAILABLE IN PAPERBACK

Baseball in April and Other Stories. San Diego: Harcourt Brace Jovanovich. *Short stories.*

A Fire in My Hands: A Book of Poems. New York: Scholastic.

Home Course in Religion: New Poems. San Francisco: Chronicle Books.

Lesser Evils: Ten Quartets. Houston: Arte Público. *Essays.*

Living Up the Street: Narrative Recollections. Portland, Oreg.: Strawberry Hill. *Essays.*

Neighborhood Odes. New York: Scholastic. *Poetry.*

Pacific Crossing. San Diego: Harcourt Brace Jovanovich. *Novel.*

A Summer Life. New York: Dell. *Essays.*

Taking Sides. San Diego: Harcourt Brace Jovanovich. *Novel.*

Who Will Know Us? San Francisco: Chronicle Books. *Poetry.*

AMY
TAN

*W*HEN AMY TAN'S parents left China, they settled in San Francisco; readers
all over the world have visited them in their new country.

*Tan was born in 1952, in Oakland, California, and now lives in San Francisco.
She attended college in Oregon first, then at California State University in San Jose,
where she took a master's degree in linguistics. In 1985, she attended a fiction
workshop at the Squaw Valley Community of Writers — and began her first novel,
which became the best-seller* The Joy Luck Club *(1989). In 1991 she followed it
with* The Kitchen God's Wife, *equally successful.* The Moon Lady *(1992) is a
children's book. "Mother Tongue" (1990) first appeared in the* Threepenny Review.

Mother Tongue

I am not a scholar of English or literature. I cannot give you much more
than personal opinions on the English language and its variations in this
country or others.

I am a writer. And by that definition, I am someone who has always
loved language. I am fascinated by language in daily life. I spend a great
deal of my time thinking about the power of language — the way it can
evoke an emotion, a visual image, a complex idea, or a simple truth. Lan-

---

Photo by Robert Foothorap

guage is the tool of my trade. And I use them all — all the Englishes I grew up with.

Recently, I was made keenly aware of the different Englishes I do use. I was giving a talk to a large group of people, the same talk I had already given to half a dozen other groups. The nature of the talk was about my writing, my life, and my book, *The Joy Luck Club*. The talk was going along well enough, until I remembered one major difference that made the whole talk sound wrong. My mother was in the room. And it was perhaps the first time she had heard me give a lengthy speech, using the kind of English I have never used with her. I was saying things like, "The intersection of memory upon imagination" and "There is an aspect of my fiction that relates to thus-and-thus" — a speech filled with carefully wrought grammatical phrases, burdened, it suddenly seemed to me, with nominalized forms, past perfect tenses, conditional phrases, all the forms of standard English that I had learned in school and through books, the forms of English I did not use at home with my mother.

Just last week, I was walking down the street with my mother, and I again found myself conscious of the English I was using, the English I do use with her. We were talking about the price of new and used furniture and I heard myself saying this: "Not waste money that way." My husband was with us as well, and he didn't notice any switch in my English. And then I realized why. It's because over the twenty years we've been together I've often used that same kind of English with him, and sometimes he even uses it with me. It has become our language of intimacy, a different sort of English that relates to family talk, the language I grew up with.

So you'll have some idea of what this family talk I heard sounds like, I'll   5
quote what my mother said during a recent conversation which I videotaped and then transcribed. During this conversation, my mother was talking about a political gangster in Shanghai who had the same last name as her family's, Du, and how the gangster in his early years wanted to be adopted by her family, which was rich by comparison. Later, the gangster became more powerful, far richer than my mother's family, and one day showed up at my mother's wedding to pay his respects. Here's what she said in part:

"Du Yusong having business like fruit stand. Like off the street kind. He is Du like Du Zong — but not Tsung-ming Island people. The local people call putong, the river east side, he belong to that side local people. That man want to ask Du Zong father take him in like become own family. Du Zong father wasn't look down on him, but didn't take seriously, until that man big like become a mafia. Now important person, very hard inviting him. Chinese way, came only to show respect, don't stay for dinner. Respect for making big celebration, he shows up. Mean give lots of respect. Chinese custom. Chinese social life that way. If too important won't have to stay too long. He come to my wedding. I didn't see, I heard it. I gone to boy's side, they have YMCA dinner. Chinese age I was nineteen."

You should know that my mother's expressive command of English belies how much she actually understands. She reads the *Forbes* report, listens to *Wall Street Week,* converses daily with her stockbroker, reads all of

Shirley MacLaine's books with ease — all kinds of things I can't begin to understand. Yet some of my friends tell me they understand 50 percent of what my mother says. Some say they understand 80 to 90 percent. Some say they understand none of it, as if she were speaking pure Chinese. But to me, my mother's English is perfectly clear, perfectly natural. It's my mother's tongue. Her language, as I hear it, is vivid, direct, full of observation and imagery. That was the language that helped shape the way I saw things, expressed things, made sense of the world.

Lately, I've been giving more thought to the kind of English my mother speaks. Like others, I have described it to people as "broken" or "fractured" English. But I wince when I say that. It has always bothered me that I can think of no way to describe it other than "broken," as if it were damaged and needed to be fixed, as if it lacked a certain wholeness and soundness. I've heard other terms used, "limited English," for example. But they seem just as bad, as if everything is limited, including people's perceptions of the limited English speaker.

I know this for a fact, because when I was growing up, my mother's "limited" English limited *my* perception of her. I was ashamed of her English. I believed that her English reflected the quality of what she had to say. That is, because she expressed them imperfectly her thoughts were imperfect. And I had plenty of empirical evidence to support me: the fact that people in department stores, at banks, and at restaurants did not take her seriously, did not give her good service, pretended not to understand her, or even acted as if they did not hear her.

My mother has long realized the limitations of her English as well. When I was fifteen, she used to have me call people on the phone to pretend I was she. In this guise, I was forced to ask for information or even to complain and yell at people who had been rude to her. One time it was a call to her stockbroker in New York. She had cashed out her small portfolio and it just so happened we were going to go to New York the next week, our very first trip outside California. I had to get on the phone and say in an adolescent voice that was not very convincing, "This is Mrs. Tan."

And my mother was standing in the back whispering loudly, "Why he don't send me check, already two weeks late. So mad he lie to me, losing me money."

And then I said in perfect English, "Yes, I'm getting rather concerned. You had agreed to send the check two weeks ago, but it hasn't arrived."

Then she began to talk more loudly. "What he want, I come to New York tell him front of his boss, you cheating me?" And I was trying to calm her down, make her be quiet, while telling the stockbroker, "I can't tolerate any more excuses. If I don't receive the check immediately, I am going to have to speak to your manager when I'm in New York next week." And sure enough, the following week there we were in front of this astonished stockbroker, and I was sitting there red-faced and quiet, and my mother, the real Mrs. Tan, was shouting at his boss in her impeccable broken English.

10

We used a similar routine five days ago, for a situation that was far less humorous. My mother had gone to the hospital for an appointment, to find out about a benign brain tumor a CAT scan had revealed a month ago. She said she had spoken very good English, her best English, no mistakes. Still, she said, the hospital did not apologize when they said they had lost the CAT scan and she had come for nothing. She said they did not seem to have any sympathy when she told them she was anxious to know the exact diagnosis, since her husband and son had both died of brain tumors. She said they would not give her any more information until the next time and she would have to make another appointment for that. So she said she would not leave until the doctor called her daughter. She wouldn't budge. And when the doctor finally called her daughter, me, who spoke in perfect English — lo and behold — we had assurances the CAT scan would be found, promises that a conference call on Monday would be held, and apologies for any suffering my mother had gone through for a most regrettable mistake.

I think my mother's English almost had an effect on limiting my possibilities in life as well. Sociologists and linguists probably will tell you that a person's developing language skills are more influenced by peers. But I do think that the language spoken in the family, especially in immigrant families which are more insular, plays a large role in shaping the language of the child. And I believe that it affected my results on achievement tests, IQ tests, and the SAT. While my English skills were never judged as poor, compared to math, English could not be considered my strong suit. In grade school I did moderately well, getting perhaps B's, sometimes B-pluses, in English and scoring perhaps in the sixtieth or seventieth percentile on achievement tests. But those scores were not good enough to override the opinion that my true abilities lay in math and science, because in those areas I achieved A's and scored in the ninetieth percentile or higher. 15

This was understandable. Math is precise; there is only one correct answer. Whereas, for me at least, the answers on English tests were always a judgment call, a matter of opinion and personal experience. Those tests were constructed around items like fill-in-the-blank sentence completion, such as, "Even though Tom was ———, Mary thought he was ———." And the correct answer always seemed to be the most bland combinations of thoughts, for example, "Even though Tom was shy, Mary thought he was charming," with the grammatical structure "even though" limiting the correct answer to some sort of semantic opposites, so you wouldn't get answers like, "Even though Tom was foolish, Mary thought he was ridiculous." Well, according to my mother, there were very few limitations as to what Tom could have been and what Mary might have thought of him. So I never did well on tests like that.

The same was true with word analogies, pairs of words in which you were supposed to find some sort of logical, semantic relationship — for example, "*Sunset* is to *nightfall* as ——— is to ———." And here you would be presented with a list of four possible pairs, one of which showed the same kind of relationship: *red* is to *stoplight, bus* is to *arrival, chills* is to *fever, yawn* is to *boring*. Well, I could never think that way. I knew what the tests were asking, but I could not block out of my mind the images already created by the first pair, "*sunset* is to *nightfall*" — and I would see a burst of colors against a darkening sky, the moon rising, the lowering of a curtain of stars. And all the other pairs of words — red, bus, stoplight, boring — just threw up a mass of confusing images, making it impossible for me to sort out something as logical as saying: "A sunset precedes nightfall" is the same as "a chill precedes a fever." The only way I would have gotten that answer right would have been to imagine an associative situation, for example, my being disobedient and staying out past sunset, catching a chill at night, which turns into feverish pneumonia as punishment, which indeed did happen to me.

I have been thinking about all this lately, about my mother's English, about achievement tests. Because lately I've been asked, as a writer, why there are not more Asian Americans represented in American literature. Why are there few Asian Americans enrolled in creative writing programs? Why do so many Chinese students go into engineering? Well, these are broad sociological questions I can't begin to answer. But I have noticed in surveys — in fact, just last week — that Asian students, as a whole, always do significantly better on math achievement tests than in English. And this makes me think that there are other Asian-American students whose English spoken in the home might also be described as "broken" or "limited." And perhaps they also have teachers who are steering them away from writing and into math and science, which is what happened to me.

Fortunately, I happen to be rebellious in nature and enjoy the challenge of disproving assumptions made about me. I became an English major my first year in college, after being enrolled as premed. I started writing nonfiction as a freelancer the week after I was told by my former boss that writing was my worst skill and I should hone my talents toward account management.

But it wasn't until 1985 that I finally began to write fiction. And at first 20 I wrote using what I thought to be wittily crafted sentences, sentences that would finally prove I had mastery over the English language. Here's an example from the first draft of a story that later made its way into *The Joy Luck Club*, but without this line: "That was my mental quandary in its nascent state." A terrible line, which I can barely pronounce.

Fortunately, for reasons I won't get into today, I later decided I should envision a reader for the stories I would write. And the reader I decided upon was my mother, because these were stories about mothers. So with this reader in mind — and in fact she did read my early drafts — I began to write stories using all the Englishes I grew up with: the English I spoke to my mother, which for lack of a better term might be described as "simple"; the English she used with me, which for lack of a better term might be described as "broken"; my translation of her Chinese, which could certainly be described as "watered down"; and what I imagined to be her translation of her Chinese if she could speak in perfect English, her internal language, and for that I sought to preserve the essence, but neither an English nor a Chinese structure. I wanted to capture what language ability tests can never reveal: her intent, her passion, her imagery, the rhythms of her speech, and the nature of her thoughts.

Apart from what any critic had to say about my writing, I knew I had succeeded where it counted when my mother finished reading my book and gave me her verdict: "So easy to read."

AFTERWORD

Ursula K. Le Guin also spoke of "the mother tongue," in her Bryn Mawr commencement address (see page 329). It is useful to compare the two uses of the phrase.

Tan speaks of "the different Englishes I do use," and gives us examples. (Remember that she has a graduate degree in linguistics.) We all use different Englishes, depending on whom we are speaking to or writing for. There is family-talk, schoolyard-talk, job-talk, book-talk, lawyer-talk. And there is always academic-talk, Tan's version of which is, "That was my mental quandary in its nascent state."

Tan's change in language or style began when she "decided I should envision a reader for the stories I would write." The task of conjuring up a reader belongs to everybody who takes up a pen. Teachers preach this gospel to students, but it is a gospel difficult for students to follow: Students envision their audience when they look to the front of the room. The teacher (with some exceptions according to pedagogic practice) is the actual audience for whom students write.

This reality leaves students small room for maneuver, practicing all their Englishes for different sets of ears — except by imagination.

BOOKS AVAILABLE IN PAPERBACK

The Joy Luck Club. New York: Random House–Vintage. *Novel.*
The Kitchen God's Wife. New York: Random House–Vintage. *Novel.*

LEWIS
THOMAS

L EWIS THOMAS (1913–1993) grew up a doctor's son on Long Island, attended Princeton University, and took his M.D. at Harvard. For most of his life, he practiced research in laboratories, more scientist than clinician, and served as administrator for medical schools and great hospitals.

For many years his publications were confined to medical journals and labored under titles like "The Physiological Disturbances Produced by Endotoxins" and "Reversible Collapse of Rabbit Ears after Intravenous Papain and Prevention of Recovery by Cortisone." Then, in 1975, he received not only a distinguished achievement award from Modern Medicine but also a National Book Award in Arts and Letters; the National Book Award is not awarded for papers on the collapse of rabbit ears.

Lewis Thomas's career as a prose stylist began with a series of columns written for the New England Journal of Medicine; he also wrote a column for Discovery, a science magazine for a general audience. He assembled five collections of essays: The Lives of a Cell: Notes of a Biology Watcher (1974); The Medusa and the Snail (1979), from which we take "The Tucson Zoo"; Late Night Thoughts on Listening to Mahler's Ninth Symphony (1984), Et Cetera, Et Cetera: Notes of a Word-Watcher (1990), and The Fragile Species (1992). In 1983 he published an autobiography called The Youngest Science: Notes of a Medicine Watcher.

Reading the autobiography, Thomas's admirers were amused and unsurprised to discover a literary past. While he was intern and resident during the Depression in the 1930s, Thomas picked up pocket money by selling poems to the Atlantic Monthly, Harper's Bazaar, and the old Saturday Evening Post. "Millennium" appeared in the Atlantic long before the atomic bomb fell on Hiroshima:

Photo by Bob Isear

It will be soft, the sound that we will hear
When we have reached the end of time and light.
A quiet, final noise within the air
Before we are returned into the night.

A sound for each to recognize and fear
In one enormous moment, as he grieves —
A sound of rustling, dry and very near,
A sudden fluttering of all the leaves.

It will be heard in all the open air
Above the fading rumble of the guns,
And we shall stand uneasily and stare,
The finally forsaken, lonely ones.

From all the distant secret places then
A little breeze will shift across the sky,
When all the earth at last is free of men
And settles with a vast and easy sigh.

Readers of The Youngest Science *learn how Thomas's enthusiasm for modern medicine and his scientific optimism took energy from recollecting his father's medical practice, at a time when doctors had little to offer patients except morphine and sympathy. His columns and essays usually reported on medical and biological science in a writerly style, a human voice. Still, Thomas's gentle and personable prose served the mind of a scientist; at times it almost turns on itself, or uses one side of itself to correct the other.*

The Tucson Zoo

Science gets most of its information by the process of reductionism, exploring the details, then the details of the details, until all the smallest bits of the structure, or the smallest parts of the mechanism, are laid out for counting and scrutiny. Only when this is done can the investigation be extended to encompass the whole organism or the entire system. So we say.

Sometimes it seems that we take a loss, working this way. Much of today's public anxiety about science is the apprehension that we may forever be overlooking the whole by an endless, obsessive preoccupation with the parts. I had a brief, personal experience of this misgiving one afternoon in Tucson, where I had time on my hands and visited the zoo, just outside the city. The designers there have cut a deep pathway between two small artificial ponds, walled by clear glass, so when you stand in the center of the path you can look into the depths of each pool, and at the same time you can regard the surface. In one pool, on the right side of the path, is a family of otters; on the other side, a family of beavers. Within just a few feet from your face, on either side, beavers and otters are at play, underwater and on the surface, swimming toward your face and then away, more filled with life than any creatures I have ever seen before, in all my days. Except for the glass, you could reach across and touch them.

I was transfixed. As I now recall it, there was only one sensation in my head: pure elation mixed with amazement at such perfection. Swept off my feet, I floated from one side to the other, swiveling my brain, staring astounded at the beavers, then at the otters. I could hear shouts across my corpus callosum, from one hemisphere to the other. I remember thinking, *mind/* with what was left in charge of my consciousness, that I wanted no part of *brain* the science of beavers and otters; I wanted never to know how they performed their marvels; I wished for no news about the physiology of their breathing, the coordination of their muscles, their vision, their endocrine systems, their digestive tracts. I hoped never to have to think of them as collections of cells. All I asked for was the full hairy complexity, then in front of my eyes, of whole, intact beavers and otters in motion.

It lasted, I regret to say, for only a few minutes, and then I was back in the late twentieth century, reductionist as ever, wondering about the details by force of habit, but not, this time, the details of otters and beavers. Instead, me. Something worth remembering had happened in my mind, I was certain of that; I would have put it somewhere in the brain stem; maybe this was my limbic system at work. I became a behavioral scientist, an experimental psychologist, an ethologist, and in the instant I lost all the wonder and the sense of being overwhelmed. I was flattened.

But I came away from the zoo with something, a piece of news about myself: I am coded, somehow, for otters and beavers. I exhibit instinctive behavior in their presence, when they are displayed close at hand behind glass, simultaneously below water and at the surface. I have receptors for this display. Beavers and otters possess a "releaser" for me, in the terminology of ethology, and the releasing was my experience. What was released? Behavior. What behavior? Standing, swiveling flabbergasted, feeling exultation and a rush of friendship. I could not, as the result of the transaction, tell you anything more about beavers and otters than you already know. I learned nothing new about them. Only about me, and I suspect also about you, maybe about human beings at large: We are endowed with genes which code out our reaction to beavers and otters, maybe our reaction to each other as well. We are stamped with stereotyped, unalterable patterns of response, ready to be released. And the behavior released in us, by such confrontations, is, essentially, a surprised affection. It is compulsory behavior and we can avoid it only by straining with the full power of our conscious minds, making up conscious excuses all the way. Left to ourselves, mechanistic and autonomic, we hanker for friends.

Everyone says, stay away from ants. They have no lessons for us; they are crazy little instruments, inhuman, incapable of controlling themselves, lacking manners, lacking souls. When they are massed together, all touching, exchanging bits of information held in their jaws like memoranda, they become a single animal. Look out for that. It is a debasement, a loss of individuality, a violation of human nature, an unnatural act.

Sometimes people argue this point of view seriously and with deep thought. Be individuals, solitary and selfish, is the message. Altruism, a jargon word for what used to be called love, is worse than weakness, it is sin, a violation of nature. Be separate. Do not be a social animal. But this is a hard argument to make convincingly when you have to depend on language to make it. You have to print up leaflets or publish books and get them bought and sent around, you have to turn up on television and catch the attention of millions of other human beings all at once, and then you have to say to all of them, all at once, all collected and paying attention: Be solitary; do not depend on each other. You can't do this and keep a straight face.

Maybe altruism is our most primitive attribute, out of reach, beyond our control. Or perhaps it is immediately at hand, waiting to be released, disguised now, in our mind of civilization, as affection or friendship or attachment. I don't see why it should be unreasonable for all human beings to have strands of DNA coiled up in chromosomes, coding out instincts for usefulness and helpfulness. Usefulness may turn out to be the hardest test of fitness for survival, more important than aggression, more effective, in the long run, than grabbiness. If this is the sort of information biological science holds for the future, applying to us as well as to ants, then I am all for science.

One thing I'd like to know most of all: When those ants have made the Hill, and are all there, touching and exchanging, and the whole mass begins to behave like a single huge creature, and *thinks*, what on earth is that thought? And while you're at it, I'd like to know a second thing: When it happens, does any single ant know about it? Does his hair stand on end?

AFTERWORD

"Instead, me." Lewis Thomas makes a transition from observing the behavior of beavers and otters to observing the behavior of Lewis Thomas. He does it, elegantly, by means of a two-word sentence which follows a sentence of forty-two words and precedes a sentence of thirty-one words — providing rhythmic variation, simple sandwiched by complex. Of course the two-word sentence is incomplete; many teachers, for good reason, ask their students to avoid incomplete sentences until they approach the skillful control of a Lewis Thomas.

Really, the essayist has all along reported not on beavers or otters but on Lewis Thomas, for it was his "mechanistic and autonomic" reaction to the animals that he revealed, not the animals themselves. Thus the essay discovers, at the moment of this transition, that its subject is not what it thought its subject was: The essay's shape is the plot of its thought.

Perhaps "Instead, me" should be scrolled onto the essayist's coat of arms. Beginning with Montaigne, the essayist's subject has been me. The assumption is implicit: If we understand one human being (possibly the one we stand closest to) we learn about all other human beings, for each man and woman potentially contains every man and woman. Lewis Thomas admires Montaigne and has written about the great inventor of the essay, who once said, "Each man bears the form of man's entire estate."

BOOKS AVAILABLE IN PAPERBACK

Et Cetera, Et Cetera: Notes of a Word-Watcher. New York: Penguin. *Essays.*

The Fragile Species. New York: Macmillan. *Essays.*

Late Night Thoughts on Listening to Mahler's Ninth Symphony. New York: Bantam. *Essays.*

The Lives of a Cell: Notes of a Biology Watcher. New York: Penguin. *Essays.*

The Youngest Science: Notes of a Medicine Watcher. New York: Bantam. *Nonfiction.*

MARIANNA
DE MARCO
TORGOVNICK

*M*ARIANNA *De MARCO TORGOVNICK (b. 1949) grew up, as she tells us, in the largely Italian-American neighborhood of Bensonhurst in Brooklyn, New York, daughter of Salvatore De Marco and Rose Cozzitorto. She attended New York University, took a Ph.D. at Columbia, and is now professor of English at Duke University.*

She has written Closure in the Novel *(1981),* The Visual Arts, Pictorialism, and the Novel: James, Lawrence, and Woolf *(1985), and* Gone Primitive: Savage Intellects, Modern Lives *(1985). Of her critical work, she writes, "My own work repeatedly investigates the ways that art imitates/influences life and life imitates/influences art." The essay is an art form, though sometimes we need reminding. When Torgovnick undertakes this essay, she uses reminiscence to investigate social influence and imitation firsthand.*

On Being White, Female,
and Born in Bensonhurst

The Mafia protects the neighborhood, our fathers say, with that peculiar satisfied pride with which law-abiding Italian Americans refer to the Mafia: The Mafia protects the neighborhood from "the coloreds." In the fifties and sixties, I heard that information repeated, in whispers, in neighborhood parks and in the yard at school in Bensonhurst. The same information probably passes today in the parks (the word now "blacks," not "coloreds") but perhaps no longer in the schoolyards. From buses each morning, from neighborhoods outside Bensonhurst, spill children of all colors and backgrounds — American black, West Indian black, Hispanic, and Asian. But the blacks are the only ones especially marked for notice. Bensonhurst is no longer entirely protected from "the coloreds." But in a deeper sense, at least for Italian Americans, Bensonhurst never changes.

Italian-American life continues pretty much as I remember it. Families with young children live side by side with older couples whose children are long gone to the suburbs. Many of those families live "down the block" from the last generation or, sometimes still, live together with parents or grandparents. When a young family leaves, as sometimes happens, for Long Island or New Jersey or (very common now) for Staten Island, another arrives, without any special effort being required, from Italy or a poorer neighborhood in New York. They fill the neat but anonymous houses that make up the mostly tree-lined streets: two-, three-, or four-family houses for the most part (this is a working, lower- to middle-middle-class area, and people need rents to pay mortgages), with a few single family or small apartment houses tossed in at random. Tomato plants, fig trees, and plaster Madonnas often decorate small but well-tended yards which face out onto the street; the grassy front lawn, like the grassy backyard, is relatively uncommon.

Crisscrossing the neighborhood and marking out ethnic zones — Italian, Irish, and Jewish, for the most part, though there are some Asian Americans and some people (usually Protestants) called simply Americans — are the great shopping streets: Eighty-sixth Street, Kings Highway, Bay Parkway, Eighteenth Avenue, each with its own distinctive character. On Eighty-sixth Street, crowds bustle along sidewalks lined with ample, packed fruit stands. Women wheeling shopping carts or baby strollers check the fruit carefully, piece by piece, and often bargain with the dealer, cajoling for a better price or letting him know that the vegetables, this time, aren't up to snuff. A few blocks down, the fruit stands are gone and the streets are lined with clothing and record shops, mobbed by teenagers. Occasionally, the el rumbles overhead, a few stops out of Coney Island on its way to the city, a trip of around one hour.

On summer nights, neighbors congregate on stoops which during the day serve as play yards for children. Air conditioning exists everywhere in Bensonhurst, but people still sit outside in the summer — to supervise children, to gossip, to stare at strangers. *"Buona sera,"* I say, or *"Buona notte,"* as I am ritually presented to Sal and Lily and Louie, the neighbors sitting on the stoop. *"Grazie,"* I say when they praise my children or my appearance. It's the only time I use Italian, which I learned at high school, although my parents (both second-generation Italian Americans, my father Sicilian, my mother Calabrian) speak it at home to each other but never to me or my brother. My accent is the Tuscan accent taught at school, not the southern Italian accents of my parents and the neighbors.

It's important to greet and please the neighbors; any break in this decorum would seriously offend and aggrieve my parents. For the neighbors are the stern arbiters of conduct in Bensonhurst. Does Mary keep a clean house? Did Gina wear black long enough after her mother's death? Was the food good at Tony's wedding? The neighbors know and pass judgment. Any news of family scandal (my brother's divorce, for example) provokes from my mother the agonized words: "But what will I *tell* people?" I sometimes collaborate in devising a plausible script.

A large sign on the church I attended as a child sums up for me the ethos of Bensonhurst. The sign urges contributions to the church building fund with the message, in huge letters: "EACH YEAR ST. SIMON AND JUDE SAVES THIS NEIGHBORHOOD ONE MILLION DOLLARS IN TAXES." Passing the church on the way from largely Jewish and middle-class Sheepshead Bay (where my in-laws live) to Bensonhurst, year after year, my husband and I look for the sign and laugh at the crass level of its pitch, its utter lack of attention to things spiritual. But we also understand exactly the values it represents.

In the summer of 1989, my parents were visiting me at my house in Durham, North Carolina, from the apartment in Bensonhurst where they have lived since 1942: three small rooms, rent-controlled, floor clean enough to eat off, every corner and crevice known and organized. My parents' longevity in a single apartment is unusual even for Bensonhurst, but not that unusual; many people live for decades in the same place or move within a ten-block radius. When I lived in this apartment, there were four rooms; one has since been ceded to a demanding landlord, one of the various landlords who have haunted my parents' life and must always be appeased lest the ultimate threat — removal from the rent-controlled apartment — be brought into play. That summer, during their visit, on August 23 (my younger daughter's birthday) a shocking, disturbing, news report issued from the neighborhood: It had become another Howard Beach.

Three black men, walking casually through the streets at night, were attacked by a group of whites. One was shot dead, mistaken, as it turned out, for another black youth who was dating a white, although part-

Hispanic, girl in the neighborhood. It all made sense: the crudely protective men, expecting to see a black arriving at the girl's house and overreacting; the rebellious girl dating the outsider boy; the black dead as a sacrifice to the feelings of the neighborhood.

I might have felt outrage, I might have felt guilt or shame, I might have despised the people among whom I grew up. In a way I felt all four emotions when I heard the news. I expect that there were many people in Bensonhurst who felt the same rush of emotions. But mostly I felt that, given the setup, this was the only way things could have happened. I detested the racial killing, but I also understood it. Those streets, which should be public property available to all, belong to the neighborhood. All the people sitting on the stoops on August 23 knew that as well as they knew their own names. The black men walking through probably knew it too — though their casual walk sought to deny the fact that, for the neighbors, even the simple act of blacks walking through the neighborhood would be seen as invasion.

Italian Americans in Bensonhurst are notable for their cohesiveness and provinciality; the slightest pressure turns those qualities into prejudice and racism. Their cohesiveness is based on the stable economic and ethical level that links generation to generation, keeping Italian Americans in Bensonhurst and the Italian-American community alive as the Jewish-American community of my youth is no longer alive. (Its young people routinely moved to the suburbs or beyond and were never replaced, so that Jews in Bensonhurst today are almost all very old people.) Their provinciality results from the Italian Americans' devotion to jealous distinctions and discriminations. Jews are suspect, but (the old Italian women admit) "they make good husbands." The Irish are okay, fellow Catholics, but not really "like us"; they make bad husbands because they drink and gamble. Even Italians come in varieties, by region (Sicilian, Calabrian, Neapolitan, very rarely any region further north) and by history in this country (the newly arrived and ridiculed "gaffoon" versus the second or third generation).

Bensonhurst is a neighborhood dedicated to believing that its values are the only values; it tends toward certain forms of inertia. When my parents visit me in Durham, they routinely take chairs from the kitchen and sit out on the lawn in front of the house, not on the chairs on the back deck; then they complain that the streets are too quiet. When they walk around my neighborhood (these De Marcos who have friends named Travaglianti and Occhipinti), they look at the mailboxes and report that my neighbors have strange names. Prices at my local supermarket are compared, in unbelievable detail, with prices on Eighty-sixth Street. Any rearrangement of my kitchen since their last visit is registered and criticized. Difference is not only unwelcome, it is unacceptable. One of the most characteristic things my mother ever said was in response to my plans for renovating my house in Durham. When she heard my plans, she looked around, crossed her arms, and said, "If it was me, I wouldn't change nothing." My father once asked me to level with him about a Jewish boyfriend who lived in a different part of the neighborhood, reacting to his Jewishness, but even more to the fact

10

that he often wore Bermuda shorts: "Tell me something, Marianna. Is he a Communist?" Such are the standards of normality and political thinking in Bensonhurst.

I often think that one important difference between Italian Americans in New York neighborhoods like Bensonhurst and Italian Americans elsewhere is that the others moved on — to upstate New York, to Pennsylvania, to the Midwest. Though they frequently settled in communities of fellow Italians, they did move on. Bensonhurst Italian Americans seem to have felt that one large move, over the ocean, was enough. Future moves could be only local: from the Lower East Side, for example, to Brooklyn, or from one part of Brooklyn to another. Bensonhurst was for many of these people the summa of expectations. If their America were to be drawn as a *New Yorker* cover, Manhattan itself would be tiny in proportion to Bensonhurst and to its satellites, Staten Island, New Jersey, and Long Island.

"Oh, no," my father says when he hears the news about the shooting. Though he still refers to blacks as "coloreds," he's not really a racist and is upset that this innocent youth was shot in his neighborhood. He has no trouble acknowledging the wrongness of the death. But then, like all the news accounts, he turns to the fact, repeated over and over, that the blacks had been on their way to look at a used car when they encountered the hostile mob of whites. The explanation is right before him but, "Yeah," he says, still shaking his head, "yeah, but what were they *doing* there? They didn't belong."

Over the next few days, the television news is even more disturbing. Rows of screaming Italians lining the streets, most of them looking like my relatives. I focus especially on one woman who resembles almost completely my mother: stocky but not fat, midseventies but well preserved, full face showing only minimal wrinkles, ample steel-gray hair neatly if rigidly coiffed in a modified beehive hairdo left over from the sixties. She shakes her fist at the camera, protesting the arrest of the Italian-American youths in the neighborhood and the incursion of more blacks into the neighborhood, protesting the shooting. I look a little nervously at my mother (the parent I resemble), but she has not even noticed the woman and stares impassively at the television.

What has Bensonhurst to do with what I teach today and write? Why did I need to write about this killing in Bensonhurst, but not in the manner of a news account or a statistical sociological analysis? Within days of hearing the news, I began to plan this essay, to tell the world what I knew, even though I was aware that I could publish the piece only someplace my parents or their neighbors would never see or hear about it. I sometimes think that I looked around from my baby carriage and decided that someday, the sooner the better, I would get out of Bensonhurst. Now, much to my surprise, Bensonhurst — the antipodes of the intellectual life I sought, the least interesting of places — had become a respectable intellectual topic. People would be willing to hear about Bensonhurst — and all by the dubious virtue of a racial killing in the streets.

The story as I would have to tell it would be to some extent a class narrative: about the difference between working class and upper middle class, dependence and a profession, Bensonhurst and a posh suburb. But I need to make it clear that I do not imagine myself as writing from a position of enormous self-satisfaction, or even enormous distance. You can take the girl out of Bensonhurst (that much is clear), but you may not be able to take Bensonhurst out of the girl. And upward mobility is not the essence of the story, though it is an important marker and symbol.

In Durham today, I live in a twelve-room house surrounded by an acre of trees. When I sit on my back deck on summer evenings, no houses are visible through the trees. I have a guaranteed income, teaching English at an excellent university, removed by my years of education from the funda-mental economic and social conditions of Bensonhurst. The one time my mother ever expressed pleasure at my work was when I got tenure, what my father still calls, with no irony intended, "ten years." "What does that mean?" my mother asked when she heard the news. Then she reached back into her experience as a garment worker, subject to periodic layoffs. "Does it mean they can't fire you just for nothing and can't lay you off?" When I said that was exactly what it means, she said, "Very good. Congratulations. That's *wonderful*." I was free from the *padrones*, from the network of petty anxieties that had formed, in large part, her very existence. Of course, I wasn't really free of petty anxieties: Would my salary increase keep pace with my colleagues', how would my office compare, would this essay be accepted for publication, am I happy? The line between these worries and my mother's is the line between the working class and the upper middle class.

But getting out of Bensonhurst never meant to me a big house, or nice clothes, or a large income. And it never meant feeling good about looking down on what I left behind or hiding my background. Getting out of Bensonhurst meant freedom — to experiment, to grow, to change. It also meant knowledge in some grand, abstract way. All the material possessions I have acquired, I acquired simply along the way — and for the first twelve years after I left Bensonhurst, I chose to acquire almost nothing at all. Now, as I write about the neighborhood, I recognize that although I've come far in physical and material distance, the emotional distance is harder to gauge. Bensonhurst has everything to do with who I am and even with what I write. Occasionally I get reminded of my roots, of their simultaneously choking and nutritive power.

Scene one: It's after a lecture at Duke, given by a visiting professor from a major university. The lecture was long and a little dull and — bad luck — I had agreed to be one of the people having dinner with the lecturer after-ward. We settle into our table at the restaurant: this man, me, the head of the comparative literature program (also a professor of German), and a couple I like who teach French, the husband at my university, the wife at one nearby. The conversation is sluggish, as it often is when a stranger, like the visiting professor, has to be assimilated into a group, so I ask the visitor a question to personalize things a bit. "How did you get interested in what you do? What made you become a professor of German?" The man gets going and begins talking about how it was really unlikely that he, a nice Jewish boy from Bensonhurst, would have chosen, in the mid-fifties, to study German. Unlikely indeed.

I remember seeing *Judgment at Nuremberg* in a local movie theater and having a woman in the row in back of me get hysterical when some clips of a concentration camp were shown. "My God," she screamed in a European accent, "look at what they did. Murderers, MURDERERS!" — and she had to be supported out by her family. I couldn't see, in the dark, whether her arm bore the neatly tattooed numbers that the arms of some of my classmates' parents did — and that always affected me with a thrill of horror. Ten years older than me, this man had lived more directly through those feelings, lived with and *among* those feelings. The first chance he got, he chose to study German. I myself have twice chosen not to visit Germany, but I could understand an urge to identify with the Other as a way of getting out of the neighborhood.

At the dinner, the memory about the movie pops into my mind but I pick up instead on the Bensonhurst — I'm also from there, but Italian American. Like a flash, he asks something I haven't been asked in years: Where did I go to high school and (a more common question) what was my maiden name? I went to Lafayette High School, I say, and my name was De Marco. Everything changes: his facial expression, his posture, his accent, his voice. "Soo, Dee Maw-ko," he says, "dun anything wrong at school today — got enny pink slips? Wanna meet me later at the parrk or maybe bye the Baye?" When I laugh, recognizing the stereotype that Italians get pink slips for misconduct at school and the notorious chemistry between Italian women and Jewish men, he says, back in his elegant voice: "My God, for a minute I felt like I was turning into a werewolf."

It's odd that although I can remember almost nothing else about this man — his face, his body type, even his name — I remember this lapse into his "real self" with enormous vividness. I am especially struck by how easily he was able to slip into the old, generic Brooklyn accent. I myself have no memory of ever speaking in that accent, though I also have no memory of trying not to speak it, except for teaching myself, carefully, to say "oil" rather than "earl."

But the surprises aren't over. The female French professor, whom I have known for at least five years, reveals for the first time that she is also from the neighborhood, though she lived across the other side of Kings Highway, went to a different, more elite high school, and was Irish American. Three of six professors, sitting at an eclectic vegetarian restaurant in Durham, all from Bensonhurst — a neighborhood where (I swear) you couldn't get the *New York Times* at any of the local stores.

Scene two: I still live in Bensonhurst. I'm waiting for my parents to return from a conference at my school, where they've been summoned to discuss my transition from elementary to junior high school. I am already a full year younger than any of my classmates, having skipped a grade, a not uncommon occurrence for "gifted" youngsters. Now the school is worried about putting me in an accelerated track through junior high, since that would make me two years younger. A compromise was reached: I would be put in a special program for gifted children, but one that took three, not two, years. It sounds okay.

Three years later, another wait. My parents have gone to school this time 25 to make another decision. Lafayette High School has three tracks: academic, for potentially college-bound kids; secretarial, mostly for Italian-American girls or girls with low aptitude-test scores (the high school is de facto segregated, so none of the tracks is as yet racially coded, though they are coded by ethnic group and gender); and vocational, mostly for boys with the same attributes, ethnic or intellectual. Although my scores are superb, the guidance counselor has recommended the secretarial track; when I protested, the conference with my parents was arranged. My mother's preference is clear: the secretarial track — college is for boys; I will need to make a "good living" until I marry and have children. My father also prefers the secretarial track, but he wavers, half proud of my aberrantly high scores, half worried. I press the attack, saying that if I were Jewish I would have been placed, without question, in the academic track. I tell him I have sneaked a peek at my files and know that my IQ is at genius level. I am allowed to insist on the change into the academic track.

What I did, and I was ashamed of it even then, was to play upon my father's competitive feelings with Jews: His daughter could and should be as good as theirs. In the bank where he was a messenger, and at the insurance company where he worked in the mailroom, my father worked with Jews, who were almost always his immediate supervisors. Several times, my father was offered the supervisory job but turned it down after long conversations with my mother about the dangers of making a change, the difficulty of giving orders to friends. After her work in the local garment shop, after cooking dinner and washing the floor each night, my mother often did piecework making bows; sometimes I would help her for fun, but it *wasn't* fun, and I was free to stop while she continued for long, tedious hours to increase the family income. Once a week, her part-time boss, Dave, would come by to pick up the boxes of bows. Short, round, with his shirttails sloppily tucked into his pants and a cigar almost always dangling from his lips, Dave was a stereotyped Jew but also, my parents always said, a nice guy, a decent man.

Years later, similar choices come up, and I show the same assertiveness I showed with my father, the same ability to deal for survival, but tinged with Bensonhurst caution. Where will I go to college? Not to Brooklyn College, the flagship of the city system — I know that, but don't press the invitations I have received to apply to prestigious schools outside of New York. The choice comes down to two: Barnard, which gives me a full scholarship, minus five hundred dollars a year that all scholarship students are expected to contribute from summer earnings, or New York University, which offers me one thousand dollars above tuition as a bribe. I waver. My parents stand firm: They are already losing money by letting me go to college; I owe it to the family to contribute the extra thousand dollars plus my summer earnings. Besides, my mother adds, harping on a favorite theme, there are no boys at Barnard; at NYU I'm more likely to meet someone to marry. I go to NYU and do marry in my senior year, but he is someone I didn't meet at college. I was secretly relieved, I now think (though at the time I thought I was just placating my parents' conventionality), to be out of the marriage sweepstakes.

The first boy who ever asked me for a date was Robert Lubitz, in eighth grade: tall and skinny to my average height and teenage chubbiness. I turned him down, thinking we would make a ridiculous couple. Day after day, I cast my eyes at stylish Juliano, the class cutup; day after day, I captivated Robert Lubitz. Occasionally, one of my brother's Italian-American friends would ask me out, and I would go, often to ROTC dances. My specialty was making political remarks so shocking that the guys rarely asked me again. After a while I recognized destiny: The Jewish man was a passport out of Bensonhurst. I of course did marry a Jewish man, who gave me my freedom and, very important, helped remove me from the expectations of Bensonhurst. Though raised in a largely Jewish section of Brooklyn, he had gone to college in Ohio and knew how important it was, as he put it, "to get past the Brooklyn Bridge." We met on neutral ground, in Central Park, at a performance of Shakespeare. The Jewish-Italian marriage is a common enough catastrophe in Bensonhurst for my parents to have accepted, even welcomed, mine — though my parents continued to treat my husband like an outsider for the first twenty years ("Now, Marianna. Here's what's going on with you brother. But don't tell-a you husband").

Along the way I make other choices, more fully marked by Bensonhurst cautiousness. I am attracted to journalism or the arts as careers, but the prospects for income seem iffy. I choose instead to imagine myself as a teacher. Only the availability of NDEA fellowships when I graduate, with their generous terms, propels me from high school teaching (a thought I never much relished) to college teaching (which seems like a brave new world). Within the college teaching profession, I choose offbeat specializations: the novel, interdisciplinary approaches (not something clear and clubby like Milton or the eighteenth century). Eventually I write the book I like best about primitive others as they figure within Western obsessions: My identification with "the Other," my sense of being "Other," surfaces at last. I avoid all mentoring structures for a long time but accept aid when it comes to me on the basis of what I perceive to be merit. I'm still, deep down, Italian-American Bensonhurst, though by this time I'm a lot of other things as well.

Scene three: In the summer of 1988, a little more than a year before the 30 shooting in Bensonhurst, my father woke up trembling and in what appeared to be a fit. Hospitalization revealed that he had a pocket of blood on his brain, a frequent consequence of falls for older people. About a year earlier, I had stayed home, using my children as an excuse, when my aunt, my father's much loved sister, died, missing her funeral; only now does my mother tell me how much my father resented my taking his suggestion that I stay home. Now, confronted with what is described as brain surgery but turns out to be less dramatic than it sounds, I fly home immediately.

My brother drives three hours back and forth from New Jersey every day to chauffeur me and my mother to the hospital: He is being a fine Italian-American son. For the first time in years, we have long conversations alone. He is two years older than I am, a chemical engineer who has also left the neighborhood but has remained closer to its values, with a suburban, Republican inflection. He talks a lot about New York, saying that (except for neighborhoods like Bensonhurst) it's a "third-world city now." It's the summer of the Tawana Brawley incident, when Brawley accused white men of abducting her and smearing racial slurs on her body with her own excrement. My brother is filled with dislike for Al Sharpton and Brawley's other vocal supporters in the black community — not because they're black, he says, but because they're troublemakers, stirring things up. The city is drenched in racial hatred that makes itself felt in the halls of the hospital: Italians and Jews in the beds and as doctors; blacks as nurses and orderlies.

This is the first time since I left New York in 1975 that I have visited Brooklyn without once getting into Manhattan. It's the first time I have spent several days alone with my mother, living in her apartment in Bensonhurst. My every move is scrutinized and commented on. I feel like I am going to go crazy.

Finally, it's clear that my father is going to be fine, and I can go home. She insists on accompanying me to the travel agent to get my ticket for home, even though I really want to be alone. The agency (a Mafia front?) has no one who knows how to ticket me for the exotic destination of North Carolina and no computer for doing so. The one person who can perform this feat by hand is out. I have to kill time for an hour and suggest to my mother that she go home, to be there for my brother when he arrives from Jersey. We stop in a Pork Store, where I buy a stash of cheeses, sausages, and other delicacies unavailable in Durham. My mother walks home with the shopping bags, and I'm on my own.

More than anything I want a kind of *sorbetto* or ice I remember from my childhood, a *cremolata*, almond-vanilla-flavored with large chunks of nuts. I pop into the local bakery (at the unlikely hour of 11 A.M.) and ask for a *cremolata*, usually eaten after dinner. The woman — a younger version of my mother — refuses: They haven't made a fresh ice yet, and what's left from the day before is too icy, no good. I explain that I'm about to get on a plane for North Carolina and want that ice, good or not. But she has her standards and holds her ground, even though North Carolina has about the same status in her mind as Timbuktu and she knows I will be banished, perhaps forever, from the land of *cremolata*.

Then, while I'm taking a walk, enjoying my solitude, I have another idea. 35 On the block behind my parents' house, there's a club for men, for men from a particular town or region in Italy: six or seven tables, some on the sidewalk beneath a garish red, green, and white sign; no women allowed or welcome unless they're with men, and no women at all during the day when the real business of the club — a game of cards for old men — is in progress. Still, I know that inside the club would be coffee and a *cremolata* ice. I'm thirty-eight, well dressed, very respectable looking; I know what I want. I also know I'm not supposed to enter that club. I enter anyway, asking the teenage boy behind the counter firmly, in my most professional tones, for a *cremolata* ice. Dazzled, he complies immediately. The old men at the card table have been staring at this scene, unable to place me exactly, though my facial type is familiar. Finally, a few old men's hisses pierce the air. "*Strega*," I hear as I leave, "*mala strega*" — "witch," or "brazen whore." I have been in Bensonhurst less than a week, but I have managed to reproduce, on my final day there for this visit, the conditions of my youth. Knowing the rules, I have broken them. I shake hands with my discreetly rebellious past, still an outsider walking through the neighborhood, marked and insulted — though unlikely to be shot.

AFTERWORD

Partisan Review published this essay, not the New Yorker, Harper's, *the* Atlantic, *the* New Republic, Vanity Fair, Playboy, Lears, Vogue, *or* Esquire. *Many essays here — and in the annual* Best American Essays *volume where we found this one — come not from magazines of large circulation but from quarterlies, like the* Partisan Review, *not available on supermarket racks. We would never find this essay — nor Margaret Atwood or John Updike on the male body — in* People *or* Family Circle. *The best American essays, or most of them, appear in magazines with relatively small circulations.*

Because her place of growing up was Bensonhurst, and because in the 1990s Americans concentrate on their origins, this essay is topical. It belongs also to a genre strong in American writing — the history of childhood, the story of growing up. We are born autobiographers of infancy and adolescence. As Herman Von Kreike put it, "America invented childhood."

BOOK AVAILABLE IN PAPERBACK

Gone Primitive: Savage Intellects, Modern Lives. Chicago: University of Chicago Press. *Nonfiction.*

BARBARA W. TUCHMAN

*W*HEN WE CALL SOMEONE *a historian these days, we usually mean a professor who teaches courses in a history department. Barbara W. Tuchman (1912–1989) was a historian in an older sense: She studied the past, made her own sense of things, and wrote books to proclaim and defend her understanding. To work, she studied, consulting the documents assembled in archives and libraries. ("To a historian," she writes, "libraries are food, shelter, and even Muse.") She took notes, followed clues, organized, made judgments, and wrote narrative that allowed room for ideas and moral argument. By selection and organization of detail, she emphasized themes and showed interpretations.*

Born in New York, she graduated from Radcliffe College in 1933. Her early interests turned her Eastward, and she worked as a research assistant at the Institute of Pacific Relations. (Much later this interest found expression in her Stilwell and the American Experience in China, *which won a Pulitzer Prize in 1971.) Later in the 1930s she wrote on politics for the* Nation, *the political magazine which her father owned. Then she worked as a journalist in London and wrote about the Spanish Civil War. After Pearl Harbor she took a job with the Office of War Information in Washington.*

Perhaps because she matured in the 1930s as the world was heading toward World War II, she always attended to the origins of war. Her first publishing success was The Guns of August *(1961), about the beginnings of World War I; subsequently* The Proud Tower *(1966) described that war's antecedents in European and in American history.* Practicing History *(1981) collected articles, reviews, and talks.* The March of Folly *(1984) assembled a rogue's gallery of misguided political leadership; her subtitle indicates her melancholy range: From Troy to Vietnam. Her last book,* The First Salute *(1988), concerned the American Revolution.*

When Tuchman writes about the fourteenth century in Europe, as she does in A
Distant Mirror *(1978), she seems to leave modern history behind, but her theme is
a six-hundred-year-old reflection. It is a commonplace that history repeats itself;
Tuchman analyzing the fourteenth century writes by analogy about the twentieth.
Her pursuit of this analogy is addressed to readers of her own time; she originally
published it in 1973, during the Watergate scandal.*

History as Mirror

At a time when everyone's mind is on the explosions of the moment, it
might seem obtuse of me to discuss the fourteenth century. But I think a
backward look at that disordered, violent, bewildered, disintegrating, and
calamity-prone age can be consoling and possibly instructive in a time of
similar disarray. Reflected in a six-hundred-year-old mirror, a more revealing
image of ourselves and our species might be seen than is visible in the clutter
of circumstances under our noses. The value of historical comparison was
made keenly apparent to the French medievalist, Edouard Perroy, when he
was writing his book on the Hundred Years' War while dodging the Gestapo
in World War II. "Certain ways of behaving," he wrote, "certain reactions
against fate, throw mutual light upon each other."

Besides, if one suspects that the twentieth century's record of inhumanity
and folly represents a phase of mankind at its worst, and that our last decade
of collapsing assumptions has been one of unprecedented discomfort, it is
reassuring to discover that the human race has been in this box before —
and emerged. The historian has the comfort of knowing that man (meaning,
here and hereafter, the species, not the sex) is always capable of his worst;
has indulged in it, painfully struggled up from it, slid back, and gone on
again.

In what follows, the parallels are not always in physical events but rather
in the effect on society, and sometimes in both.

The afflictions of the fourteenth century were the classic riders of the
Apocalypse — famine, plague, war, and death, this time on a black horse.
These combined to produce an epidemic of violence, depopulation, bad
government, oppressive taxes, an accelerated breakdown of feudal bonds,
working class insurrection, monetary crisis, decline of morals and rise in
crime, decay of chivalry, the governing idea of the governing class, and
above all, corruption of society's central institution, the Church, whose loss
of authority and prestige deprived man of his accustomed guide in a darkening world.

Yet amidst the disintegration were sprouting, invisible to contemporaries,   5
the green shoots of the Renaissance to come. In human affairs as in nature,
decay is compost for new growth.

Some medievalists reject the title of decline for the fourteenth century,
asserting instead that it was the dawn of a new age. Since the processes
obviously overlap, I am not sure that the question is worth arguing, but it
becomes poignantly interesting when applied to ourselves. Do *we* walk
amidst trends of a new world without knowing it? How far ahead is the
dividing line? Or are we on it? What designation will our age earn from
historians six hundred years hence? One wishes one could make a pact with
the devil like Enoch Soames, the neglected poet in Max Beerbohm's story,
allowing us to return and look ourselves up in the library catalogue. In that
future history book, shall we find the chapter title for the twentieth century
reading Decline and Fall, or Eve of Revival?

The fourteenth century opened with a series of famines brought on when
population growth outstripped the techniques of food production. The precarious balance was tipped by a series of heavy rains and floods and by a
chilling of the climate in what has been called the Little Ice Age. Upon a
people thus weakened fell the century's central disaster, the Black Death, an
eruption of bubonic plague which swept the known world in the years
1347–1349 and carried off an estimated one-third of the population in two
and a half years. This makes it the most lethal episode known to history,
which is of some interest to an age equipped with the tools of overkill.

The plague raged at terrifying speed, increasing the impression of horror.
In a given locality it accomplished its kill within four to six months, except
in larger cities, where it struck again in spring after lying dormant in winter.
The death rate in Avignon was said to have claimed half the population, of
whom ten thousand were buried in the first six weeks in a single mass grave.
The mortality was in fact erratic. Some communities whose last survivors
fled in despair were simply wiped out and disappeared from the map
forever, leaving only a grassed-over hump as their mortal trace.

Whole families died, leaving empty houses and property as prey to
looters. Wolves came down from the mountains to attack plague-stricken
villages, crops went unharvested, dikes crumbled, salt water reinvaded and
soured the lowlands, the forest crept back, and second growth, with the
awful energy of nature unchecked, reconverted cleared land to waste. For
lack of hands to cultivate, it was thought impossible that the world could
ever regain its former prosperity.

Once the dark bubonic swellings appeared in armpit and groin, death   10
followed rapidly within one to three days, often overnight. For lack of
gravediggers, corpses piled up in the streets or were buried so hastily that
dogs dug them up and ate them. Doctors were helpless, and priests lacking
to administer that final sacrament so that people died believing they must
go to hell. No bells tolled, the dead were buried without prayers or funeral
rites or tears; families did not weep for the loss of loved ones, for everyone

expected death. Matteo Villani, taking up the chronicle of Florence from the hands of his dead brother, believed he was recording the "extermination of mankind."

People reacted variously, as they always do: Some prayed, some robbed, some tried to help, most fled if they could, others abandoned themselves to debauchery on the theory that there would be no tomorrow. On balance, the dominant reaction was fear and a desire to save one's own skin regardless of the closest ties. "A father did not visit his son, nor the son his father; charity was dead," wrote one physician, and that was not an isolated observation. Boccaccio in his famous account reports that "kinsfolk held aloof, brother was forsaken by brother . . . often times husband by wife; nay what is more, and scarcely to be believed, fathers and mothers were found to abandon their own children to their fate, untended, unvisited as if they had been strangers."

"Men grew bold," wrote another chronicler, "in their indulgence in pleasure. . . . No fear of God or law of man deterred a criminal. Seeing that all perished alike, they reflected that offenses against human or Divine law would bring no punishment for no one would live long enough to be held to account." This is an accurate summary, but it was written by Thucydides about the Plague of Athens in the fifth century B.C. — which indicates a certain permanence of human behavior.

The nightmare of the plague was compounded for the fourteenth century by the awful mystery of its cause. The idea of disease carried by insect bite was undreamed of. Fleas and rats, which were in fact the carriers, are not mentioned in the plague writings. Contagion could be observed but not explained and thus seemed doubly sinister. The medical faculty of the University of Paris favored a theory of poisonous air spread by a conjunction of the planets, but the general and fundamental belief, made official by a papal bull, was that the pestilence was divine punishment for man's sins. Such horror could only be caused by the wrath of God. "In the year of our Lord, 1348," sadly wrote a professor of law at the University of Pisa, "the hostility of God was greater than the hostility of men."

That belief enhanced the sense of guilt, or rather the consciousness of sin (guilt, I suspect, is modern; sin is medieval), which was always so close to the surface throughout the Middle Ages. Out of the effort to appease divine wrath came the flagellants, a morbid frenzy of self-punishment that almost at once found a better object in the Jews.

A storm of pogroms followed in the track of the Black Death, widely 15 stimulated by the flagellants, who often rushed straight for the Jewish quarter, even in towns which had not yet suffered the plague. As outsiders within the unity of Christendom the Jews were natural persons to suspect of evil design on the Christian world. They were accused of poisoning the wells. Although the Pope condemned the attacks as inspired by "that liar the devil," pointing out that Jews died of plague like everyone else, the populace wanted victims, and fell upon them in three hundred communities throughout Europe. Slaughtered and burned alive, the entire colonies of Frankfurt,

Cologne, Mainz, and other towns of Germany and the Lowlands were exterminated, despite the restraining efforts of town authorities. Elsewhere the Jews were expelled by judicial process after confession of well-poisoning was extracted by torture. In every case their goods and property, whether looted or confiscated, ended in the hands of the persecutors. The process was lucrative, as it was to be again in our time under the Nazis, although the fourteenth century had no gold teeth to rob from the corpses. Where survivors slowly returned and the communities revived, it was on worse terms than before and in walled isolation. This was the beginning of the ghetto.

Men of the fourteenth century were particularly vulnerable because of the loss of credibility by the Church, which alone could absolve sin and offer salvation from hell. When the papal schism dating from 1378 divided the Church under two popes, it brought the highest authority in society into disrepute, a situation with which we are familiar. The schism was the second great calamity of the time, displaying before all the world the unedifying spectacle of twin vicars of God, each trying to bump the other off the chair of St. Peter, each appointing his own college of cardinals, each collecting tithes and revenues and excommunicating the partisans of his rival. No conflict of ideology was involved; the split arose from a simple squabble for the office of the papacy and remained no more than that for the fifty years the schism lasted. Plunged in this scandal, the Church lost moral authority, the more so as its two halves scrambled in the political arena for support. Kingdoms, principalities, even towns, took sides, finding new cause for the endless wars that scourged the times.

The Church's corruption by worldliness long antedated the schism. By the fourteenth century the papal court at Avignon was called Babylon and rivaled temporal courts in luxury and magnificence. Its bureaucracy was enormous and its upkeep mired in a commercial traffic in spiritual things. Pardons, indulgences, prayers, every benefice and bishopric, everything the Church had or was, from cardinal's hat to pilgrim's relic, everything that represented man's relation to God, was for sale. Today it is the processes of government that are for sale, especially the electoral process, which is as vital to our political security as salvation was to the emotional security of the fourteenth century.

Men still craved God and spun off from the Church in sects and heresies, seeking to purify the realm of the spirit. They too yearned for a greening of the system. The yearning, and disgust with the Establishment, produced freak orders of mystics who lived in coeducational communes, rejected marriage, and glorified sexual indulgence. Passionate reformers ranged from St. Catherine of Siena, who scolded everyone in the hierarchy from the popes down, to John Wycliffe, who plowed the soil of Protestant revolt. Both strove to renew the Church, which for so long had been the only institution to give order and meaning to the untidy business of living on earth. When in the last quarter of the century the schism brought the Church into scorn and ridicule and fratricidal war, serious men took alarm. The University of Paris made strenuous and ceaseless efforts to find a remedy, finally demanding submission of the conflict to a supreme Council of the Church whose object should be not only reunification but reform.

Without reform, said the University's theologians in their letter to the popes, the damaging effect of the current scandal could be irreversible. In words that could have been addressed to our own secular potentate although he is — happily — not double, they wrote, "The Church will suffer for your overconfidence if you repent too late of having neglected reform. If you postpone it longer the harm will be incurable. Do you think people will suffer forever from your bad government? Who do you think can endure, amid so many abuses . . . your elevation of men without literacy or virtue to the most eminent positions?" The echo sounds over the gulf of six hundred years with a timeliness almost supernatural.

When the twin popes failed to respond, pressure at last brought about a series of Church councils which endeavored to limit and constitutionalize the powers of the papacy. After a thirty-year struggle, the councils succeeded in ending the schism but the papacy resisted reform. The decades of debate only served to prove that the institution could not be reformed from within. Eighty years of mounting protest were to pass before pressure produced Luther and the great crack. 20

Despite the parallel with the present struggle between Congress and the presidency, there is no historical law that says the outcome must necessarily be the same. The American presidency at age two hundred is not a massive rock of ages embedded in a thousand years of acceptance as was the medieval Church, and should be easier to reform. One can wish for Congress a better result than the councils had in the effort to curb the executive — or at least one can hope.

The more important parallel lies in the decay of public confidence in our governing institutions, as the fourteenth-century public lost confidence in the Church. Who believes today in the integrity of government? — or of business, or of law or justice or labor unions or the military or the police? Even physicians, the last of the admired, are now in disfavor. I have a theory that the credibility vacuum owes something to our nurture in that conspiracy of fables called advertising, which we daily absorb without believing. Since public affairs and ideas and candidates are now presented to us as a form of advertising, we automatically suspend belief or suspect fraud as soon as we recognize the familiar slickness. I realize, of course, that the roots of disbelief go down to deeper ground. Meanwhile the effect is a loss of trust in all authority which leaves us guideless and dismayed and cynical — even as in the fourteenth century.

Over that whole century hung the smoke of war — dominated by the Anglo-French conflict known to us, though fortunately not to them, as the Hundred Years' War. (With the clock still ticking in Indochina, one wonders how many years there are still to go in that conflict.) Fought on French soil and extending into Flanders and Spain, the Hundred Years' War actually

lasted for more than a century, from 1337 to 1453. In addition, the English
fought the Scots; the French fought incessant civil wars against Gascons,
Bretons, Normans, and Navarrese; the Italian republics fought each other —
Florence against Pisa, Venice against Genoa, Milan against everybody; the
kingdom of Naples and Sicily was fought over by claimants from Hungary
to Aragon; the papacy fought a war that included unbridled massacre to
reconquer the Papal States; the Savoyards fought the Lombards; the Swiss
fought the Austrians; the tangled wars of Bohemia, Poland, and the German
Empire defy listing; crusades were launched against the Saracens, and to fill
up any pauses the Teutonic Knights conducted annual campaigns against
pagan Lithuania which other knights could join for extra practice. Fighting
was the function of the Second Estate, that is, of the landed nobles and
knights. A knight without a war or tournament to go to felt as restless as a
man who cannot go to the office.

Every one of these conflicts threw off Free Companies of mercenaries,
organized for brigandage under a professional captain, which became an
evil of the period as malignant as the plague. In the money economy of the
fourteenth century, armed forces were no longer feudal levies serving under
a vassal's obligation who went home after forty days, but were recruited
bodies who served for pay. Since this was at great cost to the sovereign, he
cut off the payroll as soon as he safely could during halts of truce or
negotiation. Thrown on their own resources and having acquired a taste for
plunder, the men-at-arms banded together in the Free Companies, whose
savage success swelled their ranks with landless knights and squires and
roving adventurers.

The companies contracted their services to whatever ruler was in need 25
of troops, and between contracts held up towns for huge ransom, ravaged
the countryside, and burned, pillaged, raped, and slaughtered their way
back and forth across Europe. No one was safe, no town or village knew
when it might be attacked. The leaders, prototypes of the *condottieri* in Italy,
became powers and made fortunes and even became respectable like Sir
John Hawkwood, commander of the famous White Company. Smaller
bands, called in France the *tards-venus* (latecomers), scavenged like jackals,
living off the land, plundering, killing, carrying off women, torturing peasants for their small horde of grain or townsmen for their hidden goods, and
burning, always burning. They set fire to whatever they left behind, farm-
houses, vineyards, abbeys, in a kind of madness to destroy the very sources
off which they lived, or would live tomorrow. Destruction and cruelty became self-engendering, not merely for loot but almost one might say for
sport. The phenomenon is not peculiar to any one time or people, as we
know from the experience of our own century, but in the fourteenth century
it seems to have reached a degree and extent beyond explanation.

It must be added that in practice and often personnel the Free Companies
were hardly distinguishable from the troops of organized official wars.
About 80 percent of the activity of a declared war consisted of raids of
plunder and burning through enemy territory. That paragon of chivalry, the

Black Prince, could well have earned his name from the blackened ruins he left across France. His baggage train and men-at-arms were often so heavily laden with loot that they moved as slowly as a woman's litter.

The saddest aspect of the Hundred Years' War was the persistent but vain efforts of the belligerents themselves to stop it. As in our case, it spread political damage at home, and the cost was appalling. Moreover it harmed the relations of all the powers at a time when they were anxious to unite to repel the infidel at the gates. For Christendom was now on the defensive against the encroaching Turks. For that reason the Church, too, tried to end the war that was keeping Europe at odds. On the very morning of the fatal battle of Poitiers, two cardinals hurried with offers and counter-offers between the two armed camps, trying in vain to prevent the clash. During periods of truce the parties held long parleys lasting months and sometimes years in the effort to negotiate a definitive peace. It always eluded them, failing over questions of prestige, or put off by the feeling of whichever side held a slight advantage that one more push would bring the desired gains.

All this took place under a code of chivalry whose creed was honor, loyalty, and courtesy and whose purpose, like that of every social code evolved by man in his long search for order, was to civilize and supply a pattern of rules. A knight's task under the code was to uphold the Church, defend his land and vassals, maintain the peace of his province, protect the weak and guard the poor from injustice, shed his blood for his comrade, and lay down his life if needs must. For the land-owning warrior class, chivalry was their ideology, their politics, their system — what democracy is to us or Marxism to the Communists.

Originating out of feudal needs, it was already slipping into anachronism by the fourteenth century because the development of monarchy and a royal bureaucracy was taking away the knight's functions, economic facts were forcing him to commute labor dues for money, and a rival element was appearing in the urban magnates. Even his military prowess was being nullified by trained bodies of English longbowmen and Swiss pikemen, nonmembers of the warrior class who in feudal theory had no business in battle at all.

Yet in decadence chivalry threw its brightest light; never were its cere- 30 monies more brilliant, its jousts and tournaments so brave, its apparel so splendid, its manners so gay and amorous, its entertainments so festive, its self-glorification more eloquent. The gentry elaborated the forms of chivalry just *because* institutions around them were crumbling. They clung to what gave their status meaning in a desperate embrace of the past. This is the time when the Order of the Garter was founded by the King of England, the Order of the Star by the King of France, the Golden Fleece by the Duke of Burgundy — in deliberate imitation of King Arthur's Knights of the Round Table.

The rules still worked well enough among themselves, with occasional notorious exceptions such as Charles of Navarre, a bad man appropriately known as Charles the Bad. Whenever necessity required him to swear loyal reconciliation and fealty to the King of France, his mortal enemy, he promptly engaged in treacherous intrigues with the King of England, leaving his knightly oaths to become, in the White House word, inoperative. On the whole, however, the nobility laid great stress on high standards of honor. It was vis-à-vis the Third Estate that chivalry fell so far short of the theory. Yet it remained an ideal of human relations, as Christianity remained an ideal of faith, that kept men reaching for the unattainable. The effort of society is always toward order, away from anarchy. Sometimes it moves forward, sometimes it slips back. Which is the direction of one's own time may be obscure.

The fourteenth century was further afflicted by a series of convulsions and upheavals in the working class, both urban and rural. Causes were various: the cost of constant war was thrown upon the people in hearth taxes, salt taxes, sales taxes, and debasement of coinage. In France the failure of the knights to protect the populace from incessant ravaging was a factor. It exacerbated the peasants' misery, giving it the energy of anger which erupted in the ferocious mid-century rising called the *Jacquerie*. Shortage of labor caused by the plague had temporarily brought higher wages and rising expectations. When these were met, especially in England, by statutes clamping wages at preplague levels, the result was the historic Peasants' Revolt of 1381. In the towns, capitalism was widening the gap between masters and artisans, producing the sustained weavers' revolts in the cloth towns of Flanders and major outbreaks in Florence and Paris. In Paris, too, the merchant class rose against the royal councillors, whom they despised as both corrupt and incompetent. To frighten the regent into submission, they murdered his two chief councillors in his presence.

All these struggles had one thing in common: They were doomed. United against a common threat, the ruling class could summon greater strength than its antagonists and acted to suppress insurrection with savagery equal to the fury from below. Yet discontent had found its voice; dissent and rejection of authority for the first time in the Middle Ages became a social force. Demagogues and determined leaders, reformers and agitators came to the surface. Though all were killed, several by mobs of their own followers, the uprisings they led were the beginning of modern, conscious, class war.

Meanwhile, over the second half-century, the plague returned with lesser virulence at intervals of every twelve to fifteen years. It is hardly to be wondered that people of the time saw man's fate as an endless succession of evils. He must indeed be wicked and his enemy Satan finally triumphant. According to a popular belief at the end of the century, no one since the beginning of the schism had entered Paradise.

Pessimism was a mark of the age and the *Danse Macabre* or Dance of Death its most vivid expression. Performed at occasions of popular drama and public sermons, it was an actual dance or pantomime in which a figure from every walk of life — king, clerk, lawyer, friar, goldsmith, bailiff, and so on — confronts the loathsome corpse he must become. In the accompanying verses and illustrations which have survived, the theme repeats itself over and over: the end of all life is putrefaction and the grave; no one escapes; no matter what beauty or kingly power or poor man's misery has been the lot in life, all end alike as food for worms. Death is not treated poetically as the soul's flight to reunion with God; it is a skeleton grinning at the vanity of life.

Life as well as death was viewed with disgust. The vices and corruptions of the age, a low opinion of one's fellowmen, and nostalgia for the well-ordered past were the favorite themes of literary men. Even Boccaccio in his later works became ill-tempered. "All good customs fail," laments Christine de Pisan of France, "and virtues are held at little worth." Eustache Deschamps complains that "the child of today has become a ruffian. . . . People are gluttons and drunkards, haughty of heart, caring for nought, not honor nor goodness nor kindness," and he ends each verse with the refrain, "Time past had virtue and righteousness but today reigns only vice." In England John Gower denounces Rome for simony, Lollards for heresy, clergy and monks for idleness and lust, kings, nobles, and knights for self-indulgence and rapine, the law for bribery, merchants for usury and fraud, the commons for ignorance, and in general the sins of perjury, lechery, avarice, and pride as displayed in extravagant fashions.

These last did indeed, as in all distracted times, reflect a reaching for the absurd, especially in the long pointed shoes which kept getting longer until the points had to be tied up around the knee, and the young men's doublets which kept getting shorter until they revealed the buttocks, to the censure of moralists and snickers of the crowd. Leaving miniskirts to the males, the ladies inexplicably adopted a fashion of gowns and posture designed to make them look pregnant.

Self-disgust, it seems to me, has reappeared in our time, not without cause. The succession of events since 1914 has disqualified belief in moral progress, and pollution of the physical world is our bubonic plague. Like the fourteenth century, we have lost confidence in man's capacity to control his fate and even in his capacity to be good. So we have a literature of the antihero aimlessly wandering among the perverse, absurd, and depraved; we have porn and pop and blank canvases and anti-music designed to deafen. I am not sure whether in all this the artists are expressing contempt for their fellowman or the loud laugh that bespeaks emptiness of feeling, but whatever the message, it has a faint ring of the *Danse Macabre.*

Historians until recently have hurried over the fourteenth century because like most people they prefer not to deal with failure. But it would be a mistake to imply that it was solid gloom. Seen from inside, especially from a position of privilege, it had beauties and wonders, and the ferment itself was exciting. "In these fifty years," said the renowned Comte de Foix to the chronicler Froissart in the year 1389, "there have been more feats of arms and more marvels in the world than in the three hundred years before." The Count himself, a famous huntsman, was known as Phoebus for his personal beauty and splendid court.

The streets of cities were bright with colored clothes: crimson fur-lined 40
gowns of merchants, parti-colored velvets and silks of a nobleman's retinue,
in sky blue and fawn or two shades of scarlet or it might be the all-emerald
liveries of the Green Count of Savoy. Street sounds were those of human
voices: criers of news and official announcements, shopkeepers in their
doorways and itinerant vendors crying fresh eggs, charcoal at a penny a
sack, candlewicks "brighter than the stars," cakes and waffles, mushrooms,
hot baths. Mountebanks entertained the public in the town square or village
green with tricks and magic and trained animals. Jongleurs sang ballads of
adventure in Saracen lands. After church on Sundays, laborers gathered in
cookshops and taverns; burghers promenaded in their gardens or visited
their vineyards outside the city walls. Church bells marked the eight times
of day from Matins through Vespers, when shops closed, work ceased,
silence succeeded bustle, and the darkness of unlit night descended.

The gaudy extravagance of noble life was awesome. Now and then its
patronage brought forth works of eternal beauty like the exquisite illumi-
nated Books of Hours commissioned by the Duc de Berry. More often it was
pure ostentation and conspicuous consumption. Charles V of France owned
forty-seven jeweled and golden crowns and sixty-three complete sets of
chapel furnishings, including vestments, gold crucifixes, altarpieces, reli-
quaries, and prayer books. Jewels and cloth of gold marked every occasion
and every occasion was pretext for a spectacle — a grand procession, or
ceremonial welcome to a visiting prince, a tournament or entertainment with
music, and dancing by the light of great torches. When Gian Galeazzo
Visconti, ruler of Milan, gave a wedding banquet for his daughter, eighteen
double courses were served, each of fish and meat, including trout, quail,
herons, eels, sturgeon, and suckling pig spouting fire. The gifts presented
after *each* course to several hundred guests included greyhounds in gem-
studded velvet collars, hawks in tinkling silver bells, suits of armor, rolls of
silk and brocade, garments trimmed with pearls and ermine, fully capari-
soned warhorses, and twelve fat oxen. For the entry into Paris of the new
Queen, Isabel of Bavaria, the entire length of the Rue St. Denis was hung
with a canopy representing the firmament twinkling with stars from which
sweetly singing angels descended bearing a crown, and fountains ran with
wine, distributed to the people in golden cups by lovely maidens wearing
caps of solid gold.

One wonders where all the money came from for such luxury and
festivity in a time of devastation. What taxes could burned-out and destitute
people pay? This is a puzzle until one remembers that the Aga Khan got to
be the richest man in the world on the backs of the poorest people, and that
disaster is never as pervasive as it seems from recorded accounts. It is one
of the pitfalls for historians that the very fact of being on the record makes
a happening appear to have been continuous and all-inclusive, whereas in
reality it is more likely to have been sporadic both in time and place. Besides,
persistence of the normal is usually greater than the effect of disturbance, as
we know from our own times. After absorbing the daily paper and weekly

magazine, one expects to face a world consisting entirely of strikes, crimes, power shortages, broken water mains, stalled trains, school shutdowns, Black Panthers, addicts, transvestites, rapists, and militant lesbians. The fact is that one can come home in the evening — on a lucky day — without having encountered more than two or three of these phenomena. This has led me to formulate Tuchman's Law, as follows: "The fact of being reported increases the *apparent* extent of a deplorable development by a factor of ten." (I snatch the figure from the air and will leave it to the quantifiers to justify.)

The astonishing fact is that except for Boccaccio, to whom we owe the most vivid account, the Black Death was virtually ignored by the great writers of the time. Petrarch, who was forty-four when it happened, mentions it only as the occasion for the death of Laura; Chaucer, from what I have read, passes it over in silence; Jean Froissart, the Herodotus of his time, gives it no more than one casual paragraph, and even that second Isaiah, the author of *Piers Plowman*, who might have been expected to make it central to his theme of woe, uses it only incidentally. One could argue that in 1348 Chaucer was only eight or nine years old and Froissart ten or eleven and the unknown Langland probably of the same vintage, but that is old enough to absorb and remember a great catastrophe, especially when they lived through several returns of the plague as grown men.

Perhaps this tells us that disaster, once survived, leaves less track than one supposed, or that man's instinct for living pushes it down below the surface, or simply that his recuperative powers are remarkable. Or was it just an accident of personality? Is it significant or just chance that Chaucer, the greatest writer of his age, was so uncharacteristic of it in sanguine temperament and good-humored view of his fellow creatures?

As for Froissart, never was a man more in love with his age. To him it appeared as a marvelous pageant of glittering armor and the beauty of emblazoned banners fluttering in the breeze and the clear shrill call of the trumpet. Still believing, still enraptured by the chivalric ideal, he reports savagery, treachery, limitless greed, and the pitiless slaughter of the poor when driven to revolt as minor stumbles in the grand adventure of valor and honor. Yet near the end, even Froissart could not hide from himself the decay made plain by a dissolute court, venality in high places, and a knighthood that kept losing battles. In 1397, the year he turned sixty, the defeat and massacre of the flower of chivalry at the hands of the Turks in the battle of Nicopolis set the seal on the incompetence of his heroes. Lastly, the murder of a King in England shocked him deeply, not for any love of Richard II but because the act was subversive of the whole order that sustained his world. As in Watergate, the underside had rolled to the surface all too visibly. Froissart had not the heart to continue and brought his chronicle to an end.

The sad century closed with a meeting between King Charles VI of France and the Emperor Wenceslaus, the one intermittently mad and the other regularly drunk. They met at Reims in 1397 to consult on means of ending the papal schism, but whenever Charles had a lucid interval,

Wenceslaus was in a stupor and so the conference, proving fruitless, was called off.

It makes an artistic ending. Yet in that same year Johann Gutenberg, who was to change the world, was born. In the next century appeared Joan of Arc, embodying the new spirit of nationalism, still pure like mountain water before it runs downhill; and Columbus, who opened a new hemisphere; and Copernicus, who revolutionized the concept of the earth's relation to the universe; and Michelangelo, whose sculptured visions gave men a new status; in those proud, superb, unconquered figures, the human being, not God, was captain.

As our century enters its final quarter, I am not persuaded, despite the signs, that the end is necessarily doom. The doomsayers work by extrapolation; they take a trend and extend it, forgetting that the doom factor sooner or later generates a coping mechanism. I have a rule for this situation too, which is absolute: You cannot extrapolate any series in which the human element intrudes; history, that is, the human narrative, never follows, and will always fool, the scientific curve. I cannot tell you what twists it will take, but I expect, that like our ancestors, we, too, will muddle through.

AFTERWORD

In this essay Tuchman uses a technique that can serve for exploration and exposition of many subjects. It resembles analogy, where X is continually discussed in terms of Y, although X and Y are as different as chickens and baseball. Tuchman's technique is parallelism: finding the similarities in dissimilar things (people, activities, arts, eras) of the same class. Parallelism is comparison and contrast, extended as analogy extends metaphor. One may parallel whole eras or politicians of different eras; or two scientists or a scientist and an artist; or two sports or a sport and a different pastime.

When we speak of parallelism we speak of something large enough to shape a whole essay and important enough to render that shape significant. Parallelism without import makes for hollow essays, mere skeletal frames to hang details on. The rule of thumb, for successful parallelism, resembles the cases of analogy and metaphor: Comparisons that work best combine the greatest improbability with the greatest reality of resolution.

BOOKS AVAILABLE IN PAPERBACK

Bible and Sword: England and Palestine from the Bronze Age to Balfour. New York: Ballantine. *Nonfiction.*

A Distant Mirror: The Calamitous Fourteenth Century. New York: Ballantine. *Nonfiction.*

The First Salute: A View of the American Revolution. New York: Ballantine. *Nonfiction.*

The Guns of August. New York: Bantam. *Nonfiction.*

The March of Folly: From Troy to Vietnam. New York: Ballantine. *Nonfiction.*

Notes from China. New York: Macmillan-Collier. *Nonfiction.*

Practicing History: Selected Essays. New York: Ballantine.

The Proud Tower: A Portrait of the World Before the War, 1890–1914. New York: Bantam. *Nonfiction.*

Stilwell and the American Experience in China, 1911–1945. New York: Bantam. *Nonfiction.*

The Zimmerman Telegram. New York: Ballantine. *Nonfiction.*

JOHN
UPDIKE

*J*OHN UPDIKE *(b. 1932) grew up in Pennsylvania and went to Harvard, where he helped to edit the humor magazine, the* Lampoon. *On a fellowship year at Oxford, Updike sold a poem to the* New Yorker *and began his long relationship with that magazine. For a year or two he worked on the staff, contributing to "Talk of the Town." When he quit to freelance, he continued to write stories, poems, reviews, and articles for the* New Yorker. The Same Door *(1959), his first collection of stories, appeared in the same year as* The Poorhouse Fair, *his first novel.*

Updike is a triple threat, writing superb essays as well as fiction and poetry. In 1993 he issued his Collected Poems — *from which Garrison Keillor likes to read on National Public Radio. He has published a volume of autobiography and three miscellaneous essay collections.*

Doubtless Updike is at his best as a novelist. Most recently he published Brazil *(1994) and* Memories of the Ford Administration *(1992). Many readers like best his tetralogy about Rabbit Angstrom, beginning with* Rabbit, Run *(1960) and ending with* Rabbit at Rest *in 1990. In all his work, Updike has been concerned with our sexuality. When the* Michigan Quarterly Review *published an issue on the female body in 1989, he was quick to supply an essay, later reprinted in an annual* Best American Essays *volume. This essay — like Margaret Atwood's on page 29 — comes from a subsequent issue of* MQR *about the male body.*

The Disposable Rocket

Inhabiting a male body is like having a bank account; as long as it's healthy, you don't think much about it. Compared to the female body, it is a low-maintenance proposition: a shower now and then, trim the fingernails every ten days, a haircut once a month. Oh yes, shaving — scraping or buzzing away at your face every morning. Byron, in *Don Juan*, thought the repeated nuisance of shaving balanced out the periodic agony, for females, of childbirth. Women are, his lines tell us,

> Condemn'd to child-bed, as men for their sins
> Have shaving too entail'd upon their chins, —
>
> A daily plague, which in the aggregate
> May average on the whole with parturition.

From the standpoint of reproduction, the male body is a delivery system, as the female is a mazy device for retention. Once the delivery is made, men feel a faint but distinct falling-off of interest. Yet against the enduring female heroics of birth and nurture should be set the male's superhuman frenzy to deliver his goods: He vaults walls, skips sleep, risks wallet, health, and his political future all to ram home his seed into the gut of the chosen woman. The sense of the chase lives in him as the key to life. His body is, like a delivery rocket that falls away in space, a disposable means. Men put their bodies at risk to experience the release from gravity.

When my tenancy of a male body was fairly new — of six or so years' duration — I used to jump and fall just for the joy of it. Falling — backwards, or down stairs — became a specialty of mine, an attention-getting stunt I was still practicing into my thirties, at suburban parties. Falling is, after all, a kind of flying, though of briefer duration than would be ideal. My impulse to hurl myself from high windows and the edges of cliffs belongs to my body, not my mind, which resists the siren call of the chasm with all its might; the interior struggle knocks the wind from my lungs and tightens my scrotum and gives any trip to Europe, with its Alps, castle parapets, and gargoyled cathedral lookouts, a flavor of nightmare. Falling, strangely, no longer figures in my dreams, as it often did when I was a boy and my subconscious was more honest with me. An airplane, that necessary evil, turns the earth into a map so quickly the brain turns aloof and calm; still, I marvel that there is no end of young men willing to become jet pilots.

Any accounting of male-female differences must include the male's superior recklessness, a drive not, I think, toward death, as the darker feminist cosmogonies would have it, but to test the limits, to see what the traffic will bear — a kind of mechanic's curiosity. The number of men who do lasting damage to their young bodies is striking; war and car accidents aside, secondary-school sports, with the approval of parents and the encouragement of brutish coaches, take a fearful toll of skulls and knees. We were made for combat, back in the postsimian, East-African days, and the bumping, the whacking, the breathlessness, the pain-smothering adrenaline rush form a cumbersome and unfashionable bliss, but bliss nevertheless. Take your body to the edge, and see if it flies.

The male sense of space must differ from that of the female, who has such interesting, active, and significant inner space. The space that interests men is outer. The fly ball high against the sky, the long pass spiraling overhead, the jet fighter like a scarcely visible pinpoint nozzle laying down its vapor trail at forty thousand feet, the gazelle haunch flickering just beyond arrow-reach, the uncountable stars sprinkled on their great black wheel, the horizon, the mountaintop, the quasar — these bring portents with them and awaken a sense of relation with the invisible, with the empty. The ideal male body is taut with lines of potential force, a diagram extending outward; the ideal female body curves around centers of repose. Of course, no one is ideal, and the sexes are somewhat androgynous subdivisions of a species: Diana the huntress is a more trendy body type nowadays than languid, overweight Venus, and polymorphous Dionysius poses for more underwear ads than Mars. Relatively, though, men's bodies, however elegant, are designed for covering territory, for moving on.

An erection, too, defies gravity, flirts with it precariously. It extends the   5
diagram of outward direction into downright detachability — objective in the case of the sperm, subjective in the case of the testicles and penis. Men's bodies, at this juncture, feel only partly theirs; a demon of sorts has been attached to their lower torsos, whose performance is erratic and whose errands seem, at times, ridiculous. It is like having a (much) smaller brother toward whom you feel both fond and impatient; if he is you, it is you in curiously simplified and ignoble form. This sense, of the male body being two of them, is acknowledged in verbal love play and erotic writing, where the penis is playfully given a pet name, an individuation not even the rarest rapture grants a vagina. Here, where maleness gathers to a quintessence of itself, there can be no insincerity, there can be no hiding; for sheer nakedness, there is nothing like a hopeful phallus; its aggressive shape is indivisible from its tender-skinned vulnerability. The act of intercourse, from the point of view of a consenting female, has an element of mothering, of enwrapment, of merciful concealment, even. The male body, for this interval, is tucked out of harm's way.

To inhabit a male body, then, is to feel somewhat detached from it. It is not an enemy, but not entirely a friend. Our being seems to lie not in cells and muscles but in the traces that our thoughts and actions inscribe on the air. The male body skims the surface of nature's deeps wherein the blood and pain and mysterious cravings of women perpetuate the species. Participating less in nature's processes than the female body, the male body gives the impression — false — of being exempt from time. Its powers of strength and reach descend in early adolescence, along with acne and sweaty feet, and depart, in imperceptible increments, after thirty or so. It surprises me to discover, when I remove my shoes and socks, the same paper-white, hairless ankles that struck me as pathetic when I observed them on my father. I felt betrayed when, in some tumble of touch football twenty years ago, I heard my tibia snap; and when, between two reading engagements in Cleveland, my appendix tried to burst; and when, the other day, not for the first time, there arose to my nostrils out my own body the musty attic smell my grandfather's body had.

A man's body does not betray its tenant as rapidly as a woman's. Never as fine and lovely, it has less distance to fall; what rugged beauty it has is wrinkleproof. It keeps its capability of procreation indecently long. Unless intense athletic demands are made upon it, the thing serves well enough to sixty, which is my age now. From here on, it's chancy. There are no breasts or ovaries to admit cancer to the male body, but the prostate, that awkwardly located little source of seminal fluid, shows the strain of sexual function with fits of hysterical cell replication, and all that male-bonding beer and potato chips add up in the coronary arteries. A writer, whose physical equipment can be minimal as long as it gets him to the desk, the lectern, and New York City once in a while, cannot but be grateful to his body, especially to his eyes, those tender and intricate sites where the brain extrudes from the skull, and to his hands, which hold the pen or tap the keyboard. His body has been, not himself exactly, but a close pal, potbellied and balding like most of his other pals now. A man and his body are like a boy and the buddy who has a driver's license and the use of his father's car for the evening; one goes along, gratefully, for the ride.

AFTERWORD

The contrast with Margaret Atwood's essay, written for the same issue of the same magazine (see page 29), is almost too good. Look at the opening analogies of the two authors: Atwood makes women into an invaded landscape, Updike into the vastness of space; Updike concentrates on his rocket, Atwood on her landmass. One could assemble evidence that the authors must *have conspired to write overlapping pieces. Imagine John Updike reading Margaret Atwood's paragraphs, smiling, snorting, and reaching for a pencil; equally, think of Margaret Atwood reading John Updike's words, shaking her head: "He actually* says *that!"*

BOOKS AVAILABLE IN PAPERBACK

Bech: A Book. New York: Random House–Vintage. *Short stories.*

Bech is Back. New York: Fawcett Books. *Short stories.*

Brazil. New York: Fawcett Books. *Novel.*

The Centaur. New York: Fawcett Books. *Novel.*

The Coup. New York: Fawcett Books. *Novel.*

Couples. New York: Fawcett Books. *Novel.*

Hugging the Shore: Essays and Criticism. New York: Random House–Vintage.

Marry Me! A Romance. New York: Fawcett Books. *Novel.*

Memories of the Ford Administration. New York: Fawcett Books. *Novel.*

A Month of Sundays. New York: Fawcett Books. *Novel.*

Museums and Women and Other Stories. New York: Random House–Vintage. *Short stories.*

The Music School. New York: Random House–Vintage. *Short stories.*

Of the Farm. New York: Fawcett Books. *Novel.*

Pigeon Feathers and Other Stories. New York: Fawcett Books. *Short stories.*

Problems and Other Stories. New York: Fawcett Books. *Short stories.*

Rabbit at Rest. New York: Fawcett Books. *Novel.*

Rabbit Is Rich. New York: Fawcett Books. *Novel.*

Rabbit Redux. New York: Fawcett Books. *Novel.*

Rabbit Run. New York: Fawcett Books. *Novel.*

Roger's Version. New York: Fawcett Books. *Novel.*

S. New York: Fawcett Books. *Novel.*

The Same Door: Short Stories. New York: Random House–Vintage.

Self-Consciousness: Memoirs. New York: Fawcett Books. *Nonfiction.*

Too Far to Go: The Maple Stories. New York: Fawcett Books. *Short stories.*

Trust Me: Short Stories. New York: Fawcett Books. *Short stories.*

The Witches of Eastwick. New York: Fawcett Books. *Novel.*

GORE
VIDAL

G ORE VIDAL (b. 1925) entered the army after graduating from Phillips Exeter
Academy and never attended college. He published his first novel the year he
turned twenty-one. Since then, he has run for Congress, quarreled on television with
William Buckley and Norman Mailer, written a thousand books, and lived in Europe.
In 1992 he played the part of a senator in the film Bob Roberts.

Vidal writes plays, screenplays, essays, and chiefly novels — including Julian
(1964), Myra Breckinridge (1968), and Live from Golgotha (1992). Frequently,
his novels are created out of history and politics together with imagination — in
particular his series of novels that comprises a fictional history of the United States,
including Burr (1973) and Lincoln (1984). In 1993 he won the National Book
Award for United States: Essays 1952–1992. In those forty years, Vidal occupied
or invented many states — of mind, of cantankerous opinion, of outrage. This
collection of essays occupies 1,271 pages.

Certainly a model for the young Vidal was H. L. Mencken (1880–1956) —
newspaperman, editor, writer, iconoclast, student of language. When Gore Vidal
appreciates — with his own characteristic mordant skill — a careful, humorous,
biting writer of the past, the reader enjoys two wits for the price of one.

_____ Photo by Jane Bown

H. L. Mencken
the Journalist

1

After politics, journalism has always been the preferred career of the ambitious but lazy second-rater. American exceptions to mediocrity's leaden mean: From column A, there was Franklin D. Roosevelt; from column B, H. L. Mencken.

Although Henry Louis Mencken was a magazine editor (*The Smart Set, American Mercury*), a literary critic, an expositor of Nietzsche, and a school-of-Samuel-Johnson compiler of *The American Language,* he never ceased to be a journalist for the Sunpapers in his hometown of Baltimore, where he was born in 1880 and where he died in 1956. From 1906 to 1948, he was connected with the *Baltimore Sun,* as a columnist, feature writer, editor. He was the most influential journalist of his day; he was also the wittiest.

As a working journalist, Mencken's lifelong subject was nothing less than Freedom's land and Bravery's home, the United States where flourished such gorgeous clowns as Calvin Coolidge, and "The Great Croon of Croons," Franklin D. Roosevelt, the not-so-great Great Commoner, William Jennings Bryan, and many, many others. But if only God could have invented such a cast, it was Mencken who proved to be God's most attentive and appreciative drama critic. It was Mencken who described the show. He reveled in absurdity; found no bonnet entirely beeless. He loved the national bores for their own sweet sake.

As he contemplated the meager lives of our dull presidents, he wrote: "There comes a day of public ceremonial, and a chance to make a speech. . . . A million voters with IQs below 60 have their ears glued to the radio. It takes four days' hard work to concoct a speech without a sensible word in it. Next a dam must be opened somewhere. Four dry senators get drunk and make a painful scene. The presidential automobile runs over a dog. It rains."

American journalism's golden (a kinder adjective than "yellow") age   5 coincided with Mencken's career; that is, from century's turn to midcentury's television. During this period, there was still a public educational system and although Mencken often laughs at the boobs out there, the average person could probably get through a newspaper without numb lips. Today, half the American population no longer reads newspapers: Plainly, they are the clever half.

For Mencken, the old-time journalist, or "newsie," was a combination of François Villon° and Shane.° He was "wildcattish." He was freelance, a knight for hire. In 1927, Mencken was already looking back nostalgically to the time when a journalist "used to make as much as a bartender or a police sergeant," now "he makes as much as the average doctor or lawyer, and his wife, if he has one, maybe has social ambitions." Today, of course, the "journalist" is often paid movie-star prices for movie-star appearances on television or along the lecture circuit, and he needs no wife to inspire him to a cozy lunch *à deux* with Nancy Reagan or Barbara Bush.

Mencken did acknowledge that, even then, some journalists liked to mingle with the wealthy and the powerful but, for him, there was always a greater fascination in those lower depths where dwell bartenders and police sergeants.

Mencken's ideal popular paper for that vast public which "gets all its news by listening" (today one would change "listening" to "staring" — at television), would be "printed throughout, as First Readers are printed, in words of one syllable. It should avoid every idea that is beyond the understanding of a boy of ten" on the ground that "all ideas are beyond them. They can grasp only events. But they will heed only those events that are presented as drama with one side clearly right and the other clearly wrong. They can no more imagine neutrality than they can imagine the fourth dimension." Thus, Mencken anticipates not only the television news program but the television political campaign with its combative thirty-second spot commercials and sound bites. Movies were already showing the way, and Mencken acknowledged the wisdom of the early movie magnates whose simpleminded screened *agons*° had made them rich. Unfortunately, once rich, they pined for culture, against which Mencken sternly warns with his famous injunction: "No one in this world, so far as I know — and I have researched the records for years, and employed agents to help me — has ever lost money by underestimating the intelligence of the great masses of the plain people. Nor has anyone ever lost public office thereby."

Today, Mencken's boisterous style and deadpan hyperboles are very difficult even for "educated" Americans to deal with, and Sanskrit to the generality. Although every American has a sense of humor — it is his birthright and encoded somewhere in the Constitution — few Americans have ever been able to cope with wit or irony and even the simplest jokes often cause unease, especially today when every phrase must be examined for covert sexism, racism, ageism.

American character (which does and does not exist) fascinated Mencken, 10 who observed, in 1918, that the universal image of Uncle Sam the money-

---

François Villon   Accomplished French poet (1431– ca. 1463) who was banished from Paris for, among other things, robbery and fatally stabbing a priest.

Shane   Title character of a 1953 western; he saves a homestead family from a land baron and his hired gun.

agons   Literary conflicts.

grubber was mistaken. "The character that actually marks off the American is not money-hunger at all; it was what might be called, at the risk of misunderstanding, social aspiration." For the American, money plays only a part in moving upward "to break down some barrier of caste, to secure the acceptance of his better." "Unlike Europe, no one has a station," [so far as he knows, of course: Class is a national dirty secret] "unless he makes it for himself." Of course Mencken lived in simpler times. For the American of 1918 "There is always something just behind him and tantalizing him, menacing him and causing him to sweat."

Mencken quotes Wendell Phillips: "More than any other people, we Americans are afraid of one another." Mencken acknowledges this truth, and he puts it down to the desire to conform, which means howling with the rest of the mindless pack as it careens from nowhere to nowhere in pursuit of such instant-enemies of the week as Gadhafi, Noriega, Saddam, put in place by our packmeisters, successively, like that mechanical rabbit used to keep racing dogs on course. For this sense of collective security, the individual must sacrifice himself in order "to belong to something larger and safer than he is," and he can "work off steam within prudent limits. Beyond lie the national taboos. Beyond lies true independence and the heavy penalties that go therewith."

A century earlier, that shrewd passerby, Tocqueville, also noted the force of the majority on the individual to conform. But Mencken was obliged to live a lifetime in such a society and so, unlike the French penologist, he can present data from inside the slammer: "The taboos that I have mentioned are extraordinarily harsh and numerous. They stand around nearly every subject that is genuinely important to man: They hedge in free opinion and experimentation on all sides. Consider, for example, the matter of religion. It is debated freely and furiously in almost every country in the world save the United States," but here the critic is silenced. "The result is that all religions are equally safeguarded against criticism, and that all of them lose vitality. We protect the status quo, and so make steady war upon revision and improvement."

In August 1925, Mencken meditated on how Europeans view Americans, and how they noted "our growing impatience with the free play of ideas, our increasing tendency to reduce all virtues to the single one of conformity, our relentless and all pervading standardization. . . . Europe doesn't fear our military or economic prowess, rather it is Henry Ford that gives them the shivers. . . . By Americanization it means Fordization — and not only in industry but also in politics, art, and even religion." Nor is this simply the spontaneous power of public opinion; it is the deliberate power of the state brought into play. "No other nation of today is so rigorously policed. The lust to standardize and regulate extends to the most trivial minutia of private life."

At the time that Mencken wrote this alcohol had been prohibited by law to the American people, as well as almost every form of sex, disturbing reading matter, and so on. Mencken also adverts to the Scopes trial of that year, whose verdict forbade the teaching of Darwin's theory of evolution in the schools of Christian Tennessee. This trial convinced thoughtful Europeans that Americanism was "a conspiracy of dull and unimaginative men, fortuitously made powerful, against all the ideas and ideals that seem sound to their betters," leading the Europeans to suspect "that a nation cherishing such notions and feelings, and with the money and the men to enforce them, deserved to be watched very carefully."

2

As a first-generation American, Mencken liked playing the vaudeville German, with a passion for beer, Brahms, German culture. "My grandfather made a mistake when he came to America, and I have always lived in the wrong country." Like so many *echt°*-Americans, Mencken deeply resented the British. Not only did he share in the tribal dislike of Teuton for Anglo but he resented the ease with which the Brits manipulated American politics in their favor at the time of the two world wars. During the first world war, Mencken's pro-Germanism got him banned from the *Sun*. But despite Mencken's somewhat stagy dislike of Brits, socialism, radicals, the "Anglomaniacal" Woodrow Wilson, and the reformers Franklin and Eleanor Roosevelt, he tended to make very good *patriotic* sense of American politics.

Mencken notes that from the start of the republic, "Setting aside religion, [politics] was literally the only concern of the people. All men of ability and ambition turned to it for self-expression." This is wondrously wise and an echo of Pericles's comment that the man who thinks politics not his business has no business. In the eighteenth and early nineteenth centuries, politics drew "the best literary talent into its service — Franklin, Jefferson, and Lincoln may well stand as examples — it left the cultivation of belles lettres to women and second-rate men." Now, of course, the second-rate have taken over politics. As for beautiful letters . . .

Mencken's alarm at our system's degradation was in no way based upon a starry-eyed notion of the revered but always circumvented Constitution. Although that long-ignored primer says that only Congress may declare war, President Bush has only recently confided to us that "we have fought 204 wars of which only 5 were declared," so put that in your peace pipe and smoke it! Mencken would not have been startled. For him, "All government, in its essence, is organized exploitation, and in virtually all of its existing forms it is the implacable enemy of every industrious and well-disposed man." This must have got a good chuckle from the Baltimore burgher over his breakfast of chipped beef and scrapple.

Mencken continues. Government "invades his liberty and collars his money in order to protect him, but in actuality, it always makes a stiff profit on the exchange. This profit represents the income of the professional poli-

---

echt German: "genuine."

ticians, nine-tenths of whom are professional rogues." That was then. The rogues are smoother now and often endearing on television. They are also no longer paid for by such chickenfeed as kickbacks on city contracts. Rather, they are the proud employees of the bankers and the military industrial procurers who have bought them their offices, both square and oval. But though we are worse off than in Mencken's day, he was at least able to give one cheer for the Constitution, or at least for the idea of such a document, as a kind of stoplight: "So far you may go, but no further. No matter what excuse or provocation, you may not invade certain rights, or pass certain kinds of laws."

Inevitably, Mencken's journalism is filled with stories of how our enumerated rights are constantly being evaded or struck down because it is the reflexive tactic of the politicians "to invade the Constitution stealthily, and then wait to see what happens. If nothing happens they go on more boldly; if there is a protest they reply hotly that the Constitution is worn out and absurd, and that progress is impossible under the dead hand. This is the time to watch them especially."

Mencken also notes that in the first decade of this century there was "a 20 sudden change. . . . Holes began to be punched in the Bill of Rights, and new laws of strange and often fantastic shape began to slip through them. The hysteria of the late war completed the process. The espionage act enlarged the holes to great fissures. Citizens began to be pursued into their houses, arrested without warrants, and jailed without any form of trial. The ancient writ of habeas corpus was suspended: The Bill of Rights was boldly thrown overboard."

Although the extent of the decadence of the democratic process at our end of the century was unknown if not unsuspected to Mencken at his, he knew enough of history and its engine, entropy, to know that "no government, of its own motion, will increase its own weakness, for that would mean to acquiesce in its own destruction. . . . Governments, whatever their pretensions otherwise, try to preserve themselves by holding the individual down. . . . Government itself, indeed, may be reasonably defined as a conspiracy against him. Its one permanent aim, whatever its form, is to hobble him sufficiently to maintain itself." As a self-styled "Presbyterian Tory" (with Manichean tendencies), Mencken regarded attempts at reform as doomed while the thought of any utopian system bettering things caused him deep distress because to create Utopia you would have to enslave more and more people in order to better — while worsening — their lot.

Curiously enough, of all those good and bad Americans who shuddered at the sudden sharp wind from the east known as communism, Mencken, as early as 1930, figured that there was no way that communism could ever set up shop within our alabaster cities, much less take sickle to our fruited plains. Mencken's reasoning is exquisitely sound: "That Americans, in the mass, have anything properly described as keen wits is surely far from self-evident. On the contrary, it seems likely that, if anything, they lie below the civilized norm." Incidentally, for several decades I have been trying to convince Europe that Americans are not innately stupid but merely ignorant and that with a proper educational system, et cetera. But the more one reads Mencken, the more one eyes, suspiciously, the knuckles of his countrymen, looking to see calluses from too constant a contact with the greensward.

Mencken believes Americans to be more gullible than most people, dwelling as we do in "the home of freak economic schemes" (often, alas, contagious) and "the happy hunting ground of the most blatant and absurd sort of charlatans in politics." From this intimate knowledge of the American "mind," Mencken thought that Americans, as lovers of "the bizarre and the irrational world embrace communism with joy, just as multitudes of them, in a previous age, embraced free silver. But, as everyone knows, they will have none of it." Mencken concedes the attraction of utopias to the foreign-born and educated Americans but "two-thirds of the native-born Communists that I have encountered are so plainly *mashuggah*° that it would be flattery to call them stupid."

Mencken gives two reasons for the failure of communism/socialism to take root in the United States. The first is that Americans have long since been vaccinated by the likes of Bryan and Roosevelt (TR) against this sort of virus: In effect, the folks had been there before and they are aware of so "gross" a social and economic solution. Mencken's second reason strikes me as not only true but inspired. Americans were more sensitive to "the concrete debacle in Russia" because "they probably felt themselves, in a subtle and unconscious way, to be nearer to the Russians than any Europeans. Russia was not like Europe, but it was strangely like America. In the same way the Russians were like Americans. They, too, were naturally religious and confiding; they, too, were below the civilized average in intelligence; and they, too, believed in democracy, and were trying to give it a trial."

For Mencken, communist literature was "as childish as the literature of 25 Christian Science" while communism itself "will probably disappear altogether when the Russian experiment comes to a climax, and Bolshevism either converts itself into a sickly imitation of capitalism or blows up with a bang. The former seems more likely." This is pretty good for 1930.

As Mencken thought all government bad, it follows that he was a Jeffersonian who believed that the least we had of a bad thing the better. As "an incurable Tory in politics," he was congenitally antiliberal, though "I always give heed to them politely, for they are at least free men." Surprisingly, he has respectful words for Emma Goldman and Alexander Berkman,° victims of federal persecution (it is not taught in our schools that once upon a time, at the behest of the secretary of labor, foreign-born Americans could be

---

mashuggah   Yiddish: "foolish."
Emma Goldman and Alexander Berkman   American anarchists. Lithuanian-born Goldman (1869–1940) was imprisoned several times for agitation and obstructing the draft. Russian-born Berkman (1870–1936) was jailed for stabbing industrialist Henry Clay Frick during the Homestead labor strike and for obstructing the draft. Both were eventually deported from the United States.

deported, without due process). Mencken finds the two radicals "extremely intelligent — [and] once their aberrant political ideals are set aside they are seen to be very sharp wits. They think clearly, unsentimentally and even a bit brilliantly. They write simple, glowing and excellent English." Mencken confesses that he cannot understand how they can believe so childishly in the proletariat, but "the fact that a human brain of high amperage, otherwise highly efficient, may have a hole in it is surely not a secret. All of us, in our several ways, are illogical, irrational, almost insane." Mencken's tolerance for the bees aswarm in the bonnets of others was very great if the swarm be honest and its honey pure.

The state as hostile tropism is Mencken's central philosophic notion as a journalist. Whether the state is used to deport or imprison people for their ideas or the color of their skin (as in the case of the Nisei) or simply to harass citizens who drink whiskey, he was that malevolent state's hard critic. He illuminates our marvelous Bill of Rights, no sooner promulgated than struck with the first of those sets of alien and sedition acts that continue, in one form or another, to this day. He is very funny about the Noble Experiment to prohibit alcohol (1919–33), which made the United States the world's joke-nation, a title still unceded.

As for America's once triumphant mass-production of the automobile, he notes that this achievement promptly became a pretext for the persecution of the citizenry by creating "a body of laws which fills two courtrooms to suffocation every day (in Baltimore), and keeps three judges leaping and tugging like fire-engine horses. The situation is made more intoxicating by the fact that nine-tenths of the criminals are persons who would not otherwise fall into their toils — that the traffic regulations tap whole new categories of victims. . . . The ideal of the *polizei*, at all times and everywhere, is to get their hands upon every citizen at least once a day." Today the tobacco smoker is at risk. Tomorrow, who knows who will fall victim to the state's endless sense of fun?

3

Like all good writers, Mencken is a dramatist, at his best when he shows us the ship of state in motion on high seas while his character studies of the crew of this ship of fools still give delight though every last one now lies full fathom five. Ding dong dell.

As a reporter Mencken covered many political conventions from 1904 to 1948. As a *Baltimore Sun* columnist, he wrote about national politics whenever the spirit moved or, indeed, shoved him. In 1925, he was amused, as always, by the collapse yet again of the Liberals and their journals: "The *Nation* gradually abandons Liberalism for libertarianism. The *New Republic* hangs on, but is obviously not as vigorous and confident as it used to be." Mencken delights in "Dr. Coolidge," Liberalism's natural enemy. But then "A politician has no actual principles. He is in favor of whatever seems to him to be popular at the moment." Even so, Coolidge "believes naturally in law enforcement — by lawful means if possible: if not, by any means at hand, lawful or lawless. . . . He actually got his first considerable office . . . by posturing as a fascist of the most advanced type." This was in 1919 when Governor Coolidge of Massachusetts broke the Boston police strike and became famous.

But Coolidge is only an engaging character actor in a drama whose star throughout is William Jennings Bryan (Democratic candidate for president 1896, 1900, 1908 — spokesman or person for free silver and the common person — or man). Bryan had become famous and popular and dangerous to the status quo when he put together a huge coalition of poor farmers and poorer laborers and, in their interest, spoke against the rich and their gold standard. Bryan gave the country's ownership its first big scare since the rebellion of Daniel Shays. Alas, Mencken was not at the convention in 1896 when with a single speech ("You shall not crucify mankind upon a cross of gold!"), Bryan got the nomination at the age of thirty-six and as his friend and ally, my grandfather, used to say, "He never learned anything else ever again in his life."

As much as Mencken despised Bryan, the demagogue, he is moderately touched by Bryan's appearance at the 1904 convention "in his familiar alpaca coat and his old white string tie," looking "weak and haggard" (he was suffering from pneumonia) until he started to speak and brought down the house, yet again. Four years later he would be the doomed nominee: Four years after that, Wilson made him his secretary of state, a post he resigned when he saw that the administration was moving toward war, an act of principle that Mencken rather meanly does not credit in a man he calls "the magnificent job-seeker."

At the end, Mencken was present in Dayton, Tennessee, for the Scopes trial where the old man seemed "maleficent" to Mencken when he spoke for superstition and the literal interpretation of the Bible. Bryan and the Bible won the day, but Bryan himself was dead a few weeks later, killed, my grandmother always said, by an ungovernable passion for "chicken and rice and gravy."

For Mencken, Bryan is the id — to use Freudian jargon — of American politics: the ignorant, religious, underclass leader whose fateful and dramatic climax came in the trial to determine whether or not we are descended from monkeys. Herbert Hoover is the ego; he also represents the British interest, forever trying to draw the great stupid republic into their wars and combinations. Calvin Coolidge is a near-fascist clown, whose career is "as appalling and as fascinating as a two-headed boy." Warren G. Harding is the master of a glorious near-English in which "the relations between word and meaning have long since escaped him"; Harding's style "reminds me of a string of wet sponges; it reminds me of tattered washing on the line: It reminds me of stale bean soup, of college yells, of dogs barking idiotically through endless nights. It is so bad that a sort of grandeur creeps into it." Mencken's descriptions of these wondrous clowns are still a delight because, though the originals are long since erased from the collective "memory" of the United States of Amnesia, the types persist. "I am not," Mencken observes demurely at one point, when blood is on the walls, "a constructive critic."

For Mencken "the best of [politicians] seem to be almost as bad as the 35
worst. As private citizens they are often highly intelligent and realistic men, and admirable in every way." But because of the superstitious mass, they are not allowed to make sense. "When they accomplish anything, it is usually by accident." Even of his sometimes hero, Al Smith,° he deplored his speeches but then, "like all habitual orators, he plainly likes to make speeches, no matter how dull the subject or hot the hall."

Mencken is quite aware that behind the diverting spectacle of our politics stands the ownership of the country, Business. He understands the general preference of the Business-boss for the Lawyer-employee in politics. Partly it is because "A lawyer practicing his craft under Anglo-Saxon jurisprudence becomes a pedant almost inevitably. The system he follows is expressly designed to shut out common sense," which is just as well because "Big Business, in America, is almost wholly devoid of anything even poetically describable as public spirit. It is frankly on the make. . . . Big Business was in favor of Prohibition, believing that a sober workman would make a better slave than one with a few drinks in him. It was in favor of all the gross robberies and extortions that went on in the [First] war," and profited by the curtailment of civil liberties and so on. Coolidge was their man; so was Herbert Hoover, "the perfect self-seeker. . . . His principles are so vague that even his intimates seem unable to put them into words. . . . He knows who his masters are, and he will serve them."

Mencken is also aware that there is a small but constant resistance to the "masters," but he gives the resistance little aid or comfort. Essentially, he is on the side of Business if not Businessmen because "business is the natural art of the American people." He pities those with "believing minds" who would follow this or that demagogue, and he lived long enough to attend the 1948 convention of the Progressive Party where Henry Wallace picked up the banner marked Nay; but Mencken was put off not so much by the poignant, plaintive "nay" as he was by the colouring of the letters, red.

Even so, the Tory Mencken understood the roots of radicalism. Although "it is assumed that men become radicals because they are naturally criminal, or because they have been bribed by Russian gold," what actually moves them "is simply the conviction that the government they suffer under is unbearably and incurably corrupt. . . . The notion that a radical is one who hates his country is naive and usually idiotic. He is, more likely, one who likes his country more than the rest of us, and is thus more disturbed than the rest of us when he sees it debauched. He is not a bad citizen turning to crime; he is a good citizen driven to despair." But Mencken himself is no

---

Al Smith   Alfred Smith (1873–1944), American politician and first Roman Catholic to run for president in 1928.

radical because "I believe that all government is evil, and that trying to improve it is largely a waste of time. But that is certainly not the common American view. . . . When they see an evil they try to remedy it — by peaceful means if possible, and if not, then by force." Yet, paradoxically, Mencken can also write that "history . . . is the upward struggle of man, out of darkness and into light," presumably a struggle with ooze alone.

Eventually, Franklin Delano Roosevelt would appear to be the answer to the radicals' dream and Mencken regarded him, at the beginning, with a cold but not disapproving eye as FDR metamorphosed from a John the Baptist for Al Smith to the Christ himself, or the national *superego*. With some pleasure, Mencken described the Democratic convention that nominated FDR for vice president, largely because he bore the name of a famous Republican president. Also, he was chosen to "perfume the ticket." As "leader of the anti-Tammany Democrats in New York," he could be counted on "to exorcise the Tammany split from the party." Finally, "he is a civilized man and safely wet."

When FDR's turn came at Chicago 1932, Mencken wrote, "I can recall no 40 candidate of like importance who ever had so few fanatics whooping for him." But Mencken allowed that FDR was good on radio and he smiled a lot. By the 1940 convention, Mencken was hostile not only to the New Deal but to the approaching war. To Mencken, 1940 looked like a rerun of 1916 when Wilson had campaigned as "the man who kept us out of war." Politics being nothing if not imitative of what has worked before, he glumly observed that "Roosevelt himself has promised categorically, on at least a dozen occasions, to keep out of the war, and with the most pious and eye-rolling solemnity" even though "his foreign policy . . . has been unbrokenly devious, dishonest, and dishonorable. Claiming all the immunities of a neutral, he has misled the country into countless acts of war, and there is scarcely an article of international law that he has not violated." But Roosevelt won the election. And the war came.

Roosevelt's opponent in the election of 1940 was Wendell Willkie, an eloquent "barefoot boy," as they called him, "from Wall Street," with a Hoosier accent and considerable demagogic skills. Just before he was nominated, I shook his limp hand, and he glared at me with blind eyes in a white sweating face and croaked, "Ah'd be a lah-er if ah sed ah diduhn wanna be Prez Nigh Stays." The only occasion where I gazed as Mencken gazed upon the same political spectacle was the Republican convention at Philadelphia where Willkie was nominated. This was in June, 1940, and I was guide to my blind grandfather, former Senator T. P. Gore. A Democrat, TPG was not about to miss any convention that might be fun. On a hot evening, we rode to the convention hall in a streetcar with former vice president Charles G. Dawes, a bright, crickety little man, wearing a white straw hat. At the hall, the heat was dreadful. Young women gave out palmetto fans with "FAN FOR VAN" written on them; thus, the great moose of Michigan, Senator Arthur H. Vandenberg, majestically hurled himself into the ring. Senator Robert A. Taft was also a candidate. He was even then known as "Mr. Conservative."

Twelve years later, when he was denied the nomination in favor of D. D. Eisenhower, he let slip the terrible truth that no Republican can be nominated for president without the permission of the Chase Manhattan Bank.

We sat in the bleachers to stage left of the podium where stood the former president, Herbert Hoover, face like a rosy marshmallow. Carefully, I described the scene for my blind grandfather; he had entered political history not only as the first senator from the new state of Oklahoma but as the orator who had started the longest demonstration ever recorded at any convention (for Bryan, at Denver, 1908). TPG was one of the few speakers that Mencken could endure, noting that in 1928, when he "rose to second the nomination of his old friend, Senator Reed, there was humor in his brief speech, and also a very impressive earnestness. He won the crowd instantly and got a great round of applause. No other rhetorician came near his mark."

Hoover "stood before the mike like a schoolboy reciting a piece, and seldom varied his intonation or made a gesture." Mencken brings it all alive to me a half-century later though he finds Hoover paler than I did but then I had never seen the president before — or since. I was deeply impressed by Hoover's rigid gravitas. But my grandfather, whose wit and politics were not unlike Mencken's, after listening to the ovation for the ex-president, said, "Hoover's the only man here who doesn't know that he's finished."

As the galleries chanted, "We want Willkie," I became addicted to the convention as then practiced, and it is ironic that in 1968, thanks to some television "debates" with a right-wing publicist, I should have helped preside over the transformation of the party conventions from the comings-together of the nation's tribes to a series of low-rated TV specials. No one can now say, with Mencken, "Me, I like [conventions] because they amuse me. I never get tired of the show, . . . so unimaginably exhilarating and preposterous that one lives a gorgeous year in an hour."

4

Currently, any use of the word "race" in the United States is considered an a priori proof of the user's racism. Abstract nouns are now subject to close scrutiny to make sure that the noun's deployer is not a racist or sexist or ageist or bigot. Meanwhile, any word or phrase that might cause distress must undergo erasure while euphemism (the E- or is it the U- or Eu-word?) is the order of the day as "body bag" suddenly becomes, in Pentagonese, "human remains pouch" since "pouch" is a resolutely cheery word, suggesting cute marsupials Down Under while "bag" is a downer, as in "bag lady." Munich, appeasement, Hitler. A babble of words that no one understands now fills the airwaves, and language loses all meaning as we sink slowly, mindlessly, into herstory rather than history because most rapists are men, aren't they?

Mencken is a nice antidote. Politically, he is often right but seldom correct by today's stern standards. In a cheery way, he dislikes most minorities and if he ever had a good word to say about the majority of his countrymen, I have yet to come across it. Recently, when his diaries were published, it was discovered that He Did Not Like the Jews, and that he had said unpleasant things about them not only as individuals but In General, plainly the sign of a Hitler-Holocaust enthusiast. So shocked was everyone that even the *New York Review of Books*'s unofficial de-anti-Semitiser, Garry Wills (he salvaged Dickens, barely), has yet to come to his aid, with An Explanation. But in Mencken's private correspondence, he also snarls at black Americans, Orientals, Britons, women and WASPs, particularly the clay-eating Appalachians whom he regarded as subhuman. But private irritability is of no consequence when compared to what really matters, public action.

Far from being an anti-Semite, Mencken was one of the first journalists to denounce the persecution of the Jews in Germany at a time when the *New York Times*, say, was notoriously reticent. On November 27, 1938, Mencken writes (*Baltimore Sun*), "It is to be hoped that the poor Jews now being robbed and mauled in Germany will not take too seriously the plans of various politicians to rescue them." He then reviews the various schemes to "rescue" the Jews from the Nazis who had not yet announced their own final solution.

To the British proposal that the Jews be admitted to British Guiana, Teutonophile Mencken thinks that the *Ostjuden*° might hack it in British Guiana but not the German Jews as "they constitute an undoubtedly superior group. . . . Try to imagine a German-Jewish lawyer or insurance man, or merchant, or schoolmaster [in] a place where the climate is that of a Turkish Bath." Tanganyika he thought marginally better but still pretty bad, at least "as good as the worst parts of Mexico." He then suggests that Canada could "absorb one hundred thousand or even two hundred thousand with ease, and they would be useful acquisitions, especially in the western prairie populations, which are dominated today by a low-grade of farmers, without any adequate counterbalance of the competent middle class." Today Mencken could not write this because the Farmers' Anti-Defamation League of Saskatchewan would be offended, and his column banned in Canada. "Australia, now almost as exclusive as Sing Sing, which it somewhat resembles in population, could use quite as many [Jews] as Canada and New Zealand." The Australian government would, today, file a protest; and Mencken's column would be banned.

Then Mencken gets down to business: "The American plan for helping the refugees is less openly brutal than the British plan, but almost as insulting to them, and even more futile." After many official and unofficial condemnations of Germany, including "the Hon. Mr Roosevelt's declaration that he could scarcely believe that such things could occur in a twentieth-century civilization," the president is still not willing to relax the immigration laws or do anything "that might cause him political inconvenience." Mencken finds such "pecksniffery . . . gross and disgusting, . . . and I hope that

---

Ostjuden Eastern Jews.

American Jews will not be fetched by it." Mencken also notes how the "Aframerican press" found amazing Roosevelt's solicitousness for German Jews, so unlike his complaisance to the ongoing crimes against black Americans.

Mencken concludes: "There is only one way to help the refugees, and that is to find places for them in a country in which they can really live. Why shouldn't the United States take in a couple of hundred thousand of them, or even all of them?" He notes two popular objections. One, there is already a lot of unemployment in the United States, to which he responds that it is unlikely the Jewish immigrants will either loaf or be incompetent. Two, there is anti-Semitism of the sort then being fanned by the Ku Klux Klan but, as he observes, "not many Jews are likely to go to Mississippi or Arkansas."

I am certain that those who wish to will be able to find anti-Semitism in Mencken's proposal to admit all Jewish refugees. Certainly he *generalizes* about Jews. (How does he know that they don't *all* want to go to Mississippi?) But then perhaps the whole message is code; certainly the remark about Jewish "efficiency" is a classic blood libel.

As of 1934, Mencken was moderately impressed by Eretz Israel° and agreeably condescending to the Arabs, who "breed like flies but die in the same way." Mencken was generally approving of the European Jewish settlers, though he predictably cast a cold eye on the collectivist farms and kibbutzim. Of one of them, he wrote, presciently, "It was founded in 1921, and is still in the first flush of its success. Will it last? Probably not. As soon as its present kindergartners grow up they will begin to marry outside, and then there will be quarrels over shares, and it will no doubt go the way of Brook Farm, Amana,° and all the other predecessors." Mencken thought that there was only a fifty-fifty chance of the Jewish plantation in Palestine enduring. "On the one hand [Eretz Israel] is being planted intelligently and shows every sign of developing in a healthy manner. But on the other hand there are the Arabs — and across the Jordan there is a vast reservoir of them, all hungry, all full of enlightened self-interest. Let some catastrophe in world politics take the British cops away, and the Jews who now fatten on so many lovely farms will have to fight desperately for their property and their lives." The catastrophe came right on schedule in the form of Hitler and of such professional Jewish terrorists as Begin and Shamir.

One of the few groups that Americans are fairly free to denounce, after the Arabs, are the Japanese. Mencken was almost alert to "the yellow peril."

Eretz Israel Hebrew for "Land of Israel," referring to pre-state Israel, encompassing the current state of Israel and all lands in dispute.

Brook Farm, Amana Experimental communities settled in the mid-nineteenth century. Brook Farm (1841–1847) was a cooperative farming community in West Roxbury, Massachusetts, that failed, largely because its intellectual members were not farmers. The Amana Church Society settled in Amana, Iowa, in 1855 and had greater success, becoming a cooperative corporation in 1932 and still famous for its fine wool products.

(I use quotes to forestall the usual letters accusing me of hating all Orientals along with Mencken, when neither did nor does.) In 1939, Mencken was thinking seriously about Japan. As there is no public memory in the United States, let me remind the reader that since the Japanese victory over Russia in 1904, the United States had been preparing for a war with Japan in order to establish who would be *numero uno* not only in the Pacific but in Asia.

By 1939, Japan was busy conquering China, having acquired Korea and Manchuria, and the Nippon imperial eye was set on the southeast Asian oil fields, at the time in the hands of two "local" Asiatic powers, the British and the Dutch.

As a "racist," Mencken blithely generalized about race, a real no-no in   55
today's world where each and every one of the five billion people on our common crowded planet is a treasured and unique creation, sharing nothing at all with anyone else except, maybe, the Big Fella — I mean Big Gal — in the Sky. But generalize he did, something no longer allowed in freedom's land. Mencken writes: "The Japanese, judged by Western eyes, are an extremely homely people, and no doubt the fact has a good deal to do with their general unpopularity." Mencken thought that they looked both "sinister and ludicrous," not an encouraging or likable combination. "They look, taking one with another, like Boy Scouts with buck teeth, wearing horn-rimmed spectacles. . . . I have never met a Caucasian who professed any affection for the Japs, though there are not a few white fans for the scenery," etc. Already guilty of Racist Generalizing, Mencken proceeds, sickeningly, to grade *all* Japanese: "They are a people of very considerable talents, and will have to be reckoned with in the future history of the human race. They have long since got past the stage of sitting respectfully at the feet of the West. . . . In all the fields of human endeavor save theology, politics, and swine justice they are showing the way to their ofay mentors. They have made important durable contributions to knowledge in each and every one of the exact sciences, and they have taken such a lead in trade and industry that the only way left to beat them is to murder them." But even this solution, particularly favored by England, won't be easy because they have "a considerable knack for war."

As "nearly all white men dislike the Japs and like the Chinese," Mencken tried to give an accurate impression of our soon-to-be great adversary and, as I gaze out over the Hollywood hills towards Japanese Universal Pictures, our eventual conquerors. But accuracy in reporting on Pacific matters is always difficult because the American press have always given us a view of the Japanese that "is seldom accurate and not always honest," to say the least. As of 1939, China and Chiang Kai-shek were, as always, on the brink of victory but, somehow, Japan always won and, as Mencken remarked, "The Japs, in truth, had as sound a mandate to clean up China as the United States have had to clean up Cuba." Or Mexico, Nicaragua, Salvador, Panama, Grenada, not to mention Korea, Vietnam, Cambodia, Iran, and Iraq.

Three years later, the Japs, heavily provoked, sank the American fleet at Pearl Harbor and the great race war was on with Round One (with guns) going to the white race (1945) and Round Two (with computers) going to the yellow race (1990). Mencken was particularly good — that is prophetic — on American skulduggeries south of the border where he often visited and duly noted our eerie inability to do anything honest or even intelligent whether in Cuba or Haiti or in dealing with Nicaragua's Sandino.

Like Puck, Mencken found most mortals fools. He showed us odd glimpses of the vacuous Duke of Windsor and his Baltimore lady as well as of Rudolph Valentino whom he once entertained in what must have been an unusually alcoholic session for a young Italian. Mencken commiserated with the assault by the press on the lad's manhood and he shed a public tear at the beauty's demise not long after.

In literary matters, Mencken was a shield to the meat-and-potatoes of naturalism-realism, a sounder diet than one of, shall we say, frozen fish? He was a champion of Dreiser; a foe of censorship. He was good on Conrad but at sea with James and insensitive to Wharton. He knew cooking and provided a sound recipe for "shore soup," the crab-based glory of the eastern shore of Maryland. He was passionate about music. Disliked jazz but admired "Aframerican" musicians. Interested in architecture, he was appalled by the ugliness of American cities except for San Francisco where "There is nothing European about the way life is lived; the color is all Asiatic" because it is so happily cut off from "the rest of the dun and dour Republic." He described the average person's way of life in New York as that of a "sardine in a can" while the grass in the so-called parks "looks like embalmed sauerkraut." He hated chiropractors. He was amazed, as an editor, to find that graduates of West Point write the best English. He took a bitter pride in "the love of ugliness [that] is apparently inherent in the American people. They cherish and venerate the unspeakable."

Matthew Arnold wrote that a "style is the saying in the best way what you have to say. The what you have to say depends on your age." Mencken certainly said what he had to say about the age that he had been assigned to. When asked why, if he can find nothing to "revere" in the United States, he lived there, he replied, "Why do men go to zoos?"

Religion as generally practiced by the Americans of his day, he saw as a Great Wall of China designed to keep civilization out while barbarism might flourish within the gates. He himself was a resolute breacher of the Great Wall, and to the extent that some civilization has got through, he is one of the few Americans that we can thank. Plainly, so clear and hard a writer would not be allowed in the mainstream press of today, and those who think that they would like him back would be the first to censor and censure him.

As for Mencken himself, he wrote his own epitaph in 1921 for *Smart Set*: "If, after I depart this vale, you ever remember me and have thought to please my ghost, forgive some sinner and wink your eye at some homely girl." I realize that he has viciously used the G-word and, even worse, the long-since banned H-word. But there he is. And here we are, lucky we.

AFTERWORD

Vidal's essays usually appear in the New York Review of Books, *based on a new book or a reprint, or in the* Nation. *This essay has another provenance, beginning life as a foreword, or introduction, to a collection of Mencken's newspaper stories published in 1991. Many times, a foreword cannot exist independent of the book it introduces, and would make a poor choice for a miscellaneous collection of essays. "H. L. Mencken the Journalist" stands as an essay on its own two feet.*

It works on its own partly because its quotations substantiate its claims; the reader is not invited or compelled to turn to the quoted passage to understand what Vidal praises. This introduction resembles a review of the book that it introduces, and it is not only a foreword to Mencken's book but an homage to the man. Vidal is open in his admiration for Mencken, and makes clear by his own language, tone, wit, and sarcasm that Mencken is a model. Mencken was not a novelist, but Vidal is a journalist as well as a writer of fiction. For that matter, many feel that Vidal does his best journalism in his novels.

The subject of this essay, one could argue, is really the "American character (which does and does not exist)." Mencken and Vidal both enjoy insulting the American character. Given the popularity of Mencken in this lifetime, and Vidal's own successes, it is clear that the American character (which does and does not exist) likes to hear itself insulted. Mind you, readers who laugh at the insults feel themselves separated (by their laughter) from the character ridiculed.

In his fourth and final section, Vidal addresses recent charges of racism that assault Mencken's reputation. It is a habit of our moment to judge the political morality of past writers by present standards. This habit gives pleasure to many: First, it excuses us from reading people who lived before us, thus freeing up time for reading John Grisham and watching TV; second, it allows us to understand — what everyone everywhere always likes to know — that we are the first truly virtuous people in the history of humanity.

BOOKS AVAILABLE IN PAPERBACK

At Home: Essays 1982–1988. New York: Random House–Vintage.

The Best Man. New York: Dramatists Play Service. *Play.*

Burr. New York: Ballantine. *Novel.*

The City and the Pillar. New York: Ballantine. *Novel.*

Creation. New York: Ballantine. *Novel.*

Dark Green, Bright Red. New York: Ballantine. *Novel.*

The Decline and Fall of the American Empire. Berkeley, Calif.: Odonian Press. *Essays.*

Duluth. New York: Ballantine. *Novel.*

1876. New York: Ballantine. *Novel.*

Empire. New York: Ballantine. *Novel.*

Hollywood: A Novel of America in the 1920s. New York: Ballantine.

The Judgement of Paris. New York: Ballantine. *Novel.*

Julian. New York: Ballantine. *Novel.*

Kalki. New York: Ballantine. *Novel.*

Lincoln. New York: Ballantine. *Novel.*

Live from Golgatha: The Gospel According to Gore Vidal. New York: Penguin. *Novel.*

Messiah. New York: Ballantine. *Novel.*

Myra Breckinridge; Myron. New York: Random House–Vintage. *Novel.*

A Search for the King. New York: Ballantine. *Novel.*

A Thirsty Evil: Seven Short Stories. San Francisco: Gay Sunshine.

Two Sisters. New York: Ballantine. *Novel.*

Visit to a Small Planet. New York: Dramatists Play Service. *Play.*

Washington, D.C. New York: Ballantine. *Novel.*

Weekend. New York: Dramatists Play Service. *Play.*

Williwaw. New York: Ballantine. *Novel.*

ALICE
WALKER

*A LICE WALKER was born in Georgia (1944), the youngest of eight children in
a sharecropping family. She attended Spelman College in Atlanta, then transferred to Sarah Lawrence College in New York City, from which she graduated. She
returned to Georgia, working in the civil rights movement and beginning to write.
She taught at Jackson State College and Tougalo College in Mississippi and at
Wellesley College. Now, after many years in New York, she lives in San Francisco
and teaches at the University of California at Berkeley. Her mother still lives in
Georgia, where Alice Walker travels from California to visit her.*

*Walker has received a grant from the National Endowment for the Arts and a
fellowship from the Radcliffe Institute. She has published a biography of Langston
Hughes for young people, three books of poems, two collections of short stories, and
three novels. Her novel* The Color Purple *won the Pulitzer Prize and the American
Book Award in 1983, and she has followed it with* The Temple of My Familiar
(1989) and Possessing the Secret of Joy *(1992).*

She first collected essays (including the one that follows) in a volume called In
Search of Our Mothers' Gardens *(1983) and in 1988 added* Living by the Word:
Selected Writings, 1973–1987. *For Alice Walker's work, the most important source
has been her relationship with her mother, as she believes it is for other black women
writers. When Walker is interviewed — the success of* The Color Purple *brought
Alice Walker's name to the forefront of literary attention — she returns often to the
subject of mothers. In an article in* Ms. *magazine she recalls three gifts that her
mother gave her despite poverty (her mother worked all day in affluent kitchens and
earned less than twenty dollars a week): a sewing machine, so that the young
daughter could make her own dresses for school; at high school graduation a suitcase
for going away; and — not the least important for the young author — a typewriter.*

In Search of
Our Mothers' Gardens

I described her own nature and temperament. Told how they needed
a larger life for their expression. . . . I pointed out that in lieu of proper
channels, her emotions had overflowed into paths that dissipated
them. I talked, beautifully I thought, about an art that would be born,
an art that would open the way for women the likes of her. I asked her
to hope, and build up an inner life against the coming of that day. . . .
I sang, with a strange quiver in my voice, a promise song.

– "Avey," JEAN TOOMER, *Cane*
The poet speaking to a prostitute who falls
asleep while he's talking

When the poet Jean Toomer walked through the South in the early
twenties, he discovered a curious thing: black women whose spirituality was
so intense, so deep, so *unconscious*, they were themselves unaware of the
richness they held. They stumbled blindly through their lives: creatures so
abused and mutilated in body, so dimmed and confused by pain, that they
considered themselves unworthy even of hope. In the selfless abstractions
their bodies became to the men who used them, they became more than
"sexual objects," more even than mere women: They became "Saints." Instead of being perceived as whole persons, their bodies became shrines:
What was thought to be their minds became temples suitable for worship.
These crazy Saints stared out at the world, wildly, like lunatics — or quietly,
like suicides; and the "God" that was in their gaze was as mute as a great
stone.

Who were these Saints? These crazy, loony, pitiful women?

Some of them, without a doubt, were our mothers and grandmothers.

In the still heat of the post-Reconstruction South, this is how they seemed
to Jean Toomer: exquisite butterflies trapped in an evil honey, toiling away
their lives in an era, a century, that did not acknowledge them, except as
"the *mule* of the world." They dreamed dreams that no one knew — not even
themselves, in any coherent fashion — and saw visions no one could understand. They wandered or sat about the countryside crooning lullabies to
ghosts, and drawing the mother of Christ in charcoal on courthouse walls.

They forced their minds to desert their bodies and their striving spirits 5
sought to rise, like frail whirlwinds from the hard red clay. And when those
frail whirlwinds fell, in scattered particles, upon the ground, no one
mourned. Instead, men lit candles to celebrate the emptiness that remained,
as people do who enter a beautiful but vacant space to resurrect a God.

Our mothers and grandmothers, some of them: moving to music not yet written. And they waited.

They waited for a day when the unknown thing that was in them would be made known; but guessed, somehow in their darkness, that on the day of their revelation they would be long dead. Therefore to Toomer they walked, and even ran, in slow motion. For they were going nowhere immediate, and the future was not yet within their grasp. And men took our mothers and grandmothers, "but got no pleasure from it." So complex was their passion and their calm.

To Toomer, they lay vacant and fallow as autumn fields, with harvest time never in sight: and he saw them enter loveless marriages, without joy; and become prostitutes, without resistance; and become mothers of children, without fulfillment.

For these grandmothers and mothers of ours were not Saints, but Artists; driven to a numb and bleeding madness by the springs of creativity in them for which there was no release. They were Creators, who lived lives of spiritual waste, because they were so rich in spirituality — which is the basis of Art — that the strain of enduring their unused and unwanted talent drove them insane. Throwing away this spirituality was their pathetic attempt to lighten the soul to a weight their work-worn, sexually abused bodies could bear.

What did it mean for a black woman to be an artist in our grandmothers' time? In our great-grandmothers' day? It is a question with an answer cruel enough to stop the blood.

Did you have a genius of a great-great-grandmother who died under some ignorant and depraved white overseer's lash? Or was she required to bake biscuits for a lazy backwater tramp, when she cried out in her soul to paint watercolors of sunsets, or the rain falling on the green and peaceful pasturelands? Or was her body broken and forced to bear children (who were more often than not sold away from her) — eight, ten, fifteen, twenty children — when her one joy was the thought of modeling heroic figures of rebellion, in stone or clay?

How was the creativity of the black woman kept alive, year after year and century after century, when for most of the years black people have been in America, it was a punishable crime for a black person to read or write? And the freedom to paint, to sculpt, to expand the mind with action did not exist. Consider, if you can bear to imagine it, what might have been the result if singing, too, had been forbidden by law. Listen to the voices of Bessie Smith, Billie Holiday, Nina Simone, Roberta Flack, and Aretha Franklin, among others, and imagine those voices muzzled for life. Then you may begin to comprehend the lives of our "crazy," "Sainted" mothers and grandmothers. The agony of the lives of women who might have been Poets, Novelists, Essayists, and Short-Story Writers (over a period of centuries), who died with their real gifts stifled within them.

And, if this were the end of the story, we would have cause to cry out in my paraphrase of Okot p'Bitek's great poem:

> O, my clanswoman
> Let us all cry together!
> Come,
> Let us mourn the death of our mother,
> The death of a Queen
> The ash that was produced
> By a great fire!
> O, this homestead is utterly dead
> Close the gages
> With *lacari* thorns,
> For our mother
> The creator of the Stool is lost!
> And all the young men
> Have perished in the wilderness!

But this is not the end of the story, for all the young women — our mothers and grandmothers, *ourselves* — have not perished in the wilderness. And if we ask ourselves why, and search for and find the answer, we will know beyond all efforts to erase it from our minds, just exactly who, and of what, we black American women are.

One example, perhaps the most pathetic, most misunderstood one, can provide a backdrop for our mothers' work: Phillis Wheatley, a slave in the 1700s.

Virginia Woolf, in her book *A Room of One's Own,* wrote that in order for a woman to write fiction she must have two things, certainly: a room of her own (with key and lock) and enough money to support herself.

What then are we to make of Phillis Wheatley, a slave, who owned not even herself? This sickly, frail black girl who required a servant of her own at times — her health was so precarious — and who, had she been white, would have been easily considered the intellectual superior of all the women and most of the men in the society of her day.

Virginia Woolf wrote further, speaking of course not of our Phillis, that "any woman born with a great gift in the sixteenth century [insert "eighteenth century," insert "black woman," insert "born or made a slave"] would certainly have gone crazed, shot herself, or ended her days in some lonely cottage outside the village, half witch, half wizard [insert "Saint"], feared and mocked at. For it needs little skill and psychology to be sure that a highly gifted girl who had tried to use her gift of poetry would have been so thwarted and hindered by contrary instincts [add "chains, guns, the lash, the ownership of one's body by someone else, submission to an alien religion"], that she must have lost her health and sanity to a certainty."

The key words, as they relate to Phillis, are "contrary instincts." For when we read the poetry of Phillis Wheatley — as when we read the novels of Nella Larsen or the oddly false-sounding autobiography of that freest of all black women writers, Zora Hurston — evidence of "contrary instincts" is everywhere. Her loyalties were completely divided, as was, without question, her mind.

But how could this be otherwise? Captured at seven, a slave of wealthy, 20
doting whites who instilled in her the "savagery" of the Africa they "res-
cued" her from, . . . one wonders if she was even able to remember her
homeland as she had known it, or as it really was.

Yet, because she did try to use her gift for poetry in a world that made
her a slave, she was "so thwarted and hindered by . . . contrary instincts,
that she . . . lost her health." In the last years of her brief life, burdened not
only with the need to express her gift but also with a penniless, friendless
"freedom" and several small children for whom she was forced to do strenuous work to feed, she lost her health, certainly. Suffering from malnutrition
and neglect and who knows what mental agonies, Phillis Wheatley died.

So torn by "contrary instincts" was black, kidnapped, enslaved Phillis
that her description of "the Goddess" — as she poetically called the Liberty
she did not have — is ironically, cruelly humorous. And, in fact, has held
Phillis up to ridicule for more than a century. It is usually read prior to
hanging Phillis's memory as that of a fool. She wrote:

> The Goddess comes, she moves divinely fair,
> Olive and laurel binds her *golden* hair.
> Wherever shines this native of the skies,
> Unnumber'd charms and recent graces rise. [My italics]

It is obvious that Phillis, the slave, combed the "Goddess's" hair every
morning; prior, perhaps, to bringing in the milk, or fixing her mistress's
lunch. She took her imagery from the one thing she saw elevated above all
others.

With the benefit of hindsight we ask, "How could she?"

But at last, Phillis, we understand. No more snickering when your stiff, 25
struggling, ambivalent lines are forced on us. We know now that you were
not an idiot or a traitor; only a sickly little black girl, snatched from your
home and country and made a slave; a woman who still struggled to sing
the song that was your gift, although in a land of barbarians who praised
you for your bewildered tongue. It is not so much what you sang, as that
you kept alive, in so many of our ancestors, *the notion of song.*

Black women are called, in the folklore that so aptly identifies one's
status in society, "the *mule* of the world," because we have been handed the
burdens that everyone else — *everyone* else — refused to carry. We have also
been called "Matriarchs," "Superwomen," and "Mean and Evil Bitches." Not
to mention "Castraters" and "Sapphire's Mama." When we have pleaded
for understanding, our character has been distorted; when we have asked
for simple caring, we have been handed empty inspirational appellations,
then stuck in the farthest corner. When we have asked for love, we have
been given children. In short, even our plainer gifts, our labors of fidelity
and love, have been knocked down our throats. To be an artist and a black
woman, even today, lowers our status in many respects, rather than raises
it: And yet, artists we will be.

Therefore we must fearlessly pull out of ourselves and look at and identify with our lives the living creativity some of our great-grandmothers were not allowed to know. I stress *some* of them because it is well known that the majority of our great-grandmothers knew, even without "knowing" it, the reality of their spirituality, even if they didn't recognize it beyond what happened in the singing at church — and they never had any intention of giving it up.

How they did it — those millions of black women who were not Phillis Wheatley, or Lucy Terry or Frances Harper or Zora Hurston or Nella Larsen or Bessie Smith; or Elizabeth Catlett, or Katherine Dunham, either — brings me to the title of this essay, "In Search of Our Mothers' Gardens," which is a personal account that is yet shared, in its theme and its meaning, by all of us. I found, while thinking about the far-reaching world of the creative black woman, that often the truest answer to a question that really matters can be found very close.

In the late 1920s my mother ran away from home to marry my father. Marriage, if not running away, was expected of seventeen-year-old girls. By the time she was twenty, she had two children and was pregnant with a third. Five children later, I was born. And this is how I came to know my mother: She seemed a large, soft, loving-eyed woman who was rarely impatient in our home. Her quick, violent temper was on view only a few times a year, when she battled with the white landlord who had the misfortune to suggest to her that her children did not need to go to school.

She made all the clothes we wore, even my brothers' overalls. She made all the towels and sheets we used. She spent the summers canning vegetables and fruits. She spent the winter evenings making quilts enough to cover all our beds.

During the "working" day, she labored beside — not behind — my father in the fields. Her day began before sunup, and did not end until late at night. There was never a moment for her to sit down, undisturbed, to unravel her own private thoughts; never a time free from interruption — by work or the noisy inquiries of her many children. And yet, it is to my mother — and all our mothers who were not famous — that I went in search of the secret of what has fed that muzzled and often mutilated, but vibrant, creative spirit that the black woman has inherited, and that pops out in wild and unlikely places to this day.

But when, you will ask, did my overworked mother have time to know or care about feeding the creative spirit?

The answer is so simple that many of us have spent years discovering it. We have constantly looked high, when we should have looked high — and low.

For example: In the Smithsonian Institution in Washington, D.C., there hangs a quilt unlike any other in the world. In fanciful, inspired, and yet simple and identifiable figures, it portrays the story of the Crucifixion. It is considered rare, beyond price. Though it follows no known pattern of quilt-making, and though it is made of bits and pieces of worthless rags, it is obviously the work of a person of powerful imagination and deep spiritual feeling. Below this quilt I saw a note that says it was made by "an anonymous Black woman in Alabama, a hundred years ago."

If we could locate this "anonymous" black woman from Alabama, she 35 would turn out to be one of our grandmothers — an artist who left her mark in the only materials she could afford, and in the only medium her position in society allowed her to use.

As Virginia Woolf wrote further, in *A Room of One's Own:*

> Yet genius of a sort must have existed among women as it must have existed among the working class. [Change this to "slaves" and "the wives and daughters of sharecroppers."] Now and again an Emily Brontë or a Robert Burns [change this to "a Zora Hurston or a Richard Wright"] blazes out and proves its presence. But certainly it never got itself on to paper. When, however, one reads of a witch being ducked, of a woman possessed by devils [or "Sainthood"], of a wise woman selling herbs [our root workers], or even a very remarkable man who had a mother, then I think we are on the track of a lost novelist, a suppressed poet, or some mute and inglorious Jane Austen. . . . Indeed, I would venture to guess that Anon, who wrote so many poems without signing them, was often a woman.

And so our mothers and grandmothers have, more often than not anonymously, handed on the creative spark, the seed of the flower they themselves never hoped to see: or like a sealed letter they could not plainly read.

And so it is, certainly, with my own mother. Unlike "Ma" Rainey's songs, which retained their creator's name even while blasting forth from Bessie Smith's mouth, no song or poem will bear my mother's name. Yet so many of the stories that I write, that we all write, are my mother's stories. Only recently did I fully realize this: That through years of listening to my mother's stories of her life, I have absorbed not only the stories themselves, but something of the manner in which she spoke, something of the urgency that involves the knowledge that her stories — like her life — must be recorded. It is probably for this reason that so much of what I have written is about characters whose counterparts in real life are so much older than I am.

But the telling of these stories, which came from my mother's lips as naturally as breathing, was not the only way my mother showed herself as an artist. For stories, too, were subject to being distracted, to dying without conclusion. Dinners must be started, and cotton must be gathered before the big rains. The artist that was and is my mother showed itself to me only after many years. This is what I finally noticed:

Like Mem, a character in *The Third Life of Grange Copeland*, my mother 40 adorned with flowers whatever shabby house we were forced to live in. And not just your typical straggly country stand of zinnias, either. She planted ambitious gardens — and still does — with over fifty different varieties of plants that bloom profusely from early March until late November. Before she left home for the fields, she watered her flowers, chopped up the grass, and laid out new beds. When she returned from the fields she might divide clumps of bulbs, dig a cold pit, uproot and replant roses, or prune branches from her taller bushes or trees — until night came and it was too dark to see.

Whatever she planted grew as if by magic, and her fame as a grower of flowers spread over three counties. Because of her creativity with her flowers, even my memories of poverty are seen through a screen of blooms — sunflowers, petunias, roses, dahlias, forsythia, spirea, delphiniums, verbena . . . and on and on.

And I remember people coming to my mother's yard to be given cuttings from her flowers; I hear again the praise showered on her because whatever rocky soil she landed on, she turned into a garden. A garden so brilliant with colors, so original in its design, so magnificent with life and creativity, that to this day people drive by our house in Georgia — perfect strangers and imperfect strangers — and ask to stand or walk among my mother's art.

I notice that it is only when my mother is working in her flowers that she is radiant, almost to the point of being invisible — except as Creator: hand and eye. She is involved in work her soul must have. Ordering the universe in the image of her personal conception of Beauty.

Her face, as she prepares the Art that is her gift, is a legacy of respect she leaves to me, for all that illuminates and cherishes life. She has handed down respect for the possibilities — and the will to grasp them.

For her, so hindered and intruded upon in so many ways, being an artist 45 has still been a daily part of her life. This ability to hold on, even in very simple ways, is work black women have done for a very long time.

This poem is not enough, but it is something, for the woman who literally covered the holes in our walls with sunflowers:

> They were women then
> My mama's generation
> Husky of voice — Stout of
> Step
> With fists as well as
> Hands
> How they battered down
> Doors
> And ironed
> Starched white
> Shirts
> How they led
> Armies
> Headragged Generals
> Across mined
> Fields

> Booby-trapped
> Kitchens
> To discover books
> Desks
> A place for us
> How they knew what we
> *Must* know
> Without knowing a page
> Of it
> Themselves.

Guided by my heritage of a love of beauty and a respect for strength — in search of my mother's garden, I found my own.

And perhaps in Africa over two hundred years ago, there was just such a mother; perhaps she painted vivid and daring decorations in oranges and yellows and greens on the walls of her hut; perhaps she sang — in a voice like Roberta Flack's — *sweetly* over the compounds of her village; perhaps she wove the most stunning mats or told the most ingenious stories of all the village storytellers. Perhaps she was herself a poet — though only her daughter's name is signed to the poems that we know.

Perhaps Phillis Wheatley's mother was also an artist.

Perhaps in more than Phillis Wheatley's biological life is her mother's 50 signature made clear.

AFTERWORD

Walker's writing is lyrical, metaphorical. She leaps from place to place, making images that carry feeling, seldom telling us the names of feelings unless image and metaphor have already established the emotion. For the reader timid about metaphor, her rapid improvisations may puzzle or confound; metaphor lovers luxuriate in her vigor, intelligence, and vivacity. Look at the fifth paragraph: Spirits leaving bodies turn into whirlwinds which exhaust themselves and become dust; by implication — "mourned" — they die. These whirlwind-spirits came from the bodies of women; when they die the men don't mourn them but worship the absence they left behind.

This thinking, not entirely logical, progresses by pictures and comparisons; it is the thinking of poetry.

BOOKS AVAILABLE IN PAPERBACK

The Color Purple. San Diego: Harcourt Brace Jovanovich. *Novel.*

Good Night, Willie Lee, I'll See You in the Morning. San Diego: Harcourt Brace Jovanovich. *Poetry.*

Her Blue Body Everything We Know: Earthling Poems. San Diego: Harcourt Brace Jovanovich.

Horses Make a Landscape Look More Beautiful: Poems. San Diego: Harcourt Brace Jovanovich.

In Love and Trouble: Stories of Black Women. San Diego: Harcourt Brace Jovanovich. *Short stories.*

In Search of Our Mothers' Gardens: Womanist Prose. San Diego: Harcourt Brace Jovanovich. *Essays.*

Living by the Word: Selected Writings, 1973–1987. San Diego: Harcourt Brace Jovanovich. *Essays.*

Meridian. New York: Pocket Books. *Novel.*

Once: Poems. San Diego: Harcourt Brace Jovanovich.

Possessing the Secret of Joy. New York: Simon & Schuster. *Novel.*

Revolutionary Petunias and Other Poems. San Diego: Harcourt Brace Jovanovich.

The Temple of My Familiar. New York: Pocket Books. *Novel.*

The Third Life of Grange Copeland. New York: Pocket Books. *Novel.*

To Hell with Dying. San Diego: Harcourt Brace Jovanovich. *Nonfiction.*

You Can't Keep a Good Woman Down: Stories. San Diego: Harcourt Brace Jovanovich. *Short stories.*

EUDORA
WELTY

EUDORA WELTY (b. 1909) published her Collected Stories *in 1980, bringing together 576 pages of the short fiction for which she is celebrated. Her short stories first appeared in magazines, often the literary quarterlies, and became regular features of annual collections of the best fiction from periodicals. Two of her most enduring stories are "Why I Live at the P.O.," which shows her comic genius, and "The Worn Path," which recounts the courage and perseverance of an old black woman.*

Among her novels are Delta Wedding *(1946),* Losing Battles *(1970), and* The Optimist's Daughter *(1972), which won the Pulitzer Prize. "The Little Store" comes from* The Eye of the Story *(1978), which is a collection of her essays, most on the art of fiction. In 1983 she delivered the William E. Massey Lectures at Harvard and a year later brought them out as a volume of recollections,* One Writer's Beginnings. *She has won the Gold Medal of the National Institute of Arts and Letters, the National Medal for Literature, and the Presidential Medal of Freedom. In 1989 she departed from the word long enough to issue a collection of her photographs, called* Photographs.

Born in Jackson, Mississippi, she still resides in Jackson, Mississippi. In this small town, her observation and imagination have found all the material they require. When she writes an essay out of memory, as she does in "The Little Store," she brings to reminiscence the storyteller's skills of narration and use of significant detail. Maybe more important, she also brings the stylist's ear for rhythms of word and sentence that compel attention. Her gifts for evoking intimacy and cherished detail lead in the end to hints of the darker vision that underlies her best work.

_____ Photo by Richard O. Moore

The Little Store

Two blocks away from the Mississippi State Capitol, and on the same street with it, where our house was when I was a child growing up in Jackson, it was possible to have a little pasture behind your backyard where you could keep a Jersey cow, which we did. My mother herself milked her. A thrifty homemaker, wife, mother of three, she also did all her own cooking. And as far as I can recall, she never set foot inside a grocery store. It wasn't necessary.

For her regular needs, she stood at the telephone in our front hall and consulted with Mr. Lemly, of Lemly's Market and Grocery downtown, who took her order and sent it out on his next delivery. And since Jackson at the heart of it was still within very near reach of the open country, the blackberry lady clanged on her bucket with a quart measure at your front door in June without fail, the watermelon man rolled up to your house exactly on time for the Fourth of July, and down through the summer, the quiet of the early-morning streets was pierced by the calls of farmers driving in with their plenty. One brought his with a song, so plaintive we would sing it with him:

> "Milk, milk,
> Buttermilk,
> Snap beans — butterbeans —
> Tender okra — fresh greens . . .
> And buttermilk."

My mother considered herself pretty well prepared in her kitchen and pantry for any emergency that, in her words, might choose to present itself. But if she should, all of a sudden, need another lemon or find she was out of bread, all she had to do was call out, "Quick! Who'd like to run to the Little Store for me?"

I would.

She'd count out the change into my hand, and I was away. I'll bet the nickel that would be left over that all over the country, for those of my day, the neighborhood grocery played a similar part in our growing up.

Our store had its name — it was that of the grocer who owned it, whom I'll call Mr. Sessions — but "the Little Store" is what we called it at home. It was a block down our street toward the capitol and a half a block further, around the corner, toward the cemetery. I knew even the sidewalk to it as well as I knew my own skin. I'd skipped my jumping-rope up and down it, hopped its length through mazes of hopscotch, played jacks in its islands of shade, serpentined along it on my Princess bicycle, skated it backward and forward. In the twilight I had dragged my steamboat by its string (this was

5

610

homemade out of every new shoebox, with candle in the bottom lighted and shining through colored tissue paper pasted over windows scissored out in the shapes of the sun, moon, and stars) across every crack of the walk without letting it bump or catch fire. I'd "played out" on that street after supper with my brothers and friends as long as "first-dark" lasted; I'd caught its lightning bugs. On the first Armistice Day° (and this will set the time I'm speaking of) we made our own parade down that walk on a single velocipede — my brother pedaling, our little brother riding the handlebars, and myself standing on the back, all with arms wide, flying flags in each hand. (My father snapped that picture as we raced by. It came out blurred.)

As I set forth for the Little Store, a tune would float toward me from the house where there lived three sisters, girls in their teens, who ratted their hair over their ears, wore headbands like gladiators, and were considered to be very popular. They practiced for this in the daytime; they'd wind up the Victrola, leave the same record on they'd played before, and you'd see them bobbing past their dining-room windows while they danced with each other. Being three, they could go all day, cutting in:

> "Everybody ought to know-oh
> How to do the Tickle-Toe
> (how to do the Tickle-Toe)" —

they sang it and danced to it, and as I went by to the same song, I believed it.

A little further on, across the street, was the house where the principal of our grade school lived — lived on, even while we were having vacation. What if she would come out? She would halt me in my tracks — she had a very carrying and well-known voice in Jackson, where she'd taught almost everybody — saying "Eudora Alice Welty, spell *oblige*." *Oblige* was the word that she of course knew had kept me from making 100 on my spelling exam. She'd make me miss it again now, by boring her eyes through me from across the street. This was my vacation fantasy, one good way to scare myself on the way to the store.

Down near the corner waited the house of a little boy named Lindsey. The sidewalk here was old brick, which the roots of a giant chinaberry tree had humped up and tilted this way and that. On skates, you took it fast, in a series of skittering hops, trying not to touch ground anywhere. If the chinaberries had fallen and rolled in the cracks, it was like skating through a whole shooting match of marbles. I crossed my fingers that Lindsey wouldn't be looking.

During the big flu epidemic he and I, as it happened, were being nursed through our sieges at the same time. I'd hear my father and mother murmuring to each other, at the end of a long day, "And I wonder how poor little *Lindsey* got along today?" Just as, down the street, he no doubt would

---

the first Armistice Day November 11, 1918, marked the end of World War I. Now celebrated as Veterans Day.

611

have to hear his family saying, "And I wonder how is poor *Eudora* by now?" I got the idea that a choice was going to be made soon between poor little Lindsey and poor Eudora, and I came up with a funny poem. I wasn't prepared for it when my father told me it wasn't funny and my mother cried that if I couldn't be ashamed for myself, she'd have to be ashamed for me:

> There was a little boy and his name was Lindsey.
> He went to heaven with the influinzy.

He didn't, he survived it, poem and all, the same as I did. But his chinaberries could have brought me down in my skates in a flying act of contrition before his eyes, looking pretty funny myself, right in front of his house.

Setting out in this world, a child feels so indelible. He only comes to find out later that it's all the others along his way who are making themselves indelible to him.

Our Little Store rose right up from the sidewalk; standing in a street of family houses, it alone hadn't any yard in front, any tree or flowerbed. It was a plain frame building covered over with brick. Above the door, a little railed porch ran across on an upstairs level and four windows with shades were looking out. But I didn't catch on to those.

Running in out of the sun, you met what seemed total obscurity inside. There were almost tangible smells — licorice recently sucked in a child's cheek, dill-pickle brine that had leaked through a paper sack in a fresh trail across the wooden floor, ammonia-loaded ice that had been hoisted from wet croker sacks and slammed into the icebox with its sweet butter at the door, and perhaps the smell of still-untrapped mice.

Then through the motes of cracker dust, cornmeal dust, the Gold Dust of the Gold Dust Twins that the floor had been swept out with, the realities emerged. Shelves climbed to high reach all the way around, set out with not too much of any one thing but a lot of things — lard, molasses, vinegar, starch, matches, kerosene, Octagon soap (about a year's worth of octagon-shaped coupons cut out and saved brought a signet ring addressed to you in the mail. Furthermore, when the postman arrived at your door, he blew a whistle). It was up to you to remember what you came for, while your eye traveled from cans of sardines to ice cream salt to harmonicas to flypaper (over your head, batting around on a thread beneath the blades of the ceiling fan, stuck with its testimonial catch).

Its confusion may have been in the eye of its beholder. Enchantment is 15 cast upon you by all those things you weren't supposed to have need for, it lures you close to wooden tops you'd outgrown, boy's marbles and agates in little net pouches, small rubber balls that wouldn't bounce straight, frazzly kite-string, clay bubble-pipes that would snap off in your teeth, the stiffest scissors. You could contemplate those long narrow boxes of sparklers gathering dust while you waited for it to be the Fourth of July or Christmas, and noisemakers in the shape of tin frogs for somebody's birthday party you hadn't been invited to yet, and see that they were all marvelous.

You might not have even looked for Mr. Sessions when he came around his store cheese (as big as a doll's house) and in front of the counter looking for you. When you'd finally asked him for, and received from him in its paper bag, whatever single thing it was that you had been sent for, the nickel that was left over was yours to spend.

Down at a child's eye level, inside those glass jars with mouths in their sides through which the grocer could run his scoop or a child's hand might be invited to reach for a choice, were wineballs, all-day suckers, gumdrops, peppermints. Making a row under the glass of a counter were the Tootsie Rolls, Hershey Bars, Goo-Goo Clusters, Baby Ruths. And whatever was the name of those pastilles that came stacked in a cardboard cylinder with a cardboard lid? They were thin and dry, about the size of tiddlywinks, and in the shape of twisted rosettes. A kind of chocolate dust came out with them when you shook them out in your hand. Were they chocolate? I'd say rather they were brown. They didn't taste of anything at all, unless it was wood. Their attraction was the number you got for a nickel.

Making up your mind, you circled the store around and around, around the pickle barrel, around the tower of Cracker Jack boxes; Mr. Sessions had built it for us himself on top of a packing case, like a house of cards.

If it seemed too hot for Cracker Jacks, I might get a cold drink. Mr. Sessions might have already stationed himself by the cold-drinks barrel, like a mind reader. Deep in ice water that looked black as ink, murky shapes that would come up as Coca-Colas, Orange Crushes, and various flavors of pop, were all swimming around together. When you gave the word, Mr. Sessions plunged his bare arm in to the elbow and fished out your choice, first try. I favored a locally bottled concoction called Lake's Celery. (What else could it be called? It was made by a Mr. Lake out of celery. It was a popular drink here for years but was not known universally, as I found out when I arrived in New York and ordered one in the Astor bar.) You drank on the premises, with feet set wide apart to miss the drip, and gave him back his bottle.

But he didn't hurry you off. A standing scales was by the door, with a stack of iron weights and a brass slide on the balance arm, that would weigh you up to three hundred pounds. Mr. Sessions, whose hands were gentle and smelled of carbolic, would lift you up and set your feet on the platform, hold your loaf of bread for you, and taking his time while you stood still for him, he would make certain of what you weighed today. He could even remember what you weighed last time, so you could subtract and announce how much you'd gained. That was good-bye.

Is there always a hard way to go home? From the Little Store, you could go partway through the sewer. If your brothers had called you a scarecat, then across the next street beyond the Little Store, it was possible to enter this sewer by passing through a privet hedge, climbing down into the bed of a creek, and going into its mouth on your knees. The sewer — it might have been no more than a "storm sewer" — came out and emptied here, where Town Creek, a sandy, most often shallow little stream that ambled through Jackson on its way to the Pearl River, ran along the edge of the cemetery. You could go in darkness through this tunnel to where you next saw light (if you ever did) and climb out through the culvert at your own street corner.

I was a scarecat, all right, but I was a reader with my own refuge in storybooks. Making my way under the sidewalk, under the street and the street-car track, under the Little Store, down there in the wet dark by myself, I could be Persephone° entering into my six-month sojourn underground — though I didn't suppose Persephone had to crawl, hanging onto a loaf of bread, and come out through the teeth of an iron grating. Mother Ceres° would indeed be wondering where she could find me, and mad when she knew. "Now am I going to have to start marching to the Little Store for *myself?*"

I couldn't picture it. Indeed I'm unable today to picture the Little Store with a grown person in it, except for Mr. Sessions and the lady who helped him, who belonged there. We children thought it was ours. The happiness of errands was in part that of running for the moment away from home, a free spirit. I believed the Little Store to be a center of the outside world, and hence of happiness — as I believed what I found in the Cracker Jack box to be a genuine prize, which was as simply as I believed in the Golden Fleece.°

But a day came when I ran to the store to discover, sitting on the front step, a grown person, after all — more than a grown person. It was the Monkey Man, together with his monkey. His grinding-organ was lowered to the step beside him. In my whole life so far, I must have laid eyes on the Monkey Man no more than five or six times. An itinerant of rare and wayward appearances, he was not punctual like the Gipsies, who every year with the first cool days of fall showed up in the aisles of Woolworth's. You never knew when the Monkey Man might decide to favor Jackson, or which way he'd go. Sometimes you heard him as close as the next street, and then he didn't come up yours.

But now I saw the Monkey Man at the Little Store, where I'd never seen him before. I'd never seen him sitting down. Low on that familiar doorstep, he was not the same any longer, and neither was his monkey. They looked just like an old man and an old friend of his that wore a fez, meeting quietly together, tired, and resting with their eyes fixed on some place far away, and not the same place. Yet their romance for me didn't have it in its power to waver. I wavered. I simply didn't know how to step around them, to proceed on into the Little Store for my mother's emergency as if nothing had happened. If I could have gone in there after it, whatever it was, I would have

25

Persephone   In Greek mythology, the daughter of Zeus and Demeter. She is abducted by Pluto to reign with him in the underworld for six months of every year.
   Ceres   The Roman name for Demeter, mother of Persephone.
   Golden Fleece   In Greek mythology, the fleece of the golden ram, stolen by Jason and the Argonauts.

given it to them — putting it into the monkey's cool little fingers. I would have given them the Little Store itself.

In my memory they are still attached to the store — so are all the others. Everyone I saw on my way seemed to me then part of my errand, and in a way they were. As I myself, the free spirit, was part of it too.

All the years we lived in that house where we children were born, the same people lived in the other houses on our street too. People changed through the arithmetic of birth, marriage, and death, but not by going away. So families just accrued stories, which through the fullness of time, in those times, their own lives made. And I grew up in those.

But I didn't know there'd ever been a story at the Little Store, one that was going on while I was there. Of course, all the time the Sessions family had been living right overhead there, in the upstairs rooms behind the little railed porch and the shaded windows; but I think we children never thought of that. Did I fail to see them as a family because they weren't living in an ordinary house? Because I so seldom saw them close together, or having anything to say to each other? She sat in the back of the store, her pencil over a ledger, while he stood and waited on children to make up their minds. They worked in twin black eyeshades, held on their gray heads by elastic bands. It may be harder to recognize kindness — or unkindness either — in a face whose eyes are in shadow. His face underneath his shade was as round as the little wooden wheels in the Tinker Toy box. So was her face. I didn't know, perhaps didn't even wonder: Were they husband and wife or brother and sister? Were they father and mother? There were a few other persons, of various ages, wandering singly in by the back door and out. But none of their relationships could I imagine, when I'd never seen them sitting down together around their own table.

The possibility that they had any other life at all, anything beyond what we could see within the four walls of the Little Store, occurred to me only when tragedy struck their family. There was some act of violence. The shock to the neighborhood traveled to the children, of course; but I couldn't find out from my parents what had happened. They held it back from me, as they'd already held back many things, "until the time comes for you to know."

You could find out some of these things by looking in the unabridged dictionary and the encyclopedia — kept to hand in our dining room — but you couldn't find out there what had happened to the family who for all the years of your life had lived upstairs over the Little Store, who had never been anything but patient and kind to you, who never once had sent you away. All I ever knew was its aftermath: They were the only people ever known to me who simply vanished. At the point where their life overlapped into ours, the story broke off.

We weren't being sent to the neighborhood grocery for facts of life, or death. But of course those are what we were on the track of, anyway. With the loaf of bread and the Cracker Jack prize, I was bringing home the intimations of pride and disgrace, and rumors and early news of people coming to hurt one another, while others practiced for joy — storing up a portion for myself of the human mystery.

AFTERWORD

Criticizing writers whom we read in silence, often without moving our lips, we speak in metaphor of the author's voice, meaning the collective idiosyncracies of a writer's style. In another metaphor, we sometimes call style the writer's signature. The latter compares diction and syntax to the individual flourishes of handwriting; the former compares style to the characteristic noises of the human voicebox: accent, pitch, rhythm.

The more stylish the writer, the more do the words on the page control our hearing of them. And the best silent readers hear: When I read poetry silently for an hour or two my throat gets tired from all that squeezing. Some prose — Henry James, Ernest Hemingway, Katherine Anne Porter, Eudora Welty — tires out the throat, or the tapping foot, as much as poetry does. Try out the pacing and pitch of Welty's long, idiomatic, characteristic first sentence: The first phrase so clearly waits for its attachment, you must pitch it high; the second phrase qualifies or tags the first, dangles from it attached by a thread; we drop the pitch of our voices to indicate that this phrase only specifies the one before it; the third phrase drops down even lower, maybe taxing the range of our pitch; here we learn further the identity of this place and receive important exposition in the guise of location.

Then comes the main clause — "it was possible" — and the sentence's conclusion, which gives us the reason the sentence started, "Two blocks away from the Mississippi State Capitol." Here in the main clause the voice finds its middle range: Here we find a main verb and a qualifying clause on the same pitch level: What kind of little pasture? The kind where you would keep a Jersey cow. These eighteen words, just before the end, are the meat and potato of the sentence and make sense of the earlier anticipatory phrases that kept us waiting. The sweetest measure of voice comes last, the dessert: "which we did." After the eighteen-word main clause, here is a comic three-word, three-syllable afterthought, plunk plunk plunk — as Welty with good-humored mimetic skill works on us with the rhythms of childhood.

BOOKS AVAILABLE IN PAPERBACK

The Bride of the Innisfallen and Other Stories. San Diego: Harcourt Brace Jovanovich. *Short stories.*

The Collected Stories of Eudora Welty. San Diego: Harcourt Brace Jovanovich. *Short stories.*

A Curtain of Green and Other Stories. San Diego: Harcourt Brace Jovanovich. *Short stories.*

Delta Wedding. San Diego: Harcourt Brace Jovanovich. *Novel.*

The Eye of the Story: Selected Essays and Reviews. New York: Random House–Vintage.

The Golden Apples. San Diego: Harcourt Brace Jovanovich. *Short stories.*

Losing Battles. New York: Random House–Vintage. *Novel.*

One Writer's Beginnings. New York: Warner Books. *Nonfiction.*

The Optimist's Daughter. New York: Random House–Vintage. *Novel.*

Photographs. Jackson: University Press of Mississippi. *Art.*

The Ponder Heart. San Diego: Harcourt Brace Jovanovich. *Novel.*

The Robber Bridegroom. San Diego: Harcourt Brace Jovanovich. *Novel.*

Thirteen Stories. San Diego: Harcourt Brace Jovanovich. *Short stories.*

The Wide Net and Other Stories. San Diego: Harcourt Brace Jovanovich. *Short stories.*

Acknowledgments (continued from page iv)

James Baldwin, "If Black English Isn't a Language, Then Tell Me What Is?" Copyright © 1979 by James Baldwin. Originally published by the *New York Times,* July 29, 1979. Collected in *The Price of the Ticket,* published by St. Martin's Press. Reprinted with the permission of the James Baldwin Estate. Photograph of author used by permission of AP/Wide World Photos.

John Berger, "Her Secrets." Reprinted by permission of the author. Photograph of author used by permission of Jean Mohr.

Raymond Carver, "My Father's Life." Copyright 1984 by Tess Gallagher. Reprinted by permission of Tess Gallagher. Photograph of author © Marion Ettlinger.

Judith Ortiz Cofer, "Primary Lessons." Reprinted with permission from the publisher of *Silent Dancing: A Partial Remembrance of a Puerto Rican Childhood* (Houston: Arte Público Press–University of Houston, 1990). Photograph of author reprinted with permission from the publisher of *Silent Dancing: A Partial Remembrance of a Puerto Rican Childhood* (Houston: Arte Público Press–University of Houston, 1990).

Frank Conroy, "Think About It." Copyright © 1988 by *Harper's Magazine.* All rights reserved. Reprinted from the November issue by special permission. Photograph of author used by permission of Frank Conroy.

Malcolm Cowley, "The View from 80," from *The View from 80* by Malcolm Cowley. Copyright © 1976, 1978, 1980 by Malcolm Cowley. Used by permission of Viking Penguin, a division of Penguin Books USA, Inc. William Butler Yeats, "The Spur." Reprinted with permission of Macmillan Publishing Company from *The Poems of W. B. Yeats: A New Edition,* edited by Richard J. Finneran. Copyright 1940 by Georgie Yeats, renewed 1968 by Bertha Georgie Yeats, Michael Butler Yeats, and Anne Yeats. Excerpt from "The Tower" by William Butler Yeats. Reprinted with permission of Macmillan Publishing Company from *The Poems of W. B. Yeats: A New Edition,* edited by Richard J. Finneran. Copyright 1928 by Macmillan Publishing Company, renewed 1956 by Georgie Yeats. Photograph of author by Robert Cowley.

Joan Didion, "Holy Water," from *The White Album* by Joan Didion. Copyright © 1979 by Joan Didion. Reprinted by permission of Farrar, Straus & Giroux, Inc. Excerpt of poem by Karl Shapiro reprinted by permission of Weiser and Weiser, Inc. Excerpt of an interview with Joan Didion from *The Writer's Chapbook* by George A. Plimpton, editor. Copyright © 1989 by The Paris Review, Inc. Used by permission of Viking Penguin, a division of Penguin Books USA, Inc. Photograph of author by Quintana Roo Dunne.

Annie Dillard, "Total Eclipse," from *Teaching a Stone to Talk* by Annie Dillard. Copyright © 1982 by Annie Dillard. Reprinted by permission of HarperCollins Publishers, Inc. Photograph of author © Rollie McKenna.

E. L. Doctorow, "False Documents," from *Jack London, Hemingway, and the Constitution* by E. L. Doctorow. Copyright © 1993 by E. L. Doctorow. Reprinted by permission of Random House, Inc. Photograph of author © Nancy Crampton.

Andre Dubus, "Imperiled Men." Originally appeared in *Harper's Magazine* in 1993 under another title. Reprinted by permission of the author. Photograph of author © Marion Ettlinger.

Gerald Early, "Life with Daughters: Watching the Miss America Pageant." Reprinted by permission of the author. Photograph of author used by permission of Gerald Early.

Gretel Ehrlich, "The Solace of Open Spaces," from *The Solace of Open Spaces* by Gretel Ehrlich. Copyright © 1985 by Gretel Ehrlich. Used by permission of Viking Penguin, a division of Penguin Books USA, Inc. Photograph of author © William Webb.

Ian Frazier, "Dating Your Mom," from *Dating Your Mom* by Ian Frazier. Copyright © 1986 by Ian Frazier. Reprinted by permission of Farrar, Straus & Giroux, Inc. Photograph of author used by permission of Jerry Bauer.

Robert Frost. Reprinted with permission of Macmillan Publishing Company from Robert Frost's Introduction to *King Jasper* by Edwin Arlington Robinson. Copyright 1935 and renewed 1963 by Macmillan Publishing Company. Excerpt from the Preface to *A Way*

Out from *Selected Prose of Robert Frost*, edited by Hyde Cox and Edward Connery Lathem. © 1966, Henry Holt and Company, Inc.

Paul Fussell, "Notes on Class," from *The Boy Scout Handbook and Other Observations* by Paul Fussell. Copyright © 1982 by Paul Fussell. Reprinted by permission of Oxford University Press, Inc. Excerpt from "In Memory of W. B. Yeats," from *Collected Poems* by W. H. Auden. Copyright © 1940 and renewed 1968 by W. H. Auden. Reprinted by permission of Random House, Inc. Excerpt from "In Memory of W. B. Yeats," from *Collected Poems* by W. H. Auden, edited by Edward Mendelson, published by Faber and Faber Ltd. Reprinted by permission of the publisher. Photograph of author © 1987 Courtney Grant Winston, 70 West 83rd Street, Duplex B, New York, N.Y. 10024.

Gabriel García Márquez. Excerpt of an interview with Gabriel García Márquez from *The Writer's Chapbook* by George A. Plimpton, editor. Copyright © 1989 by The Paris Review, Inc. Used by permission of Viking Penguin, a division of Penguin Books USA, Inc.

Stephen Jay Gould, "Sex, Drugs, Disasters, and the Extinction of Dinosaurs." Copyright © 1984, 1985 by Stephen Jay Gould. Reprinted from *The Flamingo's Smile: Reflections in Natural History* by Stephen Jay Gould with the permission of W. W. Norton & Company, Inc. Originally published in *Discover,* March 1984. Photograph of author used by permission of Stephen Jay Gould.

Robert Graves and Alan Hodge. A short extract from *The Reader over Your Shoulder* by Robert Graves and Alan Hodge. Reprinted by permission of A. P. Watt Ltd. on behalf of the Trustees of the Robert Graves Copyright Trust and Jane Aiken Hodge.

Francine du Plessix Gray, "On Friendship." Copyright © 1987 by Francine du Plessix Gray. Reprinted by permission of Simon & Schuster, Inc. Excerpt of an interview with Francine du Plessix Gray from *The Writer's Chapbook* by George A. Plimpton, editor. Copyright © 1989 by The Paris Review, Inc. Used by permission of Viking Penguin, a division of Penguin Books USA, Inc. Photograph of author © Sigrid Estrada.

Donald Hall, "Ballad of the Republic." Reprinted by permission of the author. Photograph of author © Marcia Curtis.

Joy Harjo, "Family Album." Previously published in the *Progressive* and *Partial Recall: Photographs of Native North Americans* by Lucy Lippard published by The New Press, New York, 1992. Reprinted by permission of the author. Photograph of author used by permission of Paul Abdoo, Photographer/Denver, Colo.

Elizabeth Hardwick. Excerpt of an interview with Elizabeth Hardwick from *The Writer's Chapbook* by George A. Plimpton, editor. Copyright © 1989 by The Paris Review, Inc. Used by permission of Viking Penguin, a division of Penguin Books USA, Inc.

Stephen Hawking, "Is Everything Determined?" from *Black Holes and Baby Universes and Other Essays* by Stephen W. Hawking. Copyright © 1993 by Stephen W. Hawking. Used by permission of Bantam Books, a division of Bantam Doubleday Dell Publishing Group, Inc. Photograph of author used by permission of M & M Management.

Vicki Hearne, "What's Wrong with Animal Rights." Copyright © 1991 by *Harper's Magazine.* All rights reserved. Reprinted from the September issue by special permission. Adaptation of "Why Dogs Bark at Mailmen" from *Animal Happiness* by Vicki Hearne. Copyright © 1994 by Vicki Hearne. Reprinted by permission of HarperCollins Publishers, Inc. Photograph of author © Ferorelli 1994.

Ernest Hemingway, from *Death in the Afternoon* by Ernest Hemingway. Copyright 1932 by Charles Scribner's Sons; renewal copyright © 1960 by Ernest Hemingway. Reprinted with permission of Scribner's, an imprint of Simon & Schuster.

Edward Hoagland, "Learning to Eat Soup." Copyright © 1992 by Edward Hoagland. Reprinted by permission of Simon & Schuster, Inc. Excerpt from "The Choice." Reprinted with permission of Macmillan Publishing Company from *The Poems of W. B. Yeats: A New Edition*, edited by Richard J. Finneran. Copyright 1993 by Macmillan Publishing Company, renewed 1961 by Bertha Georgie Yeats. Photograph of author by Thomas Victor.

Sue Hubbell, "The Great American Pie Expedition." Copyright © 1989 by Sue Hubbell. First appeared in March 27, 1989 edition of the *New Yorker.* Excerpt from "The Bird" © 1987 Dixie Stars Music (ASCAP). All rights reserved. Used by permission. Copyright © 1987 by Songs of Polygram International, Inc. Photograph of author used by permission of Nancy Albrecht Stacel.

Molly Ivins, "Sleazy Riders," "Get a Knife, Get a Dog, but Get Rid of Guns," and "'Twas a Fine Spring Day to Air Out Attitudes," from *Nothin' but Good Times Ahead* by Molly Ivins. Copyright © 1993 by Molly Ivins. Reprinted by permission of Random House, Inc. Photograph of author © Kelly Campbell.

Diane Johnson, "Rape." Copyright © 1982 by Diane Johnson. Reprinted by permission of the Helen Brann Agency, Inc. Photograph of author © Barbara Hall.

Jamaica Kincaid, "Flowers of Evil." Copyright © 1992 Jamaica Kincaid. Reprinted by permission. Originally published in the *New Yorker*. All rights reserved. Photograph of author © Sigrid Estrada.

Maxine Hong Kingston, "No Name Woman," from *The Woman Warrior* by Maxine Hong Kingston. Copyright © 1975, 1976 by Maxine Hong Kingston. Reprinted by permission of Alfred A. Knopf, Inc. Photograph of author used by permission of Jane Scherr.

Ursula K. Le Guin, "Bryn Mawr Commencement Address," from *Dancing at the Edge of the World*. Copyright © 1986 by Ursula K. Le Guin. Used by permission of Grove/Atlantic, Inc. Joy Harjo, "The Blanket Around Her" reprinted by permission of the author. Denise Levertov, *Poems 1960–1967*. Copyright © 1960 by Denise Levertov. Reprinted by permission of New Directions Publishing Corp. Excerpt by Hélène Cixous and poems by Ursula K. Le Guin used by permission of Grove/Atlantic, Inc. Wendy Rose, "The Parts of a Poet." Reprinted by permission of Malki Museum Press. Linda Hogan, "The Woman Speaking," Green Field Review Press. Reprinted by permission of the author. Photograph of author © Marian Wood Kolisch.

Alison Lurie, "Clothing as a Sign System." Copyright © 1981 by Alison Lurie. Reprinted by permission of Melanie Jackson Agency. Photograph of author used by permission of Jimm Roberts, Orlando.

Nancy Mairs, "Carnal Acts," from *Carnal Acts* by Nancy Mairs. Copyright © 1991 by Nancy Mairs. Reprinted by permission of HarperCollins Publishers, Inc. Photograph of author by Diedre Hamill, © 1993 the *Phoenix Gazette*.

Mary McCarthy. Reprinted by permission of *Paris Review*.

John McPhee, "The Search for Marvin Gardens," from *Pieces of the Frame* by John McPhee. Copyright © 1975 by John McPhee. Reprinted by permission of Farrar, Straus & Giroux, Inc., and Macfarlane Walter & Ross, Toronto. Photograph of author © Anne Hall.

H. L. Mencken. From *The American Language* by H. L. Mencken. Copyright 1919 by Alfred A. Knopf, Inc., and renewed 1947 by H. L. Mencken. Reprinted by permission of Random House, Inc.

Naomi Shihab Nye, "Newcomers in a Troubled Land." Reprinted by permission of the author. Photograph of author used by permission of Michael Nye.

Joyce Carol Oates, "Against Nature." Copyright © 1986 by The Ontario Review, Inc. Reprinted by permission of the author and Blanche C. Gregory, Inc. Excerpt from "Sailing to Byzantium." Reprinted with permission of Macmillan Publishing Company from *The Poems of W. B. Yeats: A New Edition*, edited by Richard J. Finneran. Copyright 1928 by Macmillan Publishing Company, renewed 1956 by Georgie Yeats. Photograph of author used by permission of Joyce Carol Oates.

George Orwell, excerpt from "Politics and the English Language," by George Orwell. Copyright 1946 by Sonia Brownell Orwell and renewed 1974 by Sonia Orwell. Reprinted from his volume *Shooting an Elephant and Other Essays* by permission of Harcourt Brace & Company. Reprinted by permission of the estate of the late Sonia Brownell Orwell and Martin Secker & Warburg Ltd.

Cynthia Ozick, "The First Day of School: Washington Square, 1946," from *Metaphor and Memory* by Cynthia Ozick. Copyright © 1989 by Cynthia Ozick. Reprinted by permission of Alfred A. Knopf, Inc. Excerpt from "There's a certain Slant of light" by Emily Dickinson. Reprinted by permission of the publishers and the Trustees of Amherst College from *The Poems of Emily Dickinson*, Thomas H. Johnson, editor. Cambridge, Mass.: The Belknap Press of Harvard University Press. Copyright © 1951, 1955, 1979, 1983 by the President and Fellows of Harvard College. Photograph of author by Julius Ozick, © Cynthia Ozick.

Walker Percy, "The Loss of the Creature," from *The Message in the Bottle* by Walker Percy. Copyright © 1975 by Walker Percy. Reprinted by permission of Farrar, Straus & Giroux, Inc. Photograph of author © Nancy Crampton.

S. J. Perelman. Excerpt of an interview with S. J. Perelman from *The Writer's Chapbook* by George A. Plimpton, editor. Copyright © 1989 by The Paris Review, Inc. Used by permission of Viking Penguin, a division of Penguin Books USA, Inc.

Katherine Anne Porter. Excerpt of an interview with Katherine Anne Porter from *The Writer's Chapbook* by George A. Plimpton, editor. Copyright © 1989 by The Paris Review, Inc. Used by permission of Viking Penguin, a division of Penguin Books USA, Inc.

Ezra Pound, from *The ABC's of Reading*. Copyright © 1960 by New Directions Publishing Corp. Reprinted by permission of New Directions Publishing Corp. Ezra Pound, from *The Literary Essays of Ezra Pound*. Copyright 1935 by Ezra Pound. Reprinted by permission of New Directions Publishing Corp.

Adrienne Rich, "A Leak in History," from *What Is Found There: Notebooks on Poetry and Politics* by Adrienne Rich. Copyright © 1993 by Adrienne Rich. Reprinted by permission of the author and W. W. Norton & Company, Inc. Poem by Jacqueline Dixon-Bey and Mary Glover, "Florence Crane Women's Prison," from *Insight: Serving the Women of Florence Crane Women's Facility*. Reprinted by permission of J. Dixon-Bey and Mary Glover. Excerpt from "Konvict Kitchen" by Gloria Bolden. Reprinted by permission of Gloria Bolden. Photograph of author used by permission of Jason Langer.

Richard Rodriguez, "The Achievement of Desire," from *Hunger of Memory* by Richard Rodriguez. Copyright © 1982 by Richard Rodriguez. Reprinted by permission of David R. Godine, Publisher, Inc. Photograph of author courtesy of David R. Godine, Publisher, Inc.

Scott Russell Sanders, "Doing Time in the Thirteenth Chair." Copyright © 1983 by Scott Russell Sanders. First appeared in *The North American Review*. Reprinted by permission of the author and Virginia Kidd, Literary Agent. Photograph of author used by permission of Eva Sanders.

Randy Shilts, "Talking AIDS to Death." Reprinted by permission of Frederick Hill Associates Literary Agency. Photograph of author used by permission of James D. Wilson.

Charles Simic, "The Spider's Web." Reprinted by permission of *The New Republic*. Photograph of author copyright Miriam Berkley.

Gary Soto, "Black Hair," from *Living Up the Street* published by Dell Publishing. Copyright © 1985 by Gary Soto. Used by permission of the author. Photograph of author used by permission of Carolyn Soto.

Gertrude Stein, from *Lectures in America*. Copyright 1935 and renewed 1962 by Alice B. Toklas. Reprinted by permission of Random House, Inc.

Amy Tan, "Mother Tongue." Copyright © 1989 by Amy Tan. First appeared in *Threepenny Review*. Reprinted by permission of the author and the Sandra Dijkstra Literary Agency. Photograph of author courtesy of Robert Foothorap Company.

Lewis Thomas, "The Tucson Zoo." Copyright © 1977 by Lewis Thomas from *The Medusa and the Snail* by Lewis Thomas. Used by permission of Viking Penguin, a division of Penguin Books USA, Inc. "Millenium," from *The Youngest Science: Notes of a Medicine Watcher* by Lewis Thomas. Copyright © 1983 by Lewis Thomas. Used by permission of Viking Penguin, a division of Penguin Books USA, Inc. Photograph of author by Bob Isear.

Marianna De Marco Torgovnick, "On Being White, Female, and Born in Bensonhurst." Copyright © 1994 by Marianna De Marco Torgovnick. All rights reserved. First appeared in *Partisan Review*, Vol. LVII, No. 3, 1990. To be included in a forthcoming book published by the University of Chicago Press. Photograph of author by Stuart Torgovnick, courtesy of the University of Chicago Press.

Barbara Tuchman, "History as Mirror." Copyright © 1973 by Barbara Tuchman. Reprinted by permission of Russell & Volkening as agents for the author. Photograph of author © Rand Hendrix.

John Updike, "The Disposable Rocket." Copyright © 1993 by John Updike. Excerpt of an interview with John Updike from *The Writer's Chapbook* by George A. Plimpton, editor.

Copyright © 1989 by The Paris Review, Inc. Used by permission of Viking Penguin, a division of Penguin Books USA, Inc. Photograph of author courtesy of Alfred A. Knopf, Inc.

Gore Vidal, "H. L. Mencken the Journalist," from *United States Essays 1952–1992* by Gore Vidal. Copyright © 1993 by Gore Vidal. Reprinted by permission of Random House, Inc. Photograph of author by Jane Bown, used by permission of William Morris Agency.

Alice Walker, "In Search of Our Mothers' Gardens," from *In Search of Our Mothers' Gardens: Womanist Prose.* Copyright © 1974 by Alice Walker. Reprinted by permission of Harcourt Brace & Company. "Women" from *Revolutionary Petunias & Other Poems.* Copyright © 1970 by Alice Walker. Reprinted by permission of Harcourt Brace & Company. Photograph of author copyright © 1991 Jean Weisinger.

Eudora Welty, "The Little Store," from *The Eye of the Story: Selected Essays and Reviews* by Eudora Welty. Copyright © 1978 by Eudora Welty. Reprinted by permission of Random House, Inc. Excerpt of an interview with Eudora Welty from *The Writer's Chapbook* by George A. Plimpton, editor. Copyright © 1989 by The Paris Review, Inc. Used by permission of Viking Penguin, a division of Penguin Books USA, Inc. Photograph of author by Richard O. Moore.

E. B. White, "All Pages" from "Calculating Machine" from *The Second Tree from the Corner* by E. B. White. Copyright 1951 by E. B. White. Originally appeared in the *New Yorker.* Reprinted by permission of HarperCollins Publishers, Inc.

William Carlos Williams, *Selected Essays of William Carlos Williams.* Copyright 1954 by William Carlos Williams. Reprinted by permission of New Directions Publishing Corp.

Virginia Woolf, from *The Common Reader* by Virginia Woolf, the Estate of the Author, published by The Hogarth Press. Excerpt from *The Common Reader* by Virginia Woolf. Copyright 1925 by Harcourt Brace & Company and renewed 1953 by Leonard Woolf. Reprinted by permission of the publisher.